FEDERAL INDIAN LAW AND POLICY

AN INTRODUCTION

KEITH RICHOTTE, JR.

WEST ACADEMIC PUBLISHING

© 2020 LEG, Inc. d/b/a West Academic
    444 Cedar Street, Suite 700
    St. Paul, MN 55101
    1-877-888-1330

West, West Academic Publishing, and West Academic are trademarks of West Publishing Corporation, used under license.

Printed in the United States of America

ISBN: 978-1-64242-605-2

To my parents and grandparents,

and to Jenny and Steven

Acknowledgments

I would first like to acknowledge a number of outstanding teachers and colleagues that I have had over the years. As a student, I was able to take classes from some of the foremost minds in federal Indian law and policy, including S. James Anaya, Robert Hershey, James Hopkins, Frank Pommersheim, Alex Skibine, Gerald Torres, and Kevin Washburn. Any student would be lucky to be in a classroom with any one of these fine scholars, let alone all of them. I have also been fortunate enough to take classes with a number of the leading Indian Studies scholars of the day, including, but not limited to, Jean O'Brien and Brenda Child. I am very grateful to these individuals for their significant contributions to my education and scholarship. I am also thankful to my former colleagues at the University of North Dakota School of Law and my present colleagues in the American Studies Department at the University of North Carolina. In addition, I am also grateful to all of the wonderful people and relationships that I have been fortunate enough to build within the scholarly fields of Indian Studies more broadly and federal Indian Law and Policy more particularly. There are a lot of great people doing very valuable work for Native America and I am deeply humbled and pleased to be part of this community. Unfortunately (or fortunately?) there are too many great folks to name each one individually. Nonetheless, I must give some specific attention to two: first, Robert A. Williams, Jr. has been an amazing teacher, an exceptional mentor, and a kind friend. His scholarship has been a guiding light, as has his advice and engagement with my career. Without his efforts, this book would not exist. I am fortunate to have attended the Indigenous Peoples Law and Policy Program at the University of Arizona under his tutelage. Second, Thomas Biolsi is not only an exceptional writer and thinker, but also a kind person and friend who has gone above and beyond on my behalf. I hope to emulate both his scholarship and his generosity.

I have also been fortunate enough to have a number of terrific students and other people who have helped make this book possible. I want to thank Dr. Matthew Swiatlowski. While a graduate student at the University of North Carolina, Matt collected most of the primary sources for this book and organized and standardized the text. This thankless work made my own efforts exponentially easier, for which I am grateful. I also want to thank the students in my Fall 2018 Federal Indian Law and Policy course—Amiel Elbitar-Hartwell, Lexy Locklear, Heather Menafee, Hattie Morehead, Hannah Smith, Emily Stellman, and Raymond Tu. These students endured the first draft of this text with kindness, grace, and a willingness to offer constructive feedback. I remain pleased and impressed by the high quality of these and other students that I have been fortunate to encounter during my career.

Finally, I want to acknowledge that I have been inordinately lucky in my personal life, and I am deeply grateful for this. I have been given much in the way of opportunities and kindness—even when I probably did not deserve it—from many at many stages of my life. In addition, not every person who shares a similar beginning (divorced parents, interracial home, our family's share of other of life's problems, etc.) also gets the advantages I was given (two college-educated parents, very stable and loving grandparents, etc.). This book would not be possible without my mother and father, who both had the wisdom and patience to put up with a quiet and stubborn son. It also would not be possible without my grandparents who are the kindest and most accepting people that I know. Finally, and most important, I have Jenny and Steven, the wife and son I have always wanted.

Thank you all and I hope that this book is worthy of your contribution to it.

Summary of Contents

Table of Contents

UNIT I. THE HISTORICAL FOUNDATIONS

Table of Cases

The principal cases are in bold type.

FEDERAL INDIAN LAW AND POLICY

AN INTRODUCTION

Introduction

Welcome to the study of federal Indian law and policy. *Federal Indian Law & Policy: An Introduction* is designed for undergraduate and graduate students, instructors, and members of the public who are interested in American law that concerns the Native peoples and nations within the United States. It is also useful for law students who want to establish a basic understanding of the field before taking their studies further. The purpose of this text is to offer those without legal training or a background in this area a comprehensible, useable, and helpful look at a distinct and unique area of law. No single work can explain every aspect of the field, but this text will be of value to readers who want to know more about this important facet of Native America and it will be a good first resource for readers who hope to take their study of this area of law beyond this introductory text.

Before continuing it is important to acknowledge that the prospect of studying law and policy can seem daunting, unappealing, or even frightening for those without a legal background. Just the very thought of interacting with the law is enough to make many people avoid engaging with certain materials, discussions, topics, or avenues of research. While this feeling is certainly common, it need not be controlling nor does it accurately reflect the purpose or intention of legal texts. Despite its reputation for obliqueness and obfuscation, the law is meant to be read by the public. Judges who write court opinions are attempting to explain their positions and persuade their readers, including those without a legal background. In order to do so, judges try to be as clear and direct as possible. Written laws passed by legislatures, such as the kind you would find in the U.S. Code or state codes, are open and readily available public documents that are intended to explain to every citizen what is and is not permissible. Other legal texts are also attempts to explain or persuade and often take great pains to simply and concisely do so. With a little guidance and practice, anyone can learn to read "the law."

In order to get the most out of this text, it is useful to answer a few preliminary questions: What is Native America? What is federal Indian law? Why is federal Indian law important? How should I read this text?

WHAT IS NATIVE AMERICA?

There is no easy answer to this question and this introduction can only begin to offer a basic framework. That being noted, a few key principles will help any reader, regardless of their familiarity with Native America, to get the most out of this text.

First, Native America most directly consists of the peoples who are the descendants of the original inhabitants of the Americas, the lands these descendants claim as their own, and the social structures—such as the law, tribal affiliations, cultural practices, etc.—which shape and inform the lived experiences of these descendants. Although this explanation may seem self-evident, it quickly produces a host of complicated questions: Who can claim to be a descendant from the original inhabitants of the Americas? Who is an Indian? What is a tribe? Who gets to be a part of a tribe? What constitutes tribal land? Who gets to decide? And so on. This text will detail the answers to these and other questions that have been established in American law, but it is important to note that debates about these issues continue and that the law only offers one (albeit especially powerful) perspective.

Second, there is a tremendous amount of diversity within Native America. A useful parallel is to understand that describing something as "Native American" is equivalent to describing something as "European" or "Asian." While there is certainly a connection among all of those people or things one would consider Native American or European or Asian, there is much that makes them different as well. Recognizing those differences is critical to more fully understanding a Native American (or European or Asian) context.

Third, the diversity within Native America means different things for different groups within the realm of federal Indian law and policy. For better or worse, both federal Indian law and policy and Native America itself are regularly treated as monoliths. Sometimes this is out of necessity. Since it would be impossible to describe the particular legal history and situation for each tribal nation in a single text, and since many of these histories and situations have common themes and experiences, it is often useful to discuss federal Indian law and policy as a whole. This text generally takes this approach. Sometimes, however, this approach has been a consequence of a lack of respect of the diversity within Native America on the part of American law and policymakers.

This has often been to the detriment of particular tribal nations. Regardless of the motivation, it is best to recognize that the singular way federal Indian law and policy is regularly discussed should be treated like a tool to help one begin to understand, and not an absolute determination for all peoples at all times.

An example will help to illustrate the point. There are 573 federally recognized tribal nations in the United States as of this writing. This means that there are 573 different political contexts, histories, and relationships with the federal government. Each is unique in its own way and no single text could cover them all without resorting to a high level of generalization. Also, the designation "federally recognized" is another category unto itself that excludes the dozens of state recognized and unrecognized tribal nations that also exist. These different statuses—federally recognized, state recognized, and unrecognized—each have their own consequences under the law and the differences between these groups are discussed elsewhere in this text (see Chapter 13). Of importance for this introduction is to acknowledge this diversity and to note that this text is a useful first step—but only a first step—in determining a particular tribal nation's political situation.

Fourth, federal Indian law and policy distinguishes Native peoples and nations from other minority groups in the United States. This point will be elaborated upon further below. For now, it is important to recognize that the political context in which Native America operates makes it different from other group experiences. Put simply (and at a very high level of generality), whereas other minority groups seek to enforce and exercise their civil rights within American law and society, Native peoples and nations seek to enforce and exercise their sovereignty. Sovereignty is an important concept that is not easily defined and will be regularly encountered throughout this text. For present purposes, it suffices to define sovereignty as the ability of a group or political entity to make and enforce its own rules.

This is not to suggest that there are not any commonalities between Native peoples and other minority groups. For example, Native peoples have also fought for recognition of their civil rights within American law and society. Nor is it to make a value judgment or suggest that one group of people has had it better or worse than another group. Rather, it is to state that merely lumping Native peoples within the overarching category of "minorities" can obscure more than it aids. While the political struggle for many minority groups has been greater inclusion into American society and political systems, for Native peoples maintaining a society, land base, and political system outside of the American context has often been the dominant motivation.

Fifth, there is no single designation—such as Indian or Native American—that accurately or adequately describes Native America or the people within it. Just as important, the inability to find a proper designation is much like and reflective of the quandaries that exist within federal Indian law and policy. Put differently, often the first question that many individuals who begin a study of Native America have is how to properly refer to the people who make up Native America. What should I "call them," the new student might ask. There is no mutually agreed upon answer to this question, which can be frustrating to students. Nonetheless, the very problem itself offers an opportunity to understand the challenges that Native America faces in the law and more generally.

A number of prominent scholars have detailed how the designation "Indian" is not only a historical mistake, it is also a Western invention that reveals more about the person using the word than it does about the original inhabitants of the Americas. Other terms, such as Native American, American Indian, or Indigenous, also raise similar issues, as does the designation tribe. To illustrate the point, could anyone born in the United States accurately describe her or himself as Native American? Additionally, does the word "tribe" accurately reflect the political component of Native nationhood or does it perpetuate a designation of inferiority by obscuring that political component? Others have stated a preference for specific tribal designations instead of a more general word or term. This has some benefits but can also be problematic. For example, the author of this text is an enrolled citizen of the Turtle Mountain Band of Chippewa Indians. Yet, the word "Chippewa" has fallen somewhat out of favor, as it has been acknowledged as a corruption of the word Ojibwe or Ojibway or Ojibwa. Still others prefer the word Anishinaabe, arguing that it more accurately refers to the tribal grouping than does either Ojibwe or Chippewa.

Facing the conundrum of what to "call them" allows one to reflect on the complexity of studying Native America and to think beyond this problem as well. It creates the space to ask why identifying a proper designation is such a difficult issue and how it came to be this way. In the context of this text, it also allows one to consider how the problematic nature of even describing Native America affects law and policy. By thinking past the question of what to "call them," one can more readily see how this problem is not just one for the speaker, but for Native peoples in a contemporary setting. It also offers a ready example of how the legacy of colonialism continues to shape the present. For the purposes of this text, the words or terms Native, Indigenous, and tribal nation or Native nation are most regularly used because they tend to carry less of the distracting connotations of other words and terms. However, the primary sources regularly refer to "Indians" and this text uses different context-appropriate language in different circumstances to describe aspects of Native America.

Again, this introduction cannot adequately detail the whole of Native America. Nonetheless, the above principles provide a foundation for thinking about the subject of this text and for moving on to the next question.

WHAT IS FEDERAL INDIAN LAW?

At its most basic, federal Indian law is the collection of treaties, cases, statutes, regulations, executive orders, and other like material that concerns the Native nations and peoples of the United States. A number of law schools offer a Federal Indian Law course or courses and there are a handful of high quality casebooks for that audience. Knowing this body of law is essential to knowing Native America.

Yet, a richer understanding of federal Indian law requires a deeper conceptualization than simply listing the things that compose it. To truly appreciate the study of federal Indian law, one must approach it as two halves that make up a whole. Federal Indian law is best understood as both a discrete body of law unto itself and also as a prism. One must also recognize that federal Indian law is deeply historical and, consequently, one must appreciate the eras and policy periods that have defined this body of law.

As noted, there are a number of American federal cases, statutes, and similar material that exclusively or primarily affect Native peoples and nations. This discrete body of law, as you will see in this text, covers a wide range of subjects and significantly defines the relationship between the federal government and Native America in any number of ways that do not exist in other contexts for other peoples. For example, the Indian Child Welfare Act, passed in 1978 (see Chapter 23), authorizes tribal courts to have a great deal of influence over child placement proceedings for children who are enrolled in the tribal nation or are eligible to be enrolled. This authority can deeply affect the lives of tribal citizens, tribal communities, and non-Native parents, family members, and intimate relations. Thus, one half of understanding federal Indian law is recognizing and identifying a discrete body of law that exclusively or primarily affects Native peoples and nations.

The other half of understanding federal Indian law is to conceptualize it as a prism that alters or changes everything that passes through it. Much like light is bent and changed when passed through a prism, American law takes on a different form when filtered through Native America. Thus, other bodies of American law that are not exclusively or primarily concerned with Native peoples and nations are nonetheless altered when they encounter Native America. For example, contract law can take on different dimensions if a contract is signed with a tribal nation or on reservation lands and any entity contracting with a tribal nation would be wise to have some knowledge of the doctrine of sovereign immunity (see Chapter 21). Additionally, criminal and tort law raise a whole host of questions, beginning with issues of jurisdiction (see Chapters 18 and 19 primarily, as well as in other pertinent chapters). Put simply, American law reacts differently than it otherwise would when it encounters Native America.

By recognizing that federal Indian law is a thing unto itself and something that changes everything else that it touches, one can more fully grasp the complex, interwoven, and unique status of this body of law. However, this in itself is not enough. Perhaps more than any other field of American law, federal Indian law requires knowledge of its history and development. Federal Indian law is, in many respects, a product of its times and cannot be understood without a sufficient grounding in the history of Native American relations with the federal government. Court decisions, laws, and other choices will seem deeply counterintuitive, at best, to the student of today without any historical context. As discussed further below, when you proceed through this text, make sure to remind yourself of the policy era in which the events you read about are happening.

WHY IS FEDERAL INDIAN LAW IMPORTANT?

While every person in the United States—young or old, male or female, citizen or non-citizen, minority or majority, Native or non-Native—is affected by American law in a different way depending on their various statuses, the stated ideal is equal treatment for all. Nonetheless, Native peoples and nations are differently and uniquely situated under American law for a number of reasons. For example, most Americans are citizens of two governments: the federal government and the government of the state in which they reside. Tribal members are citizens of a third government as well: their tribal nation. This third branch of citizenship carries its own set of expectations and responsibilities. In addition, as noted above, there is a discrete body of American law that applies exclusively or primarily to Native peoples and nations. No other group of American citizens— for better or for worse—exists under such a different and acknowledged set of rules. The Indian Child Welfare Act is once again illustrative of the point. While suffering the occasional court challenge and bout of unflattering press coverage, the Indian Child Welfare Act is widely understood in American courts as valid law. Yet, there is no Latino Child Welfare Act or African-American Child Welfare

Act or any other equivalent legislation for any other racial or ethnic minority group in the United States. Just as tellingly, Americans courts would almost assuredly declare any such legislation unconstitutional. Put simply, Native peoples and nations exist under a different legal and political structure than other Americans.

There are a number of important consequences of the different legal and political structure for Native America, including consequences for many non-Natives as well. Every tribal member should have at least a basic understanding of the rights, burdens, protections, and limitations of their status under American law. Anyone who lives on or near Indian Country (which has been defined in a statute by Congress; see Chapter 13) is affected by federal Indian law, whether Native or non-Native. Anyone involved in a relationship, whether business or personal, with a Native nation or person may have to confront this body of law.

Just as importantly, federal Indian law serves as a harbinger of the larger political climate and as a testament to the strengths and weaknesses of the American experiment. In the mid-20th century, Felix Cohen, the most prominent Indian law scholar of his time and perhaps any time, wrote, "Like the miner's canary, the Indian marks the shifts from fresh air to poison gas in our political atmosphere; and our treatment of Indians ... reflects the rise and fall in our democratic faith."[1] Cohen's often-cited simile remains true today, as shifts in federal Indian law often track broader political sentiments. Similarly, how the United States has treated the original inhabitants of the Americas and how it has honored or not honored its promises to Indigenous groups—who were often among the most politically vulnerable—goes a long way in demonstrating the United States' practical commitment to pluralism, equality, the rule of law, and a number of other virtues.

The United States was built upon tribal lands. It was built through negotiation, interaction, and often coercion of tribal nations and peoples. The United States accepted continuing responsibilities to tribal nations and peoples through treaties and other means. And the United States continues to interact with tribal nations on a government-to-government basis to this day. Federal Indian law stands at the very center of the nation itself. To know federal Indian law is to know the story of the United States.

HOW SHOULD I READ THIS TEXT?

In order to get the most out of this text it is important to understand its structure, understand how to engage with the materials you will be encountering, and keep some important thoughts in mind. It is also helpful to familiarize yourself with the basic structure of the American legal system, particularly the different levels of American courts. This knowledge—which is easily attainable from a number of sources—will give you a helpful context to analyze the cases you will read in this text.

Federal Indian Law & Policy: An Introduction consists of thirty chapters and is divided into two major units: The Historical Foundations and Contemporary Native America. Unit I, The Historical Foundations, comprises the first ten chapters of the text and it establishes the necessary historical grounding to understand and interpret what is otherwise a deeply counterintuitive and confusing body of law. Unit II, Contemporary Native America, comprises the final twenty chapters of the text and it offers a wide-ranging picture of the current state of the law.

Each chapter consists of excerpts from a number of primary sources, such as cases and statutes. It is imperative to read these primary sources to understand how they create and shape the law. It is also useful to have some guidance on how to read different primary sources.

COURT OPINIONS: Written opinions, mostly from the Supreme Court, are the bulk of the primary sources that you will read. As noted above, the judges and justices who write these opinions are arguing in favor of their vision of the law and the facts of a case. Knowing this makes it easier to identify what is important in the opinions. There are three levels of comprehension when engaging with an opinion. Learning how to work through all three levels will greatly enhance your understanding of the law and what it means for Native America.

- **Determining who won the case:** This is the most basic level of comprehension and the most important to the parties involved. It does not require any specialized knowledge and is rarely, if ever, difficult to discern.

- **Determining why one party won the case:** While this level of comprehension can be more difficult than the first, it also is generally not difficult to discern. The judges who write court opinions want you to know why one party prevailed over another. As you read through a case, ask yourself what law or legal principle is most important to the writer. What is the "test" or basic question or standard that a court uses to resolve a case? What idea does she or he emphasize or return to? What is it about this law or legal principle that makes it so critical to the case?

- **Determining what the outcome means for Native America:**
  After figuring out who won the case and why that party won, it is critical
  to take a step back and consider the bigger picture. Cases have ripple
  effects that reach beyond the parties to the case and reveal underlying
  assumptions and beliefs. By taking a step back and considering what an
  opinion uncovers about American law, policy, and Native America, the
  opinion takes on a deeper dimension that is not as readily apparent when
  merely discerning why one particular party prevailed. There are many
  questions that can help you get at this bigger picture. These are just a
  few to get you started as you develop your own analytical strategies:

  o   How are Native peoples and nations described in the opinion?
  What might this reveal about the basic understanding the opinion
  writer has of Native America?

  o   Who benefits the most from the outcome of the case? How
  so?

  o   How similar or different are 20th and 21st century opinions
  from 19th century opinions? What do these similarities or
  differences mean for the development of this body of law?

  o   What is the policy era in which the case was decided? What
  else is happening in American history that might help to explain the
  case?

STATUTES AND REGULATIONS: Law students primarily read court
opinions. However, American law has become increasingly dominated by
written laws, or statutes, created and passed by legislatures. This trend applies
to federal Indian law as well. The law is also increasingly defined by
regulations established by federal agencies attempting to apply statutes on the
ground. Regulations are interpretations of statutes that governmental
agencies use to guide themselves in the application of the law. When reading
statutes and regulations, it is important to discern the purpose of them. What
are they trying to define or authorize or prohibit? To whom does it apply?
As with cases, it is also important to take a step back and consider the bigger
picture. Once you have discerned what a statute or regulation is trying to
accomplish, what does your conclusion reveal about the underlying
assumptions or beliefs about Native America? How does the law
contextualize the space in which Native nations and peoples can exercise
their sovereignty? What do the limits or possibilities of that contextualized
space reveal about the relationship between tribal nations, the federal

government, and/or the states? How is this similar or different from other policy eras?

TREATIES AND OTHER MATERIALS: The remaining primary legal materials consist of sources produced or otherwise mostly written by non-Natives. Depending on the source, the level of Native involvement will vary. For example, treaties certainly had Native involvement, but they were nonetheless written by Westerners with certain Western legal principles and concepts at the forefront. With these sources, it is important to seek out the Native presence, if any. What are Native peoples trying to accomplish with a treaty? If there is no direct Native presence or the source is attempting to define or describe Native peoples, it is important to reflect on the writer, the motivations of the writer, and the conception of Native peoples that the writer presents. How are we supposed to understand Native peoples after reading the source? How does this understanding shape the law that follows in its wake?

In addition, there is one other major question you should have in mind as you read all of the primary legal sources: **What are the non-Native interests involved?** Many find federal Indian law and policy to be both confusing and counterintuitive, especially those who do have a legal background. This is because American law regularly contradicts itself and creates new precedent when Native America is involved. By keeping the non-Indian interests in mind, what seems on the surface to be strange or out of sorts or even ridiculous often becomes much more clear. In addition, be broad in your understanding of the non-Native interests involved in a matter. These interests will obviously include those directly involved in the matter, but might also include other parties that are not directly involved, states, or the federal government itself.

Each chapter also contains supporting text and information that explains the context, meaning, and importance of the primary sources. In addition, each primary source is introduced with a small handful of questions to aid your analysis. Keep these questions in mind as well as remembering when the primary source was created, what era of federal Indian policy was in place at the time the primary source was created, and what was happening more broadly in American history at the time. By reflecting on these questions, you will more fully understand the primary source itself as well as gain a deeper insight into the bigger picture. These questions can also provoke beneficial class discussion as well.

The field of federal Indian law and policy is vast and no single text can cover every last facet. While the subject matter of the chapters is broad, as is the content within them, each chapter is also designed to be concise and accessible. Each primary source has been edited to focus on no more than one or two main ideas and each chapter elucidates a few key themes within the subject matter.

Despite this text's streamlined nature, readers of *Federal Indian Law & Policy: An Introduction* will gain a greater knowledge of a critical component of Native America. Suggested readings are provided for those who wish to explore further and every reader is encouraged to remember that the materials in this text are a beginning, not an end. Students pursuing other avenues of Indian Studies scholarship or who are simply curious about Native America will better understand their own area of study, the world in which we live, and perhaps even themselves. Students who wish to further pursue the subject matter, in law school or elsewhere, will have an invaluable foundation from which to begin their own scholarly or professional interests.

---

[1]   Felix S. Cohen, "The Erosion of Indian Rights, 1950–53: A Case Study in Bureaucracy," 62 Yale Law Journal 348, 390 (1953).

The Historical Foundations

CHAPTER 1

Pre-USA Foundations

The roots of American federal Indian law and policy are found in the earliest origins of what we now call international law. Starting in the Middle Ages through the Renaissance, the colonial empires of Europe began to spread across the globe in an effort to expand their empires. With each new voyage the whole world changed quickly and irrevocably, and the colonial powers needed not only rules to govern activities and conflicts between each other as they raced to lands they had previously not encountered, but also rules and methods for contemplating the Indigenous peoples of the lands that they "discovered."

There were already centuries of colonialism-fueled exploration, interaction, trade, warfare, and other experiences in the Americas and elsewhere around the globe before there was a United States. There are many fine books, articles, and other scholarly works that examine the colonial history of the North American continent prior to the American Revolution and that history's continuing legacy. While this text cannot do justice to the many aspects of this lengthy and complex history, a brief examination of the legal and political legacy of two of the most influential colonial forces on the North American continent—the Spanish and English—will yield a few crucial points necessary for beginning to understand federal Indian law and policy as the United States developed into its own and into the present day.

The law was an indispensable tool to the process of colonization. Rapidly developing law and legal theory offered rationales for the incursions into the lands of Indigenous peoples across the globe, and the legacy of this intellectual and legal groundwork remains central to the relationship between the colonizers and colonized today. Simply put, colonizing powers created law to justify their activities to themselves and to others.

One of the many unfortunate consequences of this colonial legal legacy has been the obscuring of Indigenous legal traditions. Indigenous peoples, in the Americas as well as elsewhere around the globe, were regularly categorized by colonial powers as inferior, savage, and without governance, religion, and other aspects of civilized life in an effort to justify the law and legal theory that the colonial powers were creating. Yet, Indigenous peoples very much had their own structures, rules, societies, methods of dispute resolution, and ways of understanding the world in which they lived and relationships that they maintained. In short, pre-contact Indigenous peoples had their own law.

This chapter will demonstrate. . .

• *The legacy of Spanish colonialism*

• *The legacy of English colonialism*

• *The existence of pre-contact Native governmental systems*

SPANISH COLONIALISM

The origins of Western conceptions of non-Western peoples can be traced back centuries before Christopher Columbus's voyages to the "New World." Nonetheless, Columbus's exploration beginning in the late fifteenth century moved Spain to the forefront of colonization in the Americas and sparked the development of a body of Spanish law to reconcile with the presence of the inhabitants of the Americas. Spain's legal developments concerning the peoples of the Americas in this era have served as the foundation for subsequent discussions even into the present day about the rights of Indigenous peoples around the world.

Sailing under the support of the Spanish crown, the Italian sailor Christopher Columbus "discovered" land in North America in October of 1492 after five weeks at sea. Columbus brought what was already a long-developing Western conception of non-Europeans when he set foot on land in what is now the Bahamas. He noted what he considered the simple and easily malleable nature of the Indigenous peoples that he met. As you read this excerpt from the journal of his first voyage, ask yourself what Columbus's description about his first encounters with Indigenous North Americans reveals about his perspective about non-Western peoples. What are the motivations for engaging in his endeavor? What potential outcomes does he envision for Indigenous peoples?

JOURNAL OF CHRISTOPHER COLUMBUS (DURING HIS FIRST VOYAGE)[1]

"I . . . gave to some of them red caps, and glass beads to put round their necks, and many other things of little value, which gave them great pleasure, and made them so much our friends that it was a marvel to see. They afterward came to the ship's boats where we were, swimming and bringing us parrots, cotton threads in skeins, darts, and many other things. . . . It appeared to me to be a race of people very poor in everything. They go naked as when their mothers bore them, and so do the women. . . . They are very well made, with very handsome bodies, and very good countenances. Their hair is short and coarse, almost like the hairs of a horse's tail. They wear the hairs brought down to the eyebrows, except a few locks behind, which they wear long and never cut. . . . They neither carry nor know anything of arms, for I showed them swords, and they took them by the blade and cut themselves through ignorance. . . . They should be good servants and intelligent, for I observed that they quickly took in what was said to them, and I believe that they would easily be made Christians, as it appeared to me that they had no religion. I, our Lord being pleased, will take hence, at the time of my departure, six natives for your Highness, that they may learn to speak."

Columbus's description of this early encounter is emblematic of two key characteristics of the colonial period, for Spain and for other colonial powers as well. First, the earliest explorers, and later colonists, were interested in exploiting the resources of the New World, including Indigenous peoples themselves. This is most obvious in Columbus's plan to "take" six of the Arawak people that he encountered with him back to Spain, clearly without any consultation or consent from those individuals or the community. Although more subtle, Columbus's repeated statements on value—such as stating that "things of little value" gave the Arawak "great pleasure" and that the Arawak were "very poor in everything"— also speak to a perspective that was focused on measuring everything, including people, in terms of their potential as resources as determined by Western markets and standards.

The second characteristic that the journal excerpt reveals is a description of Native peoples that is both contradictory and consistent at the same time. At first blush, the journal seems to offer a perplexing mix of descriptions of Native peoples. On one hand, Columbus described the Arawak in negative terms—they did not know the value of the gifts that were being exchanged, they were "very poor in everything," and they were ignorant enough to grab swords by the blade.

On the other hand, Columbus describes them in positive terms—they were generous, they were "very well made" with "handsome bodies" and "very good countenances" and they were "intelligent."

These types of contradictory descriptions became commonplace among Europeans writing about Indigenous populations. Indigenous peoples were either "noble"—generous, brave, one with nature, and so on—or "ignoble"—fierce, warlike, untrustworthy and so on. Many modern scholars have noted that European writings during this period (and well after this period) were often not particularly accurate descriptions of real Indigenous peoples, but rather vehicles for writers to advance their own agenda. For example, writers who sought to critique their own societies might point to the "noble" Indians who were supposedly more in touch with their environment and led simpler, happier lives, while writers who sought to justify the acquisition of Indigenous lands might point to the "ignoble" Indians to explain the seeming necessity of the use of force against them.

Whether "noble" or "ignoble," European descriptions of Native peoples shared one common characteristic: Indigenous peoples were regarded as simpler and less advanced than the supposedly more civilized peoples who were commentating upon them. In essence, they were either noble savages or ignoble savages, but they were certainly savages. This characteristic of European writing helps to explain the seeming contradiction in Columbus's description. It is easier to contemplate what looks like a set of oppositions if one conceptualizes it less as a rumination on a different culture of human beings and more as a cataloging of livestock. Columbus was able to reconcile these differing statements in the same way one might recognize the intelligence of a horse or dog without conceding the animal as an equal.

In response to the opportunities that it saw in the wake of Columbus's voyages, the Spanish crown sent *conquistadors*—military leaders tasked with the process of colonization—to the Americas on behalf of the crown to claim lands and resources for Spain. Aided by soldiers, missionaries, and disease that decimated Indigenous populations, the *conquistadors* often violently exerted authority over peoples and territories. Shortly after Columbus's arrival, Spain began profiting from the fruits of the Americas.

Despite the immediate desire and rush to colonize, these early explorations in the New World created a number of vexing questions for Spain: On what authority could the Spanish crown claim right to the lands and resources of the New World? What rights, if any, did the Indigenous inhabitants of the Americas hold? What process, if any, should Spanish colonizers engage in to legitimize their activities in the Americas to itself and to the rest of Christendom? Although a dominant force in global politics, Spain was not content to exhume resources from the Americas through force alone. Rather, it sought to justify its efforts at colonization through legal and moral means.

The earliest efforts at establishing a legal basis for the colonization of the Americas resulted in the *Requerimiento*. Developed in 1513, the *Requerimiento* formalized a process to assert Spanish authority in the New World. *Conquistadors* were required to read the *Requerimiento* to Indigenous peoples before engaging in any forceful action towards colonization. The *Requerimiento* offered, in theory, an Indigenous group the opportunity to follow the law as established by Western Christendom. As you read this excerpt from the *Requerimiento*, ask yourself what are the justifications that Spain sets forth for claiming a legal right to Indigenous territory. What obligations does the *Requerimiento* seek to place on Indigenous peoples? What are the consequences of non-compliance for Indigenous peoples?

THE *REQUERIMIENTO*[2]

"On the part of the King, Don Fernando, and of Doña Juana I, his daughter, Queen of Castille and León, subduers of the barbarous nations, we their servants notify and make known to you, as best we can, that the Lord our God, Living and Eternal, created the Heaven and the Earth, and one man and one woman, of whom you and we, all the men of the world, were and are descendants, and all those who come after us. But, on account of the multitude which has sprung from this man and woman in the five thousand years since the world was created, it was necessary that some men should go one way and some another, and that they should be divided into many kingdoms and provinces, for in one alone they could not be sustained.

Of all these nations God our Lord gave charge to one man. . . . And he commanded him to place his seat in Rome, as the spot most fitting to rule the world from; but also he permitted him to have his seat in any other part of the world, and to judge and govern all Christians, Moors, Jews, Gentiles, and all other sects. This man was called Pope. . . .

One of these [Popes] . . . made donation of these isles . . . to the aforesaid King and Queen and to their successors, our lords, with all that there are in these territories, as is contained in certain writings which passed upon the subject as aforesaid, which you can see if you wish.

. . . Wherefore, as best we can, we ask and require you that you consider what we have said to you, and that you take the time that shall be necessary to understand and deliberate upon it, and that you acknowledge the Church as the Ruler and Superior of the whole world, and the high priest called Pope, and in his name the King and Queen Doña Juana our lords, in his place, as superiors and lords and kings of these islands . . . by virtue of the said donation, and that you consent and give place that these religious fathers should declare and preach to you the aforesaid.

If you do so, you will do well, and that which you are obliged to do to their Highnesses, and we in their name shall receive you in all love and charity, and shall leave you your wives, and your children, and your lands, free without servitude, that you may do with them and with yourselves freely that which you like and think best, and they shall not compel you to turn Christians, unless you yourselves, when informed of the truth, should wish to be converted to our Holy Catholic Faith, as almost all the inhabitants of the rest of the islands have done. And, besides this, their Highnesses award you many privileges and exemptions and will grant you many benefits.

But, if you do not do this, and maliciously make delay in it, I certify to you that, with the help of God, we shall powerfully enter into your country, and shall make war against you in all ways and manners that we can, and shall subject you to the yoke and obedience of the Church and of their Highnesses; we shall take you and your wives and your children, and shall make slaves of them, and as such shall sell and dispose of them as their Highnesses may command; and we shall take away your goods, and shall do you all the mischief and damage that we can, as to vassals who do not obey, and refuse to receive their lord, and resist and contradict him; and we protest that the deaths and losses which shall accrue from this are your fault, and not that of their Highnesses, or ours, nor of these cavaliers who come with us. And that we have said this to you and made this Requisition, we request the notary here present to give us his testimony in writing, and we ask the rest who are present that they should be witnesses of this Requisition."

The *Requerimiento* was problematic on a number of levels and a classic example of form over function. Its major problem is also its most obvious: the document was written and spoken in Spanish, a language of which newly encountered Indigenous peoples would have had no knowledge. Additionally, even if the *Requerimiento* had been presented in a language that was intelligible to newly encountered Indigenous peoples, it concerned social and religious precepts and conceptions that were also foreign to Indigenous groups. Despite these problems, or perhaps because of them, the actual process of reading the

Requerimiento to Indigenous peoples was lax at best. When it was dutifully read (which was not always the case), it was often done so under conditions that fulfilled the letter of the law while violating its spirit. Despite its problematic nature, the *Requerimiento* was instrumental in justifying the early efforts at Spanish colonization.

Aided in great part by diseases that the Indigenous populations had yet to encounter and which decimated their populations, Spanish colonists were often (though not always) able exert force over Native populations and to claim lands throughout the Americas. As a result of these efforts, Spanish authorities instituted the *encomienda* system in the early 1500s. Whereas the *Requerimiento* offered a justification for the invasion of Indigenous lands, the *encomienda* system sought to justify the continued presence of the colonizers. Under the *encomienda* system Spanish landholders in the Americas, or *encomenderos*, were placed in charge of a number of Indigenous peoples and tasked with providing those under their charge with wages for their work, Christianity, and other aspects of Spanish civilization. In return, the *encomenderos* received labor and resources—or tribute—from their Native charges. Conceptualized as a system of *quid pro quo* in which each side profited equally, the practice on the ground was usually brutal and exploitative and the Native charges were generally regarded as slaves by the *encomenderos*.

Although Spain had adopted the *Requerimiento* and the *encomienda* system to manage its legal and moral duties to the Indigenous peoples in the Americas, debate about the rights of the inhabitants of the Americas and the responsibilities of the Spanish monarchs and *conquistadors* toward them continued throughout the sixteenth century. Perhaps the most influential scholar of this era was Franciscus (or Francisco) de Victoria, a Dominican theologian.

Regarded by many as the "father of international law," Victoria's lectures on the Indigenous peoples of the New World as well as other subject matter have contributed to his status as a critical thinker in the early colonial period whose influence continues to be felt today. He delivered his lecture, "On the Indians Lately Discovered," in 1532, in which he sought to establish a moral and legal basis for interacting with the people of the New World. More specifically, he sought to outline what rights Indigenous peoples had that were to be respected by Spain and other colonial powers and under what circumstances Spain could claim Indigenous lands and make war against Indigenous peoples. Victoria used a number of sources to ground his argument, including the Bible and the works of Aristotle, Thomas Aquinas, Pope Innocent IV, as well as other prominent philosophers who had contemplated human rights. As you read, consider both what limitations and what opportunities Victoria sought to establish for colonial engagement in the New World. Also consider what sorts of concerns that Victoria might have had in mind as he sought to bring order and lawfulness to a rapidly changing world.

ON THE INDIANS LATELY DISCOVERED[3]
Francisco de Victoria

. . . The whole of this controversy and discussion was started on account of the aborigines of the New World, commonly called Indians, who came forty years ago into the power of the Spaniards, not having been previously known to our world.

. . . For, at first sight, when we see that the whole of the business has been carried on by men who are alike well-informed and upright, we may believe that everything has been done properly and justly. But then, when we hear of so many massacres, so many plunderings of otherwise innocent men, so many princes evicted from their possession and stripped of their rule, there is certainly ground for doubting whether this is rightly or wrongly done. . . .

* * *

. . . Returning now to our main topic . . . I ask first whether the aborigines in question were true owners in both private and public law before the arrival of the Spaniards. . . . Unless the contrary is shown, they must be treated as owners and not be disturbed in their possession unless cause be shown. . . .

. . . Now, some have maintained that grace is the title to dominion and consequently that sinners, at any rate those in mortal sin, have no dominion over anything. . . .

. . . I advance the proposition that mortal sin does not hinder civil dominion and true dominion. . . .

. . . Unbelief does not prevent anyone from being a true owner. . . .

. . . From the standpoint of the divine law a heretic does not lose the ownership of his property. . . .

From all this the conclusion follows that the barbarians in question can not be barred from being true owners, alike in public and in private law, by reason of the sin of disbelief or any other mortal sin, nor does such sin entitle Christians to seize their goods and lands. . . .

It remains to ask whether the Indians lacked ownership because of want of reason or unsoundness of mind. . . .

The Indian aborigines are not barred on this ground from the exercise of true dominion. This is proved from the fact that the true state of the case is that they are not of unsound mind, but have, according to their kind, the use of reason. . . . Accordingly, I for the most part attribute their seeming so unintelligent and stupid to a bad and barbarous upbringing, for even among ourselves we find many peasants who differ little from brutes. . . .

* * *

It being premised, then, that the Indian aborigines are or were true owners, it remains to inquire by what title the Spaniards could have come into possession of them and their country. . . .

Now there are seven titles, which might be alleged, but which are not adequate, and seven or eight others, which are just and legitimate. . . . [*Victoria details the inadequate titles.*]

* * *

I will now speak of the lawful and adequate titles whereby the Indians might have come under the sway of the Spaniards. (1) The first title to be named is that of natural society and fellowship. And hereon let my first conclusion be: (2) The Spaniards have a right to travel into the lands in question and to sojourn there, provided they do no harm to the natives, and the natives may not prevent them. . . .

Second proposition: The Spaniards may lawfully carry on trade among the native Indians, so long as they do no harm to their country. . . . Neither may the native princes hinder their subjects from carrying on trade with the Spanish; nor, on the other hand, may the princes of Spain prevent commerce with the natives. . . .

Third proposition: If there are among the Indians any things which are treated as common both to citizens and to strangers, the Indians may not prevent the Spaniards from a communication and participation in them. . . . Inasmuch as things that belong to nobody are acquired by the first occupant according to the law of nations, it follows that if there be in the earth gold or in the sea pearls on in a river anything else which is not appropriated by the law of nations those will vest in the first occupant, just as the fish in the sea do. . . .

Fourth proposition: If children of any Spaniard be born there and they wish to acquire citizenship, it seems they can not be barred either from citizenship or from the advantages enjoyed by other citizens. . . .

Fifth proposition: If the Indian natives wish to prevent the Spaniards from enjoying any of their above-named rights under the law of nations . . . the Spaniards ought in the first place to use reason and persuasion in order to remove scandal. . . . But if, after this recourse to reason, the barbarians decline to agree and propose to use force, the Spaniards can defend themselves and do all that consists with their own safety, it being lawful to repel force by force. And not only so, but, if safety can not otherwise be had, they may build fortresses and defensive works, and, if they have sustained a wrong, they may follow it up with war on the authorization of their sovereign and may avail themselves of the other rights of war. . . .

It is, however, to be noted that the native being timid by nature and in other respects dull and stupid, however much the Spaniards may desire to remove their fears and reassure them with regard to peaceful dealings with each other, they may very excusably continue afraid at the sight of men strange in garb and armed and much more powerful then themselves. And therefore, if, under the influence of these fears, they unite their efforts to drive out the Spaniards or even to slay them, the Spaniards might, indeed, defend themselves but within the limits of permissible self-protection, and it would not be right for them to enforce against the natives any of the other rights of war. . . . Accordingly, the Spaniards ought to defend themselves, but so far as possible with the least damage to the natives, the war being a purely defensive one.

There is no inconsistency, indeed, in holding the war to be a just war on both sides, seeing that on one side there is right and on the other side there is invincible ignorance. . . .

Sixth proposition: If after recourse to all other measures, the Spaniards are unable to obtain safety as regards the native Indians, save by seizing their cities and reducing them to subjection, they may lawfully proceed to these extremities. . . .

Seventh proposition: If, after the Spaniards have used all diligence, both in deed and in word, to show that nothing will come from them to interfere with the peace and well-being of the aborigines, the latter nevertheless persist in their hostility and do their best to destroy the Spaniards, then they can make war on the Indians, no longer as on innocent folk, but as against forsworn enemies, and may enforce against them all the rights of war. . . .

Another possible title is by way of propagation of Christianity. In this connection let my first proposition be: Christians have a right to preach and declare the Gospel in barbarian lands. . . . Second proposition: Although this is a task common and permitted to all, yet the Pope might entrust it to the Spaniards and forbid it to all others. . . . Third proposition: If the Indians allow the Spaniards freely and without hindrance to preach the Gospel, then whether they do or do not receive the faith, this furnishes no lawful ground for making war on them and seizing in any other way their lands. . . . Fourth proposition: If the Indians—whether it be their lords or the populace—prevent the Spaniards from freely preaching the Gospel, the Spaniards, after first reasoning with them in order to remove scandal, may preach it despite their unwillingness and devote themselves to the conversion of the people in question, and if need be they may then accept or even make war, until they succeed in obtaining facilities and safety from preaching the Gospel. . . .

Another title there may be. . . If any of the native converts to Christianity be subjected to force or fear by their princes in order to make them return to idolatry, this would justify the Spaniards, should other methods fail, in making war and in compelling the barbarians by force to stop such misconduct. . . .

Another possible title is the following: Suppose a large part of the Indians were converted to Christianity . . . so long as they really were Christians, the pope might for a reasonable cause, either with or without a request from them, give them a Christian sovereign and depose their other unbelieving rulers. . . .

Another possible title is founded either on the tyranny of those who bear rule among the aborigines of America or on the tyrannical laws which work wrong to innocent folk there, such as that which allows the sacrifice of innocent people or the killing in other ways of uncondemned people for cannibalistic purposes. I assert also that without the Pope's authority the Spaniards can stop all such nefarious usages and ritual among the aborigines, being entitled to rescue innocent people from an unjust death. . . .

Another possible title is by true and voluntary choice, as if the Indians, aware alike of the prudent administration and the humanity of the Spaniards, were of their own motion, both rulers and ruled, to accept the King of Spain as their sovereign. . . .

Another title may be found in the cause of allies and friends. For as the Indians themselves sometimes wage lawful wars with one another and the side which has suffered a wrong has the right to make war, they might summon the Spaniards to help and share the rewards of victory with them. . . .

There is another title which can indeed not be asserted, but brought up for discussion, and some think it is a lawful one. I dare not affirm it at all, nor do I entirely condemn it. It is this: Although the aborigines in question are (as

> has been said above) not wholly unintelligent, yet they are little short of that condition, and so are unfit to found or administer a lawful state up to the standard required by human and civil claims. Accordingly they have no proper laws nor magistrates, and are not even capable of controlling their family affairs. . . . It might, therefore, be maintained that in their own interests the sovereigns of Spain might undertake the administration of their country, providing them with prefects and governors for their towns, and might even give them new lords, so long as this was clearly for their benefit.

Victoria helped to establish the template used by Western colonizers for wrestling with the competing interests that have come to define federal Indian law and policy in the present day. On one hand, Victoria made a powerful argument on behalf of what we now call tribal sovereignty and Indigenous rights. While careful in his criticism, Victoria nonetheless was disturbed by the reports of the actions of Spanish colonizers and gave serious contemplation to the rights of Indigenous peoples. Victoria concluded that not only did Indigenous peoples have rights that needed to be respected, but that many of the arguments in favor of the use of Spanish force to overtake Indigenous peoples and lands were invalid. For example, Indigenous peoples maintained their sovereignty despite not practicing Christianity.

On the other hand, again establishing a template that others would follow, Victoria argued that the rights of Indigenous peoples were limited by Western epistemologies that made little, if any, sense in the Indigenous context. For example, Victoria argued that Spanish colonizers were justified in using force if Indigenous peoples refused to engage in trade, limited Spanish access to "things which are treated as common both to citizens and to strangers" such as gold and pearls, or denied the Spanish the authority to preach Christianity. While Victoria attempted to soften the sharper edges of his proclamations, they nonetheless required that Indigenous peoples open their land, resources, and even themselves to the colonizers for the preferred ends of the colonizers. Failure to do so would eventually lead to the justified use of force against Indigenous peoples. In this respect, Victoria's argument does little to protect Indigenous rights. As such, it is fair to ask whether, much like the *Requerimiento*, Victoria's argument did anything more than establish a legally permissible path to continue the exploitation of the New World.

Victoria's lectures went far in establishing the groundwork for international and colonial law. Nonetheless, serious debate about the legal rights of Indigenous peoples—as well as the very nature of their humanity—continued. The most famous of example of the enduring discourse was the Valladolid Debate of 1550 between Juan Ginés de Sepúlveda and Bartolomé de las Casas. Sepúlveda, a theologian who had never been to the Americas, argued that Spanish military action in the Americas was just because the Indigenous peoples of the Americas were, by their nature, slaves who committed barbarous acts. As a consequence, it was Spain's right to conquer them and their lands. Las Casas, a Dominican friar who had been to the Americas and seen many atrocities committed against Indigenous peoples, argued that they were free beings who were capable of rationality and conversion to Christianity and against whom war could not be declared without a true just cause and respect for their rights. Although many historians believe that there was no clear winner in the debate, what is clear are the parameters of this and other debates of the time: Indigenous peoples on one side were sub-human savages whose very nature and actions permitted, and often required, brute military force and conquest of their lands; on the other side, while nonetheless savage and ignorant, Indigenous peoples were capable of rational thought and decisions and their rights in international law required respect. More succinctly, they were either noble savages or ignoble savages, with important consequences flowing from either conclusion.

The repercussions of Spanish colonialism in the New World cannot be understated. Spain left both a lasting legacy and a legal regime that continues to shape our geography, identity, and federal Indian law and policy to this day.

ENGLISH COLONIALISM

By the time that England began establishing a serious colonial presence in North America in the 1600s, a pattern of diplomacy with Indigenous peoples had already emerged. While European subjects still regularly regarded Indigenous peoples as savage and inferior to themselves, they nonetheless increasingly recognized that Indigenous peoples held at least some rights and sovereignty over their territories. This sovereignty needed to be respected, even if, for some Europeans, it was more of a sign of acquiescence to the newly developing international law than an appreciation for Indigenous sovereignty.

Treaties between tribal nations and European colonizers increasingly became a central tool for diplomacy on the North American continent (for example, the Pilgrims negotiated a treaty in 1621 with the local Wampanoags). Although English and other European commentators would often describe European claims to land in grandiose and all-encompassing terms—which left little in the way of tribal rights—the reality on the ground did not support these claims. Nor did the actions of the colonies reflect a true belief that they held a superior right to tribal lands than Indigenous peoples. European colonists needed treaties with tribal nations to protect themselves in an often-hostile environment against other colonial powers and unfriendly tribal nations. The English, in particular, desired treaties as they sought to acquire land for colonial settlements. Tribal nations, for their part, agreed to treaties to establish relations with useful trade partners and to create alliances against their own enemies.

Early treaties with the English and other European colonists regularly reflected these many interests. In addition, the process by which treaties were made also revealed a developing system of diplomacy that was neither dictated exclusively by any one side nor by a uniform standard of procedure, but was rather a product of negotiation and circumstance itself. As you read the following early colonial treaty, consider the goals that each side is seeking to achieve. What do the English want? What do the Wabanakis want? How does this document reflect the power relations between the parties to the treaty and the world in which they lived? How does the fact that it was written in English alter how we might read it?

TREATY BETWEEN THE ENGLISH AND WABANAKI[4]
September 8–19, 1685

Articles of peace agreed upon the eight day of September, in the year of our Lord, 1685, between the subjects of his majesty, king James the second, inhabiting the provinces of New-Hampshire and Maine, and the Indians inhabiting the said provinces.

It is agreed there shall be for the future, a lasting peace, friendship, and kindness, between the English and the Indians, and that no injury shall be offered by the one to the other.

That if any Englishman doth any injury to an Indian, upon complaint made to any justice of the peace, the Englishman shall be punished, and the Indian shall have present satisfaction made him. And if any Indian doth an injury to the English, or threaten to do any injury, the sagamore to whom that Indian doth belong, shall punish him in presence of one of the king's justices of the peace.

That if any other Indian shall design any mischief or harm to the English, the Indians inhabiting the aforesaid provinces shall give present notice thereof to the English, and shall assist the English.

That so long as the aforesaid Indians shall continue in friendship with the English, they shall be protected against the Mohawks, or any others, and may freely and peaceably set down by the English near any their plantations.

[*There are both English and Native signatures*]

We whose names are hereunto written, do freely consent and engage to comply and perform the within written articles, as our neighbors have done, and do further engage as followeth:

Lastly, That the Indians shall not at any time hereafter remove from any of the English plantations, with their wives and children, before they have give fair and timely notice thereof, unto the English, from whence they do so remove; and in case the said Indians shall remove with their wives and children, without such fair and timely notice given to the English, that then it shall be taken pro confesso that the Indians do intend and design war with the English, and do thereby declare that the peace is broken; and it shall and may be lawful to and for the English, or any on their behalfs, to apprehend said Indians, with their wives and children, and to use acts of hostility against them, until the sagamores shall make full satisfaction for all charge and damage that may arise thereby.

[*There are additional English and Native signatures*]

The characteristics of this treaty, including its form, are both common for the time and reveal the stakes of diplomacy for both the English and Wabanaki. The treaty began with a promise from both sides to punish wrongdoers in their own community if they commit bad acts against those of the other community. In essence, both the English and the Wabanaki committed to being good neighbors as they attempted to forge a shared living space. While those sections of the treaty were inward-looking, the next sections were outward-looking. Both communities pledged to protect each other against outsiders, particularly the Mohawks, again in an effort to preserve a shared living space.

After some signatures, there is additional language stating that Wabanakis who move from the shared living space without notice will be treated as hostiles. The nature of this language, as well as its placement after previous signatures, also testifies to some critical aspects of diplomacy in this period and for the English and Wabanaki in particular. Both the Wabanaki and the English were desirous of allies, but perhaps most particularly the English. Not knowing where their allies were at a given time was frightening enough to the English to alert their allies that they could be regarded as hostile. In short, the English felt that they were in a more precarious position than the Wabanaki. In addition, diplomacy was fluid and needed to respond to changing circumstances. The placement of this additional language as well as the additional signatures makes clear that it was negotiated after the main body of the treaty. Conversations continued and there was enough desire within both parties to quickly amend the document.

Treaty making was not one-sided during this period, nor was it uniform or unalterable. Rather, it was the product of communities coming together and looking out for themselves and each other. It was not the singular imposition of a colonial force, but the negotiation between parties that had both much to gain and much to lose during the early colonial era. Although the tone and substance of treaties would gradually change once the United States became the dominant military force on the North American continent, their history, particularly with the English, reveals the necessity of diplomacy for the colonizers.

NATIVE GOVERNANCE

While European colonists routinely described Indigenous peoples as savage and uncivilized, tribal nations had very sophisticated modes of government, law, and self-regulation prior to and after contact. Generally dissimilar to European models and often not obvious to European observers, tribal methods of governance functioned well for the communities that they served. However, like European nations, tribal nations had rules and structures that members of the nations understood, generally abided by, and passed down through generations. Also like European (and Asian and African) nations, there was and is much diversity within Native America and it is impossible to identify one system or method that accurately or appropriately describes the governance structure of all tribal nations. Each tribal grouping expressed its sovereignty in its own way; although both individual autonomy and familial and clan connections were often highly regarded and respected among many tribal nations.

Perhaps the most famous example of Native governance during the colonial era was the Haudenosaunee, also known as the Iroquois Confederacy. Already hundreds of years old prior to sustained contact with European colonists, the Haudenosaunee originally consisted of five powerful northeastern tribal nations centered near the eastern Great Lakes—the Mohawk, Onondaga, Oneida, Seneca, and Cayuga. A sixth nation, the Tuscarora, joined later. Iroquois historical sources explain that the Haudenosaunee was formed to prevent the constant warfare among the constituent nations and to provide protection against other common enemies. Within the Haudenosaunee, each nation maintained its autonomy concerning internal affairs. However, they came together in council on matters concerning the greater whole, with each nation playing a different and unique role within the confederacy. Some scholars have argued that the Haudenosaunee influenced the American founding fathers as they sought to establish a new political order in the wake of the American Revolution.

The Haudenosaunee was organized under the Gayanashagowa, or the Great Binding Law. Iroquois historical sources explain that an unusually powerful man, Dekanahwideh, led the five nations together and established the Iroquois Confederacy under the Great Binding Law. The Gayanashagowa created a council in which each of the five nations had a responsibility. The Onondaga representatives organized the council. When there was a subject of debate it was first discussed among the representatives of the "Older Brothers"—the Mohawk and the Seneca. Then the subject passed to the representatives of the "Younger Brothers"—the Oneida and Cayuga. If consensus was not reached between the Older Brothers and Younger Brothers, the Onondaga sought to moderate a compromise. Discussion continued until a consensus was reached.

Originally promulgated through oral tradition and wampum beads, the Gayanashagowa was eventually written and translated into English. In this excerpt the representatives of the tribal nation are referred to as "lords." In 1900 several prominent members of the Haudenosaunee organized to produce a tribally-centered English language version of the Gayanashagowa. As you read this excerpt of the Gayanashagowa, ask yourself what similarities and differences you see to the American model of government. Also consider why the English and the Wabanaki, both neighbors to the powerful Iroquois confederacy and the subject of the previous excerpt, might have been willing to engage in a treaty with each other.

GAYANASHAGOWA, THE GREAT BINDING LAW[5]

Then Dekanahwideh again said: "We have completed the Confederation of the Five Nations, now therefore it shall be that hereafter the lords who shall be appointed in the future to fill vacancies. . . .

Then Dekanahwideh further added: "I now transfer and set over to the women who have the lordships' title vested in them, that they shall in the future have the power to appoint the successors from time to time to fill vacancies caused by death or removals from whatever cause."

* * *

Then Dekanahwideh further said: "The lords have unanimously decided to spread before you on the ground this great white wampum belt Ska-no-dah-ken-rah-ko-wah and Ka-yah-ne-ren-ko-wah, which respectfully signify purity and great peace, and the lords have also laid before you this great wing, Skaweh-yeh-she-ko-wah, and whenever any dust or stain of any description falls upon the great belt of white wampum, then you shall take this great wing and sweep it clean." (Dust or stain means evil of any description which might have a tendency to cause trouble in the Confederate Council.)

Then Dekanahwideh said: "The lords of this confederacy have unanimously decided to lay by you this rod (Ska-nah-ka-res) and whenever you see any creeping thing which might have a tendency to harm our grandchildren or see a thing creeping toward the great white wampum belt (meaning the Great Peace), then you shall take this rod and pry it away with it, and if you and your colleagues fail to pry the creeping, evil thing out, you shall then call out loudly that all the Confederate Nations may hear and they will come immediately to your assistance."

Then Dekanahwideh said: "Now you, the lords of the several Confederate Nations, shall divide yourselves and sit on opposite sides of the council fire as follows: [*The division is described prior to this excerpt.*]

Then Dekanahwideh said: "We have now completed the system for our Confederate Council."

Then Dekanahwideh further said: "We now, each nation, shall adopt all the rules and regulations governing the Confederate Council which we have here made and we shall apply them to all our respective settlements and thereby we shall carry out the principles set forth in the message of Good Tidings and Peace and Power, and in dealing with the affairs of our people of the various dominions, thus we shall secure to them contentment and happiness."

* * *

Then Dekanahwideh said: "We have now completed arranging the system of our local councils and we shall hold our annual Confederate Council at the settlement of Thadodahho, the capitol or seat of government of the Five Nations' Confederacy."

Dekanahwideh said: "Now I and you lords of the Confederate Nations shall plant a tree Ska-renj-heh-se-go-wah (meaning a tall and mighty tree) and we shall call it Jo-ne-rak-deh-ke-wah (the tree of the great long leaves).

Now this tree which we have planted shall shoot forth four great, long, white roots (Jo-doh-ra-ken-rah-ko-wah). These great, long, white roots shall shoot forth one to the north and one to the south and one to the east and one to the west, and we shall place on the top of it Oh-don-yonh (an eagle) which has great power of long vision, and we shall transact all our business beneath the shade of this great tree. . . . The nations of the earth shall see it and shall accept and follow the roots and shall follow them to the tree and when they arrive here you shall receive them and shall seat them in the midst of your confederacy. The object of placing an eagle on the top of the great, tall tree is that it may watch the roots which extend to the north and to the south and to the east and to the west, and whose duty shall be to discover if any evil is approaching your confederacy, and he shall scream loudly and give the alarm and all the nations of the confederacy at once shall heed the alarm and come to the rescue."

Then Dekanahwideh again said: We shall now combine our individual power into one great power which is this confederacy and we shall therefore symbolize the union of these powers by each nation contributing one arrow, which we shall tie up together in a bundle which, when it is made and completely tied together, no one can bend or break. . . .

Then Dekanahwideh continued his address and said: We shall tie this bundle of arrows together with deer sinew which is strong, durable and lasting and then also this institution shall be strong and unchangeable. This bundle of arrows signifies that all the lords and all the warriors and all the women of the confederacy have become united as one person."

* * *

Then Dekanahwideh said: "We have now completed our power so that we the Five Nations' Confederacy shall in the future have one body, one head, and one heart."

Then he (Dekanahwideh) further said: If any evil should befall us in the future, we shall stand or fall united as one man."

As noted above, some scholars have argued that the Gayanashagowa was a model for the U.S. Constitution. While this assertion remains controversial, it is nonetheless useful to compare the two, particularly the original U.S. Constitution that came into force in 1789. What similarities do they hold? What differences are there? What insights might be gained by reflecting on the fact that the Gayanashagowa is significantly older than the U.S. Constitution? Beyond a comparison to the U.S. Constitution, what other features distinguish the Gayanashagowa? What roles do men and women play?

While the Gayanashagowa is probably the most famous example of Native law and governance prior to contact, it was and is not an outlier. Tribal nations across the Americas had their own rules, governed themselves, proscribed roles for members of the community, made alliances with other peoples, and made war as well. In short, they behaved in some similar manners to their European counterparts as well as with other peoples around the globe.

SUGGESTED READINGS

- *Savage Anxieties: The Invention of Western Civilization.* Robert A. Williams, Jr. New York: Palgrave Macmillan, 2012.

- *The White Man's Indian.* Robert F. Berkhofer, Jr. New York: Vintage Books, 1979.

- "Spanish Indian Policies." Charles Gobson. In *Handbook of North American Indians, Vol. 4, History of Indian-White Relations.* Washington D.C.: Smithsonian Institution, 2001, 96–102.

- "British Colonial Indian Treaties." Dorothy v. Jones. In *Handbook of North American Indians, Vol. 4, History of Indian-White Relations.* Washington D.C.: Smithsonian Institution, 2001, 185–194.

---

[1] Christopher Columbus, *The Journal of Christopher Columbus (during his First Voyage, 1492–93): And Documents relating to the Voyages of John Cabot and Gaspar Corte Real,* trans. Clements R. Markham, Hakluyt Society, First Series, Volume 86 (Farnham, England: Ashgate, 2010), 37–38.

[2] This translation is from Arthur Helps, *The Spanish Conquest in America, vol. 1* (New York: John Lane, 1900), 264–67.

[3] Franciscus de Victoria, *De Indis et de Ivre Belli Relections,* trans. John Pawley Bate, ed. James Brown Scott (Washington: Carnegie Institution of Washington, 1917), 115–62.

[4] Daniel R. Mandell, ed., "Treaty, English and Wabanakis," in *Early American Indian Documents, Treaties, & Laws, 1607–1789, Vol. XX New England Treaties, North and West, 1650–1776* (Bethesda, MD: University Publications of America, 2003), 42.

[5] Arthur C. Parker, *The Constitution of the Five Nations* (Albany, NY: The University of the State of New York, 1916), 97–102.

CHAPTER 2

The Early Treaty Era

In the immediate wake of the American Revolution, the recently established United States was in a precarious position and the continuation of this new political endeavor was far from assured. The Revolution did not end English, French, and other colonial interests in North America, nor did it eliminate the substantial political and military threat that tribal nations posed. A fundamentally important and necessary part of the new United States of America's daunting project of establishing its own governing structure and place in the world was to formulate a diplomatic policy as it concerned Indigenous peoples.

As with its colonial brethren, the haughty rhetoric that the new United States of America often employed about Indigenous peoples did not always match the actions on the ground. While many individual Americans in this time period continued to discount or disregard the rights, abilities, and sovereignty of Indigenous peoples and nations, the fledgling United States as a whole had to acquiesce to the international order that, over the course of centuries, established a pattern of diplomatic relations with tribal nations. Even before the American Revolution was complete, the United States began negotiating treaties with tribal nations, often merely seeking neutrality with tribal nations as the insurrectionists fought against their motherland. For this reason, the initial period of federal Indian policy, lasting approximately from 1776–1830, will be described as the Early Treaty Era.

After the American Revolution the United States began seriously considering its relationship with tribal nations not just through treaties, but also through domestic legislation and through its courts. Unsurprisingly, land and commerce were often at the heart of the causes of concern for both the United States and for tribal nations. A study of some of the most important early developments— including the first major Indian law Supreme Court case—reveals a new country attempting to come to terms with its own existence and presence on the North

American continent and its relationship with North America's Indigenous peoples.

This chapter will demonstrate...

- *The roots of American policy toward Indigenous peoples*

- *Early developments in domestic law concerning Indigenous peoples*

- *The establishment of the Doctrine of Discovery*

DEVELOPING A POLICY

Much like the colonial powers that preceded the new country, the United States developed attitudes about the Indigenous inhabitants of the Americas that, in many respects, were contradictory. On the one hand, the new American elites, politicians, and everyday citizens regularly regarded Indigenous peoples as "savages" who were not as civilized or sophisticated as themselves. According to much of the rhetoric of the times, Indigenous peoples did not cultivate or use the land properly, were slavishly devoted to pagan and heathenish religious practices, and were simpleminded and often violent by nature. On the other hand, tribal nations were significant participants in the international realm. They were indispensable trading partners and they continued to sign treaties with not only the United States, but also with the other colonial powers that remained in North America. The United States had to respect the sovereignty of tribal nations or risk devastating economic, diplomatic, and military consequences.

As it moved forward on its own, the young country had a significant dilemma on its hands: How should the United States politically engage with Native peoples and nations? To what extent was exercising military might possible, reasonable, or desirable? To what extent could "savage" peoples and nations be expected or trusted to adhere to Western conceptions of diplomacy and civilization? To what extent were tribal nations allies and partners, and to what extent were they ready and willing to become adversaries? It is worthy of note that tribal nations were asking themselves similar questions about the new Americans as well.

As the American Revolutionary War came to a close the necessity for answers to these questions became even more immediate. No longer waging war with the British, many Americans began desirously eyeing tribal lands, with some individuals (and states) attempting to purchase or otherwise make claims to those lands, creating the potential for a diplomatic crisis for the young country. In this letter from George Washington to James Duane, a New York politician and Indian commissioner, the future first President lays out a policy for the United States. As you read it, ask yourself both what the policy is and why Washington is proposing it. How does it reflect the American understanding of Indigenous peoples and how law and policy will embody that understanding? What is desirable about the course of action that Washington lays out and how does it speak to Washington's conception of Native peoples?

LETTER FROM GEORGE WASHINGTON TO JAMES DUANE[1]
September 7, 1783

Sir,

I have carefully perused the Papers which you put into my hands relating to Indian Affairs. . . .

To suffer a wide extended Country to be overrun with Land jobbers—Speculators, and Monopolizers or even with scatter'd settlers is, in my opinion, inconsistent with that wisdom & policy which our true interest dictates, or that an enlightened People ought to adopt; and besides, is pregnant of disputes, both with the Savages, and among ourselves, the evils of which are easier, to be conceived than described; and for what? but to aggrandize a few avaricious Men to the prejudice of many and the embarrassment of Government. for the People engaged in these pursuits without contributing in the smallest degree to the support of Government, or considering themselves as amenable to its Laws, will involve it by their unrestrained conduct, in inextricable perplexities, and more than probable in a great deal of Bloodshed. . . .

My ideas therefore . . . are simply these.

First and as a preliminary, that all Prisoners of whatever age or Sex, among the Indians shall be delivered up.

That the Indians should be informed, that after a Contest of eight years for Sovereignty of the Country G: Britain has ceded all the Lands of the United States. . . .

. . . But as we prefer Peace to a state of Warfare, as we consider them as a deluded People; as we perswade ourselves that they are convinced, from experience, of their error in taking up the Hatchet against us, and that their true Interest and safety must now depend upon <u>our</u> friendship. . . . We will . . .

establish a boundary line between them and us beyond which we will <u>endeavor</u> to restrain our People from Hunting or Settling, and within which they shall not come, but for the purposes of Trading, Treating, or other business unexceptionable in its nature. . . .

. . . I have every reason to believe from my enquiries, and the information I have received, that they will not suffer their Country (if it was our policy to take it before we could settle it) to be wrested from them without another struggle. That they would compromise for a part of it I have very little doubt, and that it would be the cheapest way of coming at it, I have no doubt at all. . . .

Measures of this sort would not only obtain Peace from the Indians, but would, in my opinion, be the surest means of preserving it. . . .

. . . That it is the cheapest as well as the least distressing way of dealing with them, none who are acquainted with the Nature of Indian warfare, and has ever been at the trouble of estimating the expence of one, and comparing it with the cost of purchasing their Lands, will hesitate to acknowledge. . . .

. . . These People have a disposition towards us susceptible of favorable Impressions; but as no Arts will be left unattempted by the British to withdraw them from our Interest, the prest moment should be employed by us to fix them in it, or we may loose them forever; and with them, the advantages, or disadvantages consequent of the choice they may make. . . .

. . . for I repeat it, again, and I am clear in my opinion, that policy and oeconomy point very strongly to the expediency of being upon good terms with the Indians, and the propriety of purchasing their Lands in preference to attempting to drive them by force of arms out of their Country; which as we have already experienced is like driving the Wild Beasts of the Forest which will return us soon as the pursuit is at an end and fall perhaps on those that are left there; when the gradual extension of our Settlements will as certainly cause the Savage as the Wolf to retire; both being beasts of prey tho' they differ in shape. In a word there is nothing to be obtained by an Indian War but the Soil they live on and this can be had by purchase at less expence, and without that bloodshed, and those distresses which helpless Women and Children are made partakers of in all kinds of disputes with them.

As noted in Chapter 1, colonial writers regularly described Indigenous peoples as noble or ignoble savages (sometimes concurrently within a single writing, depending on the needs of the writer). Less diametric opposites and more two sides of the same coin, both the noble and ignoble savage were bound together and primarily identified by their uncivilized, wild nature. In announcing the philosophical underpinnings of the Early Treaty Era of federal Indian policy, Washington demonstrated both the deep hold that the conception of the savage held for colonizers and also how that conception shaped policy decisions.

In the abstract, Washington's desire to pursue peace instead of warfare is admirable. Again, in the abstract, his plan appears all the more reasonable as he argued that it was the most cost effective option. The alternative to war, Washington proposed, was to purchase tribal lands through treaties. Treaties held a number of benefits, particularly as opposed to warfare. They accomplished the same ends as attempting to seize the land by force without the violence of warfare and the threat of retaliatory action, they were more cost-effective than waging war, and they could be used to create necessary alliances, particularly since the British (and other colonial forces) were seeking those same alliances.

Yet, the basis for Washington's policy argument was that Indigenous peoples were "Wild Beasts of the Forest" who will resist efforts at removing them from their territories, return to their territories once the effort to repel them has concluded, and are likely to cause mayhem and worse for colonists that seek to inhabit their former territories. Moving beyond the abstract benefits of the Early Treaty Era to the specific rationales for it, Washington's letter raises troubling questions. The foundation for Washington's argument rests on conceptualizing Native peoples as "Savage as the Wolf," as they were "beasts of prey, tho' they differ in shape." Treaties were and are fundamental to Native conceptions of sovereignty. Washington's description of Native peoples calls into question his, and consequently the federal government's, commitment to these important documents. What obligation would one expect to have to honor in a treaty with a wolf? What does Washington's rationale for treaty making suggest about his vision for Native America? Did Washington anticipate that the treaties for which he was advocating would continue to endure? Is there a way to reconcile seemingly conflicting senses of purpose: the new United States needed to treat with tribal nations, but many Americans understood tribal peoples as savages and akin to wild animals. Do Washington's rationales hold any consequence for Native peoples and treaties today, or are they otherwise neutered or mitigated by the endurance of those treaties and tribal sovereignty?

DOMESTIC LAW

As a nation, the United States generally followed Washington's vision in the Early Treaty Era of federal policy, most often engaging in treaty making instead of military actions as it continued to expand westward. Diplomacy was conducted, for the most part, through many and varied treaty negotiations in which the United States acknowledged tribal sovereignty. The Early Treaty Era was hardly devoid of violence and conflict between the United States and the many tribal nations that existed in or near it. Nonetheless, both the United States and those tribal nations with which it treated acknowledged each other through diplomatic and political means, even if sometimes wearily so.

While treaties were the dominant method for engaging with tribal nations directly during this time, the United States still had to establish rules for itself and its own citizens concerning interactions with Indigenous peoples and nations. As Washington's letter suggests, unscrupulous Whites who were hungry for land, resources, or whatever else they believed they could take from Indigenous peoples could and often did cause troubles for the American government. Federal governmental officials often had to respond to two distinct but related constituencies. First, to tribal representatives who were angered by obtrusive actions and treaty violations committed by invading Whites. Second, to American citizens who complained when tribal officials exercised their own law against them or when tribal members committed acts in which Americans believed they had been wronged. Native/non-Native interaction caused much consternation and had the potential to lead to bigger and more serious consequences, and the early federal government was deeply concerned with managing the relationship between its citizens and tribal nations. Thus, the United States routinely sought to regulate itself and its own citizenry as it concerned relations with tribal nations. A healthy portion of national policy and legislation was committed to these affairs in the Early Treaty Era.

One of the most famous pieces of legislation in the Early Treaty Era was the Northwest Ordinance. Passed in 1787, the Northwest Ordinance paved the way for greater American westward expansion and settlement into territory west of New York State and north of the Ohio River. In so doing, the federal government also announced the tenor it sought to adopt towards tribal nations during this growth, stating in the legislation that, "The utmost good faith shall always be observed towards the Indians, their lands and property shall never be taken from them without their consent, and in their property, rights and liberty, they never shall be invaded or disturbed, unless in just and lawful wars authorized by Congress, but laws founded in justice and humanity shall from time to time be made, for preventing wrongs being done to them, and for preserving peace and friendship with them. . . ."[2]

The United States has not always lived up to this lofty ideal. But in the Early Treaty Era it did attempt to regulate interactions between American citizens and tribal nations and peoples in a number of ways, particularly with regard to trade. The most prominent legislative efforts in this area were a series of laws, each referred to as the Trade and Intercourse Act or Nonintercourse Act. The original Trade and Intercourse Act was passed in 1790 and included a sunset provision which gave the law a life of two years. The law proved to be important enough that the federal government continued to pass revised versions in 1793, 1796, 1799, 1802, and 1834 before removing the sunset provision and making it permanent. Today portions of the original law and its revisions still exist in different places in the U.S. Code, although for the purposes of this chapter it is prudent to examine the excerpt as a historical document rather than a current statement of the law. As you read the excerpt from the first Trade and Intercourse Act, ask yourself what the law does. What might be the motivations behind the law? To whom does the law apply?

AN ACT TO REGULATE TRADE AND INTERCOURSE WITH THE INDIAN TRIBES

1 Stat. 137, July 22, 1790

SECTION 1. *Be it enacted by the Senate and House of Representatives of the United States of America in Congress assembled,* That no person shall be permitted to carry on any trade or intercourse with the Indian tribes, without a license for that purpose under the hand and seal of the superintendent of the department, or of such other person as the President of the United States shall appoint for that purpose; which superintendent, or other person so appointed, shall, on application, issue such license to any proper person, who shall enter into bond with one or more sureties, approved of by the superintendent, or person issuing such license, or by the President of the United States, in the penal sum of one thousand dollars, payable to the President of the United States for the time being, for the use of the United States, conditioned for the true and faithful observance of such rules, regulations and restrictions, as now are, or hereafter shall be made for the government of trade and intercourse with the Indian tribes. The said superintendents, and persons by them licensed as aforesaid, shall be governed in all things touching the said trade and intercourse, by such rules and regulations as the President shall prescribe. And no other person shall be permitted to carry on any trade or intercourse with the Indians without such license as aforesaid No license shall be granted for a longer term than two years. *Provided nevertheless,* That the President may make such order respecting the tribes surrounded in their settlements by the citizens of the United States, as to secure an intercourse without license, if he may deem it proper.

SEC. 2. *And be it further enacted,* That the superintendent, or person issuing such license, shall have full power and authority to recall all such licenses as he may have issued, if the person so licensed shall transgress any of the regulations or restrictions provided for the government of trade and intercourse with the Indian tribes, and shall put in suit such bonds as he may have taken, immediately on the breach of any condition in said bond: *Provided always,* That if it shall appear on trial, that the person from whom such license shall have been recalled, has not offended against any of the provisions of this act, or the regulations prescribed for the trade and intercourse with the Indian tribes, he shall be entitled to receive a new license.

SEC. 3. *And be it further enacted,* That every person who shall attempt to trade with the Indian tribes, or to be found in the Indian country with such merchandise in his possession as are usually vended to the Indians, without a license first had and obtained, as in this act prescribed, and being thereof convicted in any court proper to try the same, shall forfeit all the merchandise so offered for sale to the Indian tribes, or so found in the Indian country, which forfeiture shall be one half to the benefit of the person prosecuting, and the other half to the benefit of the United States.

SEC. 4. *And be it enacted and declared,* That no sale of lands made by any Indians, or any nation or tribe of Indians within the United States, shall be valid to any person or persons, or to any state, whether having the right of pre-emption to such lands or not, unless the same shall be made and duly executed at some public treaty, held under the authority of the United States.

SEC. 5. *And be it further enacted,* That if any citizen or inhabitant of the United States, or of either of the territorial districts of the United States, shall go into any town, settlement or territory belonging to any nation or tribe of Indians, and shall there commit any crime upon, or trespass against, the person or property of any peaceable and friendly Indian or Indians, which, if committed within the jurisdiction of any state, or within the jurisdiction of either of the said districts, against a citizen or white inhabitant thereof, would be punishable by the laws of such state or district, such offender or offenders shall be subject to the same punishment, and shall be proceeded against in the same manner as if the offence had been committed within the jurisdiction of the state or district to which he or they may belong, against a citizen or white inhabitant thereof.

SEC. 6. *And be it further enacted,* That for any of the crimes or offences aforesaid, the like proceedings shad be had for apprehending, imprisoning or bailing the offender, as the case may be, and for recognizing the witnesses for their appearance to testify in the case, and where the offender shall be committed, or the witnesses shall be in a district other than that in which the offence is to be tried, for the removal of the offender and the witnesses or either of them, as the case may be, to the district in which the trial is to be had, as by the act to establish the judicial courts of the United States, are directed for any crimes or offenses against the United States.

One of the striking features of the Trade and Intercourse Act is to whom it is directed and what that reveals about the historical moment. The legislation is not directed at Native peoples, nor does it attempt to govern their internal relations. Rather, it is directed at American citizens and states. The need to pass a law to regulate the behavior of individuals and states was indicative of the types of problems that the federal government was seeking to solve. During this period, traders, land speculators, and others with a range of motives were causing a fair amount of disruption between tribal nations and the new national government. In order to curb these troubling situations, the federal government crafted rules to manage how American citizens and states could engage with Native America. The Trade and Intercourse Act was intended to filter American interaction with tribal nations through the federal government to prevent wrongs committed by states and individuals in order to keep the peace during a fragile moment of American history. Section 4 of the Act is particularly noteworthy, as it would become the impetus for tribal litigation late in the 20th century (see Chapter 15).

The U.S. Constitution came into force a year before the original Trade and Intercourse Act was passed. The Constitution was the second attempt at a national government—after the Articles of Confederation—and a major rearticulation of the country's vision for itself. Although not the primary concern of those who wrote the Constitution, the American government's relationship with tribal nations was of enough national importance that the new document had to account for the presence of Indigenous peoples, sometimes directly and sometimes indirectly. As you read this excerpt from the Constitution, ask yourself how the document understands Indigenous peoples and the federal government's relationship to them.

U.S. CONSTITUTION

Article I, Section 2

Clause 1: The House of Representatives shall be composed of Members chosen every second Year by the People of the several States. . . .

Clause 3: Representatives and direct Taxes shall be apportioned among the several States which may be included within this Union, according to their respective Numbers, which shall be determined by adding to the whole Number of free Persons, including those bound to Service for a Term of Years, and excluding Indians not taxed, three fifths of all other persons. . . .

Article I, Section 8

Clause 1: The Congress shall have Power. . . .

Clause 3: To regulate Commerce with foreign Nations, and among the several States, and with the Indian Tribes. . . .

Article II, Section 2

Clause 2: [The President] shall have Power, by and with the Advice and Consent of the Senate, to make Treaties. . .

Article VI, Clause 2

This Constitution, and the Laws of the United States which shall be made in Pursuance thereof; and all Treaties made, or which shall be made, under the Authority of the United States, shall be the supreme Law of the Land; and the Judges in every State shall be bound thereby, any Thing in the Constitution or Laws of any State to the Contrary notwithstanding.

As the excerpt demonstrates, Indigenous peoples are only explicitly mentioned twice in the original U.S. Constitution: first "Indians not taxed" are excluded from counting toward apportionment in the House of Representatives, and then again in the famous and powerful Commerce Clause. The Treaty Power, in addition to declaring treaties as part of the "supreme Law of the Land" has also participated directly in the construction of federal Indian law. You will see reference to these sections of the U.S. Constitution in the following chapters. As you consult later chapters, it will be worth your effort to return to this excerpt of the U.S. Constitution and consider how the text of the document is understood and interpreted by the Supreme Court and other facets of the federal government.

THE SUPREME COURT

Treaties and legislation were the most plentiful ways in which the young American nation built its legal and political relationship with tribal nations in the Early Treaty Era of federal policy. However, before long American courts also began playing a hand in defining the rights and responsibilities of not only the United States toward the Indigenous peoples of the continent, but also of tribal nations themselves. John Marshall, the third Chief Justice and the most prominent jurist in American Supreme Court history, was the architect for the Court's founding interpretation of American and tribal rights. The famous "Marshall Trilogy" of Indian law cases—*Johnson v. McIntosh* (1823), *Cherokee Nation v. Georgia* (1831), and *Worcester v. Georgia* (1832)—established the parameters under which the United States would recognize and understand the scope of tribal authority from thenceforth and created principles to which American law still adheres to this day. The effects of the Marshall Trilogy for Indigenous peoples were profound both in the United States and elsewhere, as other colonial powers in other parts of the world looked to Marshall's decisions as guiding lights in their own decisions concerning Indigenous peoples. In fact, it is no exaggeration to suggest that the first case in the Marshall Trilogy, *Johnson v. McIntosh*, is the most important case to ever affect Indigenous rights across the globe.

The events leading up to *Johnson v. McIntosh* are convoluted and the product of land speculators attempting to legitimize their claims to tribal lands. For the purposes of this text it suffices to summarize the facts in brief. Both before and after the American Revolution many ambitious entrepreneurs engaged in land speculation—a process whereby an investor buys a tract of land in the hopes of selling the land at great profit in the future. A number of prominent American figures, including George Washington and John Marshall and others of their stature, engaged in the practice. The growing desire for tribal lands as the United States was beginning to expand was fueled not just by settlers who wished to establish homesteads, but also by these land speculators who saw much potential for profit and routinely argued that Indigenous peoples did not properly use their lands nor did they need all (or any) of their lands.

Prior to the American Revolution, in 1773 and 1775, representatives from the Piankeshaw and Illinois tribal nations conveyed tracts of land in what is now Indiana and Illinois to various individuals in the presence of British officials. After the American Revolution, in 1805, representatives from those same tribal nations ceded lands that encompassed the same tracts to the United States in a treaty. The United States then subsequently sold the lands in question to various individuals. Each side, the 1770s purchasers and those who bought the land from the United States after the 1805 treaty, claimed to be the rightful owner of the property in dispute.

Heirs to the 1770s purchases—Johnson—found a complicit landowner who had bought an overlapping tract of land from the United States—McIntosh—to manufacture a case. The Johnson heirs used a number of questionable (and, by today's legal standards, unethical) tricks to get their case before the Supreme Court in their effort to legitimize their land claims and finally profit on their land speculation. The question of the case was ostensibly simple: Who owned the land—the Johnson heirs or McIntosh through the United States' treaty purchase?

Under traditional property law rules the case was simple and should not have reached the Supreme Court. Under traditional property rules, a piece of property belongs to the first purchaser—in this case the Johnson heirs. However, the presence of Native interests complicated the matter, according to Marshall, and answering the seemingly simple question required wrestling with a more difficult one: Were the Indians capable of selling their land? Before you read the excerpt of the case consider the possible consequences if the answer to this second question is yes and then consider the consequences if the answer is no. As you read the case, ask yourself how John Marshall resolves this seeming dilemma and what that means for tribal nations. Also, as you read this case and others in this textbook, ask yourself what are non-Native interests at stake in the case. Does acknowledging those non-Native interests help to understand why the case was resolved in the manner in which it was resolved? Is it possible that this Court, and subsequent Supreme Court decisions are more concerned with the non-Indian interests in a case than the possible consequences to tribal nations and peoples?

JOHNSON V. MCINTOSH
21 U.S. (8 Wheat.) 543 (1823)

MR. CHIEF JUSTICE MARSHALL delivered the opinion of the Court.

* * *

. . . The inquiry . . . is, in a great measure, confined to the power of Indians to give, and of private individuals to receive, a title which can be sustained in the Courts of this country.

As the right of society, to prescribe those rules by which property may be acquired and preserved is not, and cannot be drawn into question; as the title to lands, especially, is and must be admitted to depend entirely on the law of the nation in which they lie; it will be necessary, in pursuing this inquiry, to examine, not singly those principles of abstract justice, which the Creator of all things has impressed on the mind of his creature man, and which are admitted to regulate, in a great degree, the rights of civilized nations, whose perfect independence is acknowledged; but those principles also which our own government has adopted in the particular case, and given us as the rule for our decision.

On the discovery of this immense continent, the great nations of Europe were eager to appropriate to themselves so much of it as they could respectively acquire. Its vast extent offered an ample field to the ambition and enterprise of all; and the character and religion of its inhabitants afforded an apology for considering them as a people over whom the superior genius of Europe might claim an ascendency. The potentates of the old world found no difficulty in convincing themselves that they made ample compensation to the inhabitants of the new, by bestowing on them civilization and Christianity, in exchange for unlimited independence. But, as they were all in pursuit of nearly the same object, it was necessary, in order to avoid conflicting settlements, and consequent war with each other, to establish a principle, which all should acknowledge as the law by which the right of acquisition, which they all asserted, should be regulated as between themselves. This principle was, that discovery gave title to the government by whose subjects, or by whose authority, it was made, against all other European governments, which title might be consummated by possession.

The exclusion of all other Europeans, necessarily gave to the nation making the discovery the sole right of acquiring the soil from the natives, and establishing settlements upon it. It was a right with which no Europeans could interfere. It was a right which all asserted for themselves, and to the assertion of which, by others, all assented.

Those relations which were to exist between the discoverer and the natives, were to be regulated by themselves. The rights thus acquired being exclusive, no other power could interpose between them. In the establishment of these relations, the rights of the original inhabitants were, in no instance, entirely disregarded; but were necessarily, to a considerable extent, impaired. They were admitted to be the rightful occupants of the soil, with a legal as well as just claim to retain possession of it, and to use it according to their own discretion; but their rights to complete sovereignty, as independent nations, were necessarily diminished, and their power to dispose of the soil at their own will, to whomsoever they pleased, was denied by the original fundamental principle, that discovery gave exclusive title to those who made it.

While the different nations of Europe respected the right of the natives, as occupants, they asserted the ultimate dominion to be in themselves; and claimed and exercised, as a consequence of this ultimate dominion, a power to grant the soil, while yet in possession of the natives. These grants have been understood by all, to convey a title to the grantees, subject only to the Indian right of occupancy.

The history of America, from its discovery to the present day, proves, we think, the universal recognition of these principles.

* * *

No one of the powers of Europe gave its full assent to this principle, more unequivocally than England. . . .

* * *

Thus, all the nations of Europe, who have acquired territory on this continent, have asserted in themselves, and have recognised in others, the exclusive right of the discoverer to appropriate the lands occupied by the Indians. Have the American States rejected or adopted this principle?

By the treaty which concluded the war of our revolution, Great Britain relinquished all claim, not only to the government, but to the "propriety and territorial rights of the United States," whose boundaries were fixed in the second article. By this treaty, the powers of government, and the right to soil, which had previously been in Great Britain, passed definitively to these States. We had before taken possession of them, by declaring independence; but neither the declaration of independence, nor the treaty confirming it, could give us more than that which we before possessed, or to which Great Britain was before entitled. It has never been doubted, that either the United States, or the several States, had a clear title to all the lands within the boundary lines described in the treaty, subject only to the Indian right of occupancy, and that the exclusive power to extinguish that right, was vested in that government which might constitutionally exercise it.

* * *

The United States, then, have unequivocally acceded to that great and broad rule by which its civilized inhabitants now hold this country. They hold, and assert in themselves, the title by which it was acquired. They maintain, as all others have maintained, that discovery gave an exclusive right to extinguish the Indian title of occupancy, either by purchase or by conquest. . . .

* * *

We will not enter into the controversy, whether agriculturists, merchants, and manufacturers, have a right, on abstract principles, to expel hunters from the territory they possess, or to contract their limits. Conquest gives a title which the Courts of the conqueror cannot deny, whatever the private and speculative opinions of individuals may be, respecting the original justice of the claim which has been successfully asserted. . . .

Although we do not mean to engage in the defence of those principles which Europeans have applied to Indian title, they may, we think, find some excuse, if not justification, in the character and habits of the people whose rights have been wrested from them.

The title by conquest is acquired and maintained by force. The conqueror prescribes its limits. Humanity, however, acting on public opinion, has established, as a general rule, that the conquered shall not be wantonly oppressed, and that their condition shall remain as eligible as is compatible with the objects of the conquest. Most usually, they are incorporated with the victorious nation, and become subjects or citizens of the government with which they are connected. The new and old members of the society mingle with each other; the distinction between them is gradually lost, and they make one people. Where this incorporation is practicable, humanity demands, and a wise policy requires, that the rights of the conquered to property should remain unimpaired; that the new subjects should be governed as equitably as the old, and that confidence in their security should gradually banish the painful sense of being separated from their ancient connexions, and united by force to strangers.

When the conquest is complete, and the conquered inhabitants can be blended with the conquerors, or safely governed as a distinct people, public opinion, which not even the conqueror can disregard, imposes these restraints upon him; and he cannot neglect them without injury to his fame, and hazard to his power.

But the tribes of Indians inhabiting this country were fierce savages, whose occupation was war, and whose subsistence was drawn chiefly from the forest. To leave them in possession of their country, was to leave the country a wilderness; to govern them as a distinct people, was impossible, because they were as brave and as high spirited as they were fierce, and were ready to repel by arms every attempt on their independence.

What was the inevitable consequence of this state of things? The Europeans were under the necessity either of abandoning the country, and relinquishing their pompous claims to it, or of enforcing those claims by the sword, and by the adoption of principles adapted to the condition of a people with whom it was impossible to mix, and who could not be governed as a distinct society, or of remaining in their neighbourhood, and exposing themselves and their families to the perpetual hazard of being massacred.

Frequent and bloody wars, in which the whites were not always the aggressors, unavoidably ensued. European policy, numbers, and skill, prevailed. As the white population advanced, that of the Indians necessarily receded. The country in the immediate neighbourhood of agriculturists became unfit for them. The game fled into thicker and more unbroken forests, and the Indians followed. The soil, to which the crown originally claimed title, being no longer occupied by its ancient inhabitants, was parcelled out according to the will of the sovereign power, and taken possession of by persons who claimed immediately from the crown, or mediately, through its grantees or deputies.

That law which regulates, and ought to regulate in general, the relations between the conqueror and conquered, was incapable of application to a people under such circumstances. The resort to some new and different rule, better adapted to the actual state of things, was unavoidable. Every rule which can be suggested will be found to be attended with great difficulty.

However extravagant the pretension of converting the discovery of an inhabited country into conquest may appear; if the principle has been asserted in the first instance, and afterwards sustained; if a country has been acquired and held under it; if the property of the great mass of the community originates in it, it becomes the law of the land, and cannot be questioned. So, too, with respect to the concomitant principle, that the Indian inhabitants are to be considered merely as occupants, to be protected, indeed, while in peace, in the possession of their lands, but to be deemed incapable of transferring the absolute title to others. However this restriction may be opposed to natural right, and to the usages of civilized nations, yet, if it be indispensable to that system under which the country has been settled, and be adapted to the actual condition of the two people, it may, perhaps, be supported by reason, and certainly cannot be rejected by Courts of justice.

* * *

. . . The absolute ultimate title has been considered as acquired by discovery, subject only to the Indian title of occupancy, which title the discoverers possessed the exclusive right of acquiring. . . .

Another view has been taken of this question, which deserves to be considered. The title of the crown, whatever it might be, could be acquired only by a conveyance from the crown. If an individual might extinguish the Indian title for his own benefit, or, in other words, might purchase it, still he could acquire only that title. . . . The person who purchases lands from the Indians, within their territory, incorporates himself with them, so far as respects the

> property purchased; holds their title under their protection, and subject to their laws. If they annul the grant, we know of no tribunal which can revise and set aside the proceeding. We know of no principle which can distinguish this case from a grant made to a native Indian, authorizing him to hold a particular tract of land in severalty.
>
> * * *
>
> It has never been contended, that the Indian title amounted to nothing. Their right of possession has never been questioned. The claim of government extends to the complete ultimate title, charged with this right of possession, and to the exclusive power of acquiring that right.

The "Doctrine of Discovery," as it has come to be known, established parameters for both the "discovering" nation and for tribal nations. Under this international law principle, discovering nations have rights that flow in two directions: those against other nations capable of "discovery" and those against tribal nations. Before the analysis continues, you should consider what characteristics those nations capable of "discovery" have and how they differ from characteristics that define tribal nations and Indigenous peoples. Why does Marshall make this distinction? What might this reveal to a modern reader about the origins of federal Indian law?

As explained by Marshall, under the Doctrine of Discovery a discovering nation has exclusive rights to a territory against all other colonial powers. Thus, once a colonial power has discovered a territory, it can lawfully exclude any other colonial power. Discovery also gives the discovering nation the right—again, exclusive to any other colonial power—to acquire discovered lands from the indigenous inhabitants through two means: purchase or conquest. As a matter of policy, the United States chose to purchase lands from Indigenous peoples. The United States purchased tribal lands through treaties.

As it concerned tribal nations, the Doctrine of Discovery limited but did not extinguish their rights. Tribal nations, by virtue of having been discovered, no longer possessed the full title to their lands. Rather, after Discovery tribal nations held what has been variously referred to as Indian title, aboriginal title, or occupancy. At its most basic, Indian title meant (and continues to mean) that tribal nations still possess their own lands, but their possession is subject to limitations. Most prominently, tribal nations, under Discovery, are unable to sell their lands to any entity other than the discovering nation. As a consequence, any tribal sale of tribal land to an individual is invalid. Thus, the heirs of Johnson lost their case, despite the fact that the Johnson purchase occurred before the McIntosh purchase.

It is worthy of note that no tribal nations, members, or representatives were a part of *Johnson v. McIntosh* at any stage of the litigation. This monumental decision that diminished tribal rights and political authority was made with no Native input at all. Nonetheless, *Johnson*, and the next two cases of the Marshall Trilogy—which are discussed in the next chapter—have set the foundation for Indian law since their inception.

It is also worthy of note that *Johnson* established a pattern within Supreme Court Indian law cases in which various Justices throughout the years have declared that the presence of Indigenous peoples or interests have required, as Marshall put it, "the resort to some new and different rule, better adapted to the actual state of things." As you reflect on this case and as you read others ask yourself whether the presence of Indigenous peoples and interests in these cases truly requires "new and different" rules. Why or why not? In every case? If not in every case than in which cases? To what extent has American law and history demonstrated that it needs this degree of flexibility to adapt to truly unique situations, or do such declarations merely mask an effort by judges to privilege American actions at the expense of tribal nations and peoples?

SUGGESTED READINGS

- *Conquest by Law: How the Discovery of America Dispossessed Indigenous Peoples of Their Lands*. Lindsay G. Robertson. New York: Oxford University Press, 2005.

- *Buying America From the Indians:* Johnson v. McIntosh *and the History of Native Land Rights*. Blake A. Watson. Norman, OK: University of Oklahoma Press, 2012.

- *Expansion and American Indian Policy, 1783–1812*. Reginald Horsman. East Lansing, MI: University of Michigan State Press, 1967.

---

[1] Found at Francis Paul Prucha, *Documents of United States Indian Policy, 3rd ed*. (Lincoln, NE: University of Nebraska Press, 2000), 1–2.

[2] *Journals of the Continental Congress*, 32:340–41.

CHAPTER 3

The Removal Era

In the wake of the War of 1812—sometimes called the Second War of Independence—the United States began to emerge as the dominant military force on the North American continent. Although other colonial powers and tribal nations remained formidable military foes, the balance of power was shifting to the Americans. One of the consequences of the changing power dynamics was that American thinking about Indigenous peoples began to shift as well. Before long, federal policy began to embody this change in thinking.

The most prominent metaphor used to describe federal Indian policy is that of a pendulum that swings back and forth between two extremes. On one end of the pendulum is the "assimilation" model. Under this model, federal policy encourages or otherwise directs or demands that Indigenous peoples adapt to or adopt Western ways of life. Often these efforts are employed or imposed against the wishes or desires of Indigenous peoples. The assimilation model is also characterized by the belief that it is important or otherwise necessary to recognize that Indigenous peoples cannot live separately from their non-Native neighbors and surroundings. On the other end of the pendulum is the "separatist" model. Under this model, federal policy encourages or otherwise directs or demands that there be some distance—whether physically, socially, politically, or otherwise—between Indigenous peoples and the rest of America. These efforts were also often employed or imposed against the wishes and desires of Indigenous peoples. The separatist model is also characterized by the belief that it is to the benefit of Indigenous peoples that they and their nations are provided the space to develop outside of the pressures of assimilation.

The first major swing of the pendulum that is federal Indian policy occurred in the first third of the nineteenth century. Whereas Americans in the Early Treaty Era understood themselves in relationship with tribal nations in order to protect their fledgling nation, once the power dynamics began to shift so did the thinking of the time. Americans began imagining a future in which they did not have to live with Indigenous peoples as neighbors and had access to the tribal lands that they sought. In the early decades of the nineteenth century the assimilation model of the Early Treaty Era slowly but surely gave way to the separatist model of the Removal Era, which lasted approximately from 1830–1871.

The Removal Era was also birthed by the final two cases of the famous "Marshall Trilogy" of Indian law cases—*Cherokee Nation v. Georgia* and *Worcester v. Georgia*. Coupled with *Johnson v. McIntosh* (see Chapter 2), John Marshall's opinions set forth a number of principles that have been the basis of federal Indian law to this day. It is no exaggeration to suggest that the totality of federal Indian law since these cases has been a response to the Marshall Trilogy. Understanding these principles is the first step in understanding the state of the law today.

This chapter will demonstrate. . .

- *The shift from an assimilationist policy model to a separatist policy model*

- *The development and effects of the Removal Era*

- *The principles of federal Indian law established by the Marshall Trilogy of cases*

REMOVAL

As American desire for land in the quickly expanding nation grew, pressures mounted on eastern tribal nations. Spurred by the Louisiana Purchase in 1803, the United States began rapidly adding territory and states, slowed only by tribal land claims. In this moment of American growth, the national conversation about Indigenous peoples changed. No longer were American policymakers willing to tolerate their "savage" and "uncivilized" tribal neighbors, as the necessity for cooperation and tolerance that existed in the Early Treaty Era began to ebb.

The new solution to the so-called Indian Problem was removal. The idea was simple and founded on the belief that Indigenous peoples and their non-Indigenous neighbors could not co-exist. According to the supporters of removal, the process would benefit all parties involved. The federal government would negotiate with willing tribes for their lands and acquire more space for the growing country. Willing tribal nations would be relocated west, away from the mounting pressures of settlement, with the aid of the federal government. The vast continent theoretically offered enough space for those tribal nations willing to move west, those tribal nations already out west, and the growing American population in the east. Tribal nations unwilling to remove, according to the policy's proponents, were likely either to assimilate or die out under the encroaching westward expansion.

Although the idea of removal had been a part of the national conversation as early as Thomas Jefferson's administration in the early 1800s, it became national policy under Andrew Jackson's administration, which began in 1829. Jackson, whose national reputation was built in great part through military excursions against tribal nations, ran on a platform that included removal and began petitioning Congress to pass such legislation shortly after taking office. The national debate over removal was heated, but Congress did eventually narrowly pass the Indian Removal Act in 1830. As you read the law, ask yourself what steps the removal process is supposed to take and what obligations the United States creates for itself. How does the Removal Act compare and contrast with the *Requerimiento* (see Chapter 1)?

INDIAN REMOVAL ACT
U.S. Statutes at Large, 4:411–12, May 28, 1830

Be it enacted by the Senate and House of Representatives of the United States of America, in Congress assembled, That it shall and may be lawful for the President of the United States to cause so much of any territory belonging to the United States, west of the river Mississippi, not included in any state or organized territory, and to which the Indian title has been extinguished, as he may judge necessary, to be divided into a suitable number of districts, for the reception of such tribes or nations of Indians as may choose to exchange the lands where they now reside, and remove there; and to cause each of said districts to be so described by natural or artificial marks, as to be easily distinguished from every other.

Section 2—And be it further enacted, That it shall and may be lawful for the President to exchange any or all of such districts, so to be laid off and described, with any tribe or nation within the limits of any of the states or territories, and with which the United States have existing treaties, for the whole or any part or portion of the territory claimed and occupied by such tribe or nation, within the bounds of any one or more of the states or territories, where the land claimed and occupied by the Indians, is owned by the United States, or the United States are bound to the state within which it lies to extinguish the Indian claim thereto.

Section 3—And be it further enacted, That in the making of any such exchange or exchanges, it shall and may be lawful for the President solemnly to assure the tribe or nation with which the exchange is made, that the United States will forever secure and guaranty to them, and their heirs or successors, the country so exchanged with them; and if they prefer it, that the United States will cause a patent or grant to be made and executed to them for the same: Provided always, that such lands shall revert to the United States, if the Indians become extinct, or abandon the same.

* * *

Section 5—And be it further enacted, That upon the making of any such exchange as is contemplated by this act, it shall and may be lawful for the President to cause such aid and assistance to be furnished to the emigrants as may be necessary and proper to enable them to remove to, and settle in, the country for which they may have exchanged; and also, to give them such aid and assistance as may be necessary for their support and subsistence for the first year after their removal.

Section 6—And be it further enacted, That it shall and may be lawful for the President to cause such tribe or nation to be protected, at their new residence, against all interruption or disturbance from any other tribe or nation of Indians, or from any other person or persons whatever.

Section 7—And be it further enacted, That it shall and may be lawful for the President to have the same superintendence and care over any tribe or nation in the country to which they may remove, as contemplated by this act, that he is now authorized to have over them at their present places of residence.

The text of the Removal Act describes a process that is both orderly and voluntary, and that creates a number of obligations for the federal government to removed tribal nations. What are those obligations? Is there a similar or different tenor in the removal legislation than there was with the legislation of the Early Treaty Era? What is similar and what is different, and what does this analysis reveal about the shift in the two eras? Discussed in greater detail below, it is also worthy of note at this point that the process of removal was much less orderly and voluntary than the text of the Act sets forth.

CHEROKEE NATION V. GEORGIA

The most prominent example of the resistance to and effects of the removal process is the Cherokee Nation. Traditionally located in a vast swath of the southeast, the Cherokee had regularly engaged in treaties and land cessions with the United States. One of the most important of these treaties was the Treaty of Hopewell of 1785. Important to both of the following cases, the Treaty of Hopewell ceded land and stated, among other things, that, "the contracting parties shall use their utmost endeavors to maintain the peace." By the 1820s that promise was being put to the test. Despite the increasing pressures placed upon them by American settlement, the Cherokee did not want to cede any more land. Georgia, on the other hand, was increasingly angered by the federal government's failure to live up to a pledge to acquire additional Cherokee lands within its borders and decided to take matters into its own hands. The state declared, without the consent of either the Cherokee or the federal government, that it had authority over Cherokee lands and began passing laws affecting Cherokee territory. For example, Georgia declared that all White people in Cherokee lands were subject to Georgia law and that Cherokee laws were null and void.

Faced with intensifying incursions into their homeland and sovereignty, the Cherokee sought aid from the Supreme Court through a lawsuit against the state of Georgia. The Cherokee understood that they would find no relief with a Congress that had recently passed the Removal Act and a President who supported removal policy. Thus they turned to the only federal branch of government left where they could appeal for adherence to the treaties they signed with the United States. Unfortunately for the Cherokee, they also found themselves in the middle of an American inter-governmental dispute. Georgia, taking a staunch states-rights position, declared that the Supreme Court had no authority over its sovereign decisions and did not send lawyers to argue its cause before the Supreme Court. This dispute have led many to regard this moment in American history as the biggest constitutional crisis prior to the Civil War, pitting a state and the various branches of the federal government against each other. It was under these trying conditions that John Marshall, an ardent federalist who disagreed with much of Jackson's vision for the federal government, was asked to decide the second case in his Trilogy.

In order to understand the result in the case it is necessary to know two additional pieces of information. First, it is critical to understand the concept of jurisdiction. Jurisdiction can have many permutations in American law, but at its most essential, jurisdiction concerns the scope of authority that a court (or another governmental organ) holds. In order for a court to be able to properly hear a case, it must have the jurisdiction, or the authority to hear a case. A wide range of factors can influence whether a particular court will or will not have jurisdiction over a case, including, but not limited to, the individuals or entities involved, the law that will be applied to a case, and where the activity that led to the case took place.

The main purpose that the concept of jurisdiction serves is to preserve the checks and balances between both the different branches of government and between different governments themselves. For example, if a citizen of the state of North Carolina gets into a dispute with another citizen of North Carolina within the borders of the state of North Carolina, then North Carolina state courts will almost assuredly have jurisdiction over the dispute. Virginia courts, on the other hand, will almost assuredly not have the jurisdiction to hear the dispute because it would be a violation of North Carolina's authority over its own lands and citizens. Sometimes, such as in the above example, the question of jurisdiction is relatively simple and straightforward; other times it can be very complicated. Further muddying the waters, it is sometimes possible for more than one court to have jurisdiction over a case; most commonly both a particular federal court and a particular state court might both have jurisdiction over a single incident or dispute. Nonetheless, whether the matter is simple or complicated, the first decision every court must make in every case it encounters is whether or not it has jurisdiction. If a court determines that it does not have jurisdiction, it must dismiss, or decline to hear, the case. If a court determines that it does have jurisdiction then the case can proceed to the next stages.

Second, the Supreme Court is, in almost all cases, an appellate court and has what is called appellate jurisdiction. This means that in almost all instances a lawsuit must first be heard at a lower court before it can be heard at the Supreme Court. However, the U.S. Constitution allows the Supreme Court to have original jurisdiction—it can be the first court to hear a case—in very limited circumstances. One of those circumstances is when a foreign nation sues a state.

These two pieces of information—the concept of jurisdiction and the Supreme Court's very limited authority to be the first court to hear a case—are essential to deciphering the decision in *Cherokee Nation v. Georgia*. It is also helpful, before you read the case, to familiarize yourself with the excerpt of the U.S. Constitution in Chapter 2. As you read *Cherokee Nation* ask yourself exactly what Chief Justice John Marshall decided in the majority opinion. Who won and why? Does Marshall offer a fair reading of the U.S. Constitution or is this a strained interpretation that is more responsive to the political problem that Marshall faced than the actual dispute before the Court? What are the consequences of the decision? Also ask yourself how the views in the concurrences and dissent shaped the debate and what they reflect about the understanding of tribal nations at the time the case was decided.

CHEROKEE NATION V. GEORGIA

30 U.S. (5 Pet.) 1 (1831)

MR. CHIEF JUSTICE MARSHALL delivered the opinion of the Court.

* * *

If Courts were permitted to indulge their sympathies, a case better calculated to excite them can scarcely be imagined. . . .

Before we can look into the merits of the case, a preliminary inquiry presents itself. Has this Court jurisdiction of the cause?

The third article of the Constitution describes the extent of the judicial power. The second section closes an enumeration of the cases to which it is extended, with "controversies" "between a State or the citizens thereof, and foreign states, citizens, or subjects." A subsequent clause of the same section gives the Supreme Court original jurisdiction in all cases in which a State shall be a party. The party defendant may then unquestionably be sued in this Court. May the plaintiff sue in it? Is the Cherokee Nation a foreign state in the sense in which that term is used in the Constitution?

* * *

. . . The acts of our Government plainly recognize the Cherokee Nation as a State, and the Courts are bound by those acts.

A question of much more difficulty remains. Do the Cherokees constitute a foreign state in the sense of the Constitution?

This argument is imposing, but we must examine it more closely before we yield to it. The condition of the Indians in relation to the United States is perhaps unlike that of any other two people in existence. In the general, nations not owing a common allegiance are foreign to each other. The term foreign nation is, with strict propriety, applicable by either to the other. But the relation of the Indians to the United States is marked by peculiar and cardinal distinctions which exist nowhere else.

The Indian Territory is admitted to compose a part of the United States. . . .

Though the Indians are acknowledged to have an unquestionable, and heretofore unquestioned right to the lands they occupy, until that right shall be extinguished by a voluntary cession to our government, yet it may well be doubted whether those tribes which reside within the acknowledged boundaries of the United States can, with strict accuracy, be denominated foreign nations. They may, more correctly, perhaps, be denominated domestic dependent nations. They occupy a territory to which we assert a title independent of their will, which must take effect in point of possession when their right of possession ceases. Meanwhile they are in a state of pupilage. Their relation to the United States resembles that of a ward to his guardian.

* * *

These considerations go far to support the opinion that the framers of our Constitution had not the Indian tribes in view when they opened the courts of the union to controversies between a State or the citizens thereof, and foreign states.

In considering this subject, the habits and usages of the Indians in their intercourse with their white neighbours ought not to be entirely disregarded. At the time the Constitution was framed, the idea of appealing to an American court of justice for an assertion of right or a redress of wrong had perhaps never entered the mind of an Indian or of his tribe. Their appeal was to the tomahawk, or to the Government. This was well understood by the Statesmen who framed the Constitution of the United States, and might furnish some reason for omitting to enumerate them among the parties who might sue in the courts of the union. Be this as it may, the peculiar relations between the United States and the Indians occupying our territory are such that we should feel much difficulty in considering them as designated by the term foreign state were there no other part of the Constitution which might shed light on the meaning of these words. But we think that, in construing them, considerable aid is furnished by that clause in the eighth section of the third article which empowers Congress to "regulate commerce with foreign nations, and among the several States, and with the Indian tribes."

In this clause, they are as clearly contradistinguished by a name appropriate to themselves from foreign nations as from the several States composing the union. . . . The objects to which the power of regulating commerce might be directed are divided into three distinct classes—foreign nations, the several States, and Indian tribes. When forming this article, the convention considered them as entirely distinct. We cannot assume that the distinction was lost in framing a subsequent article unless there be something in its language to authorize the assumption.

* * *

The Court has bestowed its best attention on this question, and, after mature deliberation, the majority is of opinion that an Indian tribe or Nation within the United States is not a foreign state in the sense of the Constitution, and cannot maintain an action in the Courts of the United States.

* * *

MR. JUSTICE THOMPSON, dissenting.

* * *

In the opinion pronounced by the Court, the merits of the controversy between the State of Georgia and the Cherokee Indians have not been taken into consideration. The denial of the application for an injunction has been placed solely on the ground of want of jurisdiction in this Court to grant the relief prayed for. . . .

* * *

. . . Every nation that governs itself, under what form soever, without any dependence on a foreign power is a sovereign state. Its rights are naturally the same as those of any other state. . . We ought, therefore, to reckon in the number of sovereigns those states that have bound themselves to another more powerful, although by an unequal alliance. The conditions of these unequal alliances may be infinitely varied; but whatever they are, provided the inferior ally reserves to itself the sovereignty or the right to govern its own body, it ought to be considered an independent state. Consequently, a weak state, that, in order to provide for its safety, places itself under the protection of a more powerful one without stripping itself of the right of government and sovereignty, does not cease on this account to be placed among the sovereigns who acknowledge no other power. . . .

Testing the character and condition of the Cherokee Indians by these rules, it is not perceived how it is possible to escape the conclusion that they form a sovereign state. They have always been dealt with as such by the Government of the United States, both before and since the adoption of the present Constitution. . . .

* * *

That numerous tribes of Indians, and among others the Cherokee Nation, occupied many parts of this country long before the discovery by Europeans is abundantly established by history. . . .

. . . And if the Cherokees were then a foreign nation, when or how have they lost that character, and ceased to be a distinct people, and become incorporated with any other community?

They have never been, by conquest, reduced to the situation of subjects to any conqueror, and thereby lost their separate national existence, and the rights of self-government, and become subject to the laws of the conqueror. . . .

* * *

If we look to the whole course of treatment by this country of the Indians from the year 1775 to the present . . . the conclusion appears to me irresistible that they have been regarded, by the Executive and Legislative branches of the Government, not only as sovereign and independent, but as foreign nations or tribes, not within the jurisdiction nor under the government of the States within which they were located. . . .

* * *

MR. JUSTICE JOHNSON, concurring.

* * *

. . . I cannot but think that there are strong reasons for doubting the applicability of the epithet "state" to a people so low in the grade of organized society as our Indian tribes most generally are. . . .

* * *

In the very treaty of Hopewell, the language or evidence of which is appealed to as the leading proof of the existence of this supposed State, we find the commissioners of the United States expressing themselves in these terms.

The commissioners plenipotentiary of the United States give peace to all the Cherokees, and receive them into the favour and protection of the United States on the following conditions.

This is certainly the language of sovereigns and conquerors, and not the address of equals to equals. . . . It is clear that it was intended to give them no other rights over the territory than what were needed by a race of hunters, and it is not easy to see how their advancement beyond that State of society could ever have been promoted, or, perhaps, permitted, consistently with the unquestioned rights of the States, or United States, over the territory within their limits.

* * *

Where is the rule to stop? Must every petty kraal of Indians, designating themselves a tribe or nation, and having a few hundred acres of land to hunt on exclusively, be recognized as a State?

* * *

But secondly, at what time did this people acquire the character of a State?

Certainly not by the treaty of Hopewell, for every provision of that treaty operates to strip it of its sovereign attributes, and nothing subsequent adds anything to that treaty, except using the word Nation instead of Indians. . . .

* * *

MR. JUSTICE BALDWIN, concurring.

* * *

. . . the stipulations [of the Treaty of Hopewell] are wholly inconsistent with sovereignty; the Indians acknowledge their dependent character, hold the lands they occupy as an allotment of hunting grounds; give to Congress the exclusive right of regulating their trade and managing all their affairs as they may think proper.

. . . There can be no dependence so anti-national, or so utterly subversive of national existence, as transferring to a foreign government the regulation of its trade and the management of all their affairs at their pleasure. The nation or State, tribe or village, headmen or warriors of the Cherokees, call them by what name we please, call the articles they have signed a definitive treaty or an indenture of servitude; they are not by its force or virtue a foreign state capable of calling into legitimate action the judicial power of this union, by the exercise of the original jurisdiction of this Court against a sovereign State, a component part of this nation. Unless the Constitution has imparted to the Cherokees a national character never recognized under the confederation; and which, if they ever enjoyed, was surrendered by the treaty of Hopewell, they cannot be deemed in this Court plaintiffs in such a case as this.

Reading the U.S. Constitution closely, Marshall employed what lawyers and scholars call a textual analysis to come to the determination that the drafters of the document made an important distinction between foreign nations and Indian tribes in what is known as the Commerce Clause—Article I, Section 8, Clause 3. And since Indian tribes were not properly foreign nations, but they nonetheless maintained a national character capable of engaging in treaties, Marshall described them as "domestic dependent nations." Marshall also moved beyond the text of the U.S. Constitution to support his conclusion, stating that the framers would not have fully conceptualized Indian tribes as foreign nations because, "their appeal was to the tomahawk." Consequently, Marshall's argument goes, the framers would not have opened Supreme Court jurisdiction to Indian tribes in this manner.

The Court as a whole in *Cherokee Nation* was evenly split into three perspectives—one other justice joined Marshall in declaring the Cherokee a domestic, dependent nation, two voted against recognizing the Cherokee as a nation at all, and two voted to recognize the Cherokee as a nation. The divisions on the Court reflected the heated debates about removal during the era. Although technically split into three groups of two, essentially four justices voted against the Cherokee to two in favor. Put another way, only two justices found that the Cherokee constituted a foreign nation capable of invoking the original jurisdiction of the Supreme Court, while four decided that the Cherokee did not rise to the level of nationhood capable of invoking the Supreme Court's original jurisdiction. As a consequence, the Supreme Court decided it did not have the jurisdiction to hear the case and Marshall's depiction of tribal nations as domestic dependent nations became established in American law.

Marshall's opinion is also noteworthy in his description of the relationship between the federal government and tribal nations. Marshall stated that it "resembles that of a ward to his guardian." The consequences of this assertion are more fully explored in Chapter 14. For the purposes of this chapter, it suffices to note that Marshall's guardian-ward metaphor strongly implied that the United States has obligations toward tribal nations through what we now call the trust responsibility.

While the decision momentarily prevented further conflict with Georgia and the other branches of the federal government, it continued to leave the Cherokee vulnerable to Georgia's encroachments and abuses. It also created confusion. What, exactly, is a domestic dependent nation? Scholars, lawyers, tribal nations, states, the federal government, and other interested parties have been trying to define the term ever since it was first announced by Marshall. In fact, one could make a cogent argument that the totality of federal Indian law has been little more than an attempt to define domestic dependent nationhood ever since Marshall left us with the concept.

WORCESTER V. GEORGIA

Many have suggested that Marshall's opinion in *Cherokee Nation* was less of an attempt to accurately describe the national character of Native nations and more of an attempt to sidestep the serious political crisis between the Supreme Court, the President of the United States, and a state. As noted above, this was a particularly challenging moment for the still-new United States. Also as noted above, Georgia did not send lawyers to the oral arguments for *Cherokee Nation*, claiming that the U.S. Supreme Court did not have authority over its sovereign decisions (nor did Georgia send lawyers to the oral arguments for *Worcester*). Marshall, who believed in a strong federal government and who had spent the bulk of his career transforming the Supreme Court into the powerful institution that we recognize today, knew that he would find little support from Andrew Jackson, a strong states-rights advocate, in the dispute with Georgia. Without the support of the President, Marshall seemed to have little recourse concerning Georgia's open defiance. Thus, many have speculated, Marshall essentially decided not to decide. By declaring that the Cherokee were a "domestic dependent nation," Marshall was able to throw the case out of court on jurisdictional grounds, relieving the Supreme Court of the thornier task of having to issue a ruling either in favor or against Georgia's actions not only toward the Cherokee, but also, to a great extent, toward the Supreme Court itself.

One year after *Cherokee Nation*, a new conflict arose that placed the matter before the Supreme Court yet again. Samuel Worcester, a northern missionary with strong ties to the Cherokee, was convicted and sentenced by Georgia courts to four years of hard labor for violating a state law that made it illegal for non-Cherokee to reside in Cherokee territory without a state license. Worcester appealed the conviction to the Supreme Court. Since it was an appeal, Worcester's case was not confronted with any of *Cherokee Nation*'s jurisdictional hurdles. Perhaps backed into a corner by the circumstances of the case or perhaps emboldened or otherwise provoked to take a stand, Marshall and his brethren decided the case on its merits, or according to the circumstances of the case rather than on jurisdictional or any other procedural grounds. The issue in *Worcester* was whether Georgia law that purported to reach into Cherokee territory was valid. As you read the case ask yourself how Marshall describes tribal sovereignty and the Doctrine of Discovery. Can you reconcile Marshall's descriptions of tribal sovereignty and Discovery in this case with his previous descriptions of tribal sovereignty and Discovery in *Johnson v. McIntosh* (see Chapter 2)? What are the foundational principles of federal Indian law that you can identify in the Marshall Trilogy?

WORCESTER V. GEORGIA
31 U.S. (6 Pet.) 515 (1832)

MR. CHIEF JUSTICE MARSHALL delivered the opinion of the Court.

* * *

America, separated from Europe by a wide ocean, was inhabited by a distinct people, divided into separate nations, independent of each other and of the rest of the world, having institutions of their own, and governing themselves by their own laws. It is difficult to comprehend the proposition that the inhabitants of either quarter of the globe could have rightful original claims of dominion over the inhabitants of the other, or over the lands they occupied, or that the discovery of either by the other should give the discoverer rights in the country discovered which annulled the preexisting rights of its ancient possessors.

* * *

. . . We proceed, then, to the actual state of things, having glanced at their origin, because holding it in our recollection might shed some light on existing pretensions.

The great maritime powers of Europe discovered and visited different parts of this continent at nearly the same time. The object was too immense for any one of them to grasp the whole, and the claimants were too powerful to submit to the exclusive or unreasonable pretensions of any single potentate. To avoid bloody conflicts which might terminate disastrously to all, it was necessary for the nations of Europe to establish some principle which all would acknowledge, and which should decide their respective rights as between themselves. This principle, suggested by the actual state of things, was "that discovery gave title to the government by whose subjects or by whose authority it was made against all other European governments, which title might be consummated by possession."

This principle, acknowledged by all Europeans because it was the interest of all to acknowledge it, gave to the nation making the discovery, as its inevitable consequence, the sole right of acquiring the soil and of making settlements on it. It was an exclusive principle which shut out the right of competition among those who had agreed to it, not one which could annul the previous rights of those who had not agreed to it. It regulated the right given by discovery among the European discoverers, but could not affect the rights of those already in possession, either as aboriginal occupants or as occupants by virtue of a discovery made before the memory of man. It gave the exclusive right to purchase, but did not found that right on a denial of the right of the possessor to sell.

* * *

. . . The extravagant and absurd idea that the feeble settlements made on the sea coast, or the companies under whom they were made, acquired legitimate power by them to govern the people, or occupy the lands from sea to sea did not enter the mind of any man. They were well understood to convey the title which, according to the common law of European sovereigns respecting America, they might rightfully convey, and no more. This was the exclusive right of purchasing such lands as the natives were willing to sell. The Crown could not be understood to grant what the Crown did not affect to claim; nor was it so understood.

* * *

The actual state of things and the practice of European nations on so much of the American continent as lies between the Mississippi and the Atlantic, explain their claims and the charters they granted. Their pretensions unavoidably interfered with each other; though the discovery of one was admitted by all to exclude the claim of any other, the extent of that discovery was the subject of unceasing contest. Bloody conflicts arose between them which gave importance and security to the neighbouring nations. Fierce and warlike in their character, they might be formidable enemies or effective friends. Instead of rousing their resentments by asserting claims to their lands or to dominion over their persons, their alliance was sought by flattering professions, and purchased by rich presents. The English, the French, and the Spaniards were equally competitors for their friendship and their aid. Not well acquainted with the exact meaning of words, nor supposing it to be material whether they were called the subjects or the children of their father in Europe; lavish in professions of duty and affection, in return for the rich presents they received; so long as their actual independence was untouched and their right to self-government acknowledged, they were willing to profess dependence on the power which furnished supplies of which they were in absolute need, and restrained dangerous intruders from entering their country. And this was probably the sense in which the term was understood by them.

. . . The King purchased their lands when they were willing to sell, at a price they were willing to take, but never coerced a surrender of them. He also purchased their alliance and dependence by subsidies, but never intruded into the interior of their affairs or interfered with their self-government so far as respected themselves only.

* * *

This was the settled state of things when the war of our revolution commenced. The influence of our enemy was established; her resources enabled her to keep up that influence; and the colonists had much cause for the apprehension that the Indian nations would, as the allies of Great Britain, add their arms to hers. This, as was to be expected, became an object of great solicitude to Congress. Far from advancing a claim to their lands, or asserting any right of dominion over them, Congress resolved "that the securing and preserving the friendship of the Indian nations appears to be a subject of the utmost moment to these colonies."

The early journals of Congress exhibit the most anxious desire to conciliate the Indian nations. . . .

* * *

When the United States gave peace, did they not also receive it? Were not both parties desirous of it? If we consult the history of the day, does it not inform us that the United States were at least as anxious to obtain it as the Cherokees? We may ask, further: did the Cherokees come to the seat of the American government to solicit peace, or did the American commissioners go to them to obtain it? The treaty was made at Hopewell, not at New York. . . .

* * *

The general law of European sovereigns respecting their claims in America limited the intercourse of Indians, in a great degree, to the particular potentate whose ultimate right of domain was acknowledged by the others. . . . The Indians perceived in this protection only what was beneficial to themselves—an engagement to punish aggressions on them. It involved, practically, no claim to their lands, no dominion over their persons. It merely bound the nation to the British Crown as a dependent ally claiming the protection of a powerful friend and neighbour and receiving the advantages of that protection without involving a surrender of their national character. . . .

. . . [The United States] receive the Cherokee Nation into their favor and protection. The Cherokees acknowledge themselves to be under the protection of the United States, and of no other power. Protection does not imply the destruction of the protected.

* * *

To construe the expression [in the Treaty of Hopewell] "managing all their affairs" into a surrender of self-government would be, we think, a perversion of their necessary meaning, and a departure from the construction which has been uniformly put on them. . . . This may be true as respects the regulation of their trade and as respects the regulation of all affairs connected with their trade, but cannot be true as respects the management of all their affairs. . . Such a construction would be inconsistent with the spirit of this and of all subsequent treaties, especially of those articles which recognise the right of the Cherokees to declare hostilities and to make war. It would convert a treaty of peace covertly into an act, annihilating the political existence of one of the parties. Had such a result been intended, it would have been openly avowed.

. . . [the Treaty of Hopewell's] essential articles treat the Cherokees as a nation capable of maintaining the relations of peace and war, and ascertain the boundaries between them and the United States.

* * *

From the commencement of our government, Congress has passed acts to regulate trade and intercourse with the Indians; which treat them as nations, respect their rights, and manifest a firm purpose to afford that protection which treaties stipulate. All these acts . . . manifestly consider the several Indian nations as distinct political communities, having territorial boundaries within which their authority is exclusive and having a right to all the lands within those boundaries which is not only acknowledged, but guarantied, by the United States.

* * *

The Indian nations had always been considered as distinct, independent political communities, retaining their original natural rights as the undisputed possessors of the soil from time immemorial, with the single exception of that imposed by irresistible power, which excluded them from intercourse with any other European potentate than the first discoverer of the coast of the particular region claimed, and this was a restriction which those European potentates imposed on themselves, as well as on the Indians. . . .

* * *

. . . the settled doctrine of the law of nations is that a weaker power does not surrender its independence—its right to self-government—by associating with a stronger and taking its protection. A weak State, in order to provide for its safety, may place itself under the protection of one more powerful without

> stripping itself of the right of government and ceasing to be a State. Examples of this kind are not wanting in Europe. . . .
>
> The Cherokee Nation, then, is a distinct community occupying its own territory, with boundaries accurately described, in which the laws of Georgia can have no force, and which the citizens of Georgia have no right to enter but with the assent of the Cherokees themselves, or in conformity with treaties and with the acts of Congress. The whole intercourse between the United States and this Nation, is, by our Constitution and laws, vested in the Government of the United States.
>
> * * *

THE AFTERMATH

The decision in *Worcester* was a victory for the Cherokee and remains a strong statement in favor of tribal rights and authority. *Worcester* is understood as a victory by many because it legally, if not necessarily actually, halted state incursions into tribal lands. Marshall famously declared that tribal nations were "distinct political communities" that retained their sovereignty despite agreeing to come under the protection of a more powerful sovereign. According to Marshall, had the Cherokee understood the Treaty of Hopewell as destroying their own ability to govern themselves, then, "such a result . . . would have been openly avowed." As Marshall also stated, "Protection does not imply the destruction of the protected."

In further declaring that "the laws of Georgia can have no force" in Indian Country, Marshall's opinion established that the federal government, to the exclusion of states, held the capacity to engage with tribal nations. In essence, Marshall's opinion declared that there was a solid border between state lands and tribal lands and that states could not cross that border without the permission of either the federal government or the tribal nation itself. Put another way, the federal government held the plenary power, or exclusive power—as opposed to states—to engage with Native nations.

Worcester is also well regarded by many in its attempts to mitigate the Doctrine of Discovery. According to Marshall, the notion that Discovery authorized colonizing nations to govern or otherwise rule over Indigenous peoples would have been unthinkable to the earlier generations of colonists that established themselves along the East Coast and engaged in earlier treaties. In fact, there was a reciprocity to the treaties between the United States and Native nations. As Marshall stated, "When the United States gave peace, did they not also receive it? . . . We may ask, further: did the Cherokees come to the seat of the American government to solicit peace, or did the American commissioners go to them to obtain it?" The Doctrine of Discovery, as Marshall refined it, did nothing more than allow colonizers to obtain tribal lands on those occasions when tribal nations were willing to part with it. "This was the exclusive right of purchasing such lands as the natives were willing to sell."

Despite the outcome of the case, *Worcester* did little for the Cherokee in the immediate aftermath of its announcement, nor did it resolve the tensions between the Supreme Court, the President, Georgia, and the Cherokee. While the Supreme Court ruled in favor of Cherokee Interests in *Worcester*, Marshall and the rest of the Court recognized that Georgia was likely to remain defiant of the Court's authority and that it was questionable at best as to whether Jackson would honor the ruling. Consequently, the Court did not follow the normal process of requiring federal officials to enforce the decision, avoiding a showdown with a President who was more closely aligned with Georgia's interests. Testifying to the friction of the moment, it was once widely believed that Jackson, upon learning of the decision in *Worcester*, exclaimed, "John Marshall has made his decision, now let him enforce it." Although more recent scholarship casts doubt as to whether Jackson actually said this, the spirit animating the supposed quotation encapsulated the threat the Supreme Court faced to its authority. A showdown ensued in which no action was taken, as all of the interested parties waited for someone else to make the next move. The legal impasse was only finally resolved when Samuel Worcester (and another missionary who was similarly situated) accepted a pardon from the Governor of Georgia in early 1833. With Samuel Worcester's case closed, the legal remedies available to the Cherokee had been exhausted.

In 1835, without the consent of the established leadership, a faction of the Cherokee who believed that removal was inevitable signed a removal treaty with the United States. This led to the infamous Trail of Tears, in which American soldiers forced Cherokees from their homes and ushered them westward. It is estimated that one-quarter of the over 16,000 who left the southeast on the forced march to what is now Oklahoma died along the way. Removal had other legal and political consequences as well, dividing the Cherokee into the three federally recognized Cherokee tribal nations of today: The Cherokee Nation of Oklahoma, the United Keetoowah Band of Cherokee Indians (also located in Oklahoma), and the Eastern Band of Cherokee Indians—located in North Carolina and consisting of Cherokee who, through various means, escaped removal.

While the Cherokee serve as the most prominent example of the effects of the Removal Era, it is important to note that they were not the first nor the only tribal nation to suffer removal. This systematic effort at eradicating tribal nations from what was then the United States dramatically affected a number of eastern and Midwestern tribal nations. While the Removal Act called for tribal consent before being removed, federal officials coerced or otherwise manufactured treaties to support the removal process for decades. Many Indigenous peoples were forced out of their ancestral homelands and those that stayed were often harassed or driven into hiding. It also affected Western tribal nations who were not always receptive to the new inhabitants within their lands. The devastating effects of removal dramatically altered the landscape of Native America from thenceforth.

Despite (or perhaps in addition to) this tragic history, the Marshall Trilogy continues to define federal Indian law and policy to this day. Although much has changed, the basic principles within Marshall's opinions remain touchstones for contemporary conversations about tribal sovereignty and rights. These principles—Discovery, domestic dependent nationhood, trust, and plenary power—are the essence of the Marshall Trilogy. As you make your way through additional chapters of this text, take note of how these principles have and have not changed throughout the years and throughout the subsequent eras of federal Indian policy.

SUGGESTED READINGS

- *The Cherokee Cases: Two Landmark Federal Decisions in the Fight for Sovereignty.* Jill Norgren. Norman, OK: University of Oklahoma Press, 2003.

- *The Cherokee Removal: A Brief History with Documents, 3rd ed.* Theda Perdue and Michael D. Green. Boston: Bedford/St. Martin's, 2016.

- *Encyclopedia of American Indian Removal, 2 Vol.* Daniel F. Littlefield, Jr. and James W. Parins. Santa Barbara, CA: Greenwood, 2011.

CHAPTER 4

Westward Expansion and Reservations

Removal wrought a great deal of disruption throughout Indian Country. Many tribal nations were removed from their ancestral homelands in the decades after the Removal Act of 1830, causing much suffering, strife, and misery for not just those who were removed but also for those whose own ancestral lands were now imposed upon by often unwelcome newcomers. Despite this lengthy and sustained campaign to remove tribal nations from the east, the policy of removal did not solve the "Indian Problem" for federal officials and land hungry citizens—nor did it completely eliminate Native nations from the east. Before long, American hunger for tribal lands grew stronger than could be satisfied by the rather cumbersome removal process. Making matters more difficult, the discovery of gold in California in 1848 led to a steady stream of settlers traversing and clamoring for previously undesirable tribal lands. Before long, the federal government began acquiring even greater amounts of tribal lands through treaties, accelerating the reservation system that is familiar today.

By the mid-nineteenth century, American law and policy began to slowly reflect a shifting attitude on how to address Native America. Spurred in great part by the California Gold Rush, the resulting desire for Western lands, and the establishment of a number of reservations, law and policymakers began to conceptualize tribal nations much more as a domestic concern, rather than a foreign one. This dramatic shift was slowed for a while by the Civil War, which pushed federal Indian policy to the background. Consequently, a state of near lawlessness developed in Western territories, as soldiers and settlers inflicted atrocities upon Native peoples while the federal government's attention was directed elsewhere.

After the Civil War the federal government developed a new approach that further regarded Native peoples as domestic subjects. Led in great part by President Ulysses S. Grant, the "Peace Policy" accelerated the reservation system and sought to reform the federal government's interventions into tribal life by turning over authority to interested parties of various Christian denominations. During this tumultuous time, Native peoples continued to make appeals to American courts, while those courts continued to build upon the Marshall Trilogy and slowly but steadily increase American intervention into Indian Country.

This chapter will demonstrate. . .

- *The growing American sense of Native policy as a domestic issue*

- *The beginnings of the reservation system*

- *The increasing difficulties that Natives faced when encountering American law*

SHIFTING ATTITUDES

It is difficult to discern to what extent federal policymakers ever truly regarded Removal as a permanent solution to relations with tribal nations. Temporarily expedient, the policy could not keep pace with the expanding United States and quickly began to outlive its usefulness. As the American desire for tribal lands grew, so did the need—from the American perspective—to find policy alternatives.

The United States began responding to the changing dynamics in a few key ways. First, treaties with tribal nations increasingly included reservations—lands preserved for tribal use and occupation. In general, Indian treaties had always been land sales in which tribal nations ceded territory for payment. Whereas removal treaties required that a tribal nation cede all of its land, the post-Removal treaties maintained reserved territories for tribal peoples. Like many of the big ideas in this area of law and policy, in theory reservations were to the benefit of everyone involved. American policymakers argued that tribal nations, who no longer could simply be pushed further west, would maintain enough territory to sustain themselves as well as reap the benefits of governmental aid and the influences of White civilization. The United States, on the other hand, received tribal lands that Native peoples did not, according to policymakers, need or use effectively. Although some reservations had been established prior to this period, the post-Removal decades saw the establishment of many of the reservations and the reservation system that continues to exist today. Oftentimes throughout the mid-nineteenth century, tribal nations were repeatedly approached to cede more and more land, continually shrinking reservations and putting additional strains on tribal communities.

The rhetoric and the actions on the part of the federal government began to change as well. As Removal became less and less of a realistic option, tribal peoples and nations were still considered "foreign" in the sense that they were understood as uncivilized and unable to cope in the White man's world. Yet, John Marshall's depiction of tribal nations as "domestic dependent nations" changed not just the law but perspectives as well. Policymakers began to gradually reconsider tribal issues outside of foreign policy and under a domestic policy framework.

The most telling example of this new way of thinking was the development of what is now called the Bureau of Indian Affairs—the federal governmental agency tasked with interacting with tribal nations and peoples. Somewhat haphazardly, the Secretary of War created a department he called the Bureau of Indians Affairs in 1824 without Congressional approval or formal authority. Despite its questionable origins, the bureau lived on and in 1832 Congress authorized the President to appoint a Commissioner of Indian Affairs. Two years later, in 1834, Congress more fully formalized the new bureau—which went by a few names before settling on the Bureau of Indian Affairs in 1947—creating various layers of authority in which lower level bureaucrats answered to the Commissioner of Indian Affairs who answered to the Secretary of War. In 1849, Congress established the Department of the Interior—the executive department tasked with managing land, water, wildlife, and natural resources. During its creation, Congress also transferred the Indian bureau to the Department of the Interior, where it continues to exist today.

Although the change from the War Department to the Department of the Interior had little practical effect in the administration of affairs, it nonetheless marked a monumental shift in how the United States understood tribal nations. Whereas the Department of War was deeply concerned with foreign entities, the Department of the Interior was established to manage domestic issues. Tribal nations were becoming relegated to a domestic concern. As you read this excerpt from the 1849 Annual Report of the Commissioner of Indian Affairs, ask yourself how the report reflects the changing thinking about tribal nations and what consequences it holds for tribal peoples.

1849 ANNUAL REPORT OF THE COMMISSIONER OF INDIAN AFFAIRS

Orlando Brown, Commissioner of Indian Affairs

Among the border of tribes and others with whom we have defined and fixed relations, and maintain any immediate and regular intercourse, as great a degree of peace and tranquility has prevailed as during the same length of time at any former period. They have generally conducted themselves peacefully towards our citizens, and towards each other. This circumstance speaks well for the vigilance and activity of our agents and of the military stationed in the Indian country, and attests the good efforts of the policy pursued by the government in promptly repressing any symptoms of outbreak, and compelling tribes committing outrages upon others to make ample and suitable reparation for the injury, so far as, under present circumstances, these objects can be accomplished. Nor must we overlook the influence of the good example of some of our more civilized and orderly tribes, and the happy effects of the exertions of the many excellent persons who, animated by a truly philanthropic and Christian spirit, have voluntarily banished themselves beyond the confines of civilization and all its comforts and advantages, and gone to labor zealously and disinterestedly for the temporal and spiritual welfare of an unfortunate and semi-barbarous people. Both doubtless have, in some degree, aided in securing so desirable a result.

It is impossible, however, to prevent the occurrence of occasional difficulties among our more remote border tribes, who, from their position and other circumstances, have not, as yet, sufficiently felt the influence of the policy and measure of the government for the civilization and improvement of our Indians to be induced to give up their natural habits of war and the chase. From disinclination for agricultural and other peaceful and more profitable pursuits of civilized life, they have ample time and opportunity for indulgence in those habits; and as it is in their hunting excursions—when they are beyond any supervision or control, and which bring them more or less into collisions—that difficulties most generally occur. . . . As far as possible, measures have been adopted to compel the aggressors to make reparation for the injuries inflicted by them—those receiving annuities being required to make as satisfactory a compensation in money as the case admitted. . . .

* * *

If the foregoing suggestions be carried out, a stop will in a great measure be put to tribal wars and intestine broils and difficulties; the idea of individual property and its security will be promoted, which will lead to industry and thrift; intemperance, which paralyzes the benevolent efforts of the government, of Christian associations, and of individuals, will be banished from the Indian country; and, under the effects of the other beneficial measures of policy now in operation, there would be manifest in the condition and circumstances of another generation of many of our less civilized Indians evidences of moral and social improvement, and of advancement in all the substantial elements of tribal and individual prosperity and happiness, similar to those which, to the gratification and encouragement of the philanthropist and the Christian, are conspicuously evident among some of the semi-civilized tribes. . . .

* * *

So far as information has reached this office, the Indians of the prairies who infest the two routes to our possessions west of the Rocky mountains . . . have been much less troublesome during the past season than heretofore. . . . They have been influenced in their general good conduct, however, by the expectation of some reward from the government, and not from fear—as they have not as yet felt our power, and know nothing of our greatness and resources.

These Indians, who have so long roamed free and uncontrolled over the immense prairies extending westward to the Rocky mountains, and who consider the whole country as their own, have regarded with much jealously the passing of so many of our people through it, without any recognition of their rights, or any compensation for the privilege. The great destruction of the buffalo by the emigrants has also caused much dissatisfaction among them. . . . Under these circumstances, it has been deemed expedient and advisable to take measures to bring about a proper understanding with the Indians, which will secure their good will, and prevent collisions and strife among them, by obligating each tribe to remain as much as possible within their respective districts of country, and providing that, where disputes or difficulties occur, they shall be submitted to the government, and the Indians abide by its decision. Instructions have accordingly been given to hold a treaty with the different tribes, making provision for the accomplishment of these objects, and stipulating that, for the unrestricted right of way through their country, for their good conduct towards our emigrants, and for the destruction of game unavoidably committed by them, they shall be allowed a reasonable compensation annually, to consist principally of presents of goods, stock and agricultural implements, with assistance to instruct and aid them in cultivating the soil, and in other kindred pursuits, so that they may thus be enabled to sustain themselves when the buffalo and other game shall have so far disappeared as no longer to furnish them with an adequate means of subsistence. It is also intended to bring in a delegation from the different tribes, for the purpose of visiting some of the more populous portions of the country, in order that they may acquire some knowledge of our greatness and strength, which will make a salutary impression upon them, and through them upon their brethren, and which will no doubt tend, in no slight degree, to influence them to continue peaceful relations towards the government and our citizens.

Commissioner Brown's report offers a useful glimpse into mid-nineteenth century Native America and the attitudes that were fueling the changes in federal policy. Both before and after this time, Native peoples were measured against the standard of "civilization" that was created and perpetuated by Europeans and Euro-Americans. Unsurprisingly under such a regime, tribal nations who bordered the United States and had greater interactions with Americans, according to Brown, were better behaved and more civilized because of their associations with their American neighbors, whereas more isolated Western tribal nations continued to cause trouble and behave in an uncivilized manner.

Brown credited the federal government, Christian associations, and "many excellent persons who, animated by a truly philanthropic and Christian spirit, have voluntarily banished themselves beyond the confines of civilization" for what he regarded as the positive developments in Indian Country. Tellingly, this list belies the growing efforts of the federal government and interested Americans to interject themselves within tribal communities. The separatist spirit of the Removal Era was consistently eroding as those interested in federal Indian policy were feeling increasingly compelled to engage with Native America. As the United States began to expand, so did its efforts to reach into tribal communities.

Reading between the lines, Brown's report also reveals the discontentment that many tribal nations felt as a consequence of an expanding United States. From his perspective as a federal bureaucrat, Brown described the issue in terms of needing to quell growing tribal discontent through treaty making. Nonetheless, the circumstances that led to that tribal discontent are apparent to a careful reader. Tribal lands were being trespassed upon, game was being overharvested, and there was no compensation for these hostile actions. In short, tribal nations were reacting strongly against settlers because those tribal nations were being invaded.

Brown argued for "measures to bring about a proper understanding with the Indians, which will secure their good will," through "reasonable compensation." In keeping with this reasoning, he also argued on behalf of the compensation to perpetuate the flow of settlers across tribal lands and to make up for the "destruction of game unavoidably committed by them." Brown's purpose was not to protect tribal interests, but rather to limit tribal discontent while seeking to ease the troubles caused by the invasion of tribal lands. In order to keep the peace in these changing times, intimidation was not out of the question. Brown noted that it was intended that a delegation of members of various tribal nations be brought to a "populous portion" of the United States "in order that they may acquire some knowledge of our greatness and strength." And yet, regardless of which method that Brown suggested—compensation or intimidation—the purpose was the same: to limit tribal discontent as settlers entered into their lands. Such strategies were necessary since Removal was becoming less and less of an option as Americans increasingly wanted to go where Native peoples were.

THE GOLD RUSH AND THE CIVIL WAR

American expansion and the desire for more land were exacerbated in 1848 when gold was discovered in California. Settlers began to flock west, with many heading to the West Coast but with many others also looking to establish their own homesteads along the way. As noted above, the rush of Americans put a tremendous strain on much of Native America, as large groups settlers, soldiers, and others traversed tribal lands. The federal government regularly sought out treaties to create space for settlers and to contain tribal nations in order to avoid conflict. The federal government also exercised greater military force in the newly desirable expanse, increasing both the threat of and actual incidents of violence. Tribal peoples suffered as resources became more limited and previously accessible hunting, farming, and gathering grounds became scarcer. The benefits of treaties could not offset the burdens that were increasingly placed on tribal nations.

American expansion both before and in the wake of the Gold Rush adversely affected many different tribal communities throughout Native America. However, perhaps none were more dramatically and disastrously affected by the Gold Rush itself than the tribal nations of California. A brief summation of the history reveals not only the ill effects of the rapid development of the West but also how American law was complicit in the process.

The territory that is now California was a Spanish colony and then part of Mexico for a long time before it fell into American hands in 1848 through the Treaty of Guadalupe Hidalgo. With the discovery of gold and the subsequent flood of settlers, the push to make California a state quickly developed, as did violence against Native peoples. Fueled by greed, settlers—often in organized militias—perpetrated acts of harassment, destruction, murder, and other depredations to push Native peoples off of lands they hoped to claim. The United States was unable, and perhaps unwilling, to protect Native peoples and their land claims despite pledging to do so in the Treaty of Guadalupe Hidalgo.

In 1851, the United States hastily assembled a commission to negotiate treaties with tribal nations in California. The haphazard nature of the commission and its work resulted in eighteen treaties, but the eighteen treaties were nonetheless riddled with mistakes, misidentifications, and only included a portion of the tribal nations in California. Regardless, California politicians objected to any treaties at all and the sentiment from the new state was able to kill congressional ratification of the treaties, leaving those tribal nations who signed them—and who began complying with their terms—in a no man's land of legal rights.

During this period, California also sought to exercise unlimited authority over tribal lands and peoples. This included the law excerpted below, but California's efforts extended much further as well. In his 1851 State of the State Address, Governor Peter Hardeman Burnett stated, "That a war of extermination will continue to be waged between the two races until the Indian race becomes extinct, must be expected." California engaged in various methods to bring about that extermination, including literally hunting Native peoples. As you read the excerpt of this early California law, ask yourself what rights it established for Native peoples and what rights are established against Native peoples. What recourse did Native peoples have under the law?

AN ACT FOR THE GOVERNMENT AND PROTECTION OF INDIANS

Chapter 133, Statutes of California, April 22, 1850

The people of the State of California, represented in Senate and Assembly, do enact as follows:

1. Justices of the Peace shall have jurisdiction in all cases of complaints by, for or against Indians, in their respective townships in this State.

2. Persons and proprietors of land on which Indians are residing, shall permit such Indians peaceably to reside on such lands, unmolested in the pursuit of their usual avocations for the maintenance of themselves and their families: *Provided*; the white person or proprietor in possession of lands may apply to a Justice of the Peace in the Township where the Indians reside, to set off to such Indians a certain amount of land, and, on such application, the Justice

shall set off a sufficient amount of land for the necessary wants of such Indians, including the site of their village or residence, if they so prefer it; and in no case shall such selection be made to the prejudice of such Indians, nor shall they be forced to abandon their homes or villages where they have resided for a number of years; and either party feeling themselves aggrieved, can appeal to the County Court from the decision of the Justice: and then divided, a record shall be made of the lands so set off in the Court so dividing them and the Indians shall be permitted to remain thereon until otherwise provided for.

* * *

5. Any person wishing to hire an Indian, shall go before a Justice of the Peace with the Indian, and make such contract as the Justice may approve, and the Justice shall file such contract in writing in his office, and all contracts so made shall be binding between the parties; but no contract between a white man and an Indian, for labor, shall otherwise be obligatory on the part of the Indian.

6. Complaints may be made before a Justice of the Peace, by white persons or Indians: but in no case shall a white man be convicted on any offence upon the testimony of an Indian.

7. If any person forcibly conveys an Indian from his home, or compels him to work, or perform against his will, in this State, except as provided in this Act, he or they shall, on conviction, be fined in any sum not less than fifty dollars, at the discretion of the Court or Jury.

* * *

9. It shall be the duty of the Justices of the Peace, in their respective townships, as well as all other peace officers in this State, to instruct the Indians in their neighborhood in the laws which relate to them, giving them such advice as they may deem necessary and proper; and if any tribe or village of Indians refuse or neglect to obey the laws, the Justice of the Peace may punish the guilty chiefs or principal men by reprimand or fine, or otherwise reasonably chastise them.

* * *

11. If any Indian shall commit an unlawful offence against a white person, such person shall not inflict punishment for such offence, but may, without process, take the Indian before a Justice of the Peace, and on conviction, the Indian shall be punished according to the provisions of this Act.

12. In all cases of trial between a white man and an Indian, either party may require a jury.

13. Justices may require the chiefs and influential men of any village to apprehend and bring before them or him any Indian charged or suspected of an offence.

14. When an Indian is convicted of an offence before a Justice of the Peace, punishable by fine, any white man may, by consent of the justice, give bond for said Indian, conditioned for the payment of said fine and costs, and in such case the Indian shall be compelled to work for the person so bailing, until he has discharged or cancelled the fine assessed against him: *Provided*, the person bailing shall treat the Indian humanely, and feed and clothe him properly; the allowance given for such labor shall be fixed by the Court, when the bond is taken.

15. If any person in this State shall sell, give, or furnish to any Indian, male or female, any intoxicating liquors (except when administered for sickness), for good cause shown, he, she, or they so offending shall, on conviction thereof, be fined not less than twenty dollars for each offence, or be imprisoned not less than five days, or fined and imprisoned as the Court may determine.

16. An Indian convicted of stealing horses, mules, cattle, or any valuable thing, shall be subject to receive any number of lashes not exceeding twenty-five, or shall be subject to a fine not exceeding two hundred dollars, at the discretion of the Court or jury.

17. When an Indian is sentenced to be whipped, the Justice may appoint a white man, or an Indian at his discretion, to execute the sentence in his presence, and shall not permit unnecessary cruelty in the execution of the sentence.

* * *

20. Any Indian able to work and support himself in some honest calling, not having wherewithal to maintain himself, who shall be found loitering and strolling about, or frequenting public places where liquors are sold, begging, or leading an immoral or profligate course of life, shall be liable to be arrested on the complaint of any reasonable citizen of the county, brought before the Justice of the Peace of the proper county, Mayor or Recorder of any incorporated town or city, who shall examine said accused Indian, and hear the testimony in relation thereto, and if said Justice, mayor or Recorder shall be satisfied that he is a vagrant, as above set forth, he shall make out a warrant under his hand and seal, authorizing and requiring the officer having him in charge or custody, to hire out such vagrant within twenty-four hours to the highest bidder, by public notice given as he shall direct, for the highest price

that can be had, for any term not exceeding four months; and such vagrant shall be subject to and governed by the provisions of this Act, regulating guardians and minors, during the time which he has been so hired. The money received for his hire, shall, after deducting the costs, and the necessary expense for clothing the said Indian, which may have been purchased by his employer, be, if he be without a family, paid into the County Treasury, to the credit of the Indian Fund. But if he have a family, the same shall be appropriated for their use and benefit: *Provided,* that any such vagrant, when arrested, and before judgment, may relieve himself by giving to said Justice, mayor or Recorder, a bond, with good security, conditioned that he will, for the next twelve months, conduct himself with good behavior, and betake to some honest employment for support.

In many respects, this California law appears to offer important, albeit limited, protections for tribal peoples. Among other things, it offers at least some access to land (Section 2), prohibits involuntary servitude (Sections 5 and 7), and prohibits vigilante justice (Section 11). The law also offers access to state courts to Native individuals (Section 12).

Despite the (limited) promise that it holds on its face, the law neutered itself and calls into question any and all of the protections for Native peoples that one could read into it. Section 6, while opening California courts to both "white persons and Indians," nonetheless also declared that "in no case shall a white man be convicted on any offence upon the testimony of an Indian." Since it was unlikely that tribal members would seek to resolve disputes among themselves in California courts, any case in state court was likely going to be between a White person and a Native person. And since the possibility of white persons testifying against each other was unlikely, the potential of a Native individual winning a case was remote. Thus, while announcing protections for Native persons, this early California law was little more than empty words that implicitly legalized bad behavior against them.

In the early to mid-1860s the Civil War turned the federal government's attention away from the West and from its interactions with tribal nations. Nonetheless, a number of military forts and settlements were developed in Western lands and governmental forces and settlers regularly engaged in hostilities against tribal peoples outside of the attention of those in Washington, D.C. Those governmental forces tasked with keeping the peace often harshly enforced American law against tribal peoples, or ignored it altogether when it benefitted tribal peoples. Two brief examples demonstrate the difficult circumstances in which tribal peoples found themselves and how the law was often employed against them.

The first example is the Dakota Conflict or Dakota War of 1862 (sometimes referred to as the Great Sioux Uprising in older literature). In the summer of 1862 fear, hunger, and desperation were growing among the Dakota in southwest Minnesota. They had signed treaties and were living peaceably on their reservation, but the United States was not fulfilling its obligations to provide annuities or to protect those annuities against theft and fraud when they were provided. When the Dakota complained to the Indian agent about their increasingly untenable situation, the agent told them to eat grass. Angered by this response, the repeated treaty violations they had suffered, and the starvation they were enduring on the reservation, members of the Dakota began hunting off of the reservation, a dangerous action that had resulted in punishment in the past. On the excursion they encountered settlers with whom they engaged in conflict and killed. Spurred by this encounter, the Dakota attempted to drive other settlers out of the region. For the next few months, southwest Minnesota saw a number of battles, with significant casualties on both sides. Eventually, Dakota forces were overcome and around 1700 Dakota were imprisoned in Fort Snelling, a fort located in what is now Minneapolis, Minnesota. Over 400 Dakota were put on trial and over 300 were convicted and sentenced to death, with some trials lasting less than five minutes. Eventually, President Abraham Lincoln did commute many of the sentences, but on December 26, 1862, thirty-eight Dakota were hanged. To this day it remains the largest mass execution in American history.

The second example is the Sand Creek Massacre. In November of 1864 a group of Cheyenne and Arapaho were living peacefully near Big Sandy Creek in Colorado. As a sign of peace, the encampment flew an American flag with a white flag underneath it. Assured protection by the Americans, most of the able-bodied men left the encampment to hunt for food. While they were gone, Colonel John M. Chivington, with a militia of around 700 men, approached the village. After a night of drunken revelry, Chivington ordered an attack on the village the next day. Victimizing mostly women and children, Chivington's men not only killed as many as 163 tribal persons, they mutilated and violated the bodies. Accounts of the massacre depict horrifying scenes of brutality. Not content to merely partake in the events, Chivington's men later displayed grisly trophies, such as scalps, genitalia, and fetuses before cheering crowds in Denver.

While these two events are perhaps the most famous examples of the atrocities committed against Native peoples during the Civil War, they were hardly the only ones. Both depict the lack of protection, legal and otherwise, that tribal peoples could expect from American forces in the West. Treaties did not guarantee peace, nor were the rights of tribal peoples respected. Additionally, some tribal nations participated in the Civil War. While some fought on the American side, many fought with and signed treaties with the Confederacy. Those who fought for the Confederate side often expressed anger against the unfulfilled treaty promises of the American government. For example, many Cherokee, who had suffered greatly under American law and in American courts, ended up fighting with the South. The story of Cherokee involvement in the Civil War is complex and is the result of many factors, including internal strife within the Cherokee nation. It suffices to note that the Cherokee, as well as other tribal nations that fought with the Confederacy, suffered greater losses of land and further incursions upon their sovereignty when reengaging with the Union after the war.

THE PEACE POLICY

After the Civil War, American attention in the east once again began turning to tribal peoples and issues. Many were horrified by the actions that were taking place in Indian Country and sought a new avenue for engaging with Native America. The federal government took up the issue again in earnest. Among its efforts at the time was to appoint a commission to study the "Indian Problem." As you read this excerpt from the committee's report, note the critiques that the commission makes. Who is at fault for the state of Native America? To what extent does it reflect a serious division of opinion within the federal government and the United States as a whole on how to approach Native peoples? To what extent does it challenge an assumption of white superiority? To what extent does it reinforce that assumption?

REPORT OF THE BOARD OF INDIAN COMMISSIONERS
Nov. 23, 1869

Paradoxical as it may seem, the white man has been the chief obstacle in the way of Indian civilization. The benevolent measures attempted by the government for their advancement have been almost uniformly thwarted by the agencies employed to carry them out. The soldiers, sent for their protection, too often carried demoralization and disease into their midst. The agent, appointed to be their friend and counselor, business manager, and the almoner of the government bounties, frequently went among them only to enrich himself in the shortest possible time, at the cost of the Indians; and spend the largest available sum of the government money with the least ostensible beneficial result. The general interest of the trader was opposed to their enlightenment as tending to lessen his profits. Any increase of intelligence would render them less liable to his impositions; and, if occupied in agricultural pursuits, their product of furs would be proportionally decreased. The contractor's and transporter's interests were opposed to it, for the reason that the production of agricultural products on the spot would measurably cut off their profits in furnishing army supplies. The interpreter knew that if they were taught, his occupation would be gone. The more submissive and patient the tribe, the greater number of outlaws infesting their vicinity; and all these were the missionaries teaching them the most degrading vices of which humanity is capable. If in spite of these obstacles a tribe made some progress in agriculture, or their lands became valuable from any cause, the process of civilization was summarily ended by driving them away from their homes with fire and sword, to undergo similar experiences in some new locality.

Shocked by incidents such as the Dakota Conflict, the Sand Creek Massacre, and the results of the Commission's findings, and with little appetite for additional fighting after the violence of the Civil War, the United States sought treaties of peace with tribal nations. This new "Peace Policy" was intended to quell the hostilities that had grown while Washington, D.C., was preoccupied with the Civil War, and many of the treaties of this time created reservations or portions of them that now exist in the Western United States. These treaties also often provided not only payment for the land, but also provisions for the advancement of Western civilization into Native America. For example, many treaties specified that the federal government would provide equipment and training to begin Western-style farming.

Most associated with President Ulysses S. Grant, the Peace Policy sought to root out the corruption and avarice that many believed was endemic within the Bureau of Indian Affairs. To achieve these ends, the federal government began extracting federal bureaucrats from reservations and assigning different religious denominations to administer them. The belief was that religious-minded men would better resist the temptation to exploit their positions of authority and that they would further the efforts at civilizing tribal peoples. However, the practice was not as effective as intended. Different Christian denominations often fought for control over different reservations, the people sent to administer the reservations were no better trained to handle the various challenges than other government officials, and seemingly good intentions were unable to change or better an oppressive system that did not account for the actual needs and desires of Native nations. Relatively quickly, the practice of assigning reservations to different Christian denominations began to die out. However, the legacy of this choice remains, as many Native peoples today maintain an affiliation with the Christian denomination that was assigned to their reservation.

The Peace Policy was also somewhat misleadingly named. While the federal government initiated interactions with tribal nations with whom it wanted to negotiate in a peaceful manner, the threat of force or violence was always in the background. Tribal nations who resisted the diplomatic efforts of the United States quickly faced military forces and coercion. From the federal government's perspective, Native peoples were going to engage in its version of peace, regardless of whether those Native peoples wanted to participate or not.

With Native issues back in the American spotlight, and with American attitudes about how to engage with Native peoples changing, tribal issues once again began reaching the Supreme Court on a more regular basis. The following case involves two Cherokee citizens who were growing tobacco on Cherokee lands. In 1868 Congress passed a tax on tobacco grown "within the exterior boundaries of the United States." The Cherokee citizens argued that the tax did not apply to them, since an 1866 treaty exempted Cherokee citizens from paying taxes on products they produced and sold. The question of the case was whether the Cherokee citizens were subject to the 1868 tax or whether the 1866 treaty shielded them from it.

As you read this excerpt from the Supreme Court opinion ask yourself on what basis the majority makes its decision. What is the argument that the dissent makes? How should American courts read treaties, particularly Indian treaties? How does the majority's opinion and reasoning reflect the changing attitude about how to solve the "Indian Problem"? Keep this case in mind as you read about treaties later in this text.

THE CHEROKEE TOBACCO
78 U.S. (11 Wall.) 616 (1870)

MR. JUSTICE SWAYNE stated the case and delivered the opinion of the Court.

* * *

The only question argued in this Court, and upon which our decision must depend, is the effect to be given respectively to the 107th section of the act of 1868, and the 10th article of the treaty of 1866, between the United States and the Cherokee nation of Indians.

They are as follows:

"*Section 107.* That the internal revenue laws imposing taxes on distilled spirits, fermented liquors, tobacco, snuff, and cigars, shall be construed to extend to such articles produced anywhere within the exterior boundaries of the United States, whether the same shall be within a collection district or not."

"*Article 10th.* Every Cherokee Indian and freed person residing in the Cherokee nation shall have the right to sell any products of his farm, including his or her livestock, or any merchandise or manufactured products, and to ship and drive the same to market without restraint, paying any tax thereon which is now or may be levied by the United States on the quantity sold outside of the Indian territory."

On behalf of the claimants it is contended that the 107th section was not intended to apply, and does not apply, to the country of the Cherokees, and that the immunities secured by the treaty are in full force there. The United States insist that the section applies with the same effect to the territory in question as to any state or other territory of the United States, and that to the extent of the provisions of the section, the treaty is annulled.

Considering the narrowness of the questions to be decided, a remarkable wealth of learning and ability have been expended in their discussion. The views of counsel in this Court have rarely been more elaborately presented. Nevertheless the case seems to us not difficult to be determined, and to require no very extended line of remarks to vindicate the soundness of the conclusions at which we have arrived.

In *Cherokee Nation v. Georgia,* Chief Justice Marshall, delivering the opinion of this Court, said: "The Indian territory is admitted to compose a part of the United States. In all our geographical treatises, histories, and laws it is so considered." In *United States v. Rogers,* Chief Justice Taney, also speaking for the Court, held this language: "It is our duty to expound and execute the law as we find it, and we think it too firmly and clearly established to admit of dispute that the Indian tribes residing within the territorial limits of the United States are subject to their authority, and where the country occupied by them is not within the limits of one of the states, Congress may by law punish any offense committed there, no matter whether the offender be a white man or an Indian." Both these propositions are so well settled in our jurisprudence that it would be a waste of time to discuss them or to refer to further authorities in their support. There is a long and unbroken current of legislation and adjudications, in accordance with them, and we are aware of nothing in conflict with either. . . . The language of the section is as clear and explicit as could be employed. It embraces indisputably the Indian territories. Congress not having thought proper to exclude them, it is not for this Court to make the exception. If the exemption had been intended, it would doubtless have been expressed. There being no ambiguity, there is no room for construction. It would be out of place. The section must be held to mean what the language imports. . . .

But conceding these views to be correct, it is insisted that the section cannot apply to the Cherokee nation because it is in conflict with the treaty. Undoubtedly one or the other must yield. The repugnancy is clear, and they cannot stand together.

The second section of the fourth article of the Constitution of the United States declares that, "This Constitution and the laws of the United States which shall be made in pursuance thereof, and all treaties which shall be made under the authority of the United States, shall be the supreme law of the land."

It need hardly be said that a treaty cannot change the Constitution or be held valid if it be in violation of that instrument. This results from the nature and fundamental principles of our government. The effect of treaties and acts of Congress, when in conflict, is not settled by the Constitution. But the question is not involved in any doubt as to its proper solution. A treaty may supersede a prior act of Congress, and an act of Congress may supersede a prior treaty. In the cases referred to, these principles were applied to treaties with foreign nations. Treaties with Indian nations within the jurisdiction of the United States, whatever considerations of humanity and good faith may be involved and require their faithful and good faith may be inobligatory. They have no higher sanctity, and no greater inviolability or immunity from legislative invasion can be claimed for them. The consequences in all such cases give rise to questions which must be met by the political department of the government. They are beyond the sphere of judicial cognizance. In the case under consideration, the act of Congress must prevail as if the treaty were not an element to be considered. If a wrong has been done, the power of redress is with Congress, not with the judiciary, and that body, upon being applied to, it is to be presumed, will promptly give the proper relief.

Does the section thus construed deserve the severe strictures which have been applied to it? As before remarked, it extends the revenue laws over the Indian territories only as to liquors and tobacco. In all other respects, the Indians in those territories are exempt. As regards those articles only, the same duties are exacted as from our own citizens. The burden must rest somewhere. Revenue is indispensable to meet the public necessities. Is it unreasonable that this small portion of it shall rest upon these Indians? The frauds that might otherwise be perpetrated there by others, under the guise of Indian names and simulated Indian ownership, is also a consideration not to be overlooked.

We are glad to know that there is no ground for any imputation upon the integrity or good faith of the claimants who prosecuted this writ of error. In a case not free from doubt and difficulty, they acted under a misapprehension of their legal rights.

Judgment affirmed.

MR. JUSTICE BRADLEY (with whom concurred MR. JUSTICE DAVIS), dissenting.

I dissent from the opinion of the Court just read. In my judgment it was not the intention of Congress to extend the internal revenue law to the Indian territory. That territory is an exempt jurisdiction. Whilst the United States has not relinquished its power to make such regulations as it may deem necessary in relation to that territory, and whilst Congress has occasionally passed laws affecting it, yet by repeated treaties the government has in effect stipulated that in all ordinary cases, the Indian populations shall be autonomies, invested with the power to make and execute all laws for their domestic government. Such being the case, all laws of a general character passed by Congress will be considered as not applying to the Indian territory unless expressly mentioned. An express law creating certain special rights and privileges is held never to be repealed by implication by any subsequent law couched in general terms, nor by any express repeal of all laws inconsistent with such general law, unless the language be such as clearly to indicate the intention of the legislature to effect such repeal. . . . In every case, the intent of the legislature is to be sought, and in the case of such special and local exemptions the general rule for ascertaining whether the legislature does or does not intend to repeal or affect them, is to inquire whether they are expressly named; if not expressly named, then whether the language used is such, nevertheless, as *clearly to indicate* the legislative intent to repeal or affect them.

In the case before the Court, I hold that there is nothing to indicate such a legislative intent. The language used is nothing but general language imposing a general system of requirements and penalties on the whole country. Had it been the intent of Congress to include the Indian territory, it would have been very easy to say so. Not having said so, I hold that the presumption is that Congress did not intend to include it.

The case before us is, besides, a peculiar one. The exempt jurisdiction here depends on a solemn treaty entered into between the United States government and the Cherokee nation, in which the good faith of the government is involved, and not on a mere municipal law. It is conceded that the law in question cannot be extended to the Indian territory without an implied abrogation of the treaty *pro tanto*. And the opinion of the court goes upon the principle that Congress has the power to supersede the provisions of a treaty. In such a case, there are peculiar reasons for applying with great strictness the rule that the exempt jurisdiction must be expressly mentioned in order to be affected.

This view is strengthened by the fact that there is territory within the exterior bounds of the United States to which the language of the 107th section of the recent act can apply, without applying it to the Indian territory, to-wit, the Territory of Alaska. And it does not appear by the record that there are not other districts within the general territory of the United States which are in like predicament.

The judgment, according to these views, ought to be reversed.

THE CHIEF JUSTICE, and NELSON and FIELD, JJ., did not hear the argument.

In one sense, this case is about how to read a treaty, particularly in light of subsequent legislation that is in conflict with the treaty. For a deeper discussion on this question of law, see Chapter 11.

For the purposes of this chapter, this case was another example of the American government moving away from the separatist motivations that drove the Removal Era of federal policy. In the case, a federal tax was imposed upon tribal citizens growing crops on tribal territory that was within the borders of the United States. Whereas it would be unthinkable to impose a tax on a foreign nation, *The Cherokee Tobacco* sanctioned a tax against a domestic dependent nation. The further the United States moved westward, the more questions there arose like the one presented in this case on how to engage with tribal nations and peoples that more and more found themselves within the borders of the United States.

The answers to those questions increasingly became further federal interventions into the internal relations of Native nations and the lives of Native peoples. The pendulum that is federal policy was poised to swing once again, moving from the separatism of the Removal Era of federal policy to assimilation. American law, as this and future chapters demonstrate, was a foundational component to this change.

SUGGESTED READINGS

- *Lincoln and the Indians: Civil War Policy and Politics.* David A. Nichols. St. Paul, MN: Minnesota Historical Society Press, 2012.

- *An American Genocide: The United States and the California Indian Catastrophe, 1846–1873.* Benjamin Madley. New Haven, CT: Yale University Press, 2016.

- *Crooked Paths to Allotment: The Fight over Federal Indian Policy after the Civil War.* C. Joseph Genetin-Pilawa. Chapel Hill, NC: University of North Carolina Press, 2014.

CHAPTER 5

The Allotment Era

By the 1870s the changing tides that had been building in federal Indian policy began to crest. The pendulum had fully swung from the separatist model that defined the Removal Era to an assimilation model that is best described as the Allotment Era of federal policy. Lasting from approximately 1871–1934, the Allotment Era was a significant time not just in law and policy but throughout the totality of Native America. The United States made deliberate and concerted efforts to destroy tribalism and Native ways of life in the Allotment Era and the many consequences of this period are still deeply felt today. The impact within law and policy alone are so great that it will be the subject of the next three chapters.

This period of federal policy is named after the most significant piece of American legislation to affect Indian Country during this time: the Allotment Act. The consequences of the Allotment Act, also called the Dawes Act after the Senator who sponsored it, were devastating for Indian Country. It led to massive tribal land loss, disrupted tribal patterns of land ownership and use, and created a legacy that the law, policymakers, tribal peoples and nations, and others living on and near reservations continue to have to reconcile with to this day.

As important and defining as it was and continues to be, the Allotment Act was only one piece of a larger picture of American policy in the late nineteenth and early twentieth centuries. The shift to an assimilation model was a multi-pronged effort to drastically reshape not just Indian Country but Native peoples themselves and their ways of life. The federal government engaged in a number of coercive actions in the name of civilizing Native peoples.

> *This chapter will demonstrate. . .*
>
> - *The basic structure of the Allotment Act*
>
> - *The continuing consequences of Allotment*
>
> - *Other federal efforts at destroying Native ways of life in the Allotment Era*

ALLOTMENT

The defining piece of legislation during the Allotment Era was the Allotment Act, or the General Allotment Act or Dawes Act, of 1887. The impact of the legislation cannot be understated, as it resulted in drastic change for tribal peoples and lands and continues to impact Native America and beyond to this day.

As noted in the previous chapter, by the mid-19th century, the United States began to seriously regard Native peoples and nations as a domestic concern rather than a foreign problem, radically altering how the United States addressed the "Indian Problem." The Allotment Act was a major step toward treating Native issues as domestic problems, resulting in the federal government deeply interjecting itself into tribal life. At its most basic, the Allotment Act required that previously communally held tribal lands be subdivided into individual plots and assigned to individual tribal members. In general, heads of households received 160 acres on which they were supposed to farm and develop habits of "civilized life." The federal government was also to provide tools and training to Individual Native persons to foster an agrarian, individualistic lifestyle. The allotments were to be held in trust by the United States for a period of twenty-five years. After the twenty-five year period, allottees—those who received allotments—were to become United States citizens, were to receive the land in fee (or without any restrictions on the sale or use of the land), and were to be responsible for all taxes and any other obligations of ownership of the land. Additionally, as there were often "surplus" lands on reservations once allotment had taken place, those lands were put up for sale to the non-Native public.

Allotment was, like much of federal Indian policy, supposedly an elegant solution for all involved. It joined those who wanted additional tribal lands with those who earnestly believed that it was necessary to "civilize" tribal peoples before they perished under the weight of colonization. Many policymakers and other interested parties felt that the reservation system was failing and would lead to the demise of tribal peoples as it permitted tribal peoples to maintain their "uncivilized" customs. Many also argued that Native peoples needed to be taught Western ways of life in order to survive in their rapidly changing world.

The foundational principle behind these arguments was that Native peoples and their ways of life were inferior to the Western ideal. For many who took an interest in the Native cause, the only solution was to eliminate tribal habits and replace them with the more advanced Western system. For example, the Commissioner of Indian Affairs in 1881 stated that, "It must be apparent to the most casual observer that the system of gathering the Indians in bands or tribes on reservations and carrying to them victuals and clothes, thus relieving them of the necessity of labor, never will and never can civilize them. . . . The greatest kindness the government can bestow upon the Indian is to teach him to labor for his own support, thus developing a true manhood, and, as a consequence, making him self-relying and self-supporting."[1] A high ranking member of a philanthropic group that called itself the "Friends of the Indian," stated in 1896 that, "To bring him out of savagery into citizenship we must make the Indian more intelligently selfish before we can make him unselfishly intelligent. We need to awaken in him wants. . . ."[2]

The additional benefit of allotment for many non-Natives was that it opened up even more tribal land. The argument that too few Native peoples claimed too much land was longstanding, and allotment proved to be a useful vehicle for divesting tribal nations of their territory. In fact, the allotment process was supposed to pay for itself. The expense of surveying the land and providing agricultural equipment and training was supposed to be offset by the sale of "surplus" lands. The confluence of those who wanted tribal lands and reformers who wanted to civilize Native peoples proved too much for many Native nations to repel. By the time the allotment process was officially abandoned in the 1930s, it is estimated that tribal nations and individuals lost over ninety million acres of land. In addition, the legacy of this process has complicated tribal and individual land holding ever since.

As you read this excerpt from the Allotment Act, ask yourself what process it puts in place to execute its goal. What are the consequences for those who resist? What protections are in place for allottees? In its ideal form, how is allotment supposed to operate?

ALLOTMENT ACT (DAWES ACT)

U.S. Statutes at Large 24:388 (1887)

Be it enacted by the Senate and House of Representatives of the United States of America in Congress assembled, That in all cases where any tribe or band of Indians has been, or shall hereafter be, located upon any reservation created for their use . . . the President of the United States be, and he hereby is, authorized, whenever in his opinion any reservation or any part thereof of such Indians is advantageous for agricultural and grazing purposes, to cause said reservation, or any part thereof, to be surveyed, or resurveyed if necessary, and to allot the lands in said reservation in severalty to any Indian located thereon in quantities as follows:

To each head of a family, one-quarter of a section;

To each single person over eighteen years of age, one-eighth of a section;

To each orphan child under eighteen years of age, one-eighth of a section; and

To each other single person under eighteen years now living, or who may be born prior to the date of the order of the President directing an allotment of the lands embraced in any reservation, one-sixteenth of a section:

Provided, That in case there is not sufficient land in any of said reservations to allot lands to each individual of the classes above named in quantities as above provided, the lands embraced in such reservation or reservations shall be allotted to each individual of each of said classes pro rata in accordance with the provisions of this act: And provided further, That where the treaty or act of Congress setting apart such reservation provides the allotment of lands in severalty in quantities in excess of those herein provided, the President, in making allotments upon such reservation, shall allot the lands to each individual Indian belonging thereon in quantity as specified in such treaty or act: And provided further, That when the lands allotted are only valuable for grazing purposes, an additional allotment of such grazing lands, in quantities as above provided, shall be made to each individual.

Sec. 2.   That all allotments set apart under the provisions of this act shall be selected by the Indians, heads of families selecting for their minor children, and the agents shall select for each orphan child, and in such manner as to embrace the improvements of the Indians making the selection. . . . *Provided,* That if any one entitled to an allotment shall fail to make a selection within four years after the President shall direct that allotments may be made on a particular reservation, the Secretary of the Interior may direct the agent of such tribe or band, if such there be, and if there be no agent, then a special agent appointed for that purpose, to make a selection for such Indian, which selection shall be allotted as in cases where selections are made by the Indians, and patents shall issue in like manner.

* * *

Sec. 4.   That where any Indian not residing upon a reservation, or for whose tribe no reservation has been provided by treaty, act of Congress, or executive order, shall make settlement upon any surveyed or unsurveyed lands of the United States not otherwise appropriated, he or she shall be entitled, upon application to the local land-office for the district in which the lands are located, to have the same allotted to him or her, and to his or her children, in quantities and manner as provided in this act for Indians residing upon reservations. . . .

Sec. 5.   That upon the approval of the allotments . . . the United States does and will hold the land thus allotted, for the period of twenty-five years, in trust for the sole use and benefit of the Indian to whom such allotment shall have been made, or, in case of his decease, of his heirs according to the laws of the State or Territory where such land is located, and that at the expiration of said period the United States will convey the same by patent to said Indian, or his heirs as aforesaid, in fee, discharged of said trust and free of all charge or incumbrance whatsoever: *Provided*, That the President of the United States may in any case in his discretion extend the period. . . . *And provided further*, That at any time after lands have been allotted to all the Indians of any tribe as herein provided, or sooner if in the opinion of the President it shall be for the best interests of said tribe, it shall be lawful for the Secretary of the Interior to negotiate with such Indian tribe for the purchase and release by said tribe, in conformity with the treaty or statute under which such reservation is held, of such portions of its reservation not allotted as such tribe shall, from time to time, consent to sell, on such terms and conditions as shall be considered just and equitable between the United States and said tribe of Indians, which purchase shall not be complete until ratified by Congress, and the form and manner of executing such release prescribed by Congress. . . . And the sums agreed to be paid by the United States as purchase money for any portion of any such reservation shall be held in the Treasury of the United States for the sole use of the tribe or tribes Indians; to whom such reservations belonged; and the same, with interest thereon at three per cent per annum, shall be at all times subject to appropriation by Congress for the education and civilization of such tribe or tribes of Indians or the members thereof. . . . And if any religious society or other organization is now occupying any of the public lands to which this act is applicable, for religious or educational work among the

Indians, the Secretary of the Interior is hereby authorized to confirm such occupation to such society or organization, in quantity not exceeding one hundred and sixty acres in any one tract, so long as the same shall be so occupied, on such terms as he shall deem just; but nothing herein contained shall change or alter any claim of such society for religious or educational purposes heretofore granted by law. And hereafter in the employment of Indian police, or any other employees in the public service among any of the Indian tribes or bands affected by this act, and where Indians can perform the duties required, those Indians who have availed themselves of the provisions of this act and become citizens of the United States shall be preferred.

Sec. 6. That upon the completion of said allotments and the patenting of the lands to said allottees, each and every member of the respective bands or tribes of Indians to whom allotments have been made shall have the benefit of and be subject to the laws, both civil and criminal, of the State or Territory in which they may reside; and no Territory shall pass or enforce any law denying any such Indian within its jurisdiction the equal protection of the law. And every Indian born within the territorial limits of the United States to whom allotments shall have been made under the provisions of this act, or under any law or treaty, and every Indian born within the territorial limits of the United States who has voluntarily taken up, within said limits, his residence separate and apart from any tribe of Indians therein, and has adopted the habits of civilized life, is hereby declared to be a citizen of the United States, and is entitled to all the rights, privileges, and immunities of such citizens, whether said Indian has been or not, by birth or otherwise, a member of any tribe of Indians within the territorial limits of the United States without in any manner affecting the right of any such Indian to tribal or other property.

Sec. 7. That in cases where the use of water for irrigation is necessary to render the lands within any Indian reservation available for agricultural purposes, the Secretary of the Interior be, and he is hereby, authorized to prescribe such rules and regulations as he may deem necessary to secure a just and equal distribution thereof among the Indians residing upon any such reservation. . . .

Sec. 8. That the provisions of this act shall not extend to the territory occupied by the Cherokees, Creeks, Choctaws, Chickasaws, Seminoles, and Osage, Miamis and Peorias, and Sacs and Foxes, in the Indian Territory, nor to any of the reservations of the Seneca Nation of New York Indians in the State of New York, nor to that strip of territory in the State of Nebraska adjoining the Sioux Nation on the south added by executive order.

* * *

Sec. 10. That nothing in this act contained shall be so construed to affect the right and power of Congress to grant the right of way through any lands granted to an Indian, or a tribe of Indians, for railroads or other highways, or telegraph lines, for the public use, or condemn such lands to public uses, upon making just compensation. . . .

One of the main characteristics of federal Indian policy is that, despite the seemingly all-encompassing nature of various policy eras, its application has been haphazard and uneven. For example, not all tribal nations in the east were removed during the Removal Era, and not every tribal member left her or his homeland when their tribal nation was removed. So it was with allotment. Although many reservations were allotted many were only partially so and some escaped the process altogether. Some required different allotment patterns depending on the terrain of the reservation. For example, reservations that were heavily wooded were regularly allotted differently than reservations with lands more suited for agriculture. This is another example of the diversity within Native America and the importance of learning about specific histories when studying or working with a particular tribal nation.

For the many in Native America who did endure the hardship of allotment, the dire consequences were often immediate. Instead of creating a self-sustaining class of farmers, the allotment process led to more hardship and poverty. Many tribal members tried to resist the process, refusing to farm or accept their allotment. Those who did attempt to farm were often unsuccessful. Others leased their lands to non-Native ranchers and farmers, often well below market value.

Federal policymakers were also frustrated by the consequences of allotment. As the difficulties mounted, many began arguing that the problem was not with allotment itself but with its implementation. The reasoning was that the twenty-five year trust period was too long and that it prevented those individuals who were ready to participate in American life from doing so.

In 1906 Congress responded to these arguments with the Burke Act, which amended the Allotment Act. As you read this excerpt ask yourself how does it amend the Allotment Act? What are the potential consequences of the amendment? Who is this amendment supposed to benefit?

> ## BURKE ACT
> U.S. Statutes at Large 34:182 (1906)
>
> *Be it enacted by the Senate and House of Representatives of the United States of America in Congress assembled,* That section six of [the Allotment Act] be amended to read as follows:
>
> * * *
>
> **"SEC. 6.** . . . Provided, That the Secretary of the Interior may, in his discretion, and he is hereby authorized, whenever he shall be satisfied that any Indian allottee is competent and capable of managing his or her affairs, at any time to cause to be issued to such allottee a patent in fee simple, and thereafter all restrictions as to sale, incumbrance, or taxation of said land shall be removed and said land shall not be liable to the satisfaction of any debt contracted prior to the issuing of such patent. . . .

The Burke Act amended the Allotment Act to allow the federal government, through the Secretary of the Interior, to bypass the twenty-five year trust period that shielded individual tribal allotments in the original legislation. Under the Burke Act, should the Secretary of the Interior find an individual Native person to be "competent and capable of managing his or her affairs," then the Secretary could take the land out of trust before the full twenty-five years were up. The discretion given to the Secretary of the Interior to determine the competency of individual tribal members was, when put into practice, not particularly sophisticated. Often, individual tribal members were deemed competent based solely on the degree of their White blood. Those with more European heritage were automatically considered competent, and were given their allotted lands in fee, regardless of their actual ability or desire to participate in American life. Much more vulnerable than lands that were still in trust, fee lands were often quickly lost through state taxes, to unscrupulous non-Indians, and by other means, hastening the ill effects of the Allotment Era.

THREE LINGERING CONSEQUENCES

While it did not happen everywhere and not always to the same degree everywhere it did happen, allotment touched many Native peoples and nations. It created significant problems that remain to this day. Three major issues stand out for both their immediate impact on Native America and the way those issues continue to affect the lives and well-being of Native nations and peoples to this day.

The first such issue is that many reservations are "checkerboarded," or contain different patterns of land ownership. Checkerboarded reservations generally contain lands that are held in three primary ways: (1) tribal trust land—land that remains held in trust by the United States for the tribal nation as a whole; (2) Indian fee land—land owned in fee by individual tribal members; and (3) non-Indian fee land—land owned in fee by individual non-tribal members. Fee lands, as briefly noted above, are less restricted than trust lands, creating a situation in which some reservation lands are much more highly regulated than other lands. As is discussed in later chapters, this checkerboarding continues to cause a number of problems for the individuals living on the reservation, tribal nations themselves, the states in which the reservations are located, and the federal government as well. This is particularly so when considering issues of jurisdiction.

A second major issue is particularly fraught with irony since one of the avowed purposes of allotment was to eventually remove the federal government from the "Indian business" by dividing up tribal lands and converting tribal members into individual landowners and American citizens. The process of allotment and its perpetuation required that the federal government develop an enormous bureaucracy to manage the process. Lands needed to be surveyed and recorded and even chosen for those tribal members who refused to do so for themselves. Allotments also needed to be managed during the trust period. Rents needed to be collected and kept track of for allotments that were leased. Arrangements for agricultural supplies and training needed to be secured. And heirs needed to be notified when an allottee died. These and all sorts of other problems arose in the day-to-day operations of managing allotments.

The federal bureaucrats of the Bureau of Indian Affairs were rarely properly trained for the multitude of tasks that they faced during the Allotment Era, when they wore any number of hats at a given time. In addition, corruption was rampant as money moved quickly and without much oversight. The Department of the Interior established Individual Indian Money Accounts (IIMs) to handle the different financial conditions for individuals during this era. But the mismanagement of those IIM accounts, coupled with different pockets of corruption, led to a convoluted situation in which the recordkeeping was inadequate at best. After being sued by tribal members in the late twentieth century the federal government eventually had to admit that it was unable to properly account for much of the money it held in trust for individual tribal members (see Chapter 14).

The third major issue is known as fractionalization. Often an individual allotment will have an inordinate number of owners. Tribal members who held allotments in the late nineteenth and early twentieth centuries generally did not have wills. Thus, when they died, their allotment was divided up under the laws of intestacy, or the laws of inheritance. Specific laws could vary based on a number of different circumstances; nonetheless, a brief hypothetical will demonstrate the problem that quickly developed. Imagine a parent of Generation A had four children, the members of Generation B. Generally under the law of intestacy when the parent dies each child, or member of Generation B in this example, would receive an equal share of the allotment, or a 1/4th interest. If each member of Generation B also had four children then those grandchildren, or members of Generation C, would have a 1/16th interest in the original allotment. If the same pattern continued, with each generation each producing four children, by Generation G each family member would hold a 1/1024th share of the original allotment. Since property law generally requires that all persons with any interest in a parcel of land agree to its use, many pieces of land in Indian Country are essentially unable to ever change their use or undergo any additional development.

At various times throughout the 20th and 21st centuries Congress has sought to address the fractionalization problem, without much success. The first major effort was in 1934 through the Indian Reorganization Act (see Chapter 8). However, this attempt was limited by a number of factors, including the fact that the statute did not directly address situations when tribal members died without a will. In the following years Congress passed the occasional smaller bill to handle a specific tribal nation's fractionalization dilemmas. The next major attempt was in 1983 with the Indian Land Consolidation Act (ILCA). The law created a pathway for tribal nations to manage the fractionalization problem from a number of directions, including buying highly divided lands at market value prices with the agreement of a majority of the owners and establishing restrictions on further fractionalization for land owners who died without a will.

In large part due to the legacy of the Allotment Era, the subject of land is often quite sensitive and contentious in Native America, with little in the way of consensus. Consequently, one portion of the ILCA was particularly controversial—section 207, the escheat provision. Section 207 allowed for interests in land held by an individual that were exceptionally small to pass directly to a tribal nation on the death of the owner of that interest in land in lieu of the landowners heirs. A class of would-be landowners, who otherwise would have gained fractionalized interests in land upon the passing of their relatives, sued the federal government. The would-be landowners argued that section 207 amounted to "taking" by the government and was thus unconstitutional. Under the U.S. Constitution, the federal government, even on behalf of tribal nations, cannot acquire the land of a citizen without paying "just compensation." The question of the case was whether the escheat provision established the type of taking that is prohibited by the U.S. Constitution. As you read the case, ask yourself how section 207 is supposed to accomplish its goal. How does the Supreme Court describe the problem of fractionalization? What is objectionable about the process set forth in section 207? Are there any alternatives?

HODEL V. IRVING
481 U.S. 704 (1987)

JUSTICE O'CONNOR delivered the opinion of the Court.

* * *

Towards the end of the 19th century, Congress enacted a series of land Acts which divided the communal reservations of Indian tribes into individual allotments for Indians and unallotted lands for non-Indian settlement. This legislation seems to have been in part animated by a desire to force Indians to abandon their nomadic ways in order to "speed the Indians' assimilation into American society," and in part a result of pressure to free new lands for further white settlement. . . .

The policy of allotment of Indian lands quickly proved disastrous for the Indians. Cash generated by land sales to whites was quickly dissipated, and the Indians, rather than farming the land themselves, evolved into petty landlords, leasing their allotted lands to white ranchers and farmers and living off the meager rentals. The failure of the allotment program became even clearer as successive generations came to hold the allotted lands. Thus 40-, 80-, and 160-acre parcels became splintered into multiple undivided interests in land, with some parcels having hundreds, and many parcels having dozens, of owners. Because the land was held in trust and often could not be alienated or partitioned, the fractionation problem grew and grew over time.

* * *

But the end of future allotment by itself could not prevent the further compounding of the existing problem caused by the passage of time. Ownership continued to fragment as succeeding generations came to hold the property, since, in the order of things, each property owner was apt to have more than one heir . . . not until the Indian Land Consolidation Act of 1983 did the Congress take action to ameliorate the problem of fractionated ownership of Indian lands.

Section 207 of the Indian Land Consolidation Act—the escheat provision at issue in this case—provided:

> No undivided fractional interest in any tract of trust or restricted land within a tribe's reservation or otherwise subjected to a tribe's jurisdiction shall descendent [sic] by intestacy or devise but shall escheat to that tribe if such interest represents 2 per centum or less of the total acreage in such tract and has earned to its owner less than $100 in the preceding year before it is due to escheat.

Congress made no provision for the payment of compensation to the owners of the interests covered by 207. . . . But for 207, [parcels of fractionalized] property would have passed, in the ordinary course, to appellees or those they represent.

* * *

The Congress, acting pursuant to its broad authority to regulate the descent and devise of Indian trust lands enacted 207 as a means of ameliorating, over time, the problem of extreme fractionation of certain Indian lands. By forbidding the passing on at death of small, undivided interests in Indian lands, Congress hoped that future generations of Indians would be able to make more productive use of the Indians' ancestral lands. We agree with the Government that encouraging the consolidation of Indian lands is a public purpose of high order. The fractionation problem on Indian reservations is extraordinary and may call for dramatic action to encourage consolidation. The Sisseton-Wahpeton Sioux Tribe, appearing as amicus curiae in support of the Secretary of the Interior, is a quintessential victim of fractionation. Forty-acre tracts on the Sisseton-Wahpeton Lake Traverse Reservation, leasing for about $1,000 annually, are commonly subdivided into hundreds of undivided interests, many of which generate only pennies a year in rent. The average tract has 196 owners and the average owner undivided interests in 14 tracts. The administrative headache this represents can be fathomed by examining Tract 1305, dubbed "one of the most fractionated parcels of land in the world." Tract 1305 is 40 acres and produces $1,080 in income annually. It is valued at $8,000. It has 439 owners, one-third of whom receive less than $.05 in annual rent and two-thirds of whom receive less than $1. The largest interest holder receives $82.85 annually. The common denominator used to compute fractional interests in the property is 3,394,923,840,000. The smallest heir receives $.01 every 177 years. If the tract were sold (assuming the 439 owners could agree) for its estimated $8,000 value, he would be entitled to $.000418. The administrative

The Allotment Era

costs of handling this tract are estimated by the Bureau of Indian Affairs at $17,560 annually.

This Court has held that the Government has considerable latitude in regulating property rights in ways that may adversely affect the owners. The framework for examining the question whether a regulation of property amounts to a taking requiring just compensation is firmly established and has been regularly and recently reaffirmed. As THE CHIEF JUSTICE has written:

> [T]his Court . . . has examined the 'taking' question by engaging in essentially ad hoc, factual inquiries that have identified several factors—such as the economic impact of the regulation, its interference with reasonable investment backed expectations, and the character of the governmental action—that have particular significance.

There is no question that the relative economic impact of 207 upon the owners of these property rights can be substantial. . . . Even if we accept the Government's assertion that the income generated by such parcels may be properly thought of as de minimis, their value may not be. . . . There is no question . . . that the right to pass on valuable property to one's heir's is itself a valuable right. . . .

* * *

If we were to stop our analysis at this point, we might well find 207 constitutional. But the character of the Government regulation here is extraordinary . . . the regulation here amounts to virtually the abrogation of the right to pass on a certain type of property—the small undivided interest—to one's heirs. In one form or another, the right to pass on property—to one's family in particular—has been part of the Anglo-American legal system since feudal times. . . . Even the United States concedes that total abrogation of the right to pass property is unprecedented and likely unconstitutional. . . .

In holding that complete abolition of both the descent and devise of a particular class of property may be a taking, we reaffirm the continuing vitality of the long line of cases recognizing the States', and where appropriate, the United States', broad authority to adjust the rules governing the descent and devise of property without implicating the guarantees of the Just Compensation Clause. The difference in this case is the fact that both descent and devise are completely abolished; indeed they are abolished even in circumstances when the governmental purpose sought to be advanced, consolidation of ownership of Indian lands, does not conflict with the further descent of the property.

> There is little doubt that the extreme fractionation of Indian lands is a serious public problem. It may well be appropriate for the United States to ameliorate fractionation by means of regulating the descent and devise of Indian lands. Surely it is permissible for the United States to prevent the owners of such interests from further subdividing them among future heirs on pain of escheat. It may be appropriate to minimize further compounding of the problem by abolishing the descent of such interest by rules of intestacy, thereby forcing the owners to formally designate an heir to prevent escheat to the Tribe. What is certainly not appropriate is to take the extraordinary step of abolishing both descent and devise of these property interests even when the passing of the property to the heir might result in consolidation of property. . . .

Hodel v. Irving, decided in 1987, demonstrates both the fundamental problem with fractionalization in American law and the continuing legacy of the Allotment Era. In essence, the federal government sought to argue that section 207 of the Indian Land Consolidation Act was not a "taking" under the U.S. Constitution because the income generated by certain fractions of land was so small—"de minimus"—that it was the equivalent of nothing. The Supreme Court disagreed, reasoning among other things that the value of the land itself was regularly higher than the income it generated and thus amounted to a taking. Congress amended the ILCA shortly after it was first enacted to address some of these concerns, but the Supreme Court also found these amendments unconstitutional in *Babbitt v. Youpee*.[3]

As noted by the Court in *Hodel*, the capacity to pass land on to another after death "has been part of the Anglo-American legal system since feudal times." This principle, coupled with the takings clause of the 5th Amendment and other aspects of American law, reveal the importance of individual land ownership in Western law. Under such a regime, the extreme difficulty of solving the fractionalization problem becomes apparent. American law is committed to protecting individual land ownership, even if the interest is minuscule, and even if the problem was created by the government in the first place. Congress tried again with the American Indian Probate Reform Act of 2004, which amended the ILCA. However, this new legislation was directed at how land is passed from a decedent to her/his heirs, rather than directly addressing fractionalization. Congress also appropriated a significant sum of money to buy back fractionalized lands in the wake of subsequent litigation (see Chapter 14), but the effects of those efforts are not yet fully realized. Fractionalization remains a significant problem in Indian Country.

Allotment was supposed to solve the "Indian Problem" by destroying tribalism, ending the reservation system, and creating individualistic American farmers out of tribal members. When it failed to achieve these ends the shortsighted nature of the policy became ever more apparent. There was no plan to manage difficulties such as checkerboarding, long-term trust accounts, and fractionalization because American policymakers did not anticipate that tribal nations would survive the allotting process. As tribal nations have endured so have the problems that were created by allotment. Native America continues to live with this legacy to this day.

BOARDING SCHOOLS, INDIAN POLICE, AND INDIAN COURTS

In his 1901 State of the Union Address, President Theodore Roosevelt described allotment as a "mighty pulverizing engine to break up the tribal mass." In keeping with the purposes of the Allotment Era, he also described his vision of Indian education. "In the schools the education should be elementary and largely industrial. The need of higher education among the Indians is very, very limited. On the reservations care should be taken to try to suit the teaching to the needs of the particular Indian."

Education was a major key to the civilizing project of the Allotment Era. Many "Friends of the Indian" regarded adult Native peoples as a lost cause and focused their attention on the children of tribal nations. The history of Indian education is long and complex, but for the purposes of this text it suffices to note that by the late 1870s the federal government was investing in boarding schools in which Native children were removed from their families and made to live, often very far from home, at the school. Attending a boarding school was often a traumatic experience: children were regularly forcibly removed from their families; they were often taken to schools hundreds of miles away from their homelands to discourage running away; students' hair was cut, they were forced to dress in Western-style clothing, and punished for speaking their indigenous language; communicable disease was easily passed through the cramped living conditions and many children got sick and died at school; an unfamiliar diet exacerbated certain medical issues and other stresses; training rarely if ever moved beyond that which those in charge believed Native peoples were capable of learning; many forms of abuse were common; and a myriad of other problems existed as well.

Like many of the initiatives within federal Indian law and policy, the boarding schools were drastically underfunded, often requiring the schools to farm out the children's labor to nearby farms, families, and businesses to maintain themselves.

Nonetheless, they were considered essential in the effort to civilize Native peoples. Richard Henry Pratt, a leader in the field in this period and the superintendent of perhaps the most famous boarding school, the Carlisle Indian Industrial School, explained their purpose. He stated that his goal for Native peoples was to "kill the Indian in him, and save the man."[4]

The federal government also attacked tribal ways of life on the reservation as well. During the Allotment Era the federal government established Indian police forces and Indian courts on several reservations. Staffed by tribal members themselves, both the police and the courts were extensions of the efforts to civilize Native peoples.

The Indian police were created to enforce American law and the rules and regulations established by the tribal superintendent. Indian courts were created to punish those who ran afoul of American law or the superintendent's rules. The Indian courts established in this era are sometimes called CFR courts because their guidelines were found in the Code of Federal Regulations. Some tribal nations continue to operate CFR courts today, although they have much greater control over them now than they did during the Allotment Era.

Many of the offenses handled by the police and the courts in the Allotment Era were common crimes, such as theft. However, as they were tools of the push toward civilization, both the police and courts often punished those who violated the ethos of the "progress" the federal government sought to instill within reservations. Thus, a tribal member might be punished for practicing her or his traditional religion, engaging in traditional dancing, or cohabitating without being married under Western law. Superintendents held great sway over the police and courts, sometimes accompanying police during arrests, appointing judges, or even acting as judges themselves. Although the Indian police and judges were often derided within their own community, sometimes prominent and well-respected tribal members acted in these roles. There may have been any number of reasons to do so: this was often one of the few economic opportunities on a reservation, some may have believed that the efforts toward the Western model was a positive development, and some may have decided that they could slow or mitigate the effects of the Allotment Era by operating within these positions.

In the Allotment Era there was little question among policymakers about the correctness and legality of efforts like boarding schools, the Indian police, and Indian courts. In the few occasions when the authority of the federal government was challenged, those efforts were quickly brushed aside. The following case is one of the rare examples of a legal challenge of the capacity of the federal government to legally engage in these civilizing efforts. Minnie, a member of the

Umatilla tribal nation, was jailed for adultery. Although not a violation of federal or tribal law, Minnie was nonetheless charged under rules created by the Bureau of Indian Affairs in their efforts to "civilize" the Umatilla. Clapox and a number of other tribal members broke Minnie out of the jail. After being captured, Clapox and the others essentially argued that Minnie had been unlawfully held, that the federal government did not have the authority to establish Indian courts, and that since Minnie was unlawfully held the rescuers did not violate any law by rescuing her. As you read the case ask yourself why the court came to the decision that it did? How does the court describe Indian courts? Under this decision, what is the legal status of tribal peoples and tribal nations? What protections do they have under American law?

U.S. V. CLAPOX
35 F. 575 (1888)

DEADY, J.

* * *

...Counsel for the defendants contended that the alleged rescue is not within the purview of the statute, because (1) the act for which Minnie was committed is not a crime "against the United States," but only a violation of an Indian police regulation; and (2) adultery is not a "misdemeanor" at common law, and therefore the court of Indian offenses has no jurisdiction in the premises, and the arrest of Minnie was illegal and void.

It is also doubted whether the Interior Department has authority to define "Indian offenses," or establish courts for the punishment of Indian offenders, as set forth in said rules.

And first, as to the authority of the Department in the premises.

By article 8 of the treaty of June 9, 1855, (12 St. 948) between the United States and certain tribes and bands of Indians of eastern Oregon and Washington, of which the Umatilla Indians are one, it is provided:

> The confederate bands acknowledge their dependence on the government of the United States, and engage to submit to and observe all laws, rules, and regulations which may be prescribed by the United States for the government of said Indians.

The Revised Statutes provide:

Sec. 441. "The Secretary of the Interior is charged with the supervision of the public business relating to the Indians."

Sec. 463. "The Commissioner of Indian Affairs shall, under the direction of the Secretary of the Interior, and agreeably to such regulations as the President may prescribe, have the management of all Indian affairs, and of all matters arising out of the Indian relations."

Sec. 465. "The President may prescribe such regulations as he may think fit for carrying into effect the various provisions of any act relating to Indian affairs."

By this treaty the Umatilla Indians engaged to submit to any rule that might be prescribed by the United States for their government. This obviously includes the power to organize and maintain this Indian court and police, and to specify the acts or conduct concerning which it shall have jurisdiction. This treaty is an "act" or law "relating to Indian affairs,"—the affairs of these Indians; and by said section 465 the power to prescribe a rule for carrying the same into effect is given to the President, who has exercised the same in this case through the proper instrumentality,—the Secretary of the Interior.

Then there is the general power given by said sections 441 and 463 to the President, acting through the Secretary of the Interior and the Commissioner of Indian Affairs, to make regulations for the "management of all Indian affairs, and of all matters arising out of the Indian relations."

These "courts of Indian offenses" are not the constitutional courts provided for in section 1, art. 3, Const., which congress only has the power to "ordain and establish," but mere educational and disciplinary instrumentalities, by which the government of the United States is endeavoring to improve and elevate the condition of these dependent tribes to whom it sustains the relation of guardian. In fact, the reservation itself is in the nature of a school, and the Indians are gathered there, under the charge of an agent, for the purpose of acquiring the habits, ideas, and aspirations which distinguish the civilized from the uncivilized man.

* * *

There is no doubt of the power of the United States to make these rules, nor that the President is authorized by Congress to exercise the same. . . .

* * *

But, pleasantry aside, and in conclusion, the act with which these defendants are charged is in flagrant opposition to the authority of the United

States on this reservation, and directly subversive of this laudable effort to accustom and educate these Indians in the habit and knowledge of self-government. It is therefore appropriate and needful that the power and name of the government of the United States should be invoked to restrain and punish them. . . .

The generalized, foundational question of *Clapox* has been of concern to Americans from the beginning: What is the source of the government's authority over an individual? At its most basic (and perhaps most ideal), the U.S. Constitution is a direct attempt to strike the proper balance between governmental authority and individual freedom. Thus, in some respects, *Clapox* cuts to the very core of American life and asks the very question upon which the United States sought to distinguish itself from its monarchical ancestry. Is this a legitimate use of power over an individual as defined by the U.S. Constitution and the legitimate laws that exist under it?

In addition, *Clapox* also a classic example of the perspective driving the Allotment Era. Although this was not a Supreme Court decision, and consequently carries less value as precedent, it effectively captured the tenor of the times and the complicity that American law and actors like judges had in the overall project to destroy tribal ways of life. The court characterized the efforts of the federal government as "endeavoring to improve and elevate the condition of these dependent tribes to whom it sustains the relation of guardian," and likened reservations to schools in which Native peoples were supposed to learn civilization. Despite the real world consequences that the rules and decisions that reservation superintendents made—such as time in jail—this court nonetheless found such exercises of authority legitimately within the bounds of these federal officials by essentially likening them to school detention.

Combining the central question of the case with the ethos of the times offers a particularly dire picture for Native America during the Allotment Era. The serious questions that courts and other arms of the government regularly ask about the rights of individuals were not of much concern when applied to Native peoples during this time. The broad language of the statutes and the treaty to which the *Clapox* court points, coupled with the extremely expansive reading the court gave them, left federal power essentially unchecked in Indian Country. *Clapox* helps one to understand how little protection, aid, or opportunity Native peoples would find under the law in the Allotment Era.

SUGGESTED READINGS

- *A Final Promise: The Campaign to Assimilate the Indians, 1880–1920.* Frederick E. Hoxie. Lincoln, NE: University of Nebraska Press, 1984.

- *Indian Police and Judges: Experiments in Acculturation and Control.* William T. Hagan. New Haven, CT: Yale University Press, 1966.

- *Unearthing Indian Land: Living with the Legacies of Allotment.* Kristen T. Ruppel. Tucson, AZ: University of Arizona Press, 2008.

---

[1] U.S. Bureau of Indian Affairs, *Annual Report of the Commissioner of Indian Affairs*, Volume 1881 (Washington, D.C.: GPO, 1881), 1.

[2] Merrill E. Gates, "Addresses at the Lake Mohonk Conferences," found in Francis Paul Prucha, ed., *Americanizing the American Indians: Writings by the Friends of the Indians, 1880–1900* (Cambridge, MA: Harvard University Press, 1973), 334.

[3] 519 U.S. 234 (1997).

[4] Richard H. Pratt, "The Advantages of Mingling Indians with Whites," found in Francis Paul Prucha, ed., *Americanizing the American Indians: Writings by the Friends of the Indians, 1880–1900* (Cambridge, MA: Harvard University Press, 1973), 261.

CHAPTER 6

Plenary Power I—The End of Treaties and Beginning of Criminal Law

Throughout the mid-nineteenth century American policymakers began to increasingly think about the "Indian Problem" less as an international concern and more of a domestic issue. Once this new conceptualization took greater root in the American political consciousness the results for tribal nations were dramatic. Many historians regard the Allotment Era, from 1871 to 1934, as the darkest period in American history for Native peoples. Tribal political autonomy was seriously diminished, tribal cultures and understandings were under constant assault, and Native peoples themselves were at their nadir, as the population was at its lowest since contact. By 1900 there were fewer than 250,000 in the mainland of the United States—less than one-third of one percent of the entire population.

The move from thinking about Native peoples in the international sphere to the domestic realm is readily evident in two significant areas: treaties and criminal jurisdiction. In 1871 Congress decided to "end" treaty making with Native nations. This action was not a full or complete end to negotiations with tribal peoples, nor may have its motivations been exclusively about tribal peoples. Nonetheless, it marked a major moment for policymakers and Native America. Shortly thereafter, the federal government sought to assert jurisdiction for crimes committed by Native peoples on tribal lands through the Major Crimes Act. This was one of the many incursions that the United States made directly into the lives of Native peoples in the name of civilization in the Allotment Era.

The reshaping of treaty making and criminal jurisdiction were two major pillars in the restructuring of the notion of plenary power in federal Indian law and policy. "Plenary" means absolute or unqualified, but the understanding of "plenary power" in the field of federal Indian law and policy dramatically changed in the Allotment Era. When the concept of plenary power in federal Indian law was first introduced by John Marshall in his famous trilogy of cases, the plenary power of the federal government in Indian affairs was best understood as acting against the states. The federal government was empowered to manage Indian affairs to the exclusion of the states (and thus Georgia's laws affecting the Cherokee were invalid). In the Allotment Era, however, the concept of plenary power began to change shape, taking on the meaning that the federal government had complete authority over Native peoples and nations themselves. Burdened not just with allotment, but with the growing effects of the changing nature of federal plenary power in Indian affairs, tribal nations and peoples continued to suffer.

This chapter will demonstrate. . .

- *The end of treaty making and its consequences*

- *The place of criminal law in Allotment Era efforts*

- *The origins and results of Ex parte Crow Dog*

THE END OF TREATY MAKING

While there is room for debate as to when to conceptualize the start of the Allotment Era of federal policy, many assert that it started in 1871 when Congress attached a rider to an appropriations bill that "ended" treaty making with tribal nations. Although making treaties with tribal nations had been a major aspect of American policy from the beginning, by at least the middle of the nineteenth century a number of policymakers began to argue against its necessity. One of the biggest opponents of continuing the treaty system with tribal nations was Ely Parker. A member of the Seneca nation, Parker was the first Native person to be appointed Commissioner of Indian Affairs, serving from 1869–71.

Despite being Native himself, Parker's views were very much in line with the burgeoning Allotment Era. As you read this excerpt from his 1869 Annual Commissioner of Indian Affairs report, ask yourself why Parker thought an end to treaty making was necessary. Also consider the conceptualization of Native peoples that Parker presents and how he understands the relationship between tribal nations and the federal government.

1869 ANNUAL REPORT OF THE COMMISSIONER OF INDIAN AFFAIRS

Ely S. Parker, Dec. 23, 1869

. . . It has become a matter of serious import whether the treaty system in use ought longer to be continued. In my judgment it should not. A treaty involves the idea of a compact between two or more sovereign powers, each possessing sufficient authority and force to compel a compliance, with the obligations incurred. The Indian tribes of the United States are not sovereign nations, capable of making treaties, as none of them have an organized government of such inherent strength as would secure a faithful obedience of its people in the observance of compacts of this character. They are held to be the wards of the government, and the only title the law concedes to them to the lands they occupy or claim is a mere possessory one. But, because treaties have been made with them, generally for the extinguishment of their supposed absolute title to land inhabited by them, or over which they roam, they have become falsely impressed with the notion of national independence. It is time that this idea should be dispelled, and the government cease the cruel farce of this dealing with its helpless and ignorant wards. Many good men, looking at this matter only from a Christian point of view, will perhaps say that the poor Indian has been greatly wronged and ill treated; that this whole country was once his, of which he has been despoiled, and that he has been driven from place to place until he has hardly left to him a spot to lay his head. This indeed may be philanthropic and humane, but the stern letter of the law admits of no such conclusion, and great injury has been done by the government in deluding this people into the belief of their being independent sovereignties, while they were as the same time recognized only as its dependents and wards. As civilization advances and their possessions of land are required for settlement, such legislation should be granted to them as a wise, liberal, and just government ought to extend to subjects holding their dependent relation. In regard to treaties now in force, justice and humanity require that they be promptly and faithfully executed, so that the Indians may not have cause of complaint, or reason to violate their obligations by acts of violence and robbery.

While it may not be expedient to negotiate treaties with any of the tribes hereafter, it is no doubt just that those made within the past year, and now pending before the United States Senate, should be definitely acted upon. . . .

Parker's report is useful for a number of reasons, including how it established a comparison that testifies to the law's relationship to the Allotment Era and to colonialism more generally. On one side, Parker noted that, "Many good men, looking at this matter only from a Christian point of view," might regard his call for the abolishment of treaty making as inhumane or perhaps even cruel in the wake of growing suffering and pressures in Indian Country caused by increasing White incursions and settlement. Yet, on the other side, Parker stated that such concerns were no match for "the stern letter of the law," which "admits of no such conclusion." Parker went on to suggest that treaties themselves were the real source of trouble in Indian Country.

In Parker's assessment, issues of what some would consider justice and humanity were secondary to the "stern letter of the law." Building upon John Marshall's description of tribal land rights as merely "the Indian right of occupancy" (see Chapter 2), Parker extended this line of legal reasoning to argue that tribal nations lacked sovereignty, that tribal peoples were wards of the federal government, and that treaties were a "cruel farce." The law, according to Parker as well as many others, was a byproduct of human nature that regulated the inferior status of Native peoples (as opposed to creating and perpetuating that status). Thus, one was not just right thinking but actually kinder and more compassionate to forgo what looked to the "Christian point of view" like the proper course of action—based on a sense of mutual humanity—and to adhere to the law. Parker was hardly the first or the last to make this type of argument, as law and policy have been fundamental to colonialism and the expansion of the United States from the very beginning.

Despite its long history and the fact that treaty making was monumentally important in the relationship between tribal nations and the federal government, its end was performed quickly and quietly. The 1871 Indian Appropriations Bill, in which the following rider was inserted, covers twenty-seven pages in the U.S. Statutes at Large, the official source of laws passed by Congress. This small paragraph, with its major consequences, is buried within the twenty-third of those twenty-seven pages. As you read the rider, ask yourself what the law does and does not do. Where are the consequences for the federal government's decision for tribal nations and for the federal government itself?

END OF TREATY MAKING
U.S. Statutes at Large 16:566, Mar. 3, 1871

. . . *Provided,* That hereafter no Indian nation or tribe within the territory of the United States shall be acknowledged or recognized as an independent nation, tribe, or power with whom the United States may contract by treaty: *Provided, further,* That nothing herein contained shall be construed to invalidate or impair the obligation of any treaty heretofore lawfully made and ratified with any such Indian nation or tribe.

Some scholars have argued that the decision to end treaty making was based, in large part, on a conflict within the houses of Congress. Under the U.S. Constitution, only the Senate ratifies treaties—the House of Representatives plays no part. However, only the House has the authority to originate appropriations bills, and thus holds great sway over how federal money is spent. Thus, the Senate would ratify treaties with tribal nations with no input from the House, yet the House would have to determine how to pay for annuities and other expenses incurred in the treaties. Tasked with the unpopular duty of having to allocate monies that the Senate had already spent, the House wanted to have a say in Indian treaties as well. By ending treaty making, the House was able to play a greater part in federal Indian policy.

In the short term, the "end" of treaty making did little to alter the diplomatic relations between the federal government and tribal nations. Treaties were replaced with "agreements"—documents that operate in the same way as treaties but that are required to be passed by both chambers of Congress. The federal government continued to send negotiators to Indian Country and tribal nations continued to engage in discussions with those federal negotiators, although by this period the federal government was often in a much more advantageous position to dictate the terms of an agreement. The agreement process continued for years, as did other means that the federal government employed for engaging with tribal nations. Most prominently, the President regularly continued to issue Executive Orders that established reservations and otherwise engaged with Native America. It was not until almost fifty years after treaty making ended that Congress abolished the President's authority to establish reservations by Executive Order in 1919. Thus, in one limited respect, the end of treaty making did little to actually alter the relationship between tribal nations and the federal government.

Are there any legally meaningful distinctions between treaties and agreements? This is a question that the Supreme Court has addressed. In the following case, the state of Washington sought to convict two Native individuals, a husband and a wife, for violating the state's hunting laws. The Native individuals argued that they were not subject to state law because their tribal rights to hunt were preserved through an agreement with the United States. The state of Washington countered by arguing that state law was not constricted under an agreement in the same way it would be constricted under a treaty.

Before you read the case, turn to Chapter 2 and read the excerpt of the U.S. Constitution. As you read the case, ask yourself what distinction the state of Washington tries to make between treaties and agreements. What effect does the Supreme Court give to the 1871 legislation that ended treaty making? What are the consequences for tribal nations who negotiated agreement as opposed to those who negotiated treaties?

ANTOINE V. WASHINGTON
420 U.S. 194 (1975)

MR. JUSTICE BRENNAN delivered the opinion of the Court.

The appellants, husband and wife, are Indians. They were convicted in the Superior Court of the State of Washington of the offenses of hunting and possession of deer during closed season. . . . The offenses occurred on September 11, 1971. . .on unallotted non-Indian land in what was once the north half of the Colville Indian Reservation. The Colville Confederated Tribes ceded to the United States that northern half under a congressionally ratified and adopted Agreement, dated May 9, 1891. Article 6 of that ratified Agreement provided expressly that "the right to hunt and fish in common with all other persons on lands not allotted to said Indians shall not be taken away or in anywise abridged." Appellants' defense was that congressional approval of Art. 6 excluded from the cession and retained and preserved for the Confederated Tribes the exclusive, absolute, and unrestricted rights to hunt and fish that had been part of the Indians' larger rights in the ceded portion of the reservation, thus limiting governmental regulation of the rights to federal regulation and precluding application to them of [state law]. The Supreme Court of Washington held that the Superior Court had properly rejected this defense and affirmed the convictions. . . . We reverse.

* * *

Although admitted to statehood two years earlier, the State of Washington was not a party to the 1891 Agreement. The opinion of the State Supreme Court relies upon that fact to attempt a distinction for the purposes of the

Supremacy Clause between the binding result upon the State of ratification of a [treaty] effected by concurrence of two-thirds of the Senate, and the binding result of ratification of [an agreement] effected by legislation passed by the House and the Senate. . . . The fallacy in that proposition is that a legislated ratification of an agreement between the Executive Branch and an Indian tribe is a '(Law) of the United States . . . made in Pursuance" of the Constitution and, therefore, like "all Treaties made," is made binding upon affected States by the Supremacy Clause.

The [Washington State Supreme Court] opinion seems to find support for the attempted distinction in the fact that, in 1891, the Executive Branch was not authorized to [make treaties] with Indian tribes as sovereign and independent nations. Twenty years earlier, in 1871, Congress [ended treaty making]. . . .

This meant no more, however, that . . . after 1871 relations with Indians would be governed by Acts of Congress and not by treaty. The change in no way affected Congress' plenary powers to legislate on problems of Indians, including legislating the ratification of [agreements] to which affected States were not parties. Several decisions of this Court have long settled that proposition. . . .

Once ratified by Act of Congress, the provisions of the agreements become law, and like treaties, the supreme law of the land. . . .

* * *

As the Supreme Court noted, as a purely legal matter, there is no real difference in the function of treaties as opposed to the function of agreements for Native nations. Yet, while there was little change in the immediate aftermath of the legislation and no real legal difference between treaties and agreements, symbolically and eventually pragmatically the end of treaty making was a major blow to tribal sovereignty. The 1871 rider marked a significant shift in how the federal government decided to approach Indian affairs. Treaties are bi- or multilateral events that shape and define international law. They require agreement between nations. By denying tribal nations the authority to negotiate treaties, the United States denied tribal nations the right to negotiate on their own behalf, as well as their status as international bodies. Through the rider, tribal peoples no longer had any voice in their relationship with the federal government on the international level. Rather, they increasingly became the subject of domestic legislation. Denied the right to speak for themselves through treaties and, in almost all cases, denied the right to vote or participate in American government, tribal nations and peoples became subject to the whim of American policymakers. Increasingly limited in dictating their own political (and thus their social and religious and educational, etc.) fates, tribal peoples and nations suffered and endured significant loss, while also exhibiting a tremendous amount of resilience and agency whenever possible.

Some scholars have argued that it has never been within Congress's authority to alter the treaty power. As the reasoning goes, the treaty making authority is given to the President by the U.S. Constitution and Congress overstepped its role in limiting this authority. Essentially, some argue, the rider that ended treaty making with Native nations is unconstitutional. However, there has been no major challenge to the legislation as of present. More to the point for this chapter, the Allotment Era, and the dramatic redefinition of Congressional plenary power over tribal nations and peoples, began its ascendency in earnest at the end of treaty making.

CHANGES TO CRIMINAL LAW

The perception of Native savagery continued to inform federal policymakers throughout the Allotment Era. Although Native nations and peoples engaged in their own versions of governance and law, these practices were routinely discounted or simply ignored by Americans because they did not mimic the Western model of governance and law. This was especially true in the realm of criminal law. Tribal superintendents and other observers routinely decried what they saw as both the overpunishment and underpunishment of criminals. On some occasions federal officials lamented what they regarded as extreme or cruel punishment for wrongdoers. On other occasions, they lamented what they regarded as extreme leniency for criminal behavior. The contradictory nature of the critiques left little, if any, room for Native nations to operate by their own standards and reinforced an understanding of tribal peoples as unsophisticated, uncivilized, and incapable of managing themselves.

The following excerpt from the 1849 Annual Report of the Commissioner of Indian Affairs is a representative sample of the general federal attitude toward tribal criminals and criminal prosecution. As you read it, ask yourself what solution the Commissioner of Indian Affairs proposes to resolve the problem. What is the source of the problem? What role does the Commissioner believe that the federal government should take on and why?

1849 ANNUAL REPORT OF THE COMMISSIONER OF INDIAN AFFAIRS

Orlando Brown, Commissioner of Indian Affairs

So far as I am aware, it has not been the practice to interfere in cases of difficulty between different tribes, further than to interpose, by military force or otherwise, to put a stop to them; and even the practice of compelling satisfaction for outrages to be made out of annuities is one of recent adoption. The punishment of the guilty parties by arrest and confinement may therefore be regarded as an extreme measure; but there is ample authority and justification for it, arising out of the nature of the relations between the government and the Indians, as guardian and wards.

It is to tribal and intestine wars and difficulties, as much if not more than to any other causes, that the decline and misery of the Indian race are justly to be attributed. Enmity between them is hereditary and implacable, and no occasion is omitted to indulge it, by the destruction of life and other outrages; the retaliatory law of blood, which universally prevails among the uncivilized tribes, causes it to remain unappeased and unappeasable, whether existing between different tribes or between members of the same tribe. It is, therefore, no less the dictate of humanity, than it is a high moral duty on the part of the government, to interpose its strong arm, in the most effectual manner possible, to put a stop to its lamentable and dreadful consequences, if the feeling itself cannot be eradicated. Compelling compensation to be made out of annuities, and the mere imprisonment of offenders, are not sufficient for the accomplishment of this great object. . . . [T]he only effectual remedy, and one which is loudly called for by humanity, as well as by sound policy, will be, for Congress to make provision for the trial of offenders in such cases, in some appropriate manner, and for their punishment, by death, hard labor at the military posts, or otherwise, according to the nature and aggravated character of the offence. And I would go further, and recommend that authority also be given for taking cognizance of cases of theft or robbery, and of habitual or repeated intemperance among members of a tribe; and to inflict some suitable kind of punishment as a corrective of these two evils, where they are taken notice of and properly punished by the tribe itself. They are among the greatest drawbacks to the civilization and improvement of our Indians. . . .

Commissioner Brown's suggestions were still relatively new when he proposed them in 1849. However, the sentiment that the federal government needed to do something to manage criminal issues in Indian Country continued to grow from the mid-nineteenth century through the Allotment Era. More and more members of the American government came to believe that it was necessary to enforce American criminal law in Indian Country. Those who advocated for greater federal control over Indian Country often derisively described tribal expressions of criminal law with the overly simplistic label of the, "red man's revenge." As the next section reveals, federal criminal law enforcement in Indian Country became a major aim of the proponents of the Allotment Era.

CROW DOG

By the 1880s members of the Bureau of Indian Affairs were actively engaged in trying to extend American criminal law into Indian Country. As one prominent scholar of the era described it, "BIA officials had been attempting to acquire [criminal jurisdiction] since at least 1874, because they needed the coercive power of the criminal law as one means to force the assimilation of the Indians."[1] The BIA decided to initiate a test case—a case to determine the state of the law that is otherwise unclear or that can operate as a vehicle for change—in their effort to claim criminal jurisdiction.

The BIA found their test case among the Brule Lakota on what was then the Great Sioux Reservation, primarily located in what is now western South Dakota. In August of 1881 Crow Dog killed Spotted Tail. Both men were leaders within the community and a number of different circumstances, including the federal government's interference in tribal politics, led the two men to become rivals. Crow Dog may have killed Spotted Tail for any number of reasons, including possibly reasons of a personal nature, but there was certainly a deep political element to Crow Dog's actions.

The killing caused a rift in the community that the community sought to address under its own law and procedure. The tribal nation called a council meeting and the council sent peacemakers to both families. Through the council, the peacemakers, and negotiation, the families came to a resolution. The family of Crow Dog agreed to pay, and the family of Spotted Tail agreed to accept, $600, eight horses, and a blanket. The large payment was quickly remitted and the matter was considered settled under the tribal nation's law.

While aware that the Brule Lakota had settled the matter under tribal law, the federal government nonetheless arrested Crow Dog and charged him with murder. In the Spring of 1882 Crow Dog was convicted and sentenced to hang, although many correctly anticipated that the case would reach the Supreme Court. From the BIA's perspective, any decision from the Supreme Court was likely to advance its cause. If Crow Dog lost his appeal, it would have meant that the federal government had the authority to criminally prosecute Native peoples on tribal lands. If Crow Dog won his appeal, the public outcry was likely to prompt Congress to act to grant the authority to the BIA and American courts to criminally prosecute Native peoples on tribal lands.

On a more fundamental level, the dispute was about the nature and purpose of criminal law. In order to see the difference in perspectives, it is helpful to ask what a society is trying to accomplish in its treatment of criminal offenders. At its most simplistic, the Western criminal justice model that the BIA hoped to instill in tribal communities was focused on punishment. Under this model, criminals are made to suffer a roughly equivalent amount of pain that they cause in order to deter them and others from committing crimes in the future. In the American trial court, Crow Dog was sentenced to hang for the killing of Spotted Tail. Many Americans who took note of Crow Dog's actions were appalled as what they regarded as a murderer getting off easy or even buying his way out of justice under the tribal model and celebrated the actions of the American trial court. It was, to those who discounted or disregarded tribal methodologies, further evidence of the savage and uncivilized nature of Native peoples.

However, again at its most simplistic, many tribal criminal justice systems had a different goal than Western systems. Rather than focusing on punishing the offender, many tribal criminal justice systems concentrated on making the victim as whole as possible and restoring balance and equanimity to the community. The purpose of the criminal justice system was to heal the whole community quickly, efficiently, and to the greatest satisfaction of everyone involved. Whereas many American officials regarded the payment made by Crow Dog and his family to the family of Spotted Tail as a perversion of justice or "blood money," those within the community saw it differently. It was a fairly negotiated agreement involving all of the interested parties in which Crow Dog and his family sought to make Spotted Tail's family as complete as possible in the wake of their loss. The substantial payment testified to Spotted Tail's importance, the loss that they endured, and the lengths to which Crow Dog and his family needed to go to make the community as whole as possible.

The case at the Supreme Court did not consider these larger questions about the nature of criminal justice systems. Rather, the question of the case was whether the United States had the authority to criminally prosecute a crime committed by one Native individual against another Native individual on tribal land. Certainly an American government, usually a particular state, would have had the authority to punish a tribal member who committed a crime outside of tribal lands. But was there any authority to extend American law into what was still exclusively defined as Indian Country? As you read the case, ask yourself how the Court understands tribal criminal justice systems, why the Court decided the way that it did, and what possibilities the Court creates for future actions by the American government. Also pay close attention to the language concerning the nature of Native peoples and consider the consequences of a court using the same language today. It will be important to reflect on this last point when reading more modern cases.

EX PARTE CROW DOG
109 U.S. 556 (1883)

MR. JUSTICE MATTHEWS delivered the opinion of the Court.

The petitioner is in the custody of the Marshal of the United States for the Territory of Dakota, imprisoned in the jail of Lawrence County, in the First Judicial District of that territory, under sentence of death, adjudged against him by the district court for that district, to be carried into execution January 14, 1884. That judgment was rendered upon a conviction for the murder of an Indian of the Brule Sioux band of the Sioux nation of Indians by the name of Sin-ta-ge-le-Scka, or in English, Spotted Tail, the prisoner also being an Indian of the same band and nation, and the homicide having occurred, as alleged in the indictment, in the Indian country, within a place and district of country under the exclusive jurisdiction of the United States and within the said judicial district. . . . It is claimed on behalf of the prisoner that the crime charged against him and of which he stands convicted is not an offense under the laws of the United States; that the district court had no jurisdiction to try him, and that its judgment and sentence are void. [The prisoner] therefore prays . . . that he may be delivered from an imprisonment which he asserts to be illegal.

The indictment is framed upon section 5339 of the Revised Statutes. . . . It provides that "Every person who commits murder, . . . within any fort, arsenal, dockyard, magazine, or in any other place or district of country under the exclusive jurisdiction of the United States, . . . shall suffer death."

Title XXVIII of the Revised Statutes relates to Indians. . . . The next two sections are as follows:

SEC. 2145.   Except as to crimes, the punishment of which is expressly provided for in this title, the general laws of the United States as to the punishment of crimes committed in any place within the sole and exclusive jurisdiction of the United States, except the District of Columbia, shall extend to the Indian country.

SEC. 2146.   The preceding section shall not be construed to extend to [crimes committed by one Indian against the person or property of another Indian, nor to] any Indian committing any offense in the Indian country who has been punished by the local law of the tribe, or to any case where by treaty stipulations the exclusive jurisdiction over such offenses is or may be secured to the Indian tribes respectively.

* * *

The district courts of the Territory of Dakota are invested with the same jurisdiction in all cases arising under the laws of the United States as is vested in the circuit and district courts of the United States. . . In the present case, the Sioux reservation is within the geographical limits of the Territory of Dakota, and being excepted out of it only in respect to the territorial government, the district court of that territory within the geographical boundaries of whose district it lies may exercise jurisdiction under the laws of the United States over offenses made punishable by them committed within its limits. . . .

Section 2145 of the Revised Statutes extends the general laws of the United States as to the punishment of crimes committed in any place within their sole and exclusive jurisdiction except the District of Columbia to the Indian country, and it becomes necessary, therefore, to inquire whether the locality of the homicide for which the prisoner was convicted of murder is within that description. . . .

In our opinion, [Indian Country is defined as] all the country to which the Indian title has not been extinguished within the limits of the United States, even when not within a reservation expressly set apart for the exclusive occupancy of Indians. . . .

It follows that the *locus in quo* of the alleged offense is within Indian country over which, territorially, the district court of the First Judicial District of Dakota, sitting with the authority of a circuit court of the United States, had jurisdiction.

But if § 2145 Rev.Stat., extends the act of Congress, § 5339, punishing murder, to the locality of the prisoner's offense, § 2146 expressly excepts from its operation "crimes committed by one Indian against the person or property of another Indian," an exception which includes the case of the prisoner and which, if it is effective and in force, makes his conviction illegal and void. This brings us at once to the main question of jurisdiction, deemed by Congress to be of such importance to the prisoner and the public as to justify a special appropriation for the payment of the expenses incurred on his behalf in presenting it for decision in this proceeding to this Court.

The argument in support of the jurisdiction and conviction is that the exception contained in § 2146 Rev.Stat. is repealed by the operation and legal effect of [an 1868 treaty and an 1877 Congressional Statute].

The following provisions of the treaty of 1868 are relied on:

ARTICLE I. From this time forward, all war between the parties to this agreement shall forever cease. The government of the United States desires peace, and its honor is hereby pledged to keep it. The Indians desire peace, and they now pledge their honor to maintain it.

If bad men among the whites or among other people subject to the authority of the United States shall commit any wrong upon the person or property of the Indians, the United States will, upon proof made to the agent and forwarded to the Commissioner of Indian Affairs at Washington City, proceed at once to cause the offender to be arrested and punished according to the laws of the United States and also reimburse the injured person for the loss sustained.

If bad men among the Indians shall commit a wrong or depredation upon the person or property of anyone, white, black, or Indian, subject to the authority of the United States and at peace therewith, the Indians herein named solemnly agree that they will, upon proof made to their agent and notice by him, deliver up the wrongdoer to the United States, to be tried and punished according to its laws. And in case they willfully refuse so to do, the person injured shall be reimbursed for his loss from the annuities or other moneys due or to become due to them under this or other treaties made with the United States. And the President, on advising with the Commissioner of Indian Affairs, shall prescribe rules and regulations for ascertaining damages under the provisions of this article as in his judgment may be proper. But no one sustaining loss while violating the provisions of this treaty or the laws of the United States shall be reimbursed therefor.

* * *

But it is quite clear from the context that this does not cover the present case of an alleged wrong committed by one Indian upon the person of another of the same tribe. The provision must be construed with its counterpart, just preceding it, which provides for the punishment by the United States of any bad men among the whites, or among other people subject to their authority, who shall commit any wrong upon the person or property of the Indians. Here are two parties, among whom respectively there may be individuals guilty of a wrong against one of the other—one is the party of whites and their allies, the other is the tribe of Indians with whom the treaty is made. In each case, the guilty party is to be tried and punished by the United States, and in case the offender is one of the Indians who are parties to the treaty, the agreement is that he shall be delivered up. In case of refusal, deduction is to be made from the annuities payable to the tribe, for compensation to the injured person, a provision which points quite distinctly to the conclusion that the injured person cannot himself be one of the same tribe. Similar provisions for the extradition of criminals are to be found in most of the treaties with Indian tribes as far back, at least, as that concluded at Hopewell with the Cherokees.

The second of these provisions that are supposed to justify the jurisdiction asserted in the present case is the eighth article of the agreement, embodied in the act of 1877, in which it is declared: "And Congress shall, by appropriate legislation, secure to them an orderly government; they shall be subject to the laws of the United States, and each individual shall be protected in his rights of property, person, and life."

It is equally clear, in our opinion, that these words can have no such effect as that claimed for them. The pledge to secure to these people, with whom the United States was contracting as a distinct political body, an orderly government by appropriate legislation thereafter to be framed and enacted necessarily implies, having regard to all the circumstances attending the transaction, that among the arts of civilized life which it was the very purpose of all these arrangements to introduce and naturalize among them was the highest and best of all—that of self-government, the regulation by themselves of their own domestic affairs, the maintenance of order and peace among their own members by the administration of their own laws and customs. They were nevertheless to be subject to the laws of the United States, not in the sense of citizens, but, as they had always been, as wards, subject to a guardian—not as individuals, constituted members of the political community of the United States, with a voice in the selection of representatives and the framing of the laws, but as a dependent community who were in a state of pupilage, advancing from the condition of a savage tribe to that of a people who, through the discipline of labor, and by education, it was hoped might become a self-supporting and self-governed society.

* * *

It must be remembered that the question before us is whether the express letter of § 2146 of the Revised Statutes, which excludes from the jurisdiction of the United States the case of a crime committed in the Indian country by one Indian against the person or property of another Indian, has been repealed. If not, it is in force and applies to the present case. The treaty of 1868 and the agreement and act of Congress of 1877, it is admitted, do not repeal it by any express words. What we have said is sufficient at least to show that they do not work a repeal by necessary implication. . . .

* * *

The nature and circumstances of this case strongly reinforce this rule of interpretation in its present application. It is a case involving the judgment of a court of special and limited jurisdiction, not to be assumed without clear warrant of law. It is a case of life and death. It is a case where, against an express exception in the law itself, that law, by argument and inference only, is sought to be extended over aliens and strangers; over the members of a community, separated by race, by tradition, by the instincts of a free though savage life, from the authority and power which seeks to impose upon them the restraints of an external and unknown code, and to subject them to the responsibilities of civil conduct, according to rules and penalties of which they could have no previous warning; which judges them by a standard made by others, and not for them, which takes no account of the conditions which should except them from its exactions, and makes no allowance for their inability to understand it. It tries them not by their peers, nor by the customs of their people, nor the law of their land, but by superiors of a different race, according to the law of a social state of which they have an imperfect conception and which is opposed to the traditions of their history, to the habits of their lives, to the strongest prejudices of their savage nature; one which measures the red man's revenge by the maxims of the white man's morality. . . .

To give to the clauses in the treaty of 1868 and the agreement of 1877 effect so as to uphold the jurisdiction exercised in this case would be to reverse in this instance the general policy of the government toward the Indians, as declared in many statutes and treaties and recognized in many decisions of this Court from the beginning to the present time. To justify such a departure in

> such a case requires a clear expression of the intention of Congress, and that we have not been able to find.
>
> It results that the First District Court of Dakota was without jurisdiction to find or try the indictment against the prisoner; that the conviction and sentence are void, and that his imprisonment is illegal.

On a technical level, the case turned on a reading of two federal statutes—Sections 2145 and 2146 (today known as the Indian Country Crimes Act)—and whether those statutes were altered or otherwise affected by an 1868 treaty and an 1877 agreement. The question was so important, as the Court notes, that Congress passed special legislation to pay for the legal proceedings. Sections 2145 and 2146 authorized federal criminal jurisdiction in Indian Country, but exempted, among other things, crimes committed by one Native person against another Native person. Since Crow Dog's murder of Spotted Tail fell into this exemption, the federal government argued that the 1868 treaty and the 1877 agreement repealed and/or replaced the exemption. The Court ultimately disagreed with the lawyers for the United States and found that the federal government did not have jurisdiction to punish these types of crimes. It is useful to consider both the technical aspects of the case and the spirit animating it. How does the Court read the treaty and agreement that the federal government argued repealed and/or replaced sections 2145 and 2146? Does it make a difference that the treaty and agreement were negotiated with tribal members? How does the Court characterize the importance of the case, and how does that characterization understand or regard Native peoples?

On its surface, the decision was a clear victory for Crow Dog and for tribal sovereignty. Crow Dog was not hanged and continued to exercise great influence on the reservation for the rest of his lengthy life. And Indian Country was spared, for the moment, from the growing efforts of the BIA to criminally prosecute and punish tribal members.

Nonetheless, the victory quickly proved to be hollow for Indian Country as it led to an immediate backlash. Many read the Supreme Court's language that it could find no "clear expression of Congress" in asserting jurisdiction as an open invitation to Congress to act on the manner. As some in the BIA predicted, two years after the decision in *Ex parte Crow Dog*, Congress passed the Major Crimes Act. Sometimes referred to as the Seven Major Crimes Act, the legislation extended federal jurisdiction over Indian Country over specifically enumerated "major" crimes. As you read the excerpt from the Major Crimes Act, ask yourself why these particular crimes are enumerated and not others. Is there something that sets them apart and in need of special consideration by American courts? Why or why not? Also, why were the Indian courts discussed in the previous chapter not capable of adjudicating these crimes? What can we discern from the fact that certain crimes were given by Congress to American courts whereas others were left to the Indian courts that were being established on reservations?

MAJOR CRIMES ACT
U.S. Statutes at Large 23:385, Mar. 3, 1885

...That immediately upon and after the date of the passage of this act all Indians, committing against the person or property of another Indian or other person and of the following crimes, namely, murder, manslaughter, rape, assault with intent to kill, arson, burglary, and larceny within any Territory of the United States, and either within or without an Indian reservation, shall be subject therefor to the laws of such Territory relating to said crimes, and shall be tried therefor in the same courts and in the same manner and shall be subject to the same penalties as are all other persons charged with the commission of said crimes, respectively; and the said courts are hereby given jurisdiction in all such cases; and all such Indians committing any of the above crimes against the person or property of another Indian or other person within the boundaries of any State of the United States, and within the limits of any Indian reservation, shall be subject to the same laws, tried in the same courts and in the same manner, and subject to the same penalties as are all other persons committing any of the above crimes within the exclusive jurisdiction of the United States.

For reasons that will be explained in the next chapter, the Major Crimes Act (with some amendments to expand the scope of the major crimes) remains good law to this day. The increased criminal jurisdiction was a major step in the expansion of Congressional plenary power in Indian affairs during the Allotment Era. Coupled with the end of treaty making and other projects, the federal government more and more involved itself in the lives of Native peoples while simultaneously attempting to destroy tribal nations by denying the sovereignty and authority of tribal nations to manage their own affairs. The shift in the American perspective from regarding Native issues in the international realm to relegating them to the domestic sphere resulted in an increasingly tenuous position for tribal nations and peoples as they tried to exercise their rights under the oppressive regime of increased federal plenary power. This dramatic change, most prominently visible through the end of treaty making and the expansion of criminal jurisdiction, left Native peoples and nations with little political and legal recourse. As the next chapter demonstrates, the Supreme Court was fundamental to this new American conception of Native America.

SUGGESTED READINGS

- *Crow Dog's Case: American Indian Sovereignty, Tribal Law, and United States Law in the Nineteenth Century.* Sidney L. Harring. Cambridge: Cambridge University Press, 1994.

- "Touching the Pen: Plains Indian Treaty Councils in Ethnohistorical Perspective." Raymond J. DeMallie. In *The American Indian: Past and Present, 6th Ed.* Roger L. Nichols, ed. Norman, OK: University of Oklahoma Press, 2008. 171–183.

- *American Indian Treaties: The History of a Political Anomaly.* Francis Paul Prucha. Berkeley, CA: University of California Press, 1994.

---

[1] *Crow Dog's Case: American Indian Sovereignty, Tribal Law, and United States Law in the Nineteenth Century*, Sidney L. Harring, Cambridge: Cambridge University Press, 1994, 102.

CHAPTER 7

Plenary Power II—The Constitution, Treaties, and American Citizenship

When most Americans think about their rights and where they come from, they tend to think about being American citizens and the U.S. Constitution. American citizenship, according to conventional wisdom, means that the federal and state governments (as well as fellow citizens and others) must respect certain basic standards and freedoms. Many of these standards and freedoms are established and defined by the U.S. Constitution. Perhaps some Americans, especially those who live, work, or do business abroad, also think about treaties as a source of rights. International agreements such as the Geneva Convention or NAFTA help to define what rights one can expect to enforce in different parts of the world as well as at home.

During the Allotment Era, from 1871 to 1934, the United States, and particularly the Supreme Court in three major cases, considered each of these sources of rights—the U.S. Constitution, treaties, and American citizenship—in the context of Native America. The essential question raised by each case was whether the source of rights in question limited, altered, or halted the plenary power of the United States over Native peoples. Signaling that it was leaving Indian affairs to Congress and the President, the Supreme Court found that the plenary power of the United States over Native peoples was not limited by any of these traditional sources of rights. Taking a back seat to the other branches, the Supreme Court regularly described Indian affairs as political matters that were not appropriate for litigation and best left to the political branches.

Without any identifiable source of rights under American law with which to defend themselves, Native peoples were at the mercy of federal policymakers in the Allotment Era. Plenary power took on a new meaning in Indian law and policy, as the Bureau of Indian Affairs and other reformers actively engaged in attempts to destroy tribal ways of life. Unchecked by the Supreme Court, the other branches of government were able to enact the legislation and policies described in the previous two chapters as well as others that drastically affected Indian Country. The three cases in this chapter—the Plenary Power Trilogy—paved the way for the exponential growth of Congressional interference with Native ways of life in the Allotment Era.

This chapter will demonstrate...

- *How the Supreme Court decided that the U.S. Constitution was not a check on federal plenary power in Indian Affairs*

- *How the Supreme Court decided that treaties were not a check on federal plenary power in Indian Affairs*

- *How the Supreme Court decided that American citizenship was not a check on federal plenary power in Indian Affairs*

THE CONSTITUTION

As described in the previous chapter, the Supreme Court Decision in *Crow Dog* in 1883 led to the Major Crimes Act in 1885. The Major Crimes Act authorized federal jurisdiction over certain "major" crimes committed by Native peoples on tribal lands. The law theoretically solved the issue of federal criminal jurisdiction over Native peoples in Indian Country as it concerned the so-called major crimes. But the new law raised another important question: Was it constitutional? Put differently, did Congress have the authority under the U.S. Constitution to pass a law that affected Native peoples on Native lands in this manner?

The federal government is often described as having limited and enumerated powers. The authority that the federal government can exercise is described in the U.S. Constitution. This is opposed to state governments, which have a broader range of powers, although they are also limited by the U.S. Constitution and their own state constitutions. This system is designed to keep the federal government responsible to the states and to maintain limits on the authority that the federal government can exercise over its citizens. Any law that the federal government enacts must be justified by a power granted to the federal government in the U.S. Constitution. If a law is unsupported by a power granted by the U.S. Constitution then it is deemed unconstitutional and invalid.

A challenge to the constitutionality of the Major Crimes Act quickly made its way the Supreme Court. Kagama, a tribal member, was accused along with an accomplice of killing Iyouse, also a tribal member, on tribal land in California. Subsequent scholarship has demonstrated that the Supreme Court's written opinion had, at best, a haphazard command of the facts of the case. Most glaringly, the alleged murder actually took place outside of the reservation's boundaries— as a consequence the case should have been tried in California state court, not the federal court under the Major Crimes Act.

In one very meaningful sense, the Supreme Court's misunderstanding of important details of the case is a clear example of the uphill battle that Native peoples encountered when confronting the federal government during the Allotment Era. For example, the tribal members involved were misidentified as Hupa (or Hoopa) when in fact they were Yurok. Rarely if ever recognized as individuals or members of distinct nations with unique characteristics, tribal peoples were lumped together into the monolith of "Indian" and regularly treated as indistinguishable from one another. Polices that targeted "Indians" did little to appreciate the vast diversity of Native America nor adequately address the distinct consequences that a singular policy might have in different regions among different peoples. Faced with a federal government that did not understand them, and had little incentive to learn about them as they tried to change them, tribal peoples struggled to assert themselves both individually and collectively.

Additionally, federal policy may have directly led to the dispute that was the impetus for the case. Kagama and Iyouse were regularly at odds with each other over a parcel of land that they both individually claimed. The Allotment Act and the policy of the day strongly encouraged individual land ownership, and the Indian Agent in the region had been allotting lands without the official authority to do so (and thus illegally) to tribal members during this time. Although the Indian Agent had tried to mediate between Kagama and Iyouse on a number of occasions, the dispute could not be amicably resolved. Kagama, it was alleged, stabbed Iyouse while his son and accomplice held back Iyouse's wife. Prior to the killing, the Indian Agent regularly described Kagama in terms that distinguished him as more civilized than his counterparts. The agent noted that Kagama was, "quiet, sober, and industrious," and that Kagama "endeavors to live like a white man." Were it not for Kagama's efforts to fulfill the purpose of the Allotment Era and "live like a white man," there might have been no conflict between the two parties.[1]

In another sense, the details of the case were always going to be secondary to the question of the case: was the Major Crimes Act constitutional? Had the federal government accurately identified this set of facts as not fitting under the Major Crimes Act, eventually another set of facts would have been adequate and a different test case would have reached the Supreme Court. Faced with this question, lawyers for the United States who were arguing in favor of the constitutionality of the Major Crimes Act pointed to the Commerce Clause (Art. 1, Sec. 8, Cl. 3), among other things, as the source of authority that permitted Congress to pass the Major Crimes Act. In their brief to the Supreme Court, these lawyers essentially argued that the Commerce Clause was a legitimate source of authority for the Major Crimes Act because if Native peoples were permitted to kill one another then there would be no one left with whom to engage in commerce.[2] Before you read the case, turn to Chapter 2 and read the Commerce Clause in the excerpt of the U.S. Constitution.

While the constitutionality of the Major Crimes Act is at the heart of *Kagama*, the question of the case can also be described in another way that better frames its position in federal Indian law: does the U.S. Constitution limit the plenary authority of the federal government over Native peoples and nations? As you read the case, ask yourself how the Court comes to decide on the constitutionality of the Major Crimes Act. Is the Commerce Clause an adequate source of authority? What, ultimately, is the source of authority upon which the Court makes its decision? Where is it found in the U.S. Constitution? What limits, if any, does the U.S. Constitution place on federal plenary power over tribal nations and peoples?

U.S. v. KAGAMA
118 U.S. 375 (1886)

MILLER, J.

* * *

Though there are six questions certified as the subject of difference, the point of them all is well set out in the third and sixth, which are as follows: "3. Whether the provisions of [the Major Crimes Act] making it a crime for one Indian to commit murder upon another Indian upon an Indian reservation situated wholly within the limits of a State of the Union, and making such Indian so committing the crime of murder within and upon such Indian reservation 'subject to the same laws,' and subject to be 'tried in the same courts, and in the same manner, and subject to the same penalties, as are all other persons' committing the crime of murder 'within the exclusive jurisdiction of the United States' is a constitutional and valid law of the United States." "6. Whether the courts of the United States have jurisdiction or authority to try and punish an Indian belonging to an Indian tribe, for committing the crime of murder upon another Indian belonging to the same Indian tribe, both sustaining the usual tribal relations, said crime having been committed upon an Indian reservation made and set apart for the use of the Indian tribe to which said Indians both belong."

The indictment sets out in two counts that Kagama, alias Pactah Billy, an Indian, murdered Iyouse, alias Ike, another Indian, at Humboldt County, in the State of California, within the limits of the Hoopa Valley Reservation, and it charges Mahawaha, alias Ben, also an Indian, with aiding and abetting in the murder.

* * *

[The Major Crimes Act] is clearly separable into two distinct definitions of the conditions under which Indians may be punished for the same crimes as defined by the common law. The first of these is where the offense is committed within the limits of a territorial government, whether on or off an Indian reservation. . . . It is new, because it now proposes to punish these offenses when they are committed by one Indian on the person or property of another. The second is where the offense is committed by one Indian against the person or property of another, within the limits of a State of the Union, but on an Indian reservation. . . .

. . . The constitution of the United States is almost silent in regard to the relations of the government which was established by it to the numerous tribes of Indians within its borders. . . .

The mention of Indians in the constitution which has received most attention is that found in the clause which gives Congress "power to regulate commerce with foreign nations, and among the several States, and with the Indian tribes." This clause is relied on in the argument in the present case, the proposition being that the statute under consideration is a regulation of commerce with the Indian tribes. But we think it would be a very strained construction of this clause that a system of criminal laws for Indians living peaceably in their reservations, which left out the entire code of trade and intercourse laws justly enacted under that provision, and established punishments for the common law crimes of murder, manslaughter, arson, burglary, larceny, and the like, without any reference to their relation to any kind of commerce, was authorized by the grant of power to regulate commerce with the Indian tribes. . . .

But these Indians are within the geographical limits of the United States. The soil and the people within these limits are under the political control of the government of the United States, or of the States of the Union. There exists within the broad domain of sovereignty but these two. There may be cities, counties, and other organized bodies, with limited legislative functions, but they are all derived from, or exist in, subordination to one or the other of these. . . .

* * *

The Indian reservation in the case before us is land bought by the United States from Mexico by the treaty of Guadaloupe Hidalgo, and the whole of California, with the allegiance of its inhabitants, many of whom were Indians, was transferred by that treaty to the United States. The relation of the Indian tribes living within the borders of the United States, both before and since the Revolution, to the people of the United States has always been an anomalous one, and of a complex character. . . . With the Indians themselves, these relations are equally difficult to define. They were, and always have been, regarded as having a semi-independent position when they preserved their tribal relations; not as States, not as nations, not as possessed of the full attributes of sovereignty, but as a separate people, with the power of regulating their internal and social relations, and thus far not brought under the laws of the Union or of the State within whose limits they resided.

* * *

. . . It seems to us that this is within the competency of Congress. These Indian tribes are the wards of the nation. They are communities dependent on the United States—dependent largely for their daily food; dependent for their political rights. They owe no allegiance to the States, and receive from them no protection. Because of the local ill feeling, the people of the States where they are found are often their deadliest enemies. From their very weakness and helplessness, so largely due to the course of dealing of the federal government with them, and the treaties in which it has been promised, there arises the duty of protection, and with it the power. This has always been recognized by the executive, and by Congress, and by this Court, whenever the question has arisen.

* * *

The power of the General Government over these remnants of a race once powerful, now weak and diminished in numbers, is necessary to their protection, as well as to the safety of those among whom they dwell. It must

exist in that Government, because it never has existed anywhere else; because
the theater of its exercise is within the geographical limits of the United States;
because it has never been denied; and because it alone can enforce its laws on
all the tribes.

In a typical case challenging the constitutionality of a statute, a court must
identify some source of authority within the U.S. Constitution that authorizes
Congress to enact the statute. For example, if a party were to challenge a federal
tax as unconstitutional, a court would likely point to Article I, Section 8, Clause 1
of the U.S. Constitution—the taxing and spending clause—to demonstrate that
the federal government has the authority to establish the tax. In a typical case, if a
court is not able to identify a source of authority that allows Congress to pass a
particular statute, then the statute is declared unconstitutional and void.

Federal Indian law, however, often produces cases that are not typical. In
Kagama, the lawyers for the United States pointed to the Commerce Clause as the
source of federal authority to pass the Major Crimes Act. Justice Samuel Miller's
opinion rejected this theory, stating that it would be "a very strained construction"
of a constitutional power concerning commerce to justify a criminal law statute.
Nonetheless, whereas most court cases would end at this point, without finding a
constitutional basis for the power that Congress sought to exercise, the opinion
in *Kagama* continued. Ultimately, the concern for the Supreme Court in *Kagama*
was not whether an American government actually had the authority under the
U.S. Constitution to pass a statute like the Major Crimes Act—this question was
seemingly never in doubt regardless of what the U.S. Constitution had to say on
the matter. According to Miller, this far ranging, constitutionally-untethered
authority had "always been recognized by the executive, and by Congress, and by
this Court, whenever the question has arisen." Rather, the only real question was
which American government ought to have the authority to pass a statute like the
Major Crimes Act: the federal government or the states?

By positing the only sources of authority in the matter as the federal
government or the individual states, the Supreme Court's opinion completely
excluded tribal governments from the conversation and erased them and any
recognition of their ability to manage their internal affairs from the case. With
tribal nations removed from consideration—or, perhaps more accurately, never
even considered in the first place—the Court decided it had to decide between
the federal government and individual states. Since it described states as the tribal
nations' "deadliest enemies," Miller's opinion essentially argued that the most
humane outcome was to recognize the federal government's plenary authority

over tribal nations, peoples, and matters, regardless of the lack of constitutional grounding for this authority. The Major Crimes Act and the precedent set by *Kagama* remain good law to this day.

TREATIES

Despite the nebulous state they found themselves under the U.S. Constitution after *Kagama*, Native peoples could turn to another source of authority under which they could seek to protect their rights as tribal nations and peoples: treaties. A longstanding and important method of diplomacy between tribal nations and the United States, treaties were (and are) foundational to defining the relationship between the federal government and tribal peoples. Although Congress ended treaty making with tribal nations in 1871, the legislation clearly stated that every treaty up until that point was to remain in effect—and, as described in Chapter 6, agreements, which hold the same force as treaties, continued to be negotiated and ratified well after 1871.

Native America was rapidly changing in the Allotment Era, and the *Kagama* decision left tribal peoples and nations in an increasingly vulnerable position to the federal government. Treaties undoubtedly held the most promise to protect tribal sovereignty and authority after *Kagama*. Unlike tribal peoples and nations themselves, treaties were fairly well considered and established in the U.S. Constitution. Article VI, Clause 2, also known as the Supremacy Clause, states that treaties (as well as the U.S. Constitution itself and federal laws) are the "supreme Law of the Land." With this constitutional grounding, treaties must have appeared to be a formidable source of authority for tribal sovereignty and rights.

Nonetheless, treaties were also considered by many within the federal government to be an impediment to the twin goals of the Allotment Era: civilizing tribal peoples and acquiring tribal lands. As a consequence, the federal government regularly sought to renegotiate treaties to acquire "surplus" tribal lands and to interject more efforts to destroy tribalism into Indian Country. These efforts were not always scrupulous, as the circumstances of the next case attest.

In 1867 the Kiowa and Comanche negotiated what became known as the Medicine Lodge Treaty. Later also agreed to by the Apache, the Medicine Lodge Treaty was fairly typical in that it called for peace between the tribal nations and the United States, the tribal nations ceded land for payment, and a reservation was established. The Kiowa, Comanche, and Apache also agreed to engage in some of the efforts toward "civilization," such as establishing Western style schools on the diminished tribal lands. However, in an effort to preserve their reservation from any further encroachment, the Kiowa, Comanche, and Apache also negotiated an article in the Medicine Lodge Treaty that did not allow any further cession of tribal lands unless 3/4ths of the adult male population agreed to it.

Nonetheless, the American desire for additional tribal lands grew stronger and more persistent during the Allotment Era and the federal government began sending new negotiating commissions to renegotiate with tribal peoples. Many of the treaties that the federal government sought to renegotiate were less than a generation old and tribal peoples regularly lamented the reappearance of federal negotiators, the lack of finality and security of the previously negotiated treaties, and the seeming willingness of the United States to break its promises so quickly and easily. One particularly infamous negotiating party was known as the Jerome Commission.

Nicknamed after the lead negotiator, Michigan politician David H. Jerome, the Jerome Commission (also called the Cherokee Commission) was established in 1889 and was authorized to negotiate agreements with tribal nations residing in the Oklahoma Territory. The Jerome Commission worked quickly and secured a number of agreements before turning its attention to the Kiowa, Comanche, and Apache in October of 1892. The negotiations were contentious, particularly since many tribal members spoke out in favor of the Medicine Lodge Treaty and against allotment. The Jerome Commission did eventually obtain an agreement, nicknamed the Jerome Agreement, which it quickly sent to Washington, D.C. Despite this, tribal resistance to the Jerome Agreement was immediate and vociferous. Tribal members asserted a number of allegations against the commission. Prominent leaders of the Kiowa, Comanche, and Apache— including Lone Wolf—stated, among other things, that the negotiations were held in secret and not in the open as required by law, that the interpreters were deliberately misleading the community for their own gain, that many of the signatures assenting to the Jerome Agreement were obtained through duress, and, most important, that even those signatures that were obtained were not enough to constitute the requisite 3/4ths of adult males necessary to amend the Medicine Lodge Treaty.

Tribal members and their allies were able to stave off Congressional ratification of the Jerome Agreement for a number of years, as some prominent members of the federal government, including the Commissioner of Indian Affairs, acknowledged several problems with both the agreement and the possibility of allotment for the Kiowa, Comanche, and Apache. Even the Secretary of the Interior, Ethan A. Hitchcock (eventually one of the named parties in the case), noted that allotment was not appropriate for the reservation and that the 3/4ths threshold set by the Medicine Lodge Treaty had not been met. Despite the efforts of tribal members and resistance from some within the federal government, Congress ratified the Jerome Agreement in 1900.

Led by Lone Wolf, the Kiowa, Comanche, and Apache turned to their last resort: American courts. They argued that the Jerome Agreement was invalid because it did not meet the 3/4ths threshold set by the Medicine Lodge Treaty. However, they faced difficult challenges from the start. Shortly after the Jerome Agreement was ratified, non-Natives began taking homesteads on the "surplus" land on the reservation. In essence, the tribal nations were asking the federal government to not only stop selling homesteads to settlers, but to remove those who had already taken up plots during the heart of the Allotment Era. As you read the case, ask yourself how the Supreme Court resolves the tension between tribal treaties and federal plenary power. What does the Court have to say about the questionable circumstances under which the Jerome Commission gained assent on the reservation and under which the Jerome Agreement was passed? What alternatives are available to tribal nations, according to the Court? Are they feasible?

LONE WOLF V. HITCHCOCK
187 U.S. 553 (1903)

MR. JUSTICE WHITE delivered the opinion of the Court.

* * *

. . . The twelfth article [of the Medicine Lodge Treaty] reads as follows:

Article 12. No treaty for the cession of any portion or part of the reservation herein in described, which may be held in common, shall be of any validity or force as against the said Indians unless executed and signed by at least three-fourths of all the adult male Indians occupying the same. . . .

The appellants base their right to relief on the proposition that, by the effect of the article just quoted, the confederated tribes of Kiousas, Comanches, and Apaches were vested with an interest in the lands held in common within the reservation, which interest could not be divested by Congress in any other mode than that specified in the said twelfth article, and that, as a result of the said stipulation, the interest of the Indians in the common lands fell within the protection of the Fifth Amendment to the Constitution of the United States, and such interest—indirectly, at least—came under the control of the judicial branch of the government. We are unable to yield our assent to this view.

The contention in effect ignores the status of the contracting Indians and the relation of dependency they bore and continue to bear towards the government of the United States. To uphold the claim would be to adjudge that the indirect operation of the treaty was to materially limit and qualify the controlling authority of Congress in respect to the care and protection of the Indians, and to deprive Congress, in a possible emergency, when the necessity might be urgent for a partition and disposal of the tribal lands, of all power to act, if the assent of the Indians could not be obtained.

Now it is true that, in decisions of this Court, the Indian right of occupancy of tribal lands, whether declared in a treaty or otherwise created, has been stated to be sacred, or, as sometimes expressed, as sacred as the fee of the United States in the same lands. But in none of these cases was there involved a controversy between Indians and the government respecting the power of Congress to administer the property of the Indians. . . . In one of the cited cases, it was clearly pointed out that Congress possessed a paramount power over the property of the Indians by reason of its exercise of guardianship over their interests, and that such authority might be implied, even though opposed to the strict letter of a treaty with the Indians. . . .

Plenary authority over the tribal relations of the Indians has been exercised by Congress from the beginning, and the power has always been deemed a political one, not subject to be controlled by the judicial department of the government. Until the year 1871, the policy was pursued of dealing with the Indian tribes by means of treaties, and, of course, a moral obligation rested upon Congress to act in good faith in performing the stipulations entered into on its behalf. But, as with treaties made with foreign nations, the legislative power might pass laws in conflict with treaties made with the Indians.

The power exists to abrogate the provisions of an Indian treaty, though presumably such power will be exercised only when circumstances arise which will not only justify the government in disregarding the stipulations of the treaty, but may demand, in the interest of the country and the Indians themselves, that it should do so. When, therefore, treaties were entered into between the United States and a tribe of Indians, it was never doubted that the power to abrogate existed in Congress, and that, in a contingency, such power might be availed of from considerations of governmental policy, particularly if consistent with perfect good faith towards the Indians. . . .

* * *

That Indians who had not been fully emancipated from the control and protection of the United States are subject at least so far as the tribal lands were concerned, to be controlled by direct legislation of Congress. . . .

In view of the legislative power possessed by Congress over treaties with the Indians and Indian tribal property, we may not specially consider the contentions pressed upon our notice that the signing by the Indians of the agreement of October 6, 1892, was obtained by fraudulent misrepresentations, and concealment, that the requisite three-fourths of adult male Indians had not signed, as required by the twelfth article of the treaty of 1867, and that the treaty as signed had been amended by Congress without submitting such amendments to the action of the Indians since all these matters, in any event, were solely within the domain of the legislative authority, and its action is conclusive upon the courts.

. . . In effect, the action of Congress now complained of was but . . . a mere change in the form of investment of Indian tribal property, the property of those who, as we have held, were in substantial effect the wards of the government. We must presume that Congress acted in perfect good faith in the dealings with the Indians of which complaint is made, and that the legislative branch of the government exercised its best judgment in the premises. In any event, as Congress possessed full power in the matter, the judiciary cannot question or inquire into the motives which prompted the enactment of this legislation. If injury was occasioned, which we do not wish to be understood as implying, by the use made by Congress of its power, relief must be sought by an appeal to that body for redress, and not to the courts. The legislation in question was constitutional, and the demurrer to the bill was therefore rightly sustained.

Two of the most important aspects of the Supreme Court's opinion were the increasingly all-encompassing description of Native peoples as wards of the federal government and what is known as the Political Question Doctrine. Concerning the status of Native peoples, the Court's opinion posited that not only did they "bore and continue to bear" a "state of dependency" toward the federal government, but that to decide in Lone Wolf's favor would irreparably harm the federal government's capacity to act in favor of their wards. "To uphold the claim would be to adjudge that the indirect operation of the treaty was to materially limit and qualify the controlling authority of Congress in respect to the care and protection of the Indians, and to deprive Congress, in a possible emergency, when the necessity might be urgent for a partition and disposal of the tribal lands, of all power to act, if the assent of the Indians could not be obtained." Thus, according to the Supreme Court's logic, the federal government needed the authority to alter mutually agreed upon treaty provisions without the consent of tribal peoples in order to protect Native peoples.

The facts of the case, in which the federal government obtained an agreement fraudulently, would seem to run contrary to the notion that the federal government needed such authority to protect tribal peoples, as well as basic principles of trust law, in which a guardian is significantly regulated in her/his actions on behalf of a ward. However, these potential concerns were quickly brushed aside by the Supreme Court under the Political Question Doctrine. Under this doctrine, American courts acknowledge that there are some questions of policy that are "political" in nature and that should not be addressed by courts but rather by the political branches. For example, the courts will not entertain a suit challenging the decision of the political branches to go to war, as it is up to the political branches to make those sorts of determinations. Combining the Political Question Doctrine with the exponentially expanding wardship status of Native peoples in American law, the Supreme Court removed itself as an obstacle to Congressional decisions in federal Indian policy with, among other things, a dubious historical claim: "Plenary authority over the tribal relations of the Indians has been exercised by Congress from the beginning, and the power has always been deemed a political one, not subject to be controlled by the judicial department of the government." In bowing to the increased Congressional plenary authority that it was sanctioning, the Supreme Court also disavowed any need to examine the circumstances surrounding the offending governmental actions by noting that, "We must presume that Congress acted in perfect good faith in the dealings with the Indians." Neither the Medicine Lodge Treaty nor the deceit that subsumed it were enough to provoke the Supreme Court to find any barrier to the growing plenary power of Congress.

The decision in *Lone Wolf* left tribal nations in the unenviable position of having their treaty rights altered or amended by a fickle American government yet unable to negotiate treaties after Congress ended the process in 1871. And once again, according to the Court, federal plenary authority was not constrained by a traditional source of rights against the government. Even in the heart of the Allotment Era, the decision was far from universally praised. One U.S. Senator excoriated the decision, stating that it was "the *Dred Scott* decision no. 2," and that "it practically inculcates the doctrine that the red man has no rights which the white man is bound to respect, and, that no treaty or contract made with him is binding."[3] Nonetheless, the senator's strong words, as well as other lamentations, were unable to alter what was continues to be settled law.

AMERICAN CITIZENSHIP

As noted in Chapter 1, Native America had a long interaction with several colonial powers before, and even after, the establishment of the United States. This included Spain—which had several land holdings for many years in what is now the South and Southwest of the United States—and Mexico—which claimed much of what is now the American Southwest after Spain. Both Spain and Mexico left many influences in the region, including a legal legacy that informed the next case.

Pueblo Indians of the Southwest had long had engagements with first Spain and then Mexico. As a consequence, they had encountered colonial law well before their interactions with the United States. As part of this prior colonial engagement, the King of Spain granted Pueblo peoples title to their land in 1689. In 1821 Mexico declared independence from Spain and issued the Plan of Iguala, which essentially stated, among other things, that all persons within the territorial limits of Mexico were citizens. The lands then passed to the United States through the Treaty of Guadalupe Hidalgo in 1848. As the heir to position of discoverer under the Doctrine of Discovery, the United States was beholden to respect the legal rights of Indigenous peoples that had been established under previous colonial regimes. For the Pueblo, this meant a stronger right to the land than the Indian title or occupancy announced by John Marshall, as well as citizenship.

By the time of the next case, the Pueblo were in many ways well suited to challenge the growing scope of federal plenary power over tribal peoples. Not only did they have a legal legacy that seemed to define a broad scope of rights, they were regularly lauded by federal officials as already being particularly civilized. More sedentary and agricultural than many other tribal nations, the various bands of Pueblos were routinely touted as examples of that to which other tribal peoples could aspire. In fact, in 1876 the Supreme Court went so far as to distinguish the Pueblo from their surrounding tribal nations in *U.S. v. Rogers*, stating, "The pueblo Indians, if, indeed, they can be called Indians, had nothing in common with this class."[4]

Notwithstanding the circumstances that ran in the favor of the Pueblo, the facts of the case ran counter to a major purpose of the Allotment Era and a growing trend in the United States as a whole. In 1912 Felipe Sandoval was indicted for selling liquor on the Santa Clara Pueblo in violation of federal law that prohibited alcohol on tribal lands. Although non-Native himself, Sandoval argued that federal liquor laws did not apply to the Pueblos because they owned their lands and that they were American citizens. Many in the federal government and Friends of the Indians, however, felt that alcohol was a serious roadblock on the way to civilization. Additionally, prohibition was gaining popularity politically and would become part of the U.S. Constitution by the end of the decade.

The Supreme Court regarded the citizenship status of the Pueblo as an open question. As you read the case, ask yourself to what extent the Supreme Court answers this question. How does it affect the analysis? How does the Supreme Court characterize the Pueblo? What explains the depiction of the Pueblo in this case as opposed to *Rogers*?

U.S. V. SANDOVAL
231 U.S. 28 (1913)

MR. JUSTICE VAN DEVANTER delivered the opinion of the Court.

This is a criminal prosecution for introducing intoxicating liquor into the Indian country, to-wit, the Santa Clara pueblo, in the State of New Mexico. . . .

* * *

The question to be considered, then, is whether the status of the Pueblo Indians and their lands is such that Congress competently can prohibit the introduction of intoxicating liquor into those lands notwithstanding the admission of New Mexico to statehood.

There are as many as twenty Indian pueblos scattered over the state, having an aggregate population of over 8,000. The lands belonging to the several pueblos vary in quantity, but usually embrace amount 17,000 acres, held in communal, fee simple ownership under grants from the King of Spain, made during the Spanish sovereignty, and confirmed by Congress since the acquisition of that territory by the United States. As respects six of the pueblos, one being the Santa Clara, adjacent public lands have been reserved by executive orders for the use and occupancy of the Indians.

The people of the pueblos, although sedentary, rather than nomadic, in their inclinations, and disposed to peace and industry, are nevertheless Indians in race, customs, and domestic government. Always living in separate and isolated communities, adhering to primitive modes of life, largely influenced by superstition and fetishism, and chiefly governed according to the crude customs inherited from their ancestors, they are essentially a simple, uninformed, and inferior people. Upon the termination of the Spanish sovereignty, they were given enlarged political and civil rights by Mexico, but it remains an open question whether they have become citizens of the United States. Be this as it may, they have been regarded and treated by the United States as requiring special consideration and protection, like other Indian communities. Thus, public moneys have been expended in presenting them with farming implements and utensils, and in their civilization and instruction; agents and superintendents have been provided to guard their interests; central training schools and day schools at the pueblos have been established and maintained for the education of their children; dams and irrigation works have been constructed to encourage and enable them to cultivate their lands and sustain themselves; public lands, as before indicated, have been reserved for their use and occupancy where their own lands were deemed inadequate; a special attorney has been employed since 1898 at an annual cost of $2,000, to represent them and maintain their rights, and when latterly the territory undertook to tax their lands and other property, Congress forbade such taxation. . . .

The local estimate of this people is reflected by a New Mexico statute adopted in 1854, and carried into subsequent compilations, whereby they were "excluded from the privilege of voting at the popular elections of the territory" other than the election of overseers of ditches in which they were interested, and the election of the officers of their pueblos "according to their ancient customs."

With one accord, the reports of the superintendents charged with guarding their interests show that they are dependent upon the fostering care and protection of the government, like reservation Indians in general; that, although industrially superior, they are intellectually and morally inferior to many of them, and that they are easy victims to the evils and debasing influence of intoxicants. We extract the following from published reports of the superintendents:

Albuquerque, 1904:

> While a few of these Pueblo Indians are ready for citizenship and have indicated the same by their energy and willingness to accept service from the railroad companies and elsewhere, and by accepting the benefits of schools and churches, a large percent of them are unable, and not yet enough advanced along the lines of civilization, to take upon themselves the burden of citizenship. It is my opinion that, in the event taxation is imposed, it will be but a short time before the masses of the New Mexico Pueblo Indians will become paupers.

Their lands will be sold for taxes, the whites and Mexicans will have possession of their ancient grants, and the government will be compelled to support them or witness their extermination.

Sante Fe, 1904:

The Pueblo have little or no money, and they cannot understand why they should be singled out from all other Indians and be compelled to bear burdens [territorial taxes] which they are not able to assume. . . . They will not vote, nor are they sufficiently well informed to do so intelligently.

* * *

Sante Fe, 1905:

Until the old customs and Indian practices are broken among this people, we cannot hope for a great amount of progress. The secret dance, from which all whites are excluded, is perhaps one of the greatest evils. What goes on at this time I will not attempt to say, but I firmly believe that it is little less than a ribald system of debauchery. The Catholic clergy is unable to put a stop to this evil, and know as little of same as others. The United States mails are not permitted to pass through the streets of the pueblos when one of these dances is in session; travelers are met on the outskirts of the pueblo and escorted at a safe distance around. The time must come when the Pueblos must give up these old pagan customs and become citizens in fact.

* * *

During the Spanish dominion, the Indians of the pueblos were treated as wards requiring special protection, were subjected to restraints and official supervision in the alienation of their property, and were the beneficiaries of a law declaring "that in the places and pueblos of the Indians, no wine shall enter, nor shall it be sold to them." After the Mexican succession, they were elevated to citizenship and civil rights not before enjoyed, but whether the prior tutelage and restrictions were wholly terminated has been the subject of differing opinions. . . .

* * *

But it is not necessary to dwell specially upon the legal status of this people under either Spanish or Mexican rule, for whether Indian communities within the limits of the United States may be subjected to its guardianship and protection as dependent wards turns upon other considerations. Not only does the Constitution expressly authorize Congress to regulate commerce with the Indian tribes, but long continued legislative and executive usage and an unbroken current of judicial decisions have attributed to the United States as a superior and civilized nation the power and the duty of exercising a fostering care and protection over all dependent Indian communities within its borders, whether within its original territory or territory subsequently acquired, and whether within or without the limits of a state. . . .

* * *

Of course, if it is not meant by this that Congress may bring a community or body of people within the range of this power by arbitrarily calling them an Indian tribe, but only that, in respect of distinctly Indian communities, the questions whether, to what extent, and for what time they shall be recognized and dealt with as dependent tribes requiring the guardianship and protection of the United States are to be determined by Congress, and not by the courts.

As before indicated, by a uniform course of action beginning as early as 1854 and continued up to the present time, the legislative and executive branches of the government have regarded and treated the Pueblos of New Mexico as dependent communities entitled to its aid and protection, like other Indian tribes, and, considering their Indian lineage, isolated and communal life, primitive customs and limited civilization, this assertion of guardianship over them cannot be said to be arbitrary, but must be regarded as both authorized and controlling. . . .

* * *

It is said that such legislation cannot be made to embrace the Pueblos, because they are citizens. As before stated, whether they are citizens is an open question, and we need not determine it now, because citizenship is not, in itself, an obstacle to the exercise by Congress of its power to enact laws for the benefit and protection of tribal Indians as a dependent people.

It also is said that such legislation cannot be made to include the lands of the Pueblos, because the Indians have a fee simple title. It is true that the Indians of each pueblo do have such a title to all the lands connected therewith, excepting such as are occupied under Executive orders, but it is a communal title, no individual owning any separate tract. In other words, the lands are public lands of the pueblo. . . . Considering the reasons which underlie the authority of Congress to prohibit the introduction of liquor into the Indian

> country at all, it seems plain that this authority is sufficiently comprehensive to enable Congress to apply the prohibition to the lands of the Pueblos.
>
> * * *
>
> Being a legitimate exercise of that power, the legislation in question does not encroach upon the police power of the state, or disturb the principle of equality among the states. . . .

As with *Kagama* and *Lone Wolf* before it, *Sandoval* was fueled in no small part by a perception of Native peoples as savage and prone to uncivilized manners and behavior. And as with its predecessors, another traditional source of rights under American law—this time citizenship—was brushed aside by the Supreme Court to make way for congressional plenary power. Ultimately, the Court did not decide upon the question of the citizenship status of the Pueblo. Rather, it noted that, "citizenship is not, in itself, an obstacle to the exercise by Congress of its power to enact laws for the benefit and protection of tribal Indians as a dependent people."

Much like the Marshall Trilogy, *Kagama*, *Lone Wolf*, and *Sandoval* can be considered a trilogy. The "Plenary Power Trilogy" essentially removed any typical legal barriers from the federal government's authority over tribal nations and peoples in the Allotment Era. Acting in great deference to the other branches, the Supreme Court decided that neither the U.S. Constitution, nor treaties, nor American citizenship offered any meaningful restrictions to federal efforts to destroy tribal ways of life, decrease tribal landholdings, and impose a Western version of civilization. Although—as is detailed in later chapters—the holdings in each case have been somewhat mitigated, they all remain good law and continue to be cited by American courts. The delicate balance between federal plenary power and tribal sovereignty was never more in favor of the federal government than during the Allotment Era.

In addition to being easily grouped into categories of three, the Marshall Trilogy and the Plenary Power Trilogy share another major characteristic. Both trilogies posited that tribal peoples were in a unique relationship with the federal government. As a consequence, unique solutions to the problems at hand were necessary. These solutions often violated general principals of the Western legal tradition and were almost never in the favor of tribal peoples and nations. Thus, Marshall noted that the Doctrine of Discovery was an "extravagant . . . pretension," yet nonetheless embraced it as American law. Similarly, the Court in *Kagama* claimed that, "With the Indians themselves, these relations are equally difficult to define," the Court in *Lone Wolf* stated (incorrectly) that "Plenary authority over the tribal relations of the Indians has been exercised by Congress from the beginning," and the Court in *Sandoval* argued that "long continued legislative and executive usage and an unbroken current of judicial decisions have attributed to the United States as a superior and civilized nation the power and the duty of exercising a fostering care and protection over all dependent Indian communities within its borders." Tribal nations and peoples were described first by the Marshall Trilogy continuing through the Plenary Power Trilogy as outside of the normal workings of American law. Consequently the Supreme Court from Marshall to *Kagama*, *Lone Wolf*, and *Sandoval* perpetuated a justification for the expanding federal authority over tribal nations and peoples that reached its zenith in the Allotment Era.

SUGGESTED READINGS

- "The Distorted History that Gave Rise to the 'So Called' Plenary power Doctrine: The Story of *United States v. Kagama*." Sidney L. Harring. In *Indian Law Stories*. Carole Goldberg et al., eds. New York: Foundation Press, 2011, 149–188.

- "The Apex of Congress' Plenary Power over Indian Affairs: The Story of *Lone Wolf v. Hitchcock*." Angela R. Riley. In *Indian Law Stories*. Carole Goldberg et al., eds. New York: Foundation Press, 2011, 189–228.

- "Who is an Indian? The Story of *United States v. Sandoval*." Gerald Torres. In *Indian Law Stories*. Carole Goldberg et al., eds. New York: Foundation Press, 2011, 109–145.

---

[1]   A very useful elucidation of the facts that led to this case can be found in the Sidney L. Harring's contribution to the edited volume *Indian Law Stories*, which is fully cited in the suggested readings for this chapter.

[2]   A summation of the infamous brief can be found in *American Indian Sovereignty and the U.S. Supreme Court: The Masking of Justice*. David E. Wilkins. Austin, TX: University of Texas Press, 1997, 70–71.

[3]   U.S. Congressional Record (1903), 2028.

[4]   United States v. Joseph, 94 U.S. 614, 617 (1876).

CHAPTER 8

The IRA Era

By the 1920s the problems created by the Allotment Era were becoming increasingly undeniable. Native America was in a state of crisis as land loss, disease, and other ills threatened tribal peoples and communities. The benefits that the efforts to "kill the Indian and save the man" promised not only did not accrue, they created many more difficulties than they solved. By the 1920s and 1930s those who still believed in allotment, civilization projects, boarding schools, and other disruptions and reforms to tribal ways of life were beginning to lose the debate to a new group of reformers, led by John Collier, who sought to reinvigorate and reinvest in tribal nations.

Two major blows helped usher in the end of the Allotment Era. The first, in 1928, was the publication of the Meriam Report. While never fully repudiating the Allotment Era ethos, this early publication of the Washington, D.C., think tank the Brookings Institution was highly critical of the federal government's efforts towards tribal nations and peoples and called for a number of reforms. The second was the election of Franklin Roosevelt in 1932 and Roosevelt's decision to appoint John Collier as Commissioner of Indian Affairs. Although Roosevelt did not seem to be particularly concerned with or impassioned by Native America himself, his New Deal legislation and the new spirit of American governance it fostered paved the way for a radical shift in Indian affairs. This unique moment created the opportunity for Collier, previously an outsider to Washington politics, to become Commissioner and to implement major policy reforms.

The IRA period of federal policy began in 1934 with the passage of the Indian Reorganization Act (IRA). Led by Collier, influential lawyer Felix Cohen, and others, the IRA itself and other efforts in this new policy era sought to undo the damage of the Allotment Era and to aid Native America in rebuilding itself in its own image. Lasting from 1934–1953, the IRA Era is sometimes lauded for moving federal policy away from allotment and other destructive policies and sometimes critiqued for not moving further away from the paternalistic qualities that fueled allotment in the first place.

This chapter will demonstrate. . .

- *The transition from the Allotment Era to the IRA Era through the Indian Citizenship Act*

- *The impact of the Meriam Report*

- *The framework of the Indian Reorganization Act*

AMERICAN CITIZENSHIP

One of the goals of the Allotment Era was to steadily incorporate tribal members into the greater American political body by making them American citizens. Supporters of such a move argued that it would advance tribal members further along the path toward civilization by instilling a civic responsibility. During the course of the Allotment Era, a number of tribal peoples did become citizens by a number of ways: through the allotment process, treaties, intermarriage with non-Natives, and other means. In 1919, in recognition of the significant Native participation in World War I, Congress passed a law that allowed for Native veterans to petition for American citizenship upon showing proof of an honorable discharge from the service.

By 1924 one government estimate stated that two-thirds of Native peoples were already American citizens. In that year, Congress decided to close what it regarded as a loophole by granting citizenship to all Native peoples within the United States. As with the rest of Allotment Era legislation, tribal perspectives and interests concerning American citizenship were not consulted, were ignored, or were otherwise defied. Reflecting the dismissive and paternalistic attitude of the Allotment Era, New York Representative Homer P. Snyder, the chairperson of the House Committee on Indian Affairs, stated that "the New York Indians are very much opposed to [the Citizenship Act], but I am perfectly willing to take the responsibility if the committee sees fit to agree to this."[1] As you read the Indian Citizenship Act, ask yourself what it does or does not do for tribal peoples and their rights. Why might the "New York Indians" or any other Native peoples be opposed to such legislation? Can you make arguments for and against American citizenship?

> ## INDIAN CITIZENSHIP ACT
> U.S. Statutes at Large 43:253, June 2, 1924
>
> BE IT ENACTED by the Senate and house of Representatives of the United States of America in Congress assembled, That all non citizen Indians born within the territorial limits of the United States be, and they are hereby, declared to be citizens of the United States: Provided That the granting of such citizenship shall not in any manner impair or otherwise affect the right of any Indian to tribal or other property.

The Indian Citizenship Act was one of the last major actions of the Allotment Era and is worthy of consideration both for its impact on Indian Country and as a site of comparison for what was to come in the IRA Era. Philosophically, the Allotment Era tracked a shift from regarding Indian affairs from an international concern to a domestic concern. The Indian Citizenship Act was the final major push in this vein, making all tribal members subject to the United States as citizens. In keeping with the spirit of the times, the legislation completed one of the stated goals of the Allotment Act specifically and the Era more generally not only without regard to Native views on the issue, but in open defiance to some of those views.

As you read the rest of the chapter, reflect upon the differences between the Indian Citizenship Act and the next major piece of legislation to follow ten years later, the Indian Reorganization Act. Also reflect upon the perspectives of Native peoples expressed by Representative Snyder as compared to John Collier. How do these differences define and explain the policy shift between the Allotment Era and the IRA Era? Are there any commonalities between the two periods of federal policy? Do you find yourself more in agreement with those who argue that the IRA Era was a major move away from the destructive policies and attitudes that defined the Allotment Era, or are you more in agreement with those who argue that the IRA Era was similarly paternalistic to the Allotment Era, only less overt? In essence, what can the Indian Citizenship Act tell us about the IRA?

THE MOVEMENT TOWARD CHANGE

In the mid-1920s, as calls for reform were growing louder, the Secretary of the Interior commissioned a study of federal Indian policy from the Institute for Government Research, a non-governmental organization that is now known as the Brookings Institution. Led by Lewis Meriam, an expert in government administration, a team of researchers spent two years chronicling Native America and the federal government's dealings with Native peoples. Delivered in 1928, the report, titled *The Problem of Indian Administration*, was several hundred pages long and was highly critical of governmental efforts in the Allotment Era.

The study, nicknamed and more famously known as the Meriam Report, offered overwhelming evidence that allotment and other assimilationist polices left the majority of Native peoples in poverty and suffering from other ills with little or no positive benefit to show for it. The seminal study marked a critical turning point for those who wanted to move policy in a different direction, although the report's own suggestions are regularly regarded as generally in keeping with the spirit of assimilation efforts. As you read this excerpt from the Meriam Report, ask yourself what problems it identifies in Native America and in the federal government. Also, what recommendations does the report make? Are those recommendations in keeping with the Allotment Era or do they mark a significant shift in thinking about the "Indian Problem"?

THE PROBLEM OF INDIAN ADMINISTRATION (MERIAM REPORT)
Brookings Institution, 1928

The Conditions Among the Indians. An overwhelming majority of the Indians are poor, even extremely poor, and they are not adjusted to the economic and social system of the dominant white civilization.

The poverty of the Indians and their lack of adjustment to the dominant economic and social systems produce the vicious circle ordinarily found among any people under such circumstances. Because of interrelationships, causes cannot be differentiated from effects. The only course is to state briefly the conditions found that are part of this vicious circle of poverty and maladjustment.

Health. The health of the Indians as compared with that of the general population is bad. Although accurate mortality and morbidity rates are commonly lacking, the existing evidence warrants the statement that both the general death rate and the infant mortality rate is high. . . .

Living Conditions. The prevailing living conditions among the great majority of the Indians are conducive to the development and spread of disease. With comparatively few exceptions the diet of the Indians is bad. . . .

The housing conditions are likewise conductive to bad health. . . . From the standpoint of health it is probably true that the temporary, primitive dwellings . . . were more sanitary than the permanent homes that have replaced them. . . .

Economic Conditions. The income of the typical Indian family is low and the earned income extremely low. . . . The number of Indians who are supporting themselves through their own efforts, according to what a white man would regard as the minimum standard of health and decency, is extremely small. . . .

In justice to the Indians it should be said that many of them are living on lands from which a trained and experienced white man could scarcely wrest a reasonable living. . . . Frequently the better sections of [reservation lands] have fallen into the hands of whites, and the Indians have retreated to the poorer lands remote from markets. . . .

The remoteness of their homes often prevents them from easily securing opportunities for wage earning, nor do they have many contacts with persons dwelling in urban communities where they might find employment. Even boys and girls graduating from government schools have comparatively little vocational guidance or aid in finding profitable employment. . . .

Suffering and Discontent. Some people assert that the Indians prefer to live as they do; that they are happier in their idleness and irresponsibility. . . . The survey staff found altogether too much evidence of real suffering and discontent to subscribe to the belief that the Indians are reasonably satisfied with their condition. The amount of serious illness and poverty is too great to permit of real contentment. The Indian is like the white man in his affection for his children and he feels keenly the sickness and the loss of his offspring.

The Causes of Poverty. The economic basis of the primitive culture of the Indians has been largely destroyed by the encroachment of white civilization. . . . [The Indians] are by no means yet adjusted to the new economic and social conditions that confront them.

Several past policies adopted by the government in dealing with the Indians have been of a type which, if long continued, would tend to pauperize any race. . . .

When the government adopted the policy of [allotment], the expectation was that the Indians would become farmers. . . . It almost seems as if the government assumed that some magic in individual ownership of property would in itself prove an educational civilizing factor, but unfortunately this policy has for the most part operated in the opposite direction. . . .

. . . although money was sometimes given the Indians, the general belief was that the Indians could not be trusted to spend the money for the purpose agreed upon with the agent, and therefore they must not be given opportunity to misapply it. At some agencies this practice still exists, although it gives the Indians no education in the use of money, is irritating to them, and tends to decrease responsibility and increase the pauper attitude. . . .

The Work of the Government in Behalf of the Indians. The work of the government directed toward the education and advancement of the Indian himself . . . is largely ineffective. The chief explanation of the deficiency in this work lies in the fact that the government has not appropriated enough funds to permit the Indian Service to employ an adequate personnel properly qualified for the task before it. . . .

Work for the Promotion of Health. The inadequacy of appropriations has prevented the development of an adequate system of public health administration and medical relief work for the Indians. The number of doctors, nurses, and dentists is insufficient. . . . In the case of doctors the standards set for entrance have been too low. . . . Often untrained, inexperienced field matrons are attempting to perform duties which would be fairly difficult for a well trained, experienced public health nurse. . . .

The hospitals, sanatoria, and sanatorium schools . . . must be generally characterized as lacking in personnel, equipment, management, and design.

Formal Education of Indian Children. . . .

The survey staff finds itself obligated to say frankly and unequivocally that the provisions for the care of the Indian children in boarding schools are grossly inadequate. . . .

The boarding schools are frankly supported in part by the labor of the students. Those above the fourth grade ordinarily work for half a day and go to school for half a day. . . .

. . . several of the industries taught may be called vanishing trades and others are taught in such a way that the Indian students cannot apply what they have learned in their own home and they are not far enough advanced to follow their trade in a white community in competition with white workers without a period of apprenticeship. No adequate arrangements have been made to secure for them the opportunity of apprenticeship. . . .

Family and Community Development. The Indian Service has not appreciated the fundamental importance of family life and community activities in the social and economic development of a people. . . . The long continued policy of removing Indian children from the home and placing them for years in boarding school largely disintegrates the family and interferes with developing normal family life. . . .

Both the government and the missionaries have often failed to study, understand, and take a sympathetic attitude toward Indian ways, Indian ethics, and Indian religion. . . .

Legal Protection and Advancement. Much of the best work done by the Indian Service has been in the protection and conservation of Indian property, yet this program had emphasized the property rather than the Indian. Several legal situations exist which are serious impediments to the social and economic development of the race.

Most notable is the confusion that exists as to legal jurisdiction over the restricted Indians in such important matters as crimes and misdemeanors and domestic relations. . . .

Although the Indian Service has rendered much valuable service in conserving Indian property, it has not gone far enough in protecting the individual Indian from exploitation. The explanation is in part the usual one of lack of adequate personnel, both in the Washington office and in the field. . . . There is a notable absence of adequate organization to protect the Indians in petty cases and to educate then in how to secure legal aid. . . .

Many Indian tribes still have outstanding against the government claims arising out of the old treaties and laws. The existence of these claims is a serious impediment to progress. . . .

The settlement of an old claim involves a long and extremely detailed procedure and hence is necessarily slow. The question must be raised, however, as to whether the government is pressing for their settlement with maximum promptness. The evidence suggests that material improvement is practicable. Until these claims are out of the way, not much can be expected of Indians who are placing their faith in them.

Failure to Develop Cooperative Relationships. The Indian Service has not gone far enough in developing cooperative relationships with other organizations, public and private, which can be of material aid to it in educational developmental work for the Indians. . . .

Recommendations. The fundamental requirement is that the task of the Indian Service be recognized as primarily educational, in the broadest sense of that word, and that it be made an efficient educational agency, devoting its main energies to the social and economic advancement of the Indians, so that they may be absorbed into the prevailing civilization or be fitted to live in the presence of that civilization at least in accordance with a minimum standard of health and decency. . . .

In the execution of this program scrupulous care must be exercised to respect the rights of the Indian. The phrase "rights of the Indian" is often used solely to apply to his property rights. Here it is used in a much broader sense to cover his rights as a human being in a free country. Indians are entitled to unfailing courtesy and consideration from all government employees. They should not be subjected to arbitrary action. . . .

Planning and Development Program. . . .

The survey staff, therefore, recommends that the Secretary of the Interior ask Congress for an appropriation . . . to establish, in connection with the central office but with many duties in the field, a scientific and technical Division of Planning and Development. . . .

Adequate Statistics and Records. The Division of Planning and Development just described cannot function effectively without reasonably reliable and complete data. . . . The survey staff therefore recommends the immediate creation of a position of senior statisticians in the Indian Service. . . .

Strengthening of Personnel in Immediate Contact with the Indians. . . . The Indian Service, because of low salaries and low appropriations, has been attempting to conduct its activities with a personnel inadequate in number and as a rule not possessed of the qualifications requisite for the efficient performance of their duties. Little progress can be expected until this situation has been remedied. . . .

Adequate Salaries. . . .

Better Living and Working Conditions. Persons with high qualifications cannot be expected to enter and remain in the Indian Service unless a material improvement is made in the living and working conditions. . . .

Medical Service. Adequate appropriations should be made markedly to accelerate the progress of the present administration in developing a real system of preventive medicine and public health service for the Indians. . . .

School System. . . . Whatever may have been the official governmental attitude, education for the Indian in the past has proceeded largely on the theory that it is necessary to remove the Indian child as far as possible from his home environment; whereas the modern point of view in education and social work lays stress on upbringing in the natural setting of home and family life. . . .

. . . The promising Indian boy or girl who has attended an Indian boarding school and who desires to go on with his education should not encounter any educational barrier because of the limitations of the Indian boarding schools. The faculties and their courses of study should be such that they can meet the standards set for accredited high schools. . . .

Improving General Economic Conditions. The primary object of the Indian Service in the field of general economic conditions should be to increase the amount and the productivity of Indian labor so that the Indians can support themselves adequately through earned income. . . .

The problem of inherited land should be given thorough detailed study. . . . It is doubtful if the serious nature of this problem was appreciated at the time the allotment acts were passed. . . .

The policy of individual allotment should be followed with extreme conservatism. Not accompanied by adequate instruction in the use of property, it has largely failed in the accomplishment of what was expected of it. It has resulted in much loss of land and an enormous increase in the details of administration without a compensating advance in the economic ability of the Indians. . . .

Improving Family and Community Life. The program developed for each jurisdiction should place special emphasis on family life and community activities. Experience has abundantly demonstrated that the family as a whole is the social unit of major importance in the development of a people. The importance of community activities has also been generally recognized. . . .

The program should embrace health, home making with special emphasis on diet, the use of money, the supplementing of income by home activities, and organized recreation and other community activities.

In all of these activities the Indian point of view and the Indian interests should be given major consideration. . . . There is no reason at all why the Indians should be urged to have dwellings which are replicas of what white men would build. Some of the Indian's ideas regarding outdoor rooms may be found worthy of adoption by the whites.

> *Protection of the Property Rights of Indians.* No evidence warrants a conclusion that the government of the United States can at any time in the near future relinquish its guardianship over the property of restricted Indians. . . . The legal staff of the Indian Service charged with the duty of protecting Indian rights should be materially strengthened and should be authorized to act more directly. . . .
>
> *The Settlement of Claims.* The unsettled legal claims against the government should be settled as the earliest possible date. . . .

The Meriam Report did inaugurate some immediate change from the federal government. Commissioner of Indian Affairs Charles Rhodes, who served from 1929–33, and Assistant Commissioner J. Henry Scattergood attempted to lessen the devastating effects of the Allotment Era in Indian Country and to respond to the critiques levied by the Meriam Report. Although Rhodes and Scattergood were not able to accomplish as much as they had sought, they were able to secure some important victories, including recruiting more Native people into the Bureau of Indian Affairs, fending off additional attempts to divest tribal nations of additional lands, and doubling the budget of the Bureau.

These efforts, and the spirit behind them, would find greater success with the next Presidential administration and Commissioner of Indian Affairs. A new era was dawning and the federal government was becoming increasingly receptive to rethinking its relationship with Indian Country. This included the very nature of tribal governance. Whereas the Allotment Era sought to destroy tribal nations as political units, in the wake of the Meriam Report the federal government increasingly began to recognize the utility of a functioning tribal governmental structure.

Although it did not become law, the Indian Tribal Councils Act encapsulated this new perspective. Introduced in 1932, the proposed bill sought to establish tribal councils that were responsive to the nations that they served. Some of the ideas found in the bill made their way into the Indian Reorganization Act.

As you read this excerpt from the proposed bill, ask yourself what kind of tribal governments it would have created. What responsibilities and what limitations on tribal councils under the proposed legislation are explicit and which are implicit? How would it have broken from the Allotment Era ethos and how might it have continued to perpetuate it?

INDIAN TRIBAL COUNCILS ACT

S. 3668, 72nd Cong., 1st Sess.

Be it enacted. . . . That upon filing with the Commissioner of Indian Affairs a written petition signed by at least 25 per centum of the adult members of any Indian tribe residing on any reservation under the jurisdiction of the United States, the Commissioner of Indian Affairs shall call a general election of the adult members of such tribe to be held within sixty days from the date of filing of such petition for the purpose of choosing a constitutional committee to draft a proposed constitution and by-laws for such tribe. Such committee shall consist of not less than nine members. Within sixty days after its election such committee shall call a general meeting of adult members of the tribe for the purpose of considering and acting upon a proposed constitution and by-laws for such tribe, and each adult member of the tribe shall be notified of the time and place of such general meeting. A copy of the proposed constitution and by-laws, together with a notice of such meeting shall be distributed to each adult member of the tribe at least two weeks prior to the time fixed for such general meeting. At such meeting the proposed constitution and by-laws may be adopted, amended, or rejected, in whole or in part . . . each such constitution shall provide for (1) the establishment of a tribal council of not less than ____ members and the powers to be conferred on such council; (2) a direct election of at least once each year of the members, and (3) a referendum on any question of policy on the petition of at least 15 per centum of the adult members of the tribe, the action of the adult members of the tribe on such referendum to be conclusive and binding upon the tribal council. The amount of any expenses incurred by or on behalf of any tribe carrying out the provisions of this section shall be paid out of any money in the Treasury not otherwise appropriated. There is hereby authorized to be appropriated such sum as may be necessary for such purposes.

SECTION 2. Such tribal councils shall be empowered to represent their several tribes before the Congress or the executive departments of the United States or in the courts. The expenses of any such tribal council shall be paid out of any tribal funds of its tribe, or out of any other moneys over which such council may have exclusive jurisdiction. . . .

SECTION 3. All authority vested in Indian tribes or tribal councils by existing law shall be vested exclusively in the tribal councils provided for by this act. Hereafter no tribal lands, or interest in lands, belonging to any Indian tribe, shall be sold, leased, encumbered, or in any manner disposed of, nor any permit granted therefor, nor any contract made for the use thereof, by the Secretary of the Interior, except by authority of the tribal council, by authority of the general council speaking for such tribe.

SECTION 4. Said tribal councils are hereby authorized to employ legal counsel. Such employment shall not be subject to the approval or control of the Department of the Interior, but the choice of counsel and the fixing of fees paid to such counsel shall be subject to review by the Attorney General on application of any member of the tribe.

* * *

SECTION 8. The Pueblo Tribes of the States of New Mexico and Arizona may retain their traditional customs and established tribal governments in accordance with their established customs, and all provisions of this act relating to powers and functions on the tribal councils shall, so far as consistent with such governments, apply equally to such governments.

SECTION 9. The Secretary of the Interior shall dismiss any employee or officer under his jurisdiction who shall, in any manner, either directly or indirectly, interfere with any of its members in the free exercise of the powers conferred by this act.

SECTION 10. Any employee or officer of the United States who shall, in any manner, either directly or indirectly, interfere with any tribe or any of its members in the free exercise of the powers conferred by this act shall be guilty of a misdemeanor, and shall, on conviction thereof, be punished by a fine of not more than $500 or by imprisonment for not more than six months or both.

SECTION 11. All acts or parts of act inconsistent with the provisions of this act are hereby repealed.

As noted above, the Indian Tribal Councils Act did not become law. But it does offer a compelling glimpse to the shift that was occurring in its moment. In many ways, the proposed legislation was not just a significant departure from the Allotment Era, it also would have established authority for tribal communities that had been previously unheard of and was more radical than the IRA that did eventually become law. It would have, among other things, established tribal councils while respecting the traditional governing structures of some tribal nations, protected tribal lands in the wake of allotment, and freed tribal nations to retain their own lawyers without first needing approval of the federal government.

Some of these proposals, in one form or another, made their way into the IRA. However, perhaps the most far-reaching sections of the Indian Tribal

Councils Act did not. Remarkably, the Indian Tribal Councils Act would have not merely authorized but required the Secretary of the Interior to fire any federal bureaucrat under her/his control who interfered with a tribal nation's exercise of its powers under the legislation (Section 9). Just as remarkably, it would have criminalized the offending behavior as well (Section 10). In the end, the Indian Tribal Councils Act proved to be more than Congress could swallow, but it indicated that big changes in federal Indian policy were possible.

THE IRA

Franklin Roosevelt's election in 1932 was the beginning of a major shift in American politics that affected the country as a whole, including Indian Country. Roosevelt's New Deal plan to end the Great Depression made many Americans rethink the government's place in the life of ordinary citizens and it created the space for a major shift in the goals of federal Indian policy.

The leader of this new era in Indian affairs was John Collier. Officially appointed as Commissioner of Indian Affairs in 1933, Collier served for a record twelve years in the post. A social reformer all of his life, Collier worked with immigrant communities in New York City before being introduced to Native America on a visit to Taos, New Mexico, in 1920. From that point forward, Collier worked with advocacy groups that opposed allotment and other assimilationist policy and sought to reinvigorate tribal nations and peoples. When appointed as Commissioner, Collier began an ambitious agenda to undo what he regarded as the evils of past efforts of the federal government to destroy tribal nations and ways of life.

Although Collier claimed a number of accomplishments in his many years as Commissioner, his most famous and influential victory was the Indian Reorganization Act of 1934. Collier was able to assemble a formidable team to draft the proposed legislation, including Felix Cohen, a lawyer, scholar, and member of the Solicitor's Office. Years later, Cohen would become the lead author of the first edition of the highly influential *Handbook of Federal Indian Law*, a thorough synopsis of the field that became, and remains through new editions, the standard reference for practitioners.

The original draft of the IRA was very large and sought to radically reform federal policy comprehensively through a wide range of changes and new initiatives. For example, the original draft included a provision that would have established a new branch of federal courts to hear and specialize in Native-centered cases. In addition, it would have also prevented the sale of allotted land on a reservation to any party other than the tribal nation itself, as well as a number of other features intended to preserve tribal lands and cultures.

The IRA ran into significant opposition from a number of sources, including from the members of Congress who sponsored the bill. Many "friends of the Indians" who still believed in assimilationist policies considered the IRA a significant step backwards. Federal officials who worked with tribal communities were also often resistant to trying to implement policy contrary to what they had previously sought to establish. Even many tribal members were skeptical for a number of reasons, including a general distrust of governmental officials once again promising a better life through governmental reform.

To combat this resistance Collier and his officials held a number of meetings, called Indian Congresses, across Indian Country in an effort to explain the proposed legislation to tribal members. Several Native peoples congregated at the various Indian Congresses to learn about the IRA and to express either their support or their worries and dissatisfaction with aspects of the bill. Collier and his team took these concerns seriously. At the first Indian Congress in Rapid City, South Dakota, Collier was confronted with much resistance to a provision of the proposed legislation that would have returned allotted land to the tribal nation. After listening to the concerns of several tribal members, Collier stated, "We are going to recommend to the Committees of Congress that [the controversial provisions] shall be exclusively voluntary and that the compulsion feature shall be stricken out." This concession elicited, according to the stenographer, "great applause" from the crowd.[2]

Collier and his team also regularly met with members of Congress who were concerned that the proposed bill was too dramatic of a shift from previous policy. As a result of the Indian Congresses, meetings with members of Congress and other federal officials, and the nature of the political process itself, the IRA was significantly reduced from its original size. By the time that Congress voted upon the bill it no longer contained provisions for a special federal court as well as a number of other controversial aspects that met with disapproval from Congress or Indian Country.

The smaller version of the IRA was signed into law on June 18, 1934. Although scaled back, the IRA was still a very substantial piece of legislation that sought to dramatically change the course of federal Indian policy. Perhaps the greatest evidence of the spirit that Collier and his team sought to establish is found in Section 18 in the final version of the bill. Section 18 permits tribal nations to vote upon whether to come under the auspices of the IRA. Unlike previous federal legislation, which was simply imposed on Indian Country, the IRA gave tribal nations the choice to adopt or reject it. In fact, while a number of tribal nations did adopt the IRA, a number of others either rejected it or chose not to vote on it. As you read this excerpt from the IRA, identify the major points it establishes as law. How do they change or alter what the federal government sought to accomplish during the Allotment Era? To what extent does the IRA accomplish its goal, and to what extent does it maintain a paternalistic oversight of Indian Country?

INDIAN REORGANIZATION ACT (WHEELER-HOWARD ACT)
48 Stat. 984, June 18, 1934

BE IT ENACTED by the Senate and House of Representatives of the United States of America in Congress assembled, That hereafter no land of any Indian reservation, created or set apart by treaty or agreement with the Indians, Act of Congress, Executive order, purchase, or otherwise, shall be allotted in severalty to any Indian.

Sec. 2. The existing periods of trust placed upon any Indian lands and any restriction on alienation thereof are hereby extended and continued until otherwise directed by Congress.

Sec. 3. The Secretary of the Interior, if he shall find it to be in the public interest, is hereby authorized to restore to tribal ownership the remaining surplus lands of any Indian reservation heretofore opened, or authorized to be opened, to sale, or any other form of disposal by Presidential proclamation, or by any of the public land laws of the United States; Provided, however, That valid rights or claims of any persons to any lands so withdrawn existing on the date of the withdrawal shall not be affected by this Act. . .

Sec. 4. Except as herein provided, no sale, devise, gift, exchange or other transfer of restricted Indian lands or of shares in the assets of any Indian tribe or corporation organized hereunder, shall be made or approved. . .

Sec. 5. The Secretary of the Interior is hereby authorized, in his discretion, to acquire through purchase, relinquishment, gift, exchange, or assignment, any interest in lands, water rights or surface rights to lands, within or without existing reservations, including trust or otherwise restricted allotments whether the allottee be living or deceased, for the purpose of providing lands for Indians. . . .

Title to any lands or rights acquired pursuant to this Act shall be taken in the name of the United States in trust for the Indian tribe or individual Indian for which the land is acquired, and such lands or rights shall be exempt from State and local taxation.

* * *

Sec. 7.   The Secretary of the Interior is hereby authorized to proclaim new Indian reservations on lands acquired pursuant to any authority conferred by this Act, or to add such lands to existing reservations: Provided, That lands added to existing reservations shall be designated for the exclusive use of Indians entitled by enrollment or by tribal membership to residence at such reservations shall be designated for the exclusive use of Indians entitled by enrollment or by tribal membership to residence at such reservations.

Sec. 8.   Nothing contained in this Act shall be construed to relate to Indian holdings of allotments or homesteads upon the public domain outside of the geographic boundaries of any Indian reservation now existing or established hereafter.

* * *

Sec. 12.   The Secretary of the Interior is directed to establish standards of health, age, character, experience, knowledge, and ability for Indians who maybe appointed, without regard to civil-service laws, to the various positions maintained, now or hereafter, by the Indian office, in the administrations functions or services affecting any Indian tribe. Such qualified Indians shall hereafter have the preference to appointment to vacancies in any such positions.

Sec. 13.   The provisions of this Act shall not apply to any of the Territories, colonies, or insular possessions of the United States, except that sections 9, 10, 11, 12, and 16 shall apply to the Territory of Alaska: Provided, That Sections 2, 4, 7, 16, 17, and 18 of this Act shall not apply to the following named Indian tribes, together with members of other tribes affiliated with such named located in the State of Oklahoma, as follows: Cheyenne, Arapaho, Apache, Comanche, Kiowa, Caddo, Delaware, Wichita, Osage, Kaw, Otoe, Tonkawa, Pawnee, Ponca, Shawnee, Ottawa, Quapaw, Seneca, Wyandotte, Iowa, Sac and Fox, Kickapoo, Pottawatomi, Cherokee, Chickasaw, Choctaw, Creek, and Seminole. Section 4 of this Act shall not apply to the Indians of the Klamath Reservation in Oregon.

* * *

Sec. 15. Nothing in this Act shall be construed to impair or prejudice any claim or suit of any Indian tribe against the United States. It is hereby declared to be the intent of Congress that no expenditures for the benefit of Indians made out of appropriations authorized by this Act shall be considered as offsets in any suit brought to recover upon any claim of such Indians against the United States.

Sec. 16. Any Indian tribe, or tribes, residing on the same reservation, shall have the right to organize for its common welfare, and may adopt an appropriate constitution and bylaws, which shall become effective when ratified by a majority vote of the adult members of the tribe, or of the adult Indians residing on such reservation, as the case may be, at a special election authorized by the Secretary of the Interior under such rules and regulations as he may prescribe. Such constitution and bylaws when ratified as aforesaid and approved by the Secretary of the Interior shall be revocable by an election open to the same voters and conducted in the same manner as hereinabove provided. Amendments to the constitution and bylaws may be ratified and approved by the Secretary in the same manner as the original constitution and bylaws.

In addition to all powers vested in any Indian tribe or tribal council by existing law, the constitution adopted by said tribe shall also vest in such tribe or its tribal council the following rights and powers: To employ legal counsel, the choice of counsel and fixing of fees to be subject to the approval of the Secretary of the Interior; to prevent the sale, disposition, lease, or encumbrance of tribal lands, interests in lands, or other tribal assets without the consent of the tribe; and to negotiate with the Federal, State, and local Governments. The Secretary of the Interior shall advise such tribe or its tribal council of all appropriation estimates or Federal projects for the benefit of the tribe prior to the submission of such estimates to the Bureau of the Budget and the Congress.

Sec. 17. The Secretary of the Interior may, upon petition by at least one-third of the adult Indians, issue a charter of incorporation to such tribe: Provided, That such charter shall not become operative until ratified at a special election by a majority vote of the adult Indians living on the reservation. Such charter may convey to the incorporated tribe the power to purchase, take by gift, or bequest, or otherwise, own, hold, manage, operate, and dispose of property of every description, real and personal, including the power to purchase restricted Indian lands and to issue in exchange therefor interests in corporate property, and such further powers as may be incidental to the conduct of corporate business, not inconsistent with law, but no authority shall be granted to sell, mortgage, or lease for a period exceeding ten years any of the land included in the limits of the reservation. Any charter so issued shall not be revoked or surrendered except by Act of Congress.

Sec. 18. This Act shall not apply to any reservation wherein a majority of the adult Indians, voting at a special election duly called by the Secretary of the Interior, shall vote against it application. It shall be the duty of the Secretary of the Interior, within one year after the passage and approval of this Act, to call such an election, which election shall be held by secret ballot upon thirty days' notice.

Sec. 19. The term "Indian" as used in this Act shall include all persons of Indian descent who are members of any recognized Indian tribe now under Federal jurisdiction, and all person who are descendants of such members who were, on June 1, 1934, residing within the present boundaries of any reservation, and shall further include all other persons of one-half or more Indian blood. For the purposes of this Act, Eskimos and other aboriginal peoples of Alaska shall be considered Indians. The term "tribe" wherever used in this Act shall be construed to refer to any Indian tribe, organized band, pueblo, or the Indians residing on one reservation. The words "adult Indians" wherever used in this Act shall be construed to refer to Indians who have attained the age of twenty-one years.

Perhaps the two most famous portions of the IRA are its opening, which serves as Section 1 and which ended the process of allotment, and Section 16, which established a process whereby tribal nations could organize a tribal government under a constitution. The end of allotment put a halt to the land loss that Indian Country had suffered in the Allotment Era, maintaining the integrity of remaining tribal landholdings. The purchasing authority in Section 5 furthered this goal, and tribal landholdings have increased since the passage of the IRA.

Concerning Section 16, in one sense it was redundant at best, as there was no impediment to tribal nations adopting constitutions before the IRA. Dozens of tribal nations had already adopted constitutions or documents in the nature of a constitution before the IRA. However, Section 16 was important in that it signaled the major change in federal policy that was occurring. No longer was the federal government seeking to destroy tribal governance and limit sovereignty. Rather, the federal government now sought to support institutions of tribal governance and many tribal constitutions were adopted under the legislation. A number of IRA constitutions are still in place throughout Indian Country today.

Collier and his team scored other victories during his tenure as Commissioner of Indian Affairs, including legislation that eased some of the economic crisis in

Indian Country during the Great Depression, that attempted to protect and preserve Native arts, and that further protected tribal lands and funds. Nonetheless, the IRA is still considered Collier's signature achievement and remains the subject of debate among scholars and those within Indian Country.

Some have criticized the IRA and Collier for perpetuating a paternalistic attitude under the guise of freeing Native peoples and nations from such oversight. For example, while the IRA helped to usher in a new spate of tribal constitutions, ostensibly to further tribal self-government, a number of those constitutions required that any law passed by the newly formed tribal government had to meet with approval from the Secretary of the Interior. In addition, Collier and his team have been accused of manipulating the system in favor of positive outcomes in tribal communities. Section 18, which famously allowed tribal nations to vote on whether to adopt or reject the legislation, was originally written and interpreted to mean that a majority of all eligible voters of a tribal nation had to reject the IRA in order to prevent its application on a reservation. Eligible voters who did not vote were counted as votes in favor of the IRA. Thus, if only 49% of the eligible voters on a reservation cast a ballot, and even if they all voted against the IRA, it nonetheless applied to that tribal nation. About a year after the passage of the IRA Congress amended the act so that only the ballots actually cast were counted toward the adoption or rejection of the IRA—non-voters were removed from the equation. Nonetheless, by that time a number of tribal nations had already voted under the old rules. Critics of Collier and his administration argued that the votes and the application of the IRA were compromised and that this and other actions reflected little more than another version of the same type of paternalism that characterized the Allotment Era. All told, 258 tribal nations voted on the IRA: 181 in favor and 77 against. Fourteen tribal nations did not vote and, as a consequence, were placed under the auspices of the IRA.

Others, however, have lauded Collier and the IRA. At a minimum, the IRA put an end to the devastating process of allotment in Indian Country. The destructive practice divested Native America of approximately ninety million acres of land from its inception to its end, resulting in myriad problems including serious poverty and jurisdictional quandaries. In addition, however imperfectly implemented, the IRA was guided by a spirit of tribal self-rule. Collier, certainly more so than any Commissioner before him, sought to let tribal peoples determine and create their own future even though his actions did not always match the purpose that was driving them or fit with tribal peoples' own sense of self. Collier and the IRA, as well as other legislation during this era, helped to alleviate some of the difficult conditions throughout Indian Country. Collier was also very effective at making sure that the New Deal legislation that battled the Great Depression also applied to Native America.

As noted above, a number of tribal nations continue to operate under IRA constitutions. In many respects modern tribal governance emerged from the IRA Era. While still subject to debate, the influence of Collier and the IRA remains throughout Indian Country.

SUGGESTED READINGS

- *A Fateful Time: The Background and Legislative History of the Indian Reorganization Act.* Elmer R. Rusco. Reno, NV: University of Nevada Press, 2000.

- *Organizing the Lakota: The Political Economy of the New Deal on the Pine Ridge and Rosebud Reservations.* Thomas Biolsi. Tucson, AZ: University of Arizona Press, 1992.

- *The New Deal and American Indian Tribalism: The Administration of the Indian Reorganization Act, 1934–1945.* Graham D. Taylor. Lincoln, NE: University of Nebraska Press, 1980.

---

[1] Unpublished hearings, May 19, 1924. Committee on Indian Affairs, House of Representatives.

[2] Found in *The Indian Reorganization Act: Congresses and Bills.* Vine Deloria, Jr. Norman, OK: University of Oklahoma Press, 2002, 82.

CHAPTER 9

The Termination Era

The Indian Reorganization Act was, in many ways, a consequence of a unique moment in American political history in which the federal government took on a new role and new responsibilities for the country as a whole during the Great Depression and the New Deal. This seminal period allowed federal Indian policy to dramatically shift from the Allotment Era's attempts to assimilate Native peoples and destroy tribal nationhood to new efforts to reestablish tribal governments and cultures through the IRA and other like-minded legislation and means. Yet, the moment was not to last and the IRA Era was much shorter lived than its predecessor. Before long the pendulum that is federal Indian policy shifted once again, this time from the separatism that characterized the IRA Era back to assimilation.

The death of Franklin D. Roosevelt and the end of World War II in 1945 marked the beginning of another major movement in the American political climate. The United States' new position as a superpower, the Soviet Union's rise to prominence, and the threat of global destruction from nuclear war ushered in the Cold War era of American politics, and with it a new way of conceptualizing the "Indian Problem." No longer would American politicians tolerate the separatist ideals that fueled John Collier and the IRA. Assimilation, in a new guise, once again became the dominant theme of Indian policy.

The reconceived solution to the "Indian Problem" during the Cold War came to be known as Termination. Lasting from 1953 to the mid to late 1960s, the Termination Era was, like the Allotment Era, defined by the federal government's attempts to end its political relationship with tribal nations. Although itself short-lived and generally unsuccessful in its stated goals, the Termination Era nonetheless frightened and galvanized Native America while leaving a lasting reminder of the fragile nature of federal Indian law and policy.

This chapter will demonstrate...

- *The transition from the IRA Era to the Termination Era through the Indian Claims Commission*

- *The implementation and legacies of Public Law 280 and Relocation programs*

- *A case study to understand the process, consequences, and possibilities of termination*

THE INDIAN CLAIMS COMMISSION

Although most commentators posit the beginning of the Termination Era in 1953—marked by a resolution in Congress—the winds of change were already beginning to shift by the mid-1940s after the end of World War II. During the War, the federal government largely ignored Native America, despite significant Native participation and achievement in the armed services. Tellingly, the offices of the Bureau of Indian Affairs were temporarily moved to Chicago during this time to create office space in Washington, D.C., for bureaucrats concentrating on the war effort.

After the war, Congress returned its attention to domestic issues, including those centered in Native America. Within this new environment, the federal government sought to resolve one of the longstanding difficulties that tribal nations faced: trying to adjudicate wrongs committed by the federal government through American courts—including treaty violations and other depredations.

After the American Revolution, as the United States was establishing its own court system, it adopted a doctrine of law from the English common law known as Sovereign Immunity. Under the Doctrine of Sovereign Immunity, the "sovereign" (in this case the federal government) cannot be sued in its own court unless it specifically consents to be sued. Thus, an American citizen cannot sue the United States unless the United States allows the citizen to sue it. It is important to note that the Doctrine of Sovereign Immunity also applies to states and tribal nations (see Chapter 21) in a lessened form.

Despite this rule, the federal government has often recognized that it is in its own best interests and in the interests of its citizenry to consent to be sued under a number of circumstances, and thus has regularly waived its sovereign immunity.

In 1855 Congress passed the Court of Claims Act, which established a federal court specifically charged with hearing claims against the federal government. Before long, tribal nations sought to initiate suits in the newly established Court of Claims. However, an 1863 amendment to the Act excluded tribal nations from the Court of Claims' jurisdiction.

As a consequence, any tribal nation that wanted to sue the federal government was prevented from doing so unless they could overcome a major hurdle. In order to initiate a suit against the United States in the Court of Claims after 1863, a tribal nation first had to convince Congress to pass a special jurisdictional act waiving sovereign immunity for the purposes of the suit. Even getting a bill introduced, let alone getting it passed, was an arduous task, although that hardly prevented numerous tribal nations from trying, often repeatedly. According to one estimate, from 1880 to 1946 only 134 cases involving tribal nations were decided under a special jurisdictional act, approximately two per year.[1]

A number of other problems burdened this cumbersome system. Getting a special jurisdictional act passed was just a first step. Tribal nations that cleared this hurdle still had to adjudicate their case in court, and not all won. Many cases were lost, limited, or simply dismissed based on a highly technical reading of the jurisdictional bill. And those tribal nations that overcame all of those obstacles and won their case were plagued by offsets—expenses claimed by the federal government on behalf of the tribal nation that was credited against their judgment. These offsets could drastically reduce or even completely wipe out a judgment. Thus, even those few tribal nations that overcame every hurdle and won their case could still end up with nothing to show for their hard fought victory.

In 1946 Congress, weary of the ever-increasing requests for special jurisdictional acts, passed the Indian Claims Commission Act. The new law was intended to completely and finally put an end to any and all claims made by tribal nations by streamlining a process to resolve them. As you read the excerpt from the law, ask yourself what process it establishes to resolve claims. What kind of claims can be considered? Is the desire to finalize all of the "old Indian claims" more reflective of the spirit of IRA Era's goal of reestablishing and supporting tribal governments or is it a precursor to the federal government's desire in the Termination Era to remove itself from the "Indian business"?

Indian Claims Commission Act
60 Stat. 1049, Aug. 13, 1946

BE IT ENACTED by the Senate and house of Representatives of the United States of America in Congress assembled, That there is hereby created and established an Indian Claims Commission, hereafter referred to as the Commission.

* * *

JURISDICTION

Sec. 2.   The Commission shall hear and determine the following claims against the United States on behalf of any Indian tribe, band, or other identifiable group of American Indians residing within the territorial limits of the United States or Alaska: (1) claims in law or equity arising under the Constitution, law, treaties of the United States, and Executive orders of the President; (2) all other claims in law or equity, including those sounding in tort, with respect to which the claimant would have been entitled to sue in a court of the United States if the United States was subject to suit; (3) claims which would result if the treaties, contracts, and agreements between the claimant and the United States were revised on the ground of fraud, duress, unconscionable consideration, mutual or unilateral mistake, whether of law or fact, or any other ground cognizable by a court of equity; (4) claims arising from the taking by the United States, whether as the result of a treaty of cession or otherwise, of lands owned or occupied by the claimant without payment for such lands of compensation agreed to by the claimant; and (5) claims based upon fair and honorable dealings that are not recognized by any existing rule of law or equity. . . .

All claims hereunder may be heard and determined by the Commission notwithstanding any statute of limitations or laches, but all other defenses shall be available to the United States.

In determining the quantum of relief the Commission shall make appropriate deductions for all payments made by the United States on the claim, and for all other offsets, counterclaims, and demands that would be allowable in a suit brought in the Court of Claims. . . .

* * *

PRESENTATION OF CLAIM

Sec. 10.   Any claim within the provisions of this Act may be presented to the Commission by any member of an Indian tribe, band, or other identifiable group of Indians as the representative of all its members; but wherever any tribal organization exists, recognized by the Secretary of the Interior as having authority to represent such tribe, band, or group, such organization shall be accorded the exclusive privilege of representing such Indians, unless fraud, collusion, or laches on the part of such organization be shown to the satisfaction of the Commission.

* * *

LIMITATIONS

Sec. 12. The Commission shall receive claims for a period of five years after the date of the approval of this Act and no claim existing before such date but not presented within such period may thereafter be submitted to any court or administrative agency for consideration, nor will such claim thereafter be entertained by the Congress.

NOTICE AND INVESTIGATION

Sec. 13. (a)   As soon as practicable the Commission shall send a written explanation of the provisions of this Act to the recognized head of each tribe and band . . . and to the superintendents of all Indian agencies. . . .

(b) The Commission shall establish an Investigation Division to investigate all claims referred to it by the Commission for the purpose of discovering the facts relating thereto. The Division shall make a complete and thorough search for all evidence affecting each claim. . . .

* * *

REPRESENTATION BY ATTORNEYS

Sec. 15. Each such tribe . . . may retain to represent its interests in the presentation of claims before the Commission an attorney . . . of its own selection. . . . The fees of such attorney . . . for all services rendered in prosecuting the claim in question . . . shall . . . be fixed by the Commission . . . but the amount so fixed by the Commission, exclusive of reimbursements for actual expenses, shall not exceed 10 per centum of the amount recovered in any case. . . .

The Attorney General of his assistants shall represent the United States in all claims presented to the Commission. . . .

* * *

> ## DISSOLUTION OF THE COMMISSION
>
> Sec. 23. The existence of the Commission shall terminate at the end of ten years. . . .
>
> * * *

The Commission established by the act held a lot of promise and originally garnered much support in Native America. That promise was only partially fulfilled and left many Native people with a negative view of the process. The Commission, which many hoped would be collaborative in nature, quickly came to resemble an American court, which is adversarial in nature. The Investigation Division authorized in Section 13(b) was never funded and thus never established, forcing tribal nations to hire their own experts to fortify their claims. Both the federal government and tribal nations relied on lawyers to argue their sides before the Commission, and lawyers routinely convinced tribal nations to only pursue claims that made sense to the lawyers, rather than possibilities that might have fit under the rather robust description of claims seemingly allowed under Section 2. Additionally, the only available award was money damages—returning land or other similar remedies were not possible under the law. Perhaps most disappointingly, the federal government adopted a strategy of fighting every claim to the fullest for most of the life of the Commission.

Another major problem was that the process was exceedingly slow. Although Congress originally only gave tribal nations five years to file a claim and ten years for the Commission to finish its work, the heavy volume of claims and the lack of institutional support forced Congress to extend the life of the Commission several times. Despite the fact that its work was not completely finished, the Commission finally did lapse in 1978 and the remaining cases were transferred to the Court of Claims. Considering this history, it is useful to return to one of the questions that introduced the excerpt: Does the ICC more fully fit into the IRA Era or the Termination Era of federal policy?

PUBLIC LAW 280 AND RELOCATION

The Termination Era is, quite understandably, defined by the federal government's attempts to end or "terminate" its political relationship with tribal nations. However, termination, on the whole, was relatively unsuccessful in its stated goal and other aspects of this policy era have had more far reaching and lasting legal and social effects. Two of the most prominent and important aspects of the Termination Era were Public Law 280 and Relocation.

Public Law 280, passed by Congress in 1953, transferred the federal government's jurisdiction within Indian Country to a handful of mandatory states and allowed non-mandatory states to adopt the same jurisdiction. The mandatory states were Alaska, California, Minnesota, Nebraska, Oregon, and Washington— although this is somewhat overstated. It is important to note that while most reservations and tribal nations in these states are subject to PL 280, not all are. For example, Public Law 280 applies to ten of Minnesota's eleven reservations, with the exception of the Red Lake Nation, which was exempted from the law in the original legislation.

The stated purpose of Public Law 280 was to remove the barrier between state law enforcement and tribal lands created by federal jurisdiction, although, from the federal perspective, it had the additional benefit of reducing the cost of administration to parts of Indian Country. The supposed benefits of Public Law 280 angered both the mandatory states and tribal nations affected by the legislation. States were frustrated that federal funds did not accompany the new law enforcement duties thrust upon them. Tribal nations were frustrated that they were not consulted when the legislation was passed, that they were now beholden to state law enforcement and venues that had proven hostile in the past, and that law enforcement on reservations degraded as states often did little to uphold their new obligations. A more robust discussion of Public Law 280 and its effects today can be found in Chapter 17.

Relocation is the word used to describe a group of federal programs and offices that were established all around the country with the purpose of moving tribal peoples from reservations to urban centers during this time. Beginning in the late 1940s and reaching their zenith in the mid-1950s, relocation programs originally sought to find tribal members temporary off-reservation employment, but eventually shifted their focus to providing training and finding permanent employment and housing in urban centers. The idea behind relocation programs was, much in the same vein as the Allotment Era, to remove tribal citizens from their supposedly insular reservation environments where little economic opportunity existed and to acculturate them within the larger world where greater economic opportunity existed and where they would eventually blend into the general populace.

Relocation had mixed results. The federal programs were not always properly funded, nor did its administrators always fully understand the depth of their task, often presuming that some aid finding a job and some words of encouragement were enough. Tribal peoples who did relocate often had trouble finding or keeping jobs, were forced to live in poor housing conditions in segregated neighborhoods, and suffered through isolation and loneliness in unfamiliar and inhospitable spaces. In 1953, the Bureau of Indian Affairs estimated, perhaps conservatively, that one-third of those who were relocated had returned to the reservation.[2] Yet, despite the often-trying times, many Native peoples stayed in the urban centers, resulting in a growing urban Native population. Significant Native populations can be found in places like Los Angeles, San Francisco, Chicago, and other major American cities as a direct result of Relocation.

TERMINATION

As noted above, while there were precursors foreshadowing what was to come, the Termination Era is generally regarded as beginning in earnest in 1953 with House Concurrent Resolution 108. Although not a law itself, the Resolution announced a new Congressional policy direction on the "Indian Problem."

The Termination Era was fueled, at least in part, by the Cold War. The United States and the Soviet Union sought to prove not just their governmental and military superiority during this period, but also their moral superiority. Both sides made accusations that the other oppressed its citizenry. For its part, the Soviet Union accused the United States of treating racial minorities unfairly. American politicians responded, in part, by reconceptualizing federal Indian policy. Using evocative language such as "emancipation" and "freedom" to describe their efforts, policymakers sought to remove what they characterized as the shackles of federal governmental oversight from Native America.

The main thrust of these new efforts found its fullest expression in House Concurrent Resolution 108, which, despite its name, was passed by both houses of Congress. The Resolution announced what would later come to be known as termination as the new federal policy. As you read House Concurrent Resolution 108, ask yourself what it seeks to do. How does it justify this goal? What is the appeal of this approach and what objections might be raised?

HOUSE CONCURRENT RESOLUTION 108 (TERMINATION RESOLUTION)
67 Stat. B132, Aug. 1, 1953

Whereas it is the policy of Congress, as rapidly as possible, to make the Indians within the territorial limits of the United States subject to the same laws and entitled to the same privileges and responsibilities as are applicable to other citizens of the United States, to end their status as wards of the United States, and to grant them all of the rights and prerogatives pertaining to American citizenship, and

Whereas the Indians within the territorial limits of the United States should assume their full responsibilities as American citizens: Now, therefore, be it

Resolved by the House of Representatives (the Senate concurring), That it is declared to be in the sense of Congress that, at the earliest possible time, all of the Indian tribes and the individual members thereof located within the States of California, Florida, New York, and Texas, and all of the following named Indian tribes and individuals thereof, should be freed from Federal supervision and control and from all disabilities and limitations specially applicable to Indians. The Flathead Tribe of Montana, the Klamath Tribe of Oregon, the Menominee Tribe of Wisconsin, the Potawatomie Tribe of Kansas and Nebraska, and those members of the Chippewa Tribe who are on the Turtle Mountain Reservation, North Dakota. It is further declared to be the sense of Congress that, upon the release of such tribes and individual members thereof from such disabilities and limitations, all offices of the Bureau of Indian Affairs in the States of California, Florida, New York, and Texas and all other offices of the Bureau of Indian Affairs whose primary purpose was to serve any Indian tribe or individual Indian freed from Federal supervision should be abolished. It is further declared to be the sense of Congress that the Secretary of the Interior should examine all existing legislation dealing with such Indians, and treaties between the Government of the United States and each such tribe, and report to Congress at the earliest practicable date, but not later than January 1, 1954, his recommendations for such legislation as, in his judgment, may be necessary to accomplish the purposes of this resolution.

At its heart, the purpose of House Concurrent Resolution 108 and termination was to end the political relationship between the federal government and Native nations and peoples. Terminated tribal nations had their access to federal programs and protections stripped, tribal lands lost their status as reservations, and tribal peoples on those lands became subject to all applicable state laws. The rhetoric of the time claimed that by "emancipating" Native peoples through such efforts, Native peoples would be "free" of the oppressive oversight of the federal government and would be able to finally blend in with their non-Native neighbors.

While a powerful statement about the new direction that federal Indian policy was taking, House Concurrent Resolution 108 was not a law itself but rather a statement of policy. Terminating a tribal nation involved a three-step process. First the federal government had to identify a tribal nation as ready for termination. Next, Congress had to pass a termination act for a tribal nation declaring Congress' intention to end its political relationship with the tribal nation. Finally, each termination act directed the Secretary of the Interior to create a detailed plan to manage the logistics of terminating a tribal nation. Many tribal nations were considered not yet ready for termination, and some of those who were presumed ready managed to escape for a variety of reasons. Others, however, endured the full process and were terminated.

In one respect, the Termination Era was short-lived and generally unsuccessful, particularly as compared to its closest parallel, the Allotment Era. According to one study, only 3% of tribal citizens and 3.2 % of tribal lands were affected by termination bills.[3] Yet the threat of termination in the mid-twentieth century not only frightened many tribal peoples, it spurred many to action and Native activism spanning the country began to grow. The very possibility of termination led many to speak out and become politically active. Testifying to the depth of feeling about termination that many held, Vine Deloria, Jr., perhaps the leading Native scholar and activist of the twentieth century, stated that House Concurrent Resolution 108 was "the first shot of the great twentieth century Indian war."[4]

By the end of the 1950s, momentum for termination bills and for the Era's goals was essentially gone. New administrations began pointing toward a new direction in Indian policy. But the effects of the threat of termination are still felt within Indian Country today.

THE MENOMINEE

Like a number of tribal nations and peoples, the Menominee of Wisconsin suffered termination. Also like a number of those terminated—but not all—the Menominee were able to win a restoration of their political relationship with the federal government. A brief examination of their journey offers a useful example of the Termination Era.

By the early 1950s, the Menominee were regarded as a model tribal nation by many. The tribally owned lumbering company and sawmill offered employment, resources, and other economic opportunities that provided a relatively stable environment for the tribal citizenry. Within the rhetoric and thinking of the times, many outside of the community argued that the Menominee were advanced, or civilized, enough to be freed from over-burdensome and oppressive federal governmental oversight. The Menominee were specifically enumerated in House

Concurrent Resolution 108 and were the first to receive a termination bill from Congress. As you read the Menominee Termination Act below, ask yourself what roles the tribal nation, the federal government, and the state play in the process of termination. What does this bill accomplish? What is the status of a Menominee person when the requirements of the law are complete?

MENOMINEE TERMINATION ACT

U.S. Statutes at Large, 68:250–52, June 17, 1954

Be it enacted by the Senate and House of Representatives of the United States of America in Congress assembled, That the purpose of this Act is to provide for orderly termination of Federal supervision over the property and members of the Menominee Indian Tribe of Wisconsin.

* * *

Sec. 3.   At midnight of the date of enactment of this Act the roll of the tribe . . . shall be closed and no child born thereafter shall be eligible for enrollment. . . . [T]he Secretary [of the Interior] . . . shall issue and publish in the Federal Register a Proclamation of Final Closure of the roll of the tribe and the final roll of the members. Effective upon the date of such proclamation, the rights or beneficial interests of each person whose name appears on the roll shall constitute personal property. . . . Such interests shall be distributable in accordance with the laws of the State of Wisconsin. Such interests shall be alienable only in accordance with such regulations as may be adopted by the tribe.

* * *

Sec. 7.   The tribe shall formulate and submit to the Secretary a plan or plans for the future control of the tribal property and service functions now conducted by or under the supervision of the United States, including, but not limited to, services in the fields of health, education, welfare, credit, roads, and law and order. The Secretary is authorized to provide such reasonable assistance as may be requested by officials of the tribe. . . . *Provided,* That the responsibility of the United States to furnish all such supervision and services to the tribe and to the members thereof, because of their status as Indians, shall cease on December 31, 1958, or on such earlier date as may be agreed upon by the tribe and the Secretary.

Sec. 8.   The Secretary is hereby authorized and directed to transfer to the tribe, on December 31, 1958, or on such earlier date as may be agreed upon by the tribe and the Secretary, the title to all property, real and personal, held in trust by the United States for the tribe. . . .

Sec. 9.   No distribution of the assets made under the provisions of this Act shall be subject to any Federal or State income tax. . . . Following any distribution of assets made under the provisions of this Act, such assets and any income derived therefrom in the hands of any individual, or any corporation or organization . . . shall be subject to the same taxes, State and Federal, as in the case of non-Indians. . . .

Sec. 10.   When title to the property of the tribe has been transferred . . . the Secretary shall publish in the Federal Register an appropriate proclamation of that fact. Thereafter individual members of the tribe shall not be entitled to any of the services performed by the United States for Indians because of their status as Indians, all statutes of the United States which affect Indians because of their status as Indians shall no longer be applicable to the members of the tribe, and the laws of the several States shall apply to the tribe and its members in the same manner as they apply to the other citizens or persons within their jurisdiction. Nothing in this Act shall affect the status of the members of the tribe as citizens of the United States.

* * *

Termination for the Menominee quickly proved to be a disaster. The economic and social stability that had characterized the tribal nation prior to termination rapidly dissipated, as the new political reality disrupted many facets of Menominee life and led to greatly increased poverty and land loss, among other ills.

The Menominee were not the only tribal nation to suffer under the effects of termination, and the failures of the policy were immediately evident. By the late 1950s termination began to fall out of favor. By the 1960s it was largely abandoned. Presidents Lyndon Johnson and Richard Nixon both spoke in favor of supporting tribal peoples, nationhood, and sovereignty. In the midst of the larger civil rights movement of the 1960s and 1970s, termination increasingly appeared to be a derogation of the federal government's duties to Native peoples rather than any sort of freedom from oppression.

Before long, the Menominee began to fight to regain their political relationship with the federal government and rerecognition of their sovereignty on a number of fronts. One important way the Menominee sought to preserve their sovereignty was through an acknowledgment and enforcement of their treaty rights. When the state of Wisconsin sought to extend its hunting and fishing laws over the Menominee after termination went into effect, the Menominee fought back, claiming that the federal government did not adequately compensate them for the loss of these treaty rights. In a strange turn of events, by the time the case reached the Supreme Court, both of the named parties to the case—the Menominee and the United States—were arguing that the Menominee had not actually lost those treaty rights. The state of Wisconsin was effectively the only party that was arguing that the Menominee had lost their rights. The Menominee, with the support of the United States, eventually won this fight in the Supreme Court. As you read the Supreme Court decision, ask yourself what is the basis for the Menominee claim to continued treaty rights. How does the majority opinion make the case that these treaty rights survived termination? What is the dissenting opinion's counterargument? How might the era when the case was decided have affected the outcome?

MENOMINEE TRIBE OF INDIANS V. UNITED STATES
391 U.S. 404 (1968)

MR. JUSTICE DOUGLAS delivered the opinion of the Court.

The Menominee Tribe of Indians was granted a reservation in Wisconsin by the Treaty of Wolf River in 1854. By this treaty the Menominees retroceded certain lands they had acquired under an earlier treaty and the United States confirmed to them the Wolf River Reservation "for a home, to be held as Indian lands are held." Nothing was said in the 1854 treaty about hunting and fishing rights. Yet we agree . . . that the language "to be held as Indian lands are held" includes the right to fish and to hunt. The record shows that the lands covered by the Wolf River Treaty of 1854 were selected precisely because they had an abundance of game. The essence of the Treaty of Wolf River was that the Indians were authorized to maintain on the new lands ceded to them as a reservation their way of life which included hunting and fishing. What the precise nature and extent of those hunting and fishing rights were we need not at this time determine. For the issue tendered . . . is whether those rights, whatever their precise extent, have been extinguished.

That issue arose because, beginning in 1962, Wisconsin took the position that the Menominees were subject to her hunting and fishing regulations. Wisconsin prosecuted three Menominees for violating those regulations and the Wisconsin Supreme Court held that the state regulations were valid, as the hunting and fishing rights of the Menominees had been abrogated by Congress in the Menominee Indian Termination Act of 1954.

Thereupon the tribe brought suit in the Court of Claims against the United States to recover just compensation for the loss of those hunting and fishing rights. The Court of Claims by a divided vote held that the tribe possessed hunting and fishing rights under the Wolf River Treaty; but it held, contrary to the Wisconsin Supreme Court, that those rights were not abrogated by the Termination Act of 1954. . . . On oral argument both petitioner and respondent urged that the judgment of the Court of Claims be affirmed. The State of Wisconsin appeared as amicus curiae and argued that that judgment be reserved.

In 1953 Congress by concurrent resolution instructed the Secretary of the Interior to recommend legislation for the withdrawal of federal supervision over certain American Indian tribes, including the Menominees. Several bills were offered, one for the Menominee Tribe that expressly preserved hunting and fishing rights. But the one that became the Termination Act of 1954 did not mention hunting and fishing rights. Moreover, counsel for the Menominees spoke against the bill, arguing that its silence would by implication abolish those hunting and fishing rights. It is therefore argued that they were abolished by the Termination Act.

* * *

It is therefore argued with force that the Termination Act of 1954, which became fully effective in 1961, submitted the hunting and fishing rights of the Indians to state regulation and control. We reach, however, the opposite conclusion. The same Congress that passed the Termination Act also passed Public Law 280. The latter came out of the same committees of the Senate and the House as did the Termination Act; and it was amended in a way that is critical here only two months after the Termination Act became law. As amended, Public Law 280 granted designated States, including Wisconsin, jurisdiction "over offenses committed by or against Indians in the areas of Indian country" named in the Act, which in the case of Wisconsin was described as "All Indian country within the State." But Public Law 280 went on to say that "Nothing in this section . . . shall deprive an Indian or any Indian tribe, band, or community of any right, privilege, or immunity afforded under Federal treaty, agreement, or statute with respect to hunting, trapping, or fishing or the control, licensing, or regulation thereof." That provision on its face contains no limitation; it protects any hunting, trapping, or fishing right granted by a federal treaty. Public Law 280, as amended, became the law in

1954, nearly seven years before the Termination Act became fully effective in 1961. In 1954, when Public Law 280 became effective, the Menominee Reservation was still "Indian country" within the meaning of Public Law 280.

Public Law 280 must therefore be considered in pari materia with the Termination Act. The two Acts read together mean to us that, although federal supervision of the tribe was to cease and all tribal property was to be transferred to new hands, the hunting and fishing rights granted or preserved by the Wolf River Treaty of 1854 survived the Termination Act of 1954.

This construction is in accord with the overall legislative plan. The Termination Act by its terms provided for the "orderly termination of Federal supervision over the property and members" of the tribe. The Federal Government ceded to the State of Wisconsin its power of supervision over the tribe and the reservation lands, as evident from the provision of the Termination Act that the laws of Wisconsin "shall apply to the tribe and its members in the same manner as they apply to other citizens or persons within [its] jurisdiction."

The provision of the Termination Act that "all statutes of the United States which affect Indians because of their status as Indians shall no longer be applicable to the members of the tribe" plainly refers to the termination of federal supervision. The use of the word "statutes" is potent evidence that no treaty was in mind.

We decline to construe the Termination Act as a backhanded way of abrogating the hunting and fishing rights of these Indians. While the power to abrogate those rights exists "the intention to abrogate or modify a treaty is not to be lightly imputed to the Congress."

Our conclusion is buttressed by the remarks of the legislator chiefly responsible for guiding the Termination Act to enactment, Senator Watkins, who stated upon the occasion of the signing of the bill that it "in no way violates any treaty obligation with this tribe."

We find it difficult to believe that Congress, without explicit statement, would subject the United States to a claim for compensation by destroying property rights conferred by treaty, particularly when Congress was purporting by the Termination Act to settle the Government's financial obligations toward the Indians.

* * *

MR. JUSTICE STEWART, with whom MR. JUSTICE BLACK joins, dissenting.

By the Treaty of Wolf River in 1854 the United States granted to the Menominee Tribe of Indians a reservation "to be held as Indian lands are held." As the Court says, this language unquestionably conferred special hunting and fishing rights within the boundaries of the reservation. One hundred years later, in the Menominee Indian Termination Act of 1954, Congress provided for the termination of the reservation and the transfer of title to a tribal corporation. The Act provided that upon termination of the reservation,

> [T]he laws of the several States shall apply to the tribe and its members in the same manner as they apply to other citizens or persons within their jurisdiction.

The reservation was formally terminated on April 30, 1961, seven years after the Termination Act, and the State of Wisconsin has ever since subjected the Menominees, just as any other citizens, to its hunting and fishing regulations.

The Menominees instituted this proceeding against the United States, asking compensation for the taking of their special rights. The Court of Claims denied compensation on the ground that the Termination Act had not in fact extinguished those rights, and that they remained immune from regulation by Wisconsin. The Court today agrees. I do not.

The statute is plain on its face: after termination the Menominees are fully subject to state laws just as other citizens are, and no exception is made for hunting and fishing laws. Nor does the legislative history contain any indication that Congress intended to say anything other than what the unqualified words of the statute express. In fact two bills which would have explicitly preserved hunting and fishing rights were rejected in favor of the bill ultimately adopted—a bill which was opposed by counsel for the Menominees because it failed to preserve their treaty rights.

The Court today holds that the Termination Act does not mean what it says. The Court's reason for reaching this remarkable result is that it finds "in pari materia" another statute which, I submit, has nothing whatever to do with this case.

That statute, Public Law 280, granted to certain States, including Wisconsin, general jurisdiction over "Indian country" within their boundaries. Several exceptions to the general grant were enumerated, including an exception from the grant of criminal jurisdiction for treaty-based hunting and fishing rights. But this case does not deal with state jurisdiction over Indian country; it deals with state jurisdiction over Indians after Indian country has been terminated. Whereas Public Law 280 provides for the continuation of the special hunting and fishing rights while a reservation exists, the Termination Act provides for the applicability of all state laws without exception after the reservation has disappeared.

The Termination Act by its very terms provides:

[A]ll statutes of the United States which affect Indians because of their status as Indians shall no longer be applicable to the members of the tribe. . . .

Public Law 280 is such a statute. It has no application to the Menominees now that their reservation is gone.

The 1854 Treaty granted the Menominees special hunting and fishing rights. The 1954 Termination Act, by subjecting the Menominees without exception to state law, took away those rights.

* * *

Menominee Tribe v. United States offers a useful example of how the history of federal Indian policy can impose unique difficulties on courts. By the time that *Menominee Tribe v. United States* was decided in 1968, the Termination Era was not only effectively over, it already looked like a major mistake to many. Nor did the spirit of the Termination Era fit well with the growing national concern with civil rights in the late 1960s.

Thus, the Supreme Court was faced with a difficult set of circumstances in which it had to decide *Menominee Tribe v. United States.* Those circumstances raise a number of questions and perhaps explain a majority decision that many regard as less logistically sound than the dissent. Should the Court perpetuate Termination Era policies by ruling against the Menominee in the case? What obligation, if any, does the Court have to continue or foster the spirit of old, destructive laws in a much different era? Is it the Court's right, or even its duty, to minimize the harm to vulnerable parties, like the Menominee, when public policy and sentiment has changed, or is it actually violating its institutional role when it operates outside of the most consistent and logical reading of a statute from another time? How should the Court interpret laws that were passed in the Allotment or Termination Eras that continue to exist today?

The Menominee took their fight beyond the courtroom as well, lobbying Congress for what has come to be known as Restoration, or a rerecognition of the political relationship between the tribal nation and the federal government. After years of lobbying and political pressure, the Menominee won back their status as a federally recognized tribal nation in 1973. As you read the Menominee Restoration Act, ask yourself what roles the tribal nation, the federal government, and the state play in the process of restoration. What does this bill accomplish? What is the status of a Menominee person when the requirements of the law are complete?

MENOMINEE RESTORATION ACT
87 Stat. 770, Dec. 22, 1973

* * *

Sec. 3. (a) Notwithstanding the provisions of the [Menominee Termination Act] . . . Federal recognition is hereby extended to the Menominee Indian Tribe of Wisconsin and the provisions of the [Indian Reorganization Act] . . . are made applicable to it.

(b) The [Menominee Termination Act] . . . is hereby repealed and there are hereby reinstated all rights and privileges of the tribe or its members under Federal treaty, statute, or otherwise which may have been diminished or lost pursuant to such Act.

(c) Nothing contained in this Act shall diminish any rights or privileges enjoyed by the tribe or its members now or prior to [the Menominee Termination Act] under Federal treaty, statute, or otherwise, which are not inconsistent with the provisions of this Act.

(d) Except as specifically provided in this Act, nothing contained in this Act shall alter any property rights or obligations, any contractual rights or obligations, including existing fishing rights, or any obligations for taxes already levied.

* * *

Sec. 4. (a)   Within fifteen days after the enactment of this Act, the Secretary shall announce the date of a general council meeting of the tribe to nominate candidates for election to the Menominee Restoration Committee. . . . The Menominee Restoration Committee shall represent the Menominee people in the implementation of this Act and shall have no powers other than those given to it in accordance with this Act. . . .

* * *

(c) The membership roll of the tribe which was closed [by the Menominee Termination Act] is hereby declared open. The Secretary [of the Interior], under contract with the Menominee Restoration Committee, shall proceed to make current the roll in accordance with the terms of this Act. . . . The names of any descendants of an enrollee shall be added to the roll provided such descendant possesses at least one-quarter degree Menominee Indian blood. . . .

Sec. 5. (a)   Upon request from the Menominee Restoration Committee, the Secretary shall conduct an election by secret ballot, pursuant to the provisions of the [Indian Reorganization Act] . . . for the purpose of determining the tribe's constitution and bylaws. The election shall be held within sixty days after the final certification of the tribal roll.

* * *

Sec. 6. . . (d)   The Secretary and the Menominee Restoration Committee shall consult with appropriate State and local government officials to assure that the provision of necessary governmental services is not impaired as a result of the transfer of assets provided for in this section.

(e) For the purpose of implementing subsection (d), the State of Wisconsin may establish such local governmental bodies, political subdivisions, and service arrangements as will best provide the State or local government services required by the people in the territory constituting, on the effective date of this Act, the county of Menominee.

* * *

The Menominee Restoration Act sought to achieve a difficult task: undoing nearly twenty years of history that affected the rights, obligations, and perspectives of the Menominee, the state of Wisconsin, and the federal government. The provisions of the statute attempt to strike a balance, particularly in Section 3—the Menominee are "restored" and any rights that they had or acquired both before and after termination are preserved, but any obligations that members of the Menominee accrued while terminated, including previously applicable taxes, remain in force. Is this a proper balance? Does it lean too far in favor of the Menominee or the state or even the federal government? Why or why not?

In the decades since the end of the Termination Era, some tribal nations that were terminated have been restored, in a manner similar to the Menominee. However, some have not been restored. Additionally, while the termination process itself was relatively little-used, short-lived, and more or less quickly disavowed, other aspects of the Termination Era, most particularly Public Law 280 and the effects of the Relocation programs, continue to effect Native America today.

SUGGESTED READINGS

- *Termination and Relocation: Federal Indian Policy, 1945–1960.* Donald L. Fixico. Albuquerque, NM: University of New Mexico Press, 1986.

- *Their Day In Court: A History of the Indian Claims Commission.* H.D. Rosenthal. New York: Garland Pub., 1990.

- *Captured Justice: Native Nations and Public Law 280.* Duane Champagne and Carol Goldberg. Durham, NC: Carolina Academic Press, 2012.

---

[1] *Wild Justice: The People of Geronimo v. United States.* Michael Leider and Jake Page. Norman, OK: University of Oklahoma Press, 1999, 57.

[2] *The Great Father: The United States Government and the American Indians* (abridged edition). Francis Paul Prucha. Lincoln, NB: University of Nebraska Press, 1986, 355.

[3] "The Evolution of the Termination Policy." Charles F. Wilkinson and Eric R. Biggs. 5 Am. Indian L. Rev. 139 (1977), 151.

[4] *Custer Died For Your Sins: An Indian Manifesto.* Vine Deloria, Jr. Norman, OK: University of Oklahoma Press, 1988 (1969), 62.

CHAPTER 10

The Self-Determination Era

The Termination Era was ineffective in its stated goals and, by federal policy standards, very short lived. Announced in 1953, it was essentially finished by the early 1960s. A number of changes in the greater American political landscape helped to facilitate the Termination Era's demise. One of the federal government's main proponents of Termination, Utah Senator Arthur Watkins, lost his reelection bid in 1958. As the national conversation turned ever more to civil rights and the pursuit of a fair political system for minority peoples, Termination began to look less like a humane attempt to free Native peoples from the burdens of federal oversight and more like yet another effort by the federal government to shirk responsibilities to an oppressed people. Additionally, those relatively few tribal nations that were terminated offered swift and unfortunate examples of the era's failure to solve the "Indian Problem."

Most important, Native peoples and nations grew increasingly politically active in their opposition to Termination and sought greater control over their own lives and governments. In this pivotal moment, the pendulum that is federal Indian policy began to shift once again. Although lacking the seminal moment of transition that characterized other eras (such as the Removal Act or House Concurrent Resolution 108), the assimilationist model of the Termination Era was gradually but steadily replaced with a number of efforts by the federal government to move once again toward a separatist model. Mostly through proactive legislation, the federal government began reinvesting in tribal governments in what has come to be known as the Self-Determination Era.

The Self-Determination Era—the present era of federal policy—is characterized by a number of efforts by Congress to provide opportunities for tribal governments and peoples to exercise greater control over their own lives, lands, families, and other resources. However, these efforts have not been without criticism and resistance, and they often reflect a number of unexpected quandaries in the effort to embrace and expand tribal sovereignty. Interestingly, the Supreme

Court has often been the biggest obstacle to the goals of Congress and tribal nations, as the Court has increasingly taken a role in crafting the boundaries of tribal sovereignty. Understanding the Self-Determination Era requires understanding that the continuing struggle for increased tribal sovereignty is not simply resolved by turning authority over to Native nations and peoples. The long history of federal governmental interference and undue influence over Native nations and peoples, coupled with the obligations incurred by the federal government through treaties and other means, has resulted in a massive, tangled, and often conflicting collection of purposes and goals. The Self-Determination Era is significantly defined by these contradictions.

This chapter will demonstrate. . .

- *The transition from historical to modern Indian law and policy*

- *Congressional efforts to benefit Native nations and peoples in the Self-Determination Era*

- *Unintended complications arising from Congressional efforts during the Self-Determination Era*

MODERN INDIAN LAW

The Self-Determination Era lacks the singular legislative achievement—such as the Allotment Act or the Indian Reorganization Act—that easily defines the beginning of the era and/or marks a major shift in federal policy. But if it is possible to place the change from the Termination Era to Self-Determination in a single event, then it is with the 1959 Supreme Court case *Williams v. Lee*. This decision is regarded by many scholars as the beginning of modern Indian law.

The facts of the case are deceptively simple, yet they raise fundamental issues about tribal sovereignty and the balance between various American governments. Ever since the first Trade and Intercourse Act in 1790 (see Chapter 2), the federal government has licensed and regulated non-Natives who engaged in business dealings within Indian Country. Hugh Lee, a non-Native trader, operated a store under a federal license on the Navajo reservation. Paul and Lorena Williams, two Navajo citizens, incurred debts to Lee's store that they were unable to pay back. As a consequence, Lee obtained an order from an Arizona state court authorizing the seizure of a sufficient amount of the Williams property—specifically sheep from the Williams herd—to pay off the debt. In response, the Williams, with the backing of the Navajo Nation, sued in federal court. The Williams argued that the Arizona state court did not have the authority to issue the order against them and that the proper venue was the tribal court. Thus, the question for the Supreme Court was whether the state court of Arizona had the authority to issue an order concerning a business transaction between a federally licensed trader and a Native couple that occurred on tribal lands. Put more simply, did Arizona have the right to extend its jurisdiction over the Navajo reservation in this manner?

The *Williams* court was quick to reference *Worcester v. Georgia* (see Chapter 3). Before reading *Williams v. Lee* review *Worcester*. As you read *Williams*, ask yourself what connections the opinion makes between the present case and *Worcester*. What reasoning does the Court use to make its decision? What is the standard that the court announces; what is the "test" for determining how to resolve these types of situations? How does that reasoning distinguish it from *Worcester*?

WILLIAMS V. LEE
358 U.S. 217 (1959)

MR. JUSTICE BLACK delivered the opinion of the Court.

* * *

Originally, the Indian tribes were separate nations within what is now the United States. Through conquest and treaties, they were induced to give up complete independence and the right to go to war in exchange for federal protection, aid, and grants of land. When the lands granted lay within States, these governments sometimes sought to impose their laws and courts on the Indians. Around 1830, the Georgia Legislature extended its laws to the Cherokee Reservation despite federal treaties with the Indians which set aside this land for them. The Georgia statutes forbade the Cherokees from enacting laws or holding courts and prohibited outsiders from being on the Reservation except with permission of the State Governor. The constitutionality of these laws was tested in *Worcester v. Georgia* when the State sought to punish a white man, licensed by the Federal Government to practice as a missionary among the Cherokees, for his refusal to leave the Reservation. Rendering one of his most courageous and eloquent opinions, Chief Justice Marshall held that Georgia's assertion of power was invalid.

"The Cherokee nation . . . is a distinct community, occupying its own territory . . . in which the laws of Georgia can have no force, and which the citizens of Georgia have no right to enter, but with the assent of the Cherokees themselves or in conformity with treaties, and with the acts of congress. The whole intercourse between the United States and this nation is, by our constitution and laws, vested in the government of the United States."

Despite bitter criticism and the defiance of Georgia, which refused to obey this Court's mandate in *Worcester,* the broad principles of that decision came to be accepted as law. Over the years, this Court has modified these principles in cases where essential tribal relations were not involved and where the rights of Indians would not be jeopardized, but the basic policy of *Worcester* has remained. Thus, suits by Indians against outsiders in state courts have been sanctioned. And state courts have been allowed to try non-Indians who committed crimes against each other on a reservation. But if the crime was by or against an Indian, tribal jurisdiction or that expressly conferred on other courts by Congress has remained exclusive. Essentially, absent governing Acts of Congress, the question has always been whether the state action infringed on the right of reservation Indians to make their own laws and be ruled by them.

Congress has also acted consistently upon the assumption that the States have no power to regulate the affairs of Indians on a reservation. To assure adequate government of the Indian tribes, it enacted comprehensive statutes in 1834 regulating trade with Indians and organizing a Department of Indian Affairs. Not satisfied solely with centralized government of Indians, it encouraged tribal governments and courts to become stronger and more highly organized. [*The Court then notes Public Law 280, discussed in Chapter 9, which transferred federal jurisdiction over Indian Country to certain states.*] Significantly, when Congress has wished the States to exercise this power, it has expressly granted them the jurisdiction which *Worcester v. Georgia* had denied.

No departure from the policies which have been applied to other Indians is apparent in the relationship between the United States and the Navajos. On June 1, 1868, a treaty was signed between General William T. Sherman, for the United States, and numerous chiefs and headmen of the "Navajo nation or tribe of Indians.". . . Implicit in these treaty terms, as it was in the treaties with the Cherokees involved in *Worcester v. Georgia,* was the understanding that the internal affairs of the Indians remained exclusively within the jurisdiction of whatever tribal government existed. Since then, Congress and the Bureau of Indian Affairs have assisted in strengthening the Navajo tribal government and its courts. The Tribe itself has in recent years greatly improved its legal system through increased expenditures and better trained personnel. Today the Navajo Courts of Indian Offenses exercise broad criminal and civil jurisdiction which

> covers suits by outsiders against Indian defendants. No Federal Act has given state courts jurisdiction over such controversies. . . . To date, Arizona has not accepted jurisdiction [*through Public Law 280*], possibly because the people of the State anticipate that the burdens accompanying such power might be considerable.
>
> There can be no doubt that to allow the exercise of state jurisdiction here would undermine the authority of the tribal courts over Reservation affairs, and hence would infringe on the right of the Indians to govern themselves. It is immaterial that respondent is not an Indian. He was on the Reservation, and the transaction with an Indian took place there. The cases in this Court have consistently guarded the authority of Indian governments over their reservations. Congress recognized this authority in the Navajos in the Treaty of 1868, and has done so ever since. If this power is to be taken away from them, it is for Congress to do it.

Williams v. Lee is regarded by many as the marker for modern Indian law because it reflects the contradictory principles at play in the field of Indian law and the new directions in which the law and policy were headed. On one hand, the case is a clear victory for tribal sovereignty. The Williams, and by extension the Navajo nation, were able to successfully thwart the efforts of the state of Arizona to extend its jurisdiction over tribal lands. The Supreme Court acknowledged that tribal courts were the proper venue to settle these types of disputes. It is possible to read Justice Black's opinion as a validation of tribal governance and judicial systems and as a signal for a new path of dealings with tribal nations in the wake of the Termination Era.

On the other hand, the victory for tribal sovereignty is not only far from absolute, it is possible to read it as a step backwards. Black's opinion is most famous for what has been termed the "infringement test." Under the infringement test, state law is inapplicable on tribal land if it, "infringe[s] on the right of reservation Indians to make their own laws and be ruled by them." Thus, under the infringement test, if a state law were not to intrude upon the rights of tribal nations to exercise their own governmental powers it would continue to have valid force within tribal territory.

As the opinion in *Williams v. Lee* notes, this is a change from the 1832 precedential case *Worcester v. Georgia*. In *Worcester*, Chief Justice John Marshall stated that, "The Cherokee Nation . . . is a distinct community occupying its own territory . . . in which the laws of Georgia can have no force, and which the citizens of Georgia have no right to enter but with the assent of the Cherokees themselves, or in conformity with treaties and with the acts of Congress." Under Marshall's understanding, the borders between Indian Country and the state were solid and impenetrable unless either the federal government or the tribal nation itself permitted such an intrusion. Yet, Justice Black's opinion states that "this Court has modified these principles in cases where essential tribal relations were not involved and where the rights of Indians would not be jeopardized." After *Williams v. Lee*, Marshall's solid borders were eroded and replaced with something more permeable. As a consequence, the infringement test allows for state law to reach into tribal territory as long as it does not interfere with tribal governance.

The infringement test is more complicated than Marshall's straightforward assertion that state laws can have no force in Indian Country. Without much guidance in the opinion on how to accomplish such a task, the infringement test requires courts to decide when state laws do or do not interfere with tribal governance. It also demonstrates a tension that is characteristic of the Self-Determination Era: the federal government has taken many steps to support and defend tribal sovereignty, but it has also sought to protect its own interests and the interests of states in the face of what some regard as too much tribal sovereignty. Thus, in *Williams v. Lee*, tribal courts are recognized as the appropriate forum for the dispute between the Williams and Lee, but state law is also recognized as having some authority within tribal lands.

The next case, *Morton v. Mancari*, is also characteristic of the tensions at play in the Self-Determination Era. Once again, the question of the case was deceptively simple: how should we define Indian tribes—as political entities or racial groupings? Decided in 1974, the case was initiated by non-Native employees of the Bureau of Indian Affairs (BIA)—the federal agency most responsible for maintaining the relationship between the federal government and tribal nations. The BIA had a longstanding hiring preference for Native peoples and had recently instituted a preference for promotions for Native peoples within the agency. A number of non-Native employees objected to the new preference for promotions and sued the federal government (through the Secretary of the Interior, Rogers C. B. Morton) for, among other things, a violation of the 5th Amendment right to due process. The basic argument of the non-Native employees was that they were being unfairly treated and passed over for promotions because of their race. Thus, the Supreme Court had to measure a number of competing interests against each other: tribal sovereignty, the constitutional rights of American citizens and employees of the federal government, and the federal government's responsibilities to tribal nations and peoples among others.

As you read the case, ask yourself how the Supreme Court balances these many interests. Are Indian tribes political entities or racial groupings? What is the basis for the decision? Does the fact that the BIA is involved alter the analysis? What would be the outcome if a different federal agency was involved?

MORTON V. MANCARI
417 U.S. 535 (1974)

MR. JUSTICE BLACKMUN delivered the opinion of the Court.

* * *

The federal policy of according some hiring preference to Indians in the Indian service dates at least as far back as 1834. Since that time, Congress repeatedly has enacted various preferences of the general type here at issue. The purpose of these preferences, as variously expressed in the legislative history, has been to give Indians a greater participation in their own self-government; to further the Government's trust obligation toward the Indian tribes; and to reduce the negative effect of having non-Indians administer matters that affect Indian tribal life.

The preference directly at issue here was enacted as an important part of the sweeping Indian Reorganization Act of 1934. The overriding purpose of that particular Act was to establish machinery whereby Indian tribes would be able to assume a greater degree of self-government, both politically and economically. Congress was seeking to modify the then-existing situation whereby the primarily non-Indian-staffed BIA had plenary control, for all practical purposes, over the lives and destinies of the federally recognized Indian tribes. . . .

One of the primary means by which self-government would be fostered and the Bureau made more responsive was to increase the participation of tribal Indians in the BIA operations. In order to achieve this end, it was recognized that some kind of preference and exemption from otherwise prevailing civil service requirements was necessary. . . .

Congress was well aware that the proposed preference would result in employment disadvantages within the BIA for non-Indians. Not only was this displacement unavoidable if room were to be made for Indians, but it was explicitly determined that gradual replacement of non-Indians with Indians within the Bureau was a desirable feature of the entire program for self-government. Since 1934, the BIA has implemented the preference with a fair degree of success. The percentage of Indians employed in the Bureau rose from 34% in 1934 to 57% in 1972. This reversed the former downward trend and was due, clearly, to the presence of the 1934 Act. The Commissioner's extension of the preference in 1972 to promotions within the BIA was designed to bring more Indians into positions of responsibility and, in that regard, appears to be a logical extension of the congressional intent.

* * *

We still must decide whether, as the appellees contend, the preference constitutes invidious racial discrimination in violation of the Due Process Clause of the Fifth Amendment. . . .

Resolution of the instant issue turns on the unique legal status of Indian tribes under federal law and upon the plenary power of Congress, based on a history of treaties and the assumption of a "guardian-ward" status, to legislate on behalf of federally recognized Indian tribes. The plenary power of Congress to deal with the special problems of Indians is drawn both explicitly and implicitly from the Constitution itself. Article I, § 8, cl. 3, provides Congress with the power to "regulate Commerce . . . with the Indian Tribes," and thus, to this extent, singles Indians out as a proper subject for separate legislation. Article II, § 2, cl. 2, gives the President the power, by and with the advice and consent of the Senate, to make treaties. This has often been the source of the Government's power to deal with the Indian tribes. . . .

Literally every piece of legislation dealing with Indian tribes and reservations, and certainly all legislation dealing with the BIA, single out for special treatment a constituency of tribal Indians living on or near reservations. If these laws, derived from historical relationships and explicitly designed to help only Indians, were deemed invidious racial discrimination, an entire Title of the United States Code (25 U.S.C.) would be effectively erased and the solemn commitment of the Government toward the Indians would be jeopardized.

It is in this historical and legal context that the constitutional validity of the Indian preference is to be determined. As discussed above, Congress in 1934 determined that proper fulfillment of its trust required turning over to the Indians a greater control of their own destinies. The overly paternalistic approach of prior years had proved both exploitative and destructive of Indian interests. Congress was united in the belief that institutional changes were required. An important part of the Indian Reorganization Act was the preference provision here at issue.

Contrary to the characterization made by appellees, this preference does not constitute "racial discrimination." Indeed, it is not even a "racial" preference.[24] Rather, it is an employment criterion reasonably designed to further the cause of Indian self-government and to make the BIA more responsive to the needs of its constituent groups. It is directed to participation by the governed in the governing agency. The preference is similar in kind to the constitutional requirement that a United States Senator, when elected, be "an Inhabitant of that State for which he shall be chosen," Art. I, § 3, cl. 3, or that a member of a city council reside within the city governed by the council. Congress has sought only to enable the BIA to draw more heavily from among the constituent group in staffing its projects, all of which, either directly or indirectly, affect the lives of tribal Indians. The preference, as applied, is granted to Indians not as a discrete racial group, but, rather, as members of *quasi*-sovereign tribal entities whose lives and activities are governed by the BIA in a unique fashion. *See* fn 24. In the sense that there is no other group of people favored in this manner, the legal status of the BIA is truly *sui generis*. Furthermore, the preference applies only to employment in the Indian service. The preference does not cover any other Government agency or activity, and we need not consider the obviously more difficult question that would be presented by a blanket exemption for Indians from all civil service examinations. Here, the preference is reasonably and directly related to a legitimate, nonracially based goal. This is the principal characteristic that generally is absent from proscribed forms of racial discrimination.

On numerous occasions, this Court specifically has upheld legislation that singles out Indians for particular and special treatment. This unique legal status is of long standing, and its sources are diverse. As long as the special treatment can be tied rationally to the fulfillment of Congress' unique obligation toward the Indians, such legislative judgments will not be disturbed. Here, where the preference is reasonable and rationally designed to further Indian self-government, we cannot say that Congress' classification violates due process.

A major key to comprehending both the result of the *Morton v. Mancari* and the issues it raises is Footnote 24. In order to fully understand the impact of Footnote 24, it is important to remember the question of the case—whether Indian tribes should be regarded as political entities or racial groupings. More than just a social construction or rhetorical conceit, the answer to the question was central to determining what type of law to apply in the case. Consequently, the

---

[24] The preference is not directed towards a "racial" group consisting of "Indians"; instead, it applies only to members of "federally recognized" tribes. This operates to exclude many individuals who are racially to be classified as "Indians." In this sense, the preference is political, rather than racial in nature. . . .

type of law that was to be applied would go a long way in determining the outcome of the case.

In general when a law or policy (like the promotion preference in this case) is challenged as unconstitutional, it must undergo a test to determine its constitutionality. There are two basic tests a court can use.[1] If a law distinguishes a group of people on the basis of a "suspect class" (such as race, national origin, religion, or similar categories) then the law must survive the strict scrutiny test. The strict scrutiny test asks if the law is narrowly tailored and if it furthers a compelling governmental interest. This is a very high bar to overcome and most laws measured against this test do not survive it and are declared unconstitutional. If the law does not distinguish on the basis of a suspect class, then the law only has to survive the rational basis test. The rational basis test asks if a law is rationally related to a legitimate governmental interest. This is a very low bar to overcome and most laws measured against this test easily survive it.

As a consequence, the test a court uses often determines the outcome of the case. Under this light, the stakes behind the central question of *Morton v. Mancari* are revealed. If Indian tribes were considered racial groupings—or members of a "suspect class"—then the strict scrutiny test would be applied and the promotion preference (almost assuredly) would not survive it. If Indian tribes were considered political entities then the rational basis test would be applied and the promotion preference would (almost assuredly) survive.

Footnote 24 of Justice Blackmun's opinion demonstrates why the Supreme Court decided to regard Indian tribes as political entities. The promotion preference applies to members of "federally recognized" tribes (see Chapter 13). Since it is possible to be racially Indian but not be a member of a federally recognized tribal nation, Justice Blackmun reasoned that the promotion preference was not a racial classification but a political classification. As such, the rational basis test applies and not the strict scrutiny test.

Blackmun's opinion also nodded toward two other points that help to explain the decision. First, he stated that if Indian tribes are understood as racial groupings than every law dealing with Native peoples and nations is in jeopardy. In this scenario every federal effort towards Native peoples would likely collapse and "the solemn commitment of the Government toward the Indians would be jeopardized." Second, Blackmun noted that this case concerns the BIA, the federal agency most responsible for maintaining the relationship between the federal government and tribal nations. Because the case was limited to the one federal agency designed to deal with Native peoples, it made sense to the Supreme Court to have preferences for Native peoples and allowed the Supreme Court to avoid "the obviously more difficult question that would be presented by a blanket exemption for Indians from all civil service examinations."

Ever since *Morton v. Mancari* was decided, tribal advocates have increasingly used language identifying Indian tribes as political entities to advance all sorts of causes. Often, tribal nations, peoples, and advocates will remind others of the political component of tribal existence to distinguish tribal peoples from other minority groups and explain tribal efforts and goals that would be out of place in other contexts. The acknowledgment of tribal nations as governments and political actors is not new and was not created in *Morton v. Mancari*. But the case provided a new layer of legitimacy and an intellectual basis for the justifications of federal efforts to benefit tribal peoples and nations that were distinguishable from federal efforts for other minority groups in the United States.

Yet, that intellectual basis has not gone unchallenged. Skeptics have trouble recognizing Indian tribes in purely political terms. As race is involved, and as it is most often determinative in whether one can be a citizen of a tribal nation or not, some see the language of tribes as political entities as a thin veil that unhelpfully obscures the racial nature of tribal nationhood.

There also remains the question as to just how far Blackmun and his fellow justices intended their decision to extend. To further the logic of the decision, if federally recognized Indian tribes were fully and completely understood purely and solely as political entities then why shouldn't hiring and promotion preferences extend beyond the BIA? Since the BIA is part of the Department of the Interior couldn't the hiring and promotion preference exist there as well? Considering the federal government's deep influence in criminal justice within Indian Country would a hiring preference at the Department of Justice make sense? What about the Department of Transportation? Are you willing to make the argument for hiring and promotion preferences for Native peoples in any or all of these federal agencies? Why or why not?

Like *Williams v. Lee*, *Morton v. Mancari* is regarded mostly as a victory for tribal interests. However, both cases reveal a deeper layer of complexity and difficulty that confronts Native America and the United States in the modern world. Neither is an absolute victory, and both raise difficult questions about the direction of the law and its capacity to protect and expand tribal sovereignty.

MODERN CONGRESSIONAL LEGISLATION

Other than the advances made by Native peoples and nations themselves, the greatest force for positive structural change in Indian Country during the Self-

Determination Era has been Congressional legislation. A number of federal laws in the disastrous wake of the Termination Era have rebalanced the relationship between tribal nations, the federal government, and states in an effort to foster greater tribal control over tribal lands, resources, and citizens. Some prominent examples include the Indian Civil Rights Act of 1968, which considers civil rights in the tribal context (see Chapter 22); the Indian Child Welfare Act of 1978, which considers family law matters (see Chapter 23); the Indian Gaming Regulatory Act of 1988, which considers economic development through gaming (see Chapter 24); and the Native Graves and Protection Repatriation Act of 1990, which considers appropriate practices for tribal remains (see Chapter 25). Far from exhaustive, this list offers a small glimpse into the many ways that Congressional legislation has sought to be more responsible and sensitive in several different and varied aspects of Native life.

As with the laws noted above, Congressional legislation will often directly address an issue specifically with Native America in mind. Other times, tribal nations are included as part of a larger whole. The next excerpt is an example of the latter. The Clean Water Act applies to the entire United States, but it deliberately considers the role of the legislation in Indian Country. Under the Clean Water Act, individual states have a tremendous amount of authority in determining water quality standards for their lands and for enforcement of the federal law. Tribal nations can also potentially play a major role under the legislation. As you read the excerpt, ask yourself what states are required to do under the law. What can tribal nations do under the law? What criteria do tribal nations need to fulfill to come under the law? What might those criteria reflect about Congressional understandings of Native America?

CLEAN WATER ACT
33 U.S.C.A. Ch. 26

Subch. III, § 1313

. . .

(2) Any state which . . . has adopted, pursuant to its own law, water quality standards applicable to intrastate waters shall submit such standards to the Administrator [of the Clean Water Act]. . . . Each standard shall remain in effect, in the same manner and to the same extent as any other water quality standard established under this chapter. . . .

(3)

(A) Any state which . . . has not adopted pursuant to its own laws water quality standards applicable to intrastate waters shall . . . adopt and submit such standards to the Administrator.

(B) If the Administrator determines that any such standards are consistent with the applicable requirements of this Act . . . he shall approve such standards.

(C) If the Administrator determines that any such standards are not consistent with the applicable requirements of this Act . . . he shall . . . notify the State and specify the changes to meet such requirements. If such changes are not adopted by the State . . . the Administrator shall promulgate such standards. . . .

* * *

Subch. V, § 1377

. . .

(e)   Treatment as States

The Administrator is authorized to treat an Indian tribe as a State for the purposes of [the Clean Water Act], but only if—

(1)   The Indian tribe has a governing body carrying out substantial governmental duties and powers;

(2)   The Functions to be exercised by the Indian tribe pertain to the management and protection of water resources which are held by an Indian tribe, held by the United States in trust for Indians, held by a member of an Indian tribe if such property interest is subject to a trust restriction on alienation, or otherwise within the borders of an Indian reservation; and

(3)   The Indian tribe is reasonably expected to be capable, in the Administrator's judgment, of carrying out the functions to be exercised in a manner consistent with the terms and purposes of this chapter and of all applicable regulations.

While certainly positive for Native America in many regards, the legislation of the Self-Determination Era has been much like the cases of the era in that it has raised difficult quandaries and issues, despite the legislation's beneficial intentions. The Clean Water Act offers a useful example. In one respect, the federal government's willingness to place tribal nations on the same footing as states with regard to the tremendous amount of control and authority available under the law is remarkable and unlike other policy eras. Under the Clean Water Act (and other environmental legislation with similar provisions) tribal nations can and have exercised a level of authority over their lands that has not been seen in generations. On occasion, tribal environmental requirements have even forced states with tribal lands within its borders to improve their own environmental standards.

In another respect, critics note that Congressional legislation often reveals assumptions about the inferiority of tribal peoples and forces tribal nations to conform to Western understandings of governance in order to benefit from the law. Again, the Clean Water Act is instructive. Some critics argue that positioning tribal nations on the same political level as states is actually a diminution of tribal sovereignty. Tribal nations exist outside of the American constitutional framework and have greater sovereignty than states because of their national character and treaty relationship with the federal government. By reducing tribal nations to the status of states, the deeper political character of tribal nations is neglected and tribal nations are uncomfortably and inappropriately shoehorned into the American constitutional framework. In addition, the criteria for exercising powers under the Clean Water Act continues to place more authority in the hands of federal bureaucrats than in the tribal nations themselves. In order to be regarded on the same plane as states, tribal nations must be "reasonably expected to be capable," in the "Administrator's judgment," to manage the responsibility. Thus, a tribal nation must satisfy a federal governmental actor's judgment before it can assert water quality standards on its own lands under the law.

One of the most important pieces of legislation during the Self-Determination Era, and the one that might best capture the spirit of the direction of federal policy of the times, is the Indian Self-Determination and Education Assistance Act of 1975 (ISDA). This influential legislation is most famous for allowing for the transfer of the control of federal programs from the federal government to tribal nations. Tribal nations and the federal government can negotiate "638 contracts" (nicknamed after the legislation's Public Law designation: Public Law 93–638) in which the federal government turns over federal funds designated for specific programs to the tribal government and the tribal government agrees to administer the specific programs and adhere to a number of safeguards. In essence, the federal government gives tribal nations the money it would have otherwise spent running different administrative functions so that tribal nations can complete the functions themselves.

The ISDA has been a powerful tool for tribal nations to reassert greater political and institutional authority over themselves. Through 638 contracts, tribal nations have administered a wide range of functions and initiatives within Indian Country, including, but certainly not limited to, law enforcement, housing programs, health care, drug and alcohol rehabilitation programs, education, and environmental regulation. Whether through the ISDA specifically or within the Self-Determination Era more generally, tribal nations have become more emboldened and better able to determine their own governmental and societal roles.

Despite its positive impact, the ISDA is, like the other materials in this chapter, also indicative of the possibilities, complications, and limitations of the Self-Determination Era. As with the Clean Water Act, tribal nations are subject to federal approval and scrutiny before and after receiving federal funds. The ISDA and the following case add another layer of challenge to the stated goals of the Self-Determination Era: it is one thing for Congress to pass legislation on behalf of Native America. It is another thing to persuade Congress to fund those legislative initiatives and to persuade other branches of the federal government to enforce them. One of Indian Country's major criticisms of the BIA and other federal branches and agencies has been the reluctance of those arms of the government to fulfill the promise of the Self-Determination Era by refusing to relinquish control or comply with legislative mandates intended to strengthen and benefit tribal governments. The next case reflects the tension between the potential of the ISDA and its implementation on the ground. As you read the case, ask yourself about the roles of the governments involved. Where are the gaps between what is promised and what is delivered? What are the options for tribal governments after this ruling? What are the options for the federal government after this ruling? How do both the majority and the dissent's views reflect the tensions within the Self-Determination Era?

SALAZAR V. RAMAH NAVAJO CHAPTER
567 U.S. 182 (2012)

JUSTICE SOTOMAYOR delivered the opinion of the Court.

The Indian Self-Determination and Education Assistance Act (ISDA) directs the Secretary of the Interior to enter into contracts with willing tribes, pursuant to which those tribes will provide services such as education and law enforcement that otherwise would have been provided by the Federal Government. ISDA mandates that the Secretary shall pay the full amount of "contract support costs" incurred by tribes in performing their contracts. At issue in this case is whether the Government must pay those costs when Congress appropriates sufficient funds to pay in full any individual contractor's contract support costs, but not enough funds to cover the aggregate amount due every contractor. Consistent with longstanding principles of Government contracting law, we hold that the Government must pay each tribe's contract support costs in full.

* * *

As originally enacted, ISDA required the Government to provide contracting tribes with an amount of funds equivalent to those that the Secretary "would have other-wise provided for his direct operation of the programs." It soon became apparent that this secretarial amount failed to account for the full costs to tribes of providing services. . . .

Congress included a model contract in ISDA and directed that each tribal self-determination contract "shall . . . contain, or incorporate [it] by reference." . . . the Act makes clear that if the Government fails to pay the amount contracted for, then tribal contractors are entitled to pursue "money damages" in accordance with the Contract Disputes Act.

During Fiscal Years (FYs) 1994 to 2001, respondent Tribes contracted with the Secretary of the Interior to provide services such as law enforcement, environmental protection, and agricultural assistance. The Tribes fully performed. . . .

During each relevant FY, Congress appropriated sufficient funds to pay in full any individual tribal contractor's contract support costs. Congress did not, however, appropriate sufficient funds to cover the contract support costs due all tribal contractors collectively. Between FY 1994 and 2001, appropriations covered only between 77% and 92% of tribes' aggregate contract support costs. The extent of the shortfall was not revealed until each fiscal year was well underway, at which point a tribe's performance of its contractual obligations was largely complete. Lacking funds to pay each contractor in full, the Secretary paid tribes' contract support costs on a uniform, pro rata basis. Tribes responded to these shortfalls by reducing ISDA services to tribal members, diverting tribal resources from non-ISDA programs, and forgoing opportunities to contract in furtherance of Congress' self-determination objective.

Respondent Tribes sued for breach of contract pursuant to the Contract Disputes Act, alleging that the Government failed to pay the full amount of contract support costs due from FY 1994 through 2001, as required by ISDA and their contracts. . . .

* * *

In evaluating the Government's obligation to pay tribes for contract support costs, we do not write on a clean slate. . . .

. . . [In a previous case] we stressed that the Government's obligation to pay contract support costs should be treated as an ordinary contract promise, noting that ISDA "uses the word 'contract' 426 times to describe the nature of the Government's promise." As even the Government conceded, "in the case of ordinary contracts . . . 'if the amount of an unrestricted appropriation is sufficient to fund the contract, the contractor is entitled to payment even if the agency has allocated the funds to another purpose or assumes other obligations that exhaust the funds.' " It followed, therefore, that absent "something special about the promises at issue," the Government was obligated to pay the Tribes' contract support costs in full.

We held that the mere fact that ISDA self-determination contracts are made "subject to the availability of appropriations" did not warrant a special rule. That commonplace provision, we explained, is ordinarily satisfied so long as Congress appropriates adequate legally unrestricted funds to pay the contracts at issue. Because Congress made sufficient funds legally available to the agency to pay the Tribes' contracts, it did not matter that the BIA had allocated some of those funds to serve other purposes, such that the remainder was insufficient to pay the Tribes in full. Rather, we agreed with the Tribes that "as long as Congress has appropriated sufficient legally unrestricted funds to pay the contracts at issue," the Government's promise to pay was binding.

Our conclusion . . . follow[s] directly from well-established principles of Government contracting law. When a Government contractor is one of several persons to be paid out of a larger appropriation sufficient in itself to pay the contractor, it has long been the rule that the Government is responsible to the contractor for the full amount due under the contract, even if the agency exhausts the appropriation in service of other permissible ends. That is so "even if an agency's total lump-sum appropriation is insufficient to pay all the contracts the agency has made." In such cases, "[t]he United States are as much bound by their contracts as are individuals." Although the agency itself cannot disburse funds beyond those appropriated to it, the Government's "valid obligations will remain enforceable in the courts."

This principle safeguards both the expectations of Government contractors and the long-term fiscal interests of the United States. . . . Contractors are responsible for knowing the size of the pie, not how the agency elects to slice it. Thus, so long as Congress appropriates adequate funds to cover a prospective contract, contractors need not keep track of agencies' shifting priorities and competing obligations; rather, they may trust that the Government will honor its contractual promises. In such cases, if an agency overcommits its funds such that it cannot fulfill its contractual commitments, even the Government has acknowledged that "[t]he risk of over-obligation may be found to fall on the agency," not the contractor.

The rule likewise furthers "the Government's own long-run interest as a reliable contracting partner in the myriad workaday transaction of its agencies." If the Government could be trusted to fulfill its promise to pay only when more pressing fiscal needs did not arise, would-be contractors would bargain warily—if at all—and only at a premium large enough to account for the risk of nonpayment. In short, contracting would become more cumbersome and expensive for the Government, and willing partners more scarce.

* * *

. . . We have expressly rejected the Government's argument that "the tribe should bear the risk that a total lump-sum appropriation (though sufficient to cover its own contracts) will not prove sufficient to pay all similar contracts." Rather, the tribal contractors were entitled to rely on the Government's promise to pay because they were "not chargeable with knowledge" of the BIA's administration of Congress' appropriation, "nor [could their] legal rights be affected or impaired by its maladministration or by its diversion."

* * *

This result does not leave the "not to exceed" language in Congress' appropriation without legal effect. To the contrary, it prevents the Secretary from reprogramming other funds to pay contract support costs—thereby protecting funds that Congress envisioned for other BIA programs, including tribes that choose not to enter ISDA contracts. But when an agency makes competing contractual commitments with legally available funds and then fails to pay, it is the Government that must bear the fiscal consequences, not the contractor.

* * *

As the Government points out, the state of affairs resulting in this case is the product of two congressional decisions which the BIA has found difficult to reconcile. On the one hand, Congress obligated the Secretary to accept every qualifying ISDA contract, which includes a promise of "full" funding for all contract support costs. On the other, Congress appropriated insufficient funds to pay in full each tribal contractor. The Government's frustration is understandable, but the dilemma's resolution is the responsibility of Congress.

Congress is not short of options. For instance, it could reduce the Government's financial obligation by amending ISDA to remove the statutory mandate compelling the BIA to enter into self-determination contracts, or by giving the BIA flexibility to pay less than the full amount of contract support costs. It could also pass a moratorium on the formation of new self-determination contracts, as it has done before. Or Congress could elect to make line-item appropriations, allocating funds to cover tribes' contract support costs on a contractor-by-contractor basis. On the other hand, Congress could appropriate sufficient funds to the BIA to meet the tribes' total contract support cost needs. . . .

The desirability of these options is not for us to say. We make clear only that Congress has ample means at hand to resolve the situation underlying the Tribes' suit. . . .

* * *

CHIEF JUSTICE ROBERTS, with whom JUSTICE GINSBURG, JUSTICE BREYER, and JUSTICE ALITO join, dissenting.

Today the Court concludes that the Federal Government must pay the full amount of contract support costs incurred by the respondent Tribes, regardless of whether there are any appropriated funds left for that purpose. This despite the facts that payment of such costs is "subject to the availability of appropriations," a condition expressly set forth in both the statute and the contracts providing for such payment. . . Because the Court's conclusion cannot be squared with these unambiguous restrictions on the payment of contract support costs, I respectfully dissent.

The Indian Self-Determination and Education Assistance Act provides: "Notwithstanding any other provision in [the Act], the provision of funds under this [Act] is subject to the availability of appropriations. . . ." This condition is repeated in the Tribes' contracts with the Government. The question in this case is whether appropriations were "available" during fiscal years 1994 through 2001 to pay all the contract support costs incurred by the Tribes. Only if appropriations were "available" may the Tribes hold the Government liable for the unpaid amounts.

Congress restricted the amount of funds "available" to pay the Tribes' contract support costs in two ways. First, in each annual appropriations statute for the Department of the Interior from fiscal year 1994 to 2001, Congress provided that spending on contract support costs for all tribes was "not to exceed" a certain amount. . . .

Second . . . in the very same sentence that conditions funding on the "availability of appropriations"—Congress provided that "the Secretary [of the Interior] is not required to reduce funding for programs, projects, or activities serving a tribe to make funds available to another tribe or tribal organization under [the Act].". . .

Given these express restrictions established by Congress—which no one doubts are valid—I cannot agree with the Court's conclusion that appropriations were "available" to pay the Tribes' contract support costs in full. . . .

. . . What matters is what the Secretary actually does, and once he allocates the funds to one tribe, they are not "available" to another.

* * *

It is true, as the Court notes, that each of the Tribes' contracts provides that the Act and the contract "shall be liberally construed for the benefit of the Contractor." But a provision can be construed "liberally" as opposed to "strictly" only when there is some ambiguity to construe. And here there is none. Congress spoke clearly when it said that the provision of funds was "subject to the availability of appropriations," that spending on contract support costs was "not to exceed" a specific amount, and that the Secretary was "not required" to make funds allocated for one tribe's costs "available" to another. The unambiguous meaning of these provisions is that when the Secretary has allocated the maximum amount of funds appropriated each fiscal year for contract support costs, there are no other appropriations "available" to pay any remaining costs.

* * *

Salazar v. Ramah Navajo Chapter covers a wide range of the possibilities and problems of the Self-Determination Era. The case was a victory for tribal interests and a recognition of the federal government's responsibilities to tribal nations, but it required a Supreme Court ruling to secure that recognition. It involved the ISDA, one of the strongest pieces of legislation shaping tribal governance today, but the dispute centered on the federal government's unwillingness to fulfill its contractual obligations and the promise of the ISDA. Many involved in the litigation were attempting to do their best under the circumstances—the tribal nation was administering its own affairs, the Secretary of the Interior was trying to equitably distribute a budgetary shortfall—but the end result was frustration on all sides. Lofty platitudes and aspirations were not given their full effect by a lack of resources, which resulted in all parties exerting additional resources in bringing a lawsuit to the Supreme Court. Perhaps most ominously, tribal interests won a bare majority of the Justices, continuing to cast doubt on how future cases might be decided as the composition of the Supreme Court changes.

These contradictions reflected in the final chapter of Unit I of this text are a precursor to the chapters in Unit II. The rest of this text is, in many respects, an examination of the tensions that continue to define the Self-Determination Era. As you transition from the history of federal Indian law and policy to its present articulation, it is important to remember that the answers are never easy and the solutions regularly reveal new questions and unintended consequences.

SUGGESTED READINGS

- *Blood Struggle: The Rise of Modern Indian Nations.* Charles Wilkinson. New York: W.W. Norton & Company, 2005.

- *Shadow Nations: Tribal Sovereignty and the Limits of Legal Pluralism.* N. Bruce Duthu. New York: Oxford University Press, 2013.

- *Like a Loaded Weapon: The Rehnquist Court, Indian Rights, and the Legal History of Racism in America.* Robert A. Williams, Jr. Minneapolis, MN: University of Minnesota Press, 2005.

---

[1]   There is a third test—Intermediate Scrutiny—that is most often used for laws based on gender classifications. Although vitally important to issues of American constitutional law, for the purposes of clarity and simplicity, this text will concentrate on the two tests that are most important to the analysis of *Morton v. Mancari*—Strict Scrutiny and Rational Basis.

Contemporary Native America

CHAPTER 11

Treaties and the Canons of Construction

As noted in the introduction of this text, the main characteristic that distinguishes Native America from other minority groups in the United States is the political dimension to Indianness and Native nationhood. One of the foundational pillars to this political dimension of Native identity is treaties and treaty rights. Treaties, among other things, recognize and establish the government-to-government relationship between tribal nations and the federal government, define the boundaries of tribal territories and rights, and serve as a tool and a symbol of a tribal nation's sovereignty.

The centuries-old history of treaty making between Native nations and colonizing powers holds relevance to this day, for Natives and non-Natives alike. It is not possible to do justice to this rich history in this limited space; nonetheless, identifying a few major points will frame the key questions and ideas of this chapter. The United States began diplomatic relations with tribal nations even before the Declaration of Independence. Some regard a 1778 treaty with the Lenape Nation as the first signed treaty between the United States and an Indian nation, although similar diplomatic relations occurred before that date. Nearly a century of American diplomacy with Native America through the treaty process resulted in over 500 treaties. As detailed in Chapter 6, in 1871 Congress "ended" treaty making with Native nations through a short rider on a larger appropriations bill. This legislation did not immediately mean the cessation of diplomatic relations and negotiations, however, as treaty substitutes called agreements replicated the treaty process and format for many years afterward.

This history of Indian treaties and agreements raises significant issues for the present day, particularly because the history runs along potentially contradictory lines. The 1871 rider that ended treaty making with tribal nations remains in force, which means that the federal government continues to legally declare that it will no longer engage in this form of diplomacy with Native America. Some have argued that the 1871 rider is not an appropriate exercise of Congressional authority under the U.S. Constitution, but no major challenge has been made to the legislation as of present. More to the point, the rider itself states that, "That nothing herein contained shall be construed to invalidate or impair the obligation of any treaty heretofore lawfully made and ratified with any such Indian nation or tribe." In addition, as detailed in Chapter 2, treaties made by the United States "Shall be the supreme Law of the Land," according to the U.S. Constitution. Thus, the United States, at present, will not engage in more treaties with Native nations, but the United States considers the ones that were created to still be in force and the "supreme Law of the Land." How should American courts handle issues with treaties that remain in force yet signed with political entities that are no longer regarded as able to treat with the United States?

This chapter will demonstrate. . .

- *A pattern of Supreme Court interpretation of treaties*

- *The Indian canons of construction, their strengths, and their limitations*

- *The standard for determining if a treaty has been abrogated*

READING TREATIES AND THE CANONS OF CONSTRUCTION

In the contemporary context, one of the most significant questions about treaties is how to read these important historical yet highly relevant documents. Through the years American courts have developed techniques to confront the challenge of engaging with the problems that treaties present. Courts have had to reconcile a number of mitigating factors: treaties were not written in Native languages, they were written in a different era with different understandings about language and the law, and the United States has a continuing obligation to tribal nations and peoples under the trust doctrine (see Chapter 14), to list a few.

One prominent example of the Supreme Court having to confront the challenge of reading treaties is *U.S. v. Winans*. The 1905 case concerned an 1855 treaty between the United States and the Yakama (sometimes spelled Yakima, including the 1855 treaty in question), a tribal nation in the Pacific Northwest. Under the terms of the treaty, the Yakama ceded some of their lands but reserved the right to fish on the ceded lands, "at all of the usual and accustomed places, in common with the citizens of the territory." Fishing was necessary to the survival of the Yakama, as it was for many tribal nations of the Pacific Northwest. Homesteads on the ceded land were sold to non-Natives after the treaty, and after it was admitted to the union in 1898 the state of Washington began issuing permits for fishing wheels on the ceded lands. The fishing wheels, meant for commercial use, harvested a tremendous amount of fish and left little in the way for tribal peoples. In addition, non-Native landowners often excluded tribal members from homesteads that had been part of the traditional fishing areas, further preventing tribal members from engaging in this important practice. In response, the Yakama sued a pair of brothers, Lineas and Audubon Winans, who owned a homestead and a fishing wheel on the Columbia River. The Yakama accused of the brothers of excluding them from property then owned by the brothers and what had been a usual and accustomed place for fishing. The question before the Supreme Court was how to interpret the 1855 treaty, particularly in light of the subsequent actions of the state of Washington.

As you read the case, ask yourself how the Supreme Court frames the treaty. What does the Court's characterization of the treaty mean for analyzing it? How does the Supreme Court characterize the rights of the state of Washington and non-Native landowners? How does the Supreme Court describe Native peoples and how does that description alter the analysis? What obligations does the United States have toward Native peoples and how does that affect the reading of the treaty?

U.S. v. WINANS
198 U.S. 371 (1905)

MR. JUSTICE MCKENNA delivered the opinion of the Court.

* * *

There is no substantial dispute of facts, or none that is important to our inquiry.

The treaty is as follows:

* * *

"Article III. . . .

"The exclusive right of taking fish in all the streams where running through or bordering said reservation is further secured to said confederated tribes and bands of Indians, as also the right of taking fish at all usual and accustomed places, in common with citizens of the territory, and of erecting temporary buildings for curing them, together with the privilege of hunting, gathering roots and berries, and pasturing their horses and cattle upon open and unclaimed land."

* * *

The respondents or their predecessors in title claim under patents of the United States the lands bordering on the Columbia River, and under grants from the State of Washington to the shore land which, it is alleged, fronts on the patented land. They also introduced in evidence licenses from the state to maintain devices for taking fish called fish wheels.

At the time the treaty was made, the fishing places were part of the Indian country, subject to the occupancy of the Indians, with all the rights such occupancy gave. The object of the treaty was to limit the occupancy to certain lands, and to define rights outside of them.

The pivot of the controversy is the construction of the second paragraph. Respondents contend that the words "the right of taking fish at all usual and accustomed places in common with the citizens of the territory" confer only such rights as a white man would have under the conditions of ownership of the lands bordering on the river, and under the laws of the state, and, such being the rights conferred, the respondents further contend that they have the power to exclude the Indians from the river by reason of such ownership.

* * *

. . . [W]e have said we will construe a treaty with the Indians as "that unlettered people" understood it, and "as justice and reason demand, in all cases where power is exerted by the strong over those to whom they owe care and protection," and counterpoise the inequality "by the superior justice which looks only to the substance of the right, without regard to technical rules." How the treaty in question was understood may be gathered from the circumstances.

The right to resort to the fishing places in controversy was a part of larger rights possessed by the Indians, upon the exercise of which there was not a shadow of impediment, and which were not much less necessary to the existence of the Indians than the atmosphere they breathed. New conditions came into existence, to which those rights had to be accommodated. Only a limitation of them, however, was necessary and intended, not a taking away. In other words, the treaty was not a grant of rights to the Indians, but a grant of right from them—a reservation of those not granted. And the form of the instrument and its language was adapted to that purpose. . . . There was a right outside of those boundaries reserved "in common with citizens of the territory." As a mere right, it was not exclusive in the Indians. Citizens might share it, but the Indians were secured in its enjoyment by a special provision of means for its exercise. They were given "the right of taking fish at all usual and accustomed places," and the right "of erecting temporary buildings for curing them." The contingency of the future ownership of the lands therefore was foreseen and provided for; in other words, the Indians were given a right in the land—the right of crossing it to the river—the right to occupy it to the extent and for the purpose mentioned. No other conclusion would give effect to the treaty. And the right was intended to be continuing against the United States and its grantees as well as against the state and its grantees.

The respondents urge an argument based upon the different capacities of white men and Indians to devise and make use of instrumentalities to enjoy the common right. . . .

. . . But the result does not follow that the Indians may be absolutely excluded. It needs no argument to show that the superiority of a combined harvester over the ancient sickle neither increased nor decreased rights to the use of land held in common. In the actual taking of fish, white men may not be confined to a spear or crude net, but it does not follow that they may construct and use a device which gives them exclusive possession of the fishing places, as it is admitted a fish wheel does. Besides, the fish wheel is not relied on alone. Its monopoly is made complete by a license from the state. The argument based on the inferiority of the Indians is peculiar. If the Indians had not been inferior in capacity and power, what the treaty would have been, or that there would have been any treaty, would be hard to guess.

The construction of the treaty disposes of certain subsidiary contentions of respondents. The Land Department could grant no exemptions from its provisions. It makes no difference, therefore, that the patents issued by the Department are absolute in form. They are subject to the treaty as to the other laws of the land.

* * *

The extinguishment of the Indian title, opening the land for settlement and preparing the way for future states, were appropriate to the objects for which the United States held the territory. And surely it was within the competency of the nation to secure to the Indians such a remnant of the great rights they possessed as "taking fish at all usual and accustomed places." Nor does it restrain the state unreasonably, if at all, in the regulation of the right. It only fixes in the land such easements as enable the right to be exercised.

> The license from the state which respondents plead to maintain a fishing wheel gives no power to them to exclude the Indians, nor was it intended to give such power. It was the permission of the state to use a particular device.

U.S. v. Winans is remarkable for a number of reasons, including for being a rare win for tribal interests at the Supreme Court in the Allotment Era (see Chapter 5). Most important, the opinion offered a framework for reading treaties, starting with how to conceptualize the treaty process. In the opinion's most famous phrase, Justice Joseph McKenna noted that treaties were "not a grant of rights to the Indians, but a grant of right from them." Often the public discourse on treaty rights becomes confused on this point and opponents will argue that Native nations and peoples should not be accorded "special" rights under treaties or will express dismay that Native nations were "given" those rights. However, McKenna's statement reminds the reader that treaty rights were not gifted to tribal nations but retained by them.

Resting on this foundation, McKenna detailed some the necessary facets for interpreting a treaty. The opinion stated that the Court would seek to understand the treaty in the same manner as the "unlettered" Indians would have understood it, that it was important to bear in mind the disparate power dynamics, that technicalities should not overcome the spirit of retained tribal rights, and that the surrounding circumstances and evidence could aid in construing the words of a treaty. These general principles have been further distilled into what scholars now recognize as the Indian canons of construction.

A canon of construction, in a broad sense, is a tool that a judge might use to interpret a difficult or ambiguous document of law, such as a contract, statute, or treaty. There are a fair number of general canons of construction to facilitate this process and make the business of deciphering a document easier. For example, one of the more common canons of construction is that if a word in a document of law—perhaps a contract—appears more than once, then that word carries the same meaning throughout the entire document. Another common canon is that every word in a document—perhaps a statute—has meaning and should be given effect. These helpful tools not only make it easier to interpret the law, they also promote a consistent pattern of behavior among judges and foster predictability and consistency.

Over the years American courts have developed the Indian canons of construction to aid in the particular challenges of reading and interpreting Indian treaties. Following the lead of the *Winans* court and other cases, the Indian canons of construction have been distilled into three generally accepted principles:

- Treaties must be interpreted as Indians would have understood the treaty at the time it was written

- Ambiguities in treaties must be resolved in favor of Indians

- Treaties must be liberally construed in favor of Indians

As Justice McKenna's opinion suggests, looking beyond the treaty language into the historical moment and circumstances is often necessary to give the Indian canons their full effect.

The next case, *U.S. v. Washington*, is one of the most famous treaty cases of the 20th century. Nicknamed the Boldt decision after its author, George Boldt, the opinion is lauded by tribal advocates as a landmark victory for treaty rights and an example of a proper invocation of the purpose of the Indian canons of construction. As with *Winans*, the dispute was centered in the Pacific Northwest.

The litigation was initiated in the Self-Determination Era (see Chapter 10) during a period of increased tribal interest in revitalizing treaty rights. This period, from about the early 1970s to the late 1990s, was also defined by a significant backlash against those efforts, with a number of oppositional non-Natives actively arguing or working against tribal treaty interests. Many treaty rights efforts revolved around access to natural resources, such as hunting and fishing rights, and oppositional non-Natives regularly expressed fear over the loss of those natural resources and dismay that Native peoples had access to natural resources outside of state-prescribed limits. The contentiousness was often ugly and occasionally violent. Sometimes oppositional non-Natives would blockade tribal citizens' access to sites for harvesting natural resources or hold rallies against the invocation of treaty rights in which derogatory signs and language was used. In one particularly egregious example of the tenor of the times, a Wisconsin non-Native organization began selling "treaty beer," with the intention of raising funds for a legal defense against treaty rights. Although treaty rights remain central to Native nations and opposition still exists, these types of controversies have become less prominent as cases like the Boldt decision have settled the law and as tribal nations and states have engaged in cooperative efforts to preserve and perpetuate natural resources.

The Boldt decision was, in many ways, the beginning of that explosive period. The question of the case was, in essence, what right to the off-reservation fish stock did tribal nations in Washington State reserve through their treaties? As you read the case, ask yourself how the court reads the treaty. Where do you see the presence of the Indian canons of construction? What sort of effort does it take to read the treaties in this manner? What meaning does the court find when there is a lack of information or discussion on a specific topic? How does the court characterize the Native peoples who signed the treaties?

U.S. V. WASHINGTON

384 F. Supp. 312 (1974)

BOLDT, SENIOR DISTRICT JUDGE.

In September, 1970 the United States, on its own behalf and as trustee for several Western Washington Indian Tribes . . . filed the complaint initiating this action against the State of Washington. . . .

* * *

For more than three years, at the expenditure by many people of great time, effort and expense, plaintiffs and defendants have conducted exhaustive research in anthropology, biology, fishery management and other fields of expertise, and also have made extreme efforts to find and present by witnesses and exhibits as much information as possible that pertains directly or indirectly to each issue in the case. . . . It is believed considerable historic and scientific information never before presented in a case involving treaty rights is now recorded and may prove of value in later proceedings in this case and possibly in others.

* * *

More than a century of frequent and often violent controversy between Indians and non-Indians over treaty right fishing has resulted in deep distrust and animosity on both sides. This has been inflamed by provocative, sometimes illegal, conduct of extremists on both sides and by irresponsible demonstrations instigated by non-resident opportunists.

* * *

. . . Congress chose treaties rather than conquest as the means to acquire vast Indian lands. . . . The treaties were written in English, a language unknown to most of the tribal representatives, and translated for the Indians by an interpreter in the service of the United States using Chinook Jargon, which was also unknown to some tribal representatives. Having only about three hundred words in its vocabulary, the Jargon was capable of conveying only rudimentary concepts, but not the sophisticated or implied meaning of treaty provisions about which highly learned jurists and scholars differ.

In 1899 the United States Supreme Court in considering a similar situation said:

> In construing any treaty between the United States and an Indian tribe, it must always. . . . be borne in mind that the negotiations for the treaty are conducted, on the part of the United States, an enlightened and powerful nation, by representatives skilled in diplomacy, masters of a written language, understanding the modes and forms of creating the various technical estates known to their law, and assisted by an interpreter employed by themselves; that the treaty is drawn up by them and in their own language; that the Indians, on the other hand, are a weak and dependent people, who have no written language and are wholly unfamiliar with all the forms of legal expression, and whose only knowledge of the terms in which the treaty is framed is that imparted to them by the interpreter employed by the United States; and that the treaty must therefore be construed, not according to the technical meaning of its words to learned lawyers, but in the sense in which they would naturally be understood by the Indians. . . . 'The language used in treaties with the Indians should never be construed to their prejudice.' . . . 'How the words of the treaty were understood by this unlettered people, rather than their critical meaning, should form the rule of construction.'

In 1905 the above principles were reiterated in *Winans*. . . .

* * *

. . . Reluctant to be confined to small reservation bases, the Indian negotiators insisted that their people continue to fish as they had beyond the reservation boundaries. There is no indication that the Indians intended or understood the language "in common with all citizens of the Territory" to limit their right to fish in any way. For many years following the treaties the Indians continued to fish in their customary manner and places, and although non-Indians also fished, there was no need for any restrictions on fishing.

* * *

There is neither mention nor slightest intimation in the treaties themselves, in any of the treaty negotiation records or in any other credible evidence, that the Indians who represented the tribes in the making of the treaties, at that time or any time afterward, understood or intended that the fishing rights reserved by the tribes as recorded in the above quoted language would, or ever could, authorize the "citizens of the territory" or their successors, either individually or through their territorial or state government, to qualify, restrict or in any way interfere with the full *exercise* of those rights. All of the evidence is overwhelmingly to the contrary. . . .

* * *

As stated by the United States Supreme Court in *Winans*, treaty fishing rights are personal rights held and exercised by individual tribe members. Although the exercise of that particular civil treaty right may be limited or modified in any particular or to any extent by or with authority of Congress, that the exercise of such a right may be limited in any way by the police power of a state, without having previously received authority to do so from Congress, seems to be diametrically opposed to relevant treaty law and personal civil rights decisions, particularly those of recent years.

* * *

. . . In the present case a basic question is the amount of fish the plaintiff tribes may take in off reservation fishing under the express reservation of fishing rights recorded in their treaties.

* * *

By dictionary definition and as intended and used in the Indian treaties and in this decision "in common with" means *sharing equally* the opportunity to take fish at "usual and accustomed grounds and stations"; therefore, non-treaty fishermen shall have the opportunity to take up to 50% of the harvestable number of fish that may be taken by all fishermen at usual and accustomed grounds and stations and treaty right fishermen shall have the opportunity to take up to the same percentage of harvestable fish, as stated above.

* * *

Counsel for all parties appeared and presented nearly 50 witnesses, whose testimony was reported in 4,600 pages of trial transcript, more than 350 exhibits, pretrial briefs, final oral argument . . . and post trial briefs. . . .

* * *

No formal political structure had been created by the Indians living in the Puget Sound area at the time of initial contact with the United States Government. Governor Stevens, acting upon instructions from his superiors and recommendations of his subordinates, deliberately created political entities for purposes of delegating responsibilities and negotiating treaties. In creating these entities Governor Stevens named many chiefs and sub-chiefs.

* * *

There is no record of English having been spoken at the treaty councils, but it is probable that there were Indians at each council who would have spoken or understood some English. . . . Since, however, the vast majority of Indians at the treaty councils did not speak or understand English, the treaty provisions and the remarks of the treaty commissioners were interpreted by Colonel Shaw to the Indians in the Chinook jargon and then translated into native languages by Indian interpreters. Chinook jargon, a trade medium of limited vocabulary and simple grammar, was inadequate to express precisely the legal effects of the treaties, although the general meaning of treaty language could be explained. Many of those present, however, did not understand Chinook jargon. There is no record of the Chinook jargon phrase that was actually used in the treaty negotiations to interpret the provision "The right of taking fish, at all usual and accustomed grounds and stations, is further secured to said Indians, in common with all citizens of the Territory." A dictionary of the Chinook jargon . . . indicates that the jargon contains no words or expressions that would describe any limiting interpretation on the right of taking fish.

. . . There is no discussion of the phrase in the minutes of the treaty councils, in the instructions to Stevens, or to the treaty negotiators, or in Stevens' letters of transmittal of the treaties. There appears to be no phrase in [the] Chinook jargon that would interpret the term in any exact legal sense.

Although there is no evidence of the precise understanding the Indians had of the treaty language, the treaty commissioners probably used the terms "usual and accustomed" and "in common with" in their common parlance, and the meaning of them as found in a contemporaneous dictionary most likely would be what was intended by the government representatives. . . .

The Indians who negotiated the treaties probably understood the concept of common ownership interest which could have been conveyed in Chinook jargon. The clause "usual and accustomed [fishing] grounds and stations" was all-inclusive and intended by all parties to the treaty to include reservation and off-reservation areas. The words "usual and accustomed" were probably used in their restrictive sense, not intending to include areas where use was occasional or incidental. The restrictive sense of the term "usual and accustomed" could have been conveyed in Chinook jargon.

* * *

> There is nothing in the written records of the treaty councils or other accounts of discussions with the Indians to indicate that the Indians were told that their existing fishing activities or tribal control over them would in any way be restricted or impaired by the treaty. The most that could be implied from the treaty context is that the Indians may have been told or understood that non-Indians would be allowed to take fish at the Indian fishing locations along with the Indians.

* * *

Judge Boldt's exceptionally long opinion also set forth a number of factors that various parties needed to satisfy to effectuate the decision, including requirements for the tribal nations to engage in conservation activities.

The Boldt decision maintains a well-earned reputation among tribal advocates, yet it also reflects at least one troubling aspect of the Indian canons of construction. The main concern for any party to a lawsuit is its outcome; however, the basis for the decision demands critical examination and forces difficult questions. The Boldt decision quotes from an 1899 Supreme Court opinion which characterizes the United States as an "enlightened and powerful nation," with "representatives skilled in diplomacy," and so forth. This same Supreme Court case also describes Native peoples as "unlettered," "Weak and dependent," and "wholly unfamiliar with all the forms of legal expression." Boldt himself also made the highly erroneous claim that "No formal political structure had been created," by the tribal nations in the case before also noting that representatives of the United States chose with whom they would negotiate.

The Indian canons of construction are built upon the recognition that the evidence in treaty cases that is available to American courts (or perhaps that is acceptable to those courts) tilts heavily in favor of non-Native parties. The canons serve as a valuable corrective to this issue and also serve as an opportunity to fulfill the federal government's trust obligations to Native peoples. However, courts generally find little, if any, distance between acknowledging the imbalance in available evidence and assuming the inferiority of Native peoples. Boldt, the Supreme Court opinion he quotes, and others regularly define Native peoples as unlettered, lacking in governmental structure, or weak to justify the use of the Indian canons. Thus, the Indian canons of construction can be a useful tool to win a case, but at what cost? Are Native nations and peoples forced to represent themselves as inferior or unlettered or without governmental structure to win treaty cases? If so, what are the consequences of this situation? Are the benefits of maintaining and exercising treaty rights worth reiterating and reaffirming this characterization of Native people in American law? Is there an alternative?

In addition, the Boldt decision was careful to note just how much effort went into the case. Boldt stated that in the course of more than three years both the plaintiffs and the defendants "conducted exhaustive research," not only in the law but also "anthropology, biology, fishery management and other fields of expertise," and that both sides "have made extreme efforts to find and present by witnesses and exhibits as much information as possible that pertains directly or indirectly to each issue in the case." This remarkable effort requires not only paying lawyers for their efforts but possibly also historians, anthropologists, archeologists, linguists, and experts in any number of other fields that might not normally be part of a typical court case. As a consequence, treaty rights litigation can quickly become expensive and lengthy. These obstacles can be very real and may deter a tribal nation from pursuing its treaty rights. In these instances, the Indian canons of construction may be having the opposite of their intended effect.

Finally, canons of construction, Indian or otherwise, are not laws or rules in and of themselves, but rather tools that are available to a judge who wishes to use them. They are not required by any source of authority and, while they hold some limited sway as useful, appropriate, and consistent practice, they can also be ignored or dismissed in a manner that formally recognized law cannot. The Indian canons of construction remain subject to the whims of the judges who chose to employ them or not to do so. Undeniably useful for tribal interests, the Indian canons of construction are nonetheless fragile weapons that ask significant questions about their employment.

Despite these difficulties, the canons of construction remain popular with tribal advocates and one of the most effective tools tribal nations have in American courts. In 2019, the Supreme Court once again invoked the canons of construction to decide another treaty dispute. The case, *Washington v. Cougar Den*, is also discussed in Chapter 20 for its implications in tax law. In the case, the state of Washington sought to impose a tax on the transportation of fuel within the state's borders. Cougar Den—a business owned by a tribal citizen and located on tribal land, incorporated under Yakama law, and obligated by the tribal government to obtain fuel for the tribal nation and its citizens—objected to the tax as a violation of tribal treaty rights.

For the purposes of this chapter, it is most useful to concentrate on Justice Neil Gorsuch's concurring opinion and Justice Brett Kavanaugh's dissent. As you read the case, ask yourself how both justices engage with the history that informs the treaty. How are the canons used or not used? To what extent does this case reflect both the strengths and limitations of the canons of construction?

WASHINGTON V. COUGAR DEN

139 S. Ct. 1000 (2019)

JUSTICE BREYER delivered the opinion of the Court.

* * *

The relevant treaty provides for the purchase by the United States of Yakama land. . . . [R]eserved [treaty] rights include "the right, in common with citizens of the United States, to travel upon all public highways. . . ."

* * *

. . . Here, the Yakamas' lone off-reservation act within the State is traveling along a public highway with fuel.

* * *

In our view, the State of Washington's application of the fuel tax to Cougar Den's importation of fuel is pre-empted by the treaty's reservation to the Yakama Nation of the "right, in common with the citizens of the United States, to travel upon all public highways."

* * *

JUSTICE GORSUCH, with whom JUSTICE GINSBURG joins, concurring in the judgment.

* * *

Our job here is a modest one. We are charged with adopting the interpretation most consistent with the treaty's original meeting. When we're dealing with a tribal treaty, too, we must "give effect to the terms as the Indians themselves would have understood them.". . . During the negotiations "English words were translated into Chinook jargon . . . although that was not the primary language" of the Tribe. After the parties reached agreement, the U.S. negotiators wrote the treaty in English—a language that the Yakamas couldn't read or write. . . .

. . . To some modern ears, the right to travel in common with others might seem merely a right to use the roads subject to the same taxes and regulations as everyone else. But that is not how the Yakamas understood the treaty's terms. To the Yakamas, the phrase " 'in common with'. . . implie[d] that the

Indian and non-Indian use [would] be joint but [did] not imply that the Indian use [would] be in any way restricted.". . .

Applying these factual findings to our case requires a ruling for the Yakamas. . . .

A wealth of historical evidence confirms this understanding. . . .

Everyone understood that the treaty would protect the Yakamas' preexisting right to take goods to and from market freely throughout their traditional trading area. . . .

* * *

Really, this case just tells an old and familiar story. The State of Washington includes millions of acres that the Yakamas ceded to the United States under significant pressure. In return, the government supplied a handful of modest promises. The State is now dissatisfied with the consequences of one of those promises. It is a new day, and now it wants more. But today and to its credit, the Court holds the parties to the terms of their deal. It is the least we can do.

* * *

JUSTICE KAVANAUGH, with whom JUSTICE THOMAS joins, dissenting.

. . . The treaty's "in common with" language means what it says. The treaty recognizes tribal members' right to travel on off-reservation public highways on equal terms with other U.S. citizens. Under the text of the treaty, the tribal members, like other U.S. citizens, therefore still remain subject to *nondiscriminatory* state highway regulations—that is, to regulations that apply equally to tribal members and other U.S. citizens.

* * *

. . . The treaty right to travel on public highways "in common with"—that is, on equal terms with—other U.S. citizens was important to the Yakama tribal members at the time the treaty was signed. That is because, as of 1855, States and the Federal Government sometimes required tribal members to seek permission before leaving their reservations or even prohibited tribal members from leaving their reservations altogether.

* * *

The main divide between the concurrence and the dissent is when to stop reading the treaty. For Justice Kavanaugh, the language of the treaty "means what it says." Although Kavanaugh gestures toward a historical understanding of the language of the treaty, his opinion is not grounded in the historical record, nor does he cite any of the evidence gathered in the case about how the Yakamas understood the treaty. Rather, the words of the treaty themselves are dispositive; consequently, the canons of construction are not part of the analysis.

On the other hand, Justice Gorsuch took his reading of the language of the treaty a step further, noting that "to some modern ears," the case may seem deceptively easy. However, according to Gorsuch, the manner in which the Court should read treaties requires a more deliberate engagement with how the Yakama understood the treaty. Adopting the tribal perspective, as the canons of construction require, makes the outcome clear: the tribal interests win. As Gorsuch stated, "A wealth of historical evidence confirms this understanding."

Put another way, the canons of construction were a major factor in the outcome of the case. Without them, the result looks obvious; with them, the result looks just as obvious, only for the other party. Presently, the canons of construction remain a vital force in treaty litigation. Yet, their deficiencies remain on display as well.

TREATY ABROGATION

As noted earlier in this chapter, the history of Indian treaties runs along potentially contradictory lines: Indian treaties remain in force despite Congress declaring in 1871 that it would no longer treat with tribal nations. Much has changed in the last century-and-a-half, but the political limbo in which Native nations find themselves—holders of treaty rights but unable to reassert or reinstitute the treaty process—raises another vital question in the modern context: under what circumstances can Indian treaties be abrogated, or considered null or overturned by subsequent Congressional legislation?

This question is especially fraught because tribal nations, unlike foreign nations, do not have the authority to renegotiate a treaty or engage in other remedies if an American court decides that a treaty or an aspect of a treaty has been rendered void by subsequent Congressional legislation. Does this mean that American law should evaluate these situations with special or greater care? Does the federal government's trust responsibility to Native nations require greater proof that Congress really did intend to abrogate a treaty than is otherwise required? How precise does Congress need to be in its language and intent to abrogate a treaty? American courts have long wrestled with finding a useful standard to answer these types of questions.

The next case, *U.S. v. Dion*, recognizes this history and attempts to settle these questions. Dwight Dion, Sr., a citizen of the Yankton Sioux Tribe—also known as the Ihanktonwan Nation—was arrested for hunting eagles on the reservation. He was convicted at trial for violating both the Endangered Species Act and the Eagle Protection Act. On appeal, Dion argued that an 1858 treaty between the Yankton and the United States preserved the right for tribal members to hunt and fish on tribal lands. The treaty itself does not explicitly address hunting and fishing rights, but, as the Supreme Court notes, all of the parties to the case agreed that the treaty protected those rights. Thus, the question of the case was not about how to interpret the treaty. Rather, the question of the case was whether the subsequent legislation—the Endangered Species Act and the Eagle Protection Act—abrogated or ended Dion's previously held treaty right to hunt on the reservation.

As you read the case, ask yourself what standard the Supreme Court chooses when deciding questions of Indian treaty abrogation. What alternatives does the Court consider? What justifications does the Court give for settling on the standard that it chooses? What consequences does this standard hold for tribal nations and their treaties?

U.S. v. Dion
476 U.S. 734 (1986)

JUSTICE MARSHALL delivered the opinion of the Court.

The Eagle Protection Act, by its terms, prohibits the hunting of the bald or golden eagle anywhere within the United States, except pursuant to a permit issued by the Secretary of the Interior. The Endangered Species Act imposes an equally stringent ban on the hunting of the bald eagle. The Court of Appeals for the Eighth Circuit, however . . . held that members of the Yankton Sioux Tribe have a treaty right to hunt bald and golden eagles within the Yankton Reservation for noncommercial purposes. It further held that the Eagle Protection Act and Endangered Species Act did not abrogate this treaty right. . . .

The Court of Appeals relied on an 1858 treaty signed by the United States and by representatives of the Yankton Tribe. . . . The treaty did not place any restriction on the Yanktons' hunting rights on their reserved land.

All parties to this litigation agree that the treaty rights reserved by the Yankton included the exclusive right to hunt and fish on their land. As a general rule, Indians enjoy exclusive treaty rights to hunt and fish on lands reserved to them unless such rights were clearly relinquished by treaty or have been modified by Congress. These rights need not be expressly mentioned in the treaty. Those treaty rights, however, little avail Dion if, as the Solicitor General argues, they were subsequently abrogated by Congress. We find that they were.

It is long settled that "the provisions of an act of Congress, passed in the exercise of its constitutional authority, . . . if clear and explicit, must be upheld by the courts, even in contravention of express stipulations in an earlier treaty" with a foreign power. This Court applied that rule to congressional abrogation of Indian treaties in *Lone Wolf v. Hitchcock*. . . .

We have required that Congress' intention to abrogate Indian treaty rights be clear and plain. "Absent explicit statutory language, we have been extremely reluctant to find congressional abrogation of treaty rights. . . ." We do not construe statutes as abrogating treaty rights in "a backhanded way," in the absence of explicit statement, " 'the intention to abrogate or modify a treaty is not to be lightly imputed to the Congress.' " Indian treaty rights are too fundamental to be easily cast aside.

We have enunciated, however, different standards over the years for determining how such a clear and plain intent must be demonstrated. In some cases, we have required that Congress make "express declaration" of its intent to abrogate treaty rights. In other cases, we have looked to the statute's " 'legislative history' " and " 'surrounding circumstances,' " as well as to " 'the face of the Act.' " Explicit statement by Congress is preferable for the purpose of ensuring legislative accountability for the abrogation of treaty rights. We have not rigidly interpreted that preference, however, as a per se rule; where the evidence of congressional intent to abrogate is sufficiently compelling, "the weight of authority indicates that such an intent can also be found by a reviewing court from clear and reliable evidence in the legislative history of a statute." What is essential is clear evidence that Congress actually considered the conflict between its intended action on the one hand and Indian treaty rights on the other, and chose to resolve that conflict by abrogating the treaty.

The Eagle Protection Act renders it a federal crime to "take, possess, sell, purchase, barter, offer to sell, purchase or barter, transport, export or import, at any time or in any manner any bald eagle commonly known as the American eagle or any golden eagle, alive or dead, or any part, nest, or egg thereof." The prohibition is "sweepingly framed"; the enumeration of forbidden acts is "exhaustive and careful." The Act, however, authorizes the Secretary of the Interior to permit the taking, possession, and transportation of eagles "for the religious purposes of Indian tribes," and for certain other narrow purposes, upon a determination that such taking, possession, or transportation is compatible with the preservation of the bald eagle or the golden eagle.

Congressional intent to abrogate Indian treaty rights to hunt bald and golden eagles is certainly strongly suggested on the face of the Eagle Protection Act. The provision allowing taking of eagles under permit for the religious purposes of Indian tribes is difficult to explain except as a reflection of an understanding that the statute otherwise bans the taking of eagles by Indians, a recognition that such a prohibition would cause hardship for the Indians, and a decision that that problem should be solved not by exempting Indians from the coverage of the statute, but by authorizing the Secretary to issue permits to Indians where appropriate.

The legislative history of the statute supports that view. . . .

At the Senate hearings, representatives of the Interior Department reiterated their position that, because "the golden eagle is an important part of the ceremonies and religion of many Indian tribes," the Secretary should be authorized to allow the use of eagles for religious purposes by Indian tribes. The Senate Committee agreed, and passed the House bill with an additional amendment allowing the Secretary to authorize permits for the taking of golden eagles that were preying on livestock. . . .

. . . The bill passed the Senate, and was concurred in by the House, with little further discussion.

It seems plain to us, upon reading the legislative history as a whole, that Congress in 1962 believed that it was abrogating the rights of Indians to take eagles. Indeed, the House Report cited the demand for eagle feathers for Indian religious ceremonies as one of the threats to the continued survival of the golden eagle that necessitated passage of the bill. Congress expressly chose to set in place a regime in which the Secretary of the Interior had control over Indian hunting, rather than one in which Indian on-reservation hunting was unrestricted. Congress thus considered the special cultural and religious interests of Indians, balanced those needs against the conservation purposes of the statute, and provided a specific, narrow exception that delineated the extent to which Indians would be permitted to hunt the bald and golden eagle.

* * *

Congress' 1962 action, we conclude, reflected an unmistakable and explicit legislative policy choice that Indian hunting of the bald or golden eagle, except pursuant to permit, is inconsistent with the need to preserve those species. We therefore read the statute as having abrogated that treaty right.

Dion also asserts a treaty right to take bald eagles as a defense to his Endangered Species Act prosecution. He argues that the evidence that Congress intended to abrogate treaty rights when it passed the Endangered Species Act is considerably more slim than that relating to the Eagle Protection Act. The Endangered Species Act and its legislative history, he points out, are to a great extent silent regarding Indian hunting rights. In this case, however, we need not resolve the question of whether the Congress in the Endangered Species Act abrogated Indian treaty rights. We conclude that Dion's asserted treaty defense is barred in any event.

Dion asserts that he is immune from Endangered Species Act prosecution because he possesses a treaty right to hunt and kill bald eagles. We have held, however, that Congress, in passing and amending the Eagle Protection Act, divested Dion of his treaty right to hunt bald eagles. He therefore has no treaty right to hunt bald eagles that he can assert as a defense to an Endangered Species Act charge.

Justice Thurgood Marshall's opinion in *Dion* acknowledges that the Supreme Court has used different standards in measuring treaty abrogation over the years and can be characterized as seeking a middle ground between what the Court regards as two extremes. On one side, in some previous treaty abrogation cases the Supreme Court has required Congress to offer an "express declaration" that it was abrogating certain treaty rights. This method would force Congress to definitively declare that treaty rights have been abrogated in the legislation that it passes. Although the Court suggests that this is the preferred way of accomplishing treaty abrogation, it decided not to require it in all instances. On the other side, in some previous treaty abrogation cases the Supreme Court has considered the "legislative history," "surrounding circumstances," and "face of the act." This method not only does not require a definitive declaration from Congress, it opens a tremendous amount of space for interpretation and unwarranted opportunity to find an abrogation of treaty rights.

The standard set in *Dion* asks a question that incorporates aspects of both of these two methods: Did Congress actually consider the conflict between proposed legislation and treaty rights and did Congress choose to resolve the conflict in favor of the legislation? Thus, the Supreme Court wants evidence of actual deliberation on the issue from Congress without necessarily requiring the formal step of making Congress declare its decision in the legislation itself.

While the *Dion* standard is the one currently employed by the Supreme Court in Indian treaty abrogation cases, it is worth considering the strengths and weaknesses of each of the three approaches that Marshall's opinion outlines. Does the *Dion* standard strike a proper balance between protecting treaty rights and acknowledging changing times and Congressional priorities? Consider the facts of the *Dion* case. At the time of the decision, eagles were still very much on the verge of extinction. Certainly important to Native peoples, eagles also serve as a national symbol for the United States as well. There was some question as to whether Dion was hunting eagles for religious or for commercial purposes. Congress had also established a method within the Eagle Protection Act for Native peoples to gain access to eagle feathers (although it should be noted that this method might not be able to satisfy the demand). Considering these circumstances, was the Supreme Court reasonable in finding that the treaty right to hunt on tribal land had been abrogated? Is Congress justified in protecting eagles for everybody, including Natives, even from Natives? Or is it even fair to measure tribal treaty rights against other interests when tribal nations have no recourse if treaty rights are deemed abrogated?

Would the "express declaration" be a better standard? Certainly it would eliminate any question as to the intent of Congress and force legislation to be explicit in its effect on Indian treaties. But might such a standard also have unintended consequences? Would Congress be incentivized to regularly target treaty rights in legislation to avoid any potential conflict? What about the "legislative history," "surrounding circumstances," and "face of the act" standard? It is easy to recognize how this standard might allow for too much opportunity for a court to find that a treaty has been abrogated. For example, a random statement by a single senator during a committee meeting to the effect that treaty rights will be abrogated under a proposed bill certainly counts as part of the "legislative history" of a law, even if that sentiment is not shared by other senators or Congress as a whole. Yet Native America is often critical of American courts for their unwillingness to accept a wider range of sources as evidence. Is it possible that a looser standard might allow for tribal nations and peoples to better tell their story or offer a greater level of support to their position? For example, what if a senator offered a statement during a committee meeting to the effect that she did not believe that a proposed bill affected or altered treaty rights in any way?

How to read treaties and when they are abrogated remain relevant questions because treaties remain relevant to Native peoples as well as non-Native peoples. As you will see in other chapters, the local landscape of an area can be greatly affected by treaty rights. Treaties are critical for both their practical and symbolic value to Native America and the United States as well.

SUGGESTED READINGS

- *Nation to Nation: Treaties Between the United States and American Indian Nations.* Ed. Suzan Shown Harjo. Washington D.C.: Smithsonian Books, 2014.

- *The Walleye War: The Struggle for Ojibwe Spearfishing and Treaty Rights.* Larry Nesper. Lincoln, NE: University of Nebraska Press, 2002.

- *Documents of American Indian Diplomacy: Treaties Agreements, and Conventions, 1775–1979.* Ed. by Vine Deloria, Jr. and Raymond J. Demallie. Norman, OK: University of Oklahoma Press, 1999.

CHAPTER 12

Indians and the U.S. Constitution

From the very beginning of federal Indian law through to the present day, the Supreme Court has routinely described Native peoples and their relationship with the federal government as outside of the normal course of affairs. In one of his famous opinions from his Indian trilogy of cases, John Marshall described the relationship between the United States and tribal nations as "perhaps unlike that of any other two people in existence" (see Chapter 3). Over fifty years later Justice Samuel Miller stated that "the relation of the Indian tribes living within the borders of the United States . . . has always been an anomalous one, and of a complex character" (see Chapter 7). More recently, the Supreme Court has described the "unique legal status of Indian tribes under federal law" (see Chapter 10).

Supreme Court justices regularly write about Native peoples and nations in these terms for a number of reasons, but perhaps mostly because Native peoples and nations are not fully contemplated in the U.S. Constitution. Put another way, tribal nations stand outside of the constitutional order and do not find their own authority within the document. American courts, which are used to discerning governmental authority under the U.S. Constitution, often have trouble reconciling a third governmental entity and political status within the borders of the United States.

This is not to suggest that the U.S. Constitution never has any authority over Native peoples, particularly after Congress declared that all Native peoples born in the United States were American citizens in 1924 (see Chapter 8). Rather, it is to acknowledge that the sources of authority for the United States and for tribal nations emerge from different sources of power and that the U.S. Constitution does not fully contemplate tribal sovereignty on its face.

This lack of U.S. Constitutional contemplation has had some important consequences for Native peoples. Sometimes the results have been to the detriment of individual tribal members. Nonetheless, despite regularly describing the situation as strange or unusual, American courts have routinely recognized that tribal sovereignty does not stem from the U.S. Constitution. Rather, it emanates from the community itself and it predates the U.S. Constitution. This understanding has been vital in preserving tribal authority to make and exercise law. Yet it also creates a strange circumstance in which ordinary Congressional legislation holds more authority in Indian Country than the U.S. Constitution itself. Native peoples are also put in a unique position as both citizens of the United States and of their tribal nation.

This chapter will demonstrate. . .

- *The relationship between the U.S. Constitution and Indian Country*

- *The long history of Native peoples, citizenship, and the 14th Amendment*

- *The consequences for Native individuals under this system*

TRIBAL SOVEREIGNTY AND THE U.S. CONSTITUTION

Some of the most important features of the U.S. Constitution are the protections that it provides criminal defendants. These features recognize the significant power imbalance that exists between an individual and the federal government. Some consider these protections to be the finest features of the U.S. Constitution and what sets the United States apart from other countries. It is no exaggeration to state that the U.S. Constitution is deeply concerned with the rights that individuals can exercise against the federal government.

To what extent, if any, do these features of the U.S. Constitution that protect criminal defendants extend into Indian Country? The Supreme Court answered this question in *Talton v. Mayes*, a late nineteenth century case that is something of an anomaly in the Allotment Era of federal policy (see Chapter 5). In doing so, the Supreme Court established a more fundamental principle concerning the U.S. Constitution and tribal nations. The Court recognized, as will be discussed further below, that the U.S. Constitution is not the source of authority for tribal governmental power.

The case began after the Trail of Tears (see Chapter 3), when the Cherokee who were removed to Oklahoma once again established a government under a constitution. This newly reformed Cherokee government resembled the federal government and mimicked many of its same features, including requiring that a grand jury indict a criminal defendant before further legal action could be taken by the tribal government. Under the circumstances that led to this case, Bob Talton, a Cherokee man accused of murdering another Cherokee man on Cherokee land, objected to his conviction in Cherokee court, claiming among other things that his indictment was illegal because the grand jury only consisted of five people and thus violated the 5th Amendment of the U.S. Constitution.

The question of the case was if the 5th Amendment requirements of the U.S. Constitution concerning grand juries applied to the Cherokee government. Put another way, was the U.S. Constitution the source of the Cherokee governmental authority to punish a criminal defendant? As you read the case, ask yourself where the Supreme Court locates the source of tribal authority. What role does the Constitution play within Indian Country? Where does the Cherokee government derive its authority?

TALTON V. MAYES
163 U.S. 376 (1896)

MR. JUSTICE WHITE, after stating the case, delivered the opinion of the Court.

* * *

Appellant and the person he was charged with having murdered were both Cherokee Indians, and the crime was committed within the Cherokee territory.

. . . [T]he appellant asserts 1st, that the grand jury, consisting only of five persons, was not a grand jury within the contemplation of the Fifth Amendment to the Constitution, which it is asserted is operative upon the Cherokee Nation in the exercise of its legislative authority as to purely local matters. . . . A decision as to the merits of these contentions involves a consideration of the relation of the Cherokee Nation to the United States and of the operation of the constitutional provisions relied on upon the purely local legislation of that Nation.

By treaties and statutes of the United States, the right of the Cherokee Nation to exist as an autonomous body, subject always to the paramount authority of the United States, has been recognized. And from this fact there has consequently been conceded to exist in that Nation power to make laws defining offenses and providing for the trial and punishment of those who violate them when the offenses are committed by one member of the tribe against another one of its members within the territory of the Nation.

* * *

The crime of murder committed by one Cherokee Indian upon the person of another within the jurisdiction of the Cherokee Nation is therefore clearly not an offense against the United States, but an offense against the local laws of the Cherokee Nation. Necessarily, the statutes of the United States which provide for an indictment by a grand jury and the number of persons who shall constitute such a body have no application, for such statutes relate only, if not otherwise specially provided, to grand juries impaneled for the courts of and under the laws of the United States.

The question, therefore, is does the Fifth Amendment to the Constitution apply to the local legislation of the Cherokee Nation so as to require all prosecutions for offenses committed against the laws of that Nation to be initiated by a grand jury organized in accordance with the provisions of that amendment? The solution of this question involves an inquiry as to the nature and origin of the power of local government exercised by the Cherokee Nation and recognized to exist in it by the treaties and statutes above referred to. . . . [I]t has been settled that the Fifth Amendment to the Constitution of the United States is a limitation only upon the powers of the general government— that is, that the amendment operates solely on the Constitution itself by qualifying the powers of the national government which the Constitution called into being. . . .

The case in this regard therefore depends upon whether the powers of local government exercised by the Cherokee Nation are federal powers created by and springing from the Constitution of the United States, and hence controlled by the Fifth Amendment to that Constitution, or whether they are local powers not created by the Constitution, although subject to its general provisions and the paramount authority of Congress.

The repeated adjudications of this Court have long since answered the former question in the negative. . . .

It cannot be doubted . . . that prior to the formation of the Constitution, treaties were made with the Cherokee tribes by which their autonomous existence was recognized. . . .

True it is that in many adjudications of this Court, the fact has been fully recognized that although possessed of these attributes of local self-government when exercising their tribal functions, all such rights are subject to the supreme legislative authority of the United States. . . . But the existence of the right in Congress to regulate the manner in which the local powers of the Cherokee Nation shall be exercised does not render such local powers federal powers arising from and created by the Constitution of the United States. It follows that, as the powers of local self-government enjoyed by the Cherokee Nation existed prior to the Constitution, they are not operated upon by the Fifth Amendment, which, as we have said, had for its sole object to control the powers conferred by the Constitution on the national government. . . .

Justice White's opinion makes clear that tribal governmental authority existed before the U.S. Constitution and that the U.S. Constitution is not the source of the tribal authority to exercise its criminal law over its citizens. More broadly, the limitations imposed by the U.S. Constitution on the federal government (and the states) do not apply to tribal nations. Put another way, the U.S. Constitution does not control the scope of tribal governmental authority.

This principle often seems incongruous or even frightening to those unfamiliar with Native history or peoples, particularly Americans who have come to understand their constitutional rights as inherent and unalterable. All too often, this trepidation elides into a sense or belief that tribal governments were or are lawless, unprincipled, or otherwise lacking in the structure, predictability, or reasonableness of the American legal system. This unease, and the assumptions to which it often leads, offer an opportunity to ask a deeper question: What kind of law and/or institutional structure is necessary to protect individuals from abuses of governmental authority or to otherwise establish legitimacy?

The circumstances of *Talton v. Mayes* help one to think through this deeper question. Is a written constitution absolutely necessary in order for a government to rightfully claim authority over its citizenry? The Cherokee government that tried, convicted, and eventually hanged Bob Talton has such a document. Do countries like England that lack a singular written document at the center of their government lack the authority to exercise legitimate power? Do the protections offered by a government to a citizen need to resemble or even mimic those offered by the United States under its constitution to be legitimate? If so, how closely do they have to adhere to American standards? Like the United States, the Cherokee in this instance required a grand jury before proceeding with a criminal trial. Is the number of jurors on the grand jury the critical difference between a fair and an unfair trial? Is it possible to conceptualize a fair and just system of governmental authority that does not resemble that which exists in the United States? How is one's understanding of issues of legitimacy altered by placing the U.S. Constitution at the center of one's analysis? What is the source of the anxiety that many Americans feel about tribal courts specifically or non-American courts more generally?

Despite the Supreme Court's definitive statement to the contrary in *Talton v. Mayes*, there have been subsequent assertions that tribal authority stems from the U.S. Constitution. Sometimes these challenges have come from a tribal citizen who faced the possibility of having to answer to both a tribal and the federal court system. The next case, decided over eighty years after *Talton v. Mayes*, is just such an example.

To understand the decision in the next case, *U.S. v. Wheeler*, it is necessary to know another aspect of U.S. Constitutional law. The 5th Amendment prevents the federal government from practicing what has become colloquially known as double jeopardy. The "Double Jeopardy" clause of the 5th Amendment bars the federal government from engaging in a second or subsequent criminal prosecution for a particular incident. In essence, the federal government (as well as state governments) has one chance, and only one chance, to try a criminal defendant for an alleged crime. If an individual is acquitted of an alleged crime, the government cannot try the individual again even if new evidence comes to light or the individual confesses after the trial or under any other circumstances. The Double Jeopardy clause protects citizens by alleviating any possibility that the government can keep initiating criminal prosecutions until it gains a conviction and it strongly encourages the government to gather all possible evidence, be critical in its assessment on who to try, and put together the strongest case possible if it decides to move forward with a prosecution against an individual.

Understanding the decision in *Wheeler* also requires some knowledge of the Indian Civil Rights Act of 1968 (ICRA). ICRA and its function within Native America is the subject of Chapter 22. For the purposes of this chapter, it suffices to note that Congress had, through ICRA, limited the amount of punishment that a tribal court could impose on a convicted criminal. At the time that *Wheeler* was decided a tribal court could only sentence a convicted criminal to six months in jail and/or a $500 fine (Congress has since amended ICRA to allow for a year in jail and/or a $5,000 fine, and possibly more under certain circumstances).

As you read the case ask yourself why the Supreme Court does not consider this an occasion of double jeopardy. How does the tribal-federal relationship compare to the state-federal relationship when it concerns double jeopardy? What is the source of the tribal authority to engage in criminal prosecutions of its citizens? Additionally, what might be the consequences for law enforcement, federal authority, and criminal defendants if the case were decided differently?

U.S. v. Wheeler
435 U.S. 313 (1978)

Mr. Justice Stewart delivered the opinion of the Court.

The question presented in this case is whether the Double Jeopardy Clause of the Fifth Amendment bars the prosecution of an Indian in a federal district court under the Major Crimes Act when he has previously been convicted in a tribal court of a lesser included offense arising out of the same incident.

On October 16, 1974, the respondent, a member of the Navajo Tribe, was arrested by a tribal police officer at the Bureau of Indian Affairs High School in Many Farms, Ariz. on the Navajo Indian Reservation. He was taken to the tribal jail in Chinle, Ariz., and charged with disorderly conduct, in violation of . . . the Navajo Tribal Code. On October 18, two days after his arrest, the respondent pleaded guilty to disorderly conduct and a further charge of contributing to the delinquency of a minor, in violation of . . . the Navajo Tribal Code. He was sentenced to 15 days in jail or a fine of $30 on the first charge and to 60 days in jail (to be served concurrently with the other jail term) or a fine of $120 on the second.

Over a year later, on November 19, 1975, an indictment charging the respondent with statutory rape was returned by a grand jury in the United States District Court for the District of Arizona. The respondent moved to dismiss this indictment, claiming that, since the tribal offense of contributing to the delinquency of a minor was a lesser included offense of statutory rape, the proceedings that had taken place in the Tribal Court barred a subsequent federal prosecution. . . .

In *Bartkus v. Illinois* and *Abbate v. United States* this Court reaffirmed the well-established principle that a federal prosecution does not bar a subsequent state prosecution of the same person for the same acts, and a state prosecution does not bar a federal one. The basis for this doctrine is that prosecutions under the laws of separate sovereigns do not, in the language of the Fifth Amendment, "subject [the defendant] for the same offence to be twice put in jeopardy". . . .

It was noted in *Abbate* that the "undesirable consequences" that would result from the imposition of a double jeopardy bar in such circumstances further support the "dual sovereignty" concept. Prosecution by one sovereign for a relatively minor offense might bar prosecution by the other for a much graver one, thus effectively depriving the latter of the right to enforce its own laws. . . .

* * *

The respondent contends, and the Court of Appeals held, that the "dual sovereignty" concept should not apply to successive prosecutions by an Indian tribe and the United States, because the Indian tribes are not themselves sovereigns, but derive their power to punish crimes from the Federal Government. This argument relies on the undisputed fact that Congress has plenary authority to legislate for the Indian tribes in all matters, including their form of government. Because of this all-encompassing federal power, the respondent argues that the tribes are merely "arms of the federal government" which, in the words of his brief, "owe their existence and vitality solely to the political department of the federal government."

We think that the respondent and the Court of Appeals, in relying on federal control over Indian tribes, have misconceived the distinction between those cases in which the "dual sovereignty" concept is applicable and those in which it is not. . . . [The correct distinction] was not the extent of control exercised by one prosecuting authority over the other, but rather the ultimate source of the power under which the respective prosecutions were undertaken.

* * *

It is undisputed that Indian tribes have power to enforce their criminal laws against tribe members. Although physically within the territory of the United States and subject to ultimate federal control, they nonetheless remain "a separate people, with the power of regulating their internal and social relations." Their right of internal self-government includes the right to prescribe laws applicable to tribe members and to enforce those laws by criminal sanctions. . . . [T]he controlling question in this case is the source of this power to punish tribal offenders: is it a part of inherent tribal sovereignty, or an aspect of the sovereignty of the Federal Government which has been delegated to the tribes by Congress?

The powers of Indian tribes are, in general, "inherent powers of a limited sovereignty which has never been extinguished." Before the coming of the Europeans, the tribes were self-governing sovereign political communities. Like all sovereign bodies, they then had the inherent power to prescribe laws for their members and to punish infractions of those laws.

Indian tribes are, of course, no longer "possessed of the full attributes of sovereignty." Their incorporation within the territory of the United States, and their acceptance of its protection, necessarily divested them of some aspects of the sovereignty which they had previously exercised. By specific treaty provision, they yielded up other sovereign powers; by statute, in the exercise of its plenary control, Congress has removed still others.

But our cases recognize that the Indian tribes have not given up their full sovereignty. . . . The sovereignty that the Indian tribes retain is of a unique and limited character. It exists only at the sufferance of Congress, and is subject to complete defeasance. But until Congress acts, the tribes retain their existing sovereign powers. In sum, Indian tribes still possess those aspects of sovereignty not withdrawn by treaty or statute, or by implication as a necessary result of their dependent status.

It is evident that the sovereign power to punish tribal offenders has never been given up by the Navajo Tribe, and that tribal exercise of that power today is therefore the continued exercise of retained tribal sovereignty. . . .

Similarly, statutes establishing federal criminal jurisdiction over crimes involving Indians have recognized an Indian tribe's jurisdiction over its members. . . . Thus, far from depriving Indian tribes of their sovereign power to punish offenses against tribal law by members of a tribe, Congress has repeatedly recognized that power and declined to disturb it.

Moreover, the sovereign power of a tribe to prosecute its members for tribal offenses clearly does not fall within that part of sovereignty which the Indians implicitly lost by virtue of their dependent status. . . .

* * *

That the Navajo Tribe's power to punish offenses against tribal law committed by its members is an aspect of its retained sovereignty is further supported by the absence of any federal grant of such power. If Navajo self-government were merely the exercise of delegated federal sovereignty, such a delegation should logically appear somewhere. But no provision in the relevant treaties or statutes confers the right of self-government in general, or the power to punish crimes in particular, upon the Tribe.

It is true that, in the exercise of the powers of self-government, as in all other matters, the Navajo Tribe, like all Indian tribes, remains subject to ultimate federal control. . . .

But none of these laws created the Indians' power to govern themselves and their right to punish crimes committed by tribal offenders.... That Congress has, in certain ways, regulated the manner and extent of the tribal power of self-government does not mean that Congress is the source of that power.

In sum, the power to punish offenses against tribal law committed by Tribe members, which was part of the Navajos' primeval sovereignty, has never been taken away from them, either explicitly or implicitly, and is attributable in no way to any delegation to them of federal authority. It follows that, when the Navajo Tribe exercises this power, it does so as part of its retained sovereignty, and not as an arm of the Federal Government.

The conclusion that an Indian tribe's power to punish tribal offenders is part of its own retained sovereignty is clearly reflected in a case decided by this Court more than 80 years ago, *Talton v. Mayes*....

The relevance of *Talton v. Mayes* to the present case is clear. The Court there held that, when an Indian tribe criminally punishes a tribe member for violating tribal law, the tribe acts as an independent sovereign, and not as an arm of the Federal Government. Since tribal and federal prosecutions are brought by separate sovereigns, they are not "for the same offence," and the Double Jeopardy Clause thus does not bar one when the other has occurred.

The respondent contends that, despite the fact that successive tribal and federal prosecutions are not "for the same offence," the "dual sovereignty" concept should be limited to successive state and federal prosecutions. But we cannot accept so restrictive a view of that concept, a view which, as has been noted, would require disregard of the very words of the Double Jeopardy Clause. Moreover, the same sort of "undesirable consequences" identified in *Abbate* could occur if successive tribal and federal prosecutions were barred despite the fact that tribal and federal courts are arms of separate sovereigns. Tribal courts can impose no punishment in excess of [limits set by the Indian Civil Rights Act]. On the other hand, federal jurisdiction over crimes committed by Indians includes many major offenses. Thus, when both a federal prosecution for a major crime and a tribal prosecution for a lesser included offense are possible, the defendant will often face the potential of a mild tribal punishment and a federal punishment of substantial severity. Indeed, the respondent in the present case faced the possibility of a federal sentence of 15 years in prison, but received a tribal sentence of no more than 75 days and a small fine. In such a case, the prospect of avoiding more severe federal punishment would surely motivate a member of a tribe charged with the commission of an offense to seek to stand trial first in a tribal court. Were the tribal prosecution held to bar the federal one, important federal interests in the prosecution of major offenses on Indian reservations would be frustrated.

* * *

Like many cases in the Self-Determination Era (see Chapter 10), *Wheeler* reflects potentially contradictory principles. On one hand, *Wheeler* is a clear victory for tribal sovereignty. Referencing *Talton v. Mayes*, Justice Potter Stewart's opinion once again states that tribal nations are not gifted their authority over their own people through the U.S. Constitution, nor are they merely "arms of the federal government." Rather, tribal sovereignty existed prior to the U.S. Constitution and continues to form the basis of tribal authority over its own citizens. This remains in effect despite the fact that tribal nations, "no longer [possess] 'the full attributes of sovereignty.' " The tribal authority—of the Navajo specifically in *Wheeler*—to criminally prosecute its own citizens has never been ceded in a treaty, taken by Congress, nor was it "implicitly lost by virtue of their dependent status."

On the other hand, it is possible to interpret the outcome of this case with little to no regard for tribal sovereignty at all. When reflecting upon the non-Native interests at stake, Justice Potter's opinion could be read as fundamentally concerned with preserving federal authority to punish wrongdoers above all else.

Although *Wheeler* is about the federal-tribal relationship, there is an obvious comparison to be made with the federal-state relationship. Stewart referenced that comparison (in the *Bartkus v. Illinois* and *Abbate v. United States* cases), noting that the same question has come up in the federal-state context and that there is a "well established principle" that "a federal prosecution does not bar a subsequent state prosecution of the same person for the same acts, and a state prosecution does not bar a federal one"—also referenced in the case as the "Dual Sovereignty" principle. The theory behind the Dual Sovereignty principle begins with the idea that states derive their sovereignty from their own state constitutions, not the U.S. Constitution. Since there are separate sources of authority for the two governments, one prosecution from one government is not the same as another prosecution from another government, and thus double jeopardy does not apply. Stewart wrote that to decide otherwise—to decide that states were merely extensions of the federal government and that prosecutions in one forum would bar prosecutions in the other forum under the Double Jeopardy Clause of the 5th Amendment—would lead to "undesirable consequences."

After detailing the state of tribal sovereignty and the capacity of tribal nations to criminally prosecute their own citizens, Stewart pivoted back to these "undesirable consequences." Specifically, Stewart showed concern (in both the state and tribal contexts) about the possibility of a criminal defendant pleading guilty to a lesser charge in one forum and escaping punishment in a different forum were the outcomes of these types of cases to be decided differently. This is especially so in the tribal context, where ICRA severely curtailed the scope of criminal punishments. Stewart used Anthony Wheeler, the criminal defendant in the case, to illustrate his point. Wheeler pled guilty in tribal court and was sentenced to 75 days in jail and a small fine. However, the federal charges he faced carried the possibility of 15 years in jail. Were the Supreme Court to decide that tribal sovereignty emanated from the U.S. Constitution then Anthony Wheeler and others who were similarly situated would be incentivized to plead guilty in tribal court as quickly as possible to serve their sentences under the limitations of ICRA and to avoid much harsher federal penalties. In short, a decision against tribal sovereignty would also be a decision against federal authority to effectively engage in criminal law enforcement in Indian Country.

The way in which Stewart framed the potential limitations on tribal authority is also reflective of the changing landscape for Native nations in the Self-Determination Era. As noted above, Stewart identified three potential sources of limitations on tribal sovereignty: treaties, Congressional legislation, and "by virtue of their dependent status." A few weeks before deciding *Wheeler*, the Supreme Court decided another important Indian law case, *Oliphant v. Suquamish Indian Tribe*. A fuller discussion of Oliphant can be found in Chapter 18. For the purposes of this chapter, it suffices to note that the Supreme Court decided in *Oliphant* that tribal nations did not have criminal jurisdiction over non-Natives because of their "dependent status." In *Wheeler*, however, tribal nations are not prohibited from criminal prosecutions of their own members despite their "dependent status." *Wheeler* is thus reflective of the ever-growing role that the Supreme Court has come to play in determining the scope of tribal sovereignty in the Self-Determination Era. It is a worthwhile exercise to compare and contrast the opinions in *Wheeler* and *Oliphant*.

Perhaps most important, *Wheeler* also demonstrates the frequently counterintuitive manner in which American law has engaged with Native America and the difficult questions that this area of law raises. *Talton v. Mayes* and *Wheeler* stand for the proposition that the U.S. Constitution does not control the scope of tribal governmental authority over tribal citizens, nor is it the source of tribal sovereignty. Yet, a number of cases including, *U.S. v. Kagama* (see Chapter 7), stand for the proposition that the plenary power of Congress (see Chapters 6 and 7) can limit tribal governmental authority. Thus, ordinary Congressional legislation has greater force in Indian Country than the U.S. Constitution. For example, the Bill of Rights of the U.S. Constitution does not apply of its own accord in Indian Country, but Congress has made many of the provisions of the Bill of Rights applicable to tribal governments through ICRA.

Indian Country is the only place in the United States where ordinary Congressional legislation has greater force than the U.S. Constitution. In addition, the rights under the U.S. Constitution afforded to American citizens who also happen to be tribal citizens, such as Anthony Wheeler, are not in their fullest effect in tribal court (although it must be noted that this does not mean that criminal defendants in tribal courts do not have any rights or even that they have fewer rights than they would in state or federal court). Relatedly, Congress can alter the rights of tribal citizens and nations, without regard to the U.S. Constitution, through ordinary legislation. Are any of these situations fair? If one or more are not fair, to whom are they not fair? Is there a reasonable and just solution to any of these scenarios?

This anomalous situation was created in the late nineteenth and early twentieth centuries when the Supreme Court authorized exceptional Congressional incursions into Native America without any constraint from the U.S. Constitution (see Chapter 7). Today, this extraordinary (and perhaps extra-constitutional) power, known as Congressional plenary power, is generally regarded by American courts as existing within the part of the U.S. Constitution known as the Indian Commerce Clause—Article I, Section 8, Clause 3. However, the Supreme Court actually rejected the Indian Commerce Clause as a source of authority when it was establishing the broad scope of Congressional plenary power in *Kagama*. Thus, Congressional plenary power is now regarded as having a constitutional basis even though the first case to consider this possibility (*Kagama*) rejected the very clause of the constitution on which this power supposedly rests. *Wheeler* forces us to confront this strange, contradictory history and consider the unusual possibilities and limitations in which tribal nations and peoples find themselves.

NATIVE PERSONS, CITIZENSHIP, AND THE U.S. CONSTITUTION

Perhaps more than any other issues in American history, citizenship and immigration have remained ever-present matters for debate within every period of American political discourse. While other major areas of concern have waxed and waned from public attention, who gets into the country, how many get into the country, who gets to be a citizen, and how one becomes a citizen are questions that have never been far from the minds of politicians or the general public. Defining the populace and citizenry has been a fundamental task of the American political project from its inception.

As with other areas of law, Native peoples have historically complicated the questions that Americans have asked about inclusion in the United States. Unlike immigrants, who came from elsewhere, Native peoples were already part of the territorial claims of an expanding America. It was impossible to regulate how many Native peoples were within the borders of the United States in the same way it was possible to do so for immigrants. In addition, Native peoples held their own political affiliations to their tribal nations. Thus, the questions that might normally be asked about citizenship and immigration were fundamentally altered: How should the United States regard those within the borders who were here long before there was a United States? How might these people who were already here become citizens? Are they already citizens by virtue of being born and living within the borders of the United States? In many respects, this became a moot point in 1924 when Congress declared through legislation that all Native peoples were citizens of the United States. Nonetheless, tracing the history of Native America's engagement with American citizenship is useful because it reveals more aspects of the U.S. Constitution's challenges, difficulties, and limitations when engaging with Indian Country.

The original version of the U.S. Constitution, adopted in 1787, did not speak directly to issues of citizenship, leaving it to Congress to establish the parameters of who was included in the political body and who was not. However, in the wake of the American Civil War, the United States reconsidered its national identity and criteria for citizenship. The North's victory allowed for a moment of unique political change resulting in the 13th, 14th, and 15th Amendments, also known as the Civil War or Reconstruction Amendments. The 14th Amendment openly incorporated the issue of citizenship into the U.S. Constitution.

Passed in 1868, the 14th Amendment was directed toward providing political protection for newly freed slaves. Section One stated, among other important things, that, "All persons born or naturalized in the United States, and subject to the jurisdiction thereof, are citizens of the United States and of the State wherein they reside." However, Section Two stated that, "Representatives shall be apportioned among the several States according to their respective numbers, counting the whole number of persons in each State, excluding Indians not taxed." Whereas the historical moment made clear that the body of the 14th Amendment applied to recently freed slaves, the question of where Native peoples could and did fit in the American political landscape remained an open question.

Shortly after the passage of the 14th Amendment, Congress conducted an investigation into the subject. In 1870, the Senate Committee on the Judiciary issued a report detailing the investigation's findings. In contextualizing the report, it is important to remember that the report was issued before a number of major landmarks of the Allotment Era were issued or enacted, such at the end of treaty making in 1871, the Major Crimes Act in 1885, and *U.S. v. Kagama* in 1886. Thus, Congress and the Supreme Court were to shortly address many of the issues that the report raises as the United States fully transitioned into a new, much more intrusive period of federal policy toward Indian Country. As you read the excerpt from the report, is important to keep in mind the text of sections 1 and 2 of the 14th Amendment, quoted above.

Also, as you read the excerpt, ask yourself about the motivations behind the report. What questions, beside the primary question about citizenship, is the report trying to address? How does the Senate Judiciary Committee characterize the development of the law that led to its conclusion? What can be done about it? Are there any benefits for Native peoples and nations under the committee's conclusion? What non-Native interests are being served by the committee's conclusions?

SENATE REPORT 268, 41ST CONGRESS, 3D SESSION
Dec. 14, 1870

The Committee on the Judiciary, who were instructed by resolution of the Senate, of April 7, 1870, "to inquire into and report to the Senate the effect of the fourteenth amendment to the Constitution upon the Indian tribes of the country; and whether by the provisions thereof the Indians are not citizens of the United States, and whether thereby the various treaties heretofore existing between the United States and the various Indian tribes are, or are not annulled," respectfully report:

That in the opinion of your committee the fourteenth amendment to the Constitution has no effect whatever upon the status of the Indian tribes within the limits of the United States, and does not annul the treaties previously made between them and the United States. . . .

The question is whether the Indians "are subject to the jurisdiction" of the United States, within the meaning of this amendment, and the answer can only be arrived at by determining the status of the Indian tribes at the time the amendment was adopted.

The European nations when first settling the American continent regarded discovery as the foundation of their relative rights; that is, they claimed the sovereignty of the country, including the right to extinguish the aboriginal title by purchase or conquest, without interference from any other European nation, as a consequence of discovery; but it was never pretended that discovery had any other effect as against the Indian nations inhabiting the country. Whatever may be thought of the Christianity of the Christians who established this principle, and in pursuance of it proceeded to exclude the Indians from the sovereign control of the country in which they were born, and which they and their ancestors had occupied and enjoyed, it is now too late to question its soundness, because the condition of things which has grown up under its operation its renunciation would be productive of far more harm than good. The white man's treatment of the Indian is one of the great sins of civilization, for which no single generation or nation is wholly answerable, but which it is now too late to redress. Repentance is all that is left for us; restitution is impossible. But the harsh treatment of the race by former generations should not be considered a precedent to justify the infliction of further wrongs.

The principle must now be recognized and acted upon, that the Indians, after the European discovery and settlement of their domain, lost all sovereignty over it, retaining the right of occupancy until their title to that should in some way be extinguished, and the right to regulate, without question, their domestic affairs, and make and administer their own laws, provided in the exercise of such right they should not endanger the safety of the governments established by civilized man. Beyond this limit the pretensions of European settlers never extended; but to this extent the principle referred to was recognized and enforced; and although the Indians were thus overshadowed by the assumed sovereignty of the whites, it was never claimed or pretended that they had lost their respective nationalities, their right to govern themselves, the immunity which belongs to nations in the conduct of war, or any other attribute of a separate political community.

By no nation was this doctrine more clearly declared than by England, and the English colonists immediately entered into treaties with the tribes, waged war and concluded peace with them, and in every respect recognized and treated with them in their collective and national capacity. During the Revolution Congress manifested great solicitude as to the course which might be pursued by the different Indian nations, and aimed to secure their cooperation against the British forces. And after the establishment of our independence, the same principle, as controlling the relations of the Government to the Indian tribes, was asserted and steadily maintained by . . . the United States under our present Constitution. (*Johnson vs. McIntosh*)

* * *

This subject has frequently been considered by the State and federal courts, and in every instance the exemption of the tribes from municipal jurisdiction has been recognized and declared.

* * *

In the opinion of your committee, [the materials cited in the report] all speak the same language upon this subject, and all point to the conclusion that the Indians, in tribal condition, have never been subject to the jurisdiction of the United States in the sense in which the term *jurisdiction* is employed in the fourteenth amendment to the Constitution. The Government has asserted a political supremacy over the Indians, and the [cited materials] present these tribes as "domestic, dependent nations," separated from the States of the Union within whose limits they are located, and exempt from the operation of State laws; and not otherwise subject to the control of the United States than is consistent with their character as separate political communities or states. Their right of self government, and to administer justice among themselves, after their rude fashion, even to the extent of inflicting the death penalty, has never been questioned; and while the United States have provided by law for the punishment of crimes committed by Indians straggling from their tribes, and crimes committed by Indians upon white men lawfully within the reservations, the government has carefully abstained from attempting to regulate their domestic affairs, and from punishing crimes committed by one Indian against another in the Indian Country. . . .

It is worthy of mention that those who framed the fourteenth amendment, and the Congress which proposed it, as well as the legislatures which adopted it, understood that the Indian tribes were not made citizens, but were excluded by the restricting phrase, "and subject to the jurisdiction," and that such has been the universal understanding of all our public men since that amendment became a part of the Constitution. And in the opinion of your committee, the second section of the amendment furnishes conclusive evidence of this fact, and settles the question. . . .

During the war slavery had been abolished, and the former slaves had become citizens of the United States; consequently, in determining the basis of representation in the fourteenth amendment, the clause "three-fifths of all other persons" is wholly omitted; but the clause "excluding the Indians not taxed" is retained.

> The inference is irresistible that the amendment was intended to recognize the change in the status of the former slave which had been effected during the war, while it recognizes no change in the status of the Indians. . . . *The Indians were excluded because they were not citizens.*
>
> For these reasons your committee do not hesitate to say that the Indian tribes within the limits of the United States, and the individual members of such tribes, while they adhere to and form a part of the tribes to which they belong, are not, within the meaning of the fourteenth amendment, "*subject to the jurisdiction*" of the United States; and therefore, that such Indians have not become citizens of the United States by virtue of that amendment; and if your committee are correct in this conclusion, it follows that the treaties heretofore made between the United States and the Indian tribes are not annulled by that amendment.
>
> * * *

The Senate Judiciary Committee report is noteworthy for a number of reasons, including its discussion of the development of federal Indian law. In a manner reminiscent of John Marshall in *Johnson v. McIntosh* (see Chapter 2), the report expresses regret that the Doctrine of Discovery is the foundation for the relationship between the federal government and Indian nations, stating that, "The white man's treatment of the Indian is one of the great sins of civilization." Yet, also like Marshall, the report claims that this unfortunate situation is without recourse. "Whatever may be thought of the Christianity of the Christians who established this principle . . . it is now too late to question its soundness, because the condition of things which has grown up under its operation its renunciation would be productive of far more harm than good." Additionally, blame cannot be attributed to a single actor or actors, according to the report, but the ultimate end of all of this unfortunate activity is unalterable. "[N]o single generation or nation is wholly answerable, but which it is now too late to redress. Repentance is all that is left for us; restitution is impossible."

Is it too late to rectify the wrongs of the Doctrine of Discovery? Was it too late in 1870 when the report was issued? Recall that the report was issued in the wake of the American Civil War and that the 14th Amendment sought to undo the wrongs of slavery, another centuries-old legal phenomenon in American law. If it was (understandably) worth the effort to undo the wrongs of slavery through a constitutional amendment then what makes it impossible to undo the wrongs of the Doctrine of Discovery through a different reading of that same amendment? What about a different constitutional amendment to address the Doctrine of

Discovery? What makes the Native context different and/or "impossible" to rectify?

The report is also noteworthy for its conclusion: Native peoples are not made citizens through the 14th Amendment. Among other evidence it uses to support its position, the report makes a textual analysis of the U.S. Constitution and the changes brought about by the 14th Amendment. In Article I, Section 2, Clause 3, the original U.S. Constitution adopted in 1787 included the now-infamous three-fifths clause, which counted only a fraction of slaves for the purposes of determining representation in the House of Representatives. Tellingly, the same clause also excludes "Indians not taxed" in determining representation, immediately before the three-fifths language.

The report notes that the 14th Amendment, in undoing the three-fifths clause, "wholly omitted" the offending language from the amendment. However, the 14th Amendment replicated the "Indian not taxed" language, perpetuating the exclusion of most Native persons for the purpose of determining representation. The consequences of this deliberate choice, according to the report, was obvious. "[T]he amendment was intended to recognize the change in the status of the former slave which had been effected during the war, while it recognizes no change in the status of the Indians."

More finely, the Senate Judiciary Committee's report determined, through the textual analysis of the U.S. Constitution and other evidence, that Native persons were not "subject to the jurisdiction" of the United States, and thus not made citizens by the 14th Amendment. This was far from an unfounded conclusion, and may very well have been the preferred understanding for many Native persons who were seeking to maintain their sovereignty and autonomy in the face of ever greater pressures from westward expansion. The report's determination also solved another potentially difficult situation. As the preamble notes, the question of citizenship also raised the subsequent question (at least in the minds of some American politicians and policymakers) as to the validity of treaties made between Native nations and the United States. In essence, the secondary question was whether a nation could engage in a treaty with its own citizens. This possibility would have struck most as preposterous; thus the question of citizenship called into question any further treaties, if not the entirety of the treaty process to that point. The report's conclusion avoids these quandaries.

Whatever benefits it may have provided in the moment, the consequences of the report would rapidly become apparent in the soon-to-be Allotment Era of federal Indian policy. One year after the report, in 1871, Congress declared that the United States would no longer engage in treaty making with Native nations, formally (although not informally) ending the most direct and traditional method for Native engagement in American politics. Shortly thereafter, a series of Supreme Court decisions and Congressional legislation gave rise to a seemingly limitless Congressional plenary power over Native peoples. Without the ability to engage in treaty making or to participate in the political process as citizens, Native peoples and nations had little recourse to combat the incursions that the federal government made into their lives.

Despite its authoritative tone, the Senate Judiciary Committee's report was not the final word on the subject. The question of the 14th Amendment's application to Native individuals was destined for the Supreme Court. In 1879, John Elk, a Winnebago man, decided to sever his tribal ties and live among the white population in Omaha, Nebraska. He attempted to claim United States citizenship under the 14th Amendment and vote in the 1880 election. Elk was not permitted to vote by Charles Wilkins, a registrar of voters in Omaha. Elk sued, claiming a violation of his rights as an American citizen.

The Supreme Court was split on Elk's claim. The majority of justices decided, in accordance with the Senate Judiciary Committee report, that the 14th Amendment did not automatically confer citizenship on Elk and those like him. A vigorous dissent argued that the 14th Amendment should be regarded as having conferred citizenship on Elk and those like him. As you read the decision, ask yourself what rationale the majority opinion uses to justify the outcome in the case. What is the dissent's response? What recourse does John Elk have after this decision? What constitutional rights, if any, does John Elk have?

ELK V. WILKINS

112 U.S. 94 (1884)

MR. JUSTICE GRAY delivered the opinion of the Court.

* * *

The decision of this point, as both parties assume in their briefs, depends upon the question whether the legal conclusion that under and by virtue of the Fourteenth Amendment of the Constitution the plaintiff is a citizen of the United States . . . the plaintiff is an Indian and was born in the United States and has severed his tribal relation to the Indian tribes and fully and completely surrendered himself to the jurisdiction of the United States, and still continues to be subject to the jurisdiction of the United States, and is a *bona fide* resident of the State of Nebraska and City of Omaha. . . . Though the plaintiff alleges that he "had fully and completely surrendered himself to the jurisdiction of the United States," he does not allege that the United States accepted his surrender, or that he has ever been naturalized, or taxed, or in any way recognized or treated as a citizen by the state or by the United States. Nor is it contended by his counsel that there is any statute or treaty that makes him a citizen.

The question, then, is whether an Indian, born a member of one of the Indian tribes within the United States, is, merely by reason of his birth within the United States and of his afterwards voluntarily separating himself from his tribe and taking up his residence among white citizens, a citizen of the United States within the meaning of the first section of the Fourteenth Amendment of the Constitution. . . . The Indian tribes, being within the territorial limits of the United States, were not, strictly speaking, foreign states, but they were alien nations, distinct political communities, with whom the United States might and habitually did deal as they thought fit, either through treaties made by the President and Senate or through acts of Congress in the ordinary forms of legislation. The members of those tribes owed immediate allegiance to their several tribes, and were not part of the people of the United States. They were in a dependent condition, a state of pupilage, resembling that of a ward to his guardian. . . .

The alien and dependent condition of the members of the Indian tribes could not be put off at their own will without the action or assent of the United States. They were never deemed citizens of the United States except under explicit provisions of treaty or statute to that effect either declaring a certain tribe, or such members of it as chose to remain behind on the removal of the tribe westward, to be citizens or authorizing individuals of particular tribes to become citizens on application to a court of the United States for naturalization and satisfactory proof of fitness for civilized life. . . .

* * *

. . . An emigrant from any foreign state cannot become a citizen of the United States without a formal renunciation of his old allegiance, and an acceptance by the United States of that renunciation through such form of naturalization as may be required law.

* * *

Indians born within the territorial limits of the United States, members of and owing immediate allegiance to one of the Indian tribes (an alien though dependent power), although in a geographical sense born in the United States, are no more "born in the United States and subject to the jurisdiction thereof," within the meaning of the first section of the Fourteenth Amendment, than the children of subjects of any foreign government born within the domain of that government, or the children born within the United States of ambassadors or other public ministers of foreign nations.

* * *

Such Indians, then, not being citizens by birth, can only become citizens in the second way mentioned in the Fourteenth Amendment, by being "naturalized in the United States," by or under some treaty or statute.

* * *

Since the ratification of the Fourteenth Amendment, Congress has passed several acts for naturalizing Indians of certain tribes, which would have been superfluous if they were, or might become without any action of the government, citizens of the United States. . . .

* * *

The national legislation has tended more and more toward the education and civilization of the Indians, and fitting them to be citizens. But the question whether any Indian tribes, or any members thereof, have become so far advanced in civilization that they should be let out of the state of pupilage, and admitted to the privileges and responsibilities of citizenship, is a question to be decided by the nation whose wards they are and whose citizens they seek to become, and not by each Indian for himself. . . .

* * *

MR. JUSTICE HARLAN, with whom concurred MR. JUSTICE WOODS, dissenting.

* * *

At the adoption of the Constitution there were, in many of the states, Indians, not members of any tribe, who constituted a part of the people for whose benefit the state governments were established. . . .

* * *

Prior to the adoption of the Fourteenth Amendment, numerous statutes were passed with reference to particular bodies of Indians, under which the individual members of such bodies, upon the dissolution of their tribal relations, or upon the division of their lands derived from the government, became, or were entitled to become, citizens of the United States by force alone of the statute, without observing the forms required by the naturalization laws in the case of a foreigner becoming a citizen of the United States. . . .

Legislation of this character has an important bearing upon the present question, for it shows that prior to the adoption of the Fourteenth Amendment it had often been the policy of Congress to admit persons of the Indian race to citizenship upon their ceasing to have tribal relations, and without the slightest reference to the fact that they were born in tribal relations. . . .

* * *

A careful examination of all that was said by Senators and representatives, pending the consideration by Congress of the Fourteenth Amendment, justifies us in saying that everyone who participated in the debates, whether for or against the amendment, believed that, in the form in which it was approved by Congress, it granted, and was intended to grant, national citizenship to every person of the Indian race in this country who was unconnected with any tribe, and who resided, in good faith, outside of Indian reservations and within one of the states or territories of the Union. . . .

* * *

Born, therefore, in the territory, under the dominion and within the jurisdictional limits of the United States, plaintiff has acquired, as was his undoubted right, a residence in one of the states, with her consent, and is subject to taxation and to all other burdens imposed by her upon residents of every race. If he did not acquire national citizenship on abandoning his tribe and becoming, by residence in one of the states, subject to the complete jurisdiction of the United States, then the Fourteenth Amendment has wholly failed to accomplish, in respect of the Indian race, what, we think, was intended by it, and there is still in this country a despised and rejected class of persons with no nationality whatever, who, born in our territory, owing no allegiance to any foreign power, and subject, as residents of the states, to all the burdens of government, are yet not members of any political community, nor entitled to any of the rights, privileges, or immunities of citizens of the United States.

Justice Horace Gray's majority opinion begins with two assertions about Native peoples (the latter of which became the basic assumption for many policymakers in the soon-to-come Allotment Era): first, Native persons owed their political allegiances to their tribal nations and second, they were in a state of wardship. Unable to cast off their wardship status on their own, tribal persons similarly could not assume American citizenship on their own. Using these two ideas as his basis, Gray then argued that the 14th Amendment did not apply to Native persons, analogizing it to a child of a foreign diplomat being born on American soil. Since, according to Gray, the 14th Amendment did not apply to

John Elk, and since he had not otherwise been naturalized by the United States, he was not a citizen, ineligible to vote, and was properly excluded from the election.

Justice John Marshall Harlan's dissent muddied not only the logic of the majority opinion but also of the Senate Judiciary Committee's report. According to the report, "those who framed the fourteenth amendment, and the Congress which proposed it, as well as the legislatures which adopted it, understood that the Indian tribes were not made citizens . . . and that such has been the universal understanding of all our public men since that amendment became a part of the Constitution." Yet, Harlan came to the opposite conclusion, stating that after "careful examination" that "everyone who participated in the debates . . . believed that . . . it granted, and was intended to grant, national citizenship to every person of the Indian race in this country who was unconnected with any tribe. . . ." Harlan's dissent ended by noting that the decision left John Elk a man without a nation or political allegiance.

Getting the most out of *Elk v. Wilkins* first requires recognizing that it is most useful as a historical artifact and not an accurate statement on the current state of the law. Nor was the ruling as absolute concerning American citizenship for Native peoples as it might first appear. As noted above, Congress, through legislation, declared all Native peoples in the United States citizens in 1924. This was not considered particularly radical or unusual, rather it was regarded as a measure to tie up a loose end. There were a number of ways outside of the 14th Amendment for Native individuals to become American citizens both before and after *Elk v. Wilkins*: some treaties stipulated American citizenship for Native peoples, Native women who married American men might become citizens, as might their children, the Allotment Act created a path to citizenship, and Native veterans of World War I could apply for citizenship, to name a few. The legislators who argued in favor of the Indian Citizenship Act of 1924 had estimated that approximately two-thirds of Native persons were already citizens at the time of the legislation (although this is not to suggest that those who were citizens experienced the fullest expression of their rights under this status). Today, citizenship in both a Native nation and the United States is not regarded by most as incongruous as *Elk v. Wilkins* might make it seem.

Yet *Elk v. Wilkins* remains useful because it reflects the complications and difficulty that the U.S. Constitution—and American politicians and policymakers—have had in fitting Native nations into the constitutional order. Neither a state nor a foreign nation, tribal nations disrupt the American political system and provoke questions that strike at the very heart of the American political experiment. For example, what is the proper balance between recognizing and respecting tribal sovereignty and protecting constitutional rights for individuals? To what extent, if any, can the U.S. Constitution exert its authority over another nation, even if it is a domestic dependent nation? How does an extra layer of citizenship—tribal citizenship—affect the constitutional rights of American citizens (or, in the case of John Elk, those who wanted to become American citizens)?

In one sense, the basic principle is clear: tribal nations, as has been routinely recognized by the Supreme Court, were not created by the U.S. Constitution and do not derive their authority from it. Tribal nations are not bound by the U.S. Constitution of the document's own accord, as tribal sovereignty existed before the document and is the true source of tribal governmental authority. Yet this seemingly simple principle and the history surrounding it have forced tribal nations, Native individuals, and the United States itself to wrestle with the place of tribal nations and persons in the constitutional order, especially since simple Congressional legislation has been deemed to have greater force in Indian Country than the U.S. Constitution. We continue to contemplate these questions today.

SUGGESTED READINGS

- *Broken Landscape: Indians, Indian Tribes, and the Constitution.* Frank Pommersheim. New York: Oxford University Press, 2015.

- *Tribes, Treaties, and Constitutional Tribulations.* Vine Deloria, Jr., and David E. Wilkins. Austin, TX: University of Texas Press, 1999.

- "A Possible Solution to the Problem of Diminishing Tribal Sovereignty." Hope Babcock. Volume 90, Issue 1, *North Dakota Law Review*, pg. 13.

Recognition of Nations, Individuals, and Land

Scholars and others interested in federal Indian law and policy sometimes regard Native nations, Native individuals, and Indian Country as singular, well-understood groupings. This is often a necessary consequence of confronting the varied and complicated aspects of federal Indian law and policy. There are 573 federally recognized tribal nations situated in nearly every state in the union, each with a unique history and legal status. And this count does not include the many state-recognized tribes or unrecognized tribes. Any survey of federal Indian law and policy needs to operate at a substantial level of generalization to offer an overview of the history and current status of the field. Fortunately, there is, in many instances, enough commonality among those histories and statuses to still make the effort to survey federal Indian law and policy fruitful.

Nonetheless, any person interested in studying federal Indian law and policy should also be aware of the limitations to this approach as well. For example, regarding Native nations, Native individuals, and Indian Country as singular groupings whose definitions can be assumed may be beneficial to advance a conversation, analysis, or lecture, but it also has the capacity to obscure a significant number of questions and places of contestation that can dramatically alter fundamental rights and even conceptions of oneself or others.

More directly, deciding what is a tribal nation, what is tribal land, and even who is an Indian are questions that lack easy or readily agreed upon answers. Sometimes taken for granted, such questions are actually foundational and strike at the very heart of the field of federal Indian law. When such answers are necessitated, they can significantly change any number of factors for an individual or a group. Even a cursory listing of some of the more obvious possibilities these questions evoke demonstrates just how contentious and vital this subject matter can be: access to federal funds is affected as is citizenship in a tribal nation; the capacity to engage in governmental responsibilities is at stake; access to services such as the Indian Health Service might be the difference between life and death; issues of jurisdiction are dramatically implicated.

An important corollary to these questions is who gets to decide? Again, the answer is not always obvious. For example, each tribal nation has the most authority over determining its own citizenship, yet the federal government has exercised its influence in a number of ways in this arena as well. For various reasons, the federal government has had to confront these fundamental conundrums over the years—What is a tribal nation? Who is an Indian? What is Indian Country?—and it has developed rules within the American legal system to address them.

While this chapter will describe the law of the United States concerning these issues, it is important to remember that this is simply a detailing of the current state of American law and not necessarily the final word in the bigger conversation. Native America also wrestles with these difficulties beyond the parameters of federal law. Who, for example, is an Indian is a social question, as well as a legal one.

This chapter will demonstrate. . .

- *The criteria for federal recognition as a tribal nation today*

- *How American courts decide who is an Indian*

- *How the federal government has decided what constitutes Indian Country*

NATIONS

Prior to contact, tribal nations had their own methods for determining the various political divisions within the Americas, as well as who belonged, who did not, and the alliances and enmities between various constituencies. After contact, as a result of the long colonial process, we now contemplate tribal nationhood under American law in three categories: (1) federally recognized tribal nations, (2) state recognized tribal nations, and (3) unrecognized tribes. Each has a different status under the law. Tribal nations situated in North Carolina offer useful examples of each category existing in a common space.

At its most straightforward, to be federally recognized means to be in a political relationship with the federal government. Those tribal nations that are federally recognized have, unsurprisingly, had their nationhood recognized by the federal government in some manner. Historically, recognition was accomplished through a treaty or some other similar political acknowledgment by the federal government. However, as will be discussed below, treaties were and are not the only path to federal recognition. In North Carolina there is one federally recognized tribe, the Eastern Band of Cherokee Indians. Consequently, there is only one tribal nation in North Carolina with the full range of capabilities that comes along with federal recognition. For example, the Eastern Band of Cherokee own and operate the only tribal gaming facilities in the state under the auspices of the Indian Gaming Regulatory Act and Cherokee courts have the full scope of jurisdiction under the Indian Child Welfare Act (ICWA).

At its most straightforward, to be state-recognized means to be in a political relationship with a state. In North Carolina there are eight state-recognized tribal nations, including the Eastern Band of Cherokee who are also federally recognized. The remaining seven tribal nations that are exclusively state-recognized are the Coharie, the Haliwa-Saponi, the Lumbee, the Meherrin, the Occaneechi, the Sappony, and the Waccamaw-Siouan. This type of recognition is not as expansive as federal recognition, since individual states do not have the same level of authority to engage in Indian affairs as the federal government under American law. Nonetheless, state recognition can have significant advantages for tribal nations. For example, while the seven exclusively state-recognized tribal nations of North Carolina do not have jurisdiction under ICWA, the state has passed state laws that operate in a somewhat similar manner to ICWA for those seven tribal nations.

At its most straightforward, to be unrecognized means to be without a political relationship with either the federal government or an individual state. Whereas these communities are often organized among themselves and may provide services to members of the community, they nonetheless are not authorized under either federal or state law to engage in the same activities as federally or state-recognized tribal nations. Consequently, many in this category are seeking recognition, either with the federal government, a state, or both. The Tuscarora are perhaps the most prominent example of this category in North Carolina. While the Tuscarora hold events such as food distributions days, diaper assistance programs, and cultural classes for their community, they otherwise cannot interact with either the United States or North Carolina in the same manner as recognized tribal nations within the state.

As noted above, these three categories of nationhood were developed through the colonial process and they have caused a significant amount of disruption, controversy, and dispute within Native America. Many of the state-recognized and unrecognized tribal nations have sought or are seeking federal recognition, sometimes to the chagrin of those tribal nations that are already federally recognized. There is fear among some Native peoples and communities that an increase in federally recognized tribal nations will result in fewer of the already limited federal funds that many currently recognized tribal nations rely upon, or that, particularly with the advent of tribal gaming, that some communities are seeking recognition for the wrong reasons. Some passionately argue that only those people who are enrolled in federally recognized tribal nations have a legitimate claim to Indianness. Others just as passionately wonder why so much authority is given to an outside entity, in this case the federal government, to determine what does or does not constitute a tribal nation.

There are any number of reasons that a community has either never been recognized or has lost its recognition, most often due to consequences of history or even policy, such as Termination. On occasion, some tribal nations slipped into and out of federal recognition, generally on the whims of federal bureaucrats who decided based on their own criteria whether a community was worthy of federal recognition. For many years, there was little in the way of process if a tribal nation wanted to be recognized. In 1978 the federal government, in an effort to formalize the previously ad hoc process, established acknowledgment criteria for tribal nations seeking federal recognition. In the years since they were first established, the criteria have been slightly amended a few times to respond to critiques from those concerned with federal recognition. As you read the seven acknowledgment criteria, ask yourself what sort of evidence a petitioning tribal nation needs to produce. What challenges do petitioners face?

CRITERIA FOR ACKNOWLEDGMENT AS A FEDERALLY RECOGNIZED INDIAN TRIBE
25 C.F.R. § 83.11

The criteria for acknowledgment as a federally recognized Indian tribe are delineated in paragraphs (a) through (g) of this section.

(a) *Indian entity identification.* The petitioner has been identified as an American Indian entity on a substantially continuous basis since 1900. Evidence that the group's character as an Indian entity has from time to time been denied will not be considered to be conclusive evidence that this criterion has not been met. . . .

(b) *Community.* The petitioner comprises a distinct community and demonstrates that it existed as a community from 1900 until the present. Distinct community means an entity with consistent interactions and significant social relationships within its membership and whose members are differentiated from and distinct from nonmembers. . . .

(c) *Political influence or authority.* The petitioner has maintained political influence or authority over its members as an autonomous entity from 1900 until the present. Political influence or authority means the entity uses a council, leadership, internal process, or other mechanism as a means of influencing or controlling the behavior of its members in significant respects, making decisions for the entity which substantially affect its members, and/or representing the entity in dealing with outsiders in matters of consequence.

(d) *Governing document.* The petitioner must provide:

(1) A copy of the entity's present governing document, including its membership criteria; or

(2) In the absence of a governing document, a written statement describing in full its membership criteria and current governing procedures.

(e) *Descent.* The petitioner's membership consists of individuals who descend from a historical Indian tribe (or from historical Indian tribes that combined and functioned as a single autonomous political entity). . . .

(f) *Unique membership.* The petitioner's membership is composed principally of persons who are not members of any federally recognized Indian tribe. However, a petitioner may be acknowledged even if its membership is composed principally of persons whose names have appeared on rolls of, or who have been otherwise associated with, a federally recognized Indian tribe, if the petitioner demonstrates that:

(1) It has functioned as a separate politically autonomous community by satisfying criteria in paragraphs (b) and (c) of this section; and

(2) Its members have provided written confirmation of their membership in the petitioner.

(g) *Congressional termination.* Neither the petitioner nor its members are the subject of congressional legislation that has expressly terminated or forbidden the Federal relationship. The Department must determine whether the petitioner meets this criterion, and the petitioner is not required to submit evidence to meet it.

The criteria have softened somewhat since they were first adopted in 1978. For example, the original incarnation of the rules required that a petitioning tribal nation demonstrate that it has been regarded as a political unit "from historical times." The current version only requires such identification "on a substantially continuous basis since 1900." In addition, some of the sections self-referentially require that they be "understood flexibly," in an effort to acknowledge the difficulty of obtaining the types of evidence that would satisfy the requirements of the criteria.

Nonetheless, the criteria themselves and the branch of the Bureau of Indian Affairs that examines petitions under the criteria, the Office of Federal Acknowledgment, have come under criticism by a number of parties. Even at its best, the petition process is slow, expensive, and frustrating. Many petitions have lasted upwards of thirty years and have required hundreds of hours of service from lawyers and other experts. Many have critiqued the type of evidence that the criteria calls for as well, noting that it privileges documentation from non-Native sources. Still others have noted the difficult irony of the federal government requiring evidence of tribal cohesion and unity particularly during periods of federal policy in which the federal government was trying to destroy or otherwise eliminate tribal ways of life.

Despite these challenges, many tribal entities continue to participate in the acknowledgment process, and some have been successful. And still yet, the acknowledgment process is not the only method in which to become federally recognized in the present day. Many of those that have ultimately have been rejected by the Office of Federal Acknowledgment have turned to Congress, seeking legislation that recognizes them. Some tribal nations have been successful using this method. Other tribal entities continue to contemplate going through the process. The question of who gets to be a tribal nation, and in what manner, remains open.

INDIVIDUALS

As with any subject matter that intersects with race, questions of Native identity can be fraught with many challenging issues. Similar to questions about tribal nationhood, who is an Indian, who gets to decide, and what criteria are used to decide can conjure answers that are not only emotional and deeply held but that also have meaningful, real world consequences. This is especially so as determinations of Native identity carry a distinct political element in the United States that does not exist in the same manner for members of other groups. For example, whether or not one is regarded as Native can affect one's citizenship in a tribal nation, access to health care, and what court one will face if accused of a crime, among other things.

There is no single way to which everyone ascribes to determine whether an individual can rightfully call her/himself Native, nor is this discourse limited to the law. It is a social construct as well as a legal one, and many voices are part of the conversation. Attempting to fully parse out the totality of the debate about Native identity is beyond the scope of this chapter. Rather, this chapter will limit itself to two of the more important aspects of determinations of Native identity in American law: (1) blood quantum and (2) the standard constructed by American courts to determine Native identity. Both give significant context to the larger discourse.

At its simplest, blood quantum is the measure—in fractions or percentages—of an individual's ancestry. For example, if an individual has one "full blooded" Native parent and one parent with no Native ancestry at all then that individual will have an Indian blood quantum of ½ or 50%. If that individual then produces a child with someone with no Native ancestry then that child will have an Indian blood quantum of ¼ or 25%. And so on. The following chart, once in use by the BIA, offers an example not only of how blood quantum is measured, but how complicated it can quickly get.[1]

	Non-Indian	1/16	1/8	3/16	1/4	5/16	3/8	7/16	1/2	9/16	5/8	11/16	3/4	13/16	7/8	15/16	4/4
1/16	1/32	1/16	3/32	1/8	5/32	3/16	7/32	1/4	9/32	5/16	11/32	3/8	13/32	7/16	15/32	1/2	17/32
1/8	1/16	3/32	1/8	5/32	3/16	7/32	1/4	9/32	5/16	11/32	3/8	13/32	7/16	15/32	1/2	17/32	9/16
3/16	3/32	1/8	5/32	3/16	7/32	1/4	9/32	5/16	11/32	3/8	13/32	7/16	15/32	1/2	17/32	9/16	19/32
1/4	1/8	5/32	3/16	7/32	1/4	9/32	5/16	11/32	3/8	13/32	7/16	15/32	1/2	17/32	9/16	19/32	5/8
5/16	5/32	3/16	7/32	1/4	9/32	5/16	11/32	3/8	13/32	7/16	15/32	1/2	17/32	9/16	19/32	5/8	21/32
3/8	3/16	7/32	1/4	9/32	5/16	11/32	3/8	13/32	7/16	15/32	1/2	17/32	9/16	19/32	5/8	21/32	11/16
7/16	7/32	1/4	9/32	5/16	11/32	3/8	13/32	7/16	15/32	1/2	17/32	9/16	19/32	5/8	21/32	11/16	23/32
1/2	1/4	9/32	5/16	11/32	3/8	13/32	7/16	15/32	1/2	17/32	9/16	19/32	5/8	21/32	11/16	23/32	3/4
9/16	9/32	5/16	11/32	3/8	13/32	7/16	15/32	1/2	17/32	9/16	19/32	5/8	21/32	11/16	23/32	3/4	25/32
5/8	5/16	11/32	3/8	13/32	7/16	15/32	1/2	17/32	9/16	19/32	5/8	21/32	11/16	23/32	3/4	25/32	13/16
11/16	11/32	3/8	13/32	7/16	15/32	1/2	17/32	9/16	19/32	5/8	21/32	11/16	23/32	3/4	25/32	13/16	27/32
3/4	3/8	13/32	7/16	15/32	1/2	17/32	9/16	19/32	5/8	21/32	11/16	23/32	3/4	25/32	13/16	27/32	7/8
13/16	13/32	7/16	15/32	1/2	17/32	9/16	19/32	5/8	21/32	11/16	23/32	3/4	25/32	13/16	27/32	7/8	29/32
7/8	7/16	15/32	1/2	17/32	9/16	19/32	5/8	21/32	11/16	23/32	3/4	25/32	13/16	27/32	7/8	29/32	15/16
15/16	15/32	1/2	17/32	9/16	19/32	5/8	21/32	11/16	23/32	3/4	25/32	13/16	27/32	7/8	29/32	15/16	31/32
4/4	1/2	17/32	9/16	19/32	5/8	21/32	11/16	23/32	3/4	25/32	13/16	27/32	7/8	29/32	15/16	31/32	4/4
1/32	1/64	3/64	5/64	7/64	9/64	11/64	13/64	15/64	17/64	19/64	21/64	23/64	25/64	27/64	29/64	31/64	33/64
3/32	3/64	5/64	7/64	9/64	11/64	13/64	15/64	17/64	19/64	21/64	23/64	25/64	27/64	29/64	31/64	33/64	35/64
5/32	5/64	7/64	9/64	11/64	13/64	15/64	17/64	19/64	21/64	23/64	25/64	27/64	29/64	31/64	33/64	35/64	37/64
7/32	7/64	9/64	11/64	13/64	15/64	17/64	19/64	21/64	23/64	25/64	27/64	29/64	31/64	33/64	35/64	37/64	39/64
9/32	9/64	11/64	13/64	15/64	17/64	19/64	21/64	23/64	25/64	27/64	29/64	31/64	33/64	35/64	37/64	39/64	41/64
11/32	11/64	13/64	15/64	17/64	19/64	21/64	23/64	25/64	27/64	29/64	31/64	33/64	35/64	37/64	39/64	41/64	43/64
13/32	13/64	15/64	17/64	19/64	21/64	23/64	25/64	27/64	29/64	31/64	33/64	35/64	37/64	39/64	41/64	43/64	45/64
15/32	15/64	17/64	19/64	21/64	23/64	25/64	27/64	29/64	31/64	33/64	35/64	37/64	39/64	41/64	43/64	45/64	47/64
17/32	17/64	19/64	21/64	23/64	25/64	27/64	29/64	31/64	33/64	35/64	37/64	39/64	41/64	43/64	45/64	47/64	49/64
19/32	19/64	21/64	23/64	25/64	27/64	29/64	31/64	33/64	35/64	37/64	39/64	41/64	43/64	45/64	47/64	49/64	51/64
21/32	21/64	23/64	25/64	27/64	29/64	31/64	33/64	35/64	37/64	39/64	41/64	43/64	45/64	47/64	49/64	51/64	53/64
23/32	23/64	25/64	27/64	29/64	31/64	33/64	35/64	37/64	39/64	41/64	43/64	45/64	47/64	49/64	51/64	53/64	55/64
25/32	25/64	27/64	29/64	31/64	33/64	35/64	37/64	39/64	41/64	43/64	45/64	47/64	49/64	51/64	53/64	55/64	57/64
27/32	27/64	29/64	31/64	33/64	35/64	37/64	39/64	41/64	43/64	45/64	47/64	49/64	51/64	53/64	55/64	57/64	59/64
29/32	29/64	31/64	33/64	35/64	37/64	39/64	41/64	43/64	45/64	47/64	49/64	51/64	53/64	55/64	57/64	59/64	61/64
31/32	31/64	33/64	35/64	37/64	39/64	41/64	43/64	45/64	47/64	49/64	51/64	53/64	55/64	57/64	59/64	61/64	63/64

SOURCE: Bureau of Indian Affairs, Tribal Enrollment, app. H.

Measuring Indian blood quantum came to prominence in the Allotment Era (see Chapter 5) when the differences in racial categories were deemed worthy of scientific study. Much discredited today, the science around race in the late eighteenth and early nineteenth centuries sought to understand the supposed differences in ability and civilization of various racial groupings, often through very dubious means such as measuring the circumference of skulls. Unsurprisingly, those of Western European descent were the model against which all others were measured. Whereas perhaps the occasional exceptional individual could escape the trappings of her/his race, according to the conclusions based on this discredited science, in general, members of a racial group were doomed to lesser levels of ability, intelligence, honesty, civilization, and other similar attributes based on the inherent characteristics of their race. Thus, the boarding schools of the Allotment Era regularly only taught Native youth trades such as mechanical work or cooking and sewing, since higher education was regarded as beyond their racial capabilities.

This was also a period when the science of race and American law lived in a symbiotic relationship in Indian Country and elsewhere throughout the United States. For example, several states during this period of time passed anti-miscegenation laws, prohibiting members of separate races from marrying one another, as well as other Jim Crow laws. It was also the period of the "one drop rule" in which individuals with even the slightest African heritage were considered Black in some jurisdictions.

For policymakers of the Allotment Era, blood quantum became a shorthand method for determining competency. For example, the Burke Act (see Chapter 5) authorized the Secretary of the Interior to bypass the twenty-five year trust period for allotted lands originally established in the Allotment Act for those individuals who were deemed competent. In order to execute the provisions of the law, the Secretary of the Interior established competency commissions on many reservations, with many of the commissions simply declaring that individuals with a lower Indian blood quantum were "competent" to manage their lands without the trust protection, regardless of their actual ability or desire to do so. Decisions such as these accelerated the massive land loss of the era. Determinations of blood quantum were also used to manage other matters, such as an individual's eligibility to participate in treaty annuities.

Despite its dubious origins and purpose, blood quantum has come to have a powerful hold on Indian Country. Many tribal nations require that an individual have a certain measure of Indian blood quantum and can trace their lineage from a historical tribal roll (often one established during the Allotment Era that raises its own questions of accuracy) to be eligible for enrollment in the nation. Sometimes blatantly and sometimes subtly, many people still equate a higher blood quantum with a more authentic Indianness or a greater claim to a "real" Native identity. Many Native individuals are asked about their blood quantum in casual conversations in a way that would seem awkward at best in other contexts ("How white are you?" "What is your Asian blood quantum?"). Most succinctly, the emphasis on blood quantum perpetuates an understanding of Native identity purely in racial terms, and otherwise denies or limits the political dimension of that identity that otherwise distinguishes Native peoples from other groups in the United States. Nonetheless, blood quantum remains prevalent in Native America, as alternatives, particularly in the legal realm, have not been widely adopted.

At various times federal statutes have made reference to blood quantum in defining who was an Indian, although nowadays most federal statutory definitions of "Indian" describe an individual who is "a member of an Indian tribe," as well as a few other limited circumstances. Considering their importance, it is perhaps surprising that the federal criminal statutes that directly apply in Indian Country do not define who is an Indian. Obviously such a determination is fundamental to the application of the statute. To that end, federal courts have had to design a standard to use for these criminal statutes. As you read the following case, ask yourself what is the test for making this determination. What factors does it take into account? What role does blood quantum play? Does the test offer a robust enough definition so as to satisfy critics of blood quantum?

U.S. v. CRUZ

554 F.3d 840 (2009)

REINHARDT, CIRCUIT JUDGE:

At first glance, there appears to be something odd about a court of law in a diverse nation such as ours deciding whether a specific individual is or is not "an Indian." Yet, given the long and complex relationship between the government of the United States and the sovereign tribal nations within its borders, the criminal jurisdiction of the federal government often turns on precisely this question—whether a particular individual "counts" as an Indian—and it is this question that we address once again today.

As our court has noted before, the law governing "[t]he exercise of criminal jurisdiction over Indians and Indian country [encompasses] a 'complex patchwork of federal, state, and tribal law,' which is better explained by history than by logic." From that history, and from various cases we have decided over the years, our circuit has distilled a specific test for determining whether an individual can be prosecuted by the federal government. . . . We announced that test in *United States v. Bruce*. . . . Because the evidence adduced during Christopher Cruz's trial does not satisfy any of the four factors outlined in the second prong of the *Bruce* test, we hold that . . . his conviction cannot stand. . . .

Cruz was born in 1987 to Roger Cruz and Clara Clarice Bird. His father is Hispanic and his mother is 29/64 Blackfeet Indian and 32/64 Blood Indian. The Blackfeet are a federally recognized tribe based in northern Montana; the Blood Indians are a Canadian tribe. Given his parents' heritage, Cruz is 29/128 Blackfeet Indian and 32/128 Blood Indian.

For a period of three or four years during his childhood, Cruz lived in the town of Browning, Montana on the Blackfeet Reservation. Between the age of seven and eight, he moved off the reservation and spent the next ten years living first with his father in Great Falls, Montana and subsequently with his uncle in Delano, California. Neither Great Falls nor Delano is located on an Indian reservation or otherwise located in Indian country. In 2005, Cruz returned to Montana, living for a period of time in the town of Cut Bank, which is located just outside the boundaries of the Blackfeet Reservation. Shortly before the incident underlying this case, Cruz moved back to Browning, where he rented a room at the Town Motel.

On December 21, 2006, Cruz and a group of friends spent a part of the evening drinking in his room at the Town Motel. While standing outside the motel talking on a cordless phone to his girlfriend, Cruz was approached by Eudelma White Grass, who had been drinking in a neighboring room and was heavily intoxicated. An altercation took place in which White Grass was severely injured.

Cruz was arrested and charged with "[a]ssault resulting in serious bodily injury". . . . He pled not guilty and went to trial, where his Indian status was a contested issue. . . .

* * *

A "defendant's Indian status is an essential element of [the crime] which the government must allege in the indictment and prove beyond a reasonable doubt." We recently established the test for determining an individual's Indian status. . . . The *Bruce* test requires that the Government prove two things: that the defendant has a sufficient "degree of Indian blood," and has "tribal or federal government recognition as an Indian."

Cruz concedes that he meets the first prong of the test since his blood quotient is twenty-two percent Blackfeet. Only the second prong, therefore, is at issue here. In *Bruce* we outlined four factors that govern the second prong;

those four factors are, "in declining order of importance, evidence of the following: 1) tribal enrollment; 2) government recognition formally and informally through receipt of assistance reserved only to Indians; 3) enjoyment of the benefits of tribal affiliation; and 4) social recognition as an Indian through residence on a reservation and participation in Indian social life."

Taken in the light most favorable to the government, the record reveals the following facts related to Cruz's Indian status:

1. Cruz is not an enrolled member of the Blackfeet Tribe of Indians or any other tribe.

2. Cruz has descendant status in the Blackfeet Tribe as the son of an enrolled member (his mother), which entitles him to use Indian Health Services, to receive some educational grants, and to fish and hunt on the reservation.

3. Cruz has never taken advantage of any of the benefits or services to which he is entitled as a descendant.

4. Cruz lived on the Blackfeet Reservation from the time he was four years old until he was seven or eight. He rented a room in a motel on the reservation shortly before the time of the offense.

5. As a descendant, Cruz was subject to the criminal jurisdiction of the tribal court and was at one time prosecuted in tribal court.

6. Cruz attended a public school on the reservation that is open to non-Indians and worked as a firefighter for the federal Bureau of Indian Affairs, a job that is also open to non-Indians.

7. Cruz has never participated in Indian religious ceremonies or dance festivals, has never voted in a Blackfeet tribal election, and does not have a tribal identification card.

Analyzing this evidence, it is clear that Cruz does not satisfy *any* of the four *Bruce* factors. As to the first and most important factor, it is undisputed that Cruz is not an enrolled member of the Blackfeet Tribe or any other tribe. In fact, Cruz is not even eligible to become an enrolled member of the Blackfeet Tribe. . . .

Nor is there any evidence that Cruz satisfies the second most important factor, "government recognition . . . through *receipt* of assistance reserved only to Indians." To the contrary, the only evidence in the record demonstrates that the opposite is true. . . . Testimony both from Cruz and from a government witness indicated that Cruz does not practice Indian religion, has never "in any way participated in Native religious ceremonies," does not participate in Indian cultural festivals or dance competitions, has never voted in a Blackfeet election, and does not carry a tribal identification card. The government did not present any evidence suggesting that Cruz participated in any way in Indian social life.

* * *

. . . The four factors that constitute the second *Bruce* prong are designed to "probe[ ] whether the Native American has a sufficient non-racial link to a formerly sovereign people." *Bruce* intentionally requires more than a simple blood test to determine whether someone is legally deemed an Indian. . . .

* * *

KOZINSKI, CHIEF JUDGE, dissenting:

Because defendant has the requisite amount of Indian blood, the only question is whether he has "tribal or government recognition as an Indian.". . . He plainly does. The record discloses that the Blackfeet tribal authorities have accorded Cruz "descendant" status, which entitles him to many of the benefits of tribal membership, including medical treatment at any Indian Health Service facility in the United States, certain educational grants, housing assistance and hunting and fishing privileges on the reservation.

That Cruz may not have taken advantage of these benefits doesn't matter because the test is whether the *tribal authorities* recognize him as an Indian, not whether he considers himself one. . . .

. . . *Bruce* was not announcing a rule of law; it was merely reporting what it thought other courts had done: *Bruce* did not adopt this as any sort of standard, nor did it have any cause to do so. . . . We recognized this the last time we applied the test by omitting any reference to the declining order of importance.

* * *

The majority engages in vigorous verbal calisthenics to reach a wholly counter-intuitive-and wrong-result. Along the way, it mucks up several already complex areas of the law and does grave injury to our plain error standard of review. I hasten to run in the other direction.

Cruz is not a Supreme Court opinion, and thus not as controlling as a Supreme Court opinion. Federal courts are split into thirteen circuits, twelve of which are regionally defined (and one national circuit which is designed to hear specialized cases in particular areas of law). Each circuit has several trial courts and a court of appeals. The only court higher than a circuit court of appeals is the U.S. Supreme Court. The 9th Circuit Court of Appeals issued the decision in *Cruz*. The 9th Circuit covers several Western states and has been highly influential in federal Indian law because it encompasses a large selection of tribal land and nations.

The 9th Circuit's *Bruce* test is highly influential among American courts attempting to determine questions like the one found in *Cruz* (although it is not the only federal circuit to rule on the issue or develop its own test, and eventually the Supreme Court may have to resolve the disparities between circuits). Under the *Bruce* test, the federal government must establish two things in order to prosecute an individual as a Native person: (1) the individual has a "sufficient 'degree of Indian blood' " and (2) the individual has "tribal or federal government recognition as an Indian." The majority opinion of the court further refined the second part of this test, declaring that four factors of descending importance aided in determining whether an individual was recognized as an Indian by the federal government or a tribal government (although the dissent vigorously disagreed that the points were in descending order of importance): (1) tribal enrollment; (2) government recognition formally and informally through receipt of assistance reserved only to Indians; (3) enjoyment of the benefits of tribal affiliation; and (4) social recognition as an Indian through residence on a reservation and participation in Indian social life.

The case hinged on the four factors of the second point of the *Bruce* test. The majority listed a number of facts about the defendant, Christopher Cruz, to make the argument that he was not recognized as an Indian by either the federal government or the tribal nation: he had only lived on the reservation for a short period of his life when he was very young, he did not avail himself of the benefits of a connection to the tribal nation, and he did not participate in "Indian religious ceremonies or dance festivals," among others. Perhaps most tellingly, the majority noted that the defendant was not an enrolled citizen of the Blackfeet nation, but rather a descendant. Under Blackfeet law, individuals need ¼ (or 25%) blood quantum to be eligible for citizenship. Those individuals who do not meet this requirement but who come from a parent who is a citizen are recognized under tribal law as descendants. Under Blackfeet law (and a number of other tribal nations as well) descendants enjoy many of the benefits of citizenship, such as access to health care, but lack other benefits, such as the right to vote in tribal elections.

Taking these facts as a whole, the majority opinion decided that the second part of the *Bruce* test was not satisfied, and thus the defendant was not sufficiently

Indian to be prosecuted under the federal law that would have otherwise applied. The dissent strongly disagreed, arguing that even though the defendant did not personally avail himself of the benefits of being a descendant, it did not mean that they were not available to him. Consequently, he was recognized as an Indian by the tribal nation and the second part of the *Bruce* test was satisfied.

It is useful to ask yourself which side you agree with and why. In one sense, as the majority opinion notes, the second part of the Bruce test moves beyond only using blood quantum "to determine whether someone is legally deemed an Indian." Do the factors that the court announces move sufficiently beyond blood quantum to quell the critiques of using blood quantum? Assume, for the sake of argument, that a different defendant with identical circumstances did want acknowledgment at an Indian. What would that person have to do to satisfy the standard? Would it be enough, in the eyes of the court, if this hypothetical defendant participated in "Indian religious ceremonies or dance festivals"? Why or why not? If not, what else would the hypothetical defendant need to do to assert her/his Indianness?

In addition, although all of the parties involved in this case accepted that the defendant satisfied the first part of the *Bruce* test (including the defendant himself), the case offers opportunities to raise additional questions. The defendant was noted to be 29/128 (or 22%) Blackfeet Indian. Again, everyone agreed that this was "sufficient" to satisfy the *Bruce* test. What blood quantum would be too low to be sufficient? At what point is one's ancestry too remote to count? Further complicating the matter was the fact that the defendant in the case was also descended from "Canadian" Native ancestry. Why does the court not seem to count this lineage when discussing the defendant's overall blood quantum for the purposes of the *Bruce* test?

As with tribal nationhood, the question of who gets to be an Indian, and in what manner, remains open. Blood quantum and the *Bruce* test offer some history and context into this thorny issue, and they are significant parts of American law. But they are only aspects of a larger discourse and do not provide the final word.

LAND

Sometimes, when one uses the phrase "Indian Country," one is speaking metaphorically to describe a sense of place and its ethos. Thus, one might describe the importance of sovereignty to Indian Country. Yet, in American law, "Indian Country" also has a very literal meaning. As with tribal nations and individuals, sometimes it is critical for American courts to determine the nature of a place in which an incident occurred. Making this determination can have a significant bearing on which court or courts—federal, tribal, or state—can hear a case.

"Indian Country" was defined in a statute adopted by Congress in 1948. As you read the statute, ask yourself what types of lands it covers. Why are there different categories? What does this reveal about land ownership for tribal peoples and nations?

INDIAN COUNTRY
18 U.S.C.A. § 1151

..."Indian country"... means (a) all land within the limits of any Indian reservation under the jurisdiction of the United States Government, notwithstanding the issuance of any patent, and, including rights-of-way running through the reservation, (b) all dependent Indian communities within the borders of the United States whether within the original or subsequently acquired territory thereof, and whether within or without the limits of a state, and (c) all Indian allotments, the Indian titles to which have not been extinguished, including rights-of-way running through the same.

Of the three categories identified under the statute, (a) and (c) are the most straightforward. Reservations are covered under (a) and individual Indian allotments are covered in (c). The "dependent Indian communities" identified in (b) tend to be more confusing.

In the following case, the 10th Circuit Court of Appeals had to decide if a strip of road on a southwestern Pueblo nestled between two non Native-owned parcels of land constituted a "dependent Indian community." The 10th Circuit encompasses much of the Southwest and Midwest and, like the 9th Circuit, has also been influential in the development of federal Indian law. Using Supreme Court precedent, the 10th Circuit's decision gives useful context to a number of things: understanding what the above statute is attempting to cover; the historical development that led to the need to identify dependent Indian communities as part of Indian Country; and how American courts make these determinations. As you read the case, ask yourself what is the standard for determining what is a dependent Indian community. How does this standard address the history it details?

U.S. v. Arrieta

436 F.3d 1246 (2006)

McConnell, Circuit Judge.

The conviction in this case turns on whether a road maintained by Santa Fe County, New Mexico, lying between two parcels of land owned by non-Indians but within the exterior boundaries of the Pojoaque Pueblo, where the Pueblo's title has not been extinguished by Congress, is "Indian country" for purpose of the exercise of federal criminal jurisdiction.

I.   Factual and Procedural Background

As a result of an altercation in January 2000, a federal grand jury returned a two-count indictment against Defendant-Appellant Santo Arrieta for committing an assault against an Indian that resulted in serious bodily injury in Indian country and for using a firearm to facilitate a crime of violence. . . . The alleged crimes occurred on Shady Lane, also known as Santa Fe County Road 105 or Bouquet Lane. Shady Lane is a public road within the exterior boundaries of the Pojoaque Pueblo. It is surrounded on both sides by non-Indian owned land, and is maintained as a county road by Santa Fe County. Congress has not extinguished the Pueblo's title over the land underlying the road.

* * *

Mr. Arrieta filed a motion to dismiss his criminal indictment for lack of subject matter jurisdiction, claiming that Shady Lane is not "Indian country" as defined in 18 U.S.C. § 1151. The district court denied Mr. Arrieta's motion to dismiss, finding that Shady Lane is part of the Pojoaque Pueblo dependent Indian community and that Congress had not extinguished the Pojoaque Pueblo's title over Shady Lane. . . .

* * *

. . . Federal jurisdiction thus exists over the crimes for which Mr. Arrieta was charged only if Shady Lane—the [site] of the crime—was Indian country. . . .

* * *

The government does not contend that Shady Lane is within an Indian reservation or is an Indian allotment, but that it is part of the Pojoaque Pueblo dependent Indian community, the existence of which was recognized in *United States v. Sandoval*. Mr. Arrieta contends that the extinguishment of Pojoaque

Pueblo lands since *Sandoval* requires us to reexamine whether Shady Lane is a dependent Indian community as that phrase was defined in *Alaska v. Native Village of Venetie Tribal Government.*

1.   History of the Pueblo Lands

Title to the lands on which the Pueblo Indians reside was formally granted to them by the King of Spain in 1689. In 1848, the United States acquired the territory of New Mexico from Mexico, including the lands on which the Pueblo Indians resided. In the Treaty of Guadalupe Hidalgo, the United States agreed to protect the rights of Indians recognized by prior sovereigns. Following this agreement, Congress granted federal protection and supervision to the Pueblo Indians and their lands by extending to the Pueblo the provisions of the Indian Nonintercourse Act, which prohibits any loss or transfer of title of Indian lands except by treaty or convention.

In 1877, however, the Supreme Court held that the Pueblo Indians were not "Indian tribes" within the meaning of the Nonintercourse Act, and therefore could alienate their land without congressional approval. Although the decision was later overruled, approximately 3,000 non-Indians acquired putative title to Pueblo land between 1880 and 1910. The validity of title transferred to non-Indians came into question in 1913 when the Court held in *Sandoval* that the Pueblo are a dependent Indian community entitled to the aid and protection of the federal government and subject to congressional control. To settle the status of Pueblo lands, Congress enacted the Pueblo Lands Act of 1924 ("PLA"). The PLA established the Pueblo Lands Board ("Board") to resolve conflicting claims to Pueblo lands.

The Board issued patents to quiet title to land in favor of non-Indians who adversely possessed land and paid taxes on the land from 1889 to 1924 or who had color of title to the land from 1902 to 1924. The Pueblos' rights to such land were extinguished. The Pueblo retained title to all lands not patented to non-Indians. Consequently, pockets of privately owned, non-Indian land lie amidst Pueblo lands.

2.   The Status of Shady Lane

We turn now to the area at issue in this case, Shady Lane. The parties agree that the Pueblo has always held and continues to hold title to the land underlying Shady Lane. The parties likewise acknowledge that the lands surrounding Shady Lane were patented to non-Indians under the PLA, and that the Pojoaque Pueblo's title to those lands has been extinguished. The parties' disagreement, therefore, is not over who has title to the land, but over whether

Shady Lane can be classified as a "dependent Indian community" when it is maintained by Santa Fe County as a county road.

Two requirements must be satisfied for Indian lands to be classified as a "dependent Indian community." First, the lands must have been "set aside by the Federal Government for the use of the Indians as Indian land." This requirement guarantees that the land is actually occupied by an Indian community. Second, the lands must be "under federal superintendence." The latter requirement ensures that the community is dependent on the federal government such that the federal government and the Indians, rather than the states, exercise primary jurisdiction.

* * *

Shady Lane, as well as other lands on which the Pojoaque Pueblo reside, was specifically set aside as Indian lands by the federal government. Although the PLA extinguished the Pueblo's title over some of the land that was originally set aside for them, any land where title was not extinguished by the Board remained set aside for use by the Pueblo. Thus, the federal set-aside requirement is satisfied.

Mr. Arrieta rests his argument on the second requirement, that of federal superintendence. He contends that the fact that Shady Lane is maintained by Santa Fe County as a county road precludes our finding that requirement satisfied, despite the Supreme Court's previous holding that the Pueblo are subject to federal superintendence. His argument, however, too narrowly conceives the concept of federal superintendence. We examine the entire Indian community, not merely a stretch of road, to ascertain whether the federal set-aside and federal superintendence requirements are satisfied. Land owned by an Indian tribe within the exterior or boundaries of land granted to the tribe is necessarily part of the Indian community, even if the state performs some services and maintenance with respect to the land. Because the Pojoaque Pueblo possesses title to Shady Lane and Shady Lane is within the exterior boundaries of the Pojoaque Pueblo, it is part of the Pojoaque Pueblo community. The road, like the Pueblo, is therefore subject to federal superintendence. . . . Shady Lane, located within the exterior boundaries of the Pojoaque Pueblo land grant, is therefore Indian country. . . .

* * *

As noted by the court, there is a two-part test to determine if a parcel of land is a "dependent Indian community": (1) The lands must have been "set aside by the Federal Government for the use of the Indians as Indian land," and (2) the lands must be "under federal superintendence." In looking at the totality of the surrounding community, not just the road itself, the court found that the stretch of road did constitute a dependent Indian community. Is this a reasonable outcome? Why or why not?

The court also detailed the history of the Pueblo and its landholdings to give greater context to what constitutes a dependent Indian community. The example of the Pueblo offer a useful case study of both the diversity of colonial experiences in Native America and the need to recognize more than reservations and allotments as Indian Country. In addition, the opinion also referenced *U.S. v. Sandoval*, discussed in Chapter 7. It is worthwhile to briefly review *Sandoval* to consider it impact on this case and its continuing legacy in American law. Is this a benign reference to a case from the Allotment Era, particularly since Native interests prevailed? Or is there something troubling about American courts continuing to rely upon precedent from a time in which the federal government was seeking to destroy tribalism? Is there an alternative?

As with tribal nationhood and individual identity, issues of identifying land as Indian or non-Indian remain difficult, controversial, and open. Any scholar of federal Indian law and policy must be aware of these challenges. While American law has provided some answers to these large questions, it has done so for its own limited purposes and does not constitute the final or only word on the subject. The conversation remains open.

SUGGESTED READINGS

- *Becoming Indian: The Struggle over Cherokee Identity in the Twenty-First Century.* Circe Sturm. Santa Fe, NM: School for Advanced Research Press, 2011.

- *Forgotten Tribes: Unrecognized Indians and the Federal Acknowledgment Process.* Mark Edwin Miller. Lincoln, NE: University of Nebraska Press, 2006.

- "Indian Country, Indian Reservations, and the Importance of History in Indian Law." Marc Slonim. 45 *Gonzaga Law Review* 517 (2009–2010).

---

1   Found at http://nebula.wsimg.com/ea466d37a2cc856c9c00c50971a746a9?AccessKeyId=67F2BC04 9963B1A3F46F&disposition=0&alloworigin=1 (accessed June 3, 2018).

CHAPTER 14

Trust Responsibility

In 1785 the United States signed a treaty with the Wyandot, Delaware, Chippewa, and Ottawa nations. Article II of the treaty stated that, "The said Indian nations do acknowledge themselves and all their tribes to be under the protection of the United States and of no other sovereign whatsoever."[1] Nearly eighty years later, in 1864, the United States completed a treaty with the Klamath and others. Article 9 of that treaty stated that, "The several tribes of Indians, parties to this treaty, acknowledge their dependence on the Government of the United States . . . and they further agree that they will not communicate with or assist any persons or nation hostile to the United States. . . ."[2] The Northwest Ordinance, passed by Congress in 1787, stated, "The utmost good faith shall always be observed towards the Indians . . . laws founded in justice and humanity shall from time to time be made, for preventing wrongs being done to them, and for preserving peace and friendship with them. . . ." (See Chapter 2.) In his famous Indian Trilogy of cases, John Marshall noted in 1832 that, "From the commencement of our government, Congress has passed acts to regulate trade and intercourse with the Indians . . . and manifest a firm purpose to afford . . . protection which treaties stipulate." (See Chapter 3.)

The above examples illustrate that from the founding and from many times thereafter, each branch of the federal government has acknowledged that the United States has accepted certain commitments toward tribal nations. In general, the federal government has obligated itself to protecting tribal nations and peoples. This is, in essence, the trust doctrine (or trust responsibility or trust obligation) of federal Indian law. The federal government has declared time and time again that it must act in the best interests for Native America.

Despite the good will that the trust responsibility expresses, a number of foundational questions complicate its implementation. What does it mean to "protect" tribal nations and peoples? Who gets to decide? What if tribal nations or peoples disagree with the federal government's assessment of what is in their

285

best interest? How far do federal efforts have to go in fulfilling its trust obligation? In what circumstances is the federal government obligated by law to act (or not act) under the trust doctrine, and consequently under what circumstances is the federal government not obligated by law to do so? Is there a point when the trust doctrine inhibits or infringes on tribal sovereignty? This principle of American law has often proven to be easier to express as a truism than it has been to put into practice.

This chapter will demonstrate. . .

- *The rules and legacy established by the* Mitchell *cases*

- *The "Good Faith Effort" test to determine trust violations*

- *The* Cobell *case, its historical roots, and its reflection of the trust doctrine*

CAN YOU TRUST THE TRUST DOCTRINE?

Imagine a scenario in which the federal government and a tribal nation enter into a treaty in the late 1860s. One of the provisions of the treaty is that the federal government is required to distribute funds to tribal members on a per capita (or individual) basis every year for a period of fifty years. After fifteen years of this arrangement, the tribal council asks the federal government to distribute the annual payments to the council directly, so that the council can make the per capita payments to individual tribal members. In an effort to encourage tribal self-government, the federal government complies with the request for a period of ten years. This is in spite of the fact that the federal government knew, or should have known, that members of tribal council were corrupt and that the money was likely to be embezzled. Years later, in the early twentieth century, citizens of the tribal nation sue the federal government. The theory behind the lawsuit is that the federal government violated its trust responsibility to the tribal citizens for those ten years by turning over funds to a corrupt tribal government—which, for the purposes of this scenario, did embezzle the money. Would you rule in favor of the tribal citizens? Should the federal government be held responsible for the tribal council's mismanagement of treaty funds? Why or why not? Before deciding on an answer, it is important to reflect on the origins and purposes of the trust responsibility.

The Supreme Court confronted a similar fact pattern to the above scenario in a 1942 case, *Seminole Nation v. United States*.[3] In one sense, *Seminole Nation* expresses the strongest benefits of the trust responsibility in Indian law by placing such situations within general trust law principles. While it is not possible to describe trust law in totality in this chapter, for the present it suffices to note that American law requires a higher level of behavior from those placed in charge of another's property. In short, those in charge of a trust (like the federal government in *Seminole Nation*) not only have to take care to maintain and preserve the trust property, those in charge also have to refrain from any activities that will damage or diminish the value of trust property. Since the federal government did not live up to this standard in *Seminole Nation*, it was found liable to the tribal citizens who sued.

The protections afforded by the trust doctrine are particularly important in Indian law. The Plenary Power Trilogy of cases (see Chapter 7) limited some of the traditional sources of protection against the overarching authority of the federal government (U.S. Constitution, American citizenship, treaties). Without those traditional sources of protection, the trust responsibility is often the only barrier between tribal peoples and nations and the dominating force of the federal government. In *Seminole Nation*, the federal government was held responsible for its reckless behavior toward tribal citizens, an often all-too-rare occurrence that would not have been possible without the trust doctrine.

In another sense, *Seminole Nation* exposes the negative implications of the trust doctrine. At its simplest, a trust consists of three elements: a trustee (the one responsible for managing the trust), the beneficiary (the one who receives the benefit of the trust), and the trust corpus (the property that constitutes the trust). At a minimum, the very nature of such an arrangement strongly implies that the beneficiary is not responsible or capable enough to handle the trust corpus on her/his own. The trust corpus is best left in the hands of the trustee, presumably because the trustee is better equipped to manage the property.

The implications of the trust responsibility for Native America is in line with how federal law has traditionally regarded Native peoples. In the second case of his Indian Trilogy, *Cherokee Nation v. Georgia*, Chief Justice John Marshall stated that the relationship between the federal government and Native peoples, "resembles that of a ward to his guardian." (See Chapter 3.) Wards—typically children, individuals with developmental disabilities, and others similarly situated—are deemed incapable of managing their own affairs and are in need of a protection of a guardian. Furthering this reasoning, the Plenary Power Trilogy of cases was built on the presumption that the federal government needed expansive authority to act on behalf of the best interests of tribal peoples and nations, all while diminishing valuable protections that traditionally curb the overreach of the federal government.

Consequently, it is fair to ask whether the trust doctrine relegates tribal nations and peoples into an inescapable state of inferiority. Does the trust doctrine, with its implications, perpetuate an understanding of Native peoples as children or wards or those otherwise incapable of managing their own affairs in the modern world? *Seminole Nation* raises another troubling question: Does the trust doctrine create a disincentive for the federal government to encourage self-determination and governance? The corruption in *Seminole Nation* took place on the tribal level. The federal government's breach of duty was a result of authorizing the tribal government to administer treaty funds to its citizenry. Does the outcome of *Seminole Nation* create any incentive for the federal government to invest in tribal self-determination?

Does the trust doctrine act as an anchor, securing Native peoples to a conception of them as inferior and limiting their ability to progress, or, conversely, is it a beneficial and necessary tool to maintain balance in the disjointed field of Indian law? Are the benefits of the trust doctrine worth any burdens it carries? With this additional insight reflect again upon the decision in *Seminole Nation*. Which way would you have decided? Why?

THE *MITCHELL* CASES

One of the more difficult aspects of the trust doctrine is determining its scope. The federal government has pledged, at numerous times in numerous ways, that it will protect tribal peoples, nations, and interests. However, determining when this commitment is enforceable, as opposed to merely being aspirational or a gesture of good will, has not always been clear. For example, can a tribal nation demand adequate law enforcement on a reservation for major crimes since the federal government has given itself jurisdiction for those crimes under the Major Crimes Act (see Chapter 6)? If it cannot demand that action, can the tribal nation at least sue the federal government for failing to provide adequate law enforcement under the trust doctrine? Could a Native victim of domestic violence demand federal government protection under the trust doctrine? Does it make sense, morally, fiscally, or otherwise, to extend the trust doctrine to these scenarios?

In the early 1980s, the Supreme Court offered some clarity as to when the trust responsibility is enforceable in two cases, *Mitchell I* and *Mitchell II*. As you read the cases, ask yourself what circumstances need to be present to make the trust responsibility enforceable. Is this a reasonable application of the trust doctrine? Should it be more expansive or less so? Why?

U.S. v. Mitchell I
445 U.S. 535 (1980)

Mr. Justice Marshall delivered the opinion of the Court.

This case presents the question whether the Indian General Allotment Act of 1887 authorizes the award of money damages against the United States for alleged mismanagement of forests located on lands allotted to Indians under that Act.

In 1873, a Reservation was established by Executive Order in the State of Washington for the Quinault Tribe. Much of the land within the Reservation was forested. By 1935, acting under the authority of the General Allotment Act of 1887, the Government had allotted all of the Reservation's land in trust to individual Indians. Other enactments of Congress require the Secretary of the Interior to manage these forests, sell the timber, and pay the proceeds of such sales, less administrative expenses, to the allottees.

The respondents are 1,465 individual allottees of land contained in the Quinault Reservation, the Quinault Tribe, which now holds some allotments, and the Quinault Allottees Association, an unincorporated association formed to promote the interests of the allottees of the Quinault Reservation. In four actions consolidated in the Court of Claims, the respondents sought to recover damages from the Government for alleged mismanagement of timber resources found on the Reservation. The respondents asserted that the Government: (1) failed to obtain fair market value for timber sold; (2) failed to manage timber on a sustained-yield basis and to rehabilitate the land after logging; (3) failed to obtain payment for some merchantable timber; (4) failed to develop a proper system of roads and easements for timber operations and exacted improper charges from allottees for roads; (5) failed to pay interest on certain funds, and paid insufficient interest on other funds; and (6) exacted excessive administrative charges from allottees. The respondents contended that they were entitled to recover money damages because this alleged misconduct breached a fiduciary duty owed to them by the United States as trustee of the allotted lands under the General Allotment Act.

* * *

Section 1 of the General Allotment Act authorizes the President to allot to each Indian residing on a reservation up to 80 acres of agricultural land or 160 acres of grazing land found within the reservation. Section 5 of the Act provides that the United States shall retain title to such allotted lands in trust for the benefit of the allottees. . . .

Under § 2 of the Indian Reorganization Act of 1934 the United States now holds title to these lands indefinitely.

The Court of Claims held that the General Allotment Act creates a fiduciary duty on the part of the United States to manage timber resources properly. . . . The court held that [language in the Allotment Act] created an express trust. . . .

. . . We conclude that the Act created only a limited trust relationship between the United States and the allottee that does not impose any duty upon the Government to manage timber resources.

The Act does not unambiguously provide that the United States has undertaken full fiduciary responsibilities as to the management of allotted lands. . . . Furthermore, the legislative history of the Act plainly indicates that the trust Congress placed on allotted lands is of limited scope. Congress intended that, even during the period in which title to allotted land would remain in the United States, the allottee would occupy the land as a homestead for his personal use in agriculture or grazing. Under this scheme, then, the allottee, and not the United States, was to manage the land.

The earliest drafts of the Act provided that, during the 25-year period before the allottee would receive fee simple title, the allottee would hold title to the land subject to a restraint on alienation. On Senator Dawes' motion, this language was amended to provide that the United States would hold the land "in trust" for that period. Senator Dawes explained that the statute, as amended, would still ensure that title to the land would be transferred to the Indian allottee at the expiration of 25 years. He promoted the amendment because he feared that States might attempt to tax allotted lands if the allottees held title to them subject to a restraint on alienation. By placing title in the United States in trust for the allottee, his amendment made it "impossible to raise the question of [state] taxation." The next draft of the Act introduced in the Congress reflected this amendment, as, of course, did the Act as enacted. It is plain, then, that when Congress enacted the General Allotment Act, it intended that the United States "hold the land . . . in trust" not because it wished the Government to control use of the land and be subject to money damages for breaches of fiduciary duty, but simply because it wished to prevent alienation of the land and to ensure that allottees would be immune from state taxation.

Furthermore, events surrounding and following the passage of the General Allotment Act indicate that the Act should not be read as authorizing, much less requiring, the Government to manage timber resources for the benefit of Indian allottees. . . .

As time passed, Congress occasionally passed legislation authorizing the harvesting and sale of timber on specific reservations. . . . Congress subsequently enacted other legislation directing the Secretary on how to manage Indian timber resources.

The General Allotment Act, then, cannot be read as establishing that the United States has a fiduciary responsibility for management of allotted forest lands. Any right of the respondents to recover money damages for Government mismanagement of timber resources must be found in some source other than that Act.

At its most straightforward, in *Mitchell I* the Court found that the Allotment Act (see Chapter 5) only created a "limited" trust with tribal nations and individuals because the legislation did not "unambiguously provide that the United States has undertaken full fiduciary responsibilities as to the management of allotted lands." Put another way, the trust language in the Allotment Act was not enforceable in the manner in which the plaintiffs desired because the Allotment Act did not authorize a certain level of federal control over the property. Without that heightened level of federal control, the Court could not find enforceable trust obligations and the plaintiffs lost this round.

Nonetheless, the litigation was not over. The Court noted that if there was an enforceable trust obligation to be found, it "must be found in some source" other than the Allotment Act. This was a signal that the Court was open to the possibility that there was another source beyond the Allotment Act that might have established an enforceable trust obligation. Consequently, rather than ending the litigation, the Supreme Court remanded the case—or sent it back down to a lower court for further consideration on a particular matter or question—to see if there was a different source for federal trust obligations.

Three years later the case returned to the Supreme Court in *Mitchell II*. This time, the tribal members that brought the case argued that a collection of statutes beyond the Allotment Act created the federal control over the property necessary to establish enforceable trust obligations over the federal government. As you read the case, make note of the differences between how the Court reads the Allotment Act in *Mitchell I* and the other statutes identified in *Mitchell II*. What is significant about these differences? Where does the trust responsibility lie after these companion cases?

U.S. v. MITCHELL II
463 U.S. 206 (1983)

JUSTICE MARSHALL delivered the opinion of the Court.

The principal question in this case is whether the United States is accountable in money damages for alleged breaches of trust in connection with its management of forest resources on allotted lands of the Quinault Indian Reservation.

* * *

. . . In [an 1855] Treaty, the Indians ceded to the United States a vast tract of land on the Olympic Peninsula in the State of Washington, and the United States agreed to set aside a reservation for the Indians.

. . . President Grant issued an Executive Order on November 4, 1873, designating about 200,000 acres along the Washington coast as an Indian reservation. The vast bulk of this land consisted of rain forest covered with huge, coniferous trees.

In 1905, the Federal Government began to allot the Quinault Reservation in trust to individual Indians under the General Allotment Act of 1887. . . . By 1935, the entire Reservation had been divided into 2,340 trust allotments, most of which were 80 acres of heavily timbered land. . . .

The forest resources on the allotted lands have long been managed by the Department of the Interior, which exercises "comprehensive" control over the harvesting of Indian timber. The Secretary of the Interior has broad statutory authority over the sale of timber on reservations. . . . Under these statutes, the Secretary has promulgated detailed regulations governing the management of Indian timber. The Secretary is authorized to deduct an administrative fee for his services from the timber revenues paid to Indian allottees.

* * *

On remand, the Court of Claims . . . ruled that the timber management statutes, various federal statutes governing roadbuilding and rights of way, statutes governing Indian funds and Government fees, and regulations promulgated under these statutes imposed fiduciary duties upon the United States in its management of forested allotted lands. The court concluded that the statutes and regulations implicitly required compensation for damages sustained as a result of the Government's breach of its duties. Thus, the court held that respondents could proceed on their claims.

* * *

[In *Mitchell I*], this Court concluded that the General Allotment Act does not confer a right to recover money damages against the United States. While § 5 of the Act provided that the United States would hold land "in trust" for Indian allottees, we held that the Act creates only a limited trust relationship. . . .

Thus, for claims against the United States "founded either upon the Constitution, or any Act of Congress, or any regulation of an executive department," a court must inquire whether the source of substantive law can fairly be interpreted as mandating compensation by the Federal Government for the damages sustained. . . .

* * *

Respondents have based their money claims against the United States on various Acts of Congress and executive department regulations. . .

The Secretary of the Interior's pervasive role in the sales of timber from Indian lands began with the Act of June 25, 1910. . . .

The 1910 Act empowered the Secretary to sell timber on unallotted lands and apply the proceeds of the sales for the benefit of the Indians, and authorized the Secretary to consent to sales by allottees, with the proceeds to be paid to the allottees or disposed of for their benefit. Congress thus sought to provide for harvesting timber "in such a manner as to conserve the interests of the people on the reservations, namely, the Indians."

From the outset, the Interior Department recognized its obligation to supervise the cutting of Indian timber. In 1911, the Department's Office of Indian Affairs promulgated detailed regulations. . . .

The regulations addressed virtually every aspect of forest management. . . .

Over time, deficiencies in the Interior Department's performance of its responsibilities became apparent. Accordingly, as part of the Indian

Reorganization Act of 1934, Congress imposed even stricter duties upon the Government with respect to Indian timber management. . . .

Regulations promulgated under the Act required the preservation of Indian forest lands in a perpetually productive state, forbade the clear-cutting of large contiguous areas, called for the development of long-term working plans for all major reservations, required adequate provision for new growth when mature timber was removed, and required the regulation of run-off and the minimization of erosion. . . .

In 1964, Congress amended the timber provisions of the 1910 Act, again emphasizing the Secretary of the Interior's management duties. . . .

The timber management statutes and the regulations promulgated thereunder establish the "comprehensive" responsibilities of the Federal Government in managing the harvesting of Indian timber. The Department of the Interior—through the Bureau of Indian Affairs—"exercises literally daily supervision over the harvesting and management of tribal timber." Virtually every stage of the process is under federal control.

* * *

In [*Mitchell I*], this Court recognized that the General Allotment Act creates a trust relationship between the United States and Indian allottees, but concluded that the trust relationship was limited. We held that the Act could not be read "as establishing that the United States has a fiduciary responsibility for management of allotted forest lands." In contrast to the bare trust created by the General Allotment Act, the statutes and regulations now before us clearly give the Federal Government full responsibility to manage Indian resources and land for the benefit of the Indians. They thereby establish a fiduciary relationship and define the contours of the United States' fiduciary responsibilities.

The language of these statutory and regulatory provisions directly supports the existence of a fiduciary relationship. . . .

Moreover, a fiduciary relationship necessarily arises when the Government assumes such elaborate control over forests and property belonging to Indians. All of the necessary elements of a common law trust are present: a trustee (the United States), a beneficiary (the Indian allottees), and a trust corpus (Indian timber, lands, and funds).

* * *

> Our construction of these statutes and regulations is reinforced by the undisputed existence of a general trust relationship between the United States and the Indian people. This Court has previously emphasized "the distinctive obligation of trust incumbent upon the Government in its dealings with these dependent and sometimes exploited people." This principle has long dominated the Government's dealings with Indians.
>
> * * *
>
> We thus conclude that the statutes and regulations at issue here can fairly be interpreted as mandating compensation by the Federal Government for violations of its fiduciary responsibilities in the management of Indian property. . . .

Mitchell I and *Mitchell II* set the parameters for the trust obligation and the possibility for any recompense for tribal peoples or nations. There is a general trust relationship between the federal government and Native America that operates much like an ethical edict or guiding principle. It is not enforceable by itself, but rather should guide the behavior of those making law and policy for Native peoples. Legislation that establishes a large degree or "comprehensive" federal control over trust property can establish enforceable obligations. Legislation that lacks the large degree of federal control over trust property creates a "limited" or "bare" trust that is not enforceable through the courts.

Twenty years after *Mitchell II*, the Supreme Court once again confronted two trust doctrine cases, *U.S. v. Navaho Nation*[4] and *U.S. v. White Mountain Apache*[5]. Decided on the same day, both cases use the *Mitchell* parameters to achieve their results. These two recent cases give further understanding to the principles established in the *Mitchell* cases. Bare or limited trusts, in which the federal government might use the language of trust to describe its relationship to property but otherwise does not have significant control over that property, are not regarded as enforceable. Conversely, in those instances when the federal government has significant control over property and/or is obligated to protect the financial well-being of the property then an enforceable trust obligation is established. Both cases also strongly suggest that the purpose of the underlying legislation in question is tremendously significant. In *Mitchell I* and *Navajo Nation*, the statutes in question both sought to further tribal and/or individual control over tribal resources. The statutes in question in *Mitchell II* and *White Mountain Apache*, on the other hand, did not demonstrate that same purpose.

Having gained a better understanding of the legal standard for determining the federal government's trust responsibility, it is worthwhile to reconsider the question that drives the analysis in the first place: what is the scope of the federal government's trust obligation to Native America? The *Mitchell* cases offer an answer currently embraced by American courts, but is it a good answer? Does this standard cover enough ground, too much ground, or just the right amount? Does this understanding of the trust responsibility properly act as a useful or proper balance to the federal government's plenary authority in Indian law? Why or why not?

VIOLATIONS OF TRUST

It is one thing to decide if a trust obligation exists. It is another thing to decide if that trust obligation has been violated. While general trust law principles place a heavy burden on the entity in control of a trust to act in the best interests of the trust, it nonetheless offers some flexibility in how to act in those best interests. For example, if a trustee wants to sell some of the trust property (or invest trust funds or some other similar action) in order to grow or otherwise benefit the trust, the trustee is generally authorized to do so, even over the objections of the beneficiary. A trustee will not be held liable to a beneficiary if the investment results in a loss as long as the trustee acted in good faith.

In the next case, the federal government took on trust obligations through a treaty to what was then known as the Great Sioux Nation of the northern plains. As you read the case, ask yourself what obligations the federal government assumed. What is the test that the Court uses to determine whether there has been a violation of trust obligations? What is the dissent's objection to the majority's ruling?

U.S. v. SIOUX NATION
448 U.S. 371 (1980)

MR. JUSTICE BLACKMUN delivered the opinion of the Court.

This case concerns the Black Hills of South Dakota, the Great Sioux Reservation, and a colorful, and in many respects tragic, chapter in the history of the Nation's West.... [T]he litigation comes down to a claim of interest since 1877 on an award of over $17 million....

For over a century now, the Sioux Nation has claimed that the United States unlawfully abrogated the Fort Laramie Treaty, in Art. II of which the United States pledged that the Great Sioux Reservation, including the Black

Hills, would be "set apart for the absolute and undisturbed use and occupation of the Indians herein named.". . .

The Fort Laramie Treaty included several agreements central to the issues presented in this case. First, it established the Great Sioux Reservation. . . . The United States "solemnly agree[d]" that no unauthorized persons "shall ever be permitted to pass over, settle upon, or reside in [this] territory."

* * *

. . . Art. XII of the treaty provided:

No treaty for the cession of any portion or part of the reservation herein described which may be held in common shall be of any validity or force as against the said Indians, unless executed and signed by at least three fourths of all the adult male Indians, occupying or interested in the same.

The years following the treaty brought relative peace to the Dakotas, an era of tranquility that was disturbed, however, by renewed speculation that the Black Hills, which were included in the Great Sioux Reservation, contained vast quantities of gold and silver. In 1874, the Army planned and undertook an exploratory expedition into the Hills. . . . Lieutenant Colonel George Armstrong Custer led the expedition. . . . [A]nd, by mid-August, had confirmed the presence of gold fields in that region. . . . Custer's florid descriptions of the mineral and timber resources of the Black Hills, and the land's suitability for grazing and cultivation, also received wide circulation, and had the effect of creating an intense popular demand for the "opening" of the Hills for settlement. The only obstacle to "progress" was the Fort Laramie Treaty that reserved occupancy of the Hills to the Sioux.

Having promised the Sioux that the Black Hills were reserved to them, the United States Army was placed in the position of having to threaten military force, and occasionally to use it, to prevent prospectors and settlers from trespassing on lands reserved to the Indians. . . .

Eventually, however, the Executive Branch of the Government decided to abandon the Nation's treaty obligation to preserve the integrity of the Sioux territory. . . .

With the Army's withdrawal from its role as enforcer of the Fort Laramie Treaty, the influx of settlers into the Black Hills increased. The Government concluded that the only practical course was to secure to the citizens of the United States the right to mine the Black Hills for gold. Toward that end, the

Secretary of the Interior, in the spring of 1875, appointed a commission to negotiate with the Sioux. . . . The tribal leaders of the Sioux were aware of the mineral value of the Black Hills, and refused to sell the land for a price less than $70 million. The commission offered the Indians an annual rental of $400,000, or payment of $6 million for absolute relinquishment of the Black Hills. The negotiations broke down.

In the winter of 1875–1876, many of the Sioux were hunting in the unceded territory . . . reserved to them for that purpose. . . . On December 6, 1875, for reasons that are not entirely clear, the Commissioner of Indian Affairs sent instructions to the Indian agents on the reservation to notify those hunters that, if they did not return to the reservation agencies by January 31, 1876, they would be treated as "hostiles." Given the severity of the winter, compliance with these instructions was impossible. On February 1, the Secretary of the Interior nonetheless relinquished jurisdiction over all hostile Sioux, including those Indians exercising their treaty-protected hunting rights, to the War Department. The Army's campaign against the "hostiles" led to Sitting Bull's notable victory over Custer's forces at the battle of the Little Big Horn on June 25. That victory, of course, was short-lived, and those Indians who surrendered to the Army were returned to the reservation, and deprived of their weapons and horses, leaving them completely dependent for survival on rations provided them by the Government.

In the meantime, Congress was becoming increasingly dissatisfied with the failure of the Sioux living on the reservation to become self-sufficient. . . . In August, 1876, Congress enacted an appropriations bill providing that "hereafter there shall be no appropriation made for the subsistence" of the Sioux, unless they first relinquished their rights to the hunting grounds outside the reservation, ceded the Black Hills to the United States, and reached some accommodation with the Government that would be calculated to enable them to become self-supporting. Toward this end, Congress requested the President to appoint another commission to negotiate with the Sioux for the cession of the Black Hills.

This commission . . . arrived in the Sioux country in early September. . . . The commissioners brought with them the text of a treaty that had been prepared in advance. . . . [T]he commission ignored the stipulation of the Fort Laramie Treaty that any cession of the lands contained within the Great Sioux Reservation would have to be joined in by three-fourths of the adult males. . . . It was signed by only 10 % of the adult male Sioux population.

Congress resolved the impasse by enacting the 1876 "agreement" into law as the Act of Feb. 28, 1877 (1877 Act). . . .

The passage of the 1877 Act legitimized the settlers' invasion of the Black Hills, but, throughout the years, it has been regarded by the Sioux as a breach of this Nation's solemn obligation to reserve the Hills in perpetuity for occupation by the Indians. . . .

* * *

. . . The [Court of Claims] . . . remarked upon President Grant's duplicity in breaching the Government's treaty obligation to keep trespassers out of the Black Hills, and the pattern of duress practiced by the Government on the starving Sioux to get them to agree to the sale of the Black Hills. The court concluded:

> A more ripe and rank case of dishonorable dealings will never, in all probability, be found in our history. . . .

* * *

In reaching its conclusion that the 1877 Act effected a taking of the Black Hills for which just compensation was due the Sioux under the Fifth Amendment, the Court of Claims relied upon the "good faith effort" test developed in its earlier decision in *Three Tribes of Fort Berthold Reservation v. United States*. The *Fort Berthold* test had been designed to reconcile two lines of cases decided by this Court that seemingly were in conflict. . . .

The *Fort Berthold* test distinguishes between cases in which one or the other principle is applicable:

> It is obvious that Congress cannot simultaneously (1) act as trustee for the benefit of the Indians, exercising its plenary powers over the Indians and their property, as it thinks is in their best interests, and (2) exercise its sovereign power of eminent domain, taking the Indians' property within the meaning of the Fifth Amendment to the Constitution. In any given situation in which Congress has acted with regard to Indian people, it must have acted either in one capacity or the other. Congress can own two hats, but it cannot wear them both at the same time.

> . . . where Congress makes a good faith effort to give the Indians the full value of the land, and thus merely transmutes the property from land to money, there is no taking. This is a mere substitution of assets or change of form, and is a traditional function of a trustee.

Applying the *Fort Berthold* test to the facts of this case, the Court of Claims concluded that, in passing the 1877 Act, Congress had not made a good faith effort to give the Sioux the full value of the Black Hills. . . .

* * *

. . . We do not mean to imply that a reviewing court is to second-guess, from the perspective of hindsight, a legislative judgment that a particular measure would serve the best interests of the tribe. We do mean to require courts, in considering whether a particular congressional action was taken in pursuance of Congress' power to manage and control tribal lands for the Indians' welfare, to engage in a thorough-going and impartial examination of the historical record. A presumption of congressional good faith cannot serve to advance such an inquiry.

* * *

. . . [A[n essential element of the inquiry under the *Fort Berthold* guideline is determining the adequacy of the consideration the government gave for the Indian lands it acquired. That inquiry cannot be avoided by the government's simple assertion that it acted in good faith in its dealings with the Indians.

* * *

. . . the [Court of Claims] found, after engaging in an exhaustive review of the historical record, that neither the [1876] Commission, nor the congressional Committees that approved the 1877 Act, nor the individual legislators who spoke on its behalf on the floor of Congress ever indicated a belief that the Government's obligation to provide the Sioux with rations constituted a fair equivalent for the value of the Black Hills and the additional property rights the Indians were forced to surrender. . . .

* * *

In sum, we conclude that the legal analysis and factual findings of the Court of Claims fully support its conclusion that the terms of the 1877 Act did not effect "a mere change in the form of investment of Indian tribal property." Rather, the 1877 Act effected a taking of tribal property, property which had been set aside for the exclusive occupation of the Sioux by the Fort Laramie Treaty of 1868. That taking implied an obligation on the part of the Government to make just compensation to the Sioux Nation, and that obligation, including an award of interest, must now, at last, be paid.

* * *

MR. JUSTICE REHNQUIST, dissenting.

* * *

I think the Court today [rests its decision] largely on the basis of a view of the settlement of the American West which is not universally shared. There were undoubtedly greed, cupidity, and other less-than-admirable tactics employed by the Government during the Black Hills episode in the settlement of the West, but the Indians did not lack their share of villainy either. It seems to me quite unfair to judge by the light of "revisionist" historians or the mores of another era actions that were taken under pressure of time more than a century ago.

Different historians, not writing for the purpose of having their conclusions or observations inserted in the reports of congressional committees, have taken different positions than those expressed in some of the materials referred to in the Court's opinion. This is not unnatural, since history, no more than law, is not an exact (or, for that matter, an inexact) science.

But the inferences which the Court itself draws . . . leave a stereotyped and one-sided impression both of the settlement regarding the Black Hills portion of the Great Sioux Reservation and of the gradual expansion of the National Government. . . .

Ray Billington, a senior research associate at the Huntington Library in San Marino, Cal., since 1963, and a respected student of the settlement of the American West, emphasized in his introduction to the book Soldier and Brave (National Park Service, U.S. Dept. of the Interior 1963) that the confrontations in the West were the product of a long history, not a conniving Presidential administration:

> Three centuries of bitter Indian warfare reached a tragic climax on the plains and mountains of America's Far West. . . .

> . . . In three tragic decades, between 1860 and 1890, the Indians suffered the humiliating defeats that forced them to walk the white man's road toward civilization. Few conquered people in the history of mankind have paid so dearly for their defense of a way of life that the march of progress had outmoded. . . .

Another history highlights the cultural differences which made conflict and brutal warfare inevitable:

> The Plains Indians seldom practiced agriculture or other primitive arts, but they were fine physical specimens, and in warfare, once they

> had learned the use of the rifle, [were] much more formidable than
> the Eastern tribes who had slowly yielded to the white man. . . . They
> lived only for the day, recognized no rights of property, robbed or
> killed anyone if they thought they could get away with it, inflicted
> cruelty without a qualm, and endured torture without flinching.
>
> That there was tragedy, deception, barbarity, and virtually every other vice
> known to man in the 300-year history of the expansion of the original 13
> Colonies into a Nation which now embraces more than three million square
> miles and 50 States cannot be denied. But in a court opinion, as a historical and
> not a legal matter, both settler and Indian are entitled to the benefit of the
> Biblical adjuration: "Judge not, that ye be not judged."

The meandering and tortured history of this decades-long litigation raised a number of pertinent legal questions. For the purposes of this chapter, the case is important for two major reasons. First, Justice Harry Blackmun's majority opinion cemented what has come to be known as the "good faith effort" test in federal Indian law. As noted by the Court, the federal government can either exercise its plenary power (see Chapters 6 and 7) as a trustee for tribal nations or it can exercise its eminent domain authority over tribal lands (see Chapter 15), but it cannot do both at the same time. Put differently, the federal government can decide to sell or otherwise convert tribal lands—even over the objections of tribal members and nations or in contravention of the requirements of a treaty. But if the federal government makes this choice, then it has to make a "good faith effort to give the Indians the full value of the land." Failure to do so will result in liability for the federal government.

For reasons discussed in the following chapter, awards in these types of cases can be especially large. Yet they are not necessarily rewarding. In this particular case, part of which made its way through the Indian Claims Commission (see Chapter 8), the Sioux Nation was awarded approximately $106 million. However, the Black Hills have tremendous spiritual significance for Sioux peoples and the potential beneficiaries of the award have as yet refused the money in the hopes of gaining back the land. The monetary award continues to sit unclaimed and, with interest, is estimated to be over $1 billion.

Then Associate Justice William Rehnquist's dissent is the second major reason this case is important in Indian law. While he was the lone vote against tribal interests in what was an 8–1 case, Rehnquist's dissent raises troubling questions. For example, would Rehnquist's reasoning, language, and depictions of Native peoples, written in 1980, be out of place in the Allotment Era of the late nineteenth century or John Marshall's era in the early nineteenth century? Why or why not? For the purposes of this chapter it is also fair to ask what Rehnquist's perspective, as expressed in his dissent, would have meant for Native peoples under the trust responsibility. Earlier, this chapter considered the nature of the trust responsibility, and how it reflected upon Native peoples. Under Rehnquist's understanding, do the benefits of the trust responsibility outweigh the burdens? How should one interpret the then Associate Justice's statement, "Judge not, that ye be not judged"? What was Rehnquist's vision of the trust responsibility and what would it have meant for federal Indian law if it had won out in this case? Although his ruling did not control the outcome of this case, William Rehnquist cast a long shadow over federal Indian law during his thirty-three years on the Supreme Court. Understanding his vision of the field is useful to understanding the results in more modern cases.

THE *COBELL* LITIGATION

The federal government has not always honored its trust obligation to Native peoples. While examples of dishonorable dealings abound, none combine mismanagement, law, policy, history, and the difficulty in finding adequate solutions as prominently as the *Cobell* litigation. A brief detailing of this important saga will reveal the challenges that Native nations face in enforcing the trust responsibility, managing the legacy of federal policy, and gaining an adequate measure of justices for the failings of the federal government.

In the Allotment Era (see Chapter 5), the federal government divided communally held reservation lands into individual parcels, or allotments—such as those lands detailed in the *Mitchell* litigation in this chapter. The purpose of this endeavor was, among other reasons, to encourage Native individuals to live as individual landholders and farmers in the Western tradition. While some individuals attempted to live in the Western model, many did not. In addition, many of the parcels of divided lands were not suitable for the style of farming that the federal government sought to encourage or were otherwise inadequate for the lifestyle the federal government sought to impose on Native individuals.

As a consequence, the federal government regularly used individual allotments in ways that Native individuals chose not to or were prohibited from during the Allotment Era—renting the land, logging, etc. These parcels of land were held in trust by the federal government under the Allotment Act and the rents and other benefits from the use of the land were supposed to be for the benefit of the Native individuals for whom the federal government was holding the land in trust. To manage the vast number of tracts all across Native America that were being used under this system, the federal government established an accounting system that was intended to keep track of what was labeled Individual Indian Money (IIM).

The IIM system proved to be unwieldy and an example of the shortsightedness of the Allotment Era. The number of IIM accounts was vast, and tribal superintendents regularly complained about the work that they produced. In addition, many tribal superintendents were not adequately trained or equipped to manage the multitude of accountings produced by the IIM. Such a system also proved susceptible to corruption and embezzlement. All told, the IIM accounts created more engagement with Native America in a policy era when the federal government was attempting to end its role in Indian affairs, were inadequately administered by federal bureaucrats who may not have been competent to do the work and/or stole from the accounts, and steadily became impossible to keep track of.

In the mid-1990s a collection of Native peoples, anchored by the lead plaintiff Elouise Cobell, filed a class action lawsuit against the federal government seeking an accounting for the IIM monies. However, decades after most of the IIM accounts were first established, the federal government was in no position to render an adequate accounting. The federal government's inability to produce anything close to a full accounting, coupled with stories of the federal government engaging in obstructionist efforts even after being ordered to produce an accounting, led to a protracted litigation in which, among other things, high ranking federal officials were held in contempt of court and the website for the Department of the Interior—which houses the Bureau of Indian Affairs—was ordered to be shut down on several occasions. The original trial court judge in the case, in one of his many orders, stated that, "After all these years, our government still treats Native American Indians as if they were somehow less than deserving of the respect that should be afforded to everyone in a society where all people are supposed to be equal. . . . Alas, our 'modern' Interior department has time and again demonstrated that it is a dinosaur—the morally and culturally oblivious hand-me-down of a disgracefully racist and imperialist government that should have been buried a century ago, the last pathetic outpost of the indifference and anglocentrism we thought we had left behind."[6] Shortly after issuing this order, the original trial judge was removed from the case on the request of the United States—a highly uncommon occurrence.

The full details of the litigation and its resolution are better described elsewhere. It suffices to note that it eventually became clear to all involved that the Bureau of Indian Affairs—through the Department of the Interior—simply could not comply with federal court orders to produce an accounting for the IIM accounts and that another solution was necessary. Eventually Congress stepped in and, with negotiations among the involved parties, crafted legislation to resolve the issue. Passed in 2010, the Claims Resolution Act set aside $3.4 billion to accomplish a number of goals. Approximately $1.4 billion was devoted to settle the claims of the plaintiffs in the *Cobell* case. Another approximately $1.9 billion was devoted to a land consolidation fund to buy fractionalized land interests from tribal members (see Chapter 5). The rest was devoted to various other endeavors, such as a scholarship program, attorneys' fees, and similar matters. The final total of the Claims Resolution Act was well short of the over $46 billion that some estimated the federal government owed the plaintiffs, and some persons (including the lawyers for the plaintiffs, who sought additional attorneys' fees) objected to the settlement with their own lawsuits. However, these efforts did not meet with success and the case was finalized in 2011.

The *Cobell* litigation, coupled with the *Mitchell* cases and their progeny, are reflective of the structural and historical complications that confront the trust doctrine. Oftentimes the only defense against the plenary power of the federal government, the trust doctrine is nonetheless subject to the affirmative actions that the federal government does or does not take. It may also do more harm than is visible from the surface. Thus, it is fair to ask if the trust doctrine perpetuates an understanding of Native peoples and nations as inferior. Nonetheless, the trust doctrine remains a foundational principle of Indian law, one to which Native America often turns.

SUGGESTED READINGS

- " 'We Need Protection From Our Protectors': The Nature, Issues, and Future of the Federal Trust Responsibility to Indians." Daniel I.S.J. Rey-Bear and Matthew L.M. Fletcher. 6 *Michigan Journal of Environmental and Administrative Law* 397 (Spring 2017).

- *The Lakota and the Black Hills: The Struggle for Sacred Ground.* Jeffery Ostler. New York: Viking, 2010.

- "The *Cobell* Trust Fund Litigation and Settlement: An 'Accounting Coup.' " David E. Wilkins. In *Hollow Justice: A History of Indigenous Claims in the United States.* New Haven, CT: Yale University Press, 2013.

---

1 *Indian Affairs, Laws & Treaties, Vol. 2.* Charles J. Kappler, comp. Washington D.C.: GPO, 1904, 7.
2 Id., 867.
3 316 U.S. 286 (1942).

4   537 U.S. 488 (2003).

5   537 U.S. 465 (2003).

6   Cobell v. Norton, 229 F.R.D. 5, 7 (D. D.C. 2005).

Land I—Indian Title

At the very center of the interactions between colonizing forces and Native peoples is land. From the beginning, colonizers have wanted to acquire it and Native peoples have wanted to preserve and maintain their connections and relationship to it. Treaties, in many respects, are essentially land sales. Many of the continuing areas of dispute in federal Indian law—jurisdiction, natural resources, etc.—are a direct result over conflicts about land. Land is such a foundational part of federal Indian law that it is the subject of the next two chapters.

In the first case of his seminal trilogy, *Johnson v. McIntosh*, John Marshall integrated the Doctrine of Discovery into American law (see Chapter 2). Under the Doctrine of Discovery, Indigenous peoples are divested of the full title of their lands and retain what is known as Indian title or Indigenous title or the right to Occupancy. While Marshall gave some rough understandings as to what "Indian title" constituted, the need for further clarification continued after *Johnson v. McIntosh*. Throughout the course of American history, federal courts have had to confront a number of difficult questions. What is the scope of Indian title? How and when has it been recognized? How and when has it been taken away? What rights to tribal nations have under Indian title? What are the consequences when tribal nations reacquire previously held lands? This chapter examines some of those foundational questions and their answers in American law.

This chapter will demonstrate. . .

- *The relationship between Indian title and 5th Amendment takings*

- *The parameters under which the United States recognizes Indian title*

- *The relationship between Indian title and reacquired tribal lands*

INDIAN TITLE AND FEDERAL TAKINGS

In order to gain some understanding of the scope of Indian title, it is vital to have a sense of the federal government's relationship to land in the United States more broadly. The Takings Clause of the 5th Amendment of the U.S. Constitution, and consequently the principle of eminent domain, provide necessary context.

Depending on one's perspective, the federal government is either allowed to confiscate private property if, or prohibited from doing so unless, it satisfies two conditions: 1) The federal government pays "just compensation" for the property, and 2) the property is to be put to a public use. Also known as the eminent domain power, this highly controversial principle of American law has generated its share of litigation and acrimony. For the purposes of this chapter, it suffices to note that the federal government (and state governments) can acquire the land of a typical private landowner, even over the objections of that landowner, if the federal government pays just compensation and puts the land to a public use (such as building a road or other similar uses).

Nonetheless, a tribal nation is not a typical private landowner and Indian title is not the same type of interest in land that a typical private landowner holds. Consequently, when the federal government takes tribally held lands, a different set of questions arises. How similar or dissimilar is Indian title to the title held by a typical private landholder? Following in that same vein, does a taking of lands held under Indian title impose the same 5th Amendment requirements of just compensation and a public use? What limits, if any, are there to the eminent domain power when exercised over tribally held lands under Indian title?

The following case also introduces another challenging question to the equation: if there was a compensable taking, when did it occur? For reasons that are explained in greater detail after the case, establishing the date of a taking is fundamentally significant in its own right. As you read the case, make a timeline of the important events. Also, ask yourself why, as the opinion notes, both parties were disappointed with the result at the trial court level. How does the Court characterize Indian title? How does the Court characterize federal interests in tribal lands? Finally, also consider how the facts of the case reflect the historical moment in which they occurred.

U.S. v. SHOSHONE TRIBE
299 U.S. 476 (1937)

MR. JUSTICE CARDOZO delivered the opinion of the Court.

The Shoshone Tribe of Indians of the Wind River Reservation in Wyoming has sued the United States in the Court of Claims for the breach of treaty stipulations whereby the tribe has been permanently excluded from the possession and enjoyment of an undivided half interest in the tribal lands. . . .

The court gave judgment for the claimant. Neither party to the controversy was satisfied with the award of damages, the claimant finding it too low and the government too high. . . .

By Treaty of July 3, 1868, the Shoshone Tribe of Indians relinquished to the United States a reservation of 44,672,000 acres in Colorado, Utah, Idaho, and Wyoming, and accepted in exchange a reservation of 3,054,182 acres in Wyoming, with other benefits not now important. The United States agreed that the territory described in the treaty now generally known as the Wind River Reservation would be

> set apart for the absolute and undisturbed use and occupation of the
> Shoshone Indians . . . and for such other friendly tribes or individual
> Indians as from time to time they may be willing, with the consent of
> the United States, to admit amongst them.

Reinforcing this covenant, there was a solemn pledge of faith by the United States that no persons . . . should "ever be permitted to pass over, settle upon, or reside" in the territory so reserved. The loyalty of the Shoshone Tribe to the people of the United States has been conspicuous and unfaltering. A fidelity at least as constant and inflexible was owing in return.

In 1869, a band of the Northern Arapahoes, separating from the main body of the nation, was wandering about the country, looking for a home. The Arapahoes had been allies of the Sioux, who were the foes of the Shoshones. Nonetheless, the wanderers expressed a wish to have a refuge and a settlement

Chapter 15

on the Wind River Reservation. They came upon the reservation in 1870, and were informed by Washakie, Chief of the Shoshones, that they would be permitted to stay there for a short time while the government was seeking to place them elsewhere. After a few months, they moved away. The government had no success, however, in providing them with a satisfactory home, and they continued to cast longing eyes toward the fair and fertile acres set apart for their ancestral foes. At the instance of the Commissioner of Indian Affairs, acting in cooperation with the Secretary of the Interior, a new attempt was made in October, 1877, to bring the tribes together and relieve the growing tension developing between them. One Irwin, formerly the Indian agent on the Wind River Reservation, discussed the problem with Washakie. He said that the President had no intention of placing the Arapahoes on the Shoshone Reservation, but that the desire was merely to insure peace between the tribes and to find a place for the Arapahoes nearby, on a separate tract of land close to the eastern boundary. Washakie agreed that there should be peace, but insisted that the traditional enemies of his tribe be placed at a safe distance, predicting that close contact would bring friction and fresh hostility.

Irwin telegraphed the Commissioner of Indian Affairs at Washington on October 17, 1877: "I returned from Shoshone Agency today. Held a council and made peace between Shoshones and Arapahoes." . . . [T]he telegram, it seems, had been misunderstood by the Commissioner, for, in his annual report for 1877 he said:

> In a formal council held last month by Agent Irwin with the Shoshones, their consent to the arrangement desired by the Arapahoes was obtained, and the removal of the latter is now in progress.

Ignoring many warnings in February and later that consent had been refused, the Commissioner adhered to his erroneous assumption. The consequences of his error are visible in the events that followed.

On March 18, 1878, a band of Northern Arapahoes was brought to the Reservation of the Shoshones under military escort. . . . The unheralded arrival of the Arapahoes was the cause of much excitement. There was a council the next day at which the leader of the Arapahoes explained to Washakie that they and their horses were weary and without food, and in need of rest and care. Thereupon, Washakie agreed that they might remain for a short time to rest their horses and themselves. But the Indian Commissioner, it seems, had not brought them to the reservation for any temporary visit. On April 2, 1878, he telegraphed the agent at the reservation to furnish the Arapahoes with the necessary food and supplies. . . . The agent responded that the Shoshones looked upon the presence of the Arapahoes as "an encroachment on their rights." At the request of both tribes, he urged the calling of a council to be attended by the Department Commander, General Crook, in order that the location of the Arapahoes might be permanently settled. No reply to this request came from the Commissioner or from anyone else.

The famished Arapahoes and their horses had been fed and cared for, but they did not move away. Instead of moving away, they came in increasing numbers. As early as April 8, 1878, nearly the whole tribe was on the scene. Washakie protested to the agent. The agent at frequent intervals communicated the protests to the Commissioner. There was nothing in return but silence. Months lengthened into years, and the signs accumulated steadily that the Arapahoes were there to stay. . . . In numberless other ways, their equality of right and privilege became a postulate of daily life. At length, in August, 1891, the flame of controversy blazed forth anew. . . . In . . . August 13, 1891, the Commissioner notified the Commission:

> This office holds . . . that the Arapahoes have equal rights to the land on the said reservation which does not depend upon the further consent of the Shoshones, and you should conduct your negotiations with them upon that basis and with that understanding.

* * *

The Commissioner continued to act on the assumption that the occupancy of the Arapahoes, initiated, as we have seen, under military escort, was permanent and rightful. What is more to the point, Congress did the same. . . .

Again the government dealt with the two tribes as lawful occupants and equals. . . .

Nowhere is there a suggestion that the occupancy of the newcomers is impermanent or provisional.

[*Congress passed a jurisdictional act for the Shoshones in 1927*]

Upon these facts, the Court of Claims decided that the occupancy of the Arapahoes became definitive and permanent on August 13, 1891, when the Commissioner of Indian Affairs made public statement of his opinion that they were entitled to enjoy the reservation equally with the Shoshones. . . . As already stated, neither the claimant nor the government is content with the decision. Both agree that there was error in fixing the value of the land as of

August 13, 1891. The claimant insists that it should be reckoned as of March 3, 1927, the date of the jurisdictional act, and that compensation should be added for the value of the intermediate use and occupation. The government insists that the value should be reckoned as of March 18, 1878, when the unlawful occupancy began. The claimant makes the additional point that, irrespective of the date at which the value is computed, interest must be awarded up to the date of the judgment on the recovery allowed.

First: the Court of Claims did not err in refusing to fix the damages on the basis of the value of the land on March 3, 1927.

The claimant takes the ground that the jurisdictional act is an exercise of the power of eminent domain. The argument is that, by force of its provisions, a trespass which had been unlawful, though continuous, since March 18, 1878, was turned, as of March, 1927, into a definitive and lawful taking. But this is to mistake utterly the design and meaning of the statute. The jurisdictional act is not a taking of anything. . . .

* * *

Second: the Court of Claims erred in holding that damages should be measured as of August 13, 1891, the date of the letter from the Commissioner of Indian Affairs to the Woodruff Commission, and in failing to measure them as of 1878, the date of the unlawful entry.

The treaty of 1868 charged the government with a duty to see to it that strangers should never be permitted without the consent of the Shoshones to settle upon or reside in the Wind River Reservation. That duty was not fulfilled. Instead, the Arapahoes were brought upon the reservation with a show of military power, and kept there in defiance of the duty to expel them. . . . [The Commissioner of Indian Affairs] had made report to the Secretary of the Interior in November, 1877, that the transfer of the Arapahoes to the Wind River Reservation was a movement then in progress. He had notified the local agent in April, 1878, to indicate any other measures necessary to settle the intruders. He had turned a deaf ear to many a remonstrance by the tribe whose possession had been violated. Insofar as his own opinion and intention were facts of any moment, he had manifested them too often and too plainly, by conduct and by speech alike, to leave his attitude in doubt. . . .

* * *

Confusion is likely to result from speaking of the wrong to the Shoshones as a destruction of their title. Title in the strict sense was always in the United States, though the Shoshones had the treaty right of occupancy with all its beneficial incidents. What those incidents are, it is needless to consider now. The right of occupancy is the primary one to which the incidents attach and division of the right with strangers is an appropriation of the land ... in substance, if not in form.

Third: the claimant's damages include such additional amount beyond the value of its property rights when taken by the government as may be necessary to award of just compensation, the increment to be measured either by interest on the value or by such other standard as may be suitable in the light of all the circumstances.

... Given such a taking, the right to interest or a fair equivalent, attaches itself automatically to the right to an award of damages. ... Nor does the nature of the right divested avail to modify the rule. Power to control and manage the property and affairs of Indians in good faith for their betterment and welfare may be exerted in many ways and at times even in derogation of the provisions of a treaty. The power does not extend so far as to enable the government

> to give the tribal lands to others, or to appropriate them to its own purposes, without rendering, or assuming an obligation to render, just compensation; ... for that would not be an exercise of guardianship, but an act of confiscation.

The right of the Indians to the occupancy of the lands pledged to them may be one of occupancy only, but it is "as sacred as that of the United States to the fee."

At a fundamental level, the opinion in *Shoshone Tribe* stated that when the federal government takes land held under Indian title it must compensate the tribal nation for that taking. Despite the Court's assertion that "Title in the strict sense was always in the United States," today American law recognizes takings of Indian title as takings under the 5th Amendment. As a consequence, tribal nations who hold Indian title to land must receive just compensation when the federal government takes those lands, as like what happened to the Shoshone in this instance.

Determining that there was a taking was only the first stage of the analysis, however. It is also necessary to determine when the taking occurred for two very important reasons. First, the date that the land was taken by the federal government determines what the fair market value of the land was. Generally, when a taking occurs earlier, when the land is less developed, the fair market value is going to be less than a later taking, when the land is more developed and more valuable to prospective buyers.

The trial court determined the taking to have occurred in 1891 when the Commissioner of Indian Affairs announced that the Arapahoe had equal claim to the reservation. The federal government argued that the taking was earlier, in 1878 when the Arapahoe were brought to the reservation under military escort. The Shoshone argued that the date of the taking was in 1927 when Congress passed a special jurisdictional act, authorizing the Shoshone lawsuit. The federal government argued for the earlier date because the fair market value of the land was less in 1878 than it was in 1891. Conversely, the Shoshone argued for the later 1927 date because increased settlement, improvements to the land, greater infrastructure, and other similar incidents greatly increased the value of the taken land. The Supreme Court sided with the federal government and found the taking occurred when the Arapahoe were taken by military escort to the reservation.

Finding the taking at the earlier date was not a complete loss for the Shoshone, leading to the second important reason courts need to determine the date of a taking. Critical to this case, and in many other cases more so, the Supreme Court in *Shoshone Tribe* ruled that Indian title lands that are taken by the federal government are not only subject to payment for the taking itself, but are also subject to interest, "or a fair equivalent." Unlike many typical eminent domain cases, which tend to initiate quickly after the government announces or enacts a taking, many of the takings cases originating in Native America have historical roots. For any number of reasons, tribal nations were not able to pursue the claims when they first happened. For example, despite several complaints over the course of many years about this situation that began in 1869, the Shoshone were unable to sue the federal government until they received the special jurisdictional act in 1927 (see Chapter 8). The length of time between the taking and a ruling for a tribal nation in these types of cases has often meant that the interest on a claim can often be significantly more than just the fair market value of the land itself.

Thus, Indian title is compensable when it is taken by the federal government, and it is now recognized as a 5th Amendment taking. Interest must also be paid on a taking, often resulting in much greater financial compensation than the original taking itself. Yet, this raises another question: When can a tribal nation claim under American law that it has rightful Indian title?

RECOGNIZING INDIAN TITLE

The Court in *Shoshone Tribe* was considering the fate of what might be called recognized Indian title. As noted by the Court, the Shoshone maintained a reservation of their original ancestral lands through an 1868 treaty. In coming to that 1868 treaty, the United States recognized and affirmed the Shoshones' claim over the lands ceded in the treaty and the Shoshones' right to sell it. The treaty "recognized" the Shoshones' claim to Indian title over the land.

The process of recognition has become important in federal Indian law because it validates tribal claims to land under American law. Merely making a claim over property does not necessarily mean that others will respect that claim. For example, one might make a claim to a New York City skyscraper, Antarctica, or even the moon, yet those claims are not likely to be respected by others. By its very nature, recognition is a bi- or multi-lateral process in which one or many affirm or otherwise support the claims of another entity.

How do tribal nations acquire recognition of their land claims? Put another way, under what conditions does the federal government have to recognize a tribal nation's right to Indian title? In the mid-20th century the federal government began foresting lands in Alaska in a national forest on lands that the Tee-Hit-Ton argued that they had never ceded. Once the logging commenced, the Tee-Hit-Ton sought compensation for the taking of their timber property. As you read the next case, ask yourself what distinguishes these facts from the facts in *Shoshone Tribe*. What are the components that the Court identifies that will establish a recognition of Indian title? What is the fundamental connection between recognition and Indian title? What consequences does this ruling hold for Native America?

TEE-HIT-TON INDIANS V. U.S.
348 U.S. 272 (1955)

MR. JUSTICE REED delivered the opinion of the Court.

This case rests upon a claim under the Fifth Amendment by petitioner, an identifiable group of American Indians of between 60 and 70 individuals residing in Alaska, for compensation for a taking by the United States of certain timber from Alaskan lands allegedly belonging to the group. The area claimed is said to contain over 350,000 acres of land and 150 square miles of water. The Tee-Hit-Tons, a clan of the Tlingit Tribe, brought this suit.... The compensation claimed does not arise from any statutory direction to pay....

* * *

The Alaskan area in which petitioner claims a compensable interest is located near and within the exterior lines of the Tongass National Forest. By Joint Resolution of August 8, 1947, the Secretary of Agriculture was authorized to contract for the sale of national forest timber located within this National Forest "notwithstanding any claim of possessory rights." The Resolution defines "possessory rights," and provides for all receipts from the sale of timber to be maintained in a special account in the Treasury until the timber and land rights are finally determined. Section 3(b) of the Resolution provides:

> Nothing in this resolution shall be construed as recognizing or denying the validity of any claims of possessory rights to lands or timber within the exterior boundaries of the Tongass National Forest.

The Secretary of Agriculture, on August 20, 1951, pursuant to this authority contracted for sale to a private company of all merchantable timber in the area claimed by petitioner. This is the sale of timber which petitioner alleges constitutes a compensable taking by the United States of a portion of its proprietary interest in the land.

The problem presented is the nature of the petitioner's interest in the land, if any. Petitioner claims a "full proprietary ownership" of the land, or, in the alternative, at least a "recognized" right to unrestricted possession, occupation and use. Either ownership or recognized possession, petitioner asserts, is compensable.... It is petitioner's contention that its tribal predecessors have continually claimed, occupied, and used the land from time immemorial; that, when Russia took Alaska, the Tlingits had a well developed social order which included a concept of property ownership; that Russia, while it possessed Alaska, in no manner interfered with their claim to the land; that Congress has, by subsequent acts, confirmed and recognized petitioner's right to occupy the land permanently, and therefore the sale of the timber off such lands constitutes a taking . . . of its asserted rights in the area.

The Government denies that petitioner has any compensable interest. It asserts that the Tee-Hit-Tons' property interest, if any, is merely that of the right to the use of the land at the Government's will; that Congress has never recognized any legal interest of petitioner in the land, and therefore, without such recognition, no compensation is due the petitioner for any taking by the United States.

I.   Recognition.—The question of recognition may be disposed of shortly. Where the Congress, by treaty or other agreement, has declared that, thereafter, Indians were to hold the lands permanently, compensation must be paid for subsequent taking. The petitioner contends that Congress has sufficiently "recognized" its possessory rights in the land in question so as to make its interest compensable. Petitioner points specifically to two statutes to sustain this contention. . . .

We have carefully examined these statutes and the pertinent legislative history, and find nothing to indicate any intention by Congress to grant to the Indians any permanent rights in the lands of Alaska occupied by them by permission of Congress. . . . There is no particular form for congressional recognition of Indian right of permanent occupancy. It may be established in a variety of ways, but there must be the definite intention by congressional action or authority to accord legal rights, not merely permissive occupation.

* * *

II.   Indian Title.—(a) The nature of aboriginal Indian interest in land and the various rights as between the Indians and the United States dependent on such interest are far from novel as concerns our Indian inhabitants. It is well settled that, in all the States of the Union, the tribes who inhabited the lands of the States held claim to such lands after the coming of the white man, under what is sometimes termed original Indian title or permission from the whites to occupy. That description means mere possession not specifically recognized as ownership by Congress. After conquest, they were permitted to occupy portions of territory over which they had previously exercised "sovereignty," as we use that term. This is not a property right, but amounts to a right of occupancy which the sovereign grants and protects against intrusion by third parties, but which right of occupancy may be terminated and such lands fully disposed of by the sovereign itself without any legally enforceable obligation to compensate the Indians.

This position of the Indian has long been rationalized by the legal theory that discovery and conquest gave the conquerors sovereignty over and ownership of the lands thus obtained. The great case of *Johnson v. McIntosh* denied the power of an Indian tribe to pass their right of occupancy to another. It confirmed the practice of two hundred years of American history "that discovery gave an exclusive right to extinguish the Indian title of occupancy, either by purchase or by conquest."

* * *

No case in this Court has ever held that taking of Indian title or use by Congress required compensation. The American people have compassion for the descendants of those Indians who were deprived of their homes and hunting grounds by the drive of civilization. They seek to have the Indians share the benefits of our society as citizens of this Nation. Generous provision has been willingly made to allow tribes to recover for wrongs as a matter of grace, not because of legal liability.

* * *

. . . Indian occupation of land without government recognition of ownership creates no rights against taking or extinction by the United States protected by the Fifth Amendment or any other principle of law.

The Tee-Hit-Tons urge, however, that their stage of civilization and their concept of ownership of property takes them out of the rule applicable to the Indians of the States. . . .

In considering the character of the Tee-Hit-Tons' use of the land, the Court of Claims had before it the testimony of a single witness who was offered by plaintiff. He stated that he was the chief of the Tee-Hit-Ton tribe. He qualified as an expert on the Tlingits, a group composed of numerous interconnected tribes, including the Tee-Hit-Tons. His testimony showed that the Tee-Hit-Tons had become greatly reduced in numbers. Membership descends only through the female line. At the present time, there are only a few women of childbearing age, and to total membership of some 65.

The witness learned the alleged boundaries of the Tee-Hit-Ton area from hunting and fishing with his uncle after his return from Carlisle Indian School about 1904. From the knowledge so obtained, he outlined in red on the map, which petitioner filed as an exhibit, the territory claimed by the Tee-Hit-Tons. Use by other tribal members is sketchily asserted. . . .

* * *

The line of cases adjudicating Indian rights on American soil leads to the conclusion that Indian occupancy, not specifically recognized as ownership by action authorized by Congress, may be extinguished by the Government without compensation. Every American schoolboy knows that the savage tribes of this continent were deprived of their ancestral ranges by force and that, even when the Indians ceded millions of acres by treaty in return for blankets, food, and trinkets, it was not a sale, but the conquerors' will that deprived them of their land. . . .

In the light of the history of Indian relations in this Nation, no other course would meet the problem of the growth of the United States except to make congressional contributions for Indian lands rather than to subject the Government to an obligation to pay the value when taken with interest to the date of payment. Our conclusion does not uphold harshness as against tenderness toward the Indians, but it leaves with Congress, where it belongs, the policy of Indian gratuities for the termination of Indian occupancy of Government-owned land, rather than making compensation for its value a rigid constitutional principle.

The Court in Tee-Hit-Ton looked at two potential sources of the tribal assertion of federal recognition to their claims: statutes and Indian title. The Court fairly perfunctorily disposed of the statutes as a source of recognition. More important for this chapter, the Court also examined Indian title. At its essence, the principle established by *Tee-Hit-Ton* is that "Indian occupation of land without government recognition of ownership creates no rights against taking or extinction by the United States protected by the Fifth Amendment or any other principle of law." In short, the United States does not have to provide compensation for any takings of tribal lands that it does not recognize. There are two major ways to understand this ruling.

On one hand, this is a ruling of limited impact. By the time the case was decided in 1955 there was little if any land left in the United States that had not been recognized by the federal government and that had not either been ceded or reserved through a treaty or other similar means. Alaska, which was still a few years from being admitted to the Union when the decision was announced, posed a unique situation that is unlikely to be replicated again. In addition, Alaska Natives did eventually gain some measure of recognition and support when Congress passed the Alaska Native Claims Settlement Act in 1971 (see Chapter 28).

On the other hand, *Tee-Hit-Ton* has been excoriated by many commentators for a number of troubling aspects, including depicting Native peoples with the same rhetoric used in cases from the previous century and describing tribal rights with weaker language than that found in cases from the previous century. Perhaps the most striking elements of the opinion are the self-sustaining declarations of the opinion's correctness, the fragile state in which the Court describes tribal rights, and the lessened status the Court accords tribal expertise.

In Justice Stanley Reed's most infamous sentence, the Court stated that "Every American schoolboy knows" that Native peoples were "deprived of their ancestral ranges by force." The "blankets, food, and trinkets" that Native peoples received for their lands "was not a sale," but rather it was, "the conquerors' will that deprived them of their land." Similarly, Reed seemed to eschew any legal liability the United States might hold toward Native peoples earlier in the opinion when he wrote, "Generous provision has been willingly made to allow tribes to recover for wrongs as a matter of grace, not because of legal liability." These far-reaching statements serve primarily to justify themselves. Just as disturbingly, the Court's reliance on the discredited racial science of previous generations and the diminution of tribal sources of authority demonstrated the racialized perspective at the heart of the case.

Others have also pointed out that the result in this case, and the way the Court came to it, may have also been motivated by another concern beyond the state of the law. In a footnote in the opinion, Justice Reed wrote that, "The government pointed out that if aboriginal Indian title was compensable without specific legislation to that effect, there were claims with an estimated interest already pending . . . aggregating $9,000,000,000." This staggering sum potentially left a major impression with the Justices. Presuming that the nine billion dollar estimate was both correct and did influence the decision in this case, at what point, if any, does the potential award for a claim outweigh the justice supporting the claim?

Imagine a scenario in which an individual sues a local government for police brutality, false imprisonment, and similar claims and is able to prove several millions of dollars worth of damages. Imagine also that the sum of the damages is large enough to bankrupt the local government and threaten the welfare of several local services. Should the local government be forced to pay the award to one citizen despite the impact that it would have on the larger local community? Can a government ever create so much harm that it no longer should be financially responsible for the harm? Is it the responsibility of the courts to prevent more widespread difficulty at the expense of justice for one or a few? Is there a truly just outcome in this hypothetical?

These types of questions have fueled jurisprudential debate for many years and may very well have had an impact on the Court's decision. However, it is also worth asking if the situation in *Tee-Hit-Ton* is truly analogous to the hypothetical proposed above. Where are the similarities and the differences? Do the different fact patterns change your analysis as to the proper outcome?

According to the Court, a total of sixty-five tribal members were claiming Indian title to "350,000 acres of land and 150 square miles of water." By far the largest state by land, Alaska has proven to be resource-rich as well. Unlike the hypothetical detailed above, the Tee-Hit-Ton case alone did not pose a threat to the overall fiscal well-being of the United States. Rather, it is fair to ask whether the Justices were comfortable the possibility of so few Native peoples having access to so much wealth. Did Native America suffer an adverse ruling because mid-20th century Supreme Court Justices could not conceive of rich Indians? Is there another reason why it would not seem to matter to the Court that the tribal members occupied the land long before any colonization?

Regardless of the ruling's impetus, the end result of the case is that "every American schoolboy knows" that Indian title must first be recognized by the federal government before a tribal nation can claim a taking of that property. This is in spite of any actual possession or use of the property by tribal members. According to *Tee-Hit-Ton*, the actions of the colonized are less important to establishing their possession over property than the actions of the colonizers.

REVIVING INDIAN TITLE

In the Allotment Era tribal nations and individuals lost over ninety million acres of land—approximately the same amount of territory comprising the state of Montana. Since then, tribal nations have sought to regain portions of that territory, with some limited success. At times the federal government has been instrumental in these efforts. However, more recently, tribal nations have gained increasing economic ability to repurchase lands themselves.

Ownership of property carries with it control over the property. Yet, as many chapters in this text attest, the scope of control over tribal lands is often a question under American law. What is the status of repurchased lands? Is the land held under Indian title? Do tribal nations have the same scope of authority over repurchased lands that they do over, say, reservation lands? How can a tribal nation exert its fullest authority over repurchased lands?

In the facts of the next case—another step in a longstanding series of cases between the Oneidas and divisions of the state of New York that reached the Supreme Court—the Oneidas began purchasing parcels of land that were within the historic boundaries of the tribal reservation and presently within the city of Sherrill, NY, and surrounding areas. When the city sought to collect property taxes, the Oneida objected, arguing that the land had once again become Indian Country and could not be taxed by the city.

In order to understand the decision in the case, it is helpful to know something about the type of "relief" or judgment that courts can award. In general, there are two broad categories of relief: monetary damages and equitable relief. Monetary damages, as the name implies, are awards of money. Equitable relief, on the other hand, generally consists of orders from a court, such as injunctions, that require a party to a case to engage in action or to refrain from action. As you read the case, ask yourself how the Supreme Court describes the property that was reacquired by the Oneida. What type of relief do the Oneida seek and how does the Court respond? What doctrines or principles of law does the Court use to come to its decision? What are the consequences of those doctrines? What are the alternatives that the Supreme Court proposes? Are they viable?

CITY OF SHERRILL V. ONEIDA INDIAN NATION OF NEW YORK
544 U.S. 197 (2004)

JUSTICE GINSBURG delivered the opinion of the Court.

This case concerns properties in the city of Sherrill, New York, purchased by the Oneida Indian Nation of New York (OIN or Tribe) in 1997 and 1998. The separate parcels of land in question, once contained within the Oneidas' 300,000-acre reservation, were last possessed by the Oneidas as a tribal entity in 1805. For two centuries, governance of the area in which the properties are located has been provided by the State of New York and its county and municipal units. . . . In the instant action, OIN resists the payment of property taxes to Sherrill on the ground that OIN's acquisition of . . . discrete parcels of historic reservation land revived the Oneidas' ancient sovereignty piecemeal over each parcel. Consequently, the Tribe maintains, regulatory authority over OIN's newly purchased properties no longer resides in Sherrill.

. . . Today, we decline to project redress for the Tribe into the present and future, thereby disrupting the governance of central New York's counties and towns. Generations have passed during which non-Indians have owned and developed the area that once composed the Tribe's historic reservation. And at least since the middle years of the 19th century, most of the Oneidas have resided elsewhere. Given the longstanding, distinctly non-Indian character of the area and its inhabitants, the regulatory authority constantly exercised by New York State and its counties and towns, and the Oneidas' long delay in seeking judicial relief against parties other than the United States, we hold that the Tribe cannot unilaterally revive its ancient sovereignty, in whole or in part, over the parcels at issue. The Oneidas long ago relinquished the reins of government and cannot regain them through open-market purchases from current titleholders.

* * *

In the years after the Revolutionary War, "the State of New York came under increasingly heavy pressure to open the Oneidas' land for settlement." Reflective of that pressure, in 1788, New York State and the Oneida Nation entered into the Treaty of Fort Schuyler. . . . OIN does not here contest the legitimacy of the Fort Schuyler conveyance or the boundaries of the reserved area.

* * *

. . . In 1838, the Oneidas and the United States entered into the Treaty of Buffalo Creek, which envisioned removal of all remaining New York Indians, including the Oneidas, to Kansas. By this time, the Oneidas had sold all but 5,000 acres of their original reservation. Six hundred of their members resided in Wisconsin, while 620 remained in New York State.

* * *

The Oneidas who stayed on in New York after the proclamation of the Buffalo Creek Treaty continued to diminish in number and, during the 1840s, sold most of their remaining lands to the State. A few hundred Oneidas moved to Canada in 1842, and "by the mid-1840s, only about 200 Oneidas remained in New York State." By 1843, the New York Oneidas retained less than 1,000 acres in the State. That acreage dwindled to 350 in 1890; ultimately, by 1920, only 32 acres continued to be held by the Oneidas.

The United States eventually abandoned its efforts to remove the New York Indians to Kansas. . . .

* * *

This brings us to the present case, which concerns parcels of land in the city of Sherrill, located in Oneida County, New York. According to the 2000 census, over 99% of the population in the area is non-Indian: American Indians represent less than 1% of the city of Sherrill's population and less than 0.5% of Oneida County's population. OIN owns approximately 17,000 acres of land scattered throughout the Counties of Oneida and Madison, representing less than 1.5% of the counties' total area. OIN's predecessor, the Oneida Nation, had transferred the parcels at issue to one of its members in 1805, who sold the land to a non-Indian in 1807. The properties thereafter remained in non-Indian hands until OIN's acquisitions in 1997 and 1998 in open-market transactions. OIN now operates commercial enterprises on these parcels: a gasoline station, a convenience store, and a textile facility.

Because the parcels lie within the boundaries of the reservation originally occupied by the Oneidas, OIN maintained that the properties are exempt from taxation, and accordingly refused to pay the assessed property taxes. . . .

* * *

. . . When the Oneidas came before this Court 20 years ago . . . they sought money damages only. The Court reserved for another day the question whether "equitable considerations" should limit the relief available to the present-day Oneidas.

. . . In this action, OIN seeks declaratory and injunctive relief recognizing its present and future sovereign immunity from local taxation on parcels of land the Tribe purchased in the open market, properties that had been subject to state and local taxation for generations. We now reject the . . . theory of OIN and the United States and hold that "standards of federal Indian law and federal equity practice" preclude the Tribe from rekindling embers of sovereignty that long ago grew cold.

The appropriateness of the relief OIN here seeks must be evaluated in light of the long history of state sovereign control over the territory. . . . In fact, the United States' policy and practice through much of the early 19th century was designed to dislodge east coast lands from Indian possession. Moreover, the properties here involved have greatly increased in value since the Oneidas sold them 200 years ago. Notably, it was not until lately that the Oneidas sought to regain ancient sovereignty over land converted from wilderness to become part of cities like Sherrill.

This Court has observed in the different, but related, context of the diminishment of an Indian reservation that "[t]he longstanding assumption of jurisdiction by the State over an area that is over 90% non-Indian, both in population and in land use," may create "justifiable expectations." Similar justifiable expectations, grounded in two centuries of New York's exercise of regulatory jurisdiction, until recently uncontested by OIN, merit heavy weight here.

The wrongs of which OIN complains in this action occurred during the early years of the Republic. For the past two centuries, New York and its county and municipal units have continuously governed the territory. The Oneidas did not seek to regain possession of their aboriginal lands by court decree until the 1970's. And not until the 1990's did OIN acquire the properties in question. . . . This long lapse of time, during which the Oneidas did not seek to revive their sovereign control through equitable relief in court, and the attendant dramatic changes in the character of the properties, preclude OIN from gaining the disruptive remedy it now seeks.

* * *

... When a party belatedly asserts a right to present and future sovereign control over territory, longstanding observances and settled expectations are prime considerations. . . .

Finally, this Court has recognized the impracticability of returning to Indian control land that generations earlier passed into numerous private hands. . . .

In this case, the Court of Appeals concluded that the "impossibility" doctrine had no application because OIN acquired the land in the open market and does not seek to uproot current property owners. But the unilateral reestablishment of present and future Indian sovereign control, even over land purchased at the market price, would have disruptive practical consequences. . . . A checkerboard of alternating state and tribal jurisdiction in New York State—created unilaterally at OIN's behest—would "seriously burde[n] the administration of state and local governments" and would adversely affect landowners neighboring the tribal patches. If OIN may unilaterally reassert sovereign control and remove these parcels from the local tax rolls, little would prevent the Tribe from initiating a new generation of litigation to free the parcels from local zoning or other regulatory controls that protect all landowners in the area.

Recognizing these practical concerns, Congress has provided a mechanism for the acquisition of lands for tribal communities that takes account of the interests of others with stakes in the area's governance and well-being. [Federal law] authorizes the Secretary of the Interior to acquire land in trust for Indians and provides that the land "shall be exempt from State and local taxation." The regulations implementing [federal law] are sensitive to the complex interjurisdictional concerns that arise when a tribe seeks to regain sovereign control over territory. Before approving an acquisition, the Secretary must consider, among other things, the tribe's need for additional land; "[t]he purposes for which the land will be used"; "the impact on the State and its political subdivisions resulting from the removal of the land from the tax rolls"; and "[j]urisdictional problems and potential conflicts of land use which may arise." [Federal law] provides the proper avenue for OIN to reestablish sovereign authority over territory last held by the Oneidas 200 years ago.

... [The] distance from 1805 to the present day, the Oneidas' long delay in seeking equitable relief against New York or its local units, and developments in the city of Sherrill spanning several generations, evoke the doctrines of . . .

acquiescence and impossibility, and render inequitable the piecemeal shift in governance this suit seeks unilaterally to initiate.

As noted above, this case was one of a series between the Oneida and a division of the state of New York. In the earlier cases, the Supreme Court held that the Oneida could pursue claims against the state of New York for violations of the Trade and Intercourse Act (see Chapter 2) for illegal treaties signed between the state and the tribal nation, even though those treaties were signed in the early days of the republic. In that sense, this Oneida case is a departure from previous rulings. Whereas the earlier cases allowed old claims, with the possibility of monetary awards, to move forward, in this case the Court decided that federal law precluded the Oneida from "rekindling embers of sovereignty that long ago grew cold." The regular references to the lengthy periods of non-Native control of the land, coupled with the demographic information about the region, strongly suggest that the Court was deeply unsettled with the possibility of tribal nations asserting their own authority over land in the manner the Oneida chose. In short, money damages for past wrongs (even if those wrongs were nearly two centuries old) are allowable, but equitable relief to reassert sovereignty is not allowable.

In order to come to this decision, the Court relied, among other points of law, on the doctrines of acquiescence and impossibility. Concerning the acquiescence doctrine, Justice Ruth Bader Ginsburg noted that, in the state context, "when a party belatedly asserts a right to present and future sovereign control over territory, longstanding observances and settled expectations are prime considerations." This "helpful point of reference" ran against the Oneida's arguments, as the lands in question had long been held by non-Natives. Concerning the impossibility doctrine, the opinion noted that "the unilateral reestablishment of present and future Indian sovereign control, even over land purchased at the market price, would have disruptive practical consequences." Speculating as to the potential consequences of the opposite result in the case, Ginsburg wrote that "little would prevent the Tribe from initiating a new generation of litigation to free the parcels from local zoning or other regulatory controls that protect all landowners in the area."

There is reason to question whether either the doctrines of acquiescence or impossibility ought to apply in this situation, particularly in light of the previous Oneida Supreme Court cases that allowed the cases to move forward despite lengthy delays between the harm and the litigation. As noted earlier in this chapter, there were any number of reasons that precluded tribal nations from initiating a lawsuit at the time a harm occurred, particularly during the early years of the republic. In fact, for many years beginning in the mid-19th century, tribal nations were precluded from suing the federal government without a special jurisdictional act from Congress (see Chapter 8). Is it appropriate to equate these barriers to acquiescence? Additionally, the doctrine of impossibility is most firmly rooted in contract law and applied when changes that occur after a contract is signed make it impossible to perform the contract. For example, if A agrees to paint B's house and B's house burns down before A can paint it, A is no longer contractually bound to paint the house under the doctrine of impossibility. Is the Oneida situation analogous to the house painting situation? Have circumstances changed so dramatically that it is impossible for the Oneida to reassert the benefits of Indian title over the repurchased lands? Why or why not?

There is another potential hypocrisy at the heart of the decision. Justice Ginsburg's opinion stated that a, "checkerboard of alternating state and tribal jurisdiction in New York State—created unilaterally at OIN's behest—would 'seriously burde[n] the administration of state and local governments' and would adversely affect landowners neighboring the tribal patches." However, many reservations are similarly checkerboarded because of the federal government's efforts during the Allotment Era (see Chapter 5). If much of Native America lives under these conditions, why is it seemingly unthinkable to the Court to sanction such a scenario elsewhere in the United States?

The Court did note that, with the aid of the federal government, it was possible to accomplish what the Oneida were seeking to do on their own. Under federal law, the Secretary of the Interior is authorized to take lands into trust for Native peoples and nations. In essence, the Secretary of the Interior is authorized to reinstate Indian title on lands that have lost that character. Lands held in trust are not taxable by state and local governments—they exist in the manner that the Oneida were seeking in this litigation for the lands they repurchased. The Secretary of the Interior has taken lands into trust for tribal nations at different times, but the process can be very controversial. The most common argument against the process by states is precisely what the Oneida were hoping to accomplish—the lands would no longer be taxable. In addition, as noted in the opinion, the Secretary of the Interior has to balance a number of interests before taking lands into trust. Considering these circumstances, is this a viable alternative for the Oneida?

While this chapter gives some guidance on the subject, the full scope of Indian title remains a subject of debate and litigation. As currently constituted in American law, Indian title is very much dependent on the federal government's willingness to acknowledge and accept it, sometimes in spite of the actions of tribal nations. Nonetheless, it is a foundational aspect of federal Indian law.

SUGGESTED READINGS

- "The Doctrine of Discovery and the Elusive Definition of Indian Title." Blake A. Watson. 15 *Lewis & Clark Law Review* 995 (Winter 2011).

- "Chapter Thirteen—*Tee-Hit-Ton Indians v. United States:* Confiscating Indigenous Habitat." Walter R. Echo-Hawk. In *In the Courts of the Conqueror: The 10 Worst Indian Law Cases Ever Decided.* Golden, CO: Fulcrum, 2010.

- "*City of Sherrill v. Oneida Indian Nation of New York*: A Regretful Postscript to the Taxation Chapter in *Cohen's Handbook of Federal Indian Law.*" Sarah Krakoff. 41 *Tulsa Law Review* 5 (Fall 2005).

CHAPTER 16

Land II—Diminishment

Land is fundamentally important to tribal peoples. This is true spiritually and socially. It is also true legally as well. Land is one of the major catalysts of tribal sovereignty, as it provides a foundation both literally and figuratively. It is not impossible to engage in acts of tribal sovereignty without land, but it can be much more complicated. A recognized land base is also one of the distinguishing characteristics that makes Native peoples distinct from other racial minorities in the United States. In short, land is life.

And yet, despite—or perhaps because of—centuries of interaction, negotiation, legislation and litigation, questions of land, who controls it, and what can be done on it in the name of governance continue to persist. In the present, especially since tribal nations have increasingly sought to exercise greater sovereignty in the Self-Determination Era of federal policy, questions will sometimes rise about the status of a parcel of land within the original boundaries of a reservation. The consequences of these types of questions are great, as the status of the land will dictate which government or governments will have jurisdiction over it.

The way that American courts frame the questions about these disputed parcels of land is to ask if the reservation has been "diminished." In essence, courts are looking for evidence that the federal government has taken enough action to have eliminated Indian title over the disputed land (see Chapter 15). If the federal government has taken enough action, then the reservation has been diminished and the tribal nation no longer has control over the disputed land. If the federal government has not taken enough action, then the land remains under tribal jurisdiction. Seemingly straightforward, this analysis is deeply complicated by the history of federal policy. American courts have to interpret the words and deeds of federal officials from the Allotment Era in today's Self-Determination Era. Questions of diminishment raise further questions of fairness, expectation, and how to read actions of the past in a very different present.

This chapter will demonstrate...

- *The historical roots of questions of diminishment*

- *The standard for determining if a reservation has been diminished*

- *How the Supreme Court has weighed the factors in determining diminishment*

UNDERSTANDING DIMINISHMENT

Placing federal Indian law into policy eras, such as the Termination Era or Self-Determination Era, draws an effective roadmap for understanding many aspects of the field, including its history, development, and the general purpose of a period of interaction between Native America and the federal government. Knowing these policy eras—the subject of Unit I—increases one's capacity to fully engage with the complexities of this unusual area of American law in the present day. Nonetheless, the policy eras are only tools that allow a user to better understand the general tenor of policy and law. It would be unwise to think of them rigidly or as completely discrete. Law and policy do not change immediately at a moment when scholars, with the benefit of hindsight, recognize a shift in policy. The policy eras bleed into one another, are fuzzy around the edges, and change is slow and uneven.

By recognizing that the policy eras identified by scholars are tools for understanding and not absolute statements of facts, it becomes possible to recognize perhaps the most important lesson that each policy era can share: each has a legacy that we continue to confront to this day. And perhaps the policy era with the biggest legacy with which we still wrestle is the Allotment Era, lasting from 1871–1934. In the Allotment Era (see Chapters 5, 6, and 7), the federal government actively sought to destroy tribal nations and tribal ways of life. Many federal policymakers and philanthropists honestly and earnestly believed that Native America was nearing extinction and that the only way to save Native individuals was to "civilize" them, or make them more like their White counterparts. Attempting to reshape how Native people thought about land was central to this task.

One of the most profound consequences of the Allotment Era was allotment itself, and the massive land loss that accompanied it. Initiated by the Allotment (or Dawes) Act of 1887, the federal government began dividing tribal lands into individual units or plots. When a tribal member was assigned a plot, it was originally held in trust by the federal government for the individual (see Chapter 14). But many of these plots eventually lost their trust status and slipped from the hands of the original Native landholders to non-Natives. Also, since there were generally more plots of land within a reservation than Native individuals to whom to distribute them, the federal government began selling plots to non-Natives. Before long, many reservations became "checkerboarded"—with patches of land held in different statuses by different entities (see Chapter 5).

When examining a map, the borders of almost all Indian reservations appear to be clearly distinct. Often the reservation boundary appears to follow either a geographical feature, like a river, or otherwise a straight line following existing state or county lines. Many maps will even shade these areas, giving the impression that the Indian reservation is continuous and fills the entire space provided. While the treaties, statutes, and executive orders that create Indian reservations make it look like Indian reservations are large and continuous, in reality many of them have been divided up so that ordinary maps give a misleading impression of modern reservations.

There are unopened parts of the reservation where the land was never parceled out and accordingly the tribe owns all the land. There are also parcels opened to settlement by allotment where non Indian-owned parcels exceed those retained by the tribe or its members. For example consider the Rosebud Sioux reservation in South Dakota:

 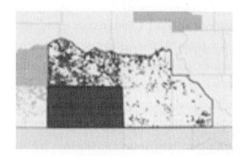

On the left is the original boundary of the reservation. In 1868 the Treaty of Fort Laramie created the great Sioux reservation, which originally included most of western South Dakota, southwestern North Dakota, and northeastern Nebraska as well as pieces of Wyoming and Montana. After years of often violent conflict, the United States forced a partition of Sioux lands in 1889 creating several reservations for the Sioux people, including the Rosebud reservation laid out in the image on the left. In a series of agreements ratified by Congress in 1904, 1907, and 1910, large parts of the original reservation were allotted, with the "surplus land" opened for settlement. As a result, the image on the right shows how much land the Rosebud Reservation lost. While present-day Todd County remained unopened to settlement, the other 2/3rds of the reservation were promptly allotted. Many reservations across the United States are checkerboarded in a similar manner as the Rosebud Reservation.

Another profound consequence of the Allotment Era was that legislation written during the era presumed a future that we do not live in today. More precisely, many involved in Indian affairs in the Allotment Era believed that reservations were soon to be relics of the past. Once allotment was accomplished and Native individuals became farmers on their own piece of land, the reasoning went, the old ways and the old borders would disappear. Native peoples would assimilate, reservations would no longer be necessary, and lands held by Native individuals would be indistinguishable from any other parcels of land in a given state. Consequently, when Congress wrote legislation concerning tribal lands, it did so with these assumptions in mind.

Both checkerboarding and Congressional legislation that did not anticipate a future when reservations continued to exist have raised questions that we must answer in the present. As noted in the previous chapter, ownership of property carries with it control over the property. But who controls a checkerboarded reservation? What are the legal effects of allotment today for reservations that look like Rosebud? At what point does the checkerboarding of a reservation and non-Native ownership of lands mean that a territory is no longer a reservation? Additionally, how should an American court read a piece of legislation from the Allotment Era in today's day and age? How does a court reconcile with the knowledge that Congress was writing legislation for a future that has not come to pass? What historical markers can a court use to guide itself, particularly when Congress never bothered to imagine the circumstances of our present?

These questions are often expressed through the language of diminishment. In essence, American courts of today are sometimes asked to consider whether the federal government of the Allotment Era was seeking to "diminish" or reduce the size of a reservation through legislation, or through what is often called a "surplus land" act or statute. For example, when Congress passed legislation allowing for the sale of "surplus" lands on allotted reservations, was Congress divesting the designated land of Native character, or was it merely allowing non-Natives to buy land on a reservation? Just as important, how does one interpret a surplus land act in a reasonable, principled way when it is fairly clear that Congress never really thought about a future that included reservations?

As you read the next case, ask yourself what standard the Court uses to make its decision. What are the factors to be considered when deciding whether a reservation has been diminished? Which factors are backward-looking and which are forward-looking? Should the Court have both forward and backward-looking considerations? Why or why not?

SOLEM V. BARTLETT
465 U.S. 463 (1984)

JUSTICE MARSHALL delivered the opinion of the Court.

On May 29, 1908, Congress authorized the Secretary of the Interior to open 1.6 million acres of the Cheyenne River Sioux Reservation for homesteading. The question presented in this case is whether that Act of Congress diminished the boundaries of the Cheyenne River Sioux Reservation or simply permitted non-Indians to settle within existing reservation boundaries.

In 1979, the State of South Dakota charged respondent John Bartlett, an enrolled member of the Cheyenne River Sioux Tribe, with attempted rape. Respondent pleaded guilty to the charge, and was sentenced to a 10-year term in the state penitentiary. . . . After exhausting state remedies, respondent filed [in federal court]. Respondent contended that the crime for which he had been convicted occurred within the Cheyenne River Sioux Reservation. . . . that, although . . . Congress opened for settlement by non-Indians the portion of the reservation on which respondent committed his crime, the opened portion nonetheless remained Indian country; and that the State therefore lacked criminal jurisdiction over respondent.

* * *

In the latter half of the 19th century, large sections of the Western States and Territories were set aside for Indian reservations. Towards the end of the century, however, Congress increasingly adhered to the view that the Indian tribes should abandon their nomadic lives on the communal reservations and settle into an agrarian economy on privately owned parcels of land. This shift was fueled in part by the belief that individualized farming would speed the Indians' assimilation into American society and in part by the continuing demand for new lands for the waves of homesteaders moving west. As a result of these combined pressures, Congress passed a series of surplus land acts at the turn of the century to force Indians onto individual allotments carved out of reservations and to open up unallotted lands for non-Indian settlement.

Initially, Congress legislated its Indian allotment program on a national scale, but by the time of the Act of May 29, 1908, Congress was dealing with the surplus land question on a reservation-by-reservation basis, with each surplus land Act employing its own statutory language, the product of a unique set of tribal negotiation and legislative compromise.

The modern legacy of the surplus land acts has been a spate of jurisdictional disputes between state and federal officials as to which sovereign has authority over lands that were opened by the acts and have since passed out of Indian ownership. As a doctrinal matter, the States have jurisdiction over unallotted opened lands if the applicable surplus land act freed that land of its reservation status and thereby diminished the reservation boundaries. On the other hand, federal, state, and tribal authorities share jurisdiction over these lands if the relevant surplus land act did not diminish the existing Indian reservation because the entire opened area is Indian country. . . .

Unfortunately, the surplus land acts themselves seldom detail whether opened lands retained reservation status or were divested of all Indian interests. When the surplus land acts were passed, the distinction seemed unimportant. The notion that reservation status of Indian lands might not be coextensive with tribal ownership was unfamiliar at the turn of the century. Indian lands were judicially defined to include only those lands in which the Indians held some form of property interest: trust lands, individual allotments, and, to a more limited degree, opened lands that had not yet been claimed by non-Indians. Only in 1948 did Congress uncouple reservation status from Indian ownership, and statutorily define Indian country to include lands held in fee by non-Indians within reservation boundaries.

Another reason why Congress did not concern itself with the effect of surplus land acts on reservation boundaries was the turn-of-the-century assumption that Indian reservations were a thing of the past. Consistent with prevailing wisdom, Members of Congress voting on the surplus land Acts believed to a man that within a short time—within a generation at most—the Indian tribes would enter traditional American society and the reservation system would cease to exist. Given this expectation, Congress naturally failed to be meticulous in clarifying whether a particular piece of legislation formally sliced a certain parcel of land off one reservation.

Although the Congress that passed the surplus land acts anticipated the imminent demise of the reservation and, in fact, passed the acts partially to facilitate the process, we have never been willing to extrapolate from this expectation a specific congressional purpose of diminishing reservations with the passage of every surplus land act. Rather, it is settled law that some surplus land acts diminished reservations, and other surplus land acts did not. The effect of any given surplus land act depends on the language of the act and the circumstances underlying its passage.

Our precedents in the area have established a fairly clean analytical structure for distinguishing those surplus land acts that diminished reservations from those acts that simply offered non-Indians the opportunity to purchase land within established reservation boundaries. The first and governing principle is that only Congress can divest a reservation of its land and diminish its boundaries. Once a block of land is set aside for an Indian reservation and no matter what happens to the title of individual plots within the area, the entire block retains its reservation status until Congress explicitly indicates otherwise.

Diminishment, moreover, will not be lightly inferred. Our analysis of surplus land acts requires that Congress clearly evince an "intent . . . to change . . . boundaries" before diminishment will be found. The most probative evidence of congressional intent is the statutory language used to open the Indian lands. Explicit reference to cession or other language evidencing the present and total surrender of all tribal interests strongly suggests that Congress meant to divest from the reservation all unallotted opened lands. When such language of cession is buttressed by an unconditional commitment from Congress to compensate the Indian tribe for its opened land, there is an almost insurmountable presumption that Congress meant for the tribe's reservation to be diminished.

. . . [H]owever, explicit language of cession and unconditional compensation are not prerequisites for a finding of diminishment. When events surrounding the passage of a surplus land act—particularly the manner in which the transaction was negotiated with the tribes involved and the tenor of legislative Reports presented to Congress—unequivocally reveal a widely held, contemporaneous understanding that the affected reservation would shrink as a result of the proposed legislation, we have been willing to infer that Congress shared the understanding that its action would diminish the reservation, notwithstanding the presence of statutory language that would otherwise suggest reservation boundaries remained unchanged. To a lesser extent, we have also looked to events that occurred after the passage of a surplus land act to decipher Congress' intentions. Congress' own treatment of the affected areas, particularly in the years immediately following the opening, has some evidentiary value, as does the manner in which the Bureau of Indian Affairs and local judicial authorities dealt with unallotted open lands.

On a more pragmatic level, we have recognized that who actually moved onto opened reservation lands is also relevant to deciding whether a surplus land act diminished a reservation. Where non-Indian settlers flooded into the opened portion of a reservation and the area has long since lost its Indian character, we have acknowledged that de facto, if not de jure, diminishment may have occurred. In addition to the obvious practical advantages of acquiescing to de facto diminishment, we look to the subsequent demographic history of opened lands as one additional clue as to what Congress expected would happen once land on a particular reservation was opened to non-Indian settlers.

* * *

We now turn to apply these principles to the Act of May 29, 1908. . . .

. . . Rather than reciting an Indian agreement to "cede, sell, relinquish and convey" the opened lands, the Cheyenne River Act simply authorizes the Secretary to "sell and dispose" of certain lands. This reference to the sale of Indian lands, coupled with the creation of Indian accounts for proceeds, suggests that the Secretary of the Interior was simply being authorized to act as the Tribe's sales agent. . . .

This case is made more difficult, however, by the presence of some language in the Cheyenne River Act that indirectly supports petitioners' view that the reservation was diminished. For instance, in a provision permitting Indians already holding an allotment on the opened lands to obtain new allotments in the unopened territories, the Act refers to the unopened territories as "within the respective reservations thus diminished." . . .

Undisputedly, the references to the opened areas as being in "the public domain" and the unopened areas as constituting "the reservation thus diminished" support petitioners' view that the Cheyenne River Act diminished the reservation. These isolated phrases, however, are hardly dispositive. And, when balanced against the Cheyenne River Act's stated and limited goal of opening up reservation lands for sale to non-Indian settlers, these two phrases cannot carry the burden of establishing an express congressional purpose to diminish. The Act of May 29, 1908, read as a whole, does not present an explicit expression of congressional intent to diminish the Cheyenne River Sioux Reservation.

The circumstances surrounding the passage of the Cheyenne River Act also fail to establish a clear congressional purpose to diminish the reservation. . . .

During his meeting with members of the Cheyenne River Tribe, [a federal official] admittedly spoke in terms of cession and the relinquishment of Indian interests in the opened territories. However, it is impossible to say that the Tribe agreed to the terms that [the federal official] presented. . . .

. . . [In] the legislative debate . . . no mention was made of the Act's effect on the reservation's boundaries or whether state or federal officials would have jurisdiction over the opened areas.

. . . Without evidence that Congress understood itself to be entering into an agreement under which the Tribe committed itself to cede and relinquish all interests in unallotted opened lands, and in the absence of some clear statement of congressional intent to alter reservation boundaries, it is impossible to infer from a few isolated and ambiguous phrases a congressional purpose to diminish the Cheyenne River Sioux Reservation.

The subsequent treatment of the Cheyenne River Sioux Reservation by Congress, courts, and the Executive is so rife with contradictions and inconsistencies as to be of no help to either side. . . .

What is clear, however, is what happened to the Cheyenne River Sioux Tribe after the Act of May 29, 1908, was passed. Most of the members of the Tribe obtained individual allotments on the lands opened by the Act. Because most of the Tribe lived on the opened territories, tribal authorities and Bureau of Indian Affairs personnel took primary responsibility for policing and supplying social services to the opened lands during the years following 1908. The strong tribal presence in the opened area has continued until the present day. Now roughly two-thirds of the Tribe's enrolled members live in the opened area. The seat of tribal government is now located in a town in the opened area, where most important tribal activities take place.

Also clear is the historical fact that the opening of the Cheyenne River Sioux Reservation was a failure. . . . Under these circumstances, it is impossible to say that the opened areas of the Cheyenne River Sioux Reservation have lost their Indian character.

Neither the Act of May 29, 1908, the circumstances surrounding its passage, nor subsequent events clearly establish that the Act diminished the Cheyenne River Sioux Reservation. The presumption that Congress did not intend to diminish the reservation therefore stands. . . .

The circumstances of the case help to explain why diminishment is such an important issue in Indian Country. The individual at the heart of the case, John

Bartlett, admitted to the charge of attempted rape. However, he objected to his state prosecution because he argued that he committed the crime on a reservation. Thus, the state did not have the jurisdiction, or the authority, to prosecute him because, in general, states do not have this type of authority on reservations. Since the Supreme Court agreed that the reservation was not diminished, the state's conviction of Bartlett was overturned. It is important to note that the decision in this case did not mean that Bartlett could not be prosecuted for his admitted crime. Rather, it meant that the state of South Dakota did not have jurisdiction over what were still reservation lands. The federal government and, to a lesser extent, the tribal nation both retained the capacity to prosecute him. Rather, the critical question in the case was whether the reservation had been diminished. Thus, questions of diminishment can determine fundamentally important issues such as which government has the authority to engage in law enforcement on a piece of land.

Solem is also noteworthy for the "fairly clean analytical structure" it identified in determining diminishment cases. According to Justice Thurgood Marshall's opinion, courts should consider three factors: 1) the language of the surplus land act; 2) the events surrounding the passage of the surplus land act, including whether the tribe gave its clear consent to the agreement before Congress enacted it and the role of the Bureau of Indian Affairs in handling the opened lands after the land was parceled out to tribal members and opened to non-Indian settlement; and 3) the existing "Indian character" of the land so as to take into account the demographics of the reservation and the expectation of the parties who actually live on the part of the reservation that was opened to settlement. The Supreme Court has returned to this analytical structure on a few occasions since *Solem*.

READING THE STATUTE

While *Solem* identifies three factors to consider when deciding whether a reservation has been diminished or not, those three factors are not weighted equally. By far, the most important factor is the language of the surplus land statutes that opened lands on reservations for non-Native purchase. As Marshall's opinion in *Solem* notes, the language of these statutes can raise an almost insurmountable presumption that the reservation had been diminished. When the statute allotting the reservation includes language of "cession" along with an unqualified commitment by the United States to pay a "sum certain" for the surplus land, the presumption is that the reservation has been diminished. Essentially, the court reasons, the United States converted the land into money in a single transaction and the tribe should not have any expectations of continuing to regulate or control land that was essentially sold to the federal government.

Consider the reasoning provided by the Supreme Court in the following case decided fourteen years after *Solem*. As you read the next case, ask yourself why the Yankton Sioux Reservation was diminished while the Cheyenne River Sioux Reservation was left intact. How is the language of the surplus land act in the following case different from the language of the act in *Solem*? Do these distinctions make sense when we, and the Court, recognize that Congress did not envision reservations continuing to exist? Why or why not?

SOUTH DAKOTA V. YANKTON SIOUX TRIBE
522 U.S. 329 (1998)

JUSTICE O'CONNOR delivered the opinion of the Court.

This case presents the question whether, in an 1894 statute that ratified an agreement for the sale of surplus tribal lands, Congress diminished the boundaries of the Yankton Sioux Reservation in South Dakota. . . . The issue we confront illustrates the jurisdictional quandaries wrought by the allotment policy: We must decide whether a landfill constructed on non-Indian fee land that falls within the boundaries of the original Yankton Reservation remains subject to federal environmental regulations. If the divestiture of Indian property in 1894 effected a diminishment of Indian territory, then the ceded lands no longer constitute "Indian country". . . and the State now has primary jurisdiction over them. In light of the operative language of the 1894 Act, and the circumstances surrounding its passage, we hold that Congress intended to diminish the Yankton Reservation and consequently that the waste site is not in Indian country.

* * *

In 1892, the Secretary of the Interior dispatched a three-member Yankton Indian Commission to Greenwood, South Dakota, to negotiate for the acquisition of . . . surplus [reservation] lands. When the Commissioners arrived on the reservation in October 1892, they informed the Tribe that they had been sent by the "Great Father" to discuss the cession of "this land that [members of the Tribe] hold in common," and they abruptly encountered opposition to the sale from traditionalist tribal leaders. In the lengthy negotiations that followed, members of the Tribe raised concerns about the suggested price per acre, the preservation of their annuities under the 1858 Treaty, and other outstanding claims against the United States, but they did not discuss the future boundaries of the reservation. Once the Commissioners garnered a measure of support for the sale of the unallotted lands, they submitted a proposed agreement to the Tribe. 1 Article I of the agreement provided that the Tribe would "cede, sell, relinquish, and convey to the United States" all of the unallotted lands on the reservation. Pursuant to Article II, the United States agreed to compensate the Tribe in a single payment of $600,000, which amounted to $3.60 per acre.

. . . On August 15, 1894, Congress finally ratified the 1892 agreement. . . .

President Cleveland issued a proclamation opening the ceded lands to settlement as of May 21, 1895, and non-Indians rapidly acquired them. By the turn of the century, 90 percent of the unallotted tracts had been settled. A majority of the individual allotments granted to members of the Tribe also were subsequently conveyed in fee by the members to non-Indians. Today, the total Indian holdings in the region consist of approximately 30,000 acres of allotted land and 6,000 acres of tribal land.

* * *

. . . In February 1992, several South Dakota counties formed the Southern Missouri Recycling and Waste Management District for the purpose of constructing a municipal solid waste disposal facility. The Waste District acquired the site for the landfill, which falls within the 1858 boundaries of the Yankton Sioux Reservation, in fee from a non-Indian. The predicate for the parties' claims in this case is that the waste site lies on land ceded in the 1894 Act, and the record supports that assumption.

* * *

When the Waste District sought a state permit for the landfill, the Yankton Tribe intervened and objected on environmental grounds, arguing that the proposed compacted clay liner was inadequate to prevent leakage. . . .

* * *

States acquired primary jurisdiction over unallotted opened lands where "the applicable surplus land Act freed that land of its reservation status and thereby diminished the reservation boundaries." In contrast, if a surplus land Act "simply offered non-Indians the opportunity to purchase land within established reservation boundaries," then the entire opened area remained Indian country. Our touchstone to determine whether a given statute diminished or retained reservation boundaries is congressional purpose. Congress possesses plenary power over Indian affairs, including the power to modify or eliminate tribal rights. Accordingly, only Congress can alter the terms of an Indian treaty by diminishing a reservation, and its intent to do so must be "clear and plain."

Here, we must determine whether Congress intended by the 1894 Act to modify the reservation set aside for the Yankton Tribe in the 1858 Treaty. Our inquiry is informed by the understanding that, at the turn of this century, Congress did not view the distinction between acquiring Indian property and assuming jurisdiction over Indian territory as a critical one ... because Congress then assumed that the reservation system would fade over time.... Thus, although "[t]he most probative evidence of diminishment is, of course, the statutory language used to open the Indian lands," we have held that we will also consider "the historical context surrounding the passage of the surplus land Acts," and, to a lesser extent, the subsequent treatment of the area in question and the pattern of settlement there. Throughout this inquiry, "we resolve any ambiguities in favor of the Indians, and we will not lightly find diminishment."

Article I of the 1894 Act provides that the Tribe will "cede, sell, relinquish, and convey to the United States all their claim, right, title, and interest in and to all the unallotted lands within the limits of the reservation"; pursuant to Article II, the United States pledges a fixed payment of $600,000 in return. This "cession" and "sum certain" language is "precisely suited" to terminating reservation status. Indeed, we have held that when a surplus land act contains both explicit language of cession, evidencing "the present and total surrender of all tribal interests," and a provision for a fixed-sum payment, representing "an unconditional commitment from Congress to compensate the Indian tribe for its opened land," a "nearly conclusive," or "almost insurmountable," presumption of diminishment arises....

The 1894 Act is also readily distinguishable from surplus land acts that the Court has interpreted as maintaining reservation boundaries ... the 1894 Act at issue here—a negotiated agreement providing for the total surrender of tribal claims in exchange for a fixed payment—bears the hallmarks of congressional intent to diminish a reservation.

* * *

Although we perceive congressional intent to diminish the reservation in the plain statutory language, we also take note of the contemporary historical context, subsequent congressional and administrative references to the reservation, and demographic trends.... In this case, although the context of the Act is not so compelling that, standing alone, it would indicate diminishment, neither does it rebut the "almost insurmountable presumption" that arises from the statute's plain terms.

The "manner in which the transaction was negotiated" with the Yankton Tribe and "the tenor of legislative Reports presented to Congress" reveal a contemporaneous understanding that the proposed legislation modified the reservation. In 1892, when the Commissioner of Indian Affairs appointed the Yankton Commission, he charged its members to "negotiate with the [Tribe] for the cession of their surplus lands" and noted that the funds exchanged for the "relinquishment" of those lands would provide a future income for the Tribe. The negotiations themselves confirm the understanding that by surrendering its interest in the unallotted lands, the Tribe would alter the reservation's character. . . .

The legislative history itself adds little . . . but the few relevant references from the floor debates support a finding of diminishment. . . .

* * *

Despite the apparent contemporaneous understanding that the 1894 Act diminished the reservation, in the years since, both Congress and the Executive Branch have described the reservation in contradictory terms and treated the region in an inconsistent manner. . . .

. . . The mixed record we are presented with "reveals no consistent, or even dominant, approach to the territory in question," and it "carries but little force" in light of the strong textual and contemporaneous evidence of diminishment. . . .

* * *

. . . The fact that the Yankton population in the region promptly and drastically declined after the 1894 Act does, however, provide "one additional clue as to what Congress expected." Today, fewer than ten percent of the 1858 reservation lands are in Indian hands, non-Indians constitute over two-thirds of the population within the 1858 boundaries, and several municipalities inside those boundaries have been incorporated under South Dakota law. The opening of the tribal casino in 1991 apparently reversed the population trend; the tribal presence in the area has steadily increased in recent years, and the advent of gaming has stimulated the local economy. In addition, some acreage within the 1858 boundaries has reverted to tribal or trust land. Nonetheless, the area remains "predominantly populated by non-Indians with only a few surviving pockets of Indian allotments," and those demographics signify a diminished reservation.

The State's assumption of jurisdiction over the territory, almost immediately after the 1894 Act and continuing virtually unchallenged to the present day, further reinforces our holding.

* * *

The allotment era has long since ended, and its guiding philosophy has been repudiated. Tribal communities struggled but endured, preserved their cultural roots, and remained, for the most part, near their historic lands. But despite the present-day understanding of a "government-to-government relationship between the United States and each Indian tribe," we must give effect to Congress' intent in passing the 1894 Act. Here . . . we believe that Congress spoke clearly, and although "[s]ome might wish [it] had spoken differently . . . we cannot remake history."

Justice O'Connor built upon the presumptive language of *Solem* to find that, unlike the surplus land act at issue in that case, in *Yankton Sioux* the United States acted more like a purchaser of the opened lands and not simply a real estate broker. It paid a "sum certain" ($600,000) for the allotted lands, essentially purchasing them in advance before it knew which lands it would be able to turn around and sell to non-Indian settlers. This "sum certain" payment coupled with a language in the agreement that the land was to be "ceded" over from the tribe to the United States was enough for the Supreme Court to conclude that the Yankton Sioux Reservation was diminished.

The *Yankton Sioux* case illustrates the importance of the diminishment question to many Indian tribes that have suffered through the allotment process. The consequence of the reservation being officially declared diminished was that the state of South Dakota was able to place a waste disposal facility on land within the original boundary of the Yankton Sioux reservation but on lands that had been opened for settlement. Because the Supreme Court recognized the reservation as diminished, the tribe had no power to zone or to otherwise regulate what happened on parcels of land no longer owned by the tribe or its members.

Unfortunately, states and tribes often have strained relationships that create odd incentives for states to single out reservations or areas surrounding reservations for the placement of unpopular but necessary land uses. This includes, but is not limited to, the storage of nuclear waste, pipelines carrying oil and gas, and, as in *Yankton Sioux*, landfills. Such projects are disproportionally located on or around tribal lands and can have significantly negative effects on the health and welfare of tribal citizens and communities. Thus, questions of diminishment are never only about land, but are also often about whether a tribal nation can protect itself against the efforts of a state to use lands close to tribal communities for potentially hazardous ends.

Both *Solem* and *Yankton Sioux* demonstrate that diminishment cases are not just about who—the state or the tribal nation—has jurisdiction, or control, over a parcel of land, but also about the extent to which the party with jurisdiction can either act affirmatively in its own interests or shield itself from the actions or decisions of other parties. Conversely, diminishment cases are also about the extent that the party without jurisdiction over a parcel of land must submit to the will of the party with jurisdiction. After *Solem*, the state could no longer enforce its criminal law over the land in question; after *Yankton Sioux*, the tribal nation could no longer regulate the landfill on the land in question.

INDIAN CHARACTER

Among the most controversial aspects of the diminishment test is the third prong—examining the present day "Indian character" of the land. The fundamental problem with this prong of the diminishment test is that it is fairly disconnected from any surplus land act that is ostensibly at the heart of diminishment cases. Since courts seek out the intent of Congress in diminishment cases, and since the results of actions do not always match the intent of those actions, any serious reliance on this prong raises major questions about how and why courts should use it. Put another way, as the demographics of Indian Country sometimes change (as happens in many spaces), why should courts consider what percentage of the population of the disputed area is Indian at the time the litigation is brought? How do present day demographics speak to the Congressional intent of surplus land acts passed up to a century ago? Also, are courts concerned only with the parts of the reservation that were allotted or can they take into account the demographics of the entire original reservation including areas that were never opened for settlement and that are controlled exclusively by the tribal nation? When the Indian population grows or falls over time should the test for diminishment also change? Placing a significant amount of emphasis on the "Indian character" requirement could open the door to lawsuits that, given changes in the Indian composition of a reservation, would invite new challenges to the status of reservations that had previously been settled by courts.

The lack of precision in the "Indian character" requirement was problematic enough that in 2016 the Supreme Court again agreed to review the test for diminishment. This time, the Omaha nation wanted to levy its alcohol licensure and tax requirements on several establishments in the city of Pender, Nebraska. Pender is within the original boundary of the Omaha nation, but is located on surplus lands opened to settlement through the allotment process. While a substantial number of Omaha Indians continue to live on the reservation, there are few tribal members and virtually no Indian land in or around the city.

In a unanimous decision written by Justice Clarence Thomas, the Supreme Court concluded that the reservation was not diminished and the Omaha tribe was not precluded from requiring businesses in Pender to maintain a tribal liquor license and collect and remit to the tribal government a tax on alcohol. As you read the next case, ask yourself how the Court regards the "Indian character" prong of the diminishment test. How does it compare with the other factors to be considered when determining if a reservation has been diminished?

NEBRASKA V. PARKER

136 S. Ct. 1072 (2016)

JUSTICE THOMAS delivered the opinion of the Court.

The village of Pender, Nebraska sits a few miles west of an abandoned right-of-way once used by the Sioux City and Nebraska Railroad Company. We must decide whether Pender and surrounding Thurston County, Nebraska, are within the boundaries of the Omaha Indian Reservation or whether the passage of an 1882 Act empowering the United States Secretary of the Interior to sell the Tribe's land west of the right-of-way "diminished" the reservation's boundaries, thereby "free[ing]" the disputed land of "its reservation status." We hold that Congress did not diminish the reservation in 1882 and that the disputed land is within the reservation's boundaries.

* * *

Then came the 1882 Act, central to the dispute between petitioners and respondents. In that Act, Congress again empowered the Secretary of the Interior "to cause to be surveyed, if necessary, and sold" more than 50,000 acres lying west of a right-of-way granted by the Tribe and approved by the Secretary of the Interior in 1880 for use by the Sioux City and Nebraska Railroad Company. . . . Once the land was appraised "in tracts of forty acres each," the Secretary was "to issue [a] proclamation" that the "lands are open for settlement under such rules and regulations as he may prescribe." Within one year of that proclamation, a nonmember could purchase up to 160 acres of land (for no less than $2.50 per acre) in cash paid to the United States, so long as the settler "occup[ied]" it, made "valuable improvements thereon," and was "a citizen of the United States, or . . . declared his intention to become such." The proceeds from any land sales, "after paying all expenses incident to and necessary for carrying out the provisions of th[e] act," were to "be placed to the credit of said Indians in the Treasury of the United States." Interest earned on the proceeds was to be "annually expended for the benefit of said Indians, under the direction of the Secretary of the Interior."

The 1882 Act also included a provision, common in the late 19th century, that enabled members of the Tribe to select individual allotments as a means of encouraging them to depart from the communal lifestyle of the reservation. . . . Members could select allotments on any part of the reservation, either east or west of the right-of-way.

After the members selected their allotments—only 10 to 15 of which were located west of the right-of-way—the Secretary proclaimed that the remaining 50,157 acres west of the right-of-way were open for settlement by nonmembers in April 1884. One of those settlers was W. E. Peebles, who "purchased a tract of 160 acres, on which he platted the townsite for Pender."

The village of Pender today numbers 1,300 residents. Most are not associated with the Omaha Tribe. Less than 2% of Omaha tribal members have lived west of the right-of-way since the early 20th century.

Despite its longstanding absence, the Tribe sought to assert jurisdiction over Pender in 2006 by subjecting Pender retailers to its newly amended Beverage Control Ordinance. The ordinance requires those retailers to obtain a liquor license (costing $500, $1,000, or $1,500 depending upon the class of license) and imposes a 10% sales tax on liquor sales. Nonmembers who violate the ordinance are subject to a $10,000 fine.

The village of Pender and Pender retailers . . . brought a federal suit against members of the Omaha Tribal Council in their official capacities to challenge the Tribe's power to impose the requirements of the Beverage Control Ordinance on nonmembers. Federal law permits the Tribe to regulate liquor sales on its reservation and in "Indian country". . . . The challengers alleged that they were neither within the boundaries of the Omaha Indian Reservation nor in Indian country and, consequently, were not bound by the ordinance.

* * *

We must determine whether Congress "diminished" the Omaha Indian Reservation in 1882. If it did so, the State now has jurisdiction over the disputed land. If Congress, on the other hand, did not diminish the reservation and instead only enabled nonmembers to purchase land within the reservation, then federal, state, and tribal authorities share jurisdiction over these "opened" but undiminished reservation lands.

The framework we employ to determine whether an Indian reservation has been diminished is well settled. "[O]nly Congress can divest a reservation of its land and diminish its boundaries," and its intent to do so must be clear. To assess whether an Act of Congress diminished a reservation, we start with the statutory text, for "[t]he most probative evidence of diminishment is, of course, the statutory language used to open the Indian lands." Under our precedents, we also "examine all the circumstances surrounding the opening of a reservation." Because of "the turn-of-the-century assumption that Indian reservations were a thing of the past," many surplus land Acts did not clearly convey "whether opened lands retained reservation status or were divested of all Indian interests." For that reason, our precedents also look to any "unequivocal evidence" of the contemporaneous and subsequent understanding of the status of the reservation by members and nonmembers, as well as the United States and the State of Nebraska.

As with any other question of statutory interpretation, we begin with the text of the 1882 Act, the most "probative evidence" of diminishment. Common textual indications of Congress' intent to diminish reservation boundaries include "[e]xplicit reference to cession or other language evidencing the present and total surrender of all tribal interests" or "an unconditional commitment from Congress to compensate the Indian tribe for its opened land." Such language "providing for the total surrender of tribal claims in exchange for a fixed payment" evinces Congress' intent to diminish a reservation, and creates "an almost insurmountable presumption that Congress meant for the tribe's reservation to be diminished," Similarly, a statutory provision restoring portions of a reservation to "the public domain" signifies diminishment. In the 19th century, to restore land to the public domain was to extinguish the land's prior use—its use, for example, as an Indian reservation—and to return it to the United States either to be sold or set aside for other public purposes.

The 1882 Act bore none of these hallmarks of diminishment. The 1882 Act empowered the Secretary to survey and appraise the disputed land, which then could be purchased in 160-acre tracts by nonmembers. . . .

* * *

We now turn to the history surrounding the passage of the 1882 Act. . . .

Petitioners rely largely on isolated statements that some legislators made about the 1882 Act. . . . Such dueling remarks by individual legislators are far from the "clear and plain" evidence of diminishment required under this Court's precedent. . . .

* * *

Finally, we consider both the subsequent demographic history of opened lands, which serves as "one additional clue as to what Congress expected would happen once land on a particular reservation was opened to non-Indian settlers," as well as the United States' "treatment of the affected areas, particularly in the years immediately following the opening," which has "some evidentiary value." Our cases suggest that such evidence might "reinforc[e]" a finding of diminishment or nondiminishment based on the text. But this Court has never relied solely on this third consideration to find diminishment.

As petitioners have discussed at length, the Tribe was almost entirely absent from the disputed territory for more than 120 years. . . .

This subsequent demographic history cannot overcome our conclusion that Congress did not intend to diminish the reservation in 1882. And it is not our role to "rewrite" the 1882 Act in light of this subsequent demographic history. After all, evidence of the changing demographics of disputed land is "the least compelling" evidence in our diminishment analysis. . . .

Evidence of the subsequent treatment of the disputed land by Government officials likewise has "limited interpretive value.". . . This "mixed record" of subsequent treatment of the disputed land cannot overcome the statutory text, which is devoid of any language indicative of Congress' intent to diminish.

Petitioners' concerns about upsetting the "justifiable expectations" of the almost exclusively non-Indian settlers who live on the land are compelling, but these expectations alone, resulting from the Tribe's failure to assert jurisdiction, cannot diminish reservation boundaries. Only Congress has the power to diminish a reservation. And though petitioners wish that Congress would have "spoken differently" in 1882, "we cannot remake history."

Justice Thomas's opinion helped to clarify that courts should place a particular emphasis on the statutory language of a surplus land act when deciding on these cases. In addition, Thomas reiterated that Congress' intent to diminish a reservation, "must be clear." While, according to Thomas, the events surrounding the passage of a surplus land act and the Indian character of the land are relevant to the final determination, these second and third factors cannot overcome statutory language that is unclear concerning Congress' intent to diminish a reservation. In fact, the importance that Justice Thomas's opinion places on the statute leave room to suggest that the Supreme Court has been trending away from truly considering the second and third factors of its "fairly clean analytical structure."

Further testifying to the importance of just the statute itself in the Court's analysis, *Nebraska v. Parker* is also noteworthy because the Omaha had not sought to exercise jurisdiction over the city of Pender for decades. Despite this, Thomas's opinion makes clear that the amount of time that has passed since a tribe was meaningfully engaged with part of its original reservation land cannot be used as definitive evidence that the reservation has been diminished. Considering this aspect of the ruling, it is worth revisiting *City of Sherrill v. Oneida Indian Nation of New York* in the previous chapter. Both cases seriously consider the passage of time, changes to the land, and the rulings' potential impact on non-Natives. Why were they decided differently?

SHARP V. MURPHY

As of this writing, another important diminishment case, *Sharp v. Murphy* (previously known as *Murphy v. Royal*) is pending before the Supreme Court. The facts of the case are similar to those in *Solem*. Patrick Murphy, a tribal citizen of the Muscogee (or Creek) Nation, was convicted of murder in Oklahoma state court and was sentenced to the death penalty. However, he argued that the crime occurred in Indian Country, and consequently, the state of Oklahoma did not have the authority to prosecute him. More specifically, Murphy argued that the Muscogee Reservation, the boundaries of which were established in an 1866 treaty with the federal government, had not been diminished and the reservation was still in existence. The 10th Circuit Court of Appeals agreed with Murphy, and overturned his state conviction, noting that, "Mr. Murphy's state conviction and death sentence are thus invalid. . . . The decision to prosecute Mr. Murphy in federal court rests with the United States. Decisions about the borders of the Creek Reservation remain with Congress."[1]

The distinguishing characteristics in *Murphy*—and presumably the reason why the Supreme Court agreed to hear the case—are the size of the disputed territory and the population that it could affect. The boundaries of the 1866 Muscogee Reservation cover a significant swath in the Eastern portion of Oklahoma, including much of the city of Tulsa. The state of Oklahoma had been exercising jurisdiction over the disputed land for decades, despite any clear evidence that it had the authority to do so.

Any student of diminishment should take note of the decision in *Murphy* once it is finally handed down, as it is likely to test the Supreme Court's commitment to the "fairly clean analytical structure" explained in *Solem* and otherwise further shape and define this area of law. Assuming the Supreme Court makes a decision on the merits of the case (as opposed to on procedural grounds or another "loophole"), it will also be important to analyze how the Court engages with the possibility of a tribal nation having jurisdiction over such a large portion of land containing such a significant non-Native population. To what extent do the non-Native interests control the outcome of the decision? Should they? Why or why not?

Murphy will also likely be important because, as tribal nations continue to reassert governing authority in the Self-Determination Era of federal policy, questions of diminishment will continue to rise. The very nature of governance is at stake when determining if lands within the borders of a reservation retain their reservation status. As the cases above attest, critical governmental functions, such as law enforcement, environmental regulation, and business regulation, are on the line. Consequently, both tribal nations and states are likely to continue to seek clarity over which party can assert jurisdiction over disputed parcels of land.

SUGGESTED READINGS

- "The Legacy of *Solem v. Bartlett*: How Courts Have Used Demographics to Bypass Congress and Erode the Basic Principles of Indian Law." Charlene Koski. 85 *Washington Law Review* 723 (November 2009).

- "*South Dakota v. Yankton Sioux Tribe*: Sewing a Patchwork Quilt of Jurisdiction." Bryan T. Andersen. 3 *Great Plains Natural Resources Journal* 99 (Fall 1998).

- "A Lack of Trust: *South Dakota v. Yankton Sioux Tribe* and the Abandonment of the Trust Doctrine in Reservation Diminishment Cases." A.J. Taylor. 73 *Washington Law Review* 1163 (October 1998).

---

[1]   866 F.3d 1164, 1233 (2017).

CHAPTER 17

Public Law 280

There is much that distinguishes the various eras of federal Indian policy from each other. Whether assimilationist or separatist in nature, each era is unique in its own way with its own purposes and goals. However, there is at least one major characteristic that each policy era shares. In each era, the federal government sought to diminish or limit or otherwise end its connections and obligations to Native peoples. As it was sometimes colloquially described by various federal officials throughout history, the federal government wanted to "get out of the Indian business."

Sometimes the federal government has sought to rid itself of its engagement with Native America more cooperatively and sometimes it has done so more unilaterally and forcefully. And sometimes tribal nations and peoples have been in favor of these efforts and sometimes they have not. For example, in today's Self-Determination Era of federal policy, the federal government will hand over federal funds to tribal nations through what are called 638 contracts so that the tribal nation can administer programs that the federal government otherwise would have administered itself without the 638 contract (see Chapter 10). These 638 contracts reduce the workload for the federal government and increase tribal control within the community. They have been a welcome development in Native America precisely because they have been cooperative measures to remove the federal government from the "Indian business."

Alternatively, the Termination Era, lasting from 1953 through the mid- to late 1960s, was defined by the federal government's unilateral and forceful efforts to divest itself of its connections to Indian Country, much to the chagrin of tribal peoples and nations (see Chapter 9). One of the most prominent and enduring ways that the federal government sought to accomplish this goal in the Termination Era was through Public Law 280. Enacted in 1953, Public Law 280 was a federal law that required certain "mandatory" states to exercise some jurisdiction over reservation lands within the states and allowed other "optional" states to adopt the same jurisdiction if the state so chose. Highly controversial within both Indian Country and the mandatory states, Public Law 280 nonetheless endures to this day.

This chapter will demonstrate. . .

- *The origins of Public Law 280*

- *The distinction between criminal and civil law under Public Law 280*

- *The standard for determining if state law applies in Indian Country in Public Law 280 states*

PUBLIC LAW 280 AND ITS ORIGINS

The Termination Era of federal policy is generally regarded to have started in 1953 when Congress passed House Concurrent Resolution 108, which announced Termination as the new national Indian policy (see Chapter 9). However, the roots of the Termination Era, and in particular Public Law 280 reach back further than that. House Concurrent Resolution 108 and Public Law 280 were the culminations of at least a decade of prior activity.

To understand Public Law 280, it is necessary to understand the Termination Era more broadly. In the wake of World War II, world politics shifted to the ideologically driven Cold War. The United States and the Soviet Union, the major forces behind the Cold War, competed with one another in a variety of arenas and in a variety of ways to assert the superiority of their political and economic systems. During this period, the Soviet Union regularly criticized the United States' treatment of its racial minorities. One of the ways that the United States responded to these criticisms was to rethink its federal Indian policy. Before long, calls to "emancipate" Native peoples from federal oversight grew into a new vision of federal Indian policy. The result was the Termination Era, in which the federal government sought, through different means, to end its political relationship with tribal nations. Although short-lived and only minimally successful in its stated goals, the Termination Era has had a profound and lasting impact on Native America. Public Law 280 is perhaps the most enduring component of the Termination Era.

One of the deepest entanglements the federal government has in Indian Country is in the area of criminal law enforcement. Since the days of *Ex parte Crow Dog* (see Chapter 6) in the late nineteenth century, the federal government has played a significant role in perpetuating a Western version of law enforcement on reservations. Congress passed the Major Crimes Act in response to *Ex parte Crow Dog*, which conferred jurisdiction to the federal government over "major" crimes committed by Natives on tribal lands. Mechanisms such as the Indian police and Indian courts were tools of assimilation and considered vital to the project of "civilizing" Native peoples in the Allotment Era. Law enforcement has been a major component of the relationship between the federal government and tribal nations for well over a century.

Nonetheless, law enforcement can be difficult, expensive, and thankless. In addition, it is also most generally a local endeavor in the United States. For example, most crimes in the United States are investigated by police officers who are employed by a state or a city, and those crimes are most often prosecuted in state or municipal court. Federal criminal jurisdiction over Indian Country is an exception to this general rule, and creates yet another difference between Indian Country and the non-Native areas that surround it. Consequently, as the federal government was beginning to rethink its relationship to Indian Country after World War II, law enforcement occasionally became a place where the federal government was willing to cede some of its authority to the states. Doing so, from the federal government's perspective, was both a pragmatic and cost-effective way to move away from the "Indian business."

In the 1940s, when the IRA Era of federal policy was beginning to transition to the Termination Era, Congress passed a handful of bills that extended state jurisdiction over tribal lands in very specific instances. Passed in 1946, the following law is one of those instances. Although it is titleless, for the purposes of this text it will be called the Devils Lake Jurisdictional Act. As you read the Devils Lake Jurisdictional Act, ask yourself what authority the law gives to the state of North Dakota. What authority does the federal government retain? What might be the motivation behind such a law? Who benefits and who is burdened by the law?

DEVILS LAKE JURISDICTION ACT

60 Stat. 229, May 31, 1946

Be it enacted by the Senate and House of Representatives of the United States of America in Congress assembled, That jurisdiction is hereby conferred on the State of North Dakota over offenses committed by or against Indians on the Devils Lake Indian Reservation in North Dakota to the same extent as its courts have jurisdiction generally over offenses committed within said state outside of Indian reservations: *Provided, however,* That nothing herein contained shall deprive the courts of the United States of jurisdiction over offenses defined by the laws of the United States committed by or against Indians on said reservation, nor shall anything herein contained deprive any Indian of any protection afforded by Federal law, contract, or treaty against the taxation or alienation of any restricted property.

This law, and the handful of other ones similar to it that were passed around the same time, were premised upon the understanding that tribal lands were lawless and that such legislation was necessary to maintain law and order. The end result, however, is a web of complications. For example, what was then called the Devils Lake Reservation—and which is now called the Spirit Lake Reservation—is one of five reservations located either wholly or partially in the state of North Dakota. Spirit Lake is the only one of the five to operate under such legislation. Thus, the state of North Dakota has, according to the law, jurisdiction over "offenses," or crimes, on the Spirit Lake Reservation, but not on any of the other four. The law reserves federal authority in certain instances as well, including the exercise of the Major Crimes Act and other similar legislation—"offenses defined by the laws of the United States." Determining which government(s)—federal, state, and/or tribal—has the authority to investigate and prosecute a crime on a reservation can be a burdensome affair that seriously inhibits law enforcement. The difficult situation is only made more so by the decisions of various participating parties. Despite the language of the act, older cases from the North Dakota Supreme Court raised the question of whether the state of North Dakota needed to consent to the federal legislation before it was in force within the state. While the state of North Dakota currently embraces jurisdiction, at least within its decisions of its courts, failure to do so for a number of years led to further confusion and strife.

These consequences notwithstanding, the Devils Lake Jurisdictional Act, and the handful of laws like it for other Native communities and states, were steppingstones to something bigger. Public Law 280 was a further extension of state jurisdiction over tribal lands. Rather than continuing to engage in piecemeal legislation, Public Law 280 broadened the scope of state jurisdiction over tribal lands to a few mandatory states with larger Native populations. This was something of a trial run for potentially more expansive legislation later to come, as Congress had considered, and rejected, similar legislation that would have affected all of Indian Country the prior year. As you read the excerpt from Public Law 280, ask yourself what type of authority the law gives to the states. What authority do tribal nations have under the law? What options are available to mandatory states? What options are available to optional states?

PUBLIC LAW 280

Pub. L. 83–280 (Amended and codified)

18 U.S.C. § 1162. STATE JURISDICTION OVER OFFENSES COMMITTED BY OR AGAINST INDIANS IN THE INDIAN COUNTRY

(a) Each of the States or Territories listed in the following table shall have jurisdiction over offenses committed by or against Indians . . . to the same extent that such State or Territory has jurisdiction over offenses committed elsewhere within the State or Territory, and the criminal laws of such State or Territory shall have the same force and effect within such Indian country as they have elsewhere within the State or Territory:

  Alaska: All Indian country within the State, except that on Annette Islands, the Metlakatla Indian community may exercise jurisdiction over offenses committed by Indians in the same manner in which such jurisdiction may be exercised by Indian tribes in Indian country over which State jurisdiction has not been extended.

  California: All Indian country within the State.

  Minnesota: All Indian country within the State, except the Red Lake Reservation.

  Nebraska: All Indian country within the State.

  Oregon: All Indian country within the State, except the Warm Springs Reservation.

  Wisconsin: All Indian country within the State.

* * *

28 U.S.C. § 1360. STATE CIVIL JURISDICTION IN ACTIONS TO WHICH INDIANS ARE PARTIES

(a)   Each of the States listed in the following table shall have jurisdiction over civil causes of action between Indians or to which Indians are parties which arise in the areas of Indian country listed opposite the name of the State to the same extent that such State has jurisdiction over other civil causes of action, and those civil laws of such State that are of general application to private persons or private property shall have the same force and effect within such Indian country as they have elsewhere within the State:

Alaska: All Indian country within the State.

California: All Indian country within the State.

Minnesota: All Indian country within the State, except the Red Lake Reservation.

Nebraska: All Indian country within the State.

Oregon: All Indian country within the State, except the Warm Springs Reservation.

Wisconsin: All Indian country within the State.

(b)   Nothing in this section shall authorize the alienation, encumbrance, or taxation of any real or personal property, including water rights, belonging to any Indian or any Indian tribe, band, or community that is held in trust by the United States or is subject to a restriction against alienation imposed by the United States; or shall authorize regulation of the use of such property in a manner inconsistent with any Federal treaty, agreement, or statute or with any regulation made pursuant thereto; or shall confer jurisdiction upon the State to adjudicate, in probate proceedings or otherwise, the ownership or right to possession of such property or any interest therein.

(c)   Any tribal ordinance or custom heretofore or hereafter adopted by an Indian tribe, band, or community in the exercise of any authority which it may possess shall, if not inconsistent with any applicable civil law of the State, be given full force and effect in the determination of civil causes of action pursuant to this section.

25 U.S.C. § 1321. ASSUMPTION BY STATE OF CRIMINAL JURISDICTION

(a)   Consent of United States

(1)   In General—The consent of the United States is hereby given to any State not having jurisdiction over criminal offenses committed by or against Indians in the areas of Indian country situated within such State to assume, with the consent of the Indian tribe occupying the particular Indian country or part thereof which could be affected by such assumption, such measure of jurisdiction over any or all of such offenses committed within such Indian country or any part thereof as may be determined by such State to the same extent that such State has jurisdiction over any such offense committed elsewhere within the State, and the criminal laws of such State shall have the same force and effect within such Indian country or part thereof as they have elsewhere within that State.

* * *

25 U.S.C. § 1322. ASSUMPTION BY STATE OF CIVIL JURISDICTION

(a)   Consent of United States; force and effect of civil laws

The consent of the United States is hereby given to any State not having jurisdiction over civil causes of action between Indians or to which Indians are parties which arise in the areas of Indian country situated within such State to assume, with the consent of the tribe occupying the particular Indian country or part thereof which would be affected by such assumption, such measure of jurisdiction over any or all such civil causes of action arising within such Indian country or any part thereof as may be determined by such State to the same extent that such State has jurisdiction over other civil causes of action, and those civil laws of such State that are of general application to private persons or private property shall have the same force and effect within such Indian country or part thereof as they have elsewhere within that State.

* * *

(c)   Force and effect of tribal ordinances or customs: Any tribal ordinance or custom heretofore or hereafter adopted by an Indian tribe, band, or community in the exercise of any authority which it may possess shall, if not inconsistent with any applicable civil law of the State, be given full force and effect in the determination of civil causes of action pursuant to this section.

> ### 25 U.S.C. § 1323. RETROCESSION OF JURISDICTION BY STATE
>
> (a)   Acceptance by United States
>
> The United States is authorized to accept a retrocession by any State of all or any measure of the criminal or civil jurisdiction, or both, acquired by [Public Law 280]. . . .
>
> * * *

From the federal government's perspective, Public Law 280 was very much in line with the goals of the Termination Era that spawned it. It removed the federal government from the "Indian business" in two significant ways. It eliminated both the bureaucracy and the cost of law enforcement within the reservation communities that were enumerated. It also allowed politicians who were sympathetic to the goals of Termination to argue that the federal government was moving closer to a legal structure in which Native peoples stood on equal footing to their non-Native neighbors within the mandatory states. The barriers that separated Native America from the rest of America, according to the argument, were crumbling and soon Native peoples would no longer be prevented from taking their rightful place in American civic life along with their neighbors in their state.

Public Law 280 was much less popular among the states and tribal nations that it affected. From the point of view of the states, Public Law 280 was little more than an unwelcome imposition and another burden on the pocketbook. Best described as an unfunded mandate, Public Law 280 required mandatory states to assume jurisdiction without providing any funding for the extra effort of doing so. Thus, Public Law 280 required the mandatory states to both accept this jurisdiction and find a way to pay for the extra law enforcement on their own. The response of mandatory states to Public Law 280 was predictably underwhelming, often with little to no effort given to exercise this new responsibility.

The tribal nations directly affected by Public Law 280 (as well as those who feared they were not far behind this trend) were equally incensed. Tribal nations in mandatory states were not given the option to consent to this new jurisdiction under the original version of the law, passed in 1953. Rather, they were simply placed under the authority of the state in which their reservation resided. States, once described by the Supreme Court as the "deadliest enemies" of tribal nations, were now in charge of law enforcement on the reservation. The new legal and jurisdictional circumstances did little to quell difficulties between tribal nations and states.

The language of the original version of Public Law 280, similar to the language found in the excerpt, authorized optional states to assume authority under the statute if the state so chose. A small handful of states chose to do so in the years after the Act's passage. These assumptions of jurisdictions were inconsistent, however, with optional states choosing certain reservation lands and not others to exercise authority, occasionally requiring tribal consent before assuming jurisdiction, and sometimes only accepting jurisdiction over certain crimes or subject matter. There is little in the way of a discernable pattern of the choices made by states concerning Public Law 280. In addition, in 1968, Public Law 280 was amended to allow states to retrocede, or give back, jurisdiction to the United States, in whole or in part. On occasion, retrocession has happened and it reflects the uneven commitment states made to the law as well as the general shifts in policy and attitude as the Termination Era morphed into the Self-Determination Era. For example, the state of Nevada, which never wholeheartedly committed to the effort, assumed Public Law 280 jurisdiction over some tribal lands within the state. In 1975 Nevada retroceded authority over every reservation but one, and in 1988 the state retroceded authority over that reservation as well. Today no tribal nations in Nevada operate under Public Law 280.

Also in 1968, when the Self-Determination Era of federal Indian policy was beginning to come into its own, Congress amended Public Law 280 to require that tribal nations consent to state jurisdiction before states could accept jurisdiction. Since Public Law 280 has been amended, no tribal nation has consented to state jurisdiction. Additionally, retrocession has increasingly occurred or been considered, and the gradual erosion of state authority under the law since its passage and persistent tribal resistance to it testify to Public Law 280's continuing unpopularity. Nonetheless, some states remain committed to jurisdiction under Public Law. For example, all of the more than 100 tribal nations in California continue to function under the legislation.

As it currently stands, the following states and reservations operate under Public Law 280 either in whole or in part:[1]

Mandatory states

Alaska—All 229 Native Villages and Tribes within the state

California—All 107 tribal nations within the state

Minnesota—Fond Du Lac Band of Minnesota Chippewa Tribe; Grand Portage Band of Minnesota Chippewa Tribe; Leech Lake Band of Minnesota Chippewa Tribe; Lower Sioux Indian Community; Mille Lacs

Band of Minnesota Chippewa Tribe; Prairie Island Indian Community; Shakopee Mdewakanton Sioux Community; Upper Sioux Community; and White Earth Band of Band of Minnesota Chippewa Tribe

Nebraska—Iowa Tribe; Ponca Tribe; Sac & Fox Nation of Missouri

Oregon—Confederated Tribes of the Coos, Lower Umpqua, and Siuslaw Indians; Confederated Tribes of the Grand Ronde Community of Oregon; Confederated Tribes of Siletz Indians; Coquille Indian Tribe; Cow Creek Band of Umpqua Indians; Fort McDermott Paiute and Shoshone Tribes; Klamath Indian Tribe

Wisconsin—Bad River Band of the Lake Superior Tribe of Chippewa Indians; Forest County Potawatomi Community; Ho-Chunk Nation; Lac Courte Oreilles Band of the Lake Superior Tribe of Chippewa Indians; Lac du Flambeau Band of the Lake Superior Tribe of Chippewa Indians; Oneida Tribe of Indians; Red Cliff Band of Lake Superior Chippewa; St. Croix Chippewa Indians; Sokaogon Chippewa Community; Stockbridge-Munsee Community

Optional states

Florida—Miccosukee Tribe of Indians; Seminole Tribe

Idaho—Coeur D'Alene Tribe; Kootenai Tribe; Nez Perce Tribe; Shoshone-Bannock Tribes

Montana—Confederated Salish & Kootenai Tribes

Washington—Confederated Tribes of the Chehalis Reservation; Confederated Tribes of the Colville Reservation; Confederated Tribes and Bands of the Yakama Nation; Cowlitz Indian Tribe; Hoh Indian Tribe; Jamestown S'Klallam Tribe; Kalispel Indian Community; Lower Elwha Tribal Community; Lummi Tribe; Makah Indian Tribe; Muckleshoot Indian Tribe; Nisqually Indian Tribe; Nooksack Indian Tribe; Port Gamble S'Klallam Tribe; Puyallup Tribe; Samish Indian Tribe; Sauk-Suiattle Indian Tribe; Shoalwater Bay Tribe; Snoqualmie Tribe; Skokomish Indian Tribe; Spokane Tribe; Squaxin Indian Tribe; Stillaguamish Tribe; Suquamish Indian Tribe; Swinomish Indians; Tulalip Tribes; Upper Skagit Indian Tribe

Note that not every tribal nation in every given state is listed. This is because Public Law 280 does not necessarily apply to every tribal nation in a given state. Often, through any number of historical circumstances, reservation lands have been excluded from the legislation. For example, although Minnesota is home to eleven reservations, Public Law 280 only applies to nine of them. Of the remaining two, Red Lake was excluded in the original bill that was passed in 1953 and Minnesota retroceded jurisdiction over Bois Forte in 1975.

It is also worth repeating two other very important points. First, not all exercises of Public Law 280 are equal. For example, the state of Idaho only accepted jurisdiction over certain subject matter. And a 1976 Supreme Court decision, *Bryan v. Itasca County* (the next case in this chapter), called into question whether Idaho really had jurisdiction over all of the limited subject matter that it claimed. Second, the long history of state and tribal resentment over the exercise of Public Law 280 continues to create confusion over which government holds what type of jurisdiction over what sort of activities. For example, most jurisdictions believe that tribal courts have concurrent, or the same, jurisdiction over crimes on reservations with states in Public Law 280 states. However, not every state shares this view.

THE SCOPE OF PUBLIC LAW 280

Despite its controversial history, Public Law 280 remains in force across a great deal of Native America. Since it remains in force, a fundamental question exists: What does the legislation do? Certainly it confers jurisdiction over tribal lands to states, but how much jurisdiction? What is the scope of the legislation? Do Public Law 280 states have unlimited authority over tribal lands? If not, where does that authority stop? And if there are limits to state jurisdiction, is there anyone covering the spaces not covered by states?

In order to understand the scope of Public Law 280 it is important to understand that one of the most important and fundamental ways that American law is divided is into two big categories: criminal law and civil law. Criminal law, sometimes also called "public law" concerns the definition of crimes and their punishment. It is sometimes called public law because the government—whether it be federal, state, or tribal—controls the activity in a criminal action. The government defines crimes, either through statute or the common law. The government also decides whom to prosecute under those laws. This is why the titles of criminal cases are usually something like "The State vs. John Doe" or "The People vs. Jane Doe." Victims of crimes will most often have very little say in the prosecution or choices made in a criminal case. For example, a victim of a crime might object to the plea bargain between a criminal defendant and a government, but if the criminal defendant and the governmental prosecutor and the courts all agree to the plea bargain, then the plea bargain will be put in force regardless of the victim's wishes. This is a brief detailing of a complicated system, but for the purposes of this chapter it suffices to know that criminal law is driven primarily by the government.

This is in distinction to civil law, which is also sometimes called "private law." Civil law concerns the disputes between private parties that can be remedied under the law. For example, imagine a scenario in which A signs a contract with B. A agrees to paint B's house for the sum of $1,000. If A paints the house but B does not pay, A can take B to court to enforce the contractual promise to pay $1,000. Again, in distinction to criminal law, the parties in a civil suit have vastly more control over the proceedings than the victim of a crime. The parties in a civil suit can decide to settle the case, take it all the way to trial, or even appeal a decision. This is why titles to civil cases are usually something like, "Smith v. Jones." This is also a brief detailing of a complicated system, but for the purposes of this chapter it suffices to know that civil law is driven primarily by the private parties involved in the incident.

It is also important to note that sometimes (although not always) a single act or incident can give rise to both criminal and civil actions. For example, if A punches B in a bar fight, A might be criminally prosecuted under the criminal laws of the government (typically state law if A and B are outside of Indian Country) prohibiting battery. Concurrently, B can sue A for committing battery against B under what is called tort law, a subset of civil law. One of the major differences, as noted above, is that B will have a significant amount of control over the direction of the civil suit, but much less control over the criminal prosecution. Thus, in the scenario from above, A might plead guilty on a lesser charge in the criminal setting to avoid the burden of a trial or jail time, yet might still be found liable for battery in civil court. Thus, civil and criminal law can operate differently even concerning the same scenario.

The distinction between criminal and civil law is important because Public Law 280 treats both types of law differently. What this text will call the criminal law section of Public Law 280—18 U.S.C. § 1162—gives a mandatory state jurisdiction over "offenses," or crimes. According to subsection (a) of the statute, state criminal law "shall have the same force and effect" within reservations lands that it has outside of the reservation.

At first glance, what this text will call the civil law section of Public Law 280—28 U.S.C. § 1360—looks remarkably similar to the language in the mandatory criminal law section. Subsection (a) of the civil law section also says that state civil law "shall have the same force and effect" within reservation lands that it has outside of the reservation.

However, subsection (b) of the civil law section creates some important distinctions.[2] Subsection (b) states that, "Nothing in this section shall authorize the alienation, encumbrance, or taxation of any real or personal property . . . belonging to any Indian or any Indian tribe, band, or community that is held in trust by the United States. . . ." It also protects treaty rights and prohibits the regulation of the use of trust property "in a manner inconsistent with any Federal treaty, agreement, or statute or with any regulation made pursuant thereto." These distinctions place limits on the civil authority of a state (i.e., taxation, regulation), as opposed to the criminal authority of the state (criminal sentences).

While Public Law 280 fairly clearly allows a state to exercise full criminal jurisdiction over reservation lands, this distinguishing language in the statute created questions about the scope of state civil jurisdiction. The Supreme Court confronted just such a question in 1976 when the state of Minnesota attempted to tax the property of Native individual residing on trust land on a reservation. The question of the case was whether Public Law 280 authorized this sort of state tax on reservation land. As you read the case, ask yourself where the Supreme Court sees the limit of state civil jurisdiction on reservations. What evidence does the Court use to come to this conclusion? What was the purpose of Public Law 280, according to the Court? How does the Court's reading of the statute further this purpose?

BRYAN V. ITASCA COUNTY

426 U.S. 373 (1976)

MR. JUSTICE BRENNAN delivered the opinion of the Court.

This case presents the question . . . whether the grant of civil jurisdiction to the States conferred by [Public Law 280] is a congressional grant of power to the States to tax reservation Indians except insofar as taxation is expressly excluded by the terms of the statute.

Petitioner Russell Bryan, an enrolled member of the Minnesota Chippewa Tribe, resides in a mobile home on land held in trust by the United States for the Chippewa Tribe on the Leech Lake Reservation in Minnesota. In June, 1972, petitioner received notices from the auditor of respondent Itasca County, Minn., that he had been assessed personal property tax liability on the mobile home totaling $147.95. Thereafter, in September, 1972, petitioner brought this suit in the Minnesota District Court seeking a declaratory judgment that the State and county were without authority to levy such a tax on personal property of a reservation Indian on the reservation, and that imposition of such a tax was contrary to federal law. . . .

* * *

[Previous cases] preclude any authority in respondent county to levy a personal property tax upon petitioner's mobile home in the absence of congressional consent. Our task therefore is to determine whether [Public Law 280] constitutes such consent.

* * *

The statute does not, in terms, provide that the tax laws of a State are among "civil laws . . . of general application to private persons or private property." The Minnesota Supreme Court concluded, however, that they were. . . .

* * *

The primary concern of Congress in enacting [Public Law 280] that emerges from its sparse legislative history was with the problem of lawlessness on certain Indian reservations, and the absence of adequate tribal institutions for law enforcement.

* * *

. . . Of special significance for our purposes, however, is the total absence of mention or discussion regarding a congressional intent to confer upon the States an authority to tax Indians or Indian property on reservations. Neither the Committee Reports nor the floor discussion in either House mentions such authority. This omission has significance in the application of the canons of construction applicable to statutes affecting Indian immunities, as some mention would normally be expected if such a sweeping change in the status of tribal government and reservation Indians had been contemplated by Congress. The only mention of taxation authority is in a colloquy between Mr. Sellery, Chief Counsel of the Bureau of Indian Affairs, and Congressman Young during House committee hearings on [Public Law 280]. That colloquy strongly suggests that Congress did not mean to grant tax authority to the States.

* * *

Piecing together as best we can the sparse legislative history of [the pertinent section of Public Law 280, it] seems to have been primarily intended to redress the lack of adequate Indian forums for resolving private legal disputes between reservation Indians, and between Indians and other private citizens, by permitting the courts of the States to decide such disputes. . . .

. . . This construction finds support in the consistent and uncontradicted references in the legislative history to "permitting" "State courts to adjudicate civil controversies" arising on Indian reservations, and the absence of anything remotely resembling an intention to confer general state civil regulatory control over Indian reservations. In short, the consistent and exclusive use of the terms "civil causes of action," "aris[ing] on," "civil laws . . . of general application to private persons or private property," and "adjudicat[ion]" in both the Act and its legislative history virtually compels our conclusion that the primary intent of [the pertinent section of Public Law 280] was to grant jurisdiction over private civil litigation involving reservation Indians in state court.

Furthermore, certain tribal reservations were completely exempted from the provisions of [Public Law 280] precisely because each had a "tribal law and order organization that functions in a reasonably satisfactory manner." Congress plainly meant only to allow state courts to decide criminal and civil matters arising on reservations not so organized. Accordingly, rather than the expansive reading given . . . by the Minnesota Supreme Court, we feel that the construction we give the section is much more consonant with the revealed congressional intent. Moreover, our construction is consistent with our prior references to [Public Law 280] as "the extension of state jurisdiction over civil causes of action by or against Indians arising in Indian country.". . .

* * *

Other considerations also support our construction. Today's congressional policy toward reservation Indians may less clearly than in 1953 favor their assimilation, but [Public Law 280] was plainly not meant to effect total assimilation. [Public Law 280] was only one of many types of assimilationist legislation under active consideration in 1953. And nothing in its legislative history remotely suggests that Congress meant the Act's extension of civil jurisdiction to the States should result in the undermining or destruction of such tribal governments as did exist and a conversion of the affected tribes into little more than " 'private, voluntary organizations,' "—a possible result if tribal governments and reservation Indians were subordinated to the full panoply of civil regulatory powers, including taxation, of state and local governments. The Act itself refutes such an inference: there is notably absent any conferral of state jurisdiction over the tribes themselves, and [another section of the Act], providing for the "full force and effect" of any tribal ordinances or customs "heretofore or hereafter adopted by an Indian tribe . . .

if not inconsistent with any applicable civil law of the State," contemplates the continuing vitality of tribal government.

Moreover, the same Congress that enacted [Public Law 280] also enacted several termination Acts—legislation which is cogent proof that Congress knew well how to express its intent directly when that intent was to subject reservation Indians to the full sweep of state laws and state taxation. . . .

* * *

Like many cases that American courts have faced and will continue to face, *Bryan v. Itasca County* required the Supreme Court to interpret and apply legislation from one policy era in a much different policy era. There are a number of challenges to this type of situation. For example, should the Court continue to enforce an existing law from the Allotment Era in today's Self-Determination Era? Is a Court obligated to strictly interpret a law regardless of its consequences because it is the law, or is a court obligated to serve a higher sense of justice? Is a court overstepping its bounds by reading older, more troublesome legislation with more modern eyes or is this precisely its role? In this instance, the Court was reading Termination Era legislation in the Self-Determination Era. In an effort to more fully understand what Congress sought to accomplish with Public Law 280 (and perhaps to better justify the decision in a new policy era), the Supreme Court examined the Act's legislative history—congressional reports, committee hearings, statements from the floor of Congress, and other like materials that give context to a statute.

Building from this legislative history as well as the words of Public Law 280 itself, the Court concluded that the purpose of the civil law section was to provide a place for tribal members to litigate their disputes where there was not already an adequate forum in which to address those disputes. As noted above, Public Law 280 was premised in great part on the belief that the tools of law enforcement, particularly Western-style courts and police, were not present or, where present, not adequate on most reservations. Unlike with the criminal law section, in which state law clearly did apply on the reservation, the civil law section was limited to making states provide a place to adjudicate civil disputes for tribal members. Since the Court found nothing more to the civil law section than the need to provide a forum for individual tribal litigants, Minnesota's tax on Bryan was not authorized under Public Law 280. The Court further justified its decision by noting that during the Termination Era, Congress was well aware of how to extend state authority over tribal lands. Since Congress had this knowledge, yet chose to use more limited language, it was another clear sign that the civil law section did not apply state law to reservations in the same way that the criminal law section did.

Just over a decade later, the Supreme Court once again confronted a case about the scope of state civil jurisdiction under Public Law 280. The next case, *California v. Cabazon Band of Mission Indians*, has been fundamental to the development of Indian gaming across the nation and will be discussed again in Chapter 24. Yet, this case is also critical to the understanding of Public Law 280 as well. California, a mandatory Public Law 280 state, was attempting to assert its jurisdiction over the Cabazon Band to prevent the tribal nation from engaging in high stakes bingo. As you read the case, ask yourself how the Court decided how it is going to decide the case. How does the Court frame the important question that will lead to the result in this and other cases? When does a state have authority to assert jurisdiction over Indian Country and when is it prohibited from doing so?

CA V. CABAZON BAND OF MISSION INDIANS
480 U.S. 202 (1987)

JUSTICE WHITE delivered the opinion of the Court.

The Cabazon and Morongo Bands of Mission Indians, federally recognized Indian Tribes, occupy reservations in Riverside County, California. Each Band, pursuant to an ordinance approved by the Secretary of the Interior, conducts bingo games on its reservation. The Cabazon Band has also opened a card club at which draw poker and other card games are played. The games are open to the public, and are played predominantly by non-Indians coming onto the reservations. The games are a major source of employment for tribal members, and the profits are the Tribes' sole source of income. The State of California seeks to apply to the two Tribes [a state statute]. That statute does not entirely prohibit the playing of bingo, but permits it when the games are operated and staffed by members of designated charitable organizations, who may not be paid for their services. Profits must be kept in special accounts and used only for charitable purposes; prizes may not exceed $250 per game. Asserting that the bingo games on the two reservations violated each of these restrictions, California insisted that the Tribes comply with state law. . . .

* * *

The Court has consistently recognized that Indian tribes retain "attributes of sovereignty over both their members and their territory," and that "tribal sovereignty is dependent on, and subordinate to, only the Federal Government, not the States." It is clear, however, that state laws may be applied to tribal Indians on their reservations if Congress has expressly so provided. Here, the State insists that Congress has . . . given its express consent [through Public Law 280]. . . .

In Pub.L. 280, Congress expressly granted six States, including California, jurisdiction over specified areas of Indian country within the States and provided for the assumption of jurisdiction by other States. In § 2, California was granted broad criminal jurisdiction over offenses committed by or against Indians within all Indian country within the State. Section 4's grant of civil jurisdiction was more limited.

In *Bryan v. Itasca County*, we interpreted § 4 to grant States jurisdiction over private civil litigation involving reservation Indians in state court, but not to grant general civil regulatory authority. We held, therefore, that Minnesota could not apply its personal property tax within the reservation. . . . The Act plainly was not intended to effect total assimilation of Indian tribes into mainstream American society. We recognized that a grant to States of general civil regulatory power over Indian reservations would result in the destruction of tribal institutions and values. Accordingly, when a State seeks to enforce a law within an Indian reservation under the authority of Pub.L. 280, it must be determined whether the law is criminal in nature, and thus fully applicable to the reservation under § 2, or civil in nature, and applicable only as it may be relevant to private civil litigation in state court.

The Minnesota personal property tax at issue in *Bryan* was unquestionably civil in nature. The California bingo statute is not so easily categorized. California law permits bingo games to be conducted only by charitable and other specified organizations, and then only by their members who may not receive any wage or profit for doing so; prizes are limited and receipts are to be segregated and used only for charitable purposes. Violation of any of these provisions is a misdemeanor. California insists that these are criminal laws which Pub.L. 280 permits it to enforce on the reservations.

* * *

. . . California does not prohibit all forms of gambling. California itself operates a state lottery, and daily encourages its citizens to participate in this state-run gambling. California also permits parimutuel horse-race betting. Although certain enumerated gambling games are prohibited under [California law], games not enumerated, including the card games played in the Cabazon card club, are permissible. The Tribes assert that more than 400 card rooms similar to the Cabazon card club flourish in California, and the State does not dispute this fact. Also, as the Court of Appeals noted, bingo is legally sponsored by many different organizations, and is widely played in California. There is no effort to forbid the playing of bingo by any member of the public over the age of 18. Indeed, the permitted bingo games must be open to the general public. Nor is there any limit on the number of games which eligible organizations may operate, the receipts which they may obtain from the games, the number of games which a participant may play, or the amount of money which a participant may spend, either per game or in total. In light of the fact that California permits a substantial amount of gambling activity, including bingo, and actually promotes gambling through its state lottery, we must conclude that California regulates, rather than prohibits, gambling in general and bingo in particular.

California argues, however, that high-stakes, unregulated bingo, the conduct which attracts organized crime, is a misdemeanor in California, and may be prohibited on Indian reservations. But that an otherwise regulatory law is enforceable by criminal as well as civil means does not necessarily convert it into a criminal law within the meaning of Pub.L. 280. Otherwise, the distinction between § 2 and § 4 of that law could easily be avoided, and total assimilation permitted. . . .

* * *

In order to determine whether a state law is going to be in force in Indian Country in a Public Law 280 state, the deciding factor, the opinion tells us, is going to be the nature of the law itself. As Justice Byron White's opinion noted, "when a State seeks to enforce a law . . . it must be determined whether the law is criminal in nature, and thus fully applicable to the reservation . . . or civil in nature, and applicable only as it may be relevant to private civil litigation in state court." In essence, if a state law is a "criminal" law, then in Public Law 280 states it will be applicable to tribal lands. If the state law is a "civil" law, then it will not be applicable to tribal lands on its own. Rather, it will only be available to individual Natives who are litigating parties in the state court forums required by Public Law 280. The final outcome in the case was somewhat complicated by the fact that California's law against high stakes bingo did carry some potential criminal penalties for its violations. But, as Court noted, merely carrying the possibility of criminal penalties does not automatically convert a civil law into a criminal law. Thus, the state can stop a customer on the way to a tribal bingo parlor for speeding, but the state cannot dictate the sizes of the prizes that the customer might win at the bingo parlor.

Decisions like *Bryan* and *Cabazon* are positives for Native America in the sense that they repel further encroachments onto tribal sovereignty. However, on the whole Public Law 280 continues to create confusion and negative consequences for tribal nations in Public Law 280 states. While Public Law 280 was supposed to improve law enforcement on tribal land by virtue of having more local authorities in charge, the opposite has been the result. Scholarship has shown that states have not effectively engaged in law enforcement and that Public Law 280 has been a hindrance to tribal sovereignty.

Nor has Public Law 280 been particularly effective in removing the federal government from the "Indian business." In 2010 the federal government authorized tribal nations under Public Law 280 to request that the federal government reassume jurisdiction over crimes within Indian Country, potentially creating a situation where three levels of government—federal, state, and tribal—would have jurisdiction over crimes.

In short, Public Law 280 has left everyone unsatisfied. Nonetheless, over sixty-five years after its passage, the law both remains in force and casts a long shadow over Indian Country.

SUGGESTED READINGS

- *Captured Justice: Native Nations and Public Law 280.* Duane Champagne and Carole Goldberg. Durham, NC: Carolina Academic Press, 2012.

- *Planting Tail Feathers: Tribal Survival and Public Law 280.* Carole Goldberg-Ambrose with the assistance of Timothy Carr Seward. Los Angeles: UCLA American Indian Studies Center, 1997.

- "Negotiating Jurisdiction: Retroceding State Authority Over Indian Country Granted by Public Law 280." Robert T. Anderson. 787 *Washington Law Review* 915 (December 2012).

---

[1] The most well regarded expert on Public Law 280 is Professor Carole Goldberg of the UCLA Law School. This list, as well as other information within this chapter, was put together primarily from two sources that Professor Goldberg has produced. First, *Captured Justice: Native Nations and Public Law 280.* Duane Champagne and Carole Goldberg. Durham, NC: Carolina Academic Press, 2012, 15–18. This source provides a more thorough history of the different maneuvers made by states and tribal nations under Public Law 280 and is highly recommended for anyone wishing to learn more. Second, the "Tribal Jurisdictional Status Analysis" page found on the Tribal Court Clearinghouse website—http://www.tribal-institute.org/lists/tjsa.htm#GROUP%203 (accessed July 1, 2018). Any errors in the list are due exclusively to the author of this text and not to Professor Goldberg or any of her collaborators.

² Similar language to subsection (b) also appears elsewhere in Public Law 280 and has been edited from the excerpt in this chapter for the sake of brevity.

Criminal Jurisdiction

In 1778 the United States and the Delaware entered into what many regard as the first written treaty between the newly formed federal government and a tribal nation. Article IV of the treaty states, "For the better security of the peace and friendship now entered into by the contracting parties, against all infractions of the same by the citizens of either party, to the prejudice of the other, neither party shall proceed to the infliction of punishment on the citizens of the other, otherwise than by securing the offender or offenders by imprisonment, or any other competent means, till a fair and impartial trial can be had by judges or juries of both parties, as near as can be to the laws, customs and usages of the contracting parties and natural justice."

This early document of diplomacy is indicative of the fact that matters of criminal law in Indian Country have been part of the engagement between the United States and tribal nations from the very beginning. As noted in the previous chapter, criminal law involves the definition of crimes and their punishment and it is controlled or directed by the government, whether that government is federal, state, or tribal. Many treaties included "bad man" clauses, which were similar to the treaty with the Delaware in that both the federal government and tribal nation agreed to give over wrongdoers for criminal prosecution in their respective home venues.

Criminal law was also, as noted elsewhere in this text, fundamental to federal efforts during various eras of federal policy. In the Allotment Era, beginning with *Ex parte Crow Dog* (see Chapter 6), the federal government assumed a level of criminal jurisdiction in Indian Country. Indian Courts, Judges, and Police were instrumental federal efforts to extend Western systems of criminal law into Indian Country during the Allotment Era. In the Termination Era, the federal government sought to turn over criminal jurisdiction to certain states through Public Law 280 (see Chapter 17).

In the Self-Determination Era of federal policy (see Chapter 10), a new set of questions concerning criminal law emerged. In essence, these questions asked over whom did tribal nations have criminal jurisdiction? Did the scope of tribal sovereignty include the ability to criminally prosecute tribal citizens? Non-Natives? Citizens of different tribal nations? In starting to answer these questions, the Supreme Court handed down *Oliphant v. Suquamish Indian Tribe*, perhaps the most influential Supreme Court case in the modern era of Indian law.

This chapter will demonstrate. . .

- *The contours of tribal criminal jurisdiction*

- *The continuing legacy of* Oliphant v. Suquamish Indian Tribe

- *The Violence Against Women Act's application in Native America*

CRIMINAL JURISDICTION OVER NON-NATIVES

One of the most positive advancements in Native America during the Self-Determination Era has been the increased proliferation and development of tribal courts. Although tribal nations have always had methods for adjudicating disputes within the community, the presence and growing sophistication of judicial systems that resemble Western counterparts (as well as bodies such as Peacemaker courts that adhere more closely to traditional systems of justice) over the last fifty years has been important and necessary (see Chapter 29). These critical institutions not only serve their particular tribal nations, they aid in developing tribal law throughout Indian Country and they are powerful tools for the expression of sovereignty.

And yet, the growth of tribal courts has created a number of questions in American law as well. As tools of sovereignty, tribal courts have regularly tested the boundaries of tribal authority within American law. American courts have shown a deep concern about the scope of tribal court authority, particularly in the criminal law realm and particularly when it concerns non-Natives.

Perhaps the most important case of modern Indian law, *Oliphant v. Suquamish Indian Tribe*, concerned tribal criminal authority over non-Natives. In 1973 the Suquamish adopted a Law and Order Code—a body of criminal law—to apply to their reservation. Later that year, as the tribal nation was celebrating a longstanding annual festival called Chief Seattle Days, Mark David Oliphant, a non-Native resident of the reservation, was arrested for disorderly conduct and resisting arrest after a drunken fight. Sometime later, Daniel Belgarde, another non-Native resident of the reservation was arrested after leading police on a high speed chase through the reservation that ended when Belgarde smashed into a tribal police car. Oliphant was Belgarde's passenger during the chase.

Both Oliphant and Belgarde were charged in tribal court and both argued that the tribal court did not have the authority to criminally try them. Both sued in federal court to try to prevent the tribal criminal cases from going forward. The question for the federal courts, and eventually the Supreme Court, was whether tribal nations had the authority to criminally prosecute non-Natives.

In order to fully understand the decision in *Oliphant*, it is extremely useful to (re)read *U.S. v. Wheeler* (see Chapter 12). Decided a little over two weeks after *Oliphant*, *Wheeler* considered the source of a tribal nation's authority to criminally prosecute its own citizens. In *Wheeler*, the Supreme Court noted that, "It is undisputed that Indian tribes have the power to enforce their criminal laws against tribe members," and that, "The powers of Indian tribes are, in general, 'inherent powers of a limited sovereignty which has never been extinguished.' " In essence, *Wheeler* stands for the proposition that tribal nations have the inherent authority to criminally prosecute their own citizens by virtue of their own sovereignty. *Wheeler* and *Oliphant* are often considered companion cases and the opinion in *Wheeler* regularly makes reference to the opinion in *Oliphant*.

Whereas *Wheeler* recognized the inherent, sovereign right of tribal nations to criminally prosecute tribal citizens, *Oliphant* asked whether that inherent, sovereign right extended to non-Natives. As you read the case, ask yourself what is the basis for the Court's decision. What evidence does the Court use to support the decision? What are the consequences of the result in the case for tribal nations and reservation communities? Also, what role does the Supreme Court cast for itself in future Indian law cases?

OLIPHANT V. SUQUAMISH INDIAN TRIBE
435 U.S. 191 (1978)

MR. JUSTICE REHNQUIST delivered the opinion of the Court.

... By the 1855 Treaty of Point Elliott the Suquamish Indian Tribe relinquished all rights that it might have had in the lands of the State of Washington and agreed to settle on a 7,276-acre reservation near Port Madison, Wash. Located on Puget Sound across from the city of Seattle, the Port

Madison Reservation is a checkerboard of tribal community land, allotted Indian lands, property held in fee simple by non-Indians, and various roads and public highways maintained by Kitsap County.

The Suquamish Indians are governed by a tribal government which, in 1973, adopted a Law and Order Code. The Code, which covers a variety of offenses from theft to rape, purports to extend the Tribe's criminal jurisdiction over both Indians and non-Indians. Proceedings are held in the Suquamish Indian Provisional Court. Pursuant to the Indian Civil Rights Act of 1968, defendants are entitled to many of the due process protections accorded to defendants in federal or state criminal proceedings. However, the guarantees are not identical. Non-Indians, for example, are excluded from Suquamish tribal court juries.

Both petitioners are non-Indian residents of the Port Madison Reservation. . .

. . . Petitioners argued that the Suquamish Indian Provisional Court does not have criminal jurisdiction over non-Indians. . . . We granted certiorari to decide whether Indian tribal courts have criminal jurisdiction over non-Indians. We decide that they do not.

Respondents do not contend that their exercise of criminal jurisdiction over non-Indians stems from affirmative congressional authorization or treaty provision. Instead, respondents urge that such jurisdiction flows automatically from the "Tribe's retained inherent powers of government over the Port Madison Indian Reservation.". . .

The Suquamish Indian Tribe does not stand alone today in its assumption of criminal jurisdiction over non-Indians. . . . Like the Suquamish these tribes claim authority to try non-Indians not on the basis of congressional statute or treaty provision, but by reason of their retained national sovereignty.

The effort by Indian tribal courts to exercise criminal jurisdiction over non-Indians, however, is a relatively new phenomenon. And where the effort has been made in the past, it has been held that the jurisdiction did not exist. Until the middle of this century, few Indian tribes maintained any semblance of a formal court system. Offenses by one Indian against another were usually handled by social and religious pressure, and not by formal judicial processes; emphasis was on restitution, rather than on punishment. In 1834, the Commissioner of Indian Affairs described the then status of Indian criminal systems. "With the exception of two or three tribes, who have within a few years past attempted to establish some few laws and regulations among themselves, the Indian tribes are without laws, and the chiefs without much authority to exercise any restraint."

... [I]t was apparently assumed that the tribes did not have criminal jurisdiction over non-Indians absent a congressional statute or treaty provision to that effect. For example, the 1830 Treaty with the Choctaw Indian Tribe, which had one of the most sophisticated of tribal structures, guaranteed to the Tribe "the jurisdiction and government of all the persons and property that may be within their limits." Despite the broad terms of this governmental guarantee, however, the Choctaws at the conclusion of this treaty provision, "express a wish that Congress may grant to the Choctaws the right of punishing by their own laws any white man who shall come into their nation, and infringe any of their national regulations."

Such a request for affirmative congressional authority is inconsistent with respondents' belief that criminal jurisdiction over non-Indians is inherent in tribal sovereignty. Faced by attempts of the Choctaw Tribe to try non-Indian offenders in the early 1800's, the United States Attorneys General also concluded that the Choctaws did not have criminal jurisdiction over non-Indians absent congressional authority. . . .

At least one court has previously considered the power of Indian courts to try non-Indians, and it also held against jurisdiction. In Ex parte Kenyon, Judge Isaac C. Parker, who as District Court Judge for the Western District of Arkansas was constantly exposed to the legal relationships between Indians and non-Indians, held that, to give an Indian tribal court "jurisdiction of the person of an offender, such offender must be an Indian." The conclusion of Judge Parker was reaffirmed only recently in a 1970 opinion of the Solicitor of the Department of the Interior.[11]

While Congress was concerned almost from its beginning with the special problems of law enforcement on the Indian reservations, it did not initially address itself to the problem of tribal jurisdiction over non-Indians. For the reasons previously stated, there was little reason to be concerned with assertions of tribal court jurisdiction over non-Indians, because of the absence of formal tribal judicial systems. . . .

* * *

It was in 1834 that Congress was first directly faced with the prospect of Indians trying non-Indians. In the Western Territory bill, Congress proposed

---

[11] The 1970 opinion of the Solicitor was withdrawn in 1974 but has not been replaced. No reason was given for the withdrawal.

to create an Indian territory beyond the western-directed destination of the settlers; the territory was to be governed by a confederation of Indian tribes and was expected ultimately to become a State of the Union. While the bill would have created a political territory with broad governing powers, Congress was careful not to give the tribes of the territory criminal jurisdiction over United States officials and citizens traveling through the area.[13]. . . .

* * *

In 1891, this Court recognized that Congress' various actions and inactions in regulating criminal jurisdiction on Indian reservations demonstrated an intent to reserve jurisdiction over non-Indians for the federal courts. In *In re Mayfield*, the Court noted that the policy of Congress had been to allow the inhabitants of the Indian country, "such power of self-government as was thought to be consistent with the safety of the white population with which they may have come in contact, and to encourage them as far as possible in raising themselves to our standard of civilization.". . .

While Congress never expressly forbade Indian tribes to impose criminal penalties on non-Indians, we now make express our implicit conclusion of nearly a century ago that Congress consistently believed this to be the necessary result of its repeated legislative actions.

In a 1960 Senate Report that body expressly confirmed its assumption that Indian tribal courts are without inherent jurisdiction to try non-Indians, and must depend on the Federal Government for protection from intruders.[15]. . . .

* * *

While not conclusive on the issue before us, the commonly shared presumption of Congress, the Executive Branch, and lower federal courts that tribal courts do not have the power to try non-Indians carries considerable weight. "Indian law" draws principally upon the treaties drawn and executed by the Executive Branch and legislation passed by Congress. These instruments, which, beyond their actual text, form the backdrop for the intricate web of judicially made Indian law, cannot be interpreted in isolation,

---

[13] . . . Even as drafted, many Congressman felt that the bill was too radical a shift in United States-Indian relations and the bill was tabled. While the Western Territory Bill was resubmitted several times in revised form, it was never passed.

[15] In 1977, a congressional Policy Review Commission . . . concluded that "[t]here is an established legal basis for tribes to exercise jurisdiction over non-Indians." However, the Commission's report does not deny that for almost 200 years before . . . the three branches of the Federal Government were in apparent agreement that Indian tribes do not have jurisdiction over non-Indians. As the Vice Chairman of the Commission, Congressman Lloyd Meads, noted in dissent, "such jurisdiction has generally not been asserted and . . . the lack of legislation on this point reflects a congressional assumption that there was no such tribal jurisdiction."

but must be read in light of the common notions of the day and the assumptions of those who drafted them.

While, in isolation, the Treaty of Point Elliott would appear to be silent as to tribal criminal jurisdiction over non-Indians, the addition of historical perspective casts substantial doubt upon the existence of such jurisdiction. In the Ninth Article, for example, the Suquamish "acknowledge their dependence on the government of the United States.". . . By acknowledging their dependence on the United States, in the Treaty of Point Elliott, the Suquamish were, in all probability, recognizing that the United States would arrest and try non-Indian intruders who came within their Reservation. Other provisions of the Treaty also point to the absence of tribal jurisdiction. . . .

By themselves, these treaty provisions would probably not be sufficient to remove criminal jurisdiction over non-Indians if the Tribe otherwise retained such jurisdiction. But an examination of our earlier precedents satisfies us that, even ignoring treaty provisions and congressional policy, Indians do not have criminal jurisdiction over non-Indians absent affirmative delegation of such power by Congress. Indian tribes do retain elements of "quasi-sovereign" authority after ceding their lands to the United States and announcing their dependence on the Federal Government. But the tribes' retained powers are not such that they are limited only by specific restrictions in treaties or congressional enactments. As the Court of Appeals recognized, Indian tribes are prohibited from exercising both those powers of autonomous states that are expressly terminated by Congress and those powers "*inconsistent with their status.*" (emphasis added).

* * *

. . . By submitting to the overriding sovereignty of the United States, Indian tribes therefore necessarily give up their power to try non-Indian citizens of the United States except in a manner acceptable to Congress. This principle would have been obvious a century ago when most Indian tribes were characterized by a "want of fixed laws [and] of competent tribunals of justice." It should be no less obvious today, even though present-day Indian tribal courts embody dramatic advances over their historical antecedents.

In *Ex parte Crow Dog*, the Court was faced with almost the inverse of the issue before us here—whether, prior to the passage of the Major Crimes Act, federal courts had jurisdiction to try Indians who had offended against fellow Indians on reservation land. In concluding that criminal jurisdiction was exclusively in the tribe, it found particular guidance in the "nature and circumstances of the case." The United States was seeking to extend United States

> law, by argument and inference only, . . . over aliens and strangers; over the members of a community separated by race [and] tradition, . . . from the authority and power which seeks to impose upon them the restraints of an external and unknown code . . .; which judges them by a standard made by others and not for them. . . . It tries them not by their peers, nor by the customs of their people, nor the law of their land, but by . . . a different race, according to the law of a social state of which they have an imperfect conception. . . .

These considerations, applied here to the non-Indian, rather than Indian, offender, speak equally strongly against the validity of respondents' contention that Indian tribes, although fully subordinated to the sovereignty of the United States, retain the power to try non-Indians according to their own customs and procedure.

* * *

In summary, respondents' position ignores that

> Indians are within the geographical limits of the United States. The soil and people within these limits are under the political control of the Government of the United States, or of the States of the Union. There exist in the broad domain of sovereignty but these two. There may be cities, counties, and other organized bodies with limited legislative functions, but they . . . exist in subordination to one or the other of these. *United States v. Kagama.*

We recognize that some Indian tribal court systems have become increasingly sophisticated, and resemble in many respects their state counterparts. We also acknowledge that, with the passage of the Indian Civil Rights Act of 1968, which extends certain basic procedural rights to anyone tried in Indian tribal court, many of the dangers that might have accompanied the exercise by tribal courts of criminal jurisdiction over non-Indians only a few decades ago have disappeared. Finally, we are not unaware of the prevalence of non-Indian crime on today's reservations which the tribes forcefully argue requires the ability to try non-Indians. But these are considerations for Congress to weigh in deciding whether Indian tribes should finally be authorized to try non-Indians. They have little relevance to the principles which lead us to conclude that Indian tribes do not have inherent jurisdiction to try and to punish non-Indians. . . .

Then Associate Justice William Rehnquist's opinion is perhaps the most influential and most maligned decision in the modern era of federal Indian law. The legal principle that emerges from Oliphant is fairly straightforward: Tribal nations do not have the inherent authority to criminally prosecute non-Natives. The reasoning and methods used to get to that principle are much less straightforward and have earned much criticism throughout Native America.

The legal principle that emerges from the case—that tribal nations do not have criminal jurisdiction over non-Natives—is built upon the assertion that the federal government has never recognized the right of tribal nations to criminally prosecute non-Natives. It is a useful exercise to go back through the opinion and identify each piece of evidence that Rehnquist uses to make this assertion, including the footnotes that give some of the pieces of evidence more context. Does this evidence lead to the conclusion that Rehnquist states that it does? What are the strengths and weaknesses of each piece of evidence? How does each apply to the Suquamish?

Another striking feature of the opinion, which many have critiqued, is the straightforward manner in which this relatively recent Supreme Court opinion cites and uses older Indian law cases. In fact, much of the resolution of *Oliphant* is built upon cases from the Allotment Era of federal policy. This raises one of the most difficult questions that American courts have to face in this field of law: To what extent is a modern day court beholden to the decisions, attitudes, and assumptions from older policy eras? Should a court in the Self-Determination Era interpret legal events and documents from, for example, the Allotment Era in the spirit of the Allotment Era or the spirit of the Self-Determination Era? Rehnquist's opinion clearly leans toward interpreting legal events in the spirit of the era from which they came, with little, if any, critical reflection on the circumstances or understandings fueling the decisions of the earlier cases.

Most prominently, Rehnquist extensively quotes from *Ex parte Crow Dog*. The excerpt in this text has replicated Rehnquist's block quote in full—the many ellipses in the excerpt also appear in the original *Oliphant* opinion. It is also a useful exercise to compare the text that Rehnquist uses with the original text from *Ex parte Crow Dog* (see Chapter 6). What does Rehnquist's edit leave out from the original *Crow Dog* text? What is the point Rehnquist is attempting to make with his use of the text from *Crow Dog*? What was the point Justice Stanley Matthews was seeking to make in the 1883 *Crow Dog* opinion? Are those two understandings, written ninety-five years apart, compatible with one another? What are the underlying ideas that fuel both of these points? What might this mean for Native America?

The *Oliphant* decision is certainly important for the principle of law that it established. However, the reason why it may very well be the most influential Indian law case of the modern era is the ultimate justification for the principle of law established in the case. The opinion noted that, "Indian tribes are prohibited from exercising . . . those powers *'inconsistent with their status'* " (emphasis in original). This assertion raises a number of important questions. Primarily, what is the status of tribal nations? And then consequently, what powers are consistent with that status and what powers are inconsistent with that status? When considering these questions, it is helpful to reflect on *Wheeler*, the companion case to *Oliphant* discussed before the excerpt. The opinion in *Wheeler* regularly referenced *Oliphant*, as both were considering somewhat similar subject matter. Whereas *Oliphant* ruled that tribal criminal jurisdiction over non-Natives was not authorized because it was "inconsistent" with their status, *Wheeler* ruled that it was "undisputed" that tribal nations could criminally prosecute their own citizens. Between the two cases, there is a limited measure of clarity about the "status" of tribal nations.

Yet, *Wheeler* to some degree and *Oliphant* particularly beg an even deeper, and perhaps more troubling, question: Who decides what is the "status" of tribal nations? In general, prior to *Oliphant*, the Supreme Court would regularly defer to the political branches of the federal government when it concerned Indian policy and the scope of tribal sovereignty, sometimes to a fault. But *Oliphant* signaled a break from that tradition. After *Oliphant*, the Supreme Court has in many instances been the branch of government that has decided the "status" of tribal nations, often to the frustration of the general spirit of the Self-Determination Era. *Oliphant* is perhaps the most important case of the modern era of Indian law because it opened the door to the increased involvement of the Supreme Court (and lower courts) in defining the boundaries of tribal sovereignty. Without any context, this development could be understood as a neutral event, or perhaps even welcome considering many appeals tribal nations have made to American courts and the difficulties that tribal nations have had with the political branches of the federal government. Yet, considering both the result in *Oliphant* and how it came about, there was much trepidation in Native America after the case. This has been particularly so since *Oliphant* also introduced the subject of race into questions about tribal jurisdiction. After *Oliphant*, any tribal government seeking to assert its criminal jurisdiction on its lands must first determine the race of the alleged criminal.

The Suquamish had developed a Law and Order Code because they, like many Native communities, suffered from a lack of adequate law enforcement.

American governments, whether either the federal government or state governments through Public Law 280 (see Chapter 17), have some form of criminal jurisdiction on tribal lands. However, Native America has routinely criticized both the federal government and the states for not providing the funds or services to properly police and serve tribal communities, especially when it came to non-Native offenders. To that end, the Suquamish, and other similarly situated tribal nations in the Self-Determination Era before *Oliphant*, had decided to make up for those deficiencies with their own laws, courts, and police.

The decision in *Oliphant* not only limited the capacity of tribal nations to police everyone on the reservation, it made the situation tribal nations like the Suquamish were trying to address even worse. Non-Native offenders on reservations began to realize that reservations could be spaces without formal consequences for their actions. Tribal governments could not arrest or prosecute non-Native offenders and states and the federal government routinely would not prosecute them.

Those most victimized by the lack of adequate law enforcement in general and even more so after *Oliphant* have been Native women, particularly as it concerns domestic and sexual violence. Matters of domestic and sexual violence traditionally have been areas that law enforcement at all levels have often been reluctant to engage with, regardless of the races or circumstances of the victims. However, Native women, especially those with non-Native partners, have been very vulnerable, as tribal nations are unable to criminally prosecute non-Native partners and states and the federal government have failed to do so. In 2007 Amnesty International published a report noting that Native women are 2.5 times more likely to be raped than other women in the United States and that 34.1% of Native women will be raped in their lifetime. The report also stated that these statistics are likely lower than the real figures as crimes of sexual violence often go unreported.[1]

Congress responded to these shocking statistics in 2013 through the reauthorization of the Violence Against Women Act (VAWA). Originally enacted by Congress in 1994, VAWA has been reauthorized on a handful of occasions since then. The purpose of the law has been to encourage greater law enforcement attention to domestic violence, and the scope of the law has expanded over time.

In general, VAWA has received bipartisan support. But in 2012 and 2013, reauthorization of the bill ran into some resistance because it was expanded to include, among other things, protections for Native women in tribal courts. For the first time since *Oliphant*, non-Natives could be subject to tribal criminal jurisdiction after the expansion of VAWA. As you read the excerpt of the law, ask yourself when tribal courts have criminal jurisdiction over non-Natives. What crimes are covered under the law? What are the exceptions even when one of those crimes is committed? What rights do the accused have under the law?

VIOLENCE AGAINST WOMEN ACT (2013 REAUTHORIZATION)
25 U.S.C.A. § 1304(b), (c) and (d)

(b) Nature of the criminal jurisdiction

(1) In general . . . the powers of self-government of a participating tribe include the inherent power of that tribe, which is hereby recognized and affirmed, to exercise special domestic violence criminal jurisdiction over all persons.

(2) Concurrent jurisdiction The exercise of special domestic violence criminal jurisdiction by a participating tribe shall be concurrent with the jurisdiction of the United States, of a State, or of both.

(3) Applicability Nothing in this section—

(A) creates or eliminates any Federal or State criminal jurisdiction over Indian country; or

(B) affects the authority of the United States or any State government that has been delegated authority by the United States to investigate and prosecute a criminal violation in Indian country.

(4) Exceptions

(A) Victim and defendant are both non-Indians

(i) In general A participating tribe may not exercise special domestic violence criminal jurisdiction over an alleged offense if neither the defendant nor the alleged victim is an Indian. . . .

(B) Defendant lacks ties to the Indian tribe A participating tribe may exercise special domestic violence criminal jurisdiction over a defendant only if the defendant—

(i) resides in the Indian country of the participating tribe;

(ii) is employed in the Indian country of the participating tribe; or

(iii) is a spouse, intimate partner, or dating partner of—

(I) a member of the participating tribe; or

(II) an Indian who resides in the Indian country of the participating tribe.

(c) Criminal conduct

A participating tribe may exercise special domestic violence criminal jurisdiction over a defendant for criminal conduct that falls into one or more of the following categories:

(1) **Domestic violence and dating violence** An act of domestic violence or dating violence that occurs in the Indian country of the participating tribe.

(2) **Violations of protection orders** An act that—

(A) occurs in the Indian country of the participating tribe; and

(B) violates the portion of a protection order that—

(i) prohibits or provides protection against violent or threatening acts or harassment against, sexual violence against, contact or communication with, or physical proximity to, another person; [and other conditions]

(d) Rights of defendants

In a criminal proceeding in which a participating tribe exercises special domestic violence criminal jurisdiction, the participating tribe shall provide to the defendant—

(1) all applicable rights under this Act;

(2) if a term of imprisonment of any length may be imposed, all rights described in [the Indian Civil Rights Act];

(3) the right to a trial by an impartial jury that is drawn from sources that—

(A) reflect a fair cross section of the community; and

(B) do not systematically exclude any distinctive group in the community, including non-Indians; and

(4) all other rights whose protection is necessary under the Constitution of the United States in order for Congress to recognize and affirm the inherent power of the participating tribe to exercise special domestic violence criminal jurisdiction over the defendant.

* * *

VAWA seeks to walk a fine line. The law does open up tribal criminal jurisdiction over non-Natives, but only over a very limited number of offenses (domestic and dating violence and violations of protection orders) and with the requirement of a number of procedural protections for the accused. It both recognizes a greater scope of tribal authority, but it also creates more federal oversight for tribal nations. Nonetheless, it has been hailed as a significant step in a positive direction by many in Indian Country and several tribal nations have initiated programs to implement the legislation. It is still too early to tell what level of impact VAWA has had in Native America, but it does represent a step away from *Oliphant* and many remain enthusiastic about its potential.

CRIMINAL JURISDICTION OVER OTHER NATIVES

Wheeler stands for the proposition that tribal nations do have the inherent authority to criminally prosecute their own citizens. *Oliphant* stands for the proposition that tribal nations do not have the inherent authority to criminally prosecute non-Natives. While covering many people, these two propositions nonetheless do not cover everybody. For example, *Wheeler* and *Oliphant* tell us that Tribal Nation A can criminally prosecute a citizen of Tribal Nation A, but not a non-Native, even if that person lives on the reservation or otherwise has close ties to the nation. Yet, what about citizens of other tribal nations? Can Tribal Nation A criminally prosecute a citizen of Tribal Nation B? Does the "status" of tribal nations allow for the criminal prosecution of non-citizen Natives?

The Supreme Court took up this question in a 1990 case, *Duro v. Reina*.[2] In the circumstances leading up to the case, Albert Duro, a citizen of the Torres-Martinez Band of the Cahuilla Mission Band of Indians, allegedly shot and killed a 14-year-old boy on the Salt River Pima-Maricopa reservation. The federal government originally arrested Duro for the alleged crime, but the charges were eventually dropped. The Salt River Pima-Maricopa Indian Community then sought to criminally prosecute Duro for the alleged crime and Duro responded by suing in federal court, arguing that the Salt River Pima-Maricopa did not have the authority to criminally prosecute him, as he was not a citizen of that nation.

Faced with the choice presented by Albert Duro's situation, the Supreme Court moved further down the path that was paved by *Oliphant*. Justice Anthony Kennedy's opinion stated that, "We think the rationale of our decisions in *Oliphant* and *Wheeler*, as well as subsequent cases, compels the conclusion that Indian tribes lack jurisdiction over persons who are not tribe members." Framing it in terms of the "status" of tribal nations, Kennedy stated that, "The areas in which such implicit divestiture of sovereignty has been held to have occurred are those involving the relations between an Indian tribe and nonmembers of the tribe." The opinion is also noteworthy for its description of tribal courts. Not unlike *Oliphant*, or even *Crow Dog*, Kennedy's opinion suggested that tribal courts were not only insufficient for the task of criminal jurisdiction over non-Natives, but that there were mysterious, unknown elements to them. "While modern tribal courts include many familiar features of the judicial process, they are influenced by the unique customs, languages, and usages of the tribes they serve. Tribal courts . . . may depend on 'unspoken practices and norms.' "

Congress acted quickly in the wake of *Duro v. Reina* and enacted what is colloquially known as the "*Duro* Fix" in 1991. In essence, Congress amended the Indian Civil Rights Act in order to reverse the decision in *Duro*. As you read the *Duro* Fix, pay special attention to the language the statute uses to give sanction to the authority of tribal nations to criminally prosecute non-citizen Natives. What is distinctive about this language? Would there have been a different way to come to the same result? Why might the drafters of this amendment chosen this particular language?

> ## "DURO FIX" (AMENDMENT TO THE INDIAN CIVIL RIGHTS ACT)
> 25 U.S.C.A. § 1301
>
> For purposes of this subchapter, the term. . . .
>
> 2) "powers of self-government" means and includes . . . the inherent power of Indian tribes, hereby recognized and affirmed, to exercise criminal jurisdiction over all Indians. . . .

The drafters of the *Duro* Fix were deliberate in stating that Congress "recognized and affirmed" the right of tribal nations to criminally prosecute non-citizen Natives, and equally deliberate in avoiding words like "delegated" or "authorized" to describe the authority held by tribal nations. If the drafters had used words like "delegated" or "authorized" then a tribal nation's authority to criminally prosecute non-citizen Natives would have been understood to have been given to them by the federal government. By using words like "recognized and affirmed," the drafters of the *Duro* Fix were signaling their belief that a tribal nation's authority to criminally prosecute non-citizen Natives derived from a tribal nation's inherent sovereignty.

The distinction was important because of what it would have meant for criminal defendants and the various levels of government attempting to prosecute them. As with *Wheeler*, the *Duro* Fix raised potential issues of double jeopardy (see Chapter 12). The "Double Jeopardy" clause of the 5th Amendment of the U.S. Constitution bars the federal government from engaging in a second or subsequent criminal prosecution for a particular incident. Consequently, if the tribal authority to criminally prosecute non-citizen Natives was given or delegated by the federal government, then when a tribal court convicted a defendant, the federal government would be prohibited from also criminally prosecuting that defendant in federal court for the same incident, and vice versa. Much like the Supreme Court in *Wheeler*, the drafters of the *Duro* Fix wanted to avoid this possibility, especially since the Indian Civil Rights Act limits the amount of punishment a tribal court can hand down (see Chapter 22). However, if a tribal government's authority to criminally prosecute a non-citizen Native was derived from its own inherent and retained sovereignty, then any potential double jeopardy problems would cease to exist. Tribal nations could prosecute a defendant for an incident under their own sovereign authority and the federal government could also prosecute for that same incident under its own authority under the U.S. Constitution. This is known as the Dual Sovereignty doctrine.

The *Duro* Fix was destined to make its way to the Supreme Court, particularly in the wake of *Oliphant*. The circumstances leading to *U.S. v. Lara*—the *Duro* Fix's challenge in the Supreme Court—were precisely of the sort that the drafters of the *Duro* Fix anticipated. Billy Jo Lara, a citizen of the Turtle Mountain Band of Chippewa Indians, lived with his spouse and children on the Spirit Lake Reservation. After Lara repeatedly caused trouble, the Spirit Lake Nation issued an order excluding Lara from the reservation. Lara ignored the order and attempted to return to the Spirit Lake Reservation. When federal officers attempted to stop Lara, he struck one of them.

As a result of the incident, the Spirit Lake Nation charged Lara for hitting the officer. Lara pled guilty and spent ninety days in jail. Shortly thereafter, the federal government also charged Lara for hitting the officer. This time, Lara objected, claiming that the *Duro* Fix was actually a delegation of authority from the federal government to tribal nations. Consequently, according to Lara, the subsequent federal charge was a violation of double jeopardy under the U.S. Constitution. The question before the Supreme Court was whether Congress had the ability to "recognize and affirm" an inherent tribal power, or whether Congress only had the ability to delegate such authority. As you read the case, ask yourself why the majority opinion decided that the *Duro* Fix was a valid exercise of Congressional power. What are the reasons? Why are there so many of them? What might the number of reasons tell one about the opinion as a whole? How does the concurrence ask one to think differently about these issues?

U.S. V. LARA
541 U.S. 193 (2004)

JUSTICE BREYER delivered the opinion of the Court.

This case concerns a congressional statute "recogniz[ing] and affirm[ing]" the "inherent" authority of a tribe to bring a criminal misdemeanor prosecution against an Indian who is not a member of that tribe—authority that this Court previously held a tribe did not possess. We must decide whether Congress has the constitutional power to relax restrictions that the political branches have, over time, placed on the exercise of a tribe's inherent legal authority. We conclude that Congress does possess this power.

* * *

The Government noted that this Court has held that an Indian tribe acts as a separate sovereign when it prosecutes its own members. The Government recognized, of course, that Lara is not one of the Spirit Lake Tribe's own members; it also recognized that, in *Duro v. Reina*, this Court had held that a tribe no longer possessed inherent or sovereign authority to prosecute a "nonmember Indian." But it pointed out that, soon after this Court decided *Duro*, Congress enacted new legislation specifically authorizing a tribe to prosecute Indian members of a different tribe. That new statute, in permitting a tribe to bring certain tribal prosecutions against nonmember Indians, does not purport to delegate the Federal Government's own federal power. Rather, it enlarges the tribes' own " 'powers of self-government' " to include "the inherent power of Indian tribes, hereby recognized and affirmed, to exercise criminal jurisdiction over all Indians," including nonmembers.

In the Government's view, given this statute, the Tribe, in prosecuting Lara, had exercised its own inherent tribal authority, not delegated federal authority; hence the "dual sovereignty" doctrine applies, and since the two prosecutions were brought by two different sovereigns, the second, federal, prosecution does not violate the Double Jeopardy Clause.

* * *

We assume, as do the parties, that Lara's double jeopardy claim turns on the answer to the "dual sovereignty" question. What is "the source of [the] power to punish" nonmember Indian offenders, "inherent tribal sovereignty" or delegated federal authority?

We also believe that Congress intended the former answer. The statute says that it "recognize[s] and affirm[s]" in each tribe the "inherent" tribal power (not delegated federal power) to prosecute nonmember Indians for misdemeanors.

                                   * * *

Thus the statute seeks to adjust the tribes' status. It relaxes the restrictions, recognized in *Duro*, that the political branches had imposed on the tribes' exercise of inherent prosecutorial power. The question before us is whether the Constitution authorizes Congress to do so. Several considerations lead us to the conclusion that Congress does possess the constitutional power to lift the restrictions on the tribes' criminal jurisdiction over nonmember Indians as the statute seeks to do.

First, the Constitution grants Congress broad general powers to legislate in respect to Indian tribes, powers that we have consistently described as "plenary and exclusive.". . .

                                   * * *

Second, Congress, with this Court's approval, has interpreted the Constitution's "plenary" grants of power as authorizing it to enact legislation that both restricts and, in turn, relaxes those restrictions on tribal sovereign authority. . . .

                                   * * *

Third, Congress' statutory goal—to modify the degree of autonomy enjoyed by a dependent sovereign that is not a State—is not an unusual legislative objective. . . .

                                   * * *

Fourth, Lara points to no explicit language in the Constitution suggesting a limitation on Congress' institutional authority to relax restrictions on tribal sovereignty previously imposed by the political branches.

Fifth, the change at issue here is a limited one. It concerns a power similar in some respects to the power to prosecute a tribe's own members—a power that this Court has called "inherent.". . .

                                   * * *

Sixth, our conclusion that Congress has the power to relax the restrictions imposed by the political branches on the tribes' inherent prosecutorial authority is consistent with our earlier cases. True, the Court held in those cases that the power to prosecute nonmembers was an aspect of the tribes' external relations and hence part of the tribal sovereignty that was divested by treaties and by Congress. But these holdings reflect the Court's view of the tribes' retained sovereign status as of the time the Court made them. They did not set forth constitutional limits that prohibit Congress from changing the relevant legal circumstances, i.e., from taking actions that modify or adjust the tribes' status.

* * *

JUSTICE THOMAS, concurring in the judgment.

As this case should make clear, the time has come to reexamine the premises and logic of our tribal sovereignty cases. It seems to me that much of the confusion reflected in our precedent arises from two largely incompatible and doubtful assumptions. First, Congress (rather than some other part of the Federal Government) can regulate virtually every aspect of the tribes without rendering tribal sovereignty a nullity. Second, the Indian tribes retain inherent sovereignty to enforce their criminal laws against their own members. These assumptions, which I must accept as the case comes to us, dictate the outcome in this case, and I therefore concur in the judgment.

I write separately principally because the Court fails to confront these tensions, a result that flows from the Court's inadequate constitutional analysis. I cannot agree with the Court, for instance, that the Constitution grants to Congress plenary power to calibrate the "metes and bounds of tribal sovereignty.". . . In my view, the tribes either are or are not separate sovereigns, and our federal Indian law cases untenably hold both positions simultaneously.

* * *

. . . To be sure, it makes sense to conceptualize the tribes as sovereigns that, due to their unique situation, cannot exercise the full measure of their sovereign powers. . . .

But I do not see how this is consistent with the apparently "undisputed fact that Congress has plenary authority to legislate for the Indian tribes in all matters, including their form of government.". . . It is quite arguably the essence of sovereignty not to exist merely at the whim of an external government.

* * *

To be sure, this does not quite suffice to demonstrate that the tribes had lost their sovereignty. After all, States retain sovereignty despite the fact that Congress can regulate States *qua* States in certain limited circumstances. But the States (unlike the tribes) are part of a constitutional framework that allocates sovereignty between the State and Federal Governments and specifically grants Congress authority to legislate with respect to them. . . .

The tribes, by contrast, are not part of this constitutional order, and their sovereignty is not guaranteed by it. . . . Federal Indian policy is, to say the least, schizophrenic. And this confusion continues to infuse federal Indian law and our cases.

I believe that we must examine more critically our tribal sovereignty case law. Both the Court and the dissent, however, compound the confusion by failing to undertake the necessary rigorous constitutional analysis. I would begin by carefully following our assumptions to their logical conclusions and by identifying the potential sources of federal power to modify tribal sovereignty.

* * *

The Court should admit that it has failed in its quest to find a source of congressional power to adjust tribal sovereignty. Such an acknowledgment might allow the Court to ask the logically antecedent question *whether* Congress (as opposed to the President) has this power. A cogent answer would serve as the foundation for the analysis of the sovereignty issues posed by this case. We might find that the Federal Government cannot regulate the tribes through ordinary domestic legislation and simultaneously maintain that the tribes are sovereigns in any meaningful sense. But until we begin to analyze these questions honestly and rigorously, the confusion that I have identified will continue to haunt our cases.

Justice Stephen Breyer's majority opinion offers six different justifications for the Supreme Court's ruling that Congress does have the authority to "recognize" powers that are inherent to sovereignty of tribal nations. It is useful to list these reasons and consider some questions. Do they fit together into a coherent whole, like pieces in a puzzle? Is each stated reason necessary to come to the conclusion that Congress can recognize this tribal power? Could any reason on its own justify the result? Could any smaller grouping of reasons justify the result? Many in Native America hailed the decision in *Lara* and its consequences for tribal sovereignty. However, few were inspired by Breyer's reasoning and the path to get to the judgment in the case.

On occasion, a secondary opinion in a case—either a concurrence or a dissent—will grow to have more influence than the majority opinion. This may one day be the fate of Justice Clarence Thomas's concurrence in *Lara*. Certainly, Thomas's concurrence caught the attention of many Indian law scholars.

Perhaps more so than any other Supreme Court justice either before or since, Thomas described the central tension at the heart of federal Indian law. Although not every commentator would describe it in such stark terms, Thomas identified two main pillars of federal Indian law: tribal sovereignty and plenary power. According to Thomas, these two pillars are inherently contradictory and cannot co-exist and the Supreme Court would do well to openly and critically examine its Indian law doctrine. Perhaps even more surprisingly, Thomas openly questioned whether there really was a constitutional basis for Congressional plenary power in Indian affairs (see Chapters 6 and 7). Without this basis, it would be fair to ask whether Congress really had any authority in this area at all. Thomas's concurrence has suggested to supporters of tribal sovereignty that they might not like the conclusion to which he would come if he were to undergo this examination. Nonetheless, Thomas argued that until the Supreme Court confronts the contradictions at its very foundation of Indian law, "the confusion that [we] have identified will continue to haunt our cases." Several have agreed with this point.

As yet, the Supreme Court has not acted upon Justice Thomas's invitation, and federal Indian law remains rooted in its traditional analytical structure. Consequently, tribal criminal jurisdiction, with some noteworthy exceptions such as VAWA, remains largely defined by *Oliphant* and *Lara*. Tribal nations have criminal jurisdiction over Natives, regardless of their tribal affiliation, but do not have criminal jurisdiction over non-Natives.

SUGGESTED READINGS

- "Mark the Plumber v. Tribal Empire, or Non-Indian Anxiety v. Tribal Sovereignty?: The Story of *Oliphant v. Suquamish Indian Tribe*." Sarah Krakoff. In *Indian Law Stories*. Carole Goldberg et al Eds. New York: Foundation Press, 2011, 261–296.

- "*United States v. Lara* as a Story of Native Agency." Bethany R. Berger. *Tulsa Law Review* 5 (Fall 2004).

- "Federal Indian Law and Tribal Criminal Justice in the Self-Determination Era." Samuel E. Ennis and Caroline P. Mayhew. 38 *American Indian Law Review* 421 (2013–2014).

1   *Maze of Injustice: The Failure to Protect Indigenous Women from Sexual Violence in the USA.* Amnesty International. https://www.amnestyusa.org/pdfs/mazeofinjustice.pdf (Accessed July 14, 2018).

2   495 U.S. 676 (1990).

CHAPTER 19

Civil Jurisdiction

On any given day there are countless incidents—some big and some small, some common and some unusual—that might give rise to a dispute that a court will have to adjudicate: Two or more vehicles get into an automobile accident; a company breaks a contractual promise to another company; two drunken patrons of a bar get into a fight. Some of these incidents may be crimes, and the appropriate government or governments might wish to prosecute them.

But several of these incidents are not crimes, or, even if they are crimes, the individuals or entities involved might want their own resolution outside of the criminal justice system as well. For example, if Company A breaks a contractual promise to Company B, it is not likely to give rise to criminal charges, yet Company B will likely want to find resolution for the promise that was broken. Additionally, if Driver Y caused an automobile accident while speeding that injures Driver Z, then the government (most likely a state government) might choose to criminally prosecute Driver Y for the speeding and the damage caused by the accident. However, the criminal prosecution of Driver Y will not result in any tangible benefit to Driver Z. Thus, Driver Z might also seek restitution from Driver Y for the injuries that Driver Z suffered. Both Company B and Driver Z might turn to the civil court system for resolution to their particular dilemmas.

What if that automobile accident or that bar fight occurs within the borders of a reservation? What if private citizens, companies, or other entities want to settle their disputes in tribal courts under tribal law? More important, what if one private party wants to use the tribal judicial system while the other party or parties to a dispute do not want to employ the tribal judicial system? Does the scope of tribal sovereignty include the authority to resolve these types of disputes in tribal court? If so, does that include those incidents when non-Natives are involved? If not, why not?

> *This chapter will demonstrate...*
>
> • *The* Montana *test for tribal civil jurisdiction*
>
> • *The differences and similarities between* Montana *and* Oliphant
>
> • *The scope and rationales for cases concerning the* Montana *test's exceptions*

THE *MONTANA* TEST

Civil law concerns the disputes between private parties that can be remedied under the law. Consequently, civil jurisdiction concerns the scope of a court's authority to hear those types of disputes. And in order to understand the scope of a tribal nation's civil jurisdiction, it is important to understand two facets of federal Indian law and policy and Native America generally: the legacy of the *Oliphant v. Suquamish Indian Tribe* case and the checkerboarding of reservation lands.

The first facet, *Oliphant*, was decided in 1978 and it dramatically changed Indian law in a number of ways (see Chapter 18). It is useful to (re)read *Oliphant* to understand the materials in the rest of this chapter. In *Oliphant*, in a widely critiqued opinion among Indian law scholars by then Associate Justice William Rehnquist, the Supreme Court decided that tribal nations could not exercise those powers "inconsistent with their status," including criminal jurisdiction over non-Natives. Among other things, the decision in *Oliphant* led to two important consequences that have shaped not just criminal jurisdiction, but civil jurisdiction as well and Indian law more broadly. First, it led to the Supreme Court increasingly determining what is and is not consistent with the "status" of tribal nations. Second, it introduced the issue of race into questions of tribal jurisdiction.

The second facet is the checkerboarding of reservation lands (see Chapters 5 and 16). Mostly as a consequence of the Allotment Era, lands within the reservation are now held in three primary ways: trust land—land that remains held in trust by the United States for the tribal nation as a whole; Indian fee land—land owned in fee by tribal members; and non-Indian fee land—land owned in fee by non-tribal members. Some reservations are heavily checkerboarded and some much less so. Yet, the introduction of non-Indian fee land—and thus more non-Native individuals—within reservation borders, coupled with the Supreme Court's interjection of race into issues of tribal authority through *Oliphant*, has raised difficult questions about tribal civil jurisdiction.

In 1981, three years after *Oliphant*, the Supreme Court considered the question of tribal civil jurisdiction over non-Natives in *Montana v. U.S.* There are a number of issues in this important and complicated case. For the purposes of this chapter, it is important to know that Crow Nation had a tribal ordinance concerning hunting and fishing on the reservation. The Crow were seeking to enforce this ordinance on non-Indian fee land within the reservation. While not as broad as *Oliphant*, *Montana* nonetheless follows in its footsteps. As you read the case, ask yourself what standard, or test, the Court announces to decide cases of this type. How is it different from *Oliphant*? How it is similar? How does the type of land at issue affect the analysis?

MONTANA V. U.S.
450 U.S. 544 (1981)

JUSTICE STEWART delivered the opinion of the Court.

This case concerns the sources and scope of the power of an Indian tribe to regulate hunting and fishing by non-Indians on lands within its reservation owned in fee simple by non-Indians. . . .

* * *

. . . Today, roughly 52 percent of the reservation is allotted to members of the Tribe and held by the United States in trust for them, 17 percent is held in trust for the Tribe itself, and approximately 28 percent is held in fee by non-Indians. The State of Montana owns in fee simple 2 percent of the reservation, the United States less than 1 percent.

. . . Since the 1950's, the Crow Tribal Council has passed several resolutions respecting hunting and fishing on the reservation, including Resolution No. 74–05, the occasion for this lawsuit. That resolution prohibits hunting and fishing within the reservation by anyone who is not a member of the Tribe. The State of Montana, however, has continued to assert its authority to regulate hunting and fishing by non-Indians within the reservation.

* * *

Though the parties in this case have raised broad questions about the power of the Tribe to regulate hunting and fishing by non-Indians on the reservation, the regulatory issue before us is a narrow one. The Court of Appeals held that the Tribe may prohibit nonmembers from hunting or fishing on land belonging to the Tribe or held by the United States in trust for the Tribe, and with this holding we can readily agree. We also agree with the Court of Appeals that if the Tribe permits nonmembers to fish or hunt on such lands, it may condition their entry by charging a fee or establishing bag and creel limits. What remains is the question of the power of the Tribe to regulate non-Indian fishing and hunting on reservation land owned in fee by nonmembers of the Tribe. . . .

* * *

. . . "[I]nherent sovereignty" is not so broad as to support the application of Resolution No. 74–05 to non-Indian lands.

This Court most recently reviewed the principles of inherent sovereignty in *United States v. Wheeler*. In that case, noting that Indian tribes are "unique aggregations possessing attributes of sovereignty over both their members and their territory," the Court upheld the power of a tribe to punish tribal members who violate tribal criminal laws. But the Court was careful to note that, through their original incorporation into the United States as well as through specific treaties and statutes, the Indian tribes have lost many of the attributes of sovereignty. The Court distinguished between those inherent powers retained by the tribes and those divested:

> The areas in which such implicit divestiture of sovereignty has been held to have occurred are those involving the relations between an Indian tribe and nonmembers of the tribe. . . .

* * *

The Court recently applied these general principles in *Oliphant v. Suquamish Indian Tribe*, rejecting a tribal claim of inherent sovereign authority to exercise criminal jurisdiction over non-Indians. . . . Though *Oliphant* only determined inherent tribal authority in criminal matters, the principles on which it relied support the general proposition that the inherent sovereign powers of an Indian tribe do not extend to the activities of nonmembers of the tribe. To be sure, Indian tribes retain inherent sovereign power to exercise some forms of civil jurisdiction over non-Indians on their reservations, even on non-Indian fee lands. A tribe may regulate, through taxation, licensing, or other means, the activities of nonmembers who enter consensual relationships with the tribe or its members, through commercial dealing, contracts, leases, or other arrangements. A tribe may also retain inherent power to exercise civil authority over the conduct of non-Indians on fee lands within its reservation when that conduct threatens or has some direct effect on the political integrity, the economic security, or the health or welfare of the tribe.

No such circumstances, however, are involved in this case. Non-Indian hunters and fishermen on non-Indian fee land do not enter any agreements or dealings with the Crow Tribe so as to subject themselves to tribal civil jurisdiction. And nothing in this case suggests that such non-Indian hunting and fishing so threaten the Tribe's political or economic security as to justify tribal regulation. . . .

Montana is similar to *Oliphant* in that both start with the presumption that jurisdiction over non-Natives is inconsistent with the "status" of tribal nations. However, whereas *Oliphant* ends with its presumption, the analysis under *Montana* is more nuanced. The opinion in *Montana* was directly concerned with non-Native fee land within the reservation, hinting at the possibility that a tribal nation might have greater authority over lands held in trust for the tribal nation. Additionally, while the opinion began with the presumption that a tribal nation was not going to have jurisdiction over non-Natives, it recognized two exceptions to this general rule: when a non-Native has entered into a "consensual relationship" with "the tribe or its members," and when the conduct of the non-Native "threatens or has some direct effect on the political integrity, the economic security, or the health or welfare of the tribe."

The original presumption and its two exceptions have come to be known as the *Montana* test.

THE FURTHER DEVELOPMENT OF THE *MONTANA* TEST

The decision in *Montana* left open a number of important questions. For example, since *Montana* concerned non-Indian fee land, what were the rules for other types of reservation lands? Additionally, what were the boundaries of the two exceptions? Put another way, what set of facts or real world situations would fit into either of the two exceptions?

In the years since *Montana*, the Supreme Court has given some additional context for understanding the *Montana* test. The next major case to offer further guidance was *Strate v. A-1 Contractors*. The facts of the case are, in many respects, unremarkable and not of the variety to typically reach the Supreme Court. Two individuals were involved in an automobile accident on a stretch of road in North Dakota. One driver, who suffered injuries, decided to sue the employer of the other driver.

The case became worthy of the Supreme Court's attention because of the location of the road and the venue in which the original suit was filed. The injured driver, Gisela Fredericks, was non-Native. But she had married a Native man, had five children who were enrolled tribal members, and lived on the Fort Berthold Reservation, where the accident took place. Fredericks sued A-1 Contractors, a non-Native company from outside of the reservation that was engaged in a business relationship with tribal nation to do some work on the reservation. The accident took place on a stretch of road on the reservation surrounded by tribal trust land in which the state of North Dakota had a right-of-way—the right to use the property of another for a limited or specific purpose. Fredericks chose to sue A-1 in tribal court. A-1 asserted that the tribal court did not have jurisdiction over the company and eventually filed suit in federal court to attempt to stop the tribal court case.

Primarily, the question before the Supreme Court was whether the tribal court had jurisdiction over A-1. Secondarily, the Court had to determine whether the *Montana* test applied to this situation and, if so, how so. As you read the case, ask yourself how the Supreme Court constructed the facts of the case. What, according to the Court, was the status of the land in question? What does that mean for the *Montana* test? What about the exceptions?

STRATE V. A-1 CONTRACTORS
520 U.S. 438 (1997)

JUSTICE GINSBURG delivered the opinion of the Court.

* * *

Our case law establishes that, absent express authorization by federal statute or treaty, tribal jurisdiction over the conduct of nonmembers exists only in limited circumstances. In *Oliphant v. Suquamish Tribe*, the Court held that Indian tribes lack criminal jurisdiction over non Indians. *Montana v. United States*, decided three years later, is the pathmarking case concerning tribal civil authority over nonmembers. . . . The *Montana* opinion added . . . that in certain circumstances, even where Congress has not expressly authorized it, tribal civil jurisdiction may encompass nonmembers. . . .

Montana thus described a general rule that . . . Indian tribes lack civil authority over the conduct of nonmembers on non Indian land within a reservation, subject to two exceptions: The first exception relates to nonmembers who enter consensual relationships with the tribe or its members;

the second concerns activity that directly affects the tribe's political integrity, economic security, health, or welfare. . . .

* * *

We consider next the argument that *Montana* does not govern this case because the land underlying the scene of the accident is held in trust for the Three Affiliated Tribes and their members. . . . We "can readily agree," in accord with *Montana*, that tribes retain considerable control over nonmember conduct on tribal land. On the particular matter before us, however . . . [t]he right of way North Dakota acquired for the State's highway renders the 6.59 mile stretch equivalent, for nonmember governance purposes, to alienated, non Indian land.

* * *

Forming part of the State's highway, the right of way is open to the public, and traffic on it is subject to the State's control. The Tribes have consented to, and received payment for, the State's use of the 6.59 mile stretch for a public highway. They have retained no gatekeeping right. So long as the stretch is maintained as part of the State's highway, the Tribes cannot assert a landowner's right to occupy and exclude. . . . We therefore align the right of way, for the purpose at hand, with land alienated to non Indians. Our decision in *Montana*, accordingly, governs this case.

* * *

The first exception to the Montana rule covers "activities of nonmembers who enter consensual relationships with the tribe or its members, through commercial dealing, contracts, leases, or other arrangements." The tortious conduct alleged in Fredericks' complaint does not fit that description. The dispute, as the Court of Appeals said, is "distinctly non tribal in nature." It "arose between two non Indians involved in [a] run of the mill [highway] accident." Although A-1 was engaged in subcontract work on the Fort Berthold Reservation, and therefore had a "consensual relationship" with the Tribes, "Gisela Fredericks was not a party to the subcontract, and the [T]ribes were strangers to the accident.". . .

The second exception to Montana's general rule concerns conduct that "threatens or has some direct effect on the political integrity, the economic security, or the health or welfare of the tribe." Undoubtedly, those who drive carelessly on a public highway running through a reservation endanger all in the vicinity, and surely jeopardize the safety of tribal members. But if Montana's

second exception requires no more, the exception would severely shrink the
rule. . . .

* * *

Justice Ruth Bader Ginsburg's opinion in *Strate* is remarkable for two things:
its deliberate analysis concluding that the stretch of road on which the accident
occurred was not tribal land and determining that the facts of the case did not
satisfy either *Montana* exception. If, according to Ginsburg, the Court understood
this type of fact pattern to threaten the "political integrity, economic security, or
the health or welfare of the tribe," then "the exception would severely shrink the
rule." As would become clear in later cases, *Strate* foreshadowed the Supreme
Court's commitment to the *Montana* test.

The Supreme Court seemed to go to some length in *Strate* to determine that
the stretch of road on the reservation was non-Indian land so that it could avoid
deciding a standard for tribal trust lands. In the next major case, *Nevada v. Hicks*,
the Court addressed the question of tribal civil jurisdiction on tribal lands directly.
In 1990 Nevada game wardens came to suspect Floyd Hicks, a citizen of the
Fallon Pauite-Shoshone Tribes, of killing a California bighorn sheep, an
endangered species. The wardens got both a state warrant and a tribal warrant to
search Hicks's property on the reservation. The wardens did not find any evidence
of wrongdoing. A year later, state game wardens again obtained both a state and
tribal warrant to search Hicks's property, again suspecting Hicks of hunting
California bighorn sheep. And once again the wardens found no evidence of
wrongdoing. Hicks, however, alleged that his property was damaged in the second
search and sued multiple parties, including the game wardens in tribal court.

Nevada v. Hicks has many aspects, but for the purposes of this chapter the
primary question was what standard, or test, should the Supreme Court use to
determine the scope of tribal civil jurisdiction for incidents that occur on tribal
trust lands? As you read the case, ask yourself how the Supreme Court frames the
status of the land in its analysis. What are the consequences for the *Montana* test?
What are the consequences for Floyd Hicks, tribal courts, and tribal sovereignty?

NEVADA V. HICKS
533 U.S. 353 (2001)

JUSTICE SCALIA delivered the opinion of the Court.

* * *

... We first inquire ... whether the Fallon Paiute-Shoshone Tribes—either as an exercise of their inherent sovereignty, or under grant of federal authority—can regulate state wardens executing a search warrant for evidence of an off-reservation crime.

Indian tribes' regulatory authority over nonmembers is governed by the principles set forth in *Montana v. United States*, which we have called the "pathmarking case" on the subject. ... Where nonmembers are concerned, the "exercise of tribal power beyond what is necessary to protect tribal self-government or to control internal relations is inconsistent with the dependent status of the tribes, and so cannot survive without express congressional delegation."

Both *Montana* and *Strate* rejected tribal authority to regulate nonmembers' activities on land over which the tribe could not "assert a landowner's right to occupy and exclude." Respondents and the United States argue that since Hicks's home and yard are on tribe-owned land within the reservation, the Tribe may make its exercise of regulatory authority over nonmembers a condition of nonmembers' entry. Not necessarily. While it is certainly true that the non-Indian ownership status of the land was central to the analysis in both *Montana* and *Strate*, the reason that was so was not that Indian ownership suspends the "general proposition" derived from *Oliphant* that "the inherent sovereign powers of an Indian tribe do not extend to the activities of nonmembers of the tribe" except to the extent "necessary to protect tribal self-government or to control internal relations.". . . The ownership status of land, in other words, is only one factor to consider in determining whether regulation of the activities of nonmembers is "necessary to protect tribal self-government or to control internal relations." It may sometimes be a dispositive factor. Hitherto, the absence of tribal ownership has been virtually conclusive of the absence of tribal civil jurisdiction. . . . But the existence of tribal ownership is not alone enough to support regulatory jurisdiction over nonmembers.

* * *

Nevada v. Hicks answered one of the questions left open by *Montana*. According to Justice Antonin Scalia's opinion, the *Montana* test applied to questions of tribal civil jurisdiction on the reservation no matter what type of land on which the conduct occurred. The status of the land, rather than determining what standard to use, became "one factor to consider" when applying the *Montana* test.

Furthermore, Scalia's opinion also strongly suggested that, under the *Montana* test, tribal nations might never have civil jurisdiction over non-Indian fee land, noting that "the absence of tribal ownership has been virtually conclusive of the absence of tribal civil jurisdiction." This point left many in Indian Country wondering if there truly was any functional difference between *Oliphant* and *Montana*. Whereas *Oliphant* prohibited any tribal criminal jurisdiction over non-Natives, *Montana* theoretically allowed for tribal civil jurisdiction over non-Natives under its two exceptions. The Supreme Court had, to that point, yet to sanction any assertion of tribal civil jurisdiction over non-Natives. Since the status of the land in *Nevada v. Hicks* did not authorize tribal civil jurisdiction, many began to wonder under what circumstances, if ever, the Supreme Court would find the exceptions in the *Montana* test applicable. Were there really any exceptions at all?

The next major Supreme Court tribal civil jurisdiction case, *Plains Commerce Bank v. Long*, also considered both the exceptions to the *Montana* test and the status of the land in question. In essence, the dispute was between a Native-owned cattle company located on the reservation and owned by spouses and tribal citizens Ronnie and Lila Long and a non-Native owned bank, Plains Commerce Bank, located outside of the reservation that had done business with the cattle company for many years. The Longs basically traded some non-Indian fee land on the reservation that they owned to the bank to manage debt that they owed the bank, with an option to repurchase the land after a couple of years. After this arrangement, the Longs asserted that the bank began treating them in a discriminatory manner and, in the wake of a particularly brutal winter, they could not pay the renegotiated loan and the bank foreclosed on the property. The bank then sold the property to other non-Natives at more favorable terms than the bank had offered the Longs. The Longs then sued the bank in tribal court and the bank eventually filed suit federal court, arguing that the tribal court did not have jurisdiction over the bank. Prior to the Supreme Court's ruling, every court, whether tribal or federal, found that the exceptions to the *Montana* test applied and that the tribal court did have jurisdiction over the bank.

As you read the case, ask yourself how the Supreme Court describes the land in dispute in this case. How does the status of the land affect the Court's reasoning? To what policy era is the Court looking for guidance when deciding the case? How does the Court contextualize tribal law and tribal courts in its ruling?

PLAINS COMMERCE BANK V. LONG
554 U.S. 316 (2008)

CHIEF JUSTICE ROBERTS delivered the opinion of the Court.

* * *

Given *Montana*'s " 'general proposition that the inherent sovereign powers of an Indian tribe do not extend to the activities of nonmembers of the tribe,' " efforts by a tribe to regulate nonmembers, especially on non-Indian fee land, are "presumptively invalid." The burden rests on the tribe to establish one of the exceptions to *Montana*'s general rule that would allow an extension of tribal authority to regulate nonmembers on non-Indian fee land. These exceptions are "limited" ones, and cannot be construed in a manner that would "swallow the rule," or "severely shrink" it. The Bank contends that neither exception authorizes tribal courts to exercise jurisdiction over the Longs' discrimination claim at issue in this case. We agree.

* * *

The status of the land is relevant "insofar as it bears on the application of . . . Montana's exceptions to [this] case." The acres at issue here were alienated from the Cheyenne River Sioux's tribal trust and converted into fee simple parcels as part of [an 1908 Act allotting the reservation]. . . .

The tribal tort law the Longs are attempting to enforce, however, operates as a restraint on alienation. It "set[s] limits on how nonmembers may engage in commercial transactions,"—and not just any transactions, but specifically nonmembers' sale of fee lands they own. . . . [The Longs] argue the regulation is fully authorized by the first *Montana* exception. They are mistaken.

Montana does not permit Indian tribes to regulate the sale of non-Indian fee land. *Montana* and its progeny permit tribal regulation of nonmember conduct inside the reservation that implicates the tribe's sovereign interests. *Montana* expressly limits its first exception to the "activities of nonmembers," allowing these to be regulated to the extent necessary "to protect tribal self-government [and] to control internal relations."

* * *

Tellingly, with only "one minor exception, we have never upheld under Montana the extension of tribal civil authority over nonmembers on non-Indian land."...

But again, whether or not we have permitted regulation of nonmember activity on non-Indian fee land in a given case, in no case have we found that *Montana* authorized a tribe to regulate the sale of such land. Rather, our *Montana* cases have always concerned nonmember conduct on the land.

The distinction between sale of the land and conduct on it is well-established in our precedent . . . and entirely logical given the limited nature of tribal sovereignty and the liberty interests of nonmembers. . . . The logic of *Montana* is that certain activities on non-Indian fee land (say, a business enterprise employing tribal members) or certain uses (say, commercial development) may intrude on the internal relations of the tribe or threaten tribal self-rule. To the extent they do, such activities or land uses may be regulated. Put another way, certain forms of nonmember behavior, even on non-Indian fee land, may sufficiently affect the tribe as to justify tribal oversight. While tribes generally have no interest in regulating the conduct of nonmembers, then, they may regulate nonmember behavior that implicates tribal governance and internal relations. . . .

. . . By definition, fee land owned by nonmembers has already been removed from the tribe's immediate control. It has already been alienated from the tribal trust. The tribe cannot justify regulation of such land's sale by reference to its power to superintend tribal land, then, because non-Indian fee parcels have ceased to be tribal land.

Nor can regulation of fee land sales be justified by the tribe's interests in protecting internal relations and self-government. Any direct harm to its political integrity that the tribe sustains as a result of fee land sale is sustained at the point the land passes from Indian to non-Indian hands. It is at that point the tribe and its members lose the ability to use the land for their purposes. Once the land has been sold in fee simple to non-Indians and passed beyond the tribe's immediate control, the mere resale of that land works no additional intrusion on tribal relations or self-government. Resale, by itself, causes no additional damage.

This is not to suggest that the sale of the land will have no impact on the tribe. The uses to which the land is put may very well change from owner to owner, and those uses may well affect the tribe and its members. . . . But the key point is that any threat to the tribe's sovereign interests flows from changed uses or nonmember activities, rather than from the mere fact of resale. The tribe is able fully to vindicate its sovereign interests in protecting its members and preserving tribal self-government by regulating nonmember activity on the land, within the limits set forth in our cases. The tribe has no independent interest in restraining alienation of the land itself, and thus, no authority to do so.

Not only is regulation of fee land sale beyond the tribe's sovereign powers, it runs the risk of subjecting nonmembers to tribal regulatory authority without commensurate consent. Tribal sovereignty, it should be remembered, is "a sovereignty outside the basic structure of the Constitution." The Bill of Rights does not apply to Indian tribes. Indian courts "differ from traditional American courts in a number of significant respects." And nonmembers have no part in tribal government—they have no say in the laws and regulations that govern tribal territory. Consequently, those laws and regulations may be fairly imposed on nonmembers only if the nonmember has consented, either expressly or by his actions. Even then, the regulation must stem from the tribe's inherent sovereign authority to set conditions on entry, preserve tribal self-government, or control internal relations.

In commenting on the policy goals Congress adopted with the General Allotment Act, we noted that "[t]here is simply no suggestion" in the history of the Act "that Congress intended that the non-Indians who would settle upon alienated allotted lands would be subject to tribal regulatory authority." In fact, we said it "defies common sense to suppose" that Congress meant to subject non-Indians to tribal jurisdiction simply by virtue of the nonmember's purchase of land in fee simple. If Congress did not anticipate tribal jurisdiction would run with the land, we see no reason why a nonmember would think so either.

The Longs point out that the Bank in this case could hardly have been surprised by the Tribe's assertion of regulatory power over the parties' business dealings. The Bank, after all, had "lengthy on-reservation commercial relationships with the Long Company.". . . But as we have emphasized repeatedly in this context, when it comes to tribal regulatory authority, it is not "in for a penny, in for a Pound." The Bank may reasonably have anticipated that its various commercial dealings with the Longs could trigger tribal authority to regulate those transactions—a question we need not and do not decide. But there is no reason the Bank should have anticipated that its general business dealings with respondents would permit the Tribe to regulate the Bank's sale of land it owned in fee simple.

Even the courts below recognized that the Longs' discrimination claim was a "novel" one. It arose "directly from Lakota tradition as embedded in Cheyenne River Sioux tradition and custom," including the Lakota "sense of justice, fair play and decency to others." The upshot was to require the Bank to offer the same terms of sale to a prospective buyer who had defaulted in several previous transactions with the Bank as it offered to a different buyer without such a history of default. This is surely not a typical regulation. But whatever the Bank anticipated, whatever "consensual relationship" may have been established through the Bank's dealing with the Longs, the jurisdictional consequences of that relationship cannot extend to the Bank's subsequent sale of its fee land.

* * *

Montana provides that, in certain circumstances, tribes may exercise authority over the conduct of nonmembers, even if that conduct takes place on non-Indian fee land. But conduct taking place on the land and the sale of the land are two very different things. The Cheyenne River Sioux Tribe lost the authority to restrain the sale of fee simple parcels inside their borders when the land was sold as part of the 1908 Allotment Act. Nothing in *Montana* gives it back.

* * *

The second exception authorizes the tribe to exercise civil jurisdiction when non-Indians' "conduct" menaces the "political integrity, the economic security, or the health or welfare of the tribe." The conduct must do more than injure the tribe, it must "imperil the subsistence" of the tribal community. One commentator has noted that "th[e] elevated threshold for application of the second *Montana* exception suggests that tribal power must be necessary to avert catastrophic consequences."

The sale of formerly Indian-owned fee land to a third party is quite possibly disappointing to the tribe, but cannot fairly be called "catastrophic" for tribal self-government. The land in question here has been owned by a non-Indian party for at least 50 years, during which time the project of tribal self-government has proceeded without interruption. The land's resale to another non-Indian hardly "imperil[s] the subsistence or welfare of the tribe." Accordingly, we hold the second Montana exception inapplicable in this case.

* * *

In terms of changing or shaping the law, Chief Justice John Roberts's opinion did not do much. It identified the *Montana* test as the appropriate standard and then applied it to the facts of the case. From one perspective, all the Supreme Court did was authorize the sale of non-Indian fee land from non-Native owner (the bank) to other non-Native owners without the sanction of the tribal court.

Nonetheless, the opinion was significant for the message that it sent to Native America. The bank had a longstanding business relationship with the Native-owned cattle company and was very familiar with the tribal court. Four separate courts—the tribal trial court, the tribal appellate court, the federal district court, and the Eighth Circuit Court of Appeals—all found that this situation satisfied the exceptions in the *Montana* test. Yet, the Supreme Court found otherwise. If these circumstances did not trigger the exceptions to the *Montana* test—if this was not a "consensual relationship" with "the tribe or its members," nor did the bank's actions affect the "political integrity, the economic security, or the health or welfare of the tribe"—then what would?

The fact that the land at issue was non-Indian fee land was significant to the *Plains Commerce Bank* decision. The Supreme Court, as Roberts's opinion describes it, was not willing to authorize the possibility that a tribal court might prevent a non-Native from selling non-Indian fee land within the reservation. Yet, it is fair to ask whether Roberts's framing truly strikes at the heart of the matter. The tribal court sought to adjudicate the bank's alleged discriminatory conduct, not the land itself. Thus, to many observers, the status of the land was not merely a "factor to be considered," but rather the dispositive factor. The line of civil jurisdiction cases, from *Montana* to *Strate* to *Nevada v. Hicks* to *Plains Commerce Bank*, have made many wonder if there is any set of circumstances under which the Supreme Court would find that a tribal nation had civil jurisdiction over conduct that occurs on non-Indian fee land within the reservation.

In addition, Roberts's opinion relied in part on two reoccurring tropes in Indian law cases that raise significant questions: uncritical acceptance of legislation and decisions from different policy eras and a significant degree of wariness of tribal courts and tribal law. As noted elsewhere in this text, one of the more difficult questions that American courts have to face is how to confront the legal events and documents from one policy era in a different policy era. Put another way, does it make sense for a court in the Self-Determination Era to continue to advance, support, or further legislation from an era when the federal government was seeking to limit or eliminate tribal sovereignty and tribal ways of life? If Roberts wrestled with these questions, it is not apparent in the opinion. Roberts noted the "policy goals Congress adopted with the General Allotment Act," in asserting that non-Natives would not have had any expectation that they would be subject to tribal court jurisdiction. Consequently, the opinion in *Plains Commerce Bank* furthers those policy goals of the Allotment Era.

The opinion also claims that the Longs' anti-discrimination claim in tribal court was "novel" and that it was based on " 'Lakota tradition as embedded in Cheyenne River Sioux tradition and custom,' including the Lakota 'sense of justice, fair play and decency to others.' " According to Roberts, "This is surely not a typical regulation." Such assertions about tribal law and courts are fairly common in Supreme Court decisions, particularly in those cases regarding tribal jurisdiction (see Chapter 18).

It is certainly possible to infer from Roberts's statements that the Supreme Court was wary of tribal law and its application. Yet, the federal government and every state have anti-discrimination laws. Presumably those laws are also based on a "sense of justice, fair play and decency to others." What makes tribal law different than American law in this regard? What basis does the Supreme Court have to be wary of tribal anti-discrimination law? Why do several Supreme Court opinions express trepidation over the potential application of tribal law to non-Natives? What justifications does Roberts offer in *Plains Commerce Bank*? Do those justifications make sense? Why or why not?

FINDING AN EXCEPTION

Plains Commerce Bank continued a trend in tribal civil jurisdictional cases that increasingly suggested that the Supreme Court was moving ever closer to simply doing away with the *Montana* test and completely prohibiting tribal civil jurisdiction over non-Natives in the same way that it had completely prohibited tribal criminal jurisdiction over non-Natives in *Oliphant*. In 2016, the Supreme Court sanctioned tribal civil jurisdiction over non-Natives for the first time in *Dollar General Corp. v. Mississippi Band of Choctaw Indians*.[1] However, the circumstances of that decision leave questions about its reach and what direction this area of law is headed.

In order to understand the Supreme Court's decision, it is necessary to read the Fifth Circuit Court of Appeals opinion, *Dolgencorp, Inc. v. Mississippi Band of Choctaw Indians*, that led to the Supreme Court's decision. A non-Native owned company operated a Dollar General franchise on tribal trust land on the reservation. The tribal nation operated a program within the community to place tribal youth in local businesses for short-term, unpaid internships. While participating in the program and on duty, a thirteen-year-old identified only as John Doe alleged that the manager of the Dollar General store molested him.

John Doe sued the manager and the company in tribal court. The company responded by suing in federal court, arguing that there was no "consensual relationship" that would satisfy the exception to the *Montana* test. As you read the case, ask yourself why the court finds that this situation does fit the exception. How does the majority opinion distinguish these facts from the ones found in *Plains Commerce Bank*? How does the dissent frame the *Montana* test?

DOLGENCORP, INC. V. MISSISSIPPI BAND OF CHOCTAW INDIANS

746 F.3d 167 (2014)

JAMES E. GRAVES, JR., CIRCUIT JUDGE:

* * *

Dolgencorp presents several arguments as to why tribal court jurisdiction over Doe's tort claims is not justified under the *Montana* consensual relationship exception.

I. Commercial relationship

. . . Dolgencorp argues that noncommercial relationships do not give rise to tribal jurisdiction under the first *Montana* exception. We decline to impose such a restriction, which does not appear to be supported by any compelling rationale. Moreover, such a requirement would be easily satisfied in this case. Although Doe worked for only a brief time at the Dollar General store and was not paid, he was essentially an unpaid intern, performing limited work in exchange for job training and experience. This is unquestionably a relationship "of a commercial nature."

II. Nexus

Dolgencorp argues that there is no nexus between its participation in the [tribal placement program] and Doe's tort claims. We disagree. The conduct for which Doe seeks to hold Dolgencorp liable is its alleged placement, in its Dollar General store located on tribal lands, of a manager who sexually assaulted Doe while he was working there. This conduct has an obvious nexus to Dolgencorp's participation in the [tribal placement program]. In essence, a tribe that has agreed to place a minor tribe member as an unpaid intern in a business located on tribal land on a reservation is attempting to regulate the safety of the child's workplace. Simply put, the tribe is protecting its own children on its own land. It is surely within the tribe's regulatory authority to insist that a child working for a local business not be sexually assaulted by the employees of the business. The fact that the regulation takes the form of a tort duty that may be vindicated by individual tribe members in tribal court makes no difference. To the extent that foreseeability is relevant to the nexus issue, as Dolgencorp suggests, it is present here. Having agreed to place a minor tribe member in a position of quasi-employment on Indian land in a reservation, it would hardly be surprising for Dolgencorp to have to answer in tribal court for harm caused to the child in the course of his employment.

Dolgencorp confuses the merits of Doe's case with the question of tribal jurisdiction. It may very well be that Dolgencorp did not do, or fail to do, anything that would cause it to be held liable to Doe. The nexus component of the tribal jurisdiction question, however, centers on the nexus between the *alleged* misconduct and the consensual action of Dolgencorp in participating in the [tribal placement program].

III. The effect of *Plains Commerce*

Dolgencorp argues that *Plains Commerce* narrowed the *Montana* consensual relationship exception, allowing tribes to regulate consensual relationships with non-members only upon a showing that the specific relationships "implicate tribal governance and internal relations." . . .

We do not interpret *Plains Commerce* to require an additional showing that one specific relationship, in itself, "intrude[s] on the internal relations of the tribe or threaten[s] self-rule." It is hard to imagine how a single employment relationship between a tribe member and a business could ever have such an impact. On the other hand, at a higher level of generality, the ability to regulate the working conditions (particularly as pertains to health and safety) of tribe members employed on reservation land is plainly central to the tribe's power of self-government. Nothing in *Plains Commerce* requires a focus on the highly specific rather than the general. . . .

* * *

JERRY E. SMITH, CIRCUIT JUDGE, dissenting:

For the first time ever, a federal court of appeals upholds Indian tribal-court tort jurisdiction over a non-Indian, based on a consensual relationship, without a finding that jurisdiction is "necessary to protect tribal self-government or to control internal relations." The majority's alarming and unprecedented holding far outpaces the Supreme Court, which has never upheld Indian jurisdiction over a nonmember defendant.

This ruling profoundly upsets the careful balance that the Supreme Court has struck between Indian tribal governance, on the one hand, and American sovereignty and the constitutional rights of U.S. citizens, on the other hand. The majority's bold announcement is conspicuous for its audacity, given that this court hears few Indian cases and decides little Indian law. I respectfully dissent.

The majority pays only lip service to, but does not heed, the Supreme Court's guidance that "exercise of tribal power beyond what is necessary to protect tribal self-government or to control internal relations is inconsistent with the dependent status of the tribes, and so cannot survive without express congressional delegation." One manifestation of that maxim is that Indian tribes lack "inherent sovereign authority to exercise criminal jurisdiction over non-Indians." Absent express congressional delegation, therefore, store manager Townsend could not have been criminally prosecuted in tribal court for the alleged molestation of John Doe.

The principle on which *Oliphant* relies, moreover, "support[s] the general proposition that the inherent sovereign powers of an Indian tribe do not extend to the activities of nonmembers of the tribe." Although the Supreme Court has not yet explicitly adopted an *Oliphant*-like rule for civil cases, it has "never held that a tribal court had jurisdiction over a nonmember defendant." It remains an open question whether there are *any* circumstances under which the Court would find that a tribal court retains civil jurisdiction over a non-Indian defendant such as Dolgencorp.

The civil action here—an ordinary tort action, despite the seriousness of the alleged offense—comes nowhere close to implicating Indian self-government or internal tribal relations. . .

"The *Montana* rule, therefore, and not its exceptions, applies to this case." Doe was free to pursue his claims in the state court open to all Mississippi tort claimants. Because Dolgencorp's conduct indisputably falls outside the Choctaw Indians' authority to "protect tribal self-government or to control internal relations," the jurisdictional inquiry should be easily and rightfully at an end.

This court therefore should reverse the district court and render judgment for Dolgencorp without reaching the first *Montana* exception. I will address it, nonetheless, because I also disagree with the majority that there was a legally sufficient nexus between Dolgencorp's participation in a short-term, unpaid internship program and the full body of Indian tort law.

Before today, no circuit court has upheld Indian-court jurisdiction, under *Montana*'s first exception, over a tort claim against a nonmember defendant....

... "*Montana's* consensual relationship exception requires that [it] have a nexus to the consensual relationship itself." The relevant consensual relationship is Dolgencorp's voluntary participation in the Youth Opportunity Program. The majority errantly contends that, "[h]aving agreed to place a minor tribe member in a position of quasi-employment on Indian land in a reservation, it would hardly be surprising for Dolgencorp to have to answer in tribal court for harm caused to the child in the course of his employment."

... There is no reason Dolgencorp should ... reasonably have anticipated that, *solely on the basis of its participation in a short-term, unpaid internship program,* it would be subject to the entire—and largely undefined—body of Indian tribal tort law. As the Supreme Court has "emphasized repeatedly in this context, when it comes to tribal regulatory authority, it is not in for a penny, in for a Pound."

The elements of Doe's claims under Indian tribal law are unknown to Dolgencorp and may very well be undiscoverable by it. Choctaw law expressly incorporates, as superior to Mississippi state law, the "customs . . . and usages of the tribes." CHOCTAW TRIBAL CODE § 1–1–4. "Where doubt arises as to the customs and usages of the Tribe, the court may request the advice of persons generally recognized in the community as being familiar with such customs and usages." Although the claims that Doe wishes to press against Dolgencorp have familiar state-law analogues, the majority's aggressive holding extends to the entire body of tribal tort law—including any novel claims recognized by the Choctaws but not by Mississippi.

Because Dolgencorp could not have anticipated that its consensual relationship with Doe would subject it to any and all tort claims actionable under tribal law, there is an insufficient nexus to satisfy *Montana*'s first exception. For the majority to hold otherwise raises serious due process concerns insofar as Dolgencorp will be forced to defend Doe's claims in an unfamiliar forum without the benefit of constitutional protections....

And finally, the majority's pronouncement is vague and unworkable in practice. On the one hand, the majority opines that "[h]aving agreed to place a minor tribe member in a position of quasi-employment on Indian land in a reservation, it would hardly be surprising for Dolgencorp to have to answer in tribal court for harm caused to the child in the course of his employment." That broad statement would authorize a tort action in Indian court if, for example, the minor had slipped on a poorly-maintained floor at the store and had cut his finger. In the majority's words, that would violate "the safety of the child's workplace."

On the other hand, the majority emphasizes that "[i]t is surely within the tribe's regulatory authority to insist that a child working for a local business not be sexually assaulted by the employees of the business." Is the majority recognizing tribal court authority over any tort related to the voluntary job-training program, or only over especially despicable incidents such as sexual assaults? What if the boy had fatally hit his head on the floor? Or would it have to be an intentional tort—a slap on the face, perhaps, for bad performance? Is the majority's unprecedented expansion of Indian-court jurisdiction limited to only highly reprehensible acts, or only to "really bad" acts, or to "sort of bad acts," or to any minor, negligent act, or only to situations in which, in the majority's words, "the tribe is protecting its own children on its own land? [sic]"

The limits to the majority's dramatic holding remain a secret. In short, the majority gives no real indication of what it means by foreseeability, which means that the next actor in the place of Dolgencorp will have no idea whether it can be subjected to the uncertainties of the Indian courts.

* * *

... The majority's stunning pronouncement expands Indian court jurisdiction over nonmember defendants far beyond the scope permitted by the Supreme Court or any other appellate authority. It is grave error from which I respectfully dissent.

The opinions in *Dolgencorp* reflect the tensions between what the dissent describes as the "careful balance that the Supreme Court has struck between Indian tribal governance ... and American sovereignty and the constitutional rights of U.S. citizens." It is useful to consider how the cases of this chapter have described this "careful balance." How is tribal sovereignty and governance described? How are the rights of U.S. citizens described? Under what circumstances has tribal sovereignty prevailed and under what circumstances has the concerns of non-Natives prevailed? How does this speak to the "careful balance" in civil jurisdictional cases? In factoring this balance, what are American courts seeking to accomplish and what are they seeking to protect against? How is tribal law characterized in these opinions? How might that speak to the results in the cases?

Two years after *Dolgencorp*, the Supreme Court handed down its decision on the matter. However, the case was decided in the period after the death of Justice Antonin Scalia when there were only eight sitting justices. The Supreme Court let the Fifth Circuit's decision stand with a single sentence: "The judgment is affirmed by an equally divided Court."

The Supreme Court's single sentence does not offer much guidance on how future cases will get resolved. The questions surrounding the *Montana* test's future remain open. Nonetheless, the *Montana* test is presently the guiding principle in tribal civil jurisdictional cases. American courts begin the analysis under the *Montana* test with the presumption that tribal nations do not have civil jurisdiction over non-Natives unless either of two exceptions are present: there is a "consensual relationship" with "the tribe or its members," or when the conduct of the non-Native "threatens or has some direct effect on the political integrity, the economic security, or the health or welfare of the tribe."

SUGGESTED READINGS

- "A Dollar For Your Thoughts: *Dollar General* and the Supreme Court's Struggle with Tribal Civil Jurisdiction." Hallie McDonald. 46 *Hofstra Law Review* 399 (Fall 2017).

- "Tribal Jurisdiction—A Historical Bargain." Matthew L.M. Fletcher and Leah K. Jurss. 76 *Maryland Law Review* 593 (2017).

- "A Unifying Theory of Tribal Civil Jurisdiction." Matthew L.M. Fletcher. 46 *Arizona State Law Journal* 779 (Fall 2014).

---

[1]   136 S.Ct. 2159 (2016).

CHAPTER 20

Taxes

There are few areas of the law that are more complicated and contentious than taxation, whether inside or outside of Indian Country. Additionally, perhaps no other subject of public life raises more questions more quickly and with more passion about what it means to be an American than taxes. There is little agreement within the public discourse about taxes, with maybe one exception: many find taxes and tax law to be particularly difficult to understand. The seemingly arcane nature of tax law is only exacerbated when Indian Country is involved. Competing sovereigns with overlapping jurisdictions further muddy the already dark waters.

Despite their troublesome nature, the deep feelings that taxes can engender and the public debate that they cause are indicative of just how important they are to the sovereigns that seek to exercise them. Taxes are fundamental to most governments to fund their functions, and thus are the very lifeblood of a government. They are necessary to maintain many of the most basic expectations we as citizens have within society. And yet, as John Marshall famously noted in one of the most important cases of his tenure, "An unlimited power to tax involves, necessarily, a power to destroy."[1]

These competing interpretations explain why the subject of taxes creates even more contention and frustration in Indian Country: whereas one sovereign sees a necessity for life, another sees an instrument of death. The strong feelings that taxes inherently produce, coupled with dense tax codes and the litigation that this subject creates, establishes what, at first, may look like an impossible area of law to understand. Yet, some basic rules are easily within reach. First, Native individuals living and working outside of Indian Country are generally subject to the same state and federal taxes as everyone else. Next, three simple, sequential questions provide some immediate clarity when seeking to decipher this subject matter within Indian Country. They are:

1.   Which sovereign is trying to tax?

2.   Which entity is the target of the tax?

3.   What other factors need to be considered?

These three sequential questions provide the necessary foundation from which to build a basic understanding of the tax law in Indian Country and determine who can tax whom. Starting your analysis with each sovereign with the potential capacity to tax Native peoples and/or Indian Country—the federal government, states, and Native nations—provides the first step on a straightforward path to understanding this area of law.

This chapter will demonstrate. . .

- *The federal authority to tax Native nations, peoples, and goods*

- *The authority of Native nations to tax those within its borders*

- *The states' limited authority to tax within Indian Country*

FEDERAL TAXATION

The original version of the U.S. Constitution, which came into force in 1789, contained two explicit references to Native peoples (see Chapter 2). The most famous of the two is the Indian Commerce Clause (see Chapters 7 and 12). However, the first explicit textual reference to Native peoples comes earlier in the document, in Article I, Section 2, Clause 3. In this first reference, "Indians not taxed" are excluded from counting toward determining the number of representatives for a state in the House of Representatives—or apportionment.

In one sense, the "Indians not taxed" reference is best understood by the company it keeps—it is immediately followed by the infamous Three-Fifths Clause, which counted three-fifths of the slave population in Southern states for the purpose of apportionment. In 1868, the post Civil War 14th Amendment changed the rules of apportionment by effectively removing the Three-Fifths Clause. Yet the "Indians not taxed" language was maintained in the Amendment. Thus, even after the Civil War, Native peoples were generally excluded from American political life. However, in another sense, it was an acknowledgment of the separate, sovereign nature of Native nationhood. At the time of the adoption of the original U.S. Constitution, and even at the time of the ratification of the

14th Amendment, very few Native individuals were taxed by the federal government or otherwise would have thought to avail themselves to the federal government beyond their rights guaranteed by treaty.

Nonetheless, even by the time of the ratification of the 14th Amendment, the federal government was increasingly regarding its interaction with Native America as a domestic issue rather than a foreign one. Consequently, the extent of the authority, if any, of the federal government to extend its tax law into Indian Country became a question for American courts, Congress, and even the Internal Revenue Service (IRS). By the mid-twentieth century some key principles were fairly well established.

Using the three sequential questions set forth above, those fairly well established principles become relatively clear. First, which sovereign is trying to tax? The United States is the sovereign, and it has significant authority to tax any entity within its borders. Second, which entity is the target of the tax? For the purposes of the immediate analysis, tribal nations are under consideration. While the broad authority of the United States to tax does include tribal nations, as a matter of general policy, the federal government does not tax the income of tribal nations—much in the same way it does not tax the income of states. The written policy of the IRS (which essentially amounts to law), states that, "Income tax statutes do not tax Indian tribes. The tribe is not a taxable entity."[2] Third, what other factors need to be considered? One potential factor is the geographic source of income—was it earned on or off reservation? Concerning a tribal nation itself (as opposed to any corporations that the tribal nation might own—which complicates the analysis), the written policy of the IRS is instructive, noting that, "Because an Indian tribe is not a taxable entity, any income earned by [the tribe], regardless of the location of the business activities that produced the income, is not subject to federal income tax."[3] Thus, tribal nations are generally not subject to federal taxes, regardless of if the tribal nation's income was generated on or off of a reservation.

What about Native individuals? Although citizens of tribal nations, they do not, as individuals, enjoy the same immunities as their tribal nations. In addition, Native individuals are also citizens of the United States. What federal taxes, if any, are they subject to?

The following case involves two Quinault (spelled Quinaielt in the case) persons: a husband and a wife. Both were described as "fullblood, noncompetent . . . Indians," even though the husband served in the armed forces in World War II. They jointly had an allotment on the reservation that was held in trust by the United States. In 1943 the federal government sold the timber on their allotment.

Sometime thereafter, the IRS demanded that the couple pay taxes on the income from the sold timber. The couple did pay and then filed a claim to get the money back, stating that they were exempt from federal taxes because, "such taxation would be in violation of the provisions of the Quinaielt Treaty, the trust patent, and the General Allotment Act."

As you read the case, ask yourself what general rule the Supreme Court establishes. What exceptions to the general rule does the Supreme Court recognize? What framework does this establish for understanding the federal government's authority to tax Native individuals?

SQUIRE V. CAPOEMAN
351 U.S. 1 (1956)

MR. CHIEF JUSTICE WARREN delivered the opinion of the Court.

* * *

The Government urges us to view this case as an ordinary tax case without regard to the treaty, relevant statutes, congressional policy concerning Indians, or the guardian-ward relationship between the United States and these particular Indians. . . .

We agree with the Government that Indians are citizens and that in ordinary affairs of life, not governed by treaties or remedial legislation, they are subject to the payment of income taxes as are other citizens. We also agree that, to be valid, exemptions to tax laws should be clearly expressed. But we cannot agree that taxability of respondents in these circumstances is unaffected by the treaty, the trust patent or the Allotment Act.

The courts below held that imposition of the tax here in question is inconsistent with the Government's promise to transfer the [land] "free of all charge or incumbrance whatsoever.". . .

. . . Congress, in an amendment to the General Allotment Act, gave additional force to the [Native couple's] position. . . .

. . . The literal language of the [Allotment Act] evinces a congressional intent to subject an Indian allotment to all taxes only after a patent in fee is issued to the allottee. This, in turn, implies that, until such time as the patent is issued, the allotment shall be free from all taxes. . . .

The wisdom of the congressional exemption from tax embodied [by the Allotment Act] is manifested by the facts of the instant case. Respondent's timber constitutes the major value of his allotted land. The Government determines the conditions under which the cutting is made. Once logged off, the land is of little value. The land no longer serves the purpose for which it was by treaty set aside to his ancestors, and for which it was allotted to him. It can no longer be adequate to his needs and serve the purpose of bringing him finally to a state of competency and independence. . . . It is unreasonable to infer that, in enacting the income tax law, Congress intended to limit or undermine the Government's undertaking. To tax respondent under these circumstances would, in the words of the court below, be "at the least, a sorry breach of faith with these Indians."

One of the unfortunate consequences of the complexity of tax law is that some people are under the mistaken impression that Native individuals do not pay any taxes whatsoever. Chief Justice Earl Warren's opinion makes clear that, in the majority of situations, Native individuals are subject to the same federal income taxes as everyone else. Typically, these federal taxes are valid regardless of where the Native individual resides or earns her/his income. However, as the opinion also makes clear, there are some important (if somewhat rare) instances in which a treaty or federal statute will exempt a Native individual from federal taxes. For the couple in the case, their status as "noncompetent" Indians under the Allotment Act negated the federal tax on the timber from their allotment.

TRIBAL TAXATION

Turning once again to the three sequential questions set forth above, it is possible to discern other fairly well established principles of tax law in Indian Country. First, which sovereign is trying to tax? Tribal nations, as sovereigns, have the same basic authority to issue taxes in the same manner as states and the federal government. The United States has long recognized this fundamental authority, which has only grown in importance as tribal governments have taken a greater role in providing services to their communities. The only real impediment to this general proposition is when federal law prohibits the tribal power to tax.

Second, which entity is the target of the tax? Different potentialities emerge under different answers to this question. If tribal citizens are the target, then tribal nations have a wide authority to tax. Many tribal nations do not exercise this authority, or only do so in a limited capacity, as they are able to fund their functions through other sources and/or do not seek to further burden what might already be an economically depressed population. Yet, even if tribal nations choose not to tax their own citizens, they still retain the authority to do so.

But what if non-Natives (or even non-citizen Natives) are the target of a tribal nation's tax? As you read the following case, ask yourself about the nature of the concerns of the non-Native companies doing business on tribal lands. What, from the non-Native companies' perspective, is the issue? How does the Supreme Court address this issue? How might the issue be perceived in the context of state or federal taxes? How does state involvement complicate the matter?

MERRION V. JICARILLA APACHE TRIBE
455 U.S. 130 (1982)

JUSTICE MARSHALL delivered the opinion of the Court.

Pursuant to long-term leases with the Jicarilla Apache Tribe, petitioners, 21 lessees, extract and produce oil and gas from the Tribe's reservation lands. . . . [P]etitioners challenge an ordinance enacted by the Tribe imposing a severance tax on "any oil and natural gas severed, saved and removed from Tribal lands.". . .

The Jicarilla Apache Tribe resides on a reservation in northwestern New Mexico. Established by Executive Order in 1887, the reservation contains 742,315 acres, all of which are held as tribal trust property. . . .

* * *

. . . Beginning in 1953, the petitioners entered into leases with the Tribe. . . . Petitioners' activities on the leased land have been subject to taxes imposed by the State of New Mexico on oil and gas severance and on oil and gas production equipment.

Pursuant to its Revised Constitution, the Tribal Council adopted an ordinance imposing a severance tax on oil and gas production on tribal land. The ordinance was approved by the Secretary [of the Interior] . . . on December 23, 1976.

* * *

Petitioners argue, and the dissent agrees, that an Indian tribe's authority to tax non-Indians who do business on the reservation stems exclusively from its power to exclude such persons from tribal lands. Because the Tribe did not initially condition the leases upon the payment of a severance tax, petitioners assert that the Tribe is without authority to impose such a tax at a later time. We disagree with the premise that the power to tax derives only from the power to exclude. Even if that premise is accepted, however, we disagree with the conclusion that the Tribe lacks the power to impose the severance tax.

* * *

. . . The power to tax is an essential attribute of Indian sovereignty because it is a necessary instrument of self-government and territorial management. This power enables a tribal government to raise revenues for its essential services. The power does not derive solely from the Indian tribe's power to exclude non-Indians from tribal lands. Instead, it derives from the tribe's general authority, as sovereign, to control economic activity within its jurisdiction, and to defray the cost of providing governmental services by requiring contributions from persons or enterprises engaged in economic activities within that jurisdiction.

The petitioners avail themselves of the "substantial privilege of carrying on business" on the reservation. They benefit from the provision of police protection and other governmental services, as well as from " 'the advantages of a civilized society' " that are assured by the existence of tribal government. Numerous other governmental entities levy a general revenue tax similar to that imposed by the Jicarilla Tribe when they provide comparable services. Under these circumstances, there is nothing exceptional in requiring petitioners to contribute through taxes to the general cost of tribal government.

As we observed in [another case], the tribe's interest in levying taxes on nonmembers to raise "revenues for essential governmental programs . . . is strongest when the revenues are derived from value generated on the reservation by activities involving the Tribes and when the taxpayer is the recipient of tribal services." This surely is the case here. The mere fact that the government imposing the tax also enjoys rents and royalties as the lessor of the mineral lands does not undermine the government's authority to impose the tax. The royalty payments from the mineral leases are paid to the Tribe in its role as partner in petitioners' commercial venture. The severance tax, in contrast, is petitioners' contribution "to the general cost of providing governmental services." State governments commonly receive both royalty payments and severance taxes from lessees of mineral lands within their borders.

Viewing the taxing power of Indian tribes as an essential instrument of self-government and territorial management has been a shared assumption of all three branches of the Federal Government. . . .

... Of course, the Tribe's authority to tax nonmembers is subject to constraints not imposed on other governmental entities: the Federal Government can take away this power. . . . These additional constraints minimize potential concern that Indian tribes will exercise the power to tax in an unfair or unprincipled manner, and ensure that any exercise of the tribal power to tax will be consistent with national policies.

* * *

Alternatively, if we accept the argument, advanced by petitioners and the dissent, that the Tribe's authority to tax derives solely from its power to exclude non-Indians from the reservation, we conclude that the Tribe has the authority to impose the severance tax challenged here. Nonmembers who lawfully enter tribal lands remain subject to the tribe's power to exclude them. This power necessarily includes the lesser power to place conditions on entry, on continued presence, or on reservation conduct, such as a tax on business activities conducted on the reservation. . . .

Most important, petitioners and the dissent confuse the Tribe's role as commercial partner with its role as sovereign. This confusion relegates the powers of sovereignty to the bargaining process undertaken in each of the sovereign's commercial agreements. It is one thing to find that the Tribe has agreed to sell the right to use the land and take from it valuable minerals; it is quite another to find that the Tribe has abandoned its sovereign powers simply because it has not expressly reserved them through a contract.

Confusing these two results denigrates Indian sovereignty. . . .

* * *

The decision in *Merrion* is a strong statement recognizing a tribal nation's authority to tax anybody, Natives and non-Natives alike. Justice Thurgood Marshall's opinion was clear to note that this authority was not given to tribal nations or otherwise delegated by the federal government, but rather it was "an essential attribute of Indian sovereignty." Also important, Marshall's opinion recognized a distinction between the tribal nation as a governmental actor and as a commercial partner, while also validating both roles and noting that the very same distinction can and does exist among the states.

The opinion in *Merrion* also indirectly considered the third sequential question—What other factors need to be considered? Marshall wrote that, "As we observed in [another case], the tribe's interest in levying taxes on nonmembers to raise 'revenues . . . is strongest when the revenues are derived from value generated on the reservation by activities involving the Tribes. . .' " Fortunately for the Jicarilla Apache, their whole reservation was held in trust and there is no question that mining creates value generated on the reservation.

Yet, not all economic activity is so directly related to tribal lands, nor are all reservations completely held in trust. Many reservations contain at least some non-Native fee land within their borders, and many are heavily "checkerboarded" (see Chapters 5 and 16). *Merrion* makes clear that tribal nations have significant authority to tax activities on tribally controlled lands. But Marshall's statement that tribal taxing authority was "strongest" under the facts of *Merrion* clearly implied that the Court could imagine a scenario in which tribal nations would have weaker claims to this authority within their borders. Perhaps unsurprisingly, considering the language of *Merrion*, the Supreme Court eventually considered the authority of tribal nations to extend their taxing powers to non-Native fee land within the reservation.

In the following case, the Navajo Nation had initiated a hotel occupancy tax, which affected a non-Native business, Atkinson Trading Company, on non-Native fee land within the borders of the reservation. While the tax was ultimately paid by the hotel customers of the Atkinson Trading Company, the business nonetheless objected to having to collect the tax on behalf of the Navajo. Every court to consider the case before the Supreme Court, including the Navajo Supreme Court and the Tenth Circuit Court of Appeals, agreed that the tribal nation had the authority to tax in this manner.

To understand the decision in *Atkinson Trading Company, Inc. v. Shirley*, it is necessary to have some knowledge of the *Montana* test. The *Montana* test is considered more fully in Chapter 19. For the purposes of this chapter, it suffices to note that the *Montana* test begins with the premise that tribal nations do not have civil jurisdiction (including taxing power) over non-Natives unless the tribal nation can demonstrate either of two exceptions: that 1) the non-Native has entered into a consensual relationship with the tribal nation or its members or 2) that the conduct of the non-Native "threatens or has some direct effect on the political integrity, the economic security, or the health or welfare of the tribe."

As you read the case, ask yourself about the application of the *Montana* test. Why is it necessary in this case? Assuming, as the Court does, that the *Montana* test is necessary, is this a principled result under it? Why or why not? Also, what are the main differences between *Atkinson* and *Merrion*? Do those differences justify the result in this case?

ATKINSON TRADING COMPANY, INC. V. SHIRLEY
532 U.S. 645 (2001)

CHIEF JUSTICE REHNQUIST delivered the opinion of the Court.

* * *

Tribal jurisdiction is limited: For powers not expressly conferred them by federal statute or treaty, Indian tribes must rely upon their retained or inherent sovereignty. In *Montana*, the most exhaustively reasoned of our modern cases addressing this latter authority, we observed that Indian tribe power over nonmembers on non-Indian fee land is sharply circumscribed. . . .

* * *

Citing our decision in *Merrion*, respondents submit that *Montana* [does] not restrict an Indian tribe's power to impose revenue-raising taxes. . . .

Merrion, however, was careful to note that an Indian tribe's inherent power to tax only extended to " 'transactions occurring on trust lands and significantly involving a tribe or its members.' " . . .

We therefore do not read *Merrion* to exempt taxation from *Montana*'s general rule that Indian tribes lack civil authority over nonmembers on non-Indian fee land. Accordingly . . . we apply *Montana* straight up. Because Congress has not authorized the Navajo Nation's hotel occupancy tax through treaty or statute, and because the incidence of the tax falls upon nonmembers on non-Indian fee land, it is incumbent upon the Navajo Nation to establish the existence of one of *Montana*'s exceptions.

Respondents argue that both petitioner and its hotel guests have entered into a consensual relationship with the Navajo Nation. . . . [R]espondents note that the Cameron Trading Post benefits from the numerous services provided by the Navajo Nation. The record reflects that the Arizona State Police and the Navajo Tribal Police patrol the portions of United States Highway 89 and Arizona Highway 64 traversing the reservation; that the Navajo Tribal Police and the Navajo Tribal Emergency Medical Services Department will respond to an emergency call from the Cameron Trading Post; and that local Arizona Fire Departments and the Navajo Tribal Fire Department provide fire protection to the area. Although we do not question the Navajo Nation's ability to charge an appropriate fee for a particular service actually rendered, we think the generalized availability of tribal services patently insufficient to sustain the Tribe's civil authority over nonmembers on non-Indian fee land.

The consensual relationship must stem from "commercial dealing, contracts, leases, or other arrangements," and a nonmember's actual or potential receipt of tribal police, fire, and medical services does not create the requisite connection. If it did, the exception would swallow the rule. . . .

* * *

Although the Court of Appeals did not reach *Montana*'s second exception, both respondents and the United States argue that the hotel occupancy tax is warranted in light of the direct effects the Cameron Trading Post has upon the Navajo Nation. . . . [R]espondents emphasize that petitioner employs almost 100 Navajo Indians; that the Cameron Trading Post derives business from tourists visiting the reservation; and that large amounts of tribal land surround petitioner's isolated property. Although we have no cause to doubt respondents' assertion that the Cameron Chapter of the Navajo Nation possesses an "overwhelming Indian character," we fail to see how petitioner's operation of a hotel on non-Indian fee land "threatens or has some direct effect on the political integrity, the economic security, or the health or welfare of the tribe."

. . . *Montana*'s second exception grants Indian tribes nothing " 'beyond what is necessary to protect tribal self-government or to control internal relations.' " Whatever effect petitioner's operation of the Cameron Trading Post might have upon surrounding Navajo land, it does not endanger the Navajo Nation's political integrity.

* * *

The decision in *Atkinson* left tribal taxing authority in much the same place as jurisdiction more broadly—tribal nations have greater authority over reservation lands that they control and less authority over lands that they do not control. Consequently, the third of the three sequential questions is generally the most important when considering tribal taxing authority—what other factors need to be considered? When contemplating tribal taxing authority the status of the land becomes central. If the tax occurs on tribally controlled lands, then American courts are more likely to support tribal taxing authority. If the tax is non-Native fee land then, according to *Atkinson*, the *Montana* test will apply. As the *Montana* test has been notoriously burdensome for tribal nations to satisfy, it is likely that the tribal tax will not find support in American courts.

STATE TAXATION

Yet another set of principles of tax law in Indian Country arises when the answer to the first sequential question—which sovereign is trying to tax?—shifts to the states. And again, different potentialities emerge with different answers to the second question—which entity is the target of the tax? As a basic rule, states do not have the authority to tax tribal nations (and, conversely, tribal nations cannot tax states). Additionally, states generally do not have the authority to tax Native individuals living and working within Indian Country, although Native individuals are subject to valid state taxes when they live and work outside of Indian Country.

But what about non-Native entities and individuals living, working, or otherwise operating in Indian Country? What reach does a state have into a reservation when trying to act upon those who are not tribal citizens? In the following case, the state of Arizona was seeking to apply a state motor carrier license tax and state fuel tax to two non-Native logging companies engaged in work exclusively on the reservation.

As you read the case, ask yourself what considerations beyond the taxes themselves are important to the Supreme Court in making its decision. How does the Court shape the third sequential question—what other factors need to be considered? Whose interests are really at stake, according to the Court? How are those competing interests measured against each other?

WHITE MOUNTAIN APACHE V. BRACKER
448 U.S. 136 (1980)

MR. JUSTICE MARSHALL delivered the opinion of the Court.

* * *

Although "[g]eneralizations on this subject have become . . . treacherous," our decisions establish several basic principles with respect to the boundaries between state regulatory authority and tribal self-government.

* * *

Congress has broad power to regulate tribal affairs under the Indian Commerce Clause. This congressional authority and the "semi-independent position" of Indian tribes have given rise to two independent but related barriers to the assertion of state regulatory authority over tribal reservations and members. First, the exercise of such authority may be preempted by federal law. Second, it may unlawfully infringe "on the right of reservation Indians to make their own laws and be ruled by them." The two barriers are independent because either, standing alone, can be a sufficient basis for holding state law inapplicable to activity undertaken on the reservation or by tribal members. They are related, however, in two important ways. The right of tribal self-government is ultimately dependent on and subject to the broad power of Congress. Even so, traditional notions of Indian self-government are so deeply engrained in our jurisprudence that they have provided an important "backdrop" against which vague or ambiguous federal enactments must always be measured.

. . . The tradition of Indian sovereignty over the reservation and tribal members must inform the determination whether the exercise of state authority has been preempted by operation of federal law. . . . We have thus rejected the proposition that, in order to find a particular state law to have been preempted by operation of federal law, an express congressional statement to that effect is required. At the same time, any applicable regulatory interest of the State must be given weight, and "automatic exemptions 'as a matter of constitutional law' " are unusual.

. . . [D]ifficult questions arise where, as here, a State asserts authority over the conduct of non-Indians engaging in activity on the reservation. In such cases, we have examined the language of the relevant federal treaties and statutes in terms of both the broad policies that underlie them and the notions of sovereignty that have developed from historical traditions of tribal independence. This inquiry is not dependent on mechanical or absolute conceptions of state or tribal sovereignty, but has called for a particularized inquiry into the nature of the state, federal, and tribal interests at stake, an inquiry designed to determine whether, in the specific context, the exercise of state authority would violate federal law.

. . . At the outset, we observe that the Federal Government's regulation of the harvesting of Indian timber is comprehensive. That regulation takes the form of Acts of Congress, detailed regulations promulgated by the Secretary of the Interior, and day-to-day supervision by the Bureau of Indian Affairs. . . . [T]he Secretary of the Interior is granted broad authority over the sale of timber on the reservation.

Timber on Indian land may be sold only with the consent of the Secretary. . . . He is authorized to promulgate regulations for the operation and management of Indian forestry units.

* * *

> Under [federal] regulations, the Bureau of Indian Affairs exercises literally daily supervision over the harvesting and management of tribal timber.
>
> * * *
>
> In these circumstances, we agree with petitioners that the federal regulatory scheme is so pervasive as to preclude the additional burdens sought to be imposed in this case. Respondents seek to apply their motor vehicle license and use fuel taxes . . . for operations that are conducted solely on Bureau and tribal roads within the reservation. There is no room for these taxes in the comprehensive federal regulatory scheme. In a variety of ways, the assessment of state taxes would obstruct federal policies. And equally important, respondents have been unable to identify any regulatory function or service performed by the State that would justify the assessment of taxes for activities on Bureau and tribal roads within the reservation.
>
> * * *
>
> . . . [T]his is not a case in which the State seeks to assess taxes in return for governmental functions it performs for those on whom the taxes fall. Nor have respondents been able to identify a legitimate regulatory interest served by the taxes they seek to impose. They refer to a general desire to raise revenue, but we are unable to discern a responsibility or service that justifies the assertion of taxes imposed for on-reservation operations conducted solely on tribal and Bureau of Indian Affairs roads.
>
> * * *
>
> Respondents' argument is reduced to a claim that they may assess taxes on non-Indians engaged in commerce on the reservation whenever there is no express congressional statement to the contrary. That is simply not the law. In a number of cases we have held that state authority over non-Indians acting on tribal reservations is preempted, even though Congress has offered no explicit statement on the subject.
>
> * * *

The decision in *Bracker* helped to cement the method that American courts use to analyze cases in which a state is seeking to tax activities within Indian Country. Rather than simply limiting state authority at the reservation border, the Supreme Court undertook a "balancing test" in which it measured the state's necessity to collect the tax on non-Natives in Indian Country against those of both the tribal nation's sovereignty and federal government's Indian law and policy goals together. Noting that this was "not a case in which [Arizona] seeks to assess taxes in return for governmental functions it performs," the Court found that the tribal and federal interests were greater than those of the state.

The decision in *Bracker* also helped to cement another principle found in this area of tax law specifically and federal Indian law more broadly—preemption. In establishing what was at stake for each sovereign, the Court gestured toward tribal sovereignty, but also described it as a "backdrop" to these types of cases. Rather, Justice Marshall's opinion was more fully concerned with the significant federal engagement with the economic activity that the state was trying to tax, noting that the federal government "exercises literally daily supervision" over the timbering that the non-Native companies performed. This "comprehensive" federal engagement excluded—or preempted—any state authority. Consequently, a state's authority to tax in Indian Country often appears to be more dependent on federal assertions of authority than anything else.

Put another way, a state will be preempted from taxing non-Natives within Indian Country if the federal government is deeply enough involved in curating the people or actions that the state seeks to tax. But when has the federal government achieved that level of involvement? And what happens when a state is authorized to tax in Indian Country, particularly as it concerns any tribal taxation over the same activity? To what extent should the consequences to the potential taxpayer be considered?

Described as the "sequel to *Merrion*" by the Supreme Court, the next case tackled these questions. A non-Native oil and gas company that was mining on the Jicarilla Apache reservation dutifully paid the tribal tax authorized by *Merrion*. The state then also required the company to pay state taxes on their mining activities. The company objected to the state taxes since it was already paying tribal taxes and brought suit against the state. As you read the case, identify the similarities and differences between this case and *Bracker*. Do these two cases offer a framework for understanding when the federal government has preempted state taxes on tribal lands? How are tribal interests described in the case? What are the consequences of the decision for both tribal nations and the non-Native businesses that engage in commerce with them?

COTTON PETROLEUM CORP. V. NM
490 U.S. 163 (1989)

JUSTICE STEVENS delivered the opinion of the Court.

* * *

Prior to 1982, Cotton paid, without objection, five different oil and gas production taxes to the State of New Mexico. The state taxes amount to about 8 percent of the value of Cotton's production. The same 8 percent is collected from producers throughout the State. Thus, on wells outside the reservation, the total tax burden is only 8 percent, while Cotton's reservation wells are taxed at a total rate of 14 percent (8 percent by the State and 6 percent by the Tribe).

* * *

. . . [I]t is well settled that, absent express congressional authorization, a State cannot tax the United States directly. It is also clear that the tax immunity of the United States is shared by the Indian tribes for whose benefit the United States holds reservation lands in trust. Under current doctrine, however, a State can impose a nondiscriminatory tax on private parties with whom the United States or an Indian tribe does business, even though the financial burden of the tax may fall on the United States or tribe. . . . Congress does, of course, retain the power to grant such immunity. Whether such immunity shall be granted is thus a question that "is essentially legislative in character."

The question for us to decide is whether Congress has acted to grant the Tribe such immunity, either expressly or by plain implication. . . .

Although determining whether federal legislation has pre-empted state taxation of lessees of Indian land is primarily an exercise in examining congressional intent, the history of tribal sovereignty serves as a necessary "backdrop" to that process. As a result, questions of pre-emption in this area are . . . not controlled by "mechanical or absolute conceptions of state or tribal sovereignty." Instead, we have applied a flexible pre-emption analysis sensitive to the particular facts and legislation involved. Each case "requires a particularized examination of the relevant state, federal, and tribal interests.". . .

. . . Most significantly, Cotton contends that the [Indian Mineral and Leasing Act of] 1938 . . . exhibits a strong federal interest in guaranteeing Indian tribes the maximum return on their oil and gas leases. Moreover, Cotton maintains that the Federal and Tribal Governments, acting pursuant to the 1938 Act, its accompanying regulations, and the Jicarilla Apache Tribal Code, exercise comprehensive regulatory control over Cotton's on-reservation activity. Cotton describes New Mexico's responsibilities, in contrast, as "significantly limited.". . . We disagree.

The 1938 Act neither expressly permits state taxation nor expressly precludes it, but rather simply provides that "unallotted lands within any Indian reservation or lands owned by any tribe . . . may, with the approval of the Secretary of the Interior, be leased for mining purposes, by authority of the tribal council. . . ." The Senate and House Reports that accompanied the Act, moreover—even when considered in their broadest possible terms—shed little light on congressional intent concerning state taxation of oil and gas produced on leased lands.

* * *

We thus agree that a purpose of the 1938 Act is to provide Indian tribes with badly needed revenue, but find no evidence for the further supposition that Congress intended to remove all barriers to profit maximization. . . .

Our review of the legislation that preceded the 1938 Act provides no additional support for Cotton's expansive view of the Act's purpose. . . .

* * *

In *Bracker*, we addressed the question whether Arizona could impose its motor carrier license and use fuel taxes on a nonmember logging company's use of roads located solely within an Indian reservation. Significantly, the roads at issue were "built, maintained, and policed exclusively by the Federal Government, the Tribe, and its contractors," and the State was "unable to identify any regulatory function or service [it] performed . . . that would justify the assessment of taxes for activities on Bureau and tribal roads within the reservation." Moreover, it was undisputed in *Bracker* that the economic burden of the taxes ultimately fell on the Tribe. Based on these facts and on our conclusion that collection of the taxes would undermine federal policy "in a context in which the Federal Government has undertaken to regulate the most minute details" of the Tribe's timber operations, we held that the taxes were pre-empted.

* * *

The factual findings . . . clearly distinguish this case from . . . *Bracker*. After conducting a trial, that court found that "New Mexico provides substantial services to both the Jicarilla Tribe and Cotton". . . . The present case is also unlike *Bracker* . . . in that the District Court found that "[n]o economic burden falls on the tribe by virtue of the state taxes," and that the Tribe could, in fact, increase its taxes without adversely affecting on-reservation oil and gas development. Finally, the District Court found that the State regulates the spacing and mechanical integrity of wells located on the reservation. Thus, although the federal and tribal regulations in this case are extensive, they are not exclusive, as were the regulations in *Bracker*. . .

We thus conclude that federal law, even when given the most generous construction, does not pre-empt New Mexico's oil and gas severance taxes. . . . It is, of course, reasonable to infer that the New Mexico taxes have at least a marginal effect on the demand for on-reservation leases, the value to the Tribe of those leases, and the ability of the Tribe to increase its tax rate. Any impairment to the federal policy favoring the exploitation of on-reservation oil and gas resources by Indian tribes that might be caused by these effects, however, is simply too indirect and too insubstantial to support Cotton's claim of pre-emption. . . .

* * *

It is, of course, true that the total taxes paid by Cotton are higher than those paid by off-reservation producers. But neither the State nor the Tribe imposes a discriminatory tax. The burdensome consequence is entirely attributable to the fact that the leases are located in an area where two governmental entities share jurisdiction. As we noted in *Merrion*, the tribal tax does "not treat minerals transported away from the reservation differently than it treats minerals that might be sold on the reservation." Similarly, the New Mexico taxes are administered in an evenhanded manner and are imposed at a uniform rate throughout the State—both on and off the reservation.

* * *

Taken together, the decisions in *Bracker* and *Cotton Petroleum* offer some guidance into how cases about state taxes on tribal lands will be decided. As noted above, the Supreme Court has developed a "balancing test" which measures the interests of the state against the combined interests of the tribal nation and the federal government. In addition, the federal government can "preempt" state incursions into Indian Country if the federal government's efforts are comprehensive enough to warrant such exclusion in the Court's eyes. Tribal sovereignty serves as a "backdrop" to the Court analysis. Consequently, the Court considers the benefits and burdens of the challenged tax to each sovereign on its face, with tribal sovereignty often treated more as something to be noted and less as a tool of analysis. In *Cotton Petroleum*, the Supreme Court found that the state tax was not preempted by federal action and that the state's interest was substantial enough to outweigh the combined tribal and federal interests.

Cotton Petroleum is also a reminder that one sovereign's authority to tax something does not have to mean that another sovereign is prevented from taxing that same thing—the most obvious examples are state and federal income taxes. The result of this particular case meant that the non-Native oil and gas company was required to pay both the 8% state tax and the 6% tribal tax, whereas companies within the state but outside of the reservation only had to pay the 8% state tax. These types of results create economic difficulties for tribal nations and the non-Natives who do business with them. Since the leases in question in *Cotton Petroleum* were taxed at a higher rate than anywhere else in the state, the non-Native companies stand to make less profit on reservation lands and tribal nations stand to make less on the leases to compensate for the diminished profits.

Ultimately, the Supreme Court acknowledged this burden that its ruling placed on tribal nations and non-Native businesses, but was unmoved by its force. As such, it raises questions about the Supreme Court's conception of tribal sovereignty and what it means in tax (and other) cases. For example, what is the relationship between a tribal nation's economic capacities and its sovereignty? Put another way, does a decision like *Cotton Petroleum*, which hampers a tribal nation's economic activity also harm its sovereignty? Why or why not? Where is the line between economic capacities and sovereignty for governments? If this ruling does limit trial sovereignty, are these limitations justified? Why or why not? Additionally, how is tribal sovereignty functioning as a "backdrop" in these cases? How does it contribute to the analysis? What factors have demonstrated to be the most important in Indian law tax cases?

Another question has arisen as tribal nations have become bigger and more sophisticated members of their economic surroundings: who actually pays a given tax? The answer to this question, and thus the answer to the second sequential question—which entity is the target of the tax?—can become cloudy as it is a common practice for businesses to pass the cost of a tax onto the consumer. To roughly demonstrate, assume that a business usually charges $100 to a consumer for a service. If a state were to institute a 6% tax for every dollar earned while performing the service, the business will then typically charge the consumer $106 for the service (plus more to make up the tax on the extra six dollars). In effect, the consumer pays the tax. Yet states, as noted above, are prohibited from directly taxing tribal nations and tribal citizens living and working on tribal lands. So what happens when a business attempts to pass the cost of a tax along to a tribal nation or a tribal citizen living and working on tribal lands? Is the state tax still valid in those circumstances? To find the answer, it is necessary to turn to the third sequential question—what other factors need to be considered?

The Supreme Court established a method for analyzing such situations in the following case. The facts of the case are fairly simple. Kansas imposed a tax on distributors of motor fuel within the state—essentially non-Native wholesale sellers of gasoline. Those distributors then passed the cost of the tax along to retailers of the motor fuel—essentially gas stations. The Prairie Band of Potawatomi, who owned a gas station on its reservation and bought fuel from the distributors, objected to the tax since they ultimately paid it through their purchase of motor fuel from the distributors. As you read the case, ask yourself what factors of analysis are most important to the Supreme Court. Who, according to the Court, pays the tax? How does the ruling in this case engage with other rulings about state taxes in Indian Country? How does the dissent characterize both the facts of the case and the ruling of the majority?

WAGNON V. PRAIRIE BAND OF POTAWATOMI INDIANS
546 U.S. 95 (2005)

JUSTICE THOMAS delivered the opinion of the Court.

... [T]he the *Bracker* interest-balancing test applies only where "a State asserts authority over the conduct of non-Indians engaging in activity on the reservation." It does not apply where, as here, a state tax is imposed on a non-Indian and arises as a result of a transaction that occurs off the reservation.

* * *

... As the Nation recognizes, under our Indian tax immunity cases, the "who" and the "where" of the challenged tax have significant consequences. We have determined that "[t]he initial and frequently dispositive question in Indian tax cases . . . is who bears the legal incidence of [the] tax". . . .

* * *

Kansas law specifies that "the incidence of [the motor fuel] tax is imposed on the distributor of the first receipt of the motor fuel." We have suggested that such "dispositive language" from the state legislature is determinative of who bears the legal incidence of a state excise tax. But even if the state legislature had not employed such "dispositive language," thereby requiring us instead to look to a "fair interpretation of the taxing statute as written and applied," we would nonetheless conclude that the legal incidence of the tax is on the distributor.

Kansas law makes clear that it is the distributor, rather than the retailer, that is liable to pay the motor fuel tax. . . . While the distributors are "entitled" to pass along the cost of the tax to downstream purchasers, they are not required to do so. In sum, the legal incidence of the Kansas motor fuel tax is on the distributor.

* * *

As written, the Kansas fuel tax provisions state that "the incidence of this tax is imposed on the distributor of the first receipt of the motor fuel and such taxes shall be paid but once. . . ." Under this provision, the distributor who initially receives the motor fuel is liable for payment of the fuel tax. . . .

* * *

Limiting the interest-balancing test exclusively to on-reservation transactions between a nontribal entity and a tribe or tribal member is consistent with our unique Indian tax immunity jurisprudence. . . .

* * *

JUSTICE GINSBURG, with whom JUSTICE KENNEDY joins, dissenting.

* * *

Both the Nation and the State have authority to tax. . . . As a practical matter however, the two tolls cannot coexist. If the Nation imposes its tax on top of Kansas' tax, then unless the Nation operates [its gas station] at a substantial loss, scarcely anyone will fill up at its pumps. Effectively double-taxed, the [gas station] must operate as an unprofitable venture, or not at all.

* * *

The Court has repeatedly applied the interest-balancing approach described in *Bracker* in evaluating claims that state taxes levied on non-Indians should be preempted because they undermine tribal and federal interests.

* * *

Balancing tests have been criticized as rudderless, affording insufficient guidance to decisionmakers. Pointed as the criticism may be, one must ask, as in life's choices generally, what is the alternative. . . . No "bright-line" test is capable of achieving such an accommodation with respect to state taxes formally imposed on non-Indians, but impacting on-reservation ventures. The one the Court adopts inevitably means, so long as the State officially places the burden on the non-Indian distributor in cases of this order, the Tribe loses. . . .

> I would adhere to precedent calling for "a particularized inquiry into the nature
> of the state, federal, and tribal interests at stake."
>
> * * *

In one sense, Justice Clarence Thomas's majority opinion sets forth a clean analytical structure for these types of cases and provides an answer to the third sequential question—what other factors need to be considered? The important elements to discern are "who" pays the tax and "where" is it paid. Or, to put it in more lawyerly language, who bears the legal incidence of the tax? Since the "who" were non-Native gasoline distributors and the "where" was off-reservation, the state tax was valid even though the tribal nation ultimately paid it. According to Thomas, the "who" and "where" questions come before the interest balancing test from *Bracker* and render the test unnecessary if the legal incidence is outside of the reservation (and not on the tribal nation directly).

In another sense, as Justice Ruth Bader Ginsburg's dissent points out, this analytical structure is not as clean as it might appear on its face and it obscures the reality on the ground. The Kansas statute in question identified the off-reservation distributors as the bearers of the legal incidence of the tax, which carried great significance with the justices in the majority. Yet, deciding these types of cases by merely identifying the legal incidence of the tax would seem to produce a situation that would allow a state to regularly tax tribal nations, albeit indirectly. Additionally, as Ginsburg points out, such decisions can have a major economic impact on tribal nations and their businesses. Her solution would be to apply *Bracker*'s interest balancing test to decide if a state tax can be validly applied.

Even after *Wagnon*, the third sequential question can remain open. In 2019 the Supreme Court decided another case with facts that were somewhat similar to *Wagnon*. Once again motor fuel was at the heart of the matter, as the state of Washington taxed importers of fuel when the fuel entered the state by highway (pipelines and water vessels were exempted from the tax). Cougar Den was a corporation owned by a Yakama tribal member, incorporated under tribal law, and designated by the tribal nation as the company to obtain fuel for the tribal nation and its members. Cougar Den argued that it was exempted from the state tax under the tribal nation's treaty with the federal government. *Washington v. Cougar Den* is also important for its understanding of the Indian canons of construction and is also considered in Chapter 11.

As you read the case, ask yourself about the various interests at play in the case. Who is trying to do what? What is the relationship between the treaty and the state tax? How does this case address the three sequential questions of this chapter?

WASHINGTON V. COUGAR DEN

139 S. Ct. 1000 (2019)

JUSTICE BREYER delivered the opinion of the Court.

* * *

The relevant treaty provides for the purchase by the United States of Yakama land. . . . [R]eserved [treaty] rights include "the right, in common with citizens of the United States, to travel upon all public highways". . . .

* * *

. . . Here, the Yakamas' lone off-reservation act within the State is traveling along a public highway with fuel.

* * *

In our view, the State of Washington's application of the fuel tax to Cougar Den's importation of fuel is pre-empted by the treaty's reservation to the Yakama Nation of the "right, in common with the citizens of the United States, to travel upon all public highways." We rest this conclusion upon three considerations taken together.

First, this Court has considered this treaty four times previously . . . each time it has stressed that the language of the treaty should be understood as bearing the meaning that the Yakamas understood it to have in 1855.

. . . The words "in common with" on their face could be read to permit application to the Yakamas of general legislation (like the legislation before us) that applies to all citizens, Yakama and non-Yakama alike. But this Court concluded the contrary because that is not what the Yakamas understood the words to mean in 1855.

* * *

Second, the historical record adopted by the agency and the courts below indicates that the right to travel includes a right to travel with goods for sale or distribution.

* * *

Third, to impose a tax upon traveling with certain goods burdens that travel.

* * *

Cougar Den moves the third sequential question—what other factors need to be considered—beyond the "who" and "where" of *Wagnon*. It demonstrates that treaty rights (and potentially other factors) can also affect taxation questions. For the Yakama, their treaty, history, and efforts in the courts led to the exclusion of state taxing authority over a Native owned business on the reservation.

As this chapter shows, the three sequential questions can offer a path for understanding an otherwise intimidating body of law. By asking who is doing the taxing, who is being taxed, and what other factors need to be considered, some easy to grasp principles emerge. These basic principles can serve as a foundation should you engage with different and deeper questions of taxation in Indian Country.

SUGGESTED READINGS

- "Taxation and Doing Business in Indian Country." Erik M. Jensen. 60 *Maine Law Review* 1 (2008).

- "The 'Who and Where' Means the State Takes All: State Taxation Crosses into Indian Country." Kelly Gaines Stoner and Casey Ross-Petherick. 30 *American Indian Law Review* 385 (2005–2006).

- "The Unfulfilled Promise of the Indian Commerce Clause and State Taxation." Richard D. Pomp. 63 *The Tax Lawyer* 897 (Summer 2010).

---

1   McCullough v. Maryland, 17 U.S. 316 (1819), 327.
2   Rev. Rul. 67–284, 1967–2 C.B. 55.
3   Rev. Rul. 94–16, 1994–1 C.B. 19.

CHAPTER 21

Sovereign Immunity

In one sense, the legal principle known as sovereign immunity is both easy to comprehend and widely accepted. Sovereign immunity is a doctrine of law that states that a sovereign—whether it be the federal government, a state, or a tribal nation—cannot be sued in its own court without its consent. It is a vestige of English common law, which the United States adopted in large part after the American Revolutionary War. As stated in one modern Supreme Court case, "The generation that designed and adopted our federal system considered immunity from private suits central to sovereign dignity. . . . Although the American people had rejected other aspects of English political theory, the doctrine that a sovereign could not be sued without its consent was universal in the States when the Constitution was drafted and ratified."[1]

In another sense, however, sovereign immunity is, at best, controversial. To many, including several prominent thinkers within the legal academy, a principle of law that inhibits the rights of a citizen to hold a government accountable in its own courts seems un-American or otherwise simply unfair. Others strongly argue that the common understanding that the United States has always accepted and revered the idea of sovereign immunity is not true. For example, the dissent in the Supreme Court case quoted above stated in response, "While sovereign immunity entered many new state legal systems as a part of the common law selectively received from England, it was not understood to be indefeasible or to have been given any such status by the new National Constitution, which did not mention it."[2]

The same basic understandings apply when sovereign immunity is considered within Indian Country: It has long been accepted that tribal nations have sovereign immunity, but the doctrine is deeply controversial. It also raises a number of questions. For example, to what extent does this European-derived rule of law speak to Indigenous governments and peoples? Is it necessary to protect sovereignty, or does it create so much fear of dealing with tribal nations that it actually inhibits the ability of tribal nations to perform in the marketplace? What happens when a tribal nation acts in a manner that many perceive as unfair yet then wants to invoke sovereign immunity as a shield against its actions?

This chapter will demonstrate. . .

- *The acknowledgment of tribal sovereign immunity in American law*

- *How tribal sovereign immunity can be waived*

- *The scope of tribal sovereign immunity*

ACKNOWLEDGING TRIBAL SOVEREIGN IMMUNITY

As noted above, the principle of sovereign immunity is an easy concept to grasp—a sovereign cannot be sued in its own courts without its consent. It acts as a shield, protecting governments from litigation. At first blush, such a rule might seem obviously unfair, since it does not allow a harmed party the same type of immediate recourse in a court that the harmed party would have against a neighbor, business, or anonymous reckless driver. However, sovereign immunity can be, and often is, waived by the governments who hold it. In fact, waiving sovereign immunity is often both a good governmental and good business practice. Governments that provide private parties a forum in their courts to resolve disputes against that government fortify a sense of fairness, demonstrate a willingness to correct wrongs, and encourage investment in and with the government. Consequently, the decision to waive sovereign immunity involves a delicate balance of a number of factors, including protecting the government (and the resources that citizens contribute to the government) from a litigious society, maintaining a system of checks and balances in which courts respect the other branches of government, and offering a recourse for legitimately aggrieved private parties. If they choose to do so, governments typically waive their sovereign immunity—or, put another way, they consent to a lawsuit—by statute or through a contract with a private party. In short, an individual cannot sue, for example, the federal government unless that individual can point to a statute, contractual clause, or other mechanism whereby the federal government has consented to the lawsuit.

Also as noted above, while the doctrine of sovereign immunity has been longstanding, even predating the United States itself, critics of the doctrine are not hard to find. These same circumstances have parallels in federal Indian law as well. Although the Supreme Court has acknowledged tribal sovereign immunity for some time, there are many—including those on the Court—who question its utility and application. Some see tribal sovereign immunity as necessary to protect tribal nations, especially since tribal nations are more economically vulnerable than states or the federal government. Others see tribal sovereign immunity as unfair to those who engage with tribal nations and an overextension of the doctrine.

In the following case, the Kiowa, a tribal nation located in Oklahoma, signed a promissory note with a non-Native business. The note itself stated that it was signed on tribal trust land, but the note was delivered to the non-Native business outside of tribal lands and payments on the note were made outside of tribal lands. The note also stated that "Nothing in this Note subjects or limits the sovereign rights of the Kiowa Tribe of Oklahoma."

At some point, the Kiowa stopped paying on the note and the non-Native company sued the tribal nation in state court. The Kiowa argued, among other things, that the non-Native company was prevented from suing the tribal nation in state court because of the tribal nation's sovereign immunity. As you read the case, ask yourself how the Court describes the historical development of tribal sovereign immunity. Why does the Court rule in the way that it does in light of this history? To whom does the majority opinion appeal? What is the most important factor for the dissent? What are the similarities and differences between the majority opinion and the dissent?

KIOWA TRIBE OF OK V. MANUFACTURING TECHNOLOGIES
523 U.S. 751 (1998)

JUSTICE KENNEDY delivered the opinion of the Court.

. . . Our case law to date often recites the rule of tribal immunity from suit. While these precedents rest on early cases that assumed immunity without extensive reasoning, we adhere to these decisions. . . .

* * *

As a matter of federal law, an Indian tribe is subject to suit only where Congress has authorized the suit or the tribe has waived its immunity. To date, our cases have sustained tribal immunity from suit without drawing a distinction based on where the tribal activities occurred. . . . Nor have we yet drawn a distinction between governmental and commercial activities of a tribe.

Though respondent asks us to confine immunity from suit to transactions on reservations and to governmental activities, our precedents have not drawn these distinctions.

* * *

. . . We have often noted, however, that the immunity possessed by Indian tribes is not coextensive with that of the States. . . . [W]e distinguished state sovereign immunity from tribal sovereign immunity, as tribes were not at the Constitutional Convention. They were thus not parties to the "mutuality of . . . concession" that "makes the States' surrender of immunity from suit by sister States plausible." So tribal immunity is a matter of federal law and is not subject to diminution by the States.

Though the doctrine of tribal immunity is settled law and controls this case, we note that it developed almost by accident. The doctrine is said by some of our own opinions to rest on the Court's opinion in *Turner v. United States*. Though *Turner* is indeed cited as authority for the immunity, examination shows it simply does not stand for that proposition. . . .

. . . *Turner*, then, is but a slender reed for supporting the principle of tribal sovereign immunity. *Turner*'s passing reference to immunity, however, did become an explicit holding that tribes had immunity from suit. We so held in [another case], saying: "These Indian Nations are exempt from suit without Congressional authorization." As sovereigns or quasi-sovereigns, the Indian Nations enjoyed immunity "from judicial attack" absent consent to be sued. Later cases, albeit with little analysis, reiterated the doctrine.

The doctrine of tribal immunity came under attack a few years ago. . . . The petitioner there asked us to abandon or at least narrow the doctrine because tribal businesses had become far removed from tribal self-governance and internal affairs. We retained the doctrine, however, on the theory that Congress had failed to abrogate it in order to promote economic development and tribal self-sufficiency. The rationale, it must be said, can be challenged as inapposite to modern, wide-ranging tribal enterprises extending well beyond traditional tribal customs and activities. JUSTICE STEVENS, in a separate opinion, criticized tribal immunity as "founded upon an anachronistic fiction" and suggested it might not extend to offreservation commercial activity.

There are reasons to doubt the wisdom of perpetuating the doctrine. At one time, the doctrine of tribal immunity from suit might have been thought necessary to protect nascent tribal governments from encroachments by States. In our interdependent and mobile society, however, tribal immunity extends beyond what is needed to safeguard tribal self-governance. This is evident when tribes take part in the Nation's commerce. Tribal enterprises now include ski resorts, gambling, and sales of cigarettes to non-Indians. In this economic context, immunity can harm those who are unaware that they are dealing with a tribe, who do not know of tribal immunity, or who have no choice in the matter, as in the case of tort victims.

These considerations might suggest a need to abrogate tribal immunity, at least as an overarching rule. Respondent does not ask us to repudiate the principle outright, but suggests instead that we confine it to reservations or to noncommercial activities. We decline to draw this distinction in this case, as we defer to the role Congress may wish to exercise in this important judgment.

* * *

. . . Congress is in a position to weigh and accommodate the competing policy concerns and reliance interests. The capacity of the Legislative Branch to address the issue by comprehensive legislation counsels some caution by us in this area. Congress "has occasionally authorized limited classes of suits against Indian tribes" and "has always been at liberty to dispense with such tribal immunity or to limit it." It has not yet done so.

In light of these concerns, we decline to revisit our case law and choose to defer to Congress. Tribes enjoy immunity from suits on contracts, whether those contracts involve governmental or commercial activities and whether they were made on or off a reservation. Congress has not abrogated this immunity, nor has petitioner waived it, so the immunity governs this case. . . .

JUSTICE STEVENS, with whom JUSTICE THOMAS and JUSTICE GINSBURG join, dissenting.

"Absent express federal law to the contrary, Indians going beyond reservation boundaries have generally been held subject to nondiscriminatory state law otherwise applicable to all citizens of the State." There is no federal statute or treaty that provides [the Kiowa] any immunity from the application of Oklahoma law to its off-reservation commercial activities. Nor, in my opinion, should this Court extend the judge-made doctrine of sovereign immunity to pre-empt the authority of the state courts to decide for themselves whether to accord such immunity to Indian tribes as a matter of comity.

* * *

> In several cases . . . we have broadly referred to the tribes' immunity from suit, but "with little analysis," and only considering controversies arising on reservation territory.
>
> . . . We have treated the doctrine of sovereign immunity . . . as settled law, but in none of our cases have we applied the doctrine to purely off-reservation conduct. . . .
>
> Three compelling reasons favor the exercise of judicial restraint.
>
> First, the law-making power that the Court has assumed belongs in the first instance to Congress. . . . The Court is . . . announcing a rule that pre-empts state power.
>
> Second, the rule is strikingly anomalous. . . .
>
> Third, the rule is unjust. . . .

The major distinction between the majority opinion and the dissent in *Kiowa Tribe* is not their levels of support for tribal sovereign immunity. Both the majority opinion and the dissent were skeptical of tribal sovereign immunity, with Justice Anthony Kennedy's majority opinion stating that it "developed almost by accident." In addition, both the majority opinion and the dissent seem disturbed by the outcome of the case, which effectively allowed the Kiowa to stop paying a loan without any recourse for the lender. Thus, the difference between those who voted in favor of the Kiowa and those who voted against them was not conditioned by tribal sovereignty or the result in the case itself. Rather, the major distinction between the majority opinion and the dissent was which branch of government ought to limit tribal sovereign immunity.

For Kennedy and the majority, Congress, as opposed to the Supreme Court, was the branch of the federal government that should decide whether or not to limit tribal sovereign immunity. Since this decision was best left to Congress, the majority opinion declined to act and the non-Native business's lawsuit against the tribal nation could not move forward. Despite the positive result for the Kiowa, Kennedy's opinion was an invitation to Congress to consider the matter, presumably to limit future situations like the case at hand.

For Justice John Paul Stevens and the rest of the dissenters, the Supreme Court would have been an appropriate venue to decide the boundaries of tribal sovereign immunity. The dissent would have placed the dispute within the confines of a trend within Indian law cases of the late twentieth and early twenty-first centuries: giving great deference to the perceived location of the dispute. According to the dissent, the dispute occurred off of tribal lands. And since, according to the dissent, the precedential cases about tribal sovereign immunity had never considered an off reservation dispute, the majority was creating a new rule to allow tribal nations to invoke sovereign immunity outside of tribal borders. Since such a rule was "strikingly anomalous" and "unjust," the dissenters would not have let the Kiowa invoke sovereign immunity.

The victory in *Kiowa Tribe* was an uneasy one for Native America. Both the majority opinion and the dissent expressed significant skepticism over tribal sovereign immunity. Yet, despite regularly appearing to be under threat, tribal sovereign immunity has remained surprisingly resilient. In 2018 the Supreme Court considered another tribal sovereign immunity case, *Upper Skagit Indian Tribe v. Lundgren,* that reflected the ongoing themes in this area of law: the continuing validity of tribal sovereign immunity, the skepticism that it faces, the ongoing threats to its existence, and the questions that it continues to raise. Ultimately, the Supreme Court remanded the case back to the Washington Supreme Court for further consideration. As of this writing the case is still pending and may very well be heard in the Supreme Court again. For the time being, it is a useful case to study to understand the present state of tribal sovereign immunity in American law.

The Upper Skagit Indian Tribe, whose people and land are located in the state of Washington, purchased approximately forty acres in 2013, seeking to add to their small reservation land base. After having the land surveyed, the Upper Skagit determined that about an acre of their newly purchased property was fenced off by some non-Native neighbors, Sharline and Ray Lundgren. The tribal nation informed the Lundgrens that it intended to tear down the old fence and build a new fence in the proper location. The Lundgrens then filed suit against the Upper Skagit in state court and the tribal nation responded by invoking its sovereign immunity from suit.

In order to understand the case, it is useful to have some knowledge of *in rem* jurisdiction. *In rem* jurisdiction concerns property, as opposed to *in personam* jurisdiction, which concerns a person or persons. Thus, a lawsuit between two participants in a bar fight would raise *in personam* issues of law and jurisdiction, whereas the dispute in Upper Skagit, which was about whether the Upper Skagit or the Lundgrens owned a parcel of land, raised *in rem* issues of law and jurisdiction.

The question in *Upper Skagit* was whether the tribal nation could invoke its sovereign immunity over a dispute over a parcel of land outside of the reservation that the tribal nation had purchased and that was not presently in trust for the tribal nation. Put another way, could the tribal nation shield itself under its sovereign immunity in an off reservation *in rem* proceeding? As you read the case, ask yourself how the Lundgrens sought to overcome tribal sovereign immunity. What are the commonalities and differences between *Upper Skagit* and *Kiowa Tribe*? Why did the majority ultimately decide to remand the case back to the Washington State Supreme Court? How might this decision offer guidance on how the Court might decide if it sees this case again—or the next tribal sovereign immunity case, for that matter? What concerns do the concurrence and dissent raise? Are they valid? Why or why not?

UPPER SKAGIT INDIAN TRIBE V. LUNDGREN
138 S.Ct. 1649 (2018)

JUSTICE GORSUCH delivered the opinion of the Court.

Lower courts disagree about the significance of our decision in County of *Yakima v. Confederated Tribes and Bands of Yakima Nation*. Some think it means Indian tribes lack sovereign immunity in *in rem* lawsuits like this one; others don't read it that way at all. We granted certiorari to set things straight.

* * *

Ultimately, the Supreme Court of Washington rejected the Tribe's claim of immunity and ruled for the Lundgrens. The court reasoned that sovereign immunity does not apply to cases where a judge "exercise[es] in rem jurisdiction" to quiet title in a parcel of land owned by a Tribe, but only to cases where a judge seeks to exercise *in personam* jurisdiction over the Tribe itself. In coming to this conclusion, the court relied in part on our decision in *Yakama*. Like some courts before it, the Washington Supreme Court read *Yakima* as distinguishing *in rem* from *in personam* lawsuits and "establish[ing] the principle that . . . courts have . . . jurisdiction over *in rem* proceedings in certain situations where claims of sovereign immunity are asserted."

That was error. *Yakima* did not address the scope of tribal sovereign immunity. Instead, it involved only a much more prosaic question of statutory interpretation concerning the Indian General Allotment Act of 1887. . . .

. . . In short, *Yakima* sought only to interpret a relic of a statute in light of a distinguishable precedent; it resolved nothing about the law of sovereign immunity.

Commendably, the Lundgrens acknowledged all this at oral argument. Instead of seeking to defend the Washington Supreme Court's reliance on *Yakima*, they now ask us to affirm their judgment on an entirely distinct alternative ground. . . . [The Lundgrens argue that] sovereigns enjoyed no immunity from actions involving immovable property located in the territory of another sovereign. . . . Relying on this line of reasoning, the Lundgrens argue, the Tribe cannot assert sovereign immunity because this suit relates to immovable property located in the State of Washington that the Tribe purchased in the "character of a private individual."

The Tribe and the federal government disagree. They note that immunity doctrines lifted from other contexts do not always neatly apply to Indian tribes. . . .

We leave it to the Washington Supreme Court to address these arguments in the first instance. . . . Determining the limits on the sovereign immunity held by Indian tribes is a grave question; the answer will affect all tribes, not just the one before us; and the alternative argument for affirmance did not emerge until late in this case. . . . This Court has often declined to take a "first view" of questions . . . and we think that course the wise one today.

* * *

CHIEF JUSTICE ROBERTS, with whom JUSTICE KENNEDY joins, concurring.

. . . What precisely is someone in the Lundgrens' position supposed to do? There should be a means of resolving a mundane dispute over property ownership, even when one of the parties to the dispute—involving non-trust, non-reservation land—is an Indian tribe. The correct answer cannot be that the tribe always wins no matter what; otherwise a tribe could wield sovereign immunity as a sword and seize property with impunity, even without a colorable claim of right.

* * *

The consequences of the Court's decision today thus seem intolerable, unless there is another means of resolving property disputes of this sort.

* * *

JUSTICE THOMAS, with whom JUSTICE ALITO joins, dissenting.

* * *

The Court easily could have resolved [this] disagreement by addressing [the Lundgrens'] alternative [argument]. Sharline and Ray Lundgren—whose family has maintained the land in question for more than 70 years—ask us to affirm based on the "immovable property" exception to sovereign immunity. That exception is settled, longstanding, and obviously applies to tribal immunity—as it does to every other type of sovereign immunity that has ever been recognized. Although the Lundgrens did not raise this argument below, we have the discretion to reach it. I would have done so.

* * *

The immovable-property exception [is longstanding]. For centuries, there has been "uniform authority in support of the view that there is no immunity from jurisdiction with respect to actions relating to immovable property."

* * *

The decision in *Upper Skagit* is much less the resolution to a dispute and more an encapsulation of how the Supreme Court understood tribal sovereign immunity at the moment of its announcement. Justice Neil Gorsuch's majority opinion is, in one sense, a strong reaffirmation of tribal sovereign immunity. It clarified that a previous case (*Yakima*) did not limit tribal sovereign immunity in the manner that some lower courts had read it to do, thereby potentially opening up more areas of protection for tribal nations. It also cautioned against unnuanced applications of Western legal doctrine to Native America.

Yet, in another sense, Gorsuch's majority opinion left the sovereign immunity of the Upper Skagit Indian Tribe, and all tribal nations, in as much question as ever. It did not foreclose the possibility that it would limit tribal sovereign immunity under the circumstances of the case. Rather, the Supreme Court decided to let the Washington Supreme Court decide first. Thus, as of this writing, the issue remains unresolved.

The concurrence and dissent also reflect some of the common considerations of the Supreme Court in tribal sovereign immunity cases specifically and Indian law cases more broadly. In his concurrence, Chief Justice John Roberts was deeply reflective on the options, or lack thereof, for the Lundgrens. He focused his concurrence on how the decision would affect them, arguing that the non-Native couple needed to have some venue to resolve the dispute. This concurrence suggests that Roberts might be willing to sacrifice tribal sovereign immunity to protect the Lundgrens and others like them. Unlike Justice Gorsuch's majority opinion, Justice Clarence Thomas's dissent was not particularly concerned with the unique application of Western legal principles in Indian Country. According to Thomas, the "immovable-property exception" to sovereign immunity—that a sovereign cannot invoke its immunity when engaged in real estate transactions outside of its own jurisdiction—should be applied to the case without any further consideration from the Washington Supreme Court. In both the concurrence and the dissent, tribal interests are found more at the periphery than at the center of the analysis.

Today, tribal sovereign immunity remains a viable and valuable aspect of tribal sovereignty more broadly. A majority of justices on the Supreme Court continue to generally vote in favor of it, despite whatever reservations some of them might have. Yet, those justices who are inclined to limit tribal sovereign immunity remain strong in numbers and continue to write against it, sometimes very forcefully. As tribal nations further develop their governments and expand their reach both inside and outside of Indian Country, questions about tribal sovereign immunity are likely to remain subjects of litigation in American courts.

WAIVING TRIBAL SOVEREIGN IMMUNITY

Also as noted above, a government's decision to waive sovereign immunity often involves a delicate balance of a number of competing interests. At a practical level, sovereign immunity might be necessary, as it might not make sense to allow every party that has a dispute with a government to take the government to court whenever she or he feels like it. For example, what would be the consequence for a government if a private citizen were able to sue that government every time she or he felt wronged by a parking ticket or had to pay a new tax? It does not take much effort to imagine that, before long, the vast bulk of governmental activities under this scenario would be directed toward defending itself in court.

Yet, there are times when a private entity is injured, financially, physically, or otherwise, by a government in a manner that is not easily remedied without the opportunity to adjudicate the matter in a court. On those occasions, the government's best choice is to waive sovereign immunity and authorize a private party to sue. For example, sometimes a government will break a contractual promise (as what happened in *Kiowa Tribe*) with a private party. Since a private party's civil or constitutional rights will likely not be at stake, that private party will only have a recourse if the government waives its sovereign immunity. Waiving sovereign immunity not only holds the government in question accountable, it promotes growth and a willingness to enter into business with the government.

The balance that any government must make in deciding to waive its sovereign immunity raises another question: How is it waived? Put another way, what condition or conditions must be satisfied to determine that a waiver has occurred? Often it is obvious, such as when a legislature passes a law waiving sovereign immunity for a specific purpose or a set of circumstances. But what about those times when it is less obvious? When will a court decide that sovereign immunity has been waived?

Four years after *Kiowa Tribe*, the Supreme Court decided its next major tribal sovereign immunity case, *C & L Enterprises v. Citizen Band Potawatomi Indian Tribe of Oklahoma*. The two cases shared some general characteristics. In both, the tribal nation contracted with a non-Native company for a business venture that was outside of reservation boundaries. In *C & L Enterprises*, the Citizen Band Potawatomi contracted with the non-Native company to do some roofing work on a tribal building. After the contract was signed but before the non-Native company could perform the work, the tribal nation decided to use different roofing materials and solicited new bids for the roofing project. The non-Native company objected and filed suit in state court. The Citizen Band Potawatomi responded to the suit by seeking to invoke its sovereign immunity.

The critical difference in *C & L Enterprises* was the language in the contract that the tribal nation signed with the non-Native company. The contract in *C & L* Enterprises had two important parts, according to the Supreme Court. The first was an arbitration clause. Arbitration clauses are agreements between contractual parties to settle disputes through a neutral, third party—known as an arbitrator—rather than through the courts. The arbitration clause in the case stated, "All claims or disputes . . . shall be decided by arbitration. . . . The award rendered by the arbitrator or arbitrators shall be final, and judgment may be entered upon it . . . in any court having jurisdiction thereof." The second important part of the contract was a choice-of-law clause. Choice-of-law clauses allow contracting parties to settle disputes under a particular jurisdiction's law (even if they live or exist outside of that jurisdiction). The choice-of-law clause in the case stated, "The contract shall be governed by the law of the place where the Project is located."

The question before the Supreme Court was whether the arbitration and choice-of-law clauses in the contract amounted to a waiver of the tribal nation's sovereign immunity. As you read the case, ask yourself what standard the Supreme Court uses to determine if the tribal nation has waived its sovereign immunity. How is the standard applied in this case? Is it fair? Why or why not? What characteristics about the contract itself also contribute to the decision? How might the decision in *Kiowa Tribe* have influenced this case? What does the result mean for tribal nations?

C & L ENTERPRISES V. CITIZEN BAND POTAWATOMI INDIAN TRIBE OF OKLAHOMA

532 U.S. 411 (2002)

JUSTICE GINSBURG delivered the opinion of the Court.

In *Kiowa Tribe of Okla. v. Manufacturing Technologies, Inc.*, this Court held that an Indian tribe is not subject to suit in a state court-even for breach of contract involving off-reservation commercial conduct-unless "Congress has authorized the suit or the tribe has waived its immunity." This case concerns the impact of an arbitration agreement on a tribe's plea of suit immunity. The document on which the case centers is a standard form construction contract signed by the parties to govern the installation of a foam roof on a building. . . . The building and land are owned by an Indian Tribe, the Citizen Potawatomi Nation (Tribe). The building is commercial, and the land is off-reservation, nontrust property. The form contract, which was proposed by the Tribe and accepted by the contractor, C & L Enterprises, Inc. (C & L), contains an arbitration clause.

* * *

The contract at issue is a standard form agreement. . . . The Tribe proposed the contract; details not set out in the form were inserted by the Tribe and its architect. Two provisions of the contract are key to this case. First, the contract contains an arbitration clause. . . .

Second, the contract includes a choice-of-law clause. . . .

* * *

Kiowa, in which we reaffirmed the doctrine of tribal immunity, involved an off-reservation, commercial agreement (a stock purchase) by a federally recognized Tribe. . . . Tribal immunity, we ruled in *Kiowa*, extends to suits on off-reservation commercial contracts. The Kiowa Tribe was immune from suit for defaulting on the promissory note, we held, because "Congress ha[d] not abrogated [the Tribe's] immunity, nor ha[d] petitioner waived it."

Like *Kiowa*, this case arises out of the breach of a commercial, off-reservation contract by a federally recognized Indian Tribe. The petitioning contractor, C & L, does not contend that Congress has abrogated tribal immunity in this setting. The question presented is whether the Tribe has waived its immunity.

To abrogate tribal immunity, Congress must "unequivocally" express that purpose. Similarly, to relinquish its immunity, a tribe's waiver must be "clear." We are satisfied that the Tribe in this case has waived, with the requisite clarity, immunity from the suit C & L brought to enforce its arbitration award.

The construction contract's provision for arbitration and related prescriptions lead us to this conclusion. The arbitration clause requires resolution of all contract-related disputes between C & L and the Tribe by binding arbitration; ensuing arbitral awards may be reduced to judgment "in accordance with applicable law in any court having jurisdiction thereof.". . .

The contract's choice-of-law clause makes it plain enough that a "court having jurisdiction" to enforce the award in question is the Oklahoma state court in which C & L filed suit. By selecting Oklahoma law ("the law of the place where the Project is located") to govern the contract, the parties have effectively consented to confirmation of the award "in accordance with" the Oklahoma Uniform Arbitration Act.

The Uniform Act in force in Oklahoma prescribes that, when "an agreement . . . provid[es] for arbitration in this state," i.e., in Oklahoma, jurisdiction to enforce the agreement vests in "any court of competent jurisdiction of this state." On any sensible reading of the Act, the District Court of Oklahoma County, a local court of general jurisdiction, fits that statutory description.

In sum, the Tribe agreed, by express contract, to adhere to certain dispute resolution procedures. In fact, the Tribe itself tendered the contract calling for those procedures.

* * *

The Tribe strenuously urges, however, that an arbitration clause simply "is not a waiver of immunity from suit." The phrase in the clause providing for enforcement of arbitration awards "in any court having jurisdiction thereof," the Tribe maintains, "begs the question of what court has jurisdiction." As counsel for the Tribe clarified at oral argument, the Tribe's answer is "no court," on earth or even on the moon. No court-federal, state, or even tribal-has jurisdiction over C & L's suit, the Tribe insists, because it has not expressly waived its sovereign immunity in any judicial forum.

Instead of waiving suit immunity in any court, the Tribe argues, the arbitration clause waives simply and only the parties' rights to a court trial of contractual disputes; under the clause, the Tribe recognizes, the parties must instead arbitrate. The clause no doubt memorializes the Tribe's commitment to adhere to the contract's dispute resolution regime. That regime has a real world objective; it is not designed for regulation of a game lacking practical consequences. And to the real world end, the contract specifically authorizes judicial enforcement of the resolution arrived at through arbitration. . . .

The Tribe also asserts that a form contract, designed principally for private parties who have no immunity to waive, cannot establish a clear waiver of tribal suit immunity. In appropriate cases, we apply "the common-law rule of contract interpretation that a court should construe ambiguous language against the interest of the party that drafted it." That rule, however, is inapposite here. The contract, as we have explained, is not ambiguous. Nor did the Tribe find itself holding the short end of [the] stick: The Tribe proposed and prepared the contract. . . .

For the reasons stated, we conclude that under the agreement the Tribe proposed and signed, the Tribe clearly consented to arbitration and to the enforcement of arbitral awards in Oklahoma state court; the Tribe thereby waived its sovereign immunity from C & L's suit.

According to the Supreme Court, "to relinquish its immunity, a tribe's waiver must be 'clear.'" In theory, such a rule prevents a tribal nation from mistakenly or thoughtlessly waiving its sovereign immunity, and thus protects and preserves that immunity. To extend the logic another step, in order for a message or statement to be "clear," there presumably has to be some intent behind it. Yet, while understanding the issue in these terms is helpful, it still does not fully answer the question. When is a message "clear," or when does it demonstrate the necessary intent? For example, if a newly licensed teenager asks to borrow the family car for a night out with friends, when is it clear that a parent has agreed to the request? Must the parent unequivocally state something to the effect of "yes, you can borrow the car"? Is the parent's intent clear if the parent merely nods without speaking? What if the parent neither speaks nor makes any other affirmative gesture and the teenager then takes the car keys and drives off? Has this parent clearly agreed to the request by not acting when the teenager started to drive off? What act or gesture or standard is necessary to determine that the parent has been clear?

The Citizen Band Potawatomi argued that no waiver of tribal sovereign immunity was valid unless it was "expressly" done so. In other words, according to the tribal nation, unless there was deliberate language in the contract to the effect that the tribal nation had waived its sovereign immunity—perhaps something like "tribal sovereign immunity is waived for the purposes of this contract"—then it remained in force. Some commentators have described these types of defenses as "magic words" arguments, in that, according to the argument, one would need specific or precise language to make something come into effect.

Justice Ruth Bader Ginsburg, who dissented in *Kiowa Tribe*, wrote the majority opinion in *C & L Enterprises* and rejected the tribal nation's "magic words" argument. For Ginsburg, the arbitration clause coupled with the choice-of-law clause in the contract provided the necessary clarity to demonstrate that the tribal nation had waived it sovereign immunity. The Court was also not moved by the tribal nation's assertion that sovereign immunity could not be waived with a "form" contract—or a contract in which much of the language is taken from a template in which the parties only fill out the pertinent details. In essence, the Citizen Band Potawatomi argued that such contracts with boilerplate language could not be a clear waiver of sovereign immunity. However, since the tribal nation was the party to propose the contract, and the tribal nation agreed to the arbitration and choice-of-law clauses in the contract that it proposed, the Court rejected this argument.

At minimum, *C & L Enterprises*, coupled with *Kiowa Tribe*, offer guidance in understanding when American courts will find waivers of tribal sovereign immunity. Waivers must be "clear," but clarity can be achieved without express language or "magic words." Beyond the basic law that they outline, the two cases perhaps also demonstrate why tribal sovereign immunity cases are troubling to a good number of justices on the Supreme Court. In both cases, it is easy to argue that the tribal nations in question were engaging in unfair business practices. Both were refusing to pay for contractually agreed upon commitments and then using sovereign immunity not as a shield against frivolous lawsuits from cranky citizens but from legitimate business dealings with non-Native companies.

The decision in *C & L Enterprises* also raises a more philosophical set of questions about tribal sovereign immunity and its future. Is it possible that the Supreme Court was willing to adopt a lesser standard than demanding express language for waivers of tribal sovereign immunity because of the Court's understanding of the behavior of the tribal nations in these cases? How might the concerns of the justices for non-Native parties affect future cases? Will a Supreme Court that has consistently shown skepticism for tribal sovereign immunity continue to uphold its application if confronted with similarly situated fact patterns in the future? How, if at all, should these decisions shape a tribal nation's behavior?

DEFINING THE SCOPE OF TRIBAL SOVEREIGN IMMUNITY

When trying to understand sovereign immunity it is easiest to start by thinking of it as a singular concept—sovereigns cannot be sued in their own courts without their consent. However, the actual application of sovereign immunity in the United States—which contains multiple sovereigns—is somewhat more nuanced than that singular concept would suggest. Each sovereign in the United States exercises a slightly different version of sovereign immunity than the others. The federal government holds the strongest version of sovereign immunity and cannot be sued without its consent.

State sovereign immunity is not quite as extensive. In general, states cannot be sued without their consent with a few exceptions: states are not immune from suits by the federal government or from other states in federal court. In *Seminole Tribe of Florida v. Florida*—a case with federal Indian law implications and discussed in greater detail in Chapter 24—the Supreme Court ruled that the federal government could not waive the sovereign immunity of states against other parties unless clearly authorized by the U.S. Constitution to do so. Tribal nations are prevented from suing states directly under state sovereign immunity; however, sometimes the federal government will sue a state on behalf of a tribal nation.

Tribal sovereign immunity is somewhat parallel to state sovereign immunity. Tribal nations cannot invoke sovereign immunity against the federal government, but they can do so against states. The critical difference, as noted in *C & L Enterprises*, is that the federal government can waive tribal sovereign immunity under its plenary power authority (see Chapters 6 and 7). Since the federal government has the authority to waive tribal sovereign immunity a related question to the one proposed by *C & L Enterprises* is raised. *C & L Enterprises* considered when courts ought to find that a tribal nation has waived its sovereign immunity, but when should courts find that the federal government has waived tribal sovereign immunity?

The Supreme Court confronted this question 2014 in *Michigan v. Bay Mills Indian Community*. This case is also noteworthy for its potential impact on tribal gaming is given further consideration in Chapter 24. The facts of the case are fairly unique. The Bay Mills Indian Community in Michigan purchased land in the state outside of the reservation and began a gaming operation on the off-reservation land, claiming that the newly purchased off-reservation land was now tribal land for the purposes of gaming. The state of Michigan sought to shut down the off-reservation gaming operation by suing the tribal nation, arguing that the federal government had waived the tribal nation's sovereign immunity through the Indian Gaming Regulatory Act (IGRA). The tribal nation argued that the federal statute had not clearly waived its sovereign immunity for these types of situations.

As you read the case, ask yourself what standard the Supreme Court uses to determine if the federal government has waived tribal sovereign immunity. How does the majority opinion understand tribal sovereign immunity more broadly? How do both the majority opinion and the dissent understand previous cases?

MI v. BAY MILLS INDIAN COMMUNITY
134 S.Ct. 2024 (2014)

JUSTICE KAGAN delivered the opinion of the Court.

* * *

The Indian Gaming Regulatory Act (IGRA or Act), creates a framework for regulating gaming activity on Indian lands. . . . A tribe may conduct such gaming on Indian lands only pursuant to, and in compliance with, a compact it has negotiated with the surrounding State. . . . Notable here, IGRA itself authorizes a State to bring suit against a tribe for certain conduct violating a compact. . . .

* * *

Indian tribes are " 'domestic dependent nations' " that exercise "inherent sovereign authority." As dependents, the tribes are subject to plenary control by Congress. And yet they remain "separate sovereigns pre-existing the Constitution." Thus, unless and "until Congress acts, the tribes retain" their historic sovereign authority.

Among the core aspects of sovereignty that tribes possess—subject, again, to congressional action—is the "common-law immunity from suit traditionally enjoyed by sovereign powers." That immunity, we have explained, is "a necessary corollary to Indian sovereignty and self-governance." And the qualified nature of Indian sovereignty modifies that principle only by placing a tribe's immunity, like its other governmental powers and attributes, in Congress's hands. Thus, we have time and again treated the "doctrine of tribal immunity [as] settled law" and dismissed any suit against a tribe absent congressional authorization (or a waiver).

In doing so, we have held that tribal immunity applies no less to suits brought by States (including in their own courts) than to those by individuals. . . . In each case, we said a State must resort to other remedies, even if they would be less "efficient." That is because, as we have often stated . . . tribal immunity "is a matter of federal law and is not subject to diminution by the States." Or as we elsewhere explained: While each State at the Constitutional Convention surrendered its immunity from suit by sister States, "it would be absurd to suggest that the tribes"—at a conference "to which they were not even parties"—similarly ceded their immunity against state-initiated suits.

Equally important here, we declined in *Kiowa* to make any exception for suits arising from a tribe's commercial activities, even when they take place off Indian lands. . . . Rather, we opted to "defer" to Congress about whether to abrogate tribal immunity for off-reservation commercial conduct.

Our decisions establish as well that such a congressional decision must be clear. The baseline position, we have often held, is tribal immunity; and "[t]o abrogate [such] immunity, Congress must 'unequivocally' express that purpose." That rule of construction reflects an enduring principle of Indian law: Although Congress has plenary authority over tribes, courts will not lightly assume that Congress in fact intends to undermine Indian self-government.

The upshot is this: Unless Congress has authorized Michigan's suit, our precedents demand that it be dismissed. And so Michigan, naturally enough, makes two arguments: first, that IGRA indeed abrogates the Tribe's immunity from the State's suit; and second, that if it does not, we should revisit—and reverse—our decision in *Kiowa*, so that tribal immunity no longer applies to claims arising from commercial activity outside Indian lands. We consider—and reject—each contention in turn.

IGRA partially abrogates tribal sovereign immunity . . . but this case, viewed most naturally, falls outside that term's ambit. The provision, as noted above, authorizes a State to sue a tribe to "[stop gaming activity] located on Indian lands and conducted in violation of any Tribal-State compact." A key phrase in that abrogation is "on Indian lands"—three words reflecting IGRA's overall scope (and repeated some two dozen times in the statute). . . . And that creates a fundamental problem for Michigan. After all, the very premise of this suit—the reason Michigan thinks Bay Mills is acting unlawfully—is that the Vanderbilt casino is outside Indian lands. By dint of that theory, a suit to enjoin gaming in Vanderbilt is correspondingly outside [IGRA's] abrogation of immunity.

* * *

. . . True enough, a State lacks the ability to sue a tribe for illegal gaming when that activity occurs off the reservation. But a State, on its own lands, has many other powers over tribal gaming that it does not possess (absent consent) in Indian territory. Unless federal law provides differently, "Indians going beyond reservation boundaries" are subject to any generally applicable state law. . . . Michigan could bring suit against tribal officials or employees (rather than the Tribe itself) seeking an injunction for, say, gambling without a license. As this Court has stated before . . . tribal immunity does not bar such a suit for injunctive relief against individuals, including tribal officers, responsible for unlawful conduct. And to the extent civil remedies proved inadequate, Michigan could resort to its criminal law, prosecuting anyone who maintains—or even frequents—an unlawful gambling establishment. . . .

Finally, if a State really wants to sue a tribe for gaming outside Indian lands, the State need only bargain for a waiver of immunity. . . .

Because IGRA's plain terms do not abrogate Bay Mills' immunity from this suit, Michigan (and the dissent) must make a more dramatic argument: that this Court should "revisit *Kiowa*'s holding" and rule that tribes "have no immunity for illegal commercial activity outside their sovereign territory.". . .

But this Court does not overturn its precedents lightly. . . .

And that is more than usually so in the circumstances here. First, *Kiowa* itself was no one-off: Rather, in rejecting the identical argument Michigan makes, our decision reaffirmed a long line of precedents, concluding that "the doctrine of tribal immunity"—without any exceptions for commercial or off-reservation conduct—"is settled law and controls this case." Second, we have relied on *Kiowa* subsequently. . . . Third, tribes across the country, as well as entities and individuals doing business with them, have for many years relied on *Kiowa* (along with its forebears and progeny), negotiating their contracts and structuring their transactions against a backdrop of tribal immunity. . . . And fourth, Congress exercises primary authority in this area and "remains free to alter what we have done"—another factor that gives "special force" to [not overturning precedent].

. . . [A]ll the State musters are retreads of assertions we have rejected before. . . .

[I]t is fundamentally Congress's job, not ours, to determine whether or how to limit tribal immunity. The special brand of sovereignty the tribes retain—both its nature and its extent—rests in the hands of Congress. *Kiowa* chose to respect that congressional responsibility. . . .

All that we said in *Kiowa* applies today, with yet one more thing: Congress has now reflected on *Kiowa* and made an initial (though of course not irrevocable) decision to retain that form of tribal immunity.

* * *

JUSTICE THOMAS, with whom JUSTICE SCALIA, JUSTICE GINSBURG, and JUSTICE ALITO join, dissenting.

In [*Kiowa*] this Court extended the judge-made doctrine of tribal sovereign immunity to bar suits arising out of an Indian tribe's commercial activities conducted outside its territory. That was error. Such an expansion of tribal immunity is unsupported by any rationale for that doctrine, inconsistent with the limits on tribal sovereignty, and an affront to state sovereignty.

That decision, wrong to begin with, has only worsened with the passage of time. . . .

There is no substantive basis for *Kiowa*'s extension of tribal immunity to off-reservation commercial acts. . . .

* * *

In the 16 years since *Kiowa*, the commercial activities of tribes have increased dramatically. . . .

As the commercial activity of tribes has proliferated, the conflict and inequities brought on by blanket tribal immunity have also increased. Tribal immunity significantly limits, and often extinguishes, the States' ability to protect their citizens and enforce the law against tribal businesses. This case is but one example. . . .

* * *

Bay Mills has a highly unusual fact pattern that is unlikely to be replicated; consequently the case is best understood for its articulation of what is necessary for federal abrogation of tribal sovereign immunity and the continuing debate among Supreme Court Justices about tribal sovereign immunity. Justice Elena Kagan's majority opinion stated that Congressional waivers of tribal sovereign immunity needed to " 'unequivocally' express that purpose." Since IGRA only spoke to activities on "Indian lands," and since Bay Mills's actions occurred outside of Indian lands, the waiver of tribal sovereign immunity did not apply to this fact pattern. Michigan, Kagan noted, would have to resort to other remedies. Justice Thomas's dissent, joined by three other members of the Court, rearticulated the reasoning of those justices who have been wary of tribal sovereign immunity. The justices who have dissented in tribal sovereign immunity cases tend to be deeply concerned with the effects of the decisions on non-Natives.

Tribal sovereign immunity, like sovereign immunity more broadly, remains an important and distinct part of American law. Yet, it also remains controversial. Tribal nations have had success in this area of litigation at the Supreme Court, but often only by the narrowest of margins. While the doctrine has proven to be resilient, perhaps this line of cases offers some guidance to tribal nations: sovereign immunity is a powerful weapon that ought to be used properly and only when necessary.

SUGGESTED READINGS

- "To Sue and Be Sued: Capacity and Immunity of American Indian Nations." Richard B. Collins. 51 *Creighton Law Review* 391 (March, 2018).

- "In Defense of Tribal Sovereign Immunity: A Pragmatic Look at the Doctrine as a Tool For Strengthening Tribal Courts." Ryan Seelau. 90 *North Dakota Law Review* 121 (2014).

- "It Wasn't an Accident: The Tribal Sovereign Immunity Story." William Wood. 62 *American University Law Review* 1587 (August, 2013).

---

[1] Alden v. Maine, 527 U.S. 706, 715–16 (1999).

[2] Id. at 762.

CHAPTER 22

The Indian Civil Rights Act

The relationship between the federal government and citizens of the United States is often described in terms of rights. Thus, the starting point for almost every political discussion in the United States is that citizens have certain rights that the government has to respect. This includes, but is not limited to, the right to peaceably assemble, the right to a speedy trial, and the right against unreasonable searches and seizures. The concept of rights stands at the very heart of how many Americans conceptualize their political identities.

But what are rights? Where do they come from? Are they universal or contextual? Are "rights" the only way to conceptualize the relationship between a government and its citizens? Perhaps most important for this chapter, to what extent does the American understanding of rights determine how tribal governments need to understand their relationship to their own citizens?

In 1968 the federal government passed one of the earliest and most influential pieces of legislation of the Self-Determination Era: the Indian Civil Rights Act (ICRA). This law required tribal governments to provide its citizens many of the same rights that are found in the Bill of Rights and the 14th Amendment. Since its passage, ICRA has significantly shaped tribal governance. Yet, the legislation has raised some important questions as well. For example, what happens if a tribal citizen alleges that her/his tribal government is in violation of ICRA? Also, is ICRA necessary? What message was the federal government sending to Native America in passing ICRA?

This chapter will demonstrate. . .

- *The scope of the Indian Civil Rights Act*

- *ICRA's application to banishment cases*

- *The scope of the 2010 Tribal Law and Order Act*

THE INDIAN CIVIL RIGHTS ACT

The story of ICRA is, in many ways, the story of American politics in its historical moment. By the 1960s civil rights was a major topic of concern in political and social circles. Minority populations had always advocated for more opportunity, inclusion, and equality throughout American history. Yet, major events, such as the Supreme Court's 1953 decision in *Brown v. Board of Education*, advanced the conversation within the majority population as well. The 1960s saw Congress pass a number of important civil rights laws, including the Civil Rights Act of 1964 and the Voting Rights Act of 1965.

Led primarily by North Carolina Senator Sam Ervin, the federal government also began contemplating civil rights in Native America during this transformative period. Ervin and others in the federal government believed that tribal citizens, who were and are also American citizens, needed additional protection for their U.S. Constitutional rights within their tribal nations. To that end, they sought to impose certain federal constitutional restrictions on tribal governments. Tribal nations and citizens responded to the proposed legislation in a variety of ways. Some were in support of it, hoping it would lead to better treatment not just on the reservation but outside of it was well. Others were neutral. And still yet many argued that the real issue was not with the underenforcement of rights at the tribal level, but rather at the federal and state levels. After over half a dozen years of hearings, debates, and drafts, Congress passed ICRA in 1968. As you read the excerpt of the law, ask yourself where ICRA parallels the U.S. Constitution's Bill of Rights. Where does it diverge? Why might Congress choose to include most, but not all, of the guarantees under the Bill of Rights in ICRA? What limits does ICRA place on a tribal government's authority to punish someone who breaks tribal law? Also, what recourse does an individual have for a violation of ICRA?

INDIAN CIVIL RIGHTS ACT

25 U.S.C.A. § 1302(a) and 25 U.S.C.A. § 1303

§ 1302.   Constitutional Rights

(a) In general

No Indian tribe in exercising powers of self-government shall—

1.   make or enforce any law prohibiting the free exercise of religion, or abridging the freedom of speech, or of the press, or the right of the people peaceably to assemble and to petition for a redress of grievances;

2.   violate the right of the people to be secure in their persons, houses, papers, and effects against unreasonable search and seizures, nor issue warrants, but upon probable cause, supported by oath or affirmation, and particularly describing the place to be searched and the person or thing to be seized;

3.   subject any person for the same offense to be twice put in jeopardy;

4.   compel any person in any criminal case to be a witness against himself;

5.   take any property for a public use without just compensation;

6.   deny to any person in a criminal proceeding the right to a speedy and public trial, to be informed of the nature and cause of the accusation, to be confronted with the witnesses against him, to have compulsory process for obtaining witnesses in his favor, and at his own expense to have the assistance of counsel for his defense;

7.   (A) require excessive bail, impose excessive fines, or inflict cruel and unusual punishments;

   (B) . . . impose for conviction of any 1 offense any penalty or punishment greater than imprisonment for a term of 1 year or a fine of $5,000, or both. . . .

8.   deny to any person within its jurisdiction the equal protection of its laws or deprive any person of liberty or property without due process of law;

9.   pass any bill of attainder or ex post facto law; or

10. deny to any person accused of an offense punishable by imprisonment the right, upon request, to a trial by jury of not less than six persons. . . .

§ 1303.   Habeas corpus

The privilege of the writ of habeas corpus shall be available to any person, in a court of the United States, to test the legality of his detention by order of an Indian tribe.

ICRA is noteworthy for both what it includes and what it does not include. Like the U.S. Constitution, ICRA is focused on the rights of the individual in relation to governmental authority. Thus, ICRA does have many of the protections found in the Bill of Rights and the 14th Amendment, including protections for freedom of speech and freedom of the press and against double jeopardy, self-incrimination, and ex post facto laws. However, the drafters of the legislation were sensitive to the context in which ICRA was going to operate. Unlike the U.S. Constitution, ICRA does not include, for example, a prohibition against the establishment of religion, nor does it require that tribal nations provide counsel for indigent criminal defendants. Excluding certain aspects of the U.S. Constitution was not a judgment value on the worth of those rights, but rather a concession to the realities of the day. For example, Native America was, in general, very poor when ICRA was passed in 1968. Had Congress required that trial nations provide counsel in tribal court for indigent criminal defendants, it likely would have seriously burdened many already-financially depressed tribal governments.

ICRA also raises deeper questions about Native America and its relationship with the federal government: was the legislation necessary? Few would argue against the protections in the Bill of Rights, and subsequently ICRA, and what they seek to accomplish. The unwanted intrusion of governmental authority into an individual's life is a fear of many, and a reality for many others—including generations of Native peoples who endured periods of policy such as the Allotment Era. Did the lack of civil rights Native individuals endured before ICRA stem from tribal governments, or from the federal government and states? If the greatest source of oppression is from outside of the tribal government, then what can ICRA reasonably accomplish? Additionally, what does the very existence of ICRA imply about tribal governments? To what extent does ICRA rely on the notion or belief that tribal governments are incapable of respecting the rights of their own people? Is an American-style conception of "rights" the only legitimate method of imagining the relationship between a government and its citizens?

Conversely, tribal governments have developed a reputation for sometimes acting corruptly, ineptly, and/or through nepotism. Whether tribal governments operate in this manner to a greater or lesser degree than any other level of American government is an open question. Regardless, this perception about tribal governments does exist. Is ICRA a useful tool to combat that perception and whatever realities that might fuel it? Is ICRA also useful in legitimizing tribal courts to the world outside of Native America? Do the benefits of ICRA outweigh whatever negative implications it might carry?

SANTA CLARA PUEBLO V. MARTINEZ

The single most important Supreme Court case to consider ICRA is *Santa Clara Pueblo v. Martinez*. Decided ten years after ICRA was passed, *Santa Clara Pueblo* has shaped how federal courts have responded to ICRA ever since.

In order to understand *Santa Clara Pueblo*, it is important to understand another aspect of American law: the writ of habeas corpus. A writ is a written order from a court commanding another individual or body to do something or refrain from doing something. Habeas corpus is a Latin phrase that translates to "that you have the body." Those who appeal to a court for a writ of habeas corpus are those who believe that they are unlawfully restrained or restricted. Thus, the writ of habeas corpus is almost always an order from a court to another to release someone from custody. The most common example of the type of person seeking a writ of habeas corpus is someone in prison, although the writ can extend further beyond just those in prison. The writ of habeas corpus is critical to understanding both ICRA and *Santa Clara Pueblo* because § 1303 of ICRA authorizes "any person" to appeal for the writ "in a court of the United States." Those arrested, detained, and/or convicted in tribal court have the capacity to file suit for a writ of habeas corpus in federal court.

Two sets of happenings led to the decision in *Santa Clara Pueblo*. First, more globally, after the passage of ICRA an increasing number of tribal members began suing their tribal governments under ICRA for all sorts of reasons. Just as important, federal courts would allow those suits to be heard in federal court, despite not having the express authorization to do so. Habeas corpus is the only express cause of action in ICRA, or the only stated authorization within the statute to bring a case involving a tribal government into a federal court. Nonetheless, federal courts were finding implied causes of action, or other authorizations outside of ICRA itself to allow a suit in federal court. For example, one federal court found that it had jurisdiction over a tribal election dispute in which two would-be candidates sued the tribal nation for not allowing them to run in a tribal election.[1] Neither would-be candidate could have seriously claimed that they were in custody, but rather they primarily made their argument on the equal protection clause of ICRA, first in tribal court and then in federal court.

The second set of happenings was more local and has moved the case's profile beyond Indian law. In 1939 the Santa Clara Pueblo passed an ordinance concerning the children of those who married outside of the tribal nation. The ordinance declared that children of men who married outside of the tribal nation were eligible for enrollment, whereas children of women who married outside of tribal nation were not eligible for enrollment. Two years, later, Julia Martinez married her husband, a Navajo. The eight children of the marriage grew up within the Pueblo and participated in many facets of tribal life within the Pueblo. Although Martinez was aware of the ordinance, she nonetheless sought tribal membership for her children, particularly to secure specialized medical treatment that was less readily available without tribal membership for a daughter in need.

How and why the situation ended up in federal court is not entirely clear. Although the tribal ordinance plainly excluded children of women who married outside of the tribal nation, the Santa Clara Pueblo regularly made arrangements to include and enroll such persons. This included accepting the fathers of such children as citizens of the tribal nation. In addition, Martinez sought membership for her children through the tribal nation in a number of ways. However, Martinez's husband refused the offer of tribal citizenship on a number of occasions, and the parties could not find a mutually agreeable solution. Martinez eventually sued the Santa Clara Pueblo in tribal court for a violation of ICRA.[2]

Although the facts of the case were rife with potential issues of great importance, the Supreme Court focused on a more structural question: Did Martinez have the right to sue in federal court in the first place? Put another way, did federal courts have the jurisdiction, or authority, to hear these types of cases? As you read the case, ask yourself how the Court decides the jurisdictional question. What evidence does the Court use to justify the decision? What questions were the lower courts asking in seeking to resolve this dispute? How might the decisions of the lower court have affected the Supreme Court?

SANTA CLARA PUEBLO V. MARTINEZ
436 U.S. 49 (1978)

MR. JUSTICE MARSHALL delivered the opinion of the Court.

This case requires us to decide whether a federal court may pass on the validity of an Indian tribe's ordinance denying membership to the children of certain female tribal members.

* * *

. . . ICRA does not expressly authorize the bringing of civil actions for declaratory or injunctive relief to enforce its substantive provisions. The threshold issue in this case is thus whether the Act may be interpreted to impliedly authorize such actions, against a tribe or its officers, in the federal courts. For the reasons set forth below, we hold that the Act cannot be so read.

* * *

Following a full trial, the District Court found for petitioners on the merits. While acknowledging the relatively recent origin of the disputed rule, the District Court nevertheless found it to reflect traditional values of patriarchy still significant in tribal life. . . .

On respondents' appeal, the Court of Appeals for the Tenth Circuit upheld the District Court's determination that [ICRA] provides a jurisdictional basis for actions. . . . The Court of Appeals disagreed, however, with the District Court's ruling on the merits. . . . Because of the ordinance's recent vintage, and because in the court's view the rule did not rationally identify those persons who were emotionally and culturally Santa Clarans, the court held that the tribe's interest in the ordinance was not substantial enough to justify its discriminatory effect.

* * *

As separate sovereigns pre-existing the Constitution, tribes have historically been regarded as unconstrained by those constitutional provisions framed specifically as limitations on federal or state authority. . . .

. . . Congress has plenary authority to limit, modify or eliminate the powers of local self-government which the tribes otherwise possess. Congress acted . . . by imposing certain restrictions upon tribal governments similar, but not identical, to those contained in the Bill of Rights and the Fourteenth Amendment. In [ICRA], the only remedial provision expressly supplied by Congress, the "privilege of the writ of habeas corpus" is made "available to any person, in a court of the United States, to test the legality of his detention by order of an Indian tribe."

* * *

. . . [W]e must bear in mind that providing a federal forum for issues arising under [ICRA] constitutes an interference with tribal autonomy and self-government beyond that created by the change in substantive law itself. . . . A fortiori, resolution in a foreign forum of intratribal disputes of a more "public" character, such as the one in this case, cannot help but unsettle a tribal government's ability to maintain authority. Although Congress clearly has power to authorize civil actions against tribal officers, and has done so with respect to habeas corpus relief in [ICRA], a proper respect both for tribal sovereignty itself and for the plenary authority of Congress in this area cautions that we tread lightly in the absence of clear indications of legislative intent.

With these considerations . . . we turn now to those factors of more general relevance in determining whether a cause of action is implicit in a statute not expressly providing one. We note at the outset that a central purpose of the ICRA . . . was to "secur[e] for the American Indian the broad constitutional rights afforded to other Americans," and thereby to "protect individual Indians from arbitrary and unjust actions of tribal governments." There is thus no doubt that respondents, American Indians living on the Santa Clara Reservation, are among the class for whose especial benefit this legislation was enacted. Moreover, we have frequently recognized the propriety of inferring a federal cause of action for the enforcement of civil rights, even when Congress has spoken in purely declarative terms. These precedents, however, are simply not dispositive here. Not only are we unpersuaded that a judicially sanctioned intrusion into tribal sovereignty is required to fulfill the purposes of the ICRA, but to the contrary, the structure of the statutory scheme and the legislative history of [ICRA] suggest that Congress' failure to provide remedies other than habeas corpus was a deliberate one.

Two distinct and competing purposes are manifest in the provisions of the ICRA: In addition to its objective of strengthening the position of individual tribal members vis-a-vis the tribe, Congress also intended to promote the well-established federal "policy of furthering Indian self-government." This commitment to the goal of tribal self-determination is demonstrated by the provisions of [ICRA] itself. . . . [R]ather than providing in wholesale fashion for the extension of constitutional requirements to tribal governments, as had been initially proposed, selectively incorporated and in some instances modified the safeguards of the Bill of Rights to fit the unique political, cultural, and economic needs of tribal governments. Thus, for example, the statute does not prohibit the establishment of religion, nor does it require jury trials in civil cases, or appointment of counsel for indigents in criminal cases.

[Other parts of] ICRA also manifest a congressional purpose to protect tribal sovereignty from undue interference. . . .

Where Congress seeks to promote dual objectives in a single statute, courts must be more than usually hesitant to infer from its silence a cause of action that, while serving one legislative purpose, will disserve the other. . . .

Moreover, contrary to the reasoning of the court below, implication of a federal remedy in addition to habeas corpus is not plainly required to give effect to Congress' objective of extending constitutional norms to tribal self-government. Tribal forums are available to vindicate rights created by the ICRA. . . Under these circumstances, we are reluctant to disturb the balance between the dual statutory objectives which Congress apparently struck in providing only for habeas corpus relief.

Our reluctance is strongly reinforced by the specific legislative history underlying [ICRA]. This history, extending over more than three years, indicates that Congress' provision for habeas corpus relief, and nothing more, reflected a considered accommodation of the competing goals of "preventing injustices perpetrated by tribal governments, on the one hand, and, on the other, avoiding undue or precipitous interference in the affairs of the Indian people."

* * *

As we have repeatedly emphasized, Congress' authority over Indian matters is extraordinarily broad, and the role of courts in adjusting relations between and among tribes and their members correspondingly restrained. Congress retains authority expressly to authorize civil actions for injunctive or other relief to redress violations of [ICRA], in the event that the tribes themselves prove deficient in applying and enforcing its substantive provisions. But unless and until Congress makes clear its intention to permit the additional intrusion on tribal sovereignty that adjudication of such actions in a federal forum would represent, we are constrained to find that [ICRA] does not impliedly authorize actions for declaratory or injunctive relief against either the tribe or its officers.

In one respect, this is a very narrow decision about jurisdiction. The Supreme Court found that ICRA only allowed a certain type of suit in federal court against tribal officials: habeas corpus. Unless a petitioner, such as Julia Martinez, was arguing that she or he was unlawfully in custody and should be released, the only appeal was to tribal court. Since Martinez was not making this type of claim, the federal court could not hear her case. The Court argued that, in limiting potential claims to habeas corpus, Congress was balancing the desire to respect the rights of American citizens and the desire to respect tribal sovereignty. Since the decision in *Santa Clara Pueblo*, ICRA cases in federal court have slowed dramatically.

Despite its limited holding, the case nonetheless did and continues to raise a number of questions about rights, equality, tribal sovereignty, and federal authority. For example, what are the limits of tribal sovereignty? In a very important respect, *Santa Clara Pueblo* is an important affirmation of tribal sovereignty. Yet, both the facts and the decision have been deeply criticized by a number of scholars. And many tribal advocates are uncomfortable with the decision's position as one of the leading Supreme Court cases to recognize and validate tribal sovereignty. Is this an acceptable exercise of tribal sovereignty? Is sovereignty defined by the capacity to make unpopular choices?

Others have argued that the tribal ordinance was in keeping with traditional practices. Yet, there are many traditional practices from around the globe that most now consider unacceptable in today's day and age. Would a ruling for Martinez have demonstrated a lack of respect for cultural difference by disrupting the choices made by a tribal nation? Or is there a baseline of basic human rights to which every government, tribal or otherwise, must adhere? If so, did the ordinance in this case violate those basic human rights? Martinez's daughter did eventually receive the specialized medical care that she needed through federal channels. Does this alter the analysis? Why or why not?

Just as important, who should enforce a citizen's rights against their government and how should they enforce them? Are federal courts adequately prepared to adjudicate these types of disputes? In *Santa Clara Pueblo*, the courts to hear the case before the Supreme Court—the district court and the court of appeals—both contemplated how the ordinance aligned with the traditional practices of the Santa Clara Pueblo. The district court, the first federal court to hear the case, ruled that the ordinance did align with the traditional practices of the tribal nation. The court of appeals ruled that it did not. Are federal courts the appropriate venue for deciding what is and is not a traditional cultural practice for a Native community?

The Supreme Court's decision in *Santa Clara Pueblo* greatly reduced the possibility of federal courts of having to make these types of determinations in the future. It also settled a major point of law concerning ICRA. Individuals who are aggrieved with a tribal nation's alleged violations of ICRA can only bring their cases to federal court under a habeas corpus petition. A federal court will not entertain any complaint outside of one alleging some form of illegal incarceration or detention by a tribal nation. Nonetheless, the philosophical questions that *Santa Clara Pueblo* have raised remain.

BANISHMENT

While those seeking to invoke ICRA violations in federal court only have habeas corpus petitions available to them, this leaves open the question as to what should be considered incarceration, detention, or some other form of physical limitation that would give rise to a writ of habeas corpus. As noted above, petitions for habeas corpus relief are made mostly by those who are in prison. Yet prisoners are not the only ones to whom this writ is available.

In recent years, a number of tribal nations have turned to the practice of banishment from the reservation as a form of punishment for a violation of tribal law. Banishment, or the complete and total removal of an individual from the community, was a traditional practice for many tribal nations as an absolute last resort against a tribal member who repeatedly and significantly harmed the community. As a formal governmental function, banishment eventually fell out of practice for most tribal nations. Yet, some have revived the practice recently and others have considered it in response to contemporary issues. For example, some tribal nations have banished citizens for repeatedly selling drugs or leading gang activity on the reservation. Banishment is also generally coupled with disenrollment from tribal rolls or a loss of tribal citizenship.

The practice of banishment is controversial for a number of reasons. Certainly the punishment itself is severe and it is legitimate to ask what crimes, if any, are commensurate with banishment. In that same vein, it is also legitimate to ask about the invocation of banishment by those in power. Put another way, is banishment always simply a criminal punishment or has it been used as a political weapon as well? In today's context, some tribal officials have been accused of using banishment for their own personal and political gain—to hoard gaming revenue, to punish political opponents or consolidate authority, or for other similar reasons.

Banishment also raises a question under federal law: Can a person who is banished by a tribal nation challenge their banishment under ICRA in a federal court? Put another way, is banishment enough of a detention or physical limitation to satisfy a habeas corpus petition? The facts of the next case raise these questions and reflect why banishment has become a controversial subject in Native America.

Late in 1991 a collection of citizens of the Tonawanda Band of Seneca Indians alleged that members of the Tonawanda Council of Chiefs—the governing structure for the tribal nation—engaged in various forms of misconduct pertaining to tribal affairs. In January of 1992 a number of the citizens who alleged the misconduct were approached at their homes by other members of the community and were presented with a notice that purported to banish them from the reservation for committing treason. The notice read in part, "It is with a great deal of sorrow that we inform you that you are now banished from the territories of the Tonawanda Band of the Seneca Nation. You are to leave now and never return. . . . You are now stripped of your Indian citizenship and permanently lose any and all rights afforded our members. YOU MUST LEAVE IMMEDIATELY AND WE WILL WALK WITH YOU TO THE OUTER BORDERS OF OUR TERRITORY." The citizens were able to escape physical removal from the reservation that day, but subsequently alleged that they became the targets of harassment, including being denied health service at the tribal clinic and being denied electrical service in their homes and businesses. In late 1992 the citizens filed a lawsuit in federal court, claiming their rights under ICRA were violated.

The resulting litigation, *Poodry v. Tonawanda Band of Seneca Indians*, reached the 2nd Circuit Court of Appeals. Although not a Supreme Court case, it is presently perhaps the foremost federal court decision on banishment and ICRA. As you read the case, ask yourself how the majority opinion defines the scope of habeas corpus. How were the citizens who alleged misconduct detained or restrained by the tribal nation? How does the majority opinion approach the tribal nation's argument that federal courts should be more receptive to the tribal nation's definition and understanding of banishment? Where does the dissent differ from the majority opinion? What does the dissent make of the rights that would be stripped from the citizens if they are banished?

POODRY V. TONAWANDA BAND OF SENECA INDIANS
85 F.3d 874 (2d Cir.) (1996)

JOSÉ A. CABRANES, CIRCUIT JUDGE:

* * *

We face here a question of federal Indian law not yet addressed by any federal court: whether an Indian stripped of tribal membership and "banished" from a reservation has recourse in a federal forum to test the legality of the tribe's actions. More specifically, the issue is whether the habeas corpus provision of [ICRA], allows a federal court to review punitive measures imposed by a tribe upon its members, when those measures involve "banishment" rather than imprisonment. We conclude that the ICRA's habeas provision affords the petitioners access to a federal court to test the legality of their "convict[ion]" and subsequent "banishment" from the reservation. . . .

* * *

. . . The thrust of the respondents' jurisdictional challenge is that the petitioners are not entitled to seek habeas relief in this case, because (1) the decision to "banish" the petitioners was "civil" in nature, and relief is available under [ICRA] only in "criminal" cases; and (2) even if the respondents could be said to have imposed "criminal" sanctions upon the petitioners in this case, habeas relief is not available because the effects of the banishment orders did not constitute severe restraints on liberty.

* * *

Santa Clara Pueblo obviously does not speak directly to the scope of [ICRA]'s habeas provision, which was a matter not raised in that case. . . . *Santa Clara Pueblo* does not resolve the jurisdictional inquiry here presented: whether the ICRA's habeas provision permits federal court review of the banishment orders.

* * *

. . . We must ascertain whether the petitioners are being "detained" within the meaning of [ICRA]. . . .

* * *

. . . It is well established that actual physical custody is not a jurisdictional prerequisite for federal habeas review. The respondents acknowledge as much, but claim that habeas review requires "restraints far more closely related to actual imprisonment than the disabilities allegedly suffered by the appellants in this case.". . .

We disagree. We begin with three decades of case law rejecting the notion that a writ of habeas corpus . . . is a formalistic remedy whose availability is strictly limited to persons in actual physical custody. . . .

. . . While the requirement of physical custody historically served to restrict access to habeas relief to those most in need of judicial attention, physical custody is no longer an adequate proxy for identifying all circumstances in which federal adjudication is necessary to guard against governmental abuse in the imposition of "severe restraints on individual liberty.". . . Thus, the inquiry into whether a petitioner has satisfied the jurisdictional prerequisites for habeas review requires a court to judge the "severity" of an actual or potential restraint on liberty. . . .

The petitioners have surely identified severe restraints on their liberty. [The tribal nation does not] appear to contest certain relevant jurisdictional facts: that the banishment notices were served upon three of the petitioners by groups of fifteen to twenty-five people demanding the petitioners' removal; that there have since been other attempts to remove the petitioners from the reservation; that certain petitioners have been threatened or assaulted by individuals purporting to act on the respondents' behalf; and that the petitioners have been denied electrical service. . . .

"Restraint" does not require "on-going supervision" or "prior approval." As long as the banishment orders stand, the petitioners may be removed from the Tonawanda Reservation at any time. That they have not been removed thus far does not render them "free" or "unrestrained." While "supervision" (or harassment) by tribal officials or others acting on their behalf may be sporadic, that only makes it all the more pernicious. . . .

Indeed, we think the existence of the orders of permanent banishment alone—even absent attempts to enforce them—would be sufficient to satisfy the jurisdictional prerequisites for habeas corpus. We deal here not with a modest fine or a short suspension of a privilege—found not to satisfy the custody requirement for habeas relief—but with the coerced and peremptory deprivation of the petitioners' membership in the tribe and their social and cultural affiliation. To determine the severity of the sanction, we need only look to the orders of banishment themselves, which suggest that banishment is imposed (without notice) only for the most severe of crimes: murder, rape, and treason. . . .

* * *

In reaching this conclusion, we recall that this is a case of first impression, and that, if not considered in due course by the Supreme Court, the holding of the case may have significance in the future. This is especially true at a time when some Indian tribal communities have achieved unusual opportunities for wealth, thereby unavoidably creating incentives for dominant elites to "banish" irksome dissidents for "treason." Be that as it may, whatever doubts we might entertain about our construction of this legislation specially crafted for the benefit of Indian tribes is assuaged by the knowledge that, if we are wrong, Congress will have ample opportunity to correct our mistake.

* * *

Finally, we address briefly a tension inevitable in any case involving questions of rights and questions of culture: whether the principles that guide our inquiry . . . must be "culturally defined" by the tribe, or whether we can approach these questions guided by general American legal norms or certain universal principles. Here, the respondents adopt a stance of cultural relativism. . . .

But we need not resolve the debate on whether basic rights can or should be culturally defined to resolve this case. . . . We need not question the power of Indian nations to govern, to establish membership criteria, to exclude outsiders, or to regulate the use of their land and resources in order to acknowledge and vindicate a federal responsibility for those American citizens subject to tribal authority when that authority imposes criminal sanctions in denial of rights guaranteed by the laws of the United States. In sum, there is simply no room in our constitutional order for the definition of basic rights on the basis of cultural affiliations, even with respect to those communities whose distinctive "sovereignty" our country has long recognized and sustained.

* * *

JACOBS, CIRCUIT JUDGE, dissenting:

In many respects, I concur in the thoughtful and learned majority opinion. . . . I respectfully dissent because I do not think these respondents have demonstrated a severe restraint on any liberty that the writ of habeas corpus protects. . . . I view the conclusion in the majority opinion—that the banishment of these petitioners is a criminal penalty—as dubious.

* * *

I conclude that, although the banishment of petitioners from the Tonawanda Band is a harsh measure, imposed here with small provocation, it cannot be deemed a restraint that habeas corpus can reach. Furthermore, I conclude that issuance of the writ here would impinge upon the tribe's power to define its membership and thereby disserves the ICRA goal of promoting tribal self-government.

* * *

. . . There is of course no doubt that the petitioners, if banished, will lose all the rights conferred by the tribal sovereignty. But the proper inquiry is whether the petitioners, if banished, will suffer a severe impairment of the liberties that are enjoyed by the American public at large.

The applicable principle is that habeas corpus responds to restraints that are "not shared by the public generally.". . .

What restraints will be brought to bear upon the petitioners after they are banished from the Tonawanda Band and its reservation? What liberties will they thereby lose? Natural born members of the Tonawanda Band are citizens of the United States. Once they exit the reservation, petitioners will be free to settle and travel where they wish, and to come and go as they please, in the same way and to the same extent as any other person in the United States. Although that freedom does not confer a right to settle or trespass on private lands, or on lands reserved to any Indian nation, the petitioners' constitutional rights will in no way be diminished after banishment; indeed, they will then enjoy important constitutional rights that are not guaranteed by the ICRA on the Tonawanda reservation. . . .

* * *

. . . Banishment is therefore a severe restraint on the liberty of one who is banished from the United States or excluded from some place within the United States that the general population has the right to be. Doubtless, petitioners could plausibly claim a severe restraint on liberty if they were facing banishment to the Tonawanda reservation. But I do not see how banishment from the Indian reservation supports habeas relief. In terms of our habeas corpus jurisdiction, banishment to the United States is a meaningless concept.

The majority opinion points out that the petitioners are complaining about several forms of restraint, of which banishment is only one, and enumerates them. In my view, these do not add up to the requisite severe restraint on liberty. . . .

* * *

I therefore conclude that the only restriction claimed by petitioners that could remotely be deemed to support habeas relief is the deprivation of their right to live in and among the Tonawanda nation (and the threat that this exclusion will be visited upon them). However, Tonawanda membership (and the concomitant right to dwell on the Tonawandas' lands) is emphatically not a right "shared by the public generally." As an Indian tribe, the Tonawanda Band retains "those aspects of sovereignty not withdrawn by treaty or statute, or by implication as a necessary result of [its] dependent status." It is well settled that a tribe may physically exclude non-members entirely or condition their presence on its reservation. Petitioners point to no provision in any treaty or statute that evidences a congressional intent to limit the Tonawanda Band's power to exclude or expel.

* * *

The result in *Poodry* strongly suggests that this area of law is not settled and that there will be more to come. The majority opinion described the attempted banishment as a "coerced and peremptory deprivation of the petitioners' membership in the tribe and their social and cultural affiliation" and found that tribal banishments fell under the umbrella of events that would allow an individual to bring a habeas corpus claim against a tribal government in federal court. Since tribal nations and politicians are increasingly engaging in banishment to punish individuals there is likely to be more federal filings for writs of habeas corpus and more federal court interpretations of ICRA and interventions into tribal politics.

The dissent in *Poodry* is also noteworthy in its description of the rights that the tribal citizens who were fighting banishment stood to lose. Unlike the majority, the dissent framed the central question of the case as "whether the petitioners, if banished, will suffer a severe impairment of the liberties that are enjoyed by the American public at large." Concluding that the tribal citizens would not suffer a severe impairment, the dissent asked, "What liberties will they thereby lose?" and concluded that habeas corpus relief was not appropriate because the tribal citizens would still be free to move or live anywhere else in the United States. According to the dissent, "banishment to the United States is a meaningless concept."

Considering the disparities between the majority opinion and the dissent, it is fair to ask what the tribal citizens did stand to lose if they were banished from the reservation and whether it should it give rise to a habeas corpus petition. According to the notice that they were served, the tribal citizens would have lost their "Indian citizenship" as well as "all rights afforded our members." This would have included any access to health care on the reservation, access to any hiring privileges, and other benefits of tribal citizenship. Since the citizens were approached by a group of people seeking to walk them to the edge of the reservation, they presumably would have lost any interest in property they had on the reservation as well as any business ventures or job opportunities on the reservation. They would have also lost access to community and ceremonial life on the reservation, as well as any treaty rights. Are there other rights or privileges of tribal citizenship that were at stake? Do these losses amount to the type of unlawful restriction that warrants a habeas corpus petition? Does the majority opinion give too much credit to the burden on the targeted individuals, who were nonetheless American citizens free to live, work, and travel anywhere else in the United States? Does the dissent not give enough credit to the harm banishment will inflict on tribal citizens?

PUNISHMENT

ICRA imposed a number of obligations and limitations on tribal nations. Yet, perhaps none was more significant than the restraint on criminal punishment. When originally passed, ICRA only allowed for a criminal sentence in tribal court of six months in jail and/or a $500 fine. ICRA was amended in 1986 to allow for the greater punishments quoted in the excerpt above: one year in jail and/or a $5,000 fine. For the drafters of ICRA, the purpose of these limits was to protect against the possibility of draconian punishments against criminal defendants in tribal courts. As with ICRA more generally, it is possible to ask to what extent these limitations rely on the notion or belief that tribal governments are incapable of respecting the rights of their own people, as opposed to evidence to support such notions or beliefs.

Regardless of their origin, the practical effect of the limitations has been to create a disincentive for tribal nations to criminally prosecute alleged wrongdoers for serious crimes. For many tribal nations the effort and expense of a difficult trial for a serious charge, particularly if it resulted in a conviction that would almost assuredly be challenged in federal court, has not been worth the effort to impose the limited sentences available under ICRA. For example, imagine a scenario in which a tribal member is accused of manslaughter, yet the federal government (or state government in a Public Law 280 state) declines to prosecute the accused, for whatever reason. Under this scenario, even if a tribal government has the resources to prosecute the accused and a sophisticated court system to manage such a trial, it might also decline to do so. The tribal nation would not only incur the expense of the initial trial, but also all subsequent trials, including any trials at the federal level should the accused decide to challenge a tribal conviction under a habeas corpus petition. And, at best, even if the accused is found guilty and the tribal nation is in full compliance with ICRA, the accused would spend, at most, one year in jail.

Yet, as tribal courts have increasingly developed and become more adept at managing a wide variety of situations, there has been a growing desire across Native America to strengthen tribal criminal justice systems and increase their capabilities. After much advocacy from tribal nations and supporters, Congress passed the Tribal Law and Order Act (TLOA) in 2010, which amended ICRA to authorize increased criminal penalties under certain circumstances. As you read the excerpt of TLOA, ask yourself how it extends the limits of criminal punishment established in ICRA. What are the maximum criminal punishments under TLOA? What circumstances are necessary to invoke TLOA? What must a tribal court provide to a criminal defendant under TLOA?

TRIBAL LAW AND ORDER ACT

25 U.S.C.A. § 1302(b), (c), (d), (e) and (f)

(b) Offenses subject to greater than 1-year imprisonment or a fine greater than $5,000

A tribal court may subject a defendant to a term of imprisonment greater than 1 year but not to exceed 3 years for any 1 offense, or a fine greater than $5,000 but not to exceed $15,000, or both, if the defendant is a person accused of a criminal offense who—

(1) has been previously convicted of the same or a comparable offense by any jurisdiction in the United States; or

(2) is being prosecuted for an offense comparable to an offense that would be punishable by more than 1 year of imprisonment if prosecuted by the United States or any of the States.

(c) Rights of defendants

In a criminal proceeding in which an Indian tribe, in exercising powers of self-government, imposes a total term of imprisonment of more than 1 year on a defendant, the Indian tribe shall—

(1) provide to the defendant the right to effective assistance of counsel at least equal to that guaranteed by the United States Constitution; and

(2) at the expense of the tribal government, provide an indigent defendant the assistance of a defense attorney licensed to practice law by any jurisdiction in the United States that applies appropriate professional licensing standards and effectively ensures the competence and professional responsibility of its licensed attorneys;

(3) require that the judge presiding over the criminal proceeding—

(A) has sufficient legal training to preside over criminal proceedings; and

(B) is licensed to practice law by any jurisdiction in the United States;

(4) prior to charging the defendant, make publicly available the criminal laws (including regulations and interpretative documents), rules of evidence, and rules of criminal procedure (including rules governing the recusal of judges in appropriate circumstances) of the tribal government; and

(5) maintain a record of the criminal proceeding, including an audio or other recording of the trial proceeding.

(d) Sentences

In the case of a defendant sentenced in accordance with subsections (b) and (c), a tribal court may require the defendant—

(1) to serve the sentence—

(A) in a tribal correctional center that has been approved by the Bureau of Indian Affairs for long-term incarceration. . . .

(B) in the nearest appropriate Federal facility, at the expense of the United States. . . .

(C) in a State or local government-approved detention or correctional center pursuant to an agreement between the Indian tribe and the State or local government; or

(D) in an alternative rehabilitation center of an Indian tribe; or

(2) to serve another alternative form of punishment, as determined by the tribal court judge pursuant to tribal law.

(e) Definition of offense

In this section, the term "offense" means a violation of a criminal law.

> **(f) Effect of section**
>
> Nothing in this section affects the obligation of the United States, or any State government that has been delegated authority by the United States, to investigate and prosecute any criminal violation in Indian country.

Like many recent pieces of legislation, TLOA reflects the tensions at the heart of the Self-Determination Era of federal policy. Many have praised TLOA for increasing the capacity of tribal nations to engage in effective criminal law enforcement on tribal lands. Under TLOA, a tribal court can sentence a convicted criminal for up to three years in jail and up to a $15,000 fine for a repeat offender and/or a serious crime that would normally carry a sentence greater than one year in other contexts. Yet, others have noted that a tribal nation can only invoke the increased punishments of TLOA if their courts closely align to American standards. Thus, any tribal court seeking to invoke TLOA needs to clear a number of hurdles, including, among others, providing counsel for indigent defendants at the expense of the tribal nation and having a presiding judge who is a licensed attorney in an American jurisdiction. In essence, tribal courts are only entrusted with this increased authority as long as they perform their functions in a manner similar to American courts with personnel trained in the same manner as American judges. Are the requirements of TLOA reasonable accommodations for tribal nations or is it another attack on tribal methodologies? Put another way, are TLOA's safeguards universal enough that they conform to traditional tribal perspectives and practices translated in the modern context, or do they force contemporary tribal judicial systems into a narrow version of engaging with criminal defendants that eschews traditional tribal perspectives and practices?

Also, reconsider the scenario presented before the excerpt of TLOA: a tribal member is accused of manslaughter and the federal government (or a state) has declined to prosecute. Would the increased punishments under TLOA incentivize a previously reluctant tribal nation to pursue prosecution? Why or why not?

ICRA is in a moment of transition, with the full effects not yet completely revealed or understood. In one sense, ICRA has remained settled and steady ever since *Santa Clara Pueblo*. Although individuals can appeal to federal courts for tribal governmental violations of ICRA, those individuals can only do so through a habeas corpus petition. Yet, ICRA is likely to receive more attention from federal courts, and perhaps even the Supreme Court, as both banishment and TLOA come into greater practice throughout Native America.

SUGGESTED READINGS

- *The Indian Civil Rights Act at Forty.* Kristen A. Carpenter, Matthew L.M. Fletcher, and Angela R. Riley, eds. Los Angeles: UCLA American Indian Studies Center, 2012.

- "Three Stories in One: The Story of *Santa Clara Pueblo v. Martinez.*" Gloria Valencia-Weber. In *Indian Law Stories.* Carole Goldberg et al. eds. New York: Foundation Press, 2011, 451–488.

- "Crime and Governance in Indian Country." Angela R. Riley. 63 *UCLA Law Review* 1564 (August 2016).

---

[1]   Howlett v. Salish and Kootenai Tribes of Flathead Reservation, Montana, 529 F.2d 233 (1976).

[2]   Perhaps the best source of information about the facts of the case is "Three Stories in One: The Story of *Santa Clara Pueblo v. Martinez.*" Gloria Valencia-Weber. In *Indian Law Stories.* Carole Goldberg et al. eds. New York: Foundation Press, 2011, 451–488. This selection is also one of the suggested readings for this chapter.

CHAPTER 23

Indian Child Welfare Act

Throughout the majority of American history, the federal government and, to a different extent, state governments have attempted to limit or eradicate tribal sovereignty, tribal nations, and Native ways of life. These attempts have been not only been directed toward the political existence of tribal nations, but on a more personal level as well. Federal and state efforts have targeted individuals and families in addition to nations and communities. Children have been at the heart of many of the attempts to reform Native America. The most notorious example of the federal government's efforts to reshape tribal families and traditions were the boarding schools of the Allotment Era of federal policy (see Chapter 5). The deleterious effects of these policy choices concerning Native families and children are still very much felt today.

The overtly coercive efforts of institutions such as boarding schools to change Native America by changing its children eventually ebbed—although a number of boarding schools existed well into the twentieth century and a few still exist today. However Native families and children remained under assault, often through less direct, yet nonetheless equally destructive, means. Native families and children became the targets of mostly well meaning but culturally insensitive social service workers who determined that Native children needed to be taken from their homes and placed in foster homes and/or placed for adoption. By the mid-1970s, the federal government estimated that 25%–35% of Native children were taken from their homes and placed elsewhere.[1]

Congress responded to this epidemic in 1978 with the passage of the Indian Child Welfare Act (ICWA). One of the signature pieces of legislation of the Self-Determination Era of federal policy, ICWA authorized tribal nations and courts to have a greater say over Native children when those children became enmeshed in the social service system. A powerful tool in service to tribal sovereignty, ICWA has nonetheless sometimes been controversial for a number of reasons, including its effect on the family law of states. In addition, any time families and children are central to legal proceedings, deep emotions will almost assuredly rise to the surface.

This chapter will demonstrate. . .

- *The purpose behind the Indian Child Welfare Act*

- *Major facets of the Indian Child Welfare Act*

- *The foundational assumptions underlying the ICWA cases that have reached the Supreme Court*

THE INDIAN CHILD WELFARE ACT

As noted above, ICWA was in response to an epidemic that plagued Native America for much of the twentieth century. Native children were being removed from their homes at an alarming rate and at a much greater proportion than other groups of children. Statistics compiled by the federal government prior to the passage of ICWA offer a shocking glimpse into the widespread nature of the problem. In Minnesota, Native children were placed outside of the home at a rate five times greater than for non-Native children; in Montana the rate was at least thirteen times greater. In South Dakota, Native children were involved in 40% of the adoptions within the state despite only accounting for 7% of the state's juvenile population. In Wisconsin, the risk of a Native child being removed from the home was 1600% greater than for a non-Native child.[2] One tribal leader, who was also the director of social services on a reservation, testifying before Congress about the conditions that tribal families faced, stated that, "General child welfare legislation, no matter how well meaning, does not address the unique legal, cultural status of Indian people. Rather, they tend to promulgate the existing problems."[3] Another tribal leader, also testifying before Congress, spoke to the threat that many Native nations and families felt as a consequence of this epidemic. "[I]f Indian families continue to be disrespected and their parental capacities challenged by non-Indian social agencies as vigorously as they have in the past, then education, the tribe, Indian culture have little meaning or future."[4]

Typically, state social workers assigned to investigate Native homes would deem them inadequate for reasons reflecting varying levels of cultural sensitivity. For example, activities that mirrored customary Native practices, such as relying on extended family to nurture and raise a child, were often treated as detrimental rather than beneficial by state social workers. The conditions of poverty that many Native people lived under also contributed to the readiness of state officials to remove Native children from their homes. And when these children were removed from their families, they were overwhelmingly placed in non-Native foster and adoptive homes. A significant segment of many generations of Native peoples were raised outside of their family and tribal contexts, leading many of those who were placed out of their homes to feel separated and isolated from both the environment in which they were raised and from their tribal context.

The federal government responded to this decades-long crisis by passing ICWA in 1978. In keeping with the spirit of the Self-Determination Era, the legislation reduces the involvement of states in legal proceedings concerning children and puts greater authority in the hands of tribal nations and tribal courts. As you read this excerpt from ICWA, ask yourself how it applies to different situations. To whom does it apply? What options do tribal nations have under the legislation? What obligations does it place on non-Natives?

INDIAN CHILD WELFARE ACT
25 U.S.C.A. §§ 1901–1963

* * *

§ 1903—Definitions

. . .

(4) "Indian child" means any unmarried person who is under the age of eighteen and is either (a) a member of an Indian tribe or (b) is eligible for membership in an Indian tribe and is the biological child of a member of an Indian tribe.

* * *

§ 1911—Indian tribe jurisdiction over Indian child custody proceedings

(a) Exclusive jurisdiction

An Indian tribe shall have jurisdiction exclusive as to any State over any child custody proceeding involving an Indian child who resides or is domiciled within the reservation of such tribe, except where such jurisdiction is otherwise vested in the State by existing Federal law. Where an Indian child is a ward of a tribal court, the Indian tribe shall retain exclusive jurisdiction, notwithstanding the residence or domicile of the child.

(b)   Transfer of proceedings; declination by tribal court

In any State court proceeding for the foster care placement of, or termination of parental rights to, an Indian child not domiciled or residing within the reservation of the Indian child's tribe, the court, in the absence of good cause to the contrary, shall transfer such proceedings to the jurisdiction of the tribe, absent objection by either parent, upon the petition of either parent or the Indian custodian or the Indian child's tribe: *Provided*, that such transfer shall be subject to the declination by the tribal court of such tribe.

(c)   State court proceedings; intervention

In any State court proceeding for the foster care placement of, or termination of parental rights to, an Indian child, the Indian custodian of the child and the Indian child's tribe shall have a right to intervene at any point in the proceeding.

(d)   Full faith and credit to public acts, records, and judicial proceedings of Indian tribes

The United States, every State, every territory or possession of the United States, and every Indian tribe shall give full faith and credit to the public acts, records, and judicial proceedings of any Indian tribe applicable to Indian child custody proceedings to the same extent that such entities give full faith and credit to the public acts, records, and judicial proceedings of any other entity.

§ 1912—Pending court proceedings

(a)   Notice. . . .

In any involuntary proceeding in a State court, where the court knows or has reason to know that an Indian child is involved, the party seeking the foster care placement of, or termination of parental rights to, an Indian child shall notify the parent or Indian custodian and the Indian child's tribe. . . .

(f)   Parental rights termination orders. . . .

No termination of parental rights may be ordered . . . in the absence of a determination . . . that the continued custody of the child by the parent or Indian custodian is likely to result in serious emotional or physical damage to the child.

* * *

§ 1914—Petition to court of competent jurisdiction to invalidate action upon showing of certain violations

Any Indian child who is the subject of any action for foster care placement or termination of parental rights under State law, any parent or Indian custodian from whose custody such child was removed, and the Indian child's tribe may petition any court of competent jurisdiction to invalidate such action upon a showing that such action violated any provisions of section 1911, 1912, and 1913 of this title.

§ 1915—Placement of Indian children

(a) Adoptive placements; preferences

In any adoptive placement of an Indian child under State law, a preference shall be given, in the absence of good cause to the contrary, to a placement with (1) a member of the child's extended family; (2) other members of the Indian child's tribe; or (3) other Indian families.

(b) Foster care or preadoptive placements; criteria; preferences

Any child accepted for foster care or preadoptive placement shall be placed in the least restrictive setting which most approximates a family and in which his special needs, if any, may be met. The child shall also be placed within reasonable proximity to his or her home, taking into account any special needs of the child. In any foster care or preadoptive placement, a preference shall be given, in the absence of good cause to the contrary, to a placement with—

> (i)   A member of the Indian child's extended family;
>
> (ii) A foster home licensed, approved, or specified by the Indian child's tribe;
>
> (iii) An Indian foster home licensed and approved by an authorized non-Indian licensing authority; or
>
> (iv) An institution for children approved by an Indian tribe or operated by an Indian organization which has a program suitable to meet the Indian child's needs

(c) Tribal resolution for different order of preference; personal preference considered. . . .

In the case of a placement under subsection (a) or (b) of this section, if the Indian child's tribe shall establish a different order of preference by resolution, the agency of court effecting the placement shall follow such order so long as the placement is the least restrictive setting appropriate to the particular needs

> of the child. . . . Where appropriate, the preference of the Indian child or parent shall be considered. . . .
>
> (d)   Social and cultural standards applicable
>
> The standards to be applied in meeting the preference requirements of this section shall be the prevailing social and cultural standards of the Indian community in which the parent or extended family resides or with which the parent or extended family members maintain social and cultural ties. . . .
>
> * * *
>
> § 1918—Reassumption of jurisdiction over child custody proceedings
>
> (a)   Petition; suitable plan; approval by Secretary
>
> Any Indian tribe which became subject to State jurisdiction pursuant to [Public Law 280], or pursuant to any other Federal law, may reassume jurisdiction over child custody proceedings. Before any Indian tribe may reassume jurisdiction over Indian child custody proceedings, such tribe shall present to the Secretary [of the Interior] for approval a petition to reassume such jurisdiction which includes a suitable plan to exercise such jurisdiction.
>
> * * *

ICWA is a comprehensive piece of legislation that seeks to enhance tribal sovereignty while still respecting the rights and choices of individuals as well as the traditional authority of states in family law matters. At its most basic, ICWA authorizes tribal courts to have significant influence over the placement proceedings—things like adoption and foster care placements—of an "Indian child." The legislation defines an "Indian child" (among other requirements) as someone under eighteen years of age who is either rerolled in a tribal nation or eligible for enrollment.

ICWA gives tribal courts exclusive jurisdiction over an Indian child who resides or is domiciled on the reservation—unless the tribal nation is subject to Public Law 280 (see Chapter 17). The rules are less straightforward if an Indian child resides or is domiciled off of the reservation. Under those circumstances, if an Indian child has become subjected to state court proceedings, the state court must transfer those proceedings to tribal court if asked to do so by a parent or guardian of the child or by the tribal nation itself. However, there are some very noteworthy exceptions to this rule: if either parent objects to such a transfer, if there is good cause not to transfer, or if the tribal nation declines jurisdiction in the matter. These exceptions attempt to balance a number of competing interests, including the desires of the parents and the traditional authority of states.

While there are a wide number of instances in which Indian children might remain under the jurisdiction of state courts, on the whole ICWA leans in favor of tribal authority and sovereignty. Even if a child placement proceeding remains in state court, ICWA authorizes that child's tribal nation to intervene—or be a party to the proceeding and have their say before the state court. It authorizes a child, parent, or custodian of a child to invalidate a state court order that was not in compliance with ICWA. The legislation also establishes preferences for the placement of an Indian child that seek to keep the child as close to the child's tribal context as possible. It even authorizes those tribal nations subject to Public Law 280 to assume authority under ICWA upon a successful petition to the Secretary of the Interior.

ICWA has not been without controversy since its inception. States have not always complied with the legislation's mandates and, on occasion, state courts have read portions of the law in ways that have attempted to limit tribal sovereignty or the scope of cases that come under ICWA. In addition, every handful of years ICWA seems to become the subject of media scrutiny, particularly when potential non-Native adoptive couples have been involved, as it regularly concerns heart-wrenching circumstances with children caught in the middle. Despite these difficulties, ICWA has been a positive force in Indian Country and has helped to slow the epidemic that spawned it. It has also created further incentive for tribal nations to develop and invest in a robust tribal court system.

ICWA AND TRIBAL COURTS

Although it has undergone extensive litigation, primarily at the tribal and state level, ICWA has only undergone serious scrutiny at the Supreme Court in two cases: *Mississippi Band of Choctaw Indians v. Holyfield* and *Adoptive Couple v. Baby Girl*, also known as the Baby Veronica case. Taken together, the cases reflect both the possibilities of ICWA and also how the facts of a case, particularly when it involves sensitive family law subject matter, can contribute to the perception of ICWA, tribal nations, parents, and even Native identity.

In order to understand the first Supreme Court case to seriously consider ICWA, *Mississippi Band v. Holyfield*, it is necessary to have a sense of how the law defines an individual's domicile. Under American law, an individual's domicile is that person's permanent residence or the place that the individual intends to return after being elsewhere. This can be, although it is not always, in distinction to an individual's present residence. An example will help illustrate the point. Many high school graduates choose to attend a university far from home. Thus, a citizen of Oregon may choose to attend an institution of higher learning in Florida. If the student does not take active steps during her years at school to become permanent resident of Florida—stay in Florida during school breaks, obtain a Florida driver's license, make plans to remain in the state after graduation, etc.—then that student's domiciliary will remain in Oregon even though the student resides in Florida.

The issue of one's domicile was central to the decision in *Mississippi Band v. Holyfield.* A Native mother of twins purposely gave birth to the children off of the reservation in an effort to secure their adoption to a specific non-Native couple. As you read the case, ask yourself about the various interests at stake. What was the biological mother of the children attempting to accomplish? What were the potential adoptive parents attempting to accomplish? What was the tribal nation attempting to accomplish? How does the Supreme Court balance these varying goals? What did the Court want to see happen with the children?

MISSISSIPPI BAND OF CHOCTAW INDIANS V. HOLYFIELD
490 U.S. 30 (1989)

JUSTICE BRENNAN delivered the opinion of the Court.

This appeal requires us to construe the provisions of the Indian Child Welfare Act that establish exclusive tribal jurisdiction over child custody proceedings involving Indian children domiciled on the tribe's reservation.

* * *

At the heart of the ICWA are its provisions concerning jurisdiction over Indian child custody proceedings. . . . Section 1911(a) establishes exclusive jurisdiction in the tribal courts for proceedings concerning an Indian child "who resides or is domiciled within the reservation of such tribe. . . ."

* * *

This case involves the status of twin babies, known for our purposes as B. B. and G. B., who were born out of wedlock on December 29, 1985. Their mother, J. B., and father, W. J., were both enrolled members of appellant Mississippi Band of Choctaw Indians (Tribe), and were residents and domiciliaries of the Choctaw Reservation in Neshoba County, Mississippi. J. B. gave birth to the twins in Gulfport, Harrison County, Mississippi, some 200 miles from the reservation. On January 10, 1986, J. B. executed a consent-to-adoption form before the Chancery Court of Harrison. W. J. signed a similar form. On January 16, appellees Orrey and Vivian Holyfield filed a petition for adoption in the same court, and the chancellor issued a Final Decree of Adoption on January 28. Despite the court's apparent awareness of the ICWA, the adoption decree contained no reference to it, nor to the infants' Indian background.

Two months later the Tribe moved in the Chancery Court to vacate the adoption decree on the ground that under the ICWA exclusive jurisdiction was vested in the tribal court. On July 14, 1986, the court overruled the motion, holding that the Tribe "never obtained exclusive jurisdiction over the children involved herein. . . ."

* * *

The meaning of "domicile" in the ICWA is, of course, a matter of Congress' intent. The ICWA itself does not define it. . . .

* * *

It remains to give content to the term "domicile" in the circumstances of the present case. The holding of the Supreme Court of Mississippi that the twin babies were not domiciled on the Choctaw Reservation appears to have rested on two findings of fact by the trial court: (1) that they had never been physically present there, and (2) that they were "voluntarily surrendered" by their parents. The question before us, therefore, is whether under the ICWA definition of "domicile" such facts suffice to render the twins nondomiciliaries of the reservation.

We have often stated that in the absence of a statutory definition we "start with the assumption that the legislative purpose is expressed by the ordinary meaning of the words used.". . . We therefore look both to the generally accepted meaning of the term "domicile" and to the purpose of the statute. . . .

"Domicile" is, of course, a concept widely used in both federal and state courts for jurisdiction and conflict-of-laws purposes, and its meaning is generally uncontroverted. "Domicile" is not necessarily synonymous with "residence," and one can reside in one place but be domiciled in another. For adults, domicile is established by physical presence in a place in connection with a certain state of mind concerning one's intent to remain there. One acquires a "domicile of origin" at birth, and that domicile continues until a new one (a "domicile of choice") is acquired. Since most minors are legally incapable of forming the requisite intent to establish a domicile, their domicile is determined by that of their parents. In the case of an illegitimate child, that has traditionally meant the domicile of its mother. Under these principles, it is entirely logical that "[o]n occasion, a child's domicile of origin will be in a place where the child has never been."

It is undisputed in this case that the domicile of the mother (as well as the father) has been, at all relevant times, on the Choctaw Reservation. Thus, it is clear that at their birth the twin babies were also domiciled on the reservation, even though they themselves had never been there. . . .

Nor can the result be any different simply because the twins were "voluntarily surrendered" by their mother. Tribal jurisdiction under 1911(a) was not meant to be defeated by the actions of individual members of the tribe, for Congress was concerned not solely about the interests of Indian children and families, but also about the impact on the tribes themselves of the large numbers of Indian children adopted by non-Indians. . . . The numerous prerogatives accorded the tribes through the ICWA's substantive provisions, must, accordingly, be seen as a means of protecting not only the interests of individual Indian children and families, but also of the tribes themselves.

In addition, it is clear that Congress' concern over the placement of Indian children in non-Indian homes was based in part on evidence of the detrimental impact on the children themselves of such placements outside their culture. Congress determined to subject such placements to the ICWA's jurisdictional and other provisions, even in cases where the parents consented to an adoption, because of concerns going beyond the wishes of individual parents. . . .

These congressional objectives make clear that a rule of domicile that would permit individual Indian parents to defeat the ICWA's jurisdictional scheme is inconsistent with what Congress intended. . . . Permitting individual members of the tribe to avoid tribal exclusive jurisdiction by the simple expedient of giving birth off the reservation would, to a large extent, nullify the purpose the ICWA was intended to accomplish. . . .

. . .Since, for purposes of the ICWA, the twin babies in this case were domiciled on the reservation when adoption proceedings were begun, the Choctaw tribal court possessed exclusive jurisdiction. . . . The Chancery Court of Harrison County was, accordingly, without jurisdiction to enter a decree of adoption. . . .

We are not unaware that over three years have passed since the twin babies were born and placed in the Holyfield home, and that a court deciding their fate today is not writing on a blank slate in the same way it would have in January 1986. Three years' development of family ties cannot be undone, and a separation at this point would doubtless cause considerable pain.

Whatever feelings we might have as to where the twins should live, however, it is not for us to decide that question. We have been asked to decide the legal question of who should make the custody determination concerning these children—not what the outcome of that determination should be. The law places that decision in the hands of the Choctaw tribal court.... It is not ours to say whether the trauma that might result from removing these children from their adoptive family should outweigh the interest of the Tribe—and perhaps the children themselves—in having them raised as part of the Choctaw community. Rather, "we must defer to the experience, wisdom, and compassion of the [Choctaw] tribal courts to fashion an appropriate remedy."

* * *

It is easy to contextualize the facts that led to *Mississippi Band v. Holyfield* as a straightforward conflict between tribal sovereignty and individual rights. Put another way, it is easy to frame the question of the case as whose decisions and authority over the twins were more important—those of the tribal nation or those of the biological mother? Certainly the Supreme Court framed it as such, noting that, "Tribal jurisdiction under [ICWA] was not meant to be defeated by the actions of individual members of the tribe." The biological mother's choices also allow such a construction of the relevant facts. She deliberately chose to give birth to the twins approximately 200 miles off of the reservation. One easy implication from the description of the facts—although Justice William Brennan's opinion never explicitly describes it as such—is that the mother engaged in this behavior to purposely avoid tribal court jurisdiction. Consequently, it is easy to read the decision as a victory for tribal sovereignty at the expense of the choices of a tribal citizen. Again, Brennan's opinion strongly gestures toward this type of reading, noting that, "Permitting individual members of the tribe to avoid tribal exclusive jurisdiction by the simple expedient of giving birth off the reservation would, to a large extent, nullify the purpose the ICWA was intended to accomplish."

Is this the only reading of this case? Perhaps more important, to what extent does this type of reading rely upon certain perceptions about the proclivities of the tribal court? Does understanding the case in the terms that the Supreme Court frames it require that we make certain assumptions about tribal courts?

Consider what ICWA requires as opposed to what it does not require. As properly noted by the Supreme Court, § 1911 of ICWA authorizes tribal courts to have exclusive jurisdiction over an Indian child, "who resides or is domiciled within the reservation." Since the twins were domiciles of the reservation—despite having never been physically present on the reservation—the tribal court had exclusive jurisdiction in the matter and the state court actions were void. In short, the Supreme Court ruled that ICWA mandated that the tribal court got to preside over the adoption of the children, not the state court.

Yet, while ICWA mandates that the tribal court has exclusive jurisdiction under these circumstances, the legislation does not direct or require the tribal court to come to any particular determinations. Although ICWA does have preferences for the placement of an Indian child, they are aimed at state courts that are engaged with a placement proceeding involving an Indian child. Tribal courts are not required by ICWA to place a child in a particular environment.

Considering this, it is useful to reconsider the supposed conflict at the heart of *Mississippi Band v. Holyfield*. As constructed by the Court (and by many readers of the opinion), the choice was between tribal sovereignty and the wishes of a tribal citizen. Yet, interpreting the facts of this case in these terms at the very least strongly implies that, had the adoption properly gone through the tribal court in the first place, the tribal court would have made a different choice about the adoptive placement of the twins than the mother made. Such a powerful implication, if not an outright assertion, demands further questions. Why is it so easy for so many readers (and, apparently, at least some Supreme Court justices) to imagine that the tribal court would have disregarded the wishes of the mother had the adoption proceedings been properly initiated in tribal court? What evidence supports this assumption? Most American courts would certainly consider the desires of a biological mother in these circumstances, especially one who went to such lengths to find a couple for her children. Why would the tribal court be different? What other assumptions must one make about tribal courts and tribal nations before imagining that the tribal court was naturally or inherently opposed to the mother's wishes in this case?

Understanding that the ruling in the case did not automatically mean that the mother's wishes were forsaken paints the case in a different light. The point of law that was decided was not about the interests of the mother against the interests of the tribal nation, but rather the jurisdiction of the tribal court as against the jurisdiction of state courts. And, in fact, when the tribal court's jurisdiction was finally recognized, the court did authorize the twins' adoption to the Holyfields.

Unfortunately, much of the public discourse outside of Indian Country about ICWA seems predicated on the underlying presumption that tribal courts will always rule in favor of tribal nations, even if it is at the expense of the best interests of the child, the desires of biological parents, and the willingness and ability of a non-Native foster or adoptive family. Ironically, this presumption often stems from the bad behavior of state courts and/or non-Native actors. On a number of occasions, state courts have not known about, misunderstood, or disregarded the mandates of ICWA. Entities such as adoption placement agencies or state social services have also sometimes been lax in their understanding and enforcement of ICWA. As such, many Indian children have continued to find themselves in state court proceedings despite ICWA. When tribal nations find out about these situations they often seek to assert their rights under the federal law. Consequently, this can result in an Indian child being in a non-Native foster home for months before a tribal nation learns about an ICWA violation and perhaps even years as the case is litigated. When tribal nations regain authority in these situations and place those children within their own social service system or place them elsewhere they are often accused of "ripping" the child away from a loving family or situation. Yet, were it not for the disregard or misunderstanding of ICWA from non-Native actors in the first place, the children would have been properly placed under the law from the beginning and further action would have been unnecessary. In essence, tribal nations are often blamed for harming children as a result of the disregard or misapplication of ICWA by non-Native actors.

ICWA AND TRIBAL PARENTS

Nearly a quarter of a century after the Supreme Court decided its first major ICWA case, it decided its second, *Adoptive Couple v. Baby Girl*. More commonly known as the "Baby Veronica" case, it received a fair amount of media attention for its heartbreaking facts. The biological father, a citizen of the Cherokee Nation of Oklahoma, was an active duty member of the military during the pertinent events. The biological mother, who is Hispanic, became pregnant shortly after the couple became engaged. Upon learning that his fiancée was pregnant, the biological father suggested that they move up the date of the wedding. The biological mother decided against marrying earlier than planned and eventually broke off the relationship. Sometime thereafter the biological mother sent a text message to the biological father asking if he would prefer to pay child support or terminate his parental rights. The biological father responded by text message by stating that he would prefer to terminate his parental rights. In later testimony, the biological father stated that he did not know that the mother was considering adoption and that he thought he was terminating his parental rights for the benefit of the birth mother.

Sometime after the biological mother broke off the relationship, she contacted an adoption agency that found an adoptive couple for the child. During the process that led to the adoptive couple gaining custody of the child, there were some efforts on the biological mother's behalf to contact the Cherokee Nation of Oklahoma, as mandated by ICWA. However, in those efforts the biological father's name was misspelled and his date of birth was incorrectly identified. As a result the Cherokee Nation of Oklahoma was unable to verify that the biological father was an enrolled citizen at that time. There was some suggestion by lower courts that ruled on the case that the biological mother may have taken steps to actually conceal the father's tribal citizenship.

Days before he was to be deployed to Iraq, the biological father signed documents that terminated his parental rights. He later testified that he did not know what he was signing and, shortly thereafter, began legal proceedings to gain custody of the child. The father alleged various violations of ICWA. A South Carolina state court agreed with the father and ordered the child, who had been living with the adoptive couple since shortly after her birth, to be given over to the biological father. The South Carolina Supreme Court affirmed the ruling and the adoptive couple appealed to the Supreme Court.

The different rulings in *Mississippi Band v. Holyfield* and *Adoptive Couple v. Baby Girl* are perhaps most reflective of the changed composition of the Supreme Court over the course of nearly twenty-five years. Nonetheless, both seem to operate from presumptions about the Native parties involved, whether those parties are courts or individuals. As you read the case, ask yourself how both the majority opinion and the dissent frame the case. What is the basis for the ruling? How, according to both the majority opinion and the dissent, does the ruling align with ICWA?

ADOPTIVE COUPLE V. BABY GIRL
570 U.S. 637 (2013)

JUSTICE ALITO delivered the opinion of the Court.

This case is about a little girl (Baby Girl) who is classified as an Indian because she is 1.2% (3/256) Cherokee. Because Baby Girl is classified in this way, the South Carolina Supreme Court held that certain provisions of the federal Indian Child Welfare Act of 1978 required her to be taken, at the age of 27 months, from the only parents she had ever known and handed over to her biological father, who had attempted to relinquish his parental rights and who had no prior contact with the child. The provisions of the federal statute at issue here do not demand this result.

* * *

It is undisputed that, had Baby Girl not been 3/256 Cherokee, Biological Father would have had no right to object to her adoption. . . .

* * *

Section 1912(f) [of ICWA] conditions the involuntary termination of parental rights on a showing regarding the merits of "*continued custody* of the child by the parent." (Emphasis added.) The adjective "continued" plainly refers to a pre-existing state. . . . The phrase "continued custody" therefore refers to custody that a parent already has (or at least had at some point in the past). As a result, § 1912(f) does not apply in cases where the Indian parent never had custody of the Indian child.

* * *

Our reading of § 1912(f) comports with the statutory text demonstrating that the primary mischief the ICWA was designed to counteract was the unwarranted *removal* of Indian children from Indian families due to the cultural insensitivity and biases of social workers and state courts. . . . In sum, when, as here, the adoption of an Indian child is voluntarily and lawfully initiated by a non-Indian parent with sole custodial rights, the ICWA's primary goal of preventing the unwarranted removal of Indian children and the dissolution of Indian families is not implicated.

* * *

Under our reading of § 1912(f), Biological Father should not have been able to invoke § 1912(f) in this case, because he had never had legal or physical custody of Baby Girl as of the time of the adoption proceedings. . . .

* * *

Consistent with the statutory text, we hold that § 1912(d) applies only in cases where an Indian family's "breakup" would be precipitated by the termination of the parent's rights. . . . But when an Indian parent abandons an Indian child prior to birth and that child has never been in the Indian parent's legal or physical custody, there is no "relationship" that would be "discontinu[ed]"—and no "effective entity" that would be "end[ed]"—by the termination of the Indian parent's rights. In such a situation, the "breakup of the Indian family" has long since occurred, and § 1912(d) is inapplicable.

* * *

The Indian Child Welfare Act was enacted to help preserve the cultural identity and heritage of Indian tribes, but under the State Supreme Court's reading, the Act would put certain vulnerable children at a great disadvantage solely because an ancestor—even a remote one—was an Indian. As the State Supreme Court read [ICWA], a biological Indian father could abandon his child in utero and refuse any support for the birth mother—perhaps contributing to the mother's decision to put the child up for adoption—and then could play his ICWA trump card at the eleventh hour to override the mother's decision and the child's best interests. If this were possible, many prospective adoptive parents would surely pause before adopting any child who might possibly qualify as an Indian under the ICWA. . . .

* * *

JUSTICE SCALIA, dissenting.

. . . I reject the conclusion that the Court draws from the words "continued custody" . . . because there is no reason that "continued" must refer to custody in the past rather than custody in the future. . . .

While I am at it, I will add one thought. The Court's opinion, it seems to me, needlessly demeans the rights of parenthood. It has been the constant practice of the common law to respect the entitlement of those who bring a child into the world to raise the child. We do not inquire whether leaving a child with his parents is "in the best interests of the child." It sometimes is not; he would be better off raised by someone else. But parents have their rights, no less than children do. This father wants to raise his daughter, and the statute amply protects his right to do so. There is no reason in law or policy to dilute that protection.

JUSTICE SOTOMAYOR, dissenting.

A casual reader of the Court's opinion could be forgiven for thinking this an easy case, one in which the text of the applicable statute clearly points the way to the only sensible result. In truth, however, the path from the text of [ICWA] the result the Court reaches is anything but clear, and its result anything but right.

The reader's first clue that the majority's supposedly straightforward reasoning is flawed is that not all Members who adopt its interpretation believe it is compelled by the text of the statute; nor are they all willing to accept the consequences it will necessarily have beyond the specific factual scenario

Indian Child Welfare Act   501

confronted here. The second clue is that the majority begins its analysis by plucking out of context a single phrase from the last clause of the last subsection of the relevant provision, and then builds its entire argument upon it. That is not how we ordinarily read statutes. The third clue is that the majority openly professes its aversion to Congress' explicitly stated purpose in enacting the statute. The majority expresses concern that reading the Act to mean what it says will make it more difficult to place Indian children in adoptive homes, but the Congress that enacted the statute announced its intent to stop "an alarmingly high percentage of Indian families [from being] broken up" by, among other things, a trend of "plac[ing] [Indian children] in non-Indian . . . adoptive homes." Policy disagreement with Congress' judgment is not a valid reason for this Court to distort the provisions of the Act. Unlike the majority, I cannot adopt a reading of ICWA that is contrary to both its text and its stated purpose. I respectfully dissent.

Beginning its reading with the last clause of § 1912(f), the majority concludes that a single phrase appearing there—"continued custody"—means that the entirety of the subsection is inapplicable to any parent, however committed, who has not previously had physical or legal custody of his child. . . .

When it excludes noncustodial biological fathers from the Act's substantive protections, this textually backward reading misapprehends ICWA's structure and scope. Moreover, notwithstanding the majority's focus on the perceived parental shortcomings of Birth Father, its reasoning necessarily extends to *all* Indian parents who have never had custody of their children, no matter how fully those parents have embraced the financial and emotional responsibilities of parenting. The majority thereby transforms a statute that was intended to provide uniform federal standards for child custody proceedings involving Indian children and their biological parents into an illogical piecemeal scheme.

* * *

The majority . . . asserts baldly that "when an Indian parent abandons an Indian child prior to birth and that child has never been in the Indian parent's legal or physical custody, there is no 'relationship' that would be 'discontinu[ed]' . . . by the termination of the Indian parent's rights." Says who? Certainly not the statute. . . . [T]he majority has no warrant to substitute its own policy views for Congress' by saying that "no 'relationship' " exists between Birth Father and Baby Girl simply because, based on the hotly contested facts of this case, it views their family bond as insufficiently substantial to deserve protection.

* * *

The entire foundation of the majority's argument that subsection (f) does not apply is the lonely phrase "continued custody." It simply cannot bear the interpretive weight the majority would place on it.

* * *

... [N]othing in the majority's reasoning limits its manufactured class of semiprotected ICWA parents to biological fathers who failed to support their child's mother during pregnancy. Its logic would apply equally to noncustodial fathers who have actively participated in their child's upbringing.

* * *

On a more general level, the majority intimates that ICWA grants Birth Father an undeserved windfall: in the majority's words, an "ICWA trump card" he can "play . . . at the eleventh hour to override the mother's decision and the child's best interests." The implicit argument is that Congress could not possibly have intended to recognize a parent-child relationship between Birth Father and Baby Girl that would have to be legally terminated (either by valid consent or involuntary termination) before the adoption could proceed.

But this supposed anomaly is illusory. In fact, the law of at least 15 States did precisely that at the time ICWA was passed. And the law of a number of States still does so. . . .

* * *

The majority also protests that a contrary result to the one it reaches would interfere with the adoption of Indian children. This claim is the most perplexing of all. A central purpose of ICWA is to "promote the stability and security of Indian . . . families," in part by countering the trend of placing "an alarmingly high percentage of [Indian] children . . . in non-Indian foster and adoptive homes and institutions." . . .

The majority may consider this scheme unwise. But no principle of construction licenses a court to interpret a statute with a view to averting the very consequences Congress expressly stated it was trying to bring about. . . .

* * *

Moreover, the majority's focus on "intact" families begs the question of what Congress set out to accomplish with ICWA. In an ideal world, perhaps all parents would be perfect. They would live up to their parental responsibilities by providing the fullest possible financial and emotional support to their children. They would never suffer mental health problems, lose their jobs, struggle with substance dependency, or encounter any of the other multitudinous personal crises that can make it difficult to meet these responsibilities. In an ideal world parents would never become estranged and leave their children caught in the middle. But we do not live in such a world. Even happy families do not always fit the custodial-parent mold for which the majority would reserve ICWA's substantive protections; unhappy families all too often do not. They are families nonetheless. Congress understood as much. ICWA's definitions of "parent" and "termination of parental rights" . . . sweep broadly. They should be honored.

* * *

. . . The majority's repeated, analytically unnecessary references to the fact that Baby Girl is 3/256 Cherokee by ancestry do nothing to elucidate. . . . I see no ground for this Court to second-guess the membership requirements of federally recognized Indian tribes, which are independent political entities. . . .

The majority's treatment of this issue, in the end, does no more than create a lingering mood of disapprobation of the criteria for membership adopted by the Cherokee Nation that, in turn, make Baby Girl an "Indian child" under the statute. . . .

* * *

The majority casts Birth Father as responsible for the painful circumstances in this case, suggesting that he intervened "at the eleventh hour to override the mother's decision and the child's best interests." I have no wish to minimize the trauma of removing a 27-month-old child from her adoptive family. It bears remembering, however, that Birth Father took action to assert his parental rights when Baby Girl was four months old, as soon as he learned of the impending adoption. As the South Carolina Supreme Court recognized, " '[h]ad the mandate of . . . ICWA been followed [in 2010], . . . much potential anguish might have been avoided. . . .' "

The majority's hollow literalism distorts the statute and ignores Congress' purpose in order to rectify a perceived wrong that, while heartbreaking at the time, was a correct application of federal law and that in any case cannot be undone. Baby Girl has now resided with her father for 18 months. However difficult it must have been for her to leave Adoptive Couple's home when she was just over 2 years old, it will be equally devastating now if, at the age of 3½,

> she is again removed from her home and sent to live halfway across the
> country. Such a fate is not foreordained, of course. But it can be said with
> certainty that the anguish this case has caused will only be compounded by
> today's decision.
>
> * * *

During the course of this saga, the child was given to the adoptive couple at birth, transferred to her biological father's custody after living with the adoptive couple for two years, and then taken from her biological father and placed back with the adoptive couple after another year and a half.

On a purely legal level, Justice Samuel Alito's majority opinion stated that the portion of ICWA that protects a Native parent's parental rights to a child is not applicable to parents who have never had custody of the child. Yet, as the dissent noted, Alito's opinion is peppered with descriptions of the father, child, and situation that suggests that factors beyond pure legal reasoning were at play. Alito stated that the biological father "attempted to relinquish his parental rights and . . . had no prior contact with the child." In another portion of the opinion (that is not part of the above excerpt), Alito noted that, "Biological Father provided no financial assistance to Birth Mother or Baby Girl, even though he had the ability to do so." Alito also began his opinion noting the low blood quantum (see Chapter 13) of the child and wrote that, "It is undisputed that, had Baby Girl not been 3/256 Cherokee, Biological Father would have had no right to object to her adoption."

It is reasonable to question, as Justice Sonia Sotomayor's dissent does, the extent to which the majority's presumptions about the parties involved—as opposed to the legislation itself—determined the outcome of this case. It is easy to read Alito's opinion as suggesting that the biological father was a deadbeat, the child was not really Native, and that the legislation had the potential to harm loving, non-Native, would-be adoptive parents. Under such a reading, it is a short step to determine that ICWA should not apply under these circumstances.

As with *Mississippi Band v. Holyfield*, *Adoptive Couple v. Baby Girl* offers the opportunity to examine the presumptions that appear to support the ruling. For example, as Sotomayor's dissent noted, the majority opinion made "repeated, analytically unnecessary references to the fact that Baby Girl is 3/256 Cherokee by ancestry." However, these references are "analytically unnecessary" only if one understands citizenship in a tribal nation in political, rather than racial, terms. If, as Alito's opinion seems to suggest, that one needs a high (or at least higher than 1.2%) degree of blood quantum to truly be Native—and thus to legitimately be under the auspices of ICWA—then the references are analytically necessary. To what extent is this ruling dependent upon defining the category of "Indian" in primarily, if not exclusively, racial terms?

Additionally, as Sotomayor also noted, "The majority . . . protests that a contrary result to the one it reaches would interfere with the adoption of Indian children [outside of the tribal nation]." Yet, as Sotomayor also pointed out, this was a feature of ICWA, not a flaw. To what extent does this ruling in this case run contrary to the purposes of ICWA? Is the majority more concerned with the potential harm to non-Native adoptive couples than the potential harm to tribal nations? Who is ICWA designed to protect? Does the majority's perception of the father ultimately dictate the outcome of the case?

ICWA remains highly contested because it often emerges from difficult circumstances that stir emotions. In 2015 the federal government issued newly revised guidelines for ICWA, and in 2016 it produced newly revised regulations. The purpose of the revised guidelines and regulations was to strengthen tribal authority over child placement proceedings and close the loopholes in ICWA that state courts had created. The full effect of the guidelines and regulations, as well as the result in *Adoptive Couple v. Baby Girl*, remains to be seen. Nonetheless, ICWA continues to be both a pillar of tribal sovereignty and a point of attack against that sovereignty.

SUGGESTED READINGS

- *Facing the Future: The Indian Child Welfare Act at Thirty*. Matthew L.M. Fletcher, Wenona T. Singel, and Kathryn E. Fort, eds. East Lansing, MI: Michigan State University Press, 2009.

- "In the Name of the Child: Race, Gender, and Economics in *Adoptive Couple v. Baby Girl.*" Bethany R. Berger. 67 *Florida Law Review* 295 (January 2015).

- " 'Indian' as a Political Classification: Reading the Tribe Back into the Indian Child Welfare Act." Allison Elder. 13 *Northwestern Journal of Law & Social Policy* 410 (Spring 2018).

[1] U.S. Congress, House. Hearings Before a Subcommittee on Indian Affairs and Public Lands. Feb. 9 and Mar. 9, 1978, 95th Cong., 2nd Sess., S. 1214. 29.

[2] Id.

[3] Id. at 66.

[4] Id. at 62.

CHAPTER 24

Indian Gaming Regulatory Act

It is no exaggeration to suggest that no other phenomenon in the Self-Determination Era has had the impact on Indian Country that gaming has. Perhaps no other case, statute, movement, social event, or other happening in the last half-century has reshaped some of the basic understandings, experiences, and questions surrounding Native peoples and nations as has gaming. Gaming is now a multibillion dollar industry within Indian Country. It has brought much needed economic relief to many reservations, and has even made a small handful of tribal nations and citizens wealthy. Interestingly, these successes have sometimes given rise to the stereotype of the "rich Indian." Yet, not all tribal nations have casinos nor do all benefit from gaming, and the variance of tribal experience is great. A small handful of tribal nations and casinos reap the most revenue, many fare anywhere from doing well to breaking even, and some tribal gaming enterprises are losing money or have failed.

Today, the Indian Gaming Regulatory Act (IGRA) stands at the very center of any analysis of tribal gaming. Passed in 1988, IGRA established the rules by which tribal nations can engage in gaming, as well as the roles the federal government and states have to play. IGRA had helped to facilitate the rapid and widespread growth of tribal gaming ventures since its passage. Yet, as discussed in greater detail further below, it has also been the source of some significant misconceptions as well. In addition to fostering the stereotype of the rich Indian, IGRA is also sometimes mistakenly credited for starting tribal gaming. In that same vein, IGRA is also mistakenly regarded by some as allowing tribal gaming, or giving tribal nations the authority to engage in gaming. In fact, IGRA was passed in an effort to regulate tribal gaming efforts that were already in existence and the statute is actually a limitation on tribal authority, not an expansion of it.

> *This chapter will demonstrate...*
>
> - *The developments leading to the Indian Gaming Regulatory Act*
>
> - *The basic structure of IGRA*
>
> - *The complications when states and tribal nations disagree over IGRA*

THE ROAD TO IGRA

As noted above, some mistakenly believe that IGRA was the start of tribal gaming in the United States. In fact, there were a number of tribal gaming operations throughout the United States before IGRA was passed in 1988 (although tribal gaming before IGRA was a very tiny fraction of what it is today), and the statute was a response to these early enterprises, not the source of them.

IGRA was also a response to a Supreme Court case, *California v. Cabazon Mission Band of Indians*. In the mid-1980s, California attempted to shut down the gaming operations of two tribal nations within its borders. Both tribal nations were engaged in high stakes bingo and one also operated a "card room" where games such as poker were played. In response to the state's efforts, both tribal nations argued that it was within their scope of sovereign authority to engage in gaming operations.

Like many cases both inside and outside of Indian law, *Cabazon* is multi-layered with many questions of law for the Supreme Court to consider. For example, *Cabazon* is also noteworthy for its implications for Public Law 280 (see Chapter 17). For the purposes of this chapter it is important to know that California was, among other things, making a public policy argument against tribal gaming. A public policy argument is a type of legal argument in which one party states that the law ought to be understood or interpreted in a certain way because it will be more beneficial for society to do so than if the law is understood or interpreted in another way. A public policy argument does not focus on the text of a statute or precedents from other cases, but rather the predicted results of the outcome of a case and what they would mean for a community or group. For example, imagine that a state law requiring children in public schools to wear a school uniform to class is challenged in court. Those in favor of the law might make the public policy argument that society benefits from the law because it prevents students from wearing inappropriate or offensive clothing, obscures class divisions and the ridicule that can often accompany them, and fosters as sense of order in the classroom. Opponents of the law might make the public policy argument that society is harmed by the law because it actually enhances class divisions since not all families can afford new or multiple uniforms, and that this level of conformity decreases a student's capacity to learn by obscuring a student's individuality.

In *Cabazon*, the state of California made—again, among other points—the public policy argument that a decision in favor of tribal gaming was bad because tribal gaming would attract organized crime and other associated vices. As you read the case, ask yourself how the Supreme Court measures California's public policy argument against the state's own practices. Whose interests, besides California's, are involved in the decision? How does the Court measure California's public policy argument against the other interests within the case? How does the Supreme Court understand tribal gaming in relation to its benefits or detriments to society?

CA V. CABAZON BAND OF MISSION INDIANS
480 U.S. 202 (1987)

JUSTICE WHITE delivered the opinion of the Court.

The Cabazon and Morongo Bands of Mission Indians, federally recognized Indian Tribes, occupy reservations in Riverside County, California. Each Band, pursuant to an ordinance approved by the Secretary of the Interior, conducts bingo games on its reservation. The Cabazon Band has also opened a card club at which draw poker and other card games are played. The games are open to the public, and are played predominantly by non-Indians coming onto the reservations. The games are a major source of employment for tribal members, and the profits are the Tribes' sole source of income. The State of California seeks to apply to the two Tribes [a state statute]. That statute does not entirely prohibit the playing of bingo, but permits it when the games are operated and staffed by members of designated charitable organizations, who may not be paid for their services. Profits must be kept in special accounts and used only for charitable purposes; prizes may not exceed $250 per game. Asserting that the bingo games on the two reservations violated each of these restrictions, California insisted that the Tribes comply with state law. . . .

* * *

. . . California law permits bingo games to be conducted only by charitable and other specified organizations, and then only by their members who may not receive any wage or profit for doing so; prizes are limited and receipts are to be segregated and used only for charitable purposes. Violation of any of these provisions is a misdemeanor. . . .

* * *

. . . California does not prohibit all forms of gambling. California itself operates a state lottery, and daily encourages its citizens to participate in this state-run gambling. California also permits parimutuel horse-race betting. Although certain enumerated gambling games are prohibited under [California law], games not enumerated, including the card games played in the Cabazon card club, are permissible. The Tribes assert that more than 400 card rooms similar to the Cabazon card club flourish in California, and the State does not dispute this fact. Also, as the Court of Appeals noted, bingo is legally sponsored by many different organizations, and is widely played in California. There is no effort to forbid the playing of bingo by any member of the public over the age of 18. Indeed, the permitted bingo games must be open to the general public. Nor is there any limit on the number of games which eligible organizations may operate, the receipts which they may obtain from the games, the number of games which a participant may play, or the amount of money which a participant may spend, either per game or in total. In light of the fact that California permits a substantial amount of gambling activity, including bingo, and actually promotes gambling through its state lottery, we must conclude that California regulates, rather than prohibits, gambling in general and bingo in particular.

* * *

. . . [The Court of Appeals] similarly concluded that bingo is not contrary to the public policy of California.

* * *

. . . [T]he Department of the Interior, which has the primary responsibility for carrying out the Federal Government's trust obligations to Indian tribes, has sought to implement [federal] policies by promoting tribal bingo enterprises. Under the Indian Financing Act of 1974, the Secretary of the Interior has made grants and has guaranteed loans for the purpose of constructing bingo facilities. The Department of Housing and Urban Development and the Department of Health and Human Services have also provided financial assistance to develop tribal gaming enterprises. Here, the Secretary of the Interior has approved tribal ordinances establishing and regulating the gaming activities involved. The Secretary has also exercised his authority to review tribal bingo management contracts . . . and has issued detailed guidelines governing that review.

These policies and actions, which demonstrate the Government's approval and active promotion of tribal bingo enterprises, are of particular relevance in this case. The Cabazon and Morongo Reservations contain no natural resources which can be exploited. The tribal games at present provide the sole source of revenues for the operation of the tribal governments and the provision of tribal services. They are also the major sources of employment on the reservations. Self-determination and economic development are not within reach if the Tribes cannot raise revenues and provide employment for their members. The Tribes' interests obviously parallel the federal interests.

California seeks to diminish the weight of these seemingly important tribal interests by asserting that the Tribes are merely marketing an exemption from state gambling laws. . . .

. . . [T]he Tribes are not merely importing a product onto the reservations for immediate resale to non-Indians. They have built modern facilities which provide recreational opportunities and ancillary services to their patrons, who do not simply drive onto the reservations, make purchases and depart, but spend extended periods of time there enjoying the services the Tribes provide. The Tribes have a strong incentive to provide comfortable, clean, and attractive facilities and well run games in order to increase attendance at the games. . . . [T]he Cabazon and Morongo Bands are generating value on the reservations through activities in which they have a substantial interest.

* * *

The sole interest asserted by the State to justify the imposition of its bingo laws on the Tribes is in preventing the infiltration of the tribal games by organized crime. . . . The State insists that the high stakes offered at tribal games are attractive to organized crime, whereas the controlled games authorized under California law are not. This is surely a legitimate concern, but we are unconvinced that it is sufficient to escape the preemptive force of federal and tribal interests apparent in this case. California does not allege any present criminal involvement in the Cabazon and Morongo enterprises, and the Ninth Circuit discerned none. . . .

We conclude that the State's interest in preventing the infiltration of the tribal bingo enterprises by organized crime does not justify state regulation of the tribal bingo enterprises in light of the compelling federal and tribal interests

> supporting them. State regulation would impermissibly infringe on tribal government. . . .

California's public policy argument failed for a number of reasons. First, the Supreme Court measured the state's argument against its own behavior. While acknowledging that protecting against organized crime is a worthwhile public policy goal, the Court nonetheless noted that California permitted multiple forms of gambling within the state. In fact, California even allowed bingo, the game at the center of the litigation. Gaming already had a significant presence in the state and the Supreme Court appeared unconvinced that the addition of tribal gaming would create the problems that the state alleged it would.

The Supreme Court also measured the state's argument against the tribal interests in engaging in gaming. In this inquiry, the Court found that the tribal interest were significant. As the Court noted, there were "no natural resources which can be exploited" on the reservation and that the gaming operations were the sole sources of income for the tribal nations. Consequently, the tribal nations had a strong incentive to "provide comfortable, clean, and attractive facilities and well run games in order to increase attendance at the games." In essence, the Court seemed to imply that the tribal nations had even more incentive to avoid organized crime than the state, as any hint of impropriety at their gaming operations was likely to hinder the only source of income for the tribal nations. Since, according to the Court, the benefit of gaming to the tribal nations was high and the state's need to regulate tribal gaming was low, the public policy argument ran in favor of the tribal nations.

The Supreme Court's analysis did not just measure state interests against tribal interests, however. The Court also considered the federal government's role in promoting tribal gaming through various means. According to the Court, "These policies and actions, which demonstrate the Government's approval and active promotion of tribal bingo enterprises, are of particular relevance in this case," because of the federal government's trust obligations to tribal nations (see Chapter 14). Since the federal government had invested in the success of the gaming operations and the tribal nations, ruling in favor of the state would have run contrary to federal policy. Taking the next logical step in this line of reasoning, any ruling contrary to federal policy would infringe upon the federal government's plenary authority in Indian affairs.

The public policy argument was just one of the many facets to the decision in *Cabazon*. Nonetheless, it was critical to the decision and an example of the type of analysis that is relatively common in the Self-Determination Era of federal policy—the balancing of state, tribal, and federal interests. In this case, the state's assertion that it needed to regulate gaming on the reservation could not hold up to the tribal and federal interests or the state's own behavior in accepting and promoting gaming within its borders. As in *Cabazon*, when a tribal nation's interests align with the federal government's interests, the tribal nation is more likely to win.

THE INDIAN GAMING REGULATORY ACT

The result in *Cabazon* caught the attention of many parties, particularly tribal nations seeking to increase economic opportunities on reservations and states that were fearful of increased gaming activities within their borders over which they would have no control. Many state officials were worried that tribal gaming would lead to the types of problems with organized crime and other vices that California had presumed would occur, albeit with little evidence to suggest that such outcomes would happen or were even likely. Congress, seeking to answer to multiple constituencies, quickly stepped in and sought to strike a balance between fostering tribal economic development and protecting state authority. A year after *Cabazon*, Congress passed IGRA.

IGRA is a lengthy piece of legislation with multiple parts that mandate a number of things concerning tribal gaming. For example, IGRA created the National Indian Gaming Commission, a federal agency that oversees the regulation and operation of tribal gaming operations. Most fundamentally, however, IGRA classified the type of gaming that could occur on tribal lands. IGRA established a three-tiered system that determined the manner in which gaming can occur. As you read this excerpt, ask yourself what those three tiers are. Who regulates each of the three tiers? What role does a state have in tribal gaming? How does the statute justify itself? What, according to the statute, is Congress trying to accomplish with IGRA?

INDIAN GAMING REGULATORY ACT
25 U.S.C.A. Ch. 29

§ 2701—Findings

The Congress finds that—

(1) Numerous Indian tribes have become engaged in or have licensed gaming activities on Indian lands as a means of generating tribal governmental revenue. . . .

(3)   Existing Federal law does not provide clear standards or regulations for the conduct of gaming on Indian lands;

(4)   A principal goal of Federal Indian policy is to promote tribal economic development, tribal self-sufficiency, and strong tribal government. . . .

§ 2702—Declaration of policy

The Purpose of this chapter is—

(1)   To provide a statutory basis for the operation of gaming by Indian tribes as a means of promoting tribal economic development, self-sufficiency, and strong tribal governments;

(2)   To provide a statutory basis for the regulation of gaming by an Indian tribe adequate to shield it from organized crime and other corrupting influences, to ensure that the Indian tribe is the primary beneficiary of the gaming operation, and to assure that gaming is conducted fairly and honestly by both the operator and players; and

(3)   To declare that the establishment of independent Federal regulatory authority for gaming on Indian lands, the establishment of Federal standards for gaming on Indian lands, and the establishment of a National Indian Gaming Commission are necessary to meet congressional concerns regarding gaming and to protect such gaming as a means of generating tribal revenue.

§ 2703—Definitions

For the purposes of this chapter—

. . .

(6)   The term "class I gaming" means social games solely for prizes of minimal value or traditional forms of Indian gaming engaged in by individuals as part of, or in connection with, tribal ceremonies or celebrations.

(7)

    (A)   The term "class II gaming" means—

        (I)   The game of chance commonly known as bingo. . . .

        (II)   Card games that—

            (I)   Are explicitly authorized by the laws of the State

            (II) Are not explicitly prohibited by the laws of the State. . . .

(B) The term "class II gaming" does not include—

(I) Any banking card games, including . . . blackjack, or

(II) Electronic . . . game[s] of chance or slot machines of any kind

. . .

(8) The term "class III gaming" means all forms of gaming that are not class I gaming or class II gaming

* * *

§ 2710—Tribal gaming ordinances

(a) Jurisdiction over class I and class II gaming activity

(1) Class I gaming on Indian lands is within the exclusive jurisdiction of the Indian tribes and shall not be subject to the provisions of this chapter.

(2) Any class II gaming on Indian lands shall continue to be within the jurisdiction of the Indian tribes, but shall be subject to the provisions of this chapter

. . .

(d) Class III gaming activities. . .

(1) Class III gaming activities shall be lawful on Indian lands only if such activities are—

(A) Authorized by [a tribal] ordinance or resolution. . . .

(B) Located in a State that permits such gaming for any purpose by any person, organization, or entity, and

(C) Conducted in conformance with a Tribal-State compact entered into by the Indian tribe and the State. . . .

* * *

Understanding the three classes of gaming is essential to understanding IGRA. Each class has a different regulatory scheme, and thus different levels of involvement from various governments. Class I gaming includes low stakes "social" games. For example, many pow-wows or tribal gatherings will include a raffle in which prizes—often works from local artisans such as quilts, shawls, or jewelry—are awarded. These games and prizes constitute Class I gaming. Under IGRA, this level of gaming is exclusively under the jurisdiction of the tribal nation. Neither the federal government nor a state has any authority over Class I gaming.

Class II gaming essentially includes games in which the "house," or the owner of the gaming operation, has no stake in the outcome of the game, but rather takes a fee from the player for operating the game. Bingo is explicitly included as a Class II game in the statute. "Banking card games" are explicitly excluded from Class II in the statute. Thus, a tribal casino that only engages in Class II gaming could operate games of bingo and/or poker, since the casino would have no interest in the outcome of the games itself, but rather would charge a fee for the bingo cards or a "rake" or small, consistent fee from each hand of poker. Yet, that casino could not operate blackjack tables, as blackjack is a "banked" card game in which the "house" plays against the player. Under IGRA, Class II gaming is under the jurisdiction of the tribal nation and the federal government through the auspices of IGRA.

Class III gaming involves any other gaming that is not Class I or Class II, and is best conceptualized as the traditional types of games one envisions when one envisions a casino. Thus, slot machines, blackjack, roulette, and other such games in which the player plays against the house are Class III games. Class III games are also the most profitable for a gaming operation, and thus also the most coveted by tribal nations and the most regulated under IGRA.

In order for a tribal nation to engage in Class III gaming, that tribal nation must negotiate a compact, or mutually binding agreement, with the state in which the tribal nation is located. The compact defines the scope of Class III gaming in which the tribal nation can engage, often in minute detail, along with any other areas of concern that might affect tribal gaming. For example, a compact might include provisions that account for additional public services incurred by the increased traffic a tribal casino might generate. Under IGRA, every level of American government—federal, tribal, and state—has some hand in regulating Class III gaming on tribal lands.

Tribal gaming exploded in the wake of IGRA. In the early days, many perceived tribal gaming and IGRA as simply another economic stimulus package intended to provide jobs to needy reservation communities. Instead, tribal gaming has become an industry measured in the billions of dollars that has reinvigorated many of the rural communities in which tribal casinos are found. Today, there are approximately 242 tribal nations operating approximately 513 gaming operations in the United States.[1] In 2017, those gaming operations generated over $32 billion.[2] That revenue is not contained to just the reservation or tribal citizens. Many tribal casinos require a greater workforce than the reservation community can sustain by itself. Thus, tribal gaming has meant economic opportunities for many non-Natives as well and also state tax revenue through those non-Native casino workers.

The structure of the statute, particularly in light of the decision in *Cabazon*, ought to dispel one of the myths surrounding IGRA. While many understand IGRA to grant tribal nations the right to engage in gaming, the opposite is true. The *Cabazon* decision (particularly since it originated in a Public Law 280 state) was a clear victory for tribal sovereignty that recognized the capacity of tribal nations to engage in gaming before IGRA. Consequently, IGRA is actually a limitation on tribal sovereignty. It forces tribal nations who wish to engage in Class II gaming to operate under the auspices of the statute and it forces those tribal nations who wish to engage in Class III gaming to negotiate with, and make certain concessions to, a state. While IGRA did set up a pathway for tribal gaming (one that many tribal nations have gone down), it did so at the expense of tribal sovereignty.

ENFORCEMENT OF IGRA

As noted above, IGRA was Congress' attempt to strike a balance between its trust responsibility to tribal nations by encouraging economic growth and the desire of states to have some say in gaming operations that did or might exist within their borders. To that end, as originally written IGRA allowed states some say over tribal gaming through compacts with tribal nations, but also required that the states negotiate "in good faith." If a state failed to negotiate in good faith, then IGRA permitted a tribal nation to sue the state in federal court, thus beginning a detailed process for remediation that is detailed in the case below. Some states objected to this provision of IGRA, arguing that it infringed on their sovereignty.

In order to comprehend the next case, it is important to know something about sovereign immunity. A principle of Western law, sovereign immunity as it is applied to tribal nations is discussed in greater detail in Chapter 21. For the purposes of this chapter, it suffices to know that sovereign immunity shields governments from lawsuits unless the government in question consents to be sued. For example, an individual cannot sue the federal government unless the federal government has passed a law consenting to be sued or otherwise allowed the type of lawsuit that the individual wishes to initiate. If the individual cannot provide proof that the federal government has consented to the type of lawsuit the individual seeks to pursue, then the case cannot be heard because of the federal government's sovereign immunity. States and tribal nations also have sovereign immunity, although they are not as fulsome as the federal government's version.

In certain instances, the federal government can limit the sovereign immunity of both states and tribal nations.

The question of the next case, *Seminole Tribe of Florida v. Florida*, was whether the federal government had the authority to waive the state's sovereign immunity under IGRA. Put differently, was the justification that the federal government put forth to waive the state's sovereign immunity under IGRA one of those certain instances in which the federal government was authorized to do so, or was it outside of the federal government's authority to waive the state's sovereign immunity under these circumstances? As you read the case, ask yourself what source of authority the federal government identifies as authorizing it to waive a state's sovereign immunity. What source of authority does the state use to argue that this is an impermissible infringement on its sovereignty? What standard, or test, does the Supreme Court use to solve these types of questions? How is the state's sovereignty conceptualized by both the majority and the dissent?

SEMINOLE TRIBE OF FLORIDA V. FLORIDA
517 U.S. 44 (1996)

CHIEF JUSTICE REHNQUIST delivered the opinion of the Court.

The Indian Gaming Regulatory Act provides that an Indian tribe may conduct certain gaming activities only in conformance with a valid compact between the tribe and the State in which the gaming activities are located. The Act, passed by Congress under the Indian Commerce Clause, imposes upon the States a duty to negotiate in good faith with an Indian tribe toward the formation of a compact, and authorizes a tribe to bring suit in federal court against a State in order to compel performance of that duty. We hold that, notwithstanding Congress' clear intent to abrogate the States' sovereign immunity, the Indian Commerce Clause does not grant Congress that power, and therefore cannot grant jurisdiction over a State that does not consent to be sued. . . .

Congress passed the Indian Gaming Regulatory Act in 1988 in order to provide a statutory basis for the operation and regulation of gaming by Indian tribes. The Act divides gaming on Indian lands into three classes—I, II, and III—and provides a different regulatory scheme for each class. Class III gaming—the type with which we are here concerned—is defined as "all forms of gaming that are not class I gaming or class II gaming," and includes such things as slot machines, casino games, banking card games, dog racing, and lotteries. It is the most heavily regulated of the three classes. . . .

* * *

The State's obligation to "negotiate with the Indian tribe in good faith," is made judicially enforceable by [IGRA]. . . .

[IGRA] describe[s] an elaborate remedial scheme designed to ensure the formation of a Tribal-State compact. A tribe that brings an action under [IGRA] must show that no Tribal-State compact has been entered and that the State failed to respond in good faith to the tribe's request to negotiate; at that point, the burden then shifts to the State to prove that it did in fact negotiate in good faith. If the district court concludes that the State has failed to negotiate in good faith toward the formation of a Tribal-State compact, then it "shall order the State and Indian tribe to conclude such a compact within a 60-day period." If no compact has been concluded 60 days after the court's order, then "the Indian tribe and the State shall each submit to a mediator appointed by the court a proposed compact that represents their last best offer for a compact." The mediator chooses from between the two proposed compacts the one "which best comports with the terms of [the Act] and any other applicable Federal law and with the findings and order of the court," and submits it to the State and the Indian tribe. If the State consents to the proposed compact within 60 days of its submission by the mediator, then the proposed compact is "treated as a Tribal-State compact. . . ." If, however, the State does not consent within that 60-day period, then the Act provides that the mediator "shall notify the Secretary [of the Interior]," and that the Secretary

> shall prescribe . . . procedures . . . under which class III gaming may be conducted on the Indian lands over which the Indian tribe has jurisdiction.

In September, 1991, the Seminole Tribe of Indians, petitioner, sued the State of Florida and its Governor, Lawton Chiles, respondents. . . . [P]etitioner alleged that respondents had "refused to enter into any negotiation for inclusion of [certain gaming activities] in a tribal-state compact," thereby violating the "requirement of good faith negotiation". . . . Respondents moved to dismiss the complaint, arguing that the suit violated the State's sovereign immunity from suit in federal court. . . .

. . . (1) Does the Eleventh Amendment prevent Congress from authorizing suits by Indian tribes against States for prospective injunctive relief to enforce legislation enacted pursuant to the Indian Commerce Clause?. . . .

The Eleventh Amendment provides:

The Judicial power of the United States shall not be construed to extend to any suit in law or equity, commenced or prosecuted against one of the United States by Citizens of another State, or by Citizens or Subjects of any Foreign State.

"[W]e have understood the Eleventh Amendment to stand not so much for what it says, but for the presupposition . . . which it confirms." That presupposition . . . has two parts: first, that each State is a sovereign entity in our federal system; and second, that " '[i]t is inherent in the nature of sovereignty not to be amenable to the suit of an individual without its consent.' " For over a century, we have reaffirmed that federal jurisdiction over suits against unconsenting States "was not contemplated by the Constitution when establishing the judicial power of the United States."

Here, petitioner has sued the State of Florida and it is undisputed that Florida has not consented to the suit. Petitioner nevertheless contends that its suit is not barred by state sovereign immunity. . . . [I]t argues that Congress, through the Act, abrogated the States' sovereign immunity. . . .

. . . In order to determine whether Congress has abrogated the States' sovereign immunity, we ask two questions: first, whether Congress has "unequivocally expresse[d] its intent to abrogate the immunity," and second, whether Congress has acted "pursuant to a valid exercise of power."

Congress' intent to abrogate the States' immunity from suit must be obvious from "a clear legislative statement.". . .

Here, we agree with the parties, with the Eleventh Circuit in the decision below, and with virtually every other court that has confronted the question that Congress has in [IGRA] provided an "unmistakably clear" statement of its intent to abrogate. . . .

* * *

Having concluded that Congress clearly intended to abrogate the States' sovereign immunity . . . we turn now to consider whether the Act was passed "pursuant to a valid exercise of power.". . .

[P]etitioner argues that the abrogation power is validly exercised here because the Act grants the States a power that they would not otherwise have, viz., some measure of authority over gaming on Indian lands. It is true enough that the Act extends to the States a power withheld from them by the Constitution. Nevertheless, we do not see how that consideration is relevant to the question whether Congress may abrogate state sovereign immunity. The Eleventh Amendment immunity may not be lifted by Congress unilaterally deciding that it will be replaced by grant of some other authority. . . .

Thus our inquiry into whether Congress has the power to abrogate unilaterally the States' immunity from suit is narrowly focused on one question: Was the Act in question passed pursuant to a constitutional provision granting Congress the power to abrogate? Previously, in conducting that inquiry, we have found authority to abrogate under only two provisions of the Constitution. [One of which was] the Fourteenth Amendment. . . .

In . . . one other case . . . a plurality of the Court found that the Interstate Commerce Clause granted Congress the power to abrogate state sovereign immunity. . . .

In arguing that Congress, through the Act, abrogated the States' sovereign immunity, petitioner does not challenge the . . . conclusion that the Act was passed pursuant to neither the Fourteenth Amendment nor the Interstate Commerce Clause. Instead, accepting . . . that the Act was passed pursuant to Congress' power under the Indian Commerce Clause, petitioner now asks us to consider whether that clause grants Congress the power to abrogate the States' sovereign immunity.

* * *

Never before [one outlying case] had we suggested that [Congress could waive state sovereign immunity] operating pursuant to any constitutional provision other than the Fourteenth Amendment. Indeed, it had seemed fundamental that Congress could not expand the jurisdiction of the federal courts [in this manner]. . . .

* * *

. . . [W]e reconfirm that the background principle of state sovereign immunity embodied in the Eleventh Amendment is not so ephemeral as to dissipate when the subject of the suit is an area, like the regulation of Indian commerce, that is under the exclusive control of the Federal Government. Even when the Constitution vests in Congress complete lawmaking authority over a particular area, the Eleventh Amendment prevents congressional authorization of suits by private parties against unconsenting States. . . .

* * *

JUSTICE STEVENS, dissenting.

* * *

The importance of the majority's decision . . . cannot be overstated. The majority's opinion does not simply preclude Congress from establishing the rather curious statutory scheme under which Indian tribes may seek the aid of a federal court to secure a State's good faith negotiations over gaming regulations. Rather, it prevents Congress from providing a federal forum for a broad range of actions against States. . . .

* * *

Fortunately, and somewhat fortuitously, a jurisdictional problem that is unmentioned by the Court may deprive its opinion of precedential significance. The Indian Gaming Regulatory Act establishes a unique set of procedures for resolving the dispute between the Tribe and the State. If each adversary adamantly adheres to its understanding of the law, if the District Court determines that the State's inflexibility constitutes a failure to negotiate in good faith, and if the State thereafter continues to insist that it is acting within its rights, the maximum sanction that the Court can impose is an order that refers the controversy to a member of the Executive Branch of the Government for resolution. As the Court of Appeals interpreted the Act, this final disposition is available even though the action against the State and its Governor may not be maintained. . . .

* * *

JUSTICE SOUTER, with whom JUSTICE GINSBURG and JUSTICE BREYER join, dissenting.

* * *

. . . [T]he power to regulate commerce with Indian Tribes has been interpreted as making "Indian relations . . . the exclusive province of federal law.". . . We have specifically held, moreover, that the states have no power to regulate gambling on Indian lands. In sum, since the States have no sovereignty in the regulation of commerce with the tribes . . . there is no source of sovereign immunity to assert in a suit based on congressional regulation of that commerce. . . .

* * *

Like a good number of cases in Indian law, *Seminole Tribe* is perhaps best understood by considering the non-Indian interests. It is, as many have noted, most centrally a case about the federal government's powers over states under the U.S. Constitution. Chief Justice William Rehnquist's majority opinion stated, in essence, that the Eleventh Amendment preserved state sovereign authority and that the Indian Commerce Clause did not authorize Congress to waive a state's sovereign immunity to allow for suits in federal court under IGRA. Both dissents argued that this was a fundamental and dangerous misreading of the U.S. Constitution.

Despite the case's reputation for being more relevant to constitutional law than Indian law, the decision did have an important impact on Indian Country. After *Seminole Nation*, tribal nations could no longer sue states in federal court under IGRA. This did not mean that the statute as a whole was invalid, as the rest of IGRA is still good law and continues to control tribal gaming. But it did remove the most powerful weapon at the disposal of tribal nations from the statute. After *Seminole Nation*, states have been able to demand greater concessions from tribal nations in their compacts. As noted by Justice John Paul Stevens dissent, there continue to be steps for tribal nations to take toward a compact without the capacity to sue the state. But those steps are more protracted and cumbersome, they require a willing partner in the federal government, and they have been and likely will continue to be challenged in the future.

In keeping with the Congressional desire to strike a balance between its trust responsibility to tribal nations and state sovereignty, IGRA also authorized states to sue tribal nations when those tribal nations engaged in unauthorized gaming on tribal lands. This waiver of tribal sovereign immunity has been less controversial because the source of federal authority to do so—plenary power—is different in scope than the federal government's authority over states under the U.S. Constitution (see Chapters 6 and 7).

The scope of this provision of IGRA has recently been tested at the Supreme Court. In a unique set of facts, a tribal nation in Michigan purchased land outside of the reservation and began a gaming operation on that land. The state sued in federal court under IGRA to stop the gaming enterprise. As with *Cabazon* and *Seminole Nation*, *Michigan v. Bay Mills Indian Community* has implications for different aspects of Indian law and American law, and the case is also considered elsewhere in this text (see Chapter 21). For the purposes of this chapter, the discussion in *Bay Mills* about IGRA is pertinent. As you read the case, ask yourself how the Supreme Court reads the text of IGRA. How does this case attend to the balance between tribal gaming and state sovereignty that Congress sought to strike in IGRA? What role does the Court see for itself in interpreting IGRA? What role does the Court see for Congress in enacting IGRA?

MI v. Bay Mills Indian Community

572 U.S. 782 (2014)

Justice Kagan delivered the opinion of the Court.

. . . Congress has not abrogated tribal sovereign immunity from a State's suit to enjoin gaming off a reservation or other Indian lands. . . .

The Indian Gaming Regulatory Act (IGRA or Act) creates a framework for regulating gaming activity on Indian lands. . . . A tribe may conduct such gaming on Indian lands only pursuant to, and in compliance with, a compact it has negotiated with the surrounding State. A compact typically prescribes rules for operating gaming, allocates law enforcement authority between the tribe and State, and provides remedies for breach of the agreement's terms. Notable here, IGRA itself authorizes a State to bring suit against a tribe for certain conduct violating a compact. . . .

Pursuant to the Act, Michigan and Bay Mills, a federally recognized Indian Tribe, entered into a compact in 1993. The compact empowers Bay Mills to conduct class III gaming on "Indian lands"; conversely, it prohibits the Tribe from doing so outside that territory. . . . Since entering into the compact, Bay Mills has operated class III gaming, as authorized, on its reservation in Michigan's Upper Peninsula.

In 2010, Bay Mills opened another class III gaming facility in Vanderbilt, a small village in Michigan's Lower Peninsula about 125 miles from the Tribe's reservation. Bay Mills had bought the Vanderbilt property with accrued interest from a federal appropriation, which Congress had made to compensate the Tribe for 19th-century takings of its ancestral lands. Congress had directed that a portion of the appropriated funds go into a "Land Trust" whose earnings the Tribe was to use to improve or purchase property. According to the legislation, any land so acquired "shall be held as Indian lands are held." Citing that provision, Bay Mills contended that the Vanderbilt property was "Indian land" under IGRA and the compact; and the Tribe thus claimed authority to operate a casino there.

Michigan disagreed: The State sued Bay Mills in federal court to enjoin operation of the new casino, alleging that the facility violated IGRA and the compact because it was located outside Indian lands. The same day Michigan filed suit, the federal Department of the Interior issued an opinion concluding (as the State's complaint said) that the Tribe's use of Land Trust earnings to purchase the Vanderbilt property did not convert it into Indian territory. . . .

* * *

Among the core aspects of sovereignty that tribes possess—subject, again, to congressional action—is the "common-law immunity from suit traditionally enjoyed by sovereign powers.". . .

* * *

. . . Unless Congress has authorized Michigan's suit, our precedents demand that it be dismissed. And so Michigan, naturally enough, makes two arguments: first, that IGRA indeed abrogates the Tribe's immunity from the State's suit. . . .

IGRA partially abrogates tribal sovereign immunity . . . but this case, viewed most naturally, falls outside that term's ambit. The provision, as noted above, authorizes a State to sue a tribe to "enjoin a class III gaming activity located on Indian lands and conducted in violation of any Tribal-State compact." A key phrase in that abrogation is "on Indian lands"—three words reflecting IGRA's overall scope (and repeated some two dozen times in the statute). A State's suit to enjoin gaming activity on Indian lands falls within [IGRA]; a similar suit to stop gaming activity off Indian lands does not. And that creates a fundamental problem for Michigan. After all, the very premise of this suit—the reason Michigan thinks Bay Mills is acting unlawfully—is that the Vanderbilt casino is outside Indian lands. By dint of that theory, a suit to enjoin gaming in Vanderbilt is correspondingly outside [IGRA]'s abrogation of immunity.

Michigan first attempts to fit this suit within [IGRA] by relocating the "class III gaming activity" to which it is objecting. True enough, Michigan states, the Vanderbilt casino lies outside Indian lands. But Bay Mills "authorized, licensed, and operated" that casino from within its own reservation. According to the State, that necessary administrative action—no less than, say, dealing craps—is "class III gaming activity," and because it occurred on Indian land, this suit to enjoin it can go forward.

But that argument comes up snake eyes, because numerous provisions of IGRA show that "class III gaming activity" means just what it sounds like— the stuff involved in playing class III games. . . .

. . . Michigan next urges us to adopt a "holistic method" of interpreting IGRA that would allow a State to sue a tribe for illegal gaming off, no less than on, Indian lands. Michigan asks here that we consider "IGRA's text and structure as a whole." But . . . Michigan fails to identify any specific textual or structural features of the statute to support its proposed result. Rather,

Michigan highlights a (purported) anomaly of the statute as written: that it enables a State to sue a tribe for illegal gaming inside, but not outside, Indian country. . . .

But this Court does not revise legislation, as Michigan proposes, just because the text as written creates an apparent anomaly as to some subject it does not address. Truth be told, such anomalies often arise from statutes. . . . This Court has no roving license, in even ordinary cases of statutory interpretation, to disregard clear language simply on the view that (in Michigan's words) Congress "must have intended" something broader. And still less do we have that warrant when the consequence would be to expand an abrogation of immunity, because (as explained earlier) "Congress must 'unequivocally' express [its] purpose" to subject a tribe to litigation.

. . . So the problem Congress set out to address in IGRA . . . arose in Indian lands alone. And the solution Congress devised, naturally enough, reflected that fact. Everything—literally everything—in IGRA affords tools (for either state or federal officials) to regulate gaming on Indian lands, and nowhere else. Small surprise that IGRA's abrogation of tribal immunity does that as well.

. . . True enough, a State lacks the ability to sue a tribe for illegal gaming when that activity occurs off the reservation. But a State, on its own lands, has many other powers over tribal gaming that it does not possess (absent consent) in Indian territory. Unless federal law provides differently, "Indians going beyond reservation boundaries" are subject to any generally applicable state law. . . .

Finally, if a State really wants to sue a tribe for gaming outside Indian lands, the State need only bargain for a waiver of immunity. Under IGRA, a State and tribe negotiating a compact "may include . . . remedies for breach of contract,"—including a provision allowing the State to bring an action against the tribe in the circumstances presented here. States have more than enough leverage to obtain such terms because a tribe cannot conduct class III gaming on its lands without a compact and cannot sue to enforce a State's duty to negotiate a compact in good faith.

* * *

. . . The abrogation of immunity in IGRA applies to gaming on, but not off, Indian lands. We will not rewrite Congress's handiwork. . . .

* * *

Bay Mills may well prove to be an outlier of a case concerning IGRA because of its unique facts (although it will likely remain important in other areas of Indian law). Whatever its overall effect on IGRA, the case is reflective of the Supreme Court's recognition that Congress was seeking to satisfy not only competing interests with IGRA, but also competing claims to sovereignty. In this instance, the Court chose to show deference to Congress, allowing that branch of the federal government to decide how, if at all, to address the issue raised in *Bay Mills*. To date, Congress has not taken additional action.

As a result of *Seminole Nation* and *Bay Mills*, tribal nations are prevented from suing states under IGRA and states are limited in when they can sue tribal nations under IGRA. This has left the state of the law in something of a position of uncertainty, with questions about what can happen when a state and a tribal nation are in conflict about Class III gaming still to be answered. Importantly, despite the limitations placed on IGRA by these recent cases, tribal gaming persists and tribal nations continue to pursue gaming operations. IGRA remains a significant presence in Native America and stands to remain so into the future. Consequently, it should also continue to produce litigation and meaningful cases for Indian Country for years to come.

SUGGESTED READINGS

- *Indian Gaming and Tribal Sovereignty: The Casino Compromise.* Steven Andrew Light and Kathryn R.L. Rand. Lawrence, KS: University of Kansas Press, 2005.

- *High Stakes: Florida Seminole Gaming and Sovereignty.* Jessica R. Cattelino. Durham, NC: Duke University Press, 2008.

- "A Pretty Smart Answer: Justifying the Secretary of the Interior's 'Seminole Fix' for the Indian Gaming Regulatory Act." Austin R. Vance. 40 *American Indian Law Review* 325 (2015–2016).

---

[1] https://www.nigc.gov/images/uploads/abc.pdf (accessed Aug. 6, 2018).

[2] https://www.nigc.gov/images/uploads/reports/Chart2017GamingRevenuesbyRange.pdf (accessed Aug. 6, 2018).

CHAPTER 25

Cultural Resources

Sovereignty, as this text seeks to make clear, is at the heart of what defines Native America. Although somewhat difficult to pinpoint with complete precision, sovereignty can, for the present purposes, be best described as the ability of a group or political entity to make and enforce its own rules. This understanding of sovereignty is inherently legal and political, and the various cases, treaties, statutes, and other primary sources in this text are all reflections of how federal Indian law and policy could be understood as one long project with the singular purpose of establishing the boundaries of tribal sovereignty. Native nations and peoples define themselves by and defend themselves under the terms of this understanding of sovereignty; it is what makes Indian Country (which is also a category of sovereignty) distinct from other minority spaces and experiences in the United States.

And yet, despite the nature of sovereignty itself, expressions of sovereignty are not always necessarily rooted in inherently political activities or actions. Many expressions of sovereignty for Native peoples and nations concern seemingly more everyday or non-political or non-legal activities. For example, many treaty rights cases emerged out of the desires of tribal peoples to hunt and fish. These seemingly non-political or non-legal triggers are a consequence of the federal government's efforts to criminalize and destroy tribal practices and ways of life during the Allotment Era of federal policy (see Chapter 5). By seeking to eradicate tribal cultural practices, the federal government and others have made those practices objects by which to measure and fight for sovereignty.

In the Self-Determination Era (see Chapter 10), the federal government has, as a general practice, sought to support those cultural practices it once tried to destroy. More specifically, Congress has passed a number of pieces of important legislation that are intended to protect tribal practices and ways of life, including in the areas of art, language, religion, and elsewhere. However, the effects of the Allotment Era are not easily erased, and many of the contemporary efforts of the federal government have run into difficult problems and significant criticism, both inside and outside of Indian Country. Tribal cultural practices remain both sources of controversy and areas in which sovereignty is tested and defined. This chapter will focus on two of the most significant areas of the crossover between law and culture in Indian Country: human and funerary remains and art.

This chapter will demonstrate. . .

- *The basic contours of the Native American Graves Protection and Repatriation Act*

- *The basic contours of the Indian Arts and Crafts Act*

- *The connections and tensions between law, culture, and sovereignty*

NAGPRA AND THE ANCIENT ONE

Native America has had a long relationship with academia, especially the social sciences, that has historically often been contentious and one-sided. In the early years, the academics that have studied Native nations and peoples were, in general, not particularly sensitive to the human beings and ways of life that they studied, nor were they always good community partners. Beginning their studies with the belief in the inherent superiority of Western ways, academics regularly dismissed or discounted tribal knowledge in favor of culturally biased interpretations and conclusions. For example, a great number of historians seeking to detail tribal nations or important events have ignored tribal oral histories and other tribally generated sources in favor of written Western sources that were problematic in their own right. Just as important, these historians focused on wars and men, regularly neglecting women, children, and everyday life. The field of anthropology was born from the study of Native peoples, yet has also come under criticism for insensitive studies that sought to define and critique Native peoples through Western cosmologies. Anthropologists have also been heavily criticized for entering into Native communities, gathering information— some of it quite sensitive—with little regard to the community's relationship to the information, using that knowledge for professional gain, and then not providing anything of value back to the community.

The often-difficult historical relationship between Native peoples and the outsiders who have studied them is perhaps best exemplified by the field of archeology. In the past, archeologists regularly held little regard for the spaces that Native peoples understood as in need of reverence. All too often, archeologists would excavate sacred sites and burial sites in their pursuit of knowledge, with little to no respect for the consequences of these actions on Native peoples. Such scholarly attitudes, coupled with a more general willingness for Western expansion and development, meant that many places and objects of great meaning and significance for Native peoples have been dug up, paved over, sold for profit, displayed or used in offensive ways, or otherwise destroyed.

Thankfully, as more Native individuals have entered into the academy in the Self-Determination Era, many of these attitudes and practices have changed. Academics, in general, have become much more sensitive to how their studies and actions affect Native individuals and communities. For example, historians tend to be more critical readers of the written Western sources upon which their predecessors once almost exclusively relied, and have been more understanding of and receptive to Native sources of information. Anthropologists now regularly collaborate with the Native communities they study, abide by the rules these communities establish, and find ways to share the fruits of their labor with those communities. Archeologists, in a practice that has become fairly standard, also follow the same procedures as anthropologists and are responsive to tribal concerns about where they can and cannot engage in excavations. In general, scholars are much more responsible than in previous generations, and academia and Native America are more inclined to create mutually beneficial partnerships than ever before.

These positive developments are a credit to the scholars who helped make them happen. But much more so, they are a credit to the Native peoples and communities who sought reform not just through the academy itself but also the law. One of the major victories for Native activists on this front was the Native American Graves Protection and Repatriation Act, or NAGPRA. Passed by Congress in 1990, NAGPRA is a federal law that seeks to undo some of the damage done to Native sacred sights and human remains by archeologists, museums, and other treasure hunters. As you read the excerpt from the statute, ask yourself how it protects tribal interests. What rights do tribal peoples and nations have under NAGPRA? Who is obligated under the law? Where does it apply? Where does NAGPRA lack coverage?

Native American Graves Protection and Repatriation Act

25 U.S.C.A. Ch. 32

§ 3001—Definitions

For purposes of this chapter, the term—

(1) "burial site" means any natural or prepared physical location, whether originally below, on, or above the surface of the earth, into which as a part of the death rite or ceremony of a culture, individual human remains are deposited. . . .

* * *

(3) "Cultural items" means human remains and—

    (A) "associated funerary objects". . . .

    (B) "unassociated funerary objects" . . .

    (C) "sacred objects". . . .

* * *

(7) "Indian tribe" means any tribe, band, nation, or other organized group or community of Indians . . . which is recognized as eligible for the special programs and services provided by the United States to Indians because of their status as Indians. . . .

(9) "Native American" means of, or relating to, a tribe, people, or culture that is indigenous to the United States.

(10) "Native Hawaiian" means any individual who is a descendant of the aboriginal people who, prior to 1778, occupied and exercised sovereignty in the area that now constitutes the State of Hawaii.

* * *

§ 3002—Ownership

(a) Native American human remains and objects

The ownership or control of Native American cultural items which are excavated or discovered on Federal or tribal lands after November 16, 1990, shall be (with priority given in the order listed)—

    (1) In the case of Native American human remains and associated funerary objects, in the lineal descendants of the Native American; or

(2)   In any case in which such lineal descendants cannot be ascertained, and in the case of unassociated funerary objects [and] sacred objects. . . .

   (A) In the Indian tribe or Native Hawaiian organization on whose tribal land such objects or remains were discovered;

   (B) In the Indian tribe or Native Hawaiian organization which has the closest cultural affiliation with such remains or objects and which, upon notice, states a claim for such remains or objects; or

   (C) If the cultural affiliation of the objects cannot be reasonably ascertained. . . .

      (1) In the Indian tribes that is recognized as aboriginally occupying the area in which the objects were discovered. . . .

      (2) If it can be shown by a preponderance of the evidence that a different tribe has a stronger cultural relationship with the remains or objects than . . . in the Indian tribe that has the strongest demonstrated relationship.

* * *

(c)   Intentional excavation and removal of Native American human remains and objects

The intentional removal from or excavation of Native American cultural items from Federal or tribal lands for purposes of discovery, study, or removal of such items is permitted only if—

   (1) Such items are excavated or removed pursuant to a permit. . . .

   (2) Such items are excavated or removed after consultation with or, in the case of tribal lands, consent of the appropriate (if any) Indian tribe or Native Hawaiian organization. . . .

(d)   Inadvertent discovery of Native American remains and objects

(1)   Any person who knows, or has reason to know, that such person has discovered Native American cultural items on Federal or tribal lands . . . shall notify, in writing, [federal officials] . . . and the appropriate Indian tribe or Native Hawaiian organization with respect to tribal lands. . . .

* * *

§ 3003—Inventory for human remains and associated funerary objects

(a)   In general

Each federal agency and each museum which has possession or control over holdings or collections of Native American human remains and associated funerary objects shall compile an inventory of such items and, to the extent possible based on information possessed by such museum or Federal agency, identify the geographical and cultural affiliation of such item.

* * *

§ 3005—Repatriation

(a)   Repatriation of Native American remains and objects possessed or controlled by Federal agencies and museums

(1)   If, pursuant to section 3003 of this title, the cultural affiliation of Native American human remains and associated funerary objects with a particular Indian tribe or Native Hawaiian organization is established, then the Federal agency or museum, upon the request of a known lineal descendent of the Native American or of the tribe or organization . . . shall expeditiously return such remains and associated funerary objects. . . .

(b)   Scientific study

If the lineal descendant, Indian tribe, or Native Hawaiian organization requests the return of culturally affiliated Native American cultural items, the Federal agency or museum shall expeditiously return such items unless such items are indispensable for completion of a specific scientific study, the outcome of which would be of major benefit to the United States. Such items shall be returned by no later than 90 days after the date on which the scientific study is completed. . . .

* * *

§ 3007—Penalty

(a)   Penalty

Any museum that fails to comply with the requirements of this chapter may be assessed a civil penalty by the Secretary of the Interior. . . . Each violation . . . shall be a separate offense.

* * *

It is difficult to understate the amount of plundering of Native burial sites that has occurred over centuries of Western colonization, the number of objects on display or otherwise in collections or non-Native hands, and the anger and sorrow this plundering and subsequent treatment of such objects has caused Native peoples. NAGPRA is a powerful rebuke to this challenging history. The statute authorizes tribal families and nations to regain control over human remains and objects that were previously removed from tribal lands and communities. It expedites this process by requiring museums and federal agencies to inventory their collections. It also prevents further excavation on tribal and federal lands without some authorization from the federal government or the interested tribal nation and penalizes those who fail to comply with the statute's orders, among other things.

Despite NAGPRA's clear edicts, the problems that the statute has sought to address have not completely dissipated and major tensions continue to exist. There remains a market for tribal items and remains. Additionally, despite the changing attitudes of many academics who study Native America, many scholars, museums, and universities have demonstrated varying degrees of willingness to abide by the law. Some institutions have found difficulty complying with NAGPRA's requirement to inventory their collections, as many objects have cloudy histories. Others have balked at the additional costs for completing such tasks. And some scholars have complained that compliance with NAGPRA would rob the world of the scholarly knowledge that could be gained with the study of such objects. While NAGPRA does allow for some scientific study, it is a narrow window that requires a "specific scientific study" that is "of major benefit to the United States." As this is a high bar to overcome, some scholars have lamented what they believe are lost opportunities to learn about the world in ways that would benefit everybody, including the tribal communities that are repatriating the objects.

Conflicts generated by NAGPRA between Native America and others holding human remains and other objects have been common, sometimes requiring years of negotiation and litigation. The most famous of these disputes concerned The Ancient One, also known as Kennewick Man.

In 1996, skeletal remains were found on the bank of the Columbia River in Kennewick, Washington. The remains quickly became of scholarly interest when early research suggested that they were approximately 8500 years old and that they did not fit the typical characteristics of the remains of the tribal peoples who originally lived in what was to become North America. Tribal nations in the Pacific Northwest argued that the remains, which they dubbed The Ancient One, were definitely Native in origin and that they needed to be returned to Native peoples under NAGPRA for a proper reburial. A small group of scholars filed a lawsuit to prevent the reburial of the remains, which also came to be known as Kennewick Man, and to authorize their studies of the remains. Their preliminary findings suggested that the skeletal remains might not have been Native American in origin. At the time the case was making its way through the courts, there was evidence that appeared to support both the tribal and the scholarly assertions of the origin of the remains.

The question of the case was whether NAGPRA applied to the remains. If NAGPRA did apply, then the remains needed to be turned over to the tribal nations that were claiming them. If NAGPRA did not apply, then the scientists were free to study them. The case made it to the Ninth Circuit Court of Appeals. As you read the case, ask yourself what information is important to the court. How does the Ninth Circuit contextualize the dispute? What standard does the court use to decide NAGPRA cases? How does the court consider the evidence submitted by the tribal nations? Are the goals of NAGPRA, balanced against the deference it does show for scientific study, satisfied in this case?

BONNICHSEN V. U.S.
367 F.3d 864 (2004)

GOULD, CIRCUIT JUDGE:

... Seeking the opportunity of study, a group of scientists as Plaintiffs in this case brought an action ... challenging various Indian tribes' claim to one of the most important American anthropological and archaeological discoveries of the late twentieth century, and challenging the Interior Department's decision honoring the tribes' claim.... From the perspective of the scientists Plaintiffs, this skeleton is an irreplaceable source of information about early New World populations that warrants careful scientific inquiry to advance knowledge of distant times. Yet, from the perspective of the intervenor-Indian tribes the skeleton is that of an ancestor who, according to the tribes' religious and social traditions, should be buried immediately without further testing.

* * *

... NAGPRA mandates a two-part analysis. The first inquiry is whether human remains are Native American within the statute's meaning. If the remains are not Native American, then NAGPRA does not apply. However, if the remains are Native American, then NAGPRA applies, triggering the second inquiry of determining which persons or tribes are most closely affiliated with the remains.

The parties dispute whether the remains of Kennewick Man constitute Native American remains within NAGPRA's meaning. NAGPRA defines human remains as "Native American" if the remains are "of, or relating to, a tribe, people, or culture that is indigenous to the United States." The text of the relevant statutory clause is written in the present tense ("of, or relating to, a tribe, people, or culture that is indigenous"). Thus the statute unambiguously requires that human remains bear some relationship to a presently existing tribe, people, or culture to be considered Native American.

* * *

Our conclusion that NAGPRA's language requires that human remains, to be considered Native American, bear some relationship to a presently existing tribe, people, or culture accords with NAGPRA's purposes. As regards newly discovered human remains, NAGPRA was enacted with two main goals: to respect the burial traditions of modern-day American Indians and to protect the dignity of the human body after death. NAGPRA was intended to benefit modern American Indians by sparing them the indignity and resentment that would be aroused by the despoiling of their ancestors' graves and the study or the display of their ancestors' remains.

Congress's purposes would not be served by requiring the transfer to modern American Indians of human remains that bear no relationship to them. Yet, that would be the result under the [tribal] construction of the statute, which would give Native American status to any remains found within the United States regardless of age and regardless of lack of connection to existing indigenous tribes. The exhumation, study, and display of ancient human remains that are unrelated to modern American Indians was not a target of Congress's aim, nor was it precluded by NAGPRA.

NAGPRA was also intended to protect the dignity of the human body after death by ensuring that Native American graves and remains be treated with respect. Congress's purpose is served by requiring the return to modern-day American Indians of human remains that bear some significant relationship to them.

* * *

... We hold that ... NAGPRA requires that human remains bear a significant relationship to a presently existing tribe, people, or culture to be considered Native American. . . .

... Under the [tribal nations'] view of NAGPRA, all graves and remains of persons, predating European settlers, that are found in the United States would be "Native American," in the sense that they presumptively would be viewed as remains of a deceased from a tribe "indigenous" to the United States, even if the tribe had ceased to exist thousands of years before the remains were found, and even if there was no showing of any relationship of the remains to some existing tribe indigenous to the United States. . . . If accepted, [this] interpretation would mean that the finding of any remains in the United States in and of itself would automatically render these remains "Native American.". . . [W]e cannot conclude that Congress intended an absurd result. . . .

* * *

The age of Kennewick Man's remains, given the limited studies to date, makes it almost impossible to establish any relationship between the remains and presently existing American Indians. At least no significant relationship has yet been shown. We cannot give credence to an interpretation of NAGPRA advanced by the government and the Tribal Claimants that would apply its provisions to remains that have at most a tenuous, unknown, and unproven connection, asserted solely because of the geographical location of the find.

* * *

The administrative record contains no evidence—let alone substantial evidence—that Kennewick Man's remains are connected by some special or significant genetic or cultural relationship to any presently existing indigenous tribe, people, or culture. An examination of the record demonstrates the absence of evidence that Kennewick Man and modern tribes share significant genetic or cultural features.

* * *

The Secretary's only evidence, perhaps, of a possible cultural relationship between Kennewick Man and modern-day American Indians comes in the form of oral histories. One [expert], Dr. Daniel Boxberger, concluded that modern day Plateau tribes' oral histories—some of which can be interpreted to refer to ancient floods, volcanic eruptions, and the like—are "highly suggestive of long-term establishment of the present-day tribes." Stated another way, Dr. Boxberger noted that oral traditions showed no necessary tale of a superseding migration with newer peoples displacing older ones. But evidence in the record demonstrates that oral histories change relatively quickly, that oral histories may be based on later observation of geological features and deduction (rather than on the first teller's witnessing ancient events), and that these oral histories might be from a culture or group other than the one to which Kennewick Man belonged. The oral traditions relied upon by the . . . expert, Dr. Boxberger, entail some published accounts of Native American folk narratives from the Columbia Plateau region, and statements from individual tribal members. But we conclude that these accounts are just not specific enough or reliable enough or relevant enough to show a significant relationship of the Tribal Claimants with Kennewick Man. Because oral accounts have been inevitably changed in context of transmission, because the traditions include myths that cannot be considered as if factual histories, because the value of such accounts is limited by concerns of authenticity, reliability, and accuracy, and because the record as a whole does not show where historical fact ends and mythic tale begins, we do not think that the oral traditions of interest to Dr. Boxberger were adequate to show the required significant relationship of the Kennewick Man's remains to the Tribal Claimants. As the district court observed, 8340 to 9200 years between the life of Kennewick Man and the present is too long a time to bridge merely with evidence of oral traditions.

* * *

At its most basic, *Bonnichsen v. U.S.* demonstrates the two-part standard that American courts use to determine if an object or human remains fall under NAGPRA. First, the court will ask if the object or remains are "Native American" as defined by the statute. If they are not "Native American" as defined by NAGPRA, then the inquiry ends and NAGPRA does not apply. In order to be "Native American" under the statute, the object or remains must "bear a significant relationship to a presently existing tribe, people, or culture." If the object or remains are "Native American," then the court asks which person or tribal nation is most clearly affiliated with them.

Beyond the law in the case, *Bonnichsen* is also useful for understanding the debate about NAGPRA as well as the difficulties that Native peoples continue to face in American courts. Despite the location of The Ancient One's remains, there was some question as to their origin as the case was being decided. Thus, as a threshold question before deciding whether NAGPRA did or did not apply, the courts in the case had to determine what sort of evidence it would use to determine how to decide whether NAGPRA applied. In making this determination, the courts rejected the oral evidence presented by the tribal nations, with the Ninth Circuit describing it as "not specific enough or reliable enough or relevant enough." As has often been the case, tribal epistemologies were not able to overcome the standards set by American courts. Consequently, the methods and knowledge produced by the scientists who wanted to study The Ancient One were given more weight and carried the day in the case.

The ruling in *Bonnichsen* was the end of the litigation and it paved the way for further testing on The Ancient One. The scientists who began the legal proceedings performed their testing in 2005 and published an edited volume about their findings in 2014. In the period after the litigation, improved testing methods for determining the origin of human remains were developed, and in 2015 a group of researchers from the University of Copenhagen determined through DNA testing that The Ancient One was more closely related to modern Native peoples than any other group. In the wake of this determination, The Ancient One was returned to a coalition of tribal nations from the region and was reburied in a private location in 2017. The Ancient One's long journey demonstrates the possibilities and difficulties that surround NAGPRA and legislation like it.

CULTURAL APPROPRIATION AND ART

One of the most deceptively pernicious and pervasive difficulties facing Native peoples historically and today is that of cultural appropriation. For centuries colonizers have adopted "Indian" images, practices, and other characteristics to suit their own ends. For example, some of the participants in one of the most famous events of the American Revolution, the Boston Tea Party, dressed up as Native peoples. These revolutionaries did so both to hide their true identities and to symbolically express their separation from England as they threw tea into the Boston Harbor, thereby appropriating an "Indian" identity as both a disguise and a symbol. Such acts of cultural appropriation, reflecting a wide range of colonial motivations but generally having little to do with actual Native peoples, have been common both before and since the Boston Tea Party. Even today Native peoples are confronted on an everyday basis by those who use "Indian" imagery to fit their own needs, often with no regard for the effects of those uses on Native America. For example, whereas it is difficult to find representations in popular culture of actual Native peoples living in the present, it is easy to find stereotypical "Indian" images in advertising, in sports, and in movies and television as well as many other places. In fact, when one begins to actively look for "Indian" imagery it becomes easy to recognize how pervasive this cultural appropriation is in the United States. There is a wide array of negative consequences to this cultural appropriation for Native peoples; this is so even if the "Indian" representation is supposed to be positive or meant innocently or even beneficially.

While cultural appropriation affects all Native peoples in one way or another, it can be particularly devastating for Native artists. Beyond the stereotypes that cultural appropriation fundamentally perpetuates, the Native art market has been regularly harmed by "Indian" art produced by non-Native individuals and companies. By the late twentieth century, the field became rife with counterfeits and imposters attempting to profit from "Indian" art. Products produced by non-Natives that were falsely represented as authentically Native drove the market down for actual Native artists, created disincentives to learn artmaking skills, furthered the acceptance of cultural appropriation, and often made Native artists feel as if they were only able to create pieces of art that fit certain predeterminations of what Native artists were expected to make.

As with NAGPRA, Native activists were able to secure legislation intended to protect Native artists and the Native art market. Also passed in 1990, the Indian Arts and Crafts Act (IACA) is similar to NAGPRA in that it limits the ability of non-Natives to engage with artifacts that are produced or otherwise belong to Native individuals and nations. As you read the statute, ask yourself how it limits non-Natives. Who can bring a claim under IACA? What are the potential penalties for violating IACA? What does IACA cover and what does it not cover?

INDIAN ARTS AND CRAFTS ACT OF 1990
25 U.S.C.A § 305, § 305a, § 305d, and § 305e

§ 305

A board is created in the Department of the Interior to be known as "Indian Arts and Crafts Board" and hereinafter referred to as the Board.

* * *

§ 305a

It shall be the function and duty of the Secretary of the Interior through the Board to promote the economic welfare of the Indian tribes and Indian individuals through the development of Indian arts and crafts and the expansion of the market for the products of Indian art and craftsmanship. In the execution of this function the Board shall have the following powers: (a) To undertake market research to determine the best opportunity for the sale of various products; (b) to engage in technical research and give technical advice and assistance...; (e) to offer assistance in the management of operating groups for the furtherance of specific projects; (f) to make recommendations to appropriate agencies for loans in furtherance of the production and sale of Indian products. ...

* * *

§ 305d—Criminal proceedings; civil actions

* * *

(b) Authority to conduct investigations

Any Federal law enforcement law officer shall have the authority to conduct an investigation relating to an alleged violation of this Act occurring within the jurisdiction of the United States

(c) Criminal proceedings

* * *

(3) Recommendations

On receiving the findings of an investigation . . . the Board may—

    (A) Recommend to the Attorney General that criminal proceedings be initiated

    (B) Provide such support to the Attorney General relating to the criminal proceedings

* * *

(d) Civil actions

In lieu of, or in addition to, any criminal proceeding . . . the Board may recommend that the Attorney General initiate a civil action. ...

§ 305e—Cause of action for misrepresentation of Indian produced goods

(a) DEFINITIONS In this section:

    (1) INDIAN The term "Indian" means an individual that—

        (A) is a member of an Indian tribe; or

        (B) is certified as an Indian artisan by an Indian tribe.

    (2) INDIAN PRODUCT The term "Indian product" has the meaning given the term in any regulation promulgated by the Secretary.

(3) INDIAN TRIBE

(A) In general The term "Indian tribe" has the meaning given [in another statute]

(B) Inclusion The term "Indian tribe" includes, for purposes of this section only, an Indian group that has been formally recognized as an Indian tribe by—

(i) a State legislature;

(ii) a State commission; or

(iii) another similar organization vested with State legislative tribal recognition authority. . . .

(b) INJUNCTIVE OR EQUITABLE RELIEF; DAMAGES A person specified in subsection (d) may, in a civil action in a court of competent jurisdiction, bring an action against a person who, directly or indirectly, offers or displays for sale or sells a good, with or without a Government trademark, in a manner that falsely suggests it is Indian produced, an Indian product, or the product of a particular Indian or Indian tribe or Indian arts and crafts organization. . . .

* * *

(d) PERSONS THAT MAY INITIATE CIVIL ACTIONS

(1) IN GENERAL A civil action under subsection (b) may be initiated by—

(A) the Attorney General, at the request of the Secretary acting on behalf of—

(i) an Indian tribe;

(ii) an Indian; or

(iii) an Indian arts and crafts organization;

(B) an Indian tribe, acting on behalf of—

(i) the Indian tribe;

(ii) a member of that Indian tribe; or

(iii) an Indian arts and crafts organization;

(C) an Indian; or

(D) an Indian arts and crafts organization.

* * *

The criminal penalties for a violation of IACA can be significant. First time violators can be fined up to $250,000 and five years in jail if the violator is an individual, or a violator can be fined up to $1,000,000 if the violator is not an individual, such as an auction house, art gallery, or other business. Repeat violators can be sentenced to up to fifteen years in jail if the violator is an individual and fined up to $5,000,000 if the violator is not an individual.[1]

IACA also establishes a federal agency, the Indian Arts and Craft Board, to further the goals of the statute. However, this board is not the only entity capable of enforcing the provisions of IACA. The statute also authorizes the attorney general of the United States to bring either a criminal charge or a civil complaint or both against an alleged violator of IACA. Somewhat uniquely, the statute also allows for a tribal nation, a Native individual, or an Indian arts and crafts organization to bring a civil complaint against an alleged violator of the IACA. This wide-ranging enforceability gives Native America an important tool to protect itself from the fraud and counterfeit product that had become rampant in the art market.

Despite its strengths and benefits for Native America, and again like NAGPRA, IACA is not without controversy. It is certainly difficult, if not impossible, for any statute to define who or what is an "Indian" or an "Indian product" with absolute certainty. Questions of identity, particularly Native identity, are inherently tricky and American law has struggled in other contexts with finding an adequate measure of Indianness (see Chapter 13). This challenge is perhaps even more so in the world of art, as artists regularly defy conventions, push boundaries, challenge traditional ways of thinking, and mix styles, techniques, and genres with regularity. Some critics of IACA have found the statutory and regulatory definitions of words and concepts such as "Indian" or "Indian product" too narrow; other critics argue that those definitions are too broad. The debate around IACA has also raised questions over just how much content a community or individual can own or keep for its own as it concerns artistic expression. For example, what claim, if any, could a tribal nation make to a certain style or design? Furthermore, is it possible that IACA violates the 1st Amendment freedom of expression of non-Indians? Put another way, is cultural appropriation constitutionally protected under the 1st Amendment?

The following case confronts some of these questions and offers guidance as to what IACA covers and what it does not cover. IACA does not define "Indian product" itself, but authorizes the Secretary of the Interior to define the term in the federal regulations that guide the application of IACA. As you read the case, ask yourself how "Indian product" is defined in the guidelines. How does this definition offer greater insight into what IACA is trying to accomplish? What is the argument of the non-Native company in the case? How does the court understand the balance between the practices that IACA is seeking to protect and the constitutional rights of non-Natives? How does the court's decision engage with the issue of cultural appropriation?

NATIVE AMERICAN ARTS, INC. V. CONTRACT SPECIALTIES, INC.

754 F.Supp.2d 386 (2010)

WILLIAM E. SMITH, DISTRICT JUDGE.

* * *

Plaintiff Native American Arts, Inc. ("NAA") is a wholly Indian-owned organization that manufactures and sells Indian arts and crafts. Defendant Contract Specialties, Inc. ("Specialties") is a Rhode Island corporation that sells arts and crafts, including those made in an Indian style. NAA has sued Specialties for violations of the [IACA] which forbids the offer or sale of a good in a manner that falsely suggests it is an Indian-made product.

The single-count complaint alleges that from March 15, 2006 onward, Specialties has advertised, marketed, and sold its non-Indian-made products nationwide in a manner that falsely suggests they are Indian-made. These products include charms, barrettes, bracelets, earrings, and various other bibelots and things, some sixty samples of which are recited in the complaint. According to the complaint, Specialties falsely suggested that its non-Indian-made products were in fact Indian-made by, among other things, advertising them using the label "Indian" and names of tribes such as "Apache," "Navajo," "Kiowa," and "Cree." These terms were used without qualifiers or disclaimers to alert potential buyers that the goods were not really made by Indians or members of these tribes.

According to the complaint, NAA and Specialties compete for the sale of similar products made in an Indian style—NAA's being authentic and Specialties' fake—such that NAA "has suffered competitive injuries as a result of" Specialties' activities. Specifically, Specialties' marketing and sales of its fake Indian-made products have allegedly eaten away at NAA's sales, driven down the price of NAA's products, and damaged NAA's goodwill and reputation. NAA contends that these actions violate the IACA. . . .

Specialties moves to dismiss the complaint because . . . (3) the IACA runs afoul of the First Amendment; and (4) the IACA contravenes the equal protection clause of the Fifth Amendment. . . .

The IACA is a truth-in-advertising statute aimed at ensuring that products marketed and sold as "Indian" are actually Indian. Congress enacted it in 1990 in response to concerns that a significant portion of the national market for "Indian" products was made up of counterfeit products, and that existing state and federal laws . . . were ineffective in curbing the flood. For example, a 1985 Commerce Department report to Congress "estimated that unmarked import imitations of Indian arts and crafts are siphoning off 10 to 20 percent of the market for genuine handicrafts produced domestically," then worth an annual $400–$800 million. Congress concluded that the influx of fake Indian products had reduced demand for the real thing, driven down the price of authentic Indian wares, tainted consumer confidence in the integrity of the market, and dissuaded young Indians from learning and practicing time-honored ways of artisanship that were an important cultural heritage. And "[w]ith Native communities plagued by unemployment and stagnant economies, the flood of fake Indian arts and crafts is decimating one of the few forms of entrepreneurship and economic development on Indian reservations."

* * *

Section 305e(b) of the IACA provides, among other things, a cause and right of action against a person who offers or sells a good in a manner that falsely suggests it is an "Indian product." The meaning of "Indian product" is determined under regulations promulgated by the Secretary of the Interior. The pertinent regulation provides, "[t]he term 'Indian product' means any art or craft product made by an Indian." Then, in a subsection entitled "Illustrations," the regulation states that the term "includes, but is not limited to . . . Art made by an Indian that is in a traditional or non-traditional style or medium."

Specialties argues that the statute and the regulation permit criminal liability "simply [for] creating artwork in the traditional or nontraditional Indian style or medium." According to Specialties, because it is not clear what a "traditional or nontraditional Indian style or medium" is, and because artistic expression is protected by the First Amendment, the statute is vague and overbroad and violative of the First Amendment.

Specialties' interpretation of the regulation is wrong. The regulation mentions art "made by an Indian that is in a traditional or non-traditional style or medium" as an "illustration" of an "Indian product,"; nowhere does it say that every product made "in a traditional or non-traditional style or medium" is, or is pretended to be, an "Indian product." Indeed, the regulation goes on to state, in a part Specialties does not quote, that "[a]n 'Indian product' under the Act does not include . . . [a] product in the style of an Indian art or craft product made by non-Indian labor." This is like saying that a Persian artifact is an artifact made by a Persian, and mentioning a Persian carpet with a rosette motif as an illustration—which certainly would not mean that every non-Persian who makes a rosette-motif carpet is trying to pass it off as a Persian carpet. There is thus no merit to Specialties' contention that a person may be liable under the IACA simply for making a product in an Indian style.

The Court has no trouble dismissing this threadbare First Amendment challenge to the IACA, as other courts have done.

Specialties [also] argues that the IACA is "race-conscious" legislation because it "grants Native Americans a right not enjoyed by other Americans, that is, a right to the protection of a special ethnic-based trademark for its style of goods that is not available to any other race or ethnicity." As such, Specialties argues, the IACA should be subjected to strict scrutiny, a test it cannot survive.

But the Supreme Court has established that statutes providing for special treatment of Indians will not be disturbed "[a]s long as the special treatment can be tied rationally to the fulfillment of Congress' unique obligation toward the Indians."

It is clear that Congress was concerned about the heavy flow of counterfeit Indian products, and attempted to stem that tide by enacting the IACA and imposing stringent damages for counterfeiting and false advertising. Thus, the IACA undoubtedly survives rational basis review. Specialties' equal protection challenge is meritless.

* * *

There are two main arguments that the non-Native company makes in this excerpt. First, according to the non-Native company, IACA violates the right to an individual's freedom of expression under the 1st Amendment. According to this reasoning, the non-Native company is under the threat of punishment for simply making products "in the traditional or nontraditional Indian style or medium." Therefore, the federal government has, according to the argument, criminalized certain types of artistic expressions. Since the 1st Amendment prohibits the federal government from limiting the free expression of individuals in this manner, the IACA is unconstitutional. In short, under the non-Native company's rationale, the federal government cannot censor art in this manner.

Describing this argument as "threadbare," the court recognized that IACA and the Secretary of the Interior's regulations do not do what the non-Native company claimed that they do. The key focal point, the court noted, is not the art itself or even the artist. It is how the art and artist is represented by the seller. The Secretary defined an "Indian product" as "any art or craft product made by an Indian." Furthermore, the Secretary's regulations go on to note that "[a] product in the style of an Indian art or craft product made by non-Indian labor" is not an "Indian product" under the statute, and thus not subject to penalty under the statute. Consequently, the act that IACA prohibits is not making art, but rather claiming that works made by non-Natives are "Indian products." Put another way, IACA does not criminalize or prohibit cultural appropriation, but it does criminalize and prohibit falsely identifying products not made by Native sources as authentically Indian art.

The second argument that the non-Native company makes in this excerpt is a challenge to the constitutionality of the IACA. According to the non-Native company, that IACA is a "race-conscious" statute that cannot survive "strict scrutiny," a high level of judicial review. Strict scrutiny is typically the test that American courts use when a statute affects a "suspect class" of people, including racial groups. The type of review that federal statutes concerning Native peoples undergo in judicial proceedings and the balance between racial and political classifications is given greater attention in Chapter 10. For the purposes of this chapter, it suffices to note that the court acknowledges that the Supreme Court has rejected strict scrutiny as the appropriate test for statutes involving Native peoples, including the IACA. Instead the court uses the "rational basis" test. Under the rational basis test, a law must be rationally related to a legitimate governmental interest to be recognized as constitutional. This is a very low barrier to cross, and, as this court determined, IACA is rationally related to the legitimate governmental pursuit of protecting the Native art market. Therefore it is constitutionally sound law.

The fight for tribal sovereignty is fought on a number of fronts and over a number of issues, including those that might seem to have little to do with law and politics at first glance. Nonetheless, these unexpected arenas can hold the most meaning for the parties involved. NAGPRA and IACA are two of the most prominent pieces of legislation of the Self-Determination Era to attempt to strengthen tribal cultural practices and identity. Both statutes and others like them are a response to the many previous efforts of the federal government and other reformers to destroy tribal ways of life, most particularly during the Allotment Era. However, both also reflect the ongoing difficulties of reaffirming tribal sovereignty within the colonial context. In addition, there are several other spaces where similar battles are taking place: "Indian" mascots, advertising, and other forms of intellectual property to name a few. As long as cultural practices and products remain tools by which to measure sovereignty, they will remain within American courtrooms and the halls of Congress.

SUGGESTED READINGS

- *Grave Injustice: The American Indian Repatriation Movement and NAGPRA.* Kathleen S. Fine-Dare. Lincoln, NE: University of Nebraska Press, 2002.

- *The Arbitrary Indian: The Indian Arts and Crafts Act of 1990.* Gail K. Sheffield. Norman, OK: University of Oklahoma Press, 1997.

- "American Indian and Tribal Intellectual Property Rights." Robert J. Miller. 13 *Tulane Journal of Technology and Intellectual Property* 179 (Fall 2010).

---

[1] 18 U.S.C.A. § 1159.

CHAPTER 26

Natural Resources

Native peoples have long been associated with a connection to the natural world. Oftentimes this connection has been described as spiritual in nature, which is certainly accurate, but which sometimes leads to overly simplistic stereotypes that can ignore a fundamental truth: Native peoples have cherished and been in connection with the natural world because the natural world has provided the resources that Native peoples have needed to survive. Put another way, the kinship that Native peoples have cultivated with the natural world has nourished the body primarily and fundamentally, as well as the soul.

To that end, Native peoples have been deeply concerned with protecting their access to the natural resources upon which they have needed to live since their first engagements with colonizers. It is why so many treaties protect access to valuable hunting and fishing grounds outside of reservations. It is also why Native peoples and nations have sought increased recognition and protection of their access to natural resources in both the courts and Congress. Tribal nations have had some success on this front and are now regularly explicitly included in federal environmental legislation.

Of course, colonizing forces have sought access to natural resources as well—it was often the impetus for colonizing in the first place. Questions over who could claim control over or access to natural resources have been a part of the engagement between Native America and colonists from the beginning. As issues of climate change and environmental law become increasingly important in today's world, these questions are likely to only become even more imperative. Water, air, land, and more remain fundamental to Native America for deeply practical as well as spiritual and religious reasons.

This chapter will demonstrate. . .

- *The basic parameters of water rights for tribal nations*

- *The impact of federal environmental legislation in Indian Country*

- *The engagement between tribal nations and states concerning natural resources*

WATER AND THE *WINTERS* DOCTRINE

Water is life. Those who have easy and affordable access to it can sometimes forget this simple truth.

As the United States rapidly expanded westward in the nineteenth century, particularly into the arid Southwest, water was often as valuable as land to the colonizers, and sometimes more so. It made settlement, agriculture, travel, and more possible. As with land, settlers wanted ownership of as much water as possible, with Native peoples and claims regularly regarded as little more than annoyances to be quickly dismissed or disregarded altogether. When the United States accelerated the creation of reservations in the second half of the nineteenth century, the purpose was to provide settlers access to water just as much as land.

Native peoples, fully understanding how important this resource was to their survival, sought to protect their own claims to water, generally first through treaties and then the courts. In the Allotment Era (see Chapter 5), the federal government was occasionally sympathetic to these efforts and sought to protect Native interests in its role under the trust responsibility (see Chapter 14).

The following case, decided in the heart of the Allotment Era, set forth one of the most important principles of federal Indian law: the *Winters* doctrine. The facts of the case are relatively simple. In 1888 the federal government established the Fort Belknap Indian Reservation—now occupied by the Nakoda and Aaniiih Nations (also known as the Assiniboine and Gros Ventre) in north central Montana, with the Milk River as its northern boundary. In 1900, non-Native settlers living outside of the reservation began diverting large amounts of water from the Milk River, leaving too little for the needs of the people of the Fort Belknap Reservation. The federal government sued the non-Native settlers on behalf of the tribal interests. As you read the case, ask yourself what fundamental principle of law the Supreme Court sets forth. What interests are at stake? What is the most important event in the case? What rationale does the Court utilize to justify the establishment of what has become known as the *Winters* doctrine?

WINTERS V. U.S.
207 U.S. 564 (1908)

Statement by MR. JUSTICE MCKENNA.

This suit was brought by the United States to restrain [non-Native settlers] from constructing or maintaining dams or reservoirs on the Milk River in the state of Montana, or in any manner preventing the water of the river or its tributaries from flowing to the Fort Belknap Indian Reservation.

* * *

[The important facts are]: On the 1st day of May 1888, a tract of land . . . was reserved and set apart "as an Indian reservation . . . known as the Fort Belknap Indian Reservation." The tract has ever since been used as an Indian reservation and as the home and abiding place of the Indians. . . .

* * *

It is alleged that, "notwithstanding the . . . rights" of the United States and the Indians to the uninterrupted flow of the waters of the river, the [non-Native settlers] . . . wrongfully entered upon the river and its tributaries above the points of the diversion of the waters of the river by the United States and the Indians, built large and substantial dams and reservoirs, and, by means of canals and ditches and water ways, have diverted the waters of the river from its channel, and have deprived the United States and the Indians of the use thereof. . . .

[The non-Native settlers argue] that the waters of the river are indispensible to [them] . . . and that if they are deprived of the waters "their lands will be ruined, it will be necessary to abandon their homes, and they will be greatly and irreparably damaged. . . .

MR. JUSTICE MCKENNA, after making the foregoing statement, delivered the opinion of the court.

* * *

The case, as we view it, turns on the agreement of May, 1888, resulting in the creation of Fort Belknap Reservation. In the construction of this agreement there are certain elements to be considered that are prominent and significant. The reservation was a part of a very much larger tract which the Indians had the right to occupy and use and which was adequate for the habits and wants of a nomadic and uncivilized people. It was the policy of the Government, it was the desire of the Indians, to change those habits and to become a pastoral and civilized people. If they should become such the original tract was too extensive, but a smaller tract would be inadequate without a change of conditions. The lands were arid and, without irrigation, were practically valueless. And yet, it is contended, the means of irrigation were deliberately given up by the Indians and deliberately accepted by the Government. The lands ceded were, it is true, also arid; and some argument may be urged, and is urged, that with their cession there was the cession of the waters, without which they would be valueless, and "civilized communities could not be established thereon." And this, it is further contended, the Indians knew, and yet made no reservation of the waters. We realize that there is a conflict of implications, but that which makes for the retention of the waters is of greater force than that which makes for their cession. The Indians had command of the lands and the waters—command of all their beneficial use, whether kept for hunting, "and grazing roving herds of stock," or turned to agriculture and the arts of civilization. Did they give up all this? Did they reduce the area of their occupation and give up the waters which made it valuable or adequate?. . . . By a rule of interpretation of agreements and treaties with the Indians, ambiguities occurring will be resolved from the standpoint of the Indians. And the rule should certainly be applied to determine between two inferences, one of which would support the purpose of the agreement and the other impair or defeat it. On account of their relations to the Government, it cannot be supposed that the Indians were alert to exclude by formal words every inference which might militate against or defeat the declared purpose of themselves and the Government, even if it could be supposed that they had the intelligence to foresee the "double sense" which might some time be urged against them.

Another contention of appellants is that if it be conceded that there was a reservation of the waters of Milk River by the agreement of 1888, yet the reservation was repealed by the admission of Montana into the Union, February 22, 1889, "upon an equal footing with the original States.". . . But to establish the repeal counsel rely substantially upon the same argument that they advance against the intention of the agreement to reserve the waters. The power of the Government to reserve the waters and exempt them from appropriation under the state laws is not denied, and could not be. That the Government did reserve them we have decided, and for a use which would be necessarily continued through years. This was done May 1, 1888, and it would be extreme to believe that within a year Congress destroyed the reservation and

> took from the Indians the consideration of their grant, leaving them a barren waste—took from them the means of continuing their old habits, yet did not leave them the power to change to new ones.
>
> * * *

Of the few victories for tribal interests at the Supreme Court in the Allotment Era, *Winters* may very well be the most important. The principle of law that emerges from this case—known as the *Winters* doctrine—is that tribal reservations of land are also reservations of water rights. This is regardless of whether the treaty, agreement, or other mechanism establishing a reservation does or does not expressly reserve those water rights. Water rights are inherently a part of the reservation that a tribal nation maintains when reserving lands.

In making this ruling the Court had to contend with the "equal footing" doctrine—a principle of American law that states that newly admitted states of the union have all of the same rights and privileges as all of the other states of the union. The equal footing doctrine has been a recurring argument in federal Indian law litigation and still occasionally makes appearances in contemporary cases. In general, states have a significant amount of authority to regulate the natural resources within their borders and the non-Native settlers argued that the state of Montana became the true holder and distributor of the water rights in question when it was admitted to the union in 1889. However, as the Court stated, "The power of the [federal] Government to reserve the waters and exempt them from appropriation under the state laws is not denied, and could not be." According to the Court, the federal government reserved those rights in 1888, when the Fort Belknap Reservation was established. Consequently, the authority over those rights was not transferred to Montana when it was admitted to the union one year later. Thus, the date upon which a reservation is established is often critical to determining if tribal water rights have been reserved.

Ever since its announcement, tribal nations have relied on the *Winters* doctrine to protect their rights and access to much needed water, particularly in the more arid Western states. The doctrine has been a critical tool for tribal interests. Yet, the decision in *Winters*—and thus the doctrine itself—is also characteristic of the troubling foundations for many of the victories for tribal nations at the Supreme Court, particularly the few that occurred in the Allotment Era. It is a double-edged sword that rests upon certain notions about the capacities of Native peoples and the obligations of the federal government.

On the one hand, *Winters* was an undeniable victory for Native America. In addition, Justice Joseph McKenna's opinion demonstrated an effective use of the

Indian canons of construction (see Chapter 11) to read the treaty in the favor of the tribal interests. On the other hand, it is easy to interpret the case as a victory for the federal government and the goals of the Allotment Era more than anything else. According to McKenna, "It was the policy of the Government, it was the desire of the Indians, to change [their tribal] habits and to become a pastoral and civilized people." It is questionable just how much the tribal peoples of the Fort Belknap Reservation desired to "become . . . pastoral and civilized." What is less questionable was the federal government's efforts to destroy Native ways of life during the Allotment Era. More specifically, the federal government sought to make farmers out of the Nakoda and Aaniiih at Fort Belknap, and of many other peoples elsewhere in Indian Country. Since significant amounts of water are critical to agriculture, it is worthy to consider how much the decision in *Winters*— and the *Winters* doctrine itself—hinges on furthering the destructive goals of the Allotment Era. While McKenna's opinion does discuss Native interpretations of agreement that led to the reservation, none of the discussion is couched in terms of tribal sovereignty. Rather, it is primarily about the need to preserve water rights for Native peoples so that they can become "civilized" farmers. The decision in *Winters* presumes that Allotment Era policies that sought to end tribal ways of life were positive or at least necessary. Under this premise, the Court made the logical leap of needing to preserve water rights for the reservation in order to turn Native individuals into farmers. To what extent, if any, does the rationale for the victory for tribal interests in *Winters* undermine the victory itself?

Despite the troubling foundation upon which it was built, *Winters* made clear that reservations of land inherently included water rights. Yet, this raises another question: how much water? Put differently, how much water can a reservation claim under the *Winters* doctrine?

The Supreme Court tackled this question in *Arizona v. California*, a decades-long dispute over access to water in the Southwest. As noted above, in general states have a tremendous amount of authority over the natural resources within their borders. However, natural resources, such as rivers, lakes, or underground reservoirs, are not always contained within a single state's borders, and the resource allocation of one state can have a significant impact on another state. Although only Arizona and California are named in the title of the case, the actual dispute—which has resulted in multiple Supreme Court and other court opinions—involved a number of states in the Southwest as well as the federal government and several tribal nations. The basic issue in the case was how to allocate water from the Colorado River and its tributaries among the interested parties. The federal Indian law aspect of the case is just one part of a multi-layered, complicated litigation.

In order to understand the result for tribal interests in this case, it is useful to have some knowledge the doctrine of equitable apportionment. This judicially created doctrine of law is meant to resolve disputes between two or more states claiming access to water that crosses state borders. If the demand for water by two or more states is greater than what the resource—typically a river—can provide, then the court must divide the resource in an equitable manner considering all of the needs of the various users.

As you read the case, ask yourself what rule the Supreme Court established for determining how much water reservations should be allocated. How does this rule compare and contrast to the doctrine of equitable apportionment? What rationale does the Court utilize for establishing this rule? How does the rule engage with the *Winters* decision and the origins of the *Winters* doctrine?

ARIZONA V. CALIFORNIA
373 U.S. 546 (1963)

MR. JUSTICE BLACK delivered the opinion of the Court.

* * *

In these proceedings, the United States has asserted claims to waters . . . for use on Indian Reservations. . . .

The Government, on behalf of five Indian Reservations in Arizona, California, and Nevada, asserted rights to water in the mainstream of the Colorado River. . . . Arizona argues that . . . the judicial doctrine of equitable apportionment should be used to divide the water between the Indians and the other people in the state of Arizona.

The last argument is easily answered. The doctrine of equitable apportionment is a method of resolving water disputes between States. . . . An Indian Reservation is not a State. And while Congress has sometimes left Indian Reservations considerable power to manage their own affairs, we are not convinced by Arizona's argument that each reservation is so much like a State that its rights to water should be determined by the doctrine of equitable apportionment. Moreover, even were we to treat an Indian Reservation like a State, equitable apportionment would still not control since, under our view, the Indian claims here are governed by the statutes and Executive Orders creating the reservations.

***

The Court in *Winters* concluded that the Government, when it created that Indian Reservation, intended to deal fairly with the Indians by reserving for them the waters without which their lands would have been useless. . . . We . . . agree that the United States did reserve the water rights for the Indians effective as of the time the Indian Reservations were created. . . .

We also agree with [an earlier judge's] conclusion as to the quantity of water intended to be reserved. [The earlier judge] found that the water was intended to satisfy the future as well as the present needs of the Indian Reservations and ruled that enough water was reserved to irrigate all the practically irrigable acreage on the reservation. Arizona, on the other hand, contends that the quantity of water reserved should be measured by the Indians' "reasonably foreseeable needs," which, in fact, means by the number of Indians. How many Indians there will be and what their future needs will be can only be guessed. We have concluded . . . that the only feasible and fair way by which reserved water for the reservations can be measured is irrigable acreage. . . .

***

Noting that a reservation was not the same as a state, Justice Hugo Black's opinion rejected the application of the doctrine of equitable apportionment for tribal lands. Rather, the Supreme Court decided that reservations are entitled to enough water to irrigate all of the "practically irrigable acreage" on the reservation. In the arid Southwest, this can be a significant amount, which has been a boon to tribal interests but has also often raised the ire of non-Native residents of the region. More theoretically, the "practically irrigable acreage" standard also harkens to the fundamental understanding in *Winters* of a reservation as a place where a Western method of agriculture is supposed to occur. Does this fundamental understanding—which has resulted in a generally positive legal standard for tribal interests—continue to reinforce the Allotment Era goals of the federal government? Or is the rule far enough removed from its theoretical origins that any negative connotations have been shed?

Disputes over water remain contentious, especially in the Southwest, and they are likely to continue in that region and in other parts of the country as well, as population growth, climate change, and other factors increase the demand. Neither the *Winters* doctrine nor the decision in *Arizona v. California* have completely eradicated challenges to tribal water rights. Nonetheless, both cases established the parameters around which those challenges are litigated.

Reservations of land inherently carry rights to water and the amount of water to which a reservation has access is measured by that reservation's practicably irrigable acreage.

FEDERAL ENVIRONMENTAL LEGISLATION

As noted in Chapter 10, during the Self-Determination Era, the federal government explicitly included tribal nations in much of the legislation intended to protect the environment. The benefits and potential drawbacks of this practice are discussed in greater detail in that chapter, and it is useful to review that section before continuing. For the purposes of this chapter, it will suffice to note that the Clean Air Act is a representative example of how tribal nations have been incorporated into major pieces of environmental legislation.

As you read this excerpt from the statute, ask yourself what it requires from a tribal nation. What standards does a tribal nation need to meet to come under the Clean Air Act? What else is required if the tribal nation meets those standards? What authority does the Administrator of the Environmental Protection Agency (EPA)—the federal agency tasked with carrying out the purposes of environmental legislation—have over tribal nations under the Act?

CLEAN AIR ACT
42 U.S.C.A §§ 7407 and 7601

§ 7407

(a) Responsibility of each State for air quality; submission of implementation plan

Each state shall have the primary responsibility for assuring air quality within the entire geographic area comprising such state by submitting an implementation plan for such State which will specify the manner in which . . . air quality standards will be achieved and maintained within [the] State.

* * *

§ 7601

(a) Regulations; delegation of powers and duties; regional officers and employees

    (1) The Administrator [of the Environmental Protection Agency] is authorized to prescribe such regulations as are necessary to carry out his functions under this chapter. . . .

(d) Tribal authority

(1) Subject to the provisions of paragraph (2), the Administrator—

(A) is authorized to treat Indian tribes as States under this chapter. . . .

(B) may provide any such Indian tribe grant and contract assistance to carry out functions provided by this chapter.

(2) The Administrator shall promulgate regulations . . . specifying those provisions of this chapter for which it is appropriate to treat Indian tribes as States. Such treatment shall be authorized only if—

(A) the Indian tribe has a governing body carrying out substantial governmental duties and powers;

(B) the functions to be exercised by the Indian tribe pertain to the management and protection of air resources within the exterior boundaries of the reservation or other areas within the tribe's jurisdiction; and

(C) the Indian tribe is reasonably expected to be capable, in the judgment of the Administrator, of carrying out the functions to be exercised in a manner consistent with the terms and purposes of this chapter and all applicable regulations.

(3) The Administrator may promulgate regulations which establish the elements of tribal implementation plans and procedures for approval or disapproval of tribal implementation plans and portions thereof.

(4) In any case in which the Administrator determines that the treatment of Indian tribes as identical to States is inappropriate or administratively infeasible, the Administrator may provide, by regulation, other means by which the Administrator will directly administer such provisions so as to achieve the appropriate purpose.

* * *

Like other pieces of environmental legislation, the Clean Air Act authorizes the federal government to treat tribes as if they were states under the statute. This authorization is subject to some noteworthy hurdles that tribal nations must overcome, including having to satisfy the judgment of the administrator of the EPA. In creating these hurdles, the Clean Air Act and similar pieces of legislation have sought to strike a balance between respecting tribal sovereignty and autonomy and recognizing that Indian Country is diverse and not all tribal nations will have the capability or want the responsibility of managing environmental matters. Should a tribal nation overcome the hurdles in the Clean Air Act, it then must, among other things, submit an implementation plan to control air quality in the same manner as a state.

The Clean Air Act, originally passed in 1963, was amended in 1990 to include the provisions that treat tribal nations like states under the statute. Under the amendments, the Administrator was required to create regulations to fulfill the obligation to treat tribal nations as states under the Act. Regulations act as an agency's guidelines on how it will interpret and enforce a law. In so doing, the EPA adopted a fairly wide scope of authority for tribal nations over lands, including over non-Native fee land within the reservation and over other areas of Indian Country not specifically within a reservation. Both the amendments that treated tribal nations as states and the regulations created by the EPA to fulfill this statutory mandate were eventually challenged in court, most prominently in *Arizona Public Service Co. v. EPA*.

In order to understand the decision in the case, it is important to have some knowledge of an important rule of administrative law: the *Chevron* doctrine. Congress passes hundreds of laws every year. Once a law is passed it is often up to the federal agencies within the Executive branch to enforce the law. With so many laws passed each year and so many more already on the books, it is inevitable that some laws will leave room for interpretation or explicitly authorize a federal agency to make certain choices. Others are simply ambiguous or otherwise difficult to interpret and apply. Consequently, federal agencies regularly have to make decisions about how to apply the law or make choices that have been purposely been left to the agency to make. Many times, a federal agency will write and publish regulations that demonstrate the agency's understanding and interpretation of a statute. When a party wants to challenge an agency's interpretation of a statute or its regulations in a lawsuit, the court will apply the *Chevron* doctrine.

Named after a famous case, the *Chevron* doctrine essentially states that if a statute is ambiguous or unclear, than a federal agency's interpretation of the statute is valid as long as the agency's interpretation is reasonable. Put another way, a court will first ask if a statute is clear or unclear concerning the point of controversy. If it is clear, than the court will follow what the statute says. If it is unclear then the court will ask if the agency's interpretation is reasonable or unreasonable. If it is reasonable (even if the court thinks the particular interpretation is unwise or bad policy) the court will let it stand. If the court finds the interpretation to be unreasonable, then the challenging party will win the case.

As you read the following case, ask yourself about the scope of the EPA's interpretation of the Clean Air Act. In what areas, under these interpretations, do tribal nations have authority to establish air quality standards? Why are these interpretations being challenged? What steps does the court take to determine a ruling in this case? How does the *Chevron* doctrine factor into the outcome of the case?

ARIZONA PUBLIC SERVICE CO. V. EPA
211 F.3d 1280 (2000)

HARRY T. EDWARDS, CHIEF JUDGE:

In 1990, Congress passed a compendium of amendments to the Clean Air Act ("CAA" or "the Act"). This case concerns those amendments that specifically address the power of Native American nations (or "tribes") to implement air quality regulations under the Act. Petitioners challenge the Environmental Protection Agency's ("EPA" or "the Agency") regulations, promulgated in 1998, implementing the 1990 Amendments. Petitioners' principal contention is that EPA has granted too much authority to tribes.

Petitioners' primary challenges focus on two issues. The first is whether Congress expressly delegated to Native American nations authority to regulate air quality on all land within reservations, including fee land held by private landowners who are not tribe members. The second is whether EPA has properly construed "reservation" to include trust lands and Pueblos.

* * *

The Act establishes a framework for a federal-state partnership to regulate air quality. The provisions of the 1990 Amendments under review, fairly read, constitute an attempt by Congress to increase the role of Native American nations in this partnership.

* * *

Importantly, the 1990 Amendments added language to the Act granting EPA the "author[ity] to treat Indian tribes as States under this chapter". . . .

The 1990 Amendments also directed EPA to promulgate regulations "specifying those provisions of this chapter for which it is appropriate to treat Indian tribes as States.". . . .

... On February 12, 1998, after receiving and responding to public comments, EPA issued [regulations]. The Agency first found that the 1990 Amendments constitute a delegation of federal authority to regulate air quality to Native American nations within the boundaries of reservations, regardless of whether the land is owned by the tribes. The Agency read the statute to support this "territorial view of tribal jurisdiction," authorizing a "tribal role for all air resources within the exterior boundaries of Indian reservations without distinguishing among various categories of onreservation land." EPA believed that this "territorial approach ... best advances rational, sound, air quality management." Thus, the Agency determined that Congress delegated to tribes the authority to regulate air quality in areas within the exterior boundaries of a reservation.

The Act does not define "reservation" for the purposes of tribal regulation. EPA interpreted "reservation" to include "trust lands that have been validly set apart for the use of a tribe even though the land has not been formally designated as a reservation." The Agency explained that this interpretation was consistent with the Supreme Court's definition of "reservation". . . .

For areas not within a "reservation," the Agency determined that a tribe would be allowed to regulate such areas if the tribe could demonstrate inherent jurisdiction over the particular non-reservation area under general principles of federal Indian law. This means that tribes may propose air quality regulations in "allotted land" and "dependent Indian communities" provided they can otherwise demonstrate inherent jurisdiction over these areas. Allotted land is land "owned by individual Indians and either held in trust by the United States or subject to a statutory restriction on alienation." Dependent Indian communities include "those tribal Indian communities under federal protection that did not originate in either a federal or tribal act of 'reserving,' or were not specifically designated a reservation."

* * *

... EPA contends that the 1990 Amendments constitute an express congressional delegation to the tribes of the authority to regulate air quality on fee lands located within the exterior boundaries of a reservation.

... Our review of the CAA indicates that EPA's interpretation comports with congressional intent.

Section 7601(d), in pertinent part, authorizes EPA to treat otherwise eligible tribes as states if "the functions to be exercised by the Indian tribe pertain to the management and protection of air resources within the exterior boundaries of the reservation or other areas within the tribe's jurisdiction." The statute's clear distinction between areas "within the exterior boundaries of the reservation" and "other areas within the tribe's jurisdiction" carries with it the implication that Congress considered the areas within the exterior boundaries of a tribe's reservation to be per se within the tribe's jurisdiction. Thus, EPA correctly interpreted § 7601(d) to express congressional intent to grant tribal jurisdiction over nonmember owned fee land within a reservation without the need to determine, on a case-specific basis, whether a tribe possesses "inherent sovereign power". . . .

Finally, we note that the legislative history of the 1990 Amendments supports EPA's interpretation. . . . The statute as finally enacted . . . treats tribes and states as equivalent if the tribe is to exercise functions "within the exterior boundaries of the reservation or other areas within the tribe's jurisdiction."

Thus, Congress moved from authorizing tribal regulation over the areas "within the tribal government's jurisdiction" (an admittedly general category) to a bifurcated classification of all areas within "the exterior boundaries of the reservation" and "other areas within the tribe's jurisdiction.". . . The fact that Congress specifically rejected language favorable to petitioners' position and enacted instead language that is consistent with EPA's interpretation only strengthens our conclusion that the Agency has correctly ascertained Congress' intent in passing the 1990 Amendments.

* * *

Given that EPA correctly interpreted § 7601(d) to expressly delegate jurisdiction to otherwise eligible tribes over all land within the exterior boundaries of reservations, including fee land, the next question is what areas are covered by a "reservation." EPA interprets "reservation" . . . to mean formally designated reservations as well as "trust lands that have been validly set apart for the use of a tribe even though the land has not been formally designated as a reservation." This includes what EPA terms "Pueblos" and tribal trust land. Pueblos are villages, primarily located in New Mexico, held by tribes in communal fee-simple ownership, originally acquired under grants from Spain and Mexico, and confirmed by Congress in the late 1800s. Petitioners ignore the status of Pueblos and concentrate their attack on EPA's interpretation of "reservation" to include tribal trust land.

* * *

We start with Chevron step one and rely on traditional principles of statutory construction to determine whether EPA's interpretation contravenes congressional intent as manifested by the 1990 Amendments. Significantly, the Act nowhere defines "reservation." Therefore, we look to the term's ordinary and natural meaning, and the context in which the term is used. And we must remain cognizant of the rule that courts construe federal statutes liberally to benefit Native American nations.

The dictionary defines "reservation" to be a "tract of public land set aside for a particular purpose (as schools, forest, or the use of Indians)." This definition surely encompasses both trust lands and formally designated reservations. Nothing in the United States Code is clearly to the contrary, for the term "reservation" has no rigid meaning as suggested by petitioners.

* * *

Aside from the statute's plain meaning and its context, other sources of statutory interpretation offer no insight into congressional intent with respect to the meaning of "reservation.". . .

Accordingly, we turn to step two of the Chevron inquiry. That is, did the Agency reasonably interpret the term "reservation" to include formal reservations, Pueblos, and trust lands? EPA supported its interpretation of "reservation" by looking to relevant case law, in particular Supreme Court precedent holding that there is no relevant distinction between tribal trust land and reservations for the purpose of tribal sovereign immunity. This view is consonant with other federal court holdings that an Indian reservation includes trust lands.

. . . In light of the ample precedent treating trust land as reservation land in other contexts, and the canon of statutory interpretation calling for statutes to be interpreted favorably towards Native American nations, we cannot condemn as unreasonable EPA's interpretation of "reservations" to include Pueblos and tribal trust land.

* * *

The dispute in *Arizona Public Service* is a product of the potential status of reservation lands as well as Supreme Court precedent that has severely limited the authority of tribal nations over non-Natives. The status of tribal lands is covered in greater detail in Chapters 5 and 16; for the purposes of this chapter it suffices to note that tribal lands can generally be held in three ways: tribal trust land, tribal fee land, and non-Native fee land. Furthermore, as discussed in greater detail in

Chapter 19, the Supreme Court has, in general, significantly limited tribal civil authority over non-Native fee lands within reservation boundaries.

With these factors in mind, the dispute in *Arizona Public Service* becomes more clear: the non-Native company challenged the EPA's broad interpretations of the scope of tribal authority under the Clean Air Act in light of other limitations that had been placed on tribal authority over reservation lands in other areas of the law. To decide whether the EPA's reading of the statute and its regulations were valid, the court had to take a step-by-step approach. First, the court had to determine whether Congress granted tribal nations the authority to regulate air quality over all lands on a reservation, including non-Native fee land. The court decided that Congress did grant this authority primarily by carefully reading the statute. Next, the court had to decide what constituted a reservation under the Act, and thus was subject to tribal air quality standards. Since "reservation" was not defined in the Clean Air Act itself, the court applied the *Chevron* doctrine to the EPA's interpretation. As "reservation" was not defined, there was some ambiguity as to its meaning and the first step of the *Chevron* doctrine was satisfied. Next, the court asked if the EPA's definition was reasonable. In finding that it was reasonable, the court noted that the EPA's definition was supported by "ample precedent."

The dispute in *Arizona Public Service* also demonstrates another pertinent point: environmental interests are one area where tribal interests have found some sustained success in American law. This is not to suggest that tribal interests always win environmental disputes, as tribal nations are often frustrated in the implementation, enforcement, and expansion of tribal environmental protections and continue to face significant resistance from non-Native interests. Additionally, the success that tribal interests have gained may very well be based, at least in part, on the stereotype of the Native as an environmentalist—a stereotype which, while ostensibly positive, is grounded in simplistic and limiting connotations of Native peoples. Nonetheless, both courts and Congress have been more understanding and accommodating to tribal concerns in the environmental realm than perhaps in any other aspect of American law.

STATE INCURSIONS

Tribal nations are not the only interested parties when it comes to preserving natural resources, which includes not just water, air, and plant life, but wildlife as well. As noted above, states have a tremendous amount of authority over the natural resources within their borders and regularly put significant effort into preserving them. In fact, many states cultivate and promote these resources to attract the travel and tourist dollars of hunters, fishers, and other outdoorspeople.

And yet, while states and tribal interests might have common interests in protecting and preserving natural resources, there has often been conflict about how to accomplish these tasks. More specifically, there have regularly been disputes over which party has had the authority, or jurisdiction, to implement rules and regulations concerning hunting and fishing over a territory. Such disputes are often a significant aspect of treaty rights litigation and other territorial boundary issues. Other factors have added to the tension. For example, as a general trend, the federal government, particularly the Supreme Court, has sanctioned increased state authority within Indian Country over the years. Consequently, states have been emboldened to extend their reach into Indian Country as the Supreme Court has defined tribal sovereignty, particularly in regards to non-Natives, more narrowly. Also, when it came to issues of natural resources (and other issues as well), many states historically exercised authority over Indian Country regardless of their legal right to do so. As tribal nations have sought to increase the scope of their own sovereignty, they have sought to exclude states from arenas in which the states have previously—often without a legal foundation—operated. In short, the issue of natural resources has been a space in which the sovereignty of differing governments has come into conflict.

In *New Mexico v. Mescalero Apache Tribe*, the Supreme Court was confronted with a state seeking to impose its hunting and fishing regulations on tribal lands. The Mescalero Apache, with the aid of the federal government, began operating a resort, which attracted tourists seeking to hunt and fish. The tribal nation had its own hunting and fishing regulations to manage on-reservation natural resources, but the state wanted to impose its own restrictions as well. As you read the case, ask yourself where the state concedes authority versus where it seeks to exercise authority. Also, what sovereigns are in conflict? How does this change the analysis?

NEW MEXICO V. MESCALERO APACHE TRIBE
462 U.S. 324 (1983)

JUSTICE MARSHALL delivered the opinion of the Court.

* * *

Anticipating a decline in the sale of lumber which has been the largest income-producing activity within the reservation, the Tribe has recently committed substantial time and resources to the development of other sources of income. The Tribe has constructed a resort complex financed principally by federal funds, and has undertaken a substantial development of the reservation's hunting and fishing resources. These efforts provide employment opportunities for members of the Tribe, and the sale of hunting and fishing licenses and related services generates income which is used to maintain the tribal government and provide services to Tribe members.

Development of the reservation's fish and wildlife resources has involved a sustained, cooperative effort by the Tribe and the Federal Government. Indeed, the reservation's fishing resources are wholly attributable to these recent efforts. . . .

The Tribe and the Federal Government jointly conduct a comprehensive fish and game management program. . . .

Numerous conflicts exist between state and tribal hunting regulations. For instance, tribal seasons and bag limits for both hunting and fishing often do not coincide with those imposed by the State. . . .

* * *

New Mexico concedes that on the reservation the Tribe exercises exclusive jurisdiction over hunting and fishing by members of the Tribe and may also regulate the hunting and fishing by nonmembers. New Mexico contends, however, that it may exercise concurrent jurisdiction over nonmembers and that therefore its regulations governing hunting and fishing throughout the State should also apply to hunting and fishing by nonmembers on the reservation. Although New Mexico does not claim that it can require the Tribe to permit nonmembers to hunt and fish on the reservation, it claims that, once the Tribe chooses to permit hunting and fishing by nonmembers, such hunting and fishing is subject to any state-imposed conditions. Under this view the State would be free to impose conditions more restrictive than the Tribe's own regulations, including an outright prohibition. The question in this case is whether the State may so restrict the Tribe's exercise of its authority.

* * *

On numerous occasions this Court has considered the question whether a State may assert authority over a reservation. . . . We long ago . . . have acknowledged certain limitations on tribal sovereignty. . . .

Nevertheless, in demarcating the respective spheres of state and tribal authority over Indian reservations, we have continued to stress that Indian tribes are unique aggregations possessing " 'attributes of sovereignty over both their members and their territory.'" Because of their sovereign status, tribes and their reservation lands are insulated in some respects by a "historic immunity from state and local control".....

The sovereignty retained by tribes includes "the power of regulating their internal and social relations." A tribe's power to prescribe the conduct of tribal members has never been doubted, and our cases establish that "'absent governing Acts of Congress,'" a State may not act in a manner that "'infringe[s] on the right of reservation Indians to make their own laws and be ruled by them.'"

... While under some circumstances a State may exercise concurrent jurisdiction over non-Indians acting on tribal reservations, such authority may be asserted only if not pre-empted by the operation of federal law.

* * *

Certain broad considerations guide our assessment of the federal and tribal interests. The traditional notions of Indian sovereignty provide a crucial "backdrop," against which any assertion of state authority must be assessed. Moreover, both the tribes and the Federal Government are firmly committed to the goal of promoting tribal self-government.... Thus, when a tribe undertakes an enterprise under the authority of federal law, an assertion of state authority must be viewed against any interference with the successful accomplishment of the federal purpose.

Our prior decisions also guide our assessment of the state interest asserted to justify state jurisdiction over a reservation. The exercise of state authority which imposes additional burdens on a tribal enterprise must ordinarily be justified by functions or services performed by the State in connection with the on-reservation activity.... A State's regulatory interest will be particularly substantial if the State can point to off-reservation effects that necessitate state intervention.

With these principles in mind, we turn to New Mexico's claim that it may superimpose its own hunting and fishing regulations on the Mescalero Apache Tribe's regulatory scheme.

It is beyond doubt that the Mescalero Apache Tribe lawfully exercises substantial control over the lands and resources of its reservation, including its wildlife....

* * *

Several considerations strongly support the . . . conclusion that the Tribe's authority to regulate hunting and fishing pre-empts state jurisdiction. It is important to emphasize that concurrent jurisdiction would effectively nullify the Tribe's authority to control hunting and fishing on the reservation. . . .

Furthermore, the exercise of concurrent state jurisdiction in this case would completely "disturb and disarrange" the comprehensive scheme of federal and tribal management established pursuant to federal law. . . .

* * *

The assertion of concurrent jurisdiction by New Mexico not only would threaten to disrupt the federal and tribal regulatory scheme, but also would threaten Congress' overriding objective of encouraging tribal self-government and economic development. . . .

The State has failed to "identify any regulatory function or service . . . that would justify" the assertion of concurrent regulatory authority. The hunting and fishing permitted by the Tribe occur entirely on the reservation. The fish and wildlife resources are either native to the reservation or were created by the joint efforts of the Tribe and the Federal Government. New Mexico does not contribute in any significant respect to the maintenance of these resources, and can point to no other "governmental functions it provides," in connection with hunting and fishing on the reservation by nonmembers that would justify the assertion of its authority.

The State also cannot point to any off-reservation effects that warrant state intervention. Some species of game never leave tribal lands, and the State points to no specific interest concerning those that occasionally do. . . . The State concedes that the Tribe's management has "not had an adverse impact on fish and wildlife outside the Reservation."

* * *

. . . Given the strong interests favoring exclusive tribal jurisdiction and the absence of state interests which justify the assertion of concurrent authority, we conclude that the application of the State's hunting and fishing laws to the reservation is pre-empted.

One particularly effective strategy for understanding the questions about jurisdiction in federal Indian law is to ask who is trying to exercise authority over whom. Once you have established the answer to this baseline question, it becomes clear which test or standard American courts are going to use to judge the exercise of that authority.

In *Mescalero Apache*, the state of New Mexico conceded that the tribal nation had the exclusive authority to regulate hunting and fishing for tribal citizens on the reservation. However, the state argued that it had concurrent jurisdiction—or an equal amount of authority as the tribal nation—over non-tribal citizens on the reservation. New Mexico's answer to the baseline question was that it was seeking to exercise authority over non-tribal citizens, primarily non-Natives who would otherwise have come under exclusive state jurisdiction outside of the reservation boundaries.

The Supreme Court, however, saw the dispute in different terms. Justice Thurgood Marshall's opinion stated that, "It is important to emphasize that concurrent jurisdiction would effectively nullify the Tribe's authority to control hunting and fishing on the reservation." As a practical matter, according to the Supreme Court's understanding of the baseline question, the state's efforts were a regulation of the tribal nation itself. Under such circumstances, unless Congress has expressly authorized a state to police or regulate a tribal nation in the manner in question, American courts will apply the infringement test. The infringement test is discussed in greater detail in Chapter 10. For the purposes of this chapter, it suffices to note, as the Court did in *Mescalero Apache*, that under the infringement test the court asks whether the state's efforts "[infringe] on the right of reservation Indians to make their own laws and be ruled by them."

While the infringement test is critical to jurisdiction cases, it is not the only measure an American court makes when considering a state's capacity to reach into Indian Country. The interests of a third sovereign, the United States, are also given great weight. The federal government has a trust responsibility to tribal nations (see Chapter 14) and has, in the Self-Determination Era, put significant resources into supporting tribal efforts at governmental and economic growth. Recognizing the federal government's role in these matters, sometimes courts will decide that federal actions have "preempted" otherwise valid state efforts. Put another way, if the goals, resources, and actions of the federal government in a particular matter are both significant and are contrary to the efforts of a state, than the federal actions will take precedence—they will "preempt" state efforts (preemption is also considered in Chapter 20).

Thus, when deciding cases where states are trying to regulate activities on a reservation, American courts will engage in a balancing test. On one side are the state's interests in regulating the activity. These interests are greatest when, as the Court notes in *Mescalero Apache*, "the State can point to off-reservation effects that necessitate state intervention." On the other side are the tribal interests, measured through the infringement test, and the federal interests, considered through the lens of preemption. In *Mescalero Apache*, the Court found that the extreme burden the New Mexico regulations would have on the tribal nation and on the federal government's interest in seeing tribal economic activity succeed were not justified by the state's relatively weak interest in enforcing state law on the reservation.

The decision in *Mescalero Apache* and cases like it have forced both tribal nations and states to reconsider their approaches to disputes over jurisdictional issues in the realm of natural resources (and elsewhere). Litigation can be time-consuming, expensive, risky, provoke animosity, and create as many problems as it solves. In addition, both tribal nations and states generally have a common goal in this area: each sovereign wants to protect its natural resources.

To that end, many tribal nations and states have begun to work in tandem with one another instead of engaging in litigation over which entity has the ultimate authority. These efforts often result in cooperative agreements— negotiated contracts in which tribal nations and states agree to share the responsibility for a major governmental effort and to respect each other's sovereignty. Cooperative agreements are not exclusive to the field of natural resources—for example, states and tribal nations have sometimes cross deputized their law enforcement officials—but it is an area in which the sovereigns involved have demonstrated an increased willingness to work with each other for the greater good. Presently, there are a number of cooperative agreements between states and tribal nations, as well as with the federal government and with other nations, to manage the environment and wildlife.

Cooperative agreements will not be suitable to every occasion. They require parties who have both enough to gain by agreeing to them and enough to lose without the assurances that they provide. They also require a level of trust that has not always been present between tribal nations and other American governments. Despite these limitations, cooperative agreements have been beneficial and continue to be promising. This is especially true in the field of natural resources, as water, air, wildlife, and more exist and move irrespective of borders. As one considers the field of federal Indian law, it is becoming increasingly important to seek out not just lines of argument in order to win a case, but also opportunities not to argue in the first place. Cooperative agreements will likely continue to grow in use and in importance, as it concerns natural resources and many other arenas of interaction with other American governments.

SUGGESTED READINGS

- *Tribal Water Rights: Essays in Contemporary Law, Policy, and Economics.* John E. Thorson, Sarah Britton, and Bonnie G. Colby, eds. Tucson, AZ: University of Arizona Press, 2006.

- "The Control of Air Pollution on Indian Reservations." Andrew W. Reitze, Jr. 46 *Environmental Law* 893 (Fall 2016).

- "Ecosystem Co-Management Plans: A Sound Approach or a Threat to Tribal Rights?" Shelly D. Stokes. 27 *Vermont Law Review* 421 (Winter 2003).

CHAPTER 27

Religion

On December 5, 1870, President Ulysses S. Grant delivered his second State of the Union Address to Congress. In the address, Grant detailed the basic framework of his newly implemented Peace Policy (see Chapter 4) toward Native America:

> The experiment of making it a missionary work was tried with a few agencies . . . and has been found to work most advantageously. . . . I determined to give all the agencies to such religious denominations as had heretofore established missionaries among the Indians, and perhaps to some other denominations who would undertake the work on the same terms—i.e., as a missionary work. The [religious] societies selected are . . . expected to watch over them and aid them as missionaries, to Christianize and civilize the Indian. . . .

In essence, Grant sought to turn over the day-to-day administration of Indian affairs to Christian missionaries. This aspect of Grant's Peace Policy toward Native America was perhaps the most extensive effort by the federal government to institutionalize a national policy to convert Native peoples to Christianity and eradicate tribal spiritual and religious practices. Yet, it was far from the only attempt to do so. For centuries before the Peace Policy and long after it various colonial forces—particularly the United States—have sought to end tribal religious practices and beliefs and replace them with their own.

These efforts have run contrary to one of the most celebrated principles of the U.S. Constitution and American life: religious freedom. The 1st Amendment protects the free exercise of religion and against the establishment of a national religion. As Justice Hugo Black stated in a noteworthy dissent, "The very reason for the First Amendment is to make the people of this country free to think, speak, write and worship as they wish, not as the Government commands."[1]

In the Self-Determination Era (see Chapter 10) Congress has taken important strides to end the destructive efforts of the past and show support for Native religious and spiritual practices. These newer efforts have eased the contradictions between federal policies and constitutional guarantees. However, it is still fair to ask whether tribal religious practices and beliefs are adequately shielded from governmental interference or even recognized today. Put another way, is the 1st Amendment—or more precisely 1st Amendment law and precedent—capable of protecting Native religions?

This chapter will demonstrate. . .

- *The basic parameters of the American Indian Religious Freedom Act*

- *The operation of 1st Amendment Free Exercise jurisprudence in Indian Country*

- *The operation of Establishment jurisprudence in Indian Country*

CONGRESSIONAL LEGISLATION

It would be difficult to overstate the degree to which the federal government has sought to coerce Native peoples into alternative behavior or otherwise radically sought to alter their lives, particularly in the Allotment Era of federal policy. Religious practices were a common target for the would-be reformers, with the federal government regularly banning dancing and other spiritual practices, criminalizing the activities of medicine men and women, and, as noted above, allowing missionaries extensive access to reservations among other efforts. Those Native individuals who persisted in their traditional practices risked suffering all sorts of sanctions, including but not limited to imprisonment and the withholding of their treaty-guaranteed rations. Nor were these isolated incidents or the product of only a few moments of misguided action or unfortunate leadership. This was a widespread and longstanding policy of the federal government. Many Native religious practices went underground, often masked as secular or Christian celebrations, in order to survive. The keepers of Native knowledge were regularly forced to live defiantly, secretively, and illegally.

The openly hostile governmental regard for Native ways of life, which had been unevenly eroding since the end of the Allotment Era, began to subside in earnest in the Self-Determination Era. In this new policy era, the federal government began seeking to support tribal nations and individuals in many walks of life. Although an improvement from past governmental actions, the federal efforts in the Self-Determination Era have not always been as extensive as Native peoples would like them to be, nor have they satisfactorily solved all of the difficulties created and perpetuated by colonialism and its legacy.

Greater attention is given to the mixed legacy of the Self-Determination Era in Chapter 10. For the purposes of this chapter, it suffices to note that the federal government sought to undo some of its previous suppression of tribal religious practices and beliefs during the Self-Determination Era. The most prominent piece of legislation in support of this new goal was the American Indian Religious Freedom Act (AIRFA), which was passed in 1978. As you read the Act, ask yourself what it does. Who and what is protected? How is it protected?

AMERICAN INDIAN RELIGIOUS FREEDOM ACT
42 U.S.C.A. § 1996

On and after August 11, 1978, it shall be the policy of the United States to protect and preserve for American Indians their inherent right of freedom to believe, express, and exercise the traditional religions of the American Indian, Eskimo, Aleut, and Native Hawaiians, including but not limited to access to sites, use and possession of sacred objects, and the freedom to worship through ceremonials and traditional rites.

Tribal nations sought protections under AIRFA in American courts after it was passed. In the following case, the court had to decide on the capacity of the AIRFA to protect tribal religious interests. In 1937 the U.S. Forest Service, an agency in the Department of Agriculture, built a ski resort in what is known as the Snow Bowl of the San Francisco Peaks. The San Francisco Peaks are part of the Coconino National Forest, which is located in Arizona and is controlled by the federal government. In 1977 the Forest Service, along with a private management company, developed a plan to expand the modest resort. As part of the expansion plan, the Forest Service drafted an Environmental Impact Statement and solicited input from the public, including from the closely located Navajo and Hopi. As the San Francisco Peaks are a place of major religious significance for both tribal nations, both the Navajo and the Hopi objected to the proposed expansion and asked for the removal of the original ski resort. The bureaucratic process took a number of twists and turns, with the Forest Service originally adopting a more limited expansion—known as the "preferred alternative"—than was originally proposed, then rejecting any expansion altogether, then finally settling on the preferred alternative. In the wake of this decision the Navajo and Hopi sued, claiming, among other things, a violation of AIRFA, objecting to any expansion of the ski resort, and requesting the removal of the ski resort altogether.

As you read the case, ask yourself how the court understands AIRFA. What requirements does AIRFA impose upon the federal government? How are the objections of the Navajo and Hopi understood? How does the ruling in the case comport with your understanding of the guarantee of free exercise of religion in the United States?

WILSON V. BLOCK
708 F.2d 735 (1983)

LUMBARD, SENIOR CIRCUIT JUDGE:

* * *

. . . The Navajo and Hopi plaintiffs contend that development of the Snow Bowl is inconsistent with their . . . right freely to hold and practice their religious beliefs. Believing the San Francisco Peaks to be sacred, they feel that development of the Peaks would be a profane act, and an affront to the deities, and that, in consequence, the Peaks would lose their healing power and otherwise cease to benefit the tribes. They contend that development would seriously impair their ability to pray and conduct ceremonies upon the Peaks, and to gather from the Peaks the sacred objects, such as fir boughs and eaglets, which are necessary to their religious practices. . .

* * *

The plaintiffs contend that AIRFA proscribes all federal land uses that conflict or interfere with traditional Indian religious beliefs or practices, unless such uses are justified by compelling governmental interests. They argue that the Snow Bowl ski resort expansion is not a compelling governmental interest, and is accordingly proscribed by AIRFA. [The trial judge] refused to give AIRFA the broad reading urged by plaintiffs. He found that AIRFA requires federal agencies to evaluate their policies and procedures with the aim of protecting Indian religious freedom, to refrain from prohibiting access, possession and use of religious objects and the performance of religious ceremonies, and to consult with Indian organizations in regard to proposed actions, but that AIRFA does not require "Native traditional religious considerations always [to] prevail to the exclusion of all else." We agree. [The trial judge's] interpretation of AIRFA is fully supported by the legislative history, and the record supports his finding of Forest Service compliance.

AIRFA affirms the protection and preservation of traditional Indian religions as a policy of the United States, but the statutory language does not indicate the extent to which Congress intended that policy to override other land use considerations. We therefore look for guidance to the legislative history. . . . [The legislative history reveals] that in AIRFA Congress addressed the unwarranted and often unintended intrusions upon Indian religious practices resulting from federal officials' ignorance and the inflexible enforcement of laws and regulations which, though intended to achieve valid secular goals, had directly affected Indian religious practices. The reports identify three areas of concern: (1) denial of access to religious sites; (2) restrictions on the possession of such substances as peyote; and (3) actual interference with religious events. The federal government, the reports note, had sometimes denied Indians access to religious sites on federal land; had failed to accommodate such federal statutes as the drug and endangered species laws to the Indians' religious needs, and had itself interfered, or permitted others to interfere, with religious observances. Thus, [a Congressional report] stated that the purpose of AIRFA is "to insure that the policies and procedures of various Federal agencies, as they may impact upon the exercise of traditional Indian religious practices, are brought into compliance with the constitutional injunction that Congress shall make no laws abridging the free exercise of religion."

It is clear . . . that AIRFA requires federal agencies to learn about, and to avoid unnecessary interference with, traditional Indian religious practices. Agencies must evaluate their policies and procedures in light of the Act's purpose, and ordinarily should consult Indian leaders before approving a project likely to affect religious practices. AIRFA does not, however, declare the protection of Indian religions to be an overriding federal policy, or grant Indian religious practitioners a veto on agency action. . . .

* * *

Thus AIRFA requires federal agencies to consider, but not necessarily to defer to, Indian religious values. It does not prohibit agencies from adopting all land uses that conflict with traditional Indian religious beliefs or practices. Instead, an agency undertaking a land use project will be in compliance with AIRFA if, in the decision-making process, it obtains and considers the views of Indian leaders, and if, in project implementation, it avoids unnecessary interference with Indian religious practices. . . .

Finally, we find that the Forest Service complied with AIRFA in the present case. Before approving the Preferred Alternative the Forest Service held many meetings with Indian religious practitioners and conducted public hearings on the Hopi and Navajo reservations at which practitioners testified. The views there expressed were discussed at length in the Final Environmental Statement and were given due consideration in the evaluation of the alternative development schemes proposed for the Snow Bowl. Development of the Snow Bowl under the Preferred Alternative will not deny the plaintiffs access to the Peaks, nor will it prevent them from collecting religious objects. The Forest Service has not burdened the plaintiffs' religious practices in any manner prohibited by AIRFA.

* * *

Wilson v. Block is a useful illustration of the limited reach of AIRFA. As noted by the court, "AIRFA requires federal agencies to consider, but not necessarily to defer to, Indian religious values." Many scholars and others have pointed out that AIRFA lacks any mechanism within its text to enforce its provisions, thus leading a number of interested parties, including the court in *Wilson v. Block*, to describe AIRFA as "policy" instead of law. The only requirement under this "policy," according to the court in *Wilson v. Block*, is that, "AIRFA requires federal agencies to learn about, and to avoid unnecessary interference with, traditional Indian religious practices." Ultimately, the court reasoned, expanding a ski resort on sacred lands (or building it in the first place) did not amount to unnecessary interference with Hopi and Navajo religious practices since it did not "deny the plaintiffs access to the Peaks" or "prevent them from collecting religious objects." *Wilson v. Block* and other cases like it have made clear that the AIRFA does little more than state that the United States will give some consideration to tribal religious practices, while not requiring it to defer to tribal religious beliefs. Nor does the statute offer tribal nations much direct recourse itself.

Subsequent litigation has also been ineffective in protecting tribal interests in the San Francisco Peaks and Snow Bowl. Twenty-five years after the decision in *Wilson v. Block*, the Ninth Circuit Court of Appeals decided *Navajo Nation v. U.S. Forest Service*.[2] The dispute in Navajo Nation concerned the use of recycled wastewater, which contained trace amounts of human waste, to create artificial snow for the ski resort. The tribal interests in the case objected to the use of the recycled wastewater on a sacred site, arguing that it desecrated the space and made it harder to engage in their religious practices. Once again, the tribal interests lost, as the court held that the recycled wastewater did not place a " 'substantial burden' on the exercise of their religion."[3]

In short, federal legislation has, from the tribal point of view, been generally ineffective in protecting tribal religious interests.

FREE EXERCISE CLAUSE

While legislation has been limited in its capacity to protect tribal religious interests, the 1st Amendment does not generally need further legislation to enforce its commands. It stands on its own against the overreach of governmental intrusions on religious practices. Disputes under the 1st Amendment are best understood as operating within two categories. One category consists of the "establishment" cases. This group will be taken up in the next section.

The second category consists of the "free exercise" cases. These cases concern the government's role in limiting or preventing an individual from freely exercising her or his religion. In general, the federal government cannot prohibit an individual from having certain religious beliefs or engaging in certain religious practices. Yet this general principle has its limits. For example, the government is authorized to prevent human sacrifice, even if human sacrifice is part of an individual's validly held religious beliefs.

Native America has raised some of the most important free exercise cases of the last half-century, which have reached far beyond Indian Country. The Supreme Court has reshaped the scope of the 1st Amendment through two prominent decisions: *Lyng v. Northwest Indian Cemetery Protective Association* and *Employment Division v. Smith*, both of which have received significant attention from scholars and other 1st Amendment advocates who do not regularly engage with federal Indian law.

The facts in *Lyng* are reminiscent of the San Francisco Peaks cases of the last section. The federal government sought to build a six-mile stretch of paved road through the Six Rivers National Forest, located in California, to connect two towns and to foster the lumbering that occurred in the forest. Prior to doing so, the U.S. Forest Service, as in *Wilson v. Block*, drafted an environmental impact statement, which noted that the area was "an integral and indispensible part of Indian religious conceptualization and practice" for the Yurok, Karok, and Tolowa tribal nations. The statement also noted that "successful use of the [area] is dependent upon and facilitated by certain qualities of the physical environment, the most important of which are privacy, silence, and an undisturbed natural setting." The statement recommended that the road not be built as it "would cause serious and irreparable damage to the sacred areas which are an integral and necessary part of the belief systems and lifeway of Northwest California Indian peoples."

The Forest Service ultimately rejected this recommendation and chose a plan for the road that did seek to make some accommodation for tribal practices, including a one-half mile protective zone around the specific sites of practice identified by statement. Nonetheless, the tribal interests sued, arguing that the timbering in the forest and the road itself would effectively prevent them from engaging in their religious practices, as it would disrupt their sacred sites and the silence and natural setting necessary to perform their tasks. The tribal interests won at the trial court level and the appellate level before reaching the Supreme Court.

To understand the decision in *Lyng*, it is useful to have some knowledge of some of the legal principles of free exercise jurisprudence. As with any area of law, free exercise cases contain a multitude of opportunities for complications. But at a very basic level, the cases proceed in the following two-step manner. First, the court asks, or, perhaps more precisely, the plaintiff has to demonstrate, that a governmental action or inaction places a substantial burden on the plaintiff's religious practices or beliefs. If there is no substantial burden then the plaintiff will not prevail. If the plaintiff can demonstrate a substantial burden then the court moves to the next step by asking if the government has a compelling interest for its action or inaction. If there is a compelling governmental interest, then the governmental action or inaction will remain constitutionally valid, regardless of the effect it has on the plaintiff's capacity to practice or believe in the way that she or he chooses. If the government's interest is not compelling, then the plaintiff will prevail. To illustrate further from a previous example, every U.S. jurisdiction makes murder illegal. These laws against murder would undoubtedly substantially burden someone who earnestly believes in human sacrifice as part of their religious beliefs. Thus, the first step in the free exercise cases would be satisfied. In general, the second step—demonstrating a "compelling" governmental interest—is very difficult. As such, it is important in facilitating the protection of religion under the U.S. Constitution. Nonetheless, the government's interest in protecting human life is compelling, and, despite the limitations it would place on someone who earnestly believes in human sacrifice as part of their religious beliefs, laws against murder would survive a 1st Amendment challenge.

As you read the case, ask yourself how both the majority opinion and dissent engage with the two-step process for free exercise cases. What is the important

---

principle guiding the majority's decision? What, according to the majority, is the government doing and/or not doing to the tribal religious interests at stake in this case? What is the dissent's response? How does the dissent's description of tribal religious practices help to demonstrate the difficulty in applying the 1st Amendment to those practices?

LYNG V. NORTHWEST INDIAN CEMETERY PROTECTIVE ASSOCIATION
485 U.S. 439 (1988)

JUSTICE O'CONNOR delivered the opinion of the Court.

* * *

The Free Exercise Clause of the First Amendment provides that "Congress shall make no law . . . prohibiting the free exercise [of religion]." It is undisputed that the Indian respondents' beliefs are sincere and that the Government's proposed actions will have severe adverse effects on the practice of their religion. Those respondents contend that the burden on their religious practices is heavy enough to violate the Free Exercise Clause unless the Government can demonstrate a compelling need to complete the . . . road or to engage in timber harvesting in the . . . area. We disagree.

* * *

. . . The crucial word in the constitutional text is "prohibit": "For the Free Exercise Clause is written in terms of what the government cannot do to the individual, not in terms of what the individual can exact from the government."

Whatever may be the exact line between unconstitutional prohibitions on the free exercise of religion and the legitimate conduct by government of its own affairs, the location of the line cannot depend on measuring the effects of a governmental action on a religious objector's spiritual development. The Government does not dispute, and we have no reason to doubt, that the logging and road-building projects at issue in this case could have devastating effects on traditional Indian religious practices. . . .

Even if we assume that we should accept the . . . prediction [that] the . . . road will "virtually destroy the . . . Indians' ability to practice their religion," the Constitution simply does not provide a principle that could justify upholding respondents' legal claims. However much we might wish that it were otherwise, government simply could not operate if it were required to satisfy every citizen's religious needs and desires. A broad range of government activities—

from social welfare programs to foreign aid to conservation projects—will always be considered essential to the spiritual well-being of some citizens, often on the basis of sincerely held religious beliefs. Others will find the very same activities deeply offensive, and perhaps incompatible with their own search for spiritual fulfillment and with the tenets of their religion. The First Amendment must apply to all citizens alike, and it can give to none of them a veto over public programs that do not prohibit the free exercise of religion. The Constitution does not, and courts cannot, offer to reconcile the various competing demands on government, many of them rooted in sincere religious belief, that inevitably arise in so diverse a society as ours. That task, to the extent that it is feasible, is for the legislatures and other institutions.

. . . Nothing in the principle for which [the tribal interests] contend . . . would distinguish this case from another lawsuit in which they (or similarly situated religious objectors) might seek to exclude all human activity but their own from sacred areas of the public lands. . . . No disrespect for these practices is implied when one notes that such beliefs could easily require *de facto* beneficial ownership of some rather spacious tracts of public property. . . .

The Constitution does not permit government to discriminate against religions that treat particular physical sites as sacred, and a law prohibiting the Indian respondents from visiting the . . . area would raise a different set of constitutional questions. Whatever rights the Indians may have to the use of the area, however, those rights do not divest the Government of its right to use what is, after all, *its* land.

* * *

JUSTICE BRENNAN, with whom JUSTICE MARSHALL and JUSTICE BLACKMUN join, dissenting.

" '[T]he Free Exercise Clause,' " the Court explains today, " 'is written in terms of what the government cannot do to the individual, not in terms of what the individual can exact from the government.' " Pledging fidelity to this unremarkable constitutional principle, the Court nevertheless concludes that even where the Government uses federal land in a manner that threatens the very existence of a Native American religion, the Government is simply not "*doing*" anything to the practitioners of that faith. Instead, the Court believes that Native Americans who request that the Government refrain from destroying their religion effectively seek to exact from the Government *de facto* beneficial ownership of federal property. These two astonishing conclusions follow naturally from the Court's determination that federal land-use decisions that render the practice of a given religion impossible do not burden that religion in a manner cognizable under the Free Exercise Clause, because such decisions neither coerce conduct inconsistent with religious belief nor penalize religious activity. The constitutional guarantee we interpret today, however, draws no such fine distinctions between types of restraints on religious exercise, but rather is directed against any form of governmental action that frustrates or inhibits religious practice. Because the Court today refuses even to acknowledge the constitutional injury respondents will suffer, and because this refusal essentially leaves Native Americans with absolutely no constitutional protection against perhaps the gravest threat to their religious practices, I dissent.

* * *

In marked contrast to traditional Western religions, the belief systems of Native Americans do not rely on doctrine, creeds, or dogmas. Established or universal truths—the mainstay of Western religions—play no part in Indian faith. . . . Where dogma lies at the heart of Western religions, Native American faith is inextricably bound to the use of land. The site-specific nature of Indian religious practice derives from the Native American perception that land is itself a sacred, living being. Rituals are performed in prescribed locations not merely as a matter of traditional orthodoxy, but because land, like all other living things, is unique, and specific sites possess different spiritual properties and significance. . . .

* * *

The critical difference between the majority opinion and the dissent in *Lyng* is how to proceed through the two-step process for free exercise cases. Justice Sandra Day O'Connor's majority opinion was primarily concerned with the nature of the governmental action, as opposed to how the tribal interests in the case have articulated how those governmental actions would affect their ability to practice their religion. In focusing the majority's attention on the nature of the governmental action, O'Connor argued that the determination in free exercise cases "cannot depend on measuring the effects of a governmental action on a religious objector's spiritual development." In other words, how a religious practitioner feels about a governmental action is not as important as what that governmental action does.

Focusing squarely on the nature of the governmental action determined the scope of the first step of the two-part process for the majority opinion. O'Connor noted that, "The crucial word in the constitutional text is 'prohibit.'" Since the building of the road did not prohibit the Native practitioners from visiting their sacred sites or holding certain beliefs it did not amount to the substantial burden necessary to move on to the second step of the two-step process. To decide otherwise, according to O'Connor, would amount to giving the beliefs of individuals too much authority over governmental action. In this case in particular, it would "divest the Government of its right to use what is, after all, *its* land."

Justice William Brennan's dissent, on the other hand, was deeply concerned with the effect that the proposed road would have for the tribal practitioners, as opposed to the nature of the governmental action. Brennan argued that the majority's conclusion that it was "simply not '*doing*' anything to the practitioners of that faith" was "astonishing" in light of the fact that the ruling would destroy the Native practitioners' ability to practice their faith. The critical line that the majority opinion drew between what the governmental action sought to do and what it actually did—simply build a road versus destroying the capacity of tribal individuals to practice their religion—was too insignificant for Brennan and his fellow dissenters.

Brennan's discussion concerning the differences between Native and Western religious systems is perhaps slightly overly generalized, but it nonetheless raises serious questions about the application of the 1st Amendment in Indian Country. Noting that Native religious practices are not driven by "doctrine, creeds, or dogmas" in the same way that Western religious practices are, Brennan recognized that "Native American faith is inextricably bound to the use of land." In short and in general, Western religious practices are not site-specific in the same way that Native religious practices often are. This fundamental difference creates important questions about the nature of religious practices and beliefs and, consequently, the 1st Amendment's capacity to cover non-Western religions. For example, if the 1st Amendment cannot protect a sacred site, as it could not in *Lyng*, can it truly protect tribal religious practices? To what extent does the 1st Amendment's protection against governmental interference with one's beliefs hold any meaning for Native America if, as Brennan stated, Native belief systems are not driven by "doctrine, creeds, or dogma"? Is the 1st Amendment only capable of protecting Western religious traditions?

Brennan's articulation of the differences between Native and Western religious systems is a useful framing device for understanding the challenges that Native practitioners face under the 1st Amendment. It is perhaps overly generalized in the sense that it does not account for the tremendous diversity in Native religious belief or the various changes since colonial contact. Not all Native peoples engage in the religious traditions of their tribal nation, nor have all of those traditions remained static. In order to understand the next case, *Employment Division v. Smith*, it is useful to know something about one of the most important developments within Native religious belief since contact—the Native American Church.

The Native American Church developed over the course of the nineteenth century and is most simply described as a mix of Christianity and traditional Native religious practices. The blend of the two can be uneven and can depend on the practitioner, but adherents to the Native American Church have found religious significance in each tradition. The most controversial aspect of the Native American Church is the sacramental use of peyote, a hallucinogen that, according to the Church's adherents, allows communication with a higher power. Under American law, peyote is considered a controlled substance and users or distributors can be criminally prosecuted. Additionally, in its early years, the Native American Church was regularly a target for non-Native reformers who sought to end tribal religious practices and a magnet for skepticism from outsiders. However, in recent decades the Native American Church has gained more acceptance, and exemptions for peyote use for bona fide practitioners have been made in federal and state law. Today only card-carrying members of the Native American Church may legally use, possess, or transport peyote.

The following case began when two members of the Native American Church, Alfred Smith and Galen Black, were fired from a private substance abuse rehabilitation clinic for failing a drug test because they used peyote. Both practitioners had been substance abusers in the past and credited the Native American Church for their recovery. After they were fired, both practitioners filed for unemployment benefits with the state of Oregon and were denied because they were fired for what was described as work-related misconduct. At the time, Oregon had not exempted the sacramental use of peyote from its criminal law. Smith and Black challenged Oregon's denial of their unemployment benefits, arguing that the denial was an infringement of their 1st Amendment right to the free exercise of their religious beliefs.

The opinion below is actually the second Supreme Court decision in this dispute, or *Smith II*. In the first decision, *Smith I*, the Supreme Court remanded the case back down to the Oregon Supreme Court for clarification about how peyote was treated under state law. As you read the case, ask yourself how the answer the Supreme Court was seeking in *Smith I* affected the outcome of *Smith II*. What is the role of the two-step process for free exercise cases in *Smith II*? How does this case compare to *Lyng*? How does the dissent's argument offer a view into what this case means for tribal religious practices and the 1st Amendment more broadly?

EMPLOYMENT DIVISION V. SMITH
494 U.S. 872 (1990)

JUSTICE SCALIA delivered the opinion of the Court.

* * *

[Smith and Black's] claim for relief rests on our decisions in [earlier cases] in which we held that a State could not condition the availability of unemployment insurance on an individual's willingness to forgo conduct required by his religion. As we observed in *Smith I*, however, the conduct at issue in those cases was not prohibited by law. We held that distinction to be critical. . . . Now that the Oregon Supreme Court has confirmed that Oregon does prohibit the religious use of peyote, we proceed to consider whether that prohibition is permissible under the Free Exercise Clause.

The Free Exercise Clause of the First Amendment . . . provides that "Congress shall make no law respecting an establishment of religion, or prohibiting the free exercise thereof. . . ." The free exercise of religion means, first and foremost, the right to believe and profess whatever religious doctrine one desires. Thus, the First Amendment obviously excludes all "governmental regulation of religious beliefs as such." The government may not compel affirmation of religious belief, punish the expression of religious doctrines it believes to be false, impose special disabilities on the basis of religious views or religious status, or lend its power to one or the other side in controversies over religious authority or dogma.

But the "exercise of religion" often involves not only belief and profession but the performance of (or abstention from) physical acts. . . . It would be true, we think (though no case of ours has involved the point), that a state would be "prohibiting the free exercise [of religion]" if it sought to ban such acts or abstentions only when they are engaged in for religious reasons, or only because of the religious belief that they display. . . .

Respondents in the present case, however, seek to carry the meaning of "prohibiting the free exercise [of religion]" one large step further. They contend that their religious motivation for using peyote places them beyond the reach of a criminal law that is not specifically directed at their religious practice, and that is concededly constitutional as applied to those who use the drug for other reasons. . . .

. . . We have never held that an individual's religious beliefs excuse him from compliance with an otherwise valid law prohibiting conduct that the State is free to regulate. . . .

Subsequent decisions have consistently held that the right of free exercise does not relieve an individual of the obligation to comply with a "valid and neutral law of general applicability on the ground that the law proscribes (or prescribes) conduct that his religion prescribes (or proscribes)."

* * *

Respondents argue that, even though exemption from generally applicable criminal laws need not automatically be extended to religiously motivated actors, at least the claim for a religious exemption must be evaluated under [the two-step process for free exercise cases]. . . .

. . . We conclude today that the sounder approach, and the approach in accord with the vast majority of our precedents, is to hold the [two-step process for free exercise cases] inapplicable to such challenges. The government's ability to enforce generally applicable prohibitions of socially harmful conduct, like its ability to carry out other aspects of public policy, "cannot depend on measuring the effects of a governmental action on a religious objector's spiritual development." . . .

* * *

JUSTICE BLACKMUN, with whom JUSTICE BRENNAN and JUSTICE MARSHALL join, dissenting.

This Court over the years painstakingly has developed [the two-step process] to test the constitutionality of a state statute that burdens the free exercise of religion. . . .

Until today, I thought this was a settled and inviolate principle of this Court's First Amendment Jurisprudence. The majority, however, perfunctorily dismisses it as a "constitutional anomaly". . . . [T]he majority is able to arrive at this view only by mischaracterizing this Court's precedents. . . . One hopes that [the] result is not a product of overreaction to the serious problems the country's drug crisis has generated.

This distorted view of our precedents leads the majority to conclude that [the two-step process] is a "luxury" that a well-ordered society cannot afford, and that the repression of minority religions is an "unavoidable consequence of democratic government." I do not believe the Founders thought their dearly bought freedom from religious persecution a "luxury," but an essential element of liberty—and they could not have thought religious intolerance "unavoidable," for they drafted the Religion Clauses precisely in order to avoid that intolerance.

* * *

Moreover ... the values and interests of those seeking a religious exemption in this case are congruent, to a great degree, with those the State seeks to promote through its drug laws. . . . Far from promoting the lawless and irresponsible use of drugs, Native American Church members' spiritual code exemplifies values that Oregon's drug laws are presumably intended to foster.

* * *

As the dissent notes, *Smith II* announced what many saw as a major shift in 1st Amendment law. It produced a legislative response from Congress, seeking to overturn the ruling of the case, and then a further response from the Supreme Court, which ruled that a portion of Congress' efforts were unconstitutional. While it is outside of the scope of this textbook to more fully trace those developments, it is necessary to know that *Smith II* changed the landscape of American law to better understand the case's meaning for Native America and federal Indian law.

In *Lyng*, the major distinction for the justices of the Supreme Court was where to stop in the two-step process for free exercise cases. In *Smith II*, the major distinction was whether the two-step process applied at all. Put another way, the question was, in essence, whether the Court had to engage in the two-step process simply because an individual made a 1st Amendment free exercise claim.

Justice Antonin Scalia's majority opinion was controversial because it limited the range of cases in which American courts had to undergo the two-step process. According to the majority, were a law to directly compel certain beliefs or punish an individual for particular actions because of their religious nature then the two-step process would certainly apply. However, according to Scalia, "the right of free exercise does not relieve an individual of the obligation to comply with a 'valid and neutral law of general applicability.'" Since Oregon's prohibition against peyote was generally applicable to everybody, and not just the practitioners of the Native American Church, there was no need to engage in the two-step process. The opinion quoted *Lyng* to come to its conclusion, and, like *Lyng*, trained its focus on the nature of the governmental action as opposed to how the governmental action would affect the tribal members' capacity to practice their religion.

Many believe that the two-step process is critical for fulfilling the 1st Amendment right to the free exercise of religion. To that end, the majority's limitation of the rule caused a strong backlash, even among the members of the Court. In his dissent, Justice Harry Blackmun noted that majority's disruption of the "settled and inviolate principle" of the two-step process could only come about by "mischaracterizing this Court's precedents." He also hinted at the possibility that the Supreme Court was overreacting to the "War on Drugs"—a major domestic policy imitative to reduce illegal drug trafficking and use that was implemented in the 1980s.

For Native America, the decision has had mixed results. It once again cast doubt on the 1st Amendment's capacity to protect tribal religious practices. Without the protection of the two-part test, a generally applicable state law that does not recognize or appreciate tribal practices might inadvertently disrupt tribal practices. Yet it also provided a pathway for at least some relief. It provoked many of the states that had not already done so to exempt sacramental peyote use from their criminal law. Nonetheless, the decision in *Smith II* forces tribal practitioners to rely much more heavily on state legislatures—which can be more or less amenable to tribal needs at any given time—and the federal government, rather than the U.S. Constitution itself, to protect their religious freedoms.

ESTABLISHMENT CASES

As noted above, 1st Amendment claims come in two categories: free exercise and establishment. Free exercise claims concern governmental interference with an individual's capacity to freely practice their religion. Establishment claims concern the prohibition against the government establishing or endorsing a particular religion, sect, or belief.

On the one hand, establishment cases pose a significant problem for tribal advocates. The federal and state governments are prohibited from offering too much support or endorsement of tribal religious beliefs or practices under the establishment clause of the 1st Amendment. Thus, states and the federal government cannot pass laws that are in support of tribal religious practices for the singular purpose of supporting those religious practices. For example, a federal law that devotes federal funds to Native American Church members for the purpose of purchasing peyote for sacramental use would violate the establishment clause.

On the other hand, tribal advocates have found their most success in protecting tribal religious practices in American courts through establishment cases, particularly as it concerns sacred sites. In addition, the federal government—despite the outcome of some of the cases in this chapter—has often been a beneficial partner in the effort to protect sacred sites. When sacred sites are located on federal land, the federal government has regularly sought to protect those spaces for tribal practitioners, establishing regulations for the use of the sites that accommodate tribal practices or otherwise limit or eliminate offensive uses of the sites. The biggest challengers to these regulations have typically been outdoor enthusiasts who have sought access to federal lands for recreational uses.

The following case illustrates both the opportunities for tribal religious practitioners and the hurdles that they have to overcome. Cave Rock, located within a national forest on the shore of Lake Tahoe in Nevada, is a sacred site for the Washoe. In the mid-1990s, the federal government—as with some of the cases above—began developing a plan for the area that sought to balance the competing interests in the land. The Forest Service eventually settled on banning rock climbing at Cave Rock. The Access Fund, an advocacy group for rock climbers, sued, arguing that the Forest Service's decision amounted to a violation of the establishment clause of the 1st Amendment.

As you read the case, ask yourself what standard the court uses to determine establishment clause cases. How does that standard affect how tribal advocates need to approach establishment cases? What role does the fact that Cave Rock is a sacred site play in the court's determination in the case? To what extent is this a victory for the Washoe?

ACCESS FUND V. DEPT. OF AGRICULTURE
499 F.3d 1036 (2007)

McKeown, Circuit Judge:

* * *

Under traditional Washoe beliefs, Cave Rock is "the most religious feature within the Washoe religion," and many Washoe compare Cave Rock to a church. Cave Rock is considered so powerful and sacred that the health and integrity of Washoe society may be jeopardized if traditional practices are not observed there. . . .

Traditional Washoe assert that Cave Rock is to be avoided by all people, except Washoe practitioners who have been called to "seek power or knowledge at the rock." The presence of others at Cave Rock, including non-Washoe, is thought to endanger the lives of all. . . .

The site is also historically and archaeologically significant. . . .

The rock also reflects developments in the history of American transportation. It has served as an evolving travel corridor that moved aboriginal peoples, early immigrants, commercial freight, and tourists along the east shore of Lake Tahoe. . . .

Since the late 1980s, Cave Rock has been a popular area for rock climbing. . . . Cave Rock's overhanging walls have become a coveted challenge for many of the world's best climbers. . . . [C]limbers drilled permanent bolts into Cave Rock itself. Climbers expanded climbing routes without Forest Service approval both inside and outside the main cave area.

In the early 1990s, unknown individuals added a masonry floor and arranged rock seating in the cave without Forest Service approval and in violation of federal regulations. . . .

The Washoe consider rock climbing a desecration of Cave Rock. . . .

* * *

The Access Fund's primary contention . . . is that the Forest Service's decision to ban climbing at Cave Rock violated the Establishment Clause. . . .

The *Lemon* test remains the benchmark to gauge whether a particular government activity violates the Establishment Clause. . . .

Under *Lemon*, an action or policy violates the Establishment Clause if (1) it has no secular purpose; (2) its principal effect is to advance religion; or (3) it involves excessive entanglement with religion. . . .

In recent years, the Supreme Court often has discussed the last two *Lemon* criteria together, asking whether the challenged governmental practice has the effect of endorsing religion. . . .

The government easily satisfies the first prong of the *Lemon* test. . . . Here, the Forest Service acted pursuant to a secular purpose—the preservation of a historic cultural area.

At every opportunity, the Forest Service reaffirmed its desire to protect Cave Rock as a cultural, historical, and archaeological monument. . . .

The Forest Service's approach during its recent environmental review also reflected these secular motivations. . . .

The Forest Service's limitation on climbing served the permissible secular goal of protecting cultural, historical and archeological features of Cave Rock. We discern no support for the claim that the Forest Service's decision was taken for the predominant purpose of advancing Washoe religion. . . .

* * *

The effect prong of *Lemon* "asks whether, irrespective of the government's actual purpose, the practice under review in fact conveys a message of endorsement or disapproval.". . .

As a practical matter, the climbing ban cannot be fairly perceived as an endorsement of Washoe religious practices. Indeed . . . the Washoe Tribe favored an alternative that would have precluded all activities inconsistent with traditional Washoe belief. This alternative would have denied non-Washoe access to the traditional cultural property and banned hiking and other recreational uses at the rock.

The Forest Service's chosen alternative not only provides for general public use and access well beyond members of the Washoe Tribe, but also permits activities that are incompatible with Washoe beliefs. When a government action . . . explicitly violates some core tenets of the religion it allegedly favors, such action will typically be considered permissible accommodation rather than impermissible endorsement.

* * *

As the court noted, establishment cases are decided under the *Lemon* test. Named after a notable Supreme Court case, the *Lemon* test asks three questions: First, does a law have a secular purpose? If a law lacks a secular purpose then it will be ruled unconstitutional. Second, is the principal effect of the law to advance religion? If so, then it will be ruled unconstitutional. Third, does the law involve an excessive entanglement with religion? Once again, if so then the law will be ruled unconstitutional. The purpose of the *Lemon* test is to distinguish between those laws which inadvertently or indirectly benefit some aspect of religion (which are valid) and those laws which are specifically directed at benefitting a religion (which are invalid).

Consequently, under the *Lemon* test, tribal advocates must demonstrate some primary secular purpose for the protection of sacred sites. Protection of a sacred site for its own sake as a sacred site would not survive the *Lemon* test. The Forest

Service in *Access Fund* was able to justify the ban on rock climbing on Cave Rock because it "served the permissible secular goal of protecting cultural, historical and archeological features of Cave Rock."

With this understanding in mind, it is useful to return to return to the fundamental question that began this chapter: Is the 1st Amendment capable of protecting Native religions? Both federal legislation and the free exercise clause of the 1st Amendment have proven to be fairly ineffectual. In fact, the Supreme Court has shrunk the scope of cases that fall under 1st Amendment protections through Indian law cases and both *Lyng* and *Smith II* suggest that the free exercise clause is severely limited in its capacity to conceptualize and protect Native religious understandings and practices. The establishment clause has been of greater use to Native interests, but it has not been without noteworthy limitations. It requires that tribal advocates connect their desired outcome to a secular purpose; the desired outcome cannot stand on its own. And the desired outcome from the tribal perspective is rarely, if ever, completely fulfilled. As noted in *Access Fund*, the Forest Service's plan, which was upheld as constitutional, included banning rock climbing on Cave Rock, yet it continued to permit "activities that are incompatible with Washoe beliefs," such as hiking and sightseeing.

The issue of governmental involvement in religious activity is, of course, neither just limited to Indian Country nor any less controversial outside of Native America. Nonetheless, the long history of governmental suppression of tribal religious beliefs and practices has raised the stakes for Native practitioners. Despite some successes and better cooperation from some federal sources in the Self-Determination era, tribal religious practices and beliefs remain in a precarious situation under the current state of 1st Amendment law.

SUGGESTED READINGS

- *Many Nations Under Many Gods: Public Land Management and American Indian Sacred Sites.* Todd Allin Morman. Norman, OK: University of Oklahoma Press, 2018.

- "Limiting Principles and Empowering Practices in American Indian Religious Freedoms." Kirsten A. Carpenter. 44 *Connecticut Law Review* 387 (December 2012).

- "Towards a Balanced Approach for the Protection of Native American Sacred Sites." Alex Tallchief Skibine. 17 *Michigan Journal of Race and Law* 269 (Spring 2012).

---

[1]   International Ass'n of Machinists v. Street, 367 U.S. 740, 788 (1961).

[2]   535 F.3d 1058 (2008).

[3]   Id. at 1063.

CHAPTER 28

Diversity in Indian Law and Indian Country

As noted in the introduction, Indian Country is an incredibly diverse place. There are, as of the publication of this text, 573 federally recognized tribal nations in thirty-six different states from Alaska to Florida and California to Maine. There are also over sixty state recognized tribal nations and many other tribal entities seeking either federal or state recognition. Also, as noted in the introduction, describing something as "Native American" is equivalent to describing something as "European" or "Asian." While there are certainly a few common characteristics for all "Native Americans" or tribal nations, there is much that distinguishes them as well. This includes their individual legal and political histories.

No single piece of writing can do complete justice to the each and every one of these legal and political histories. To that end, this text strives to describe the more common elements of federal law and policy that will be most recognizable and applicable to the most tribal nations. Nonetheless, the federal government has sometimes responded to different tribal nations in different ways at different points of history. Thus, it is important to recognize that each tribal nation has a unique set of legal and political circumstances that it must navigate.

This chapter offers three examples filtered through a state context—Oklahoma, Alaska, and Hawaii. Each example will both demonstrate the significant diversity of legal and political experiences in Indian Country and describe some of the most prominent diversions from a more typical tribal experience under American law. A full rendition of the history between each example state and Native peoples and nations within its borders is outside of the scope of this chapter. However, some major points of engagement will help to demonstrate the distinctive nature of federal Indian law for tribal nations in each state. Any student of federal Indian law and policy should have some awareness of each example's noteworthiness within the field as well as the need to be attuned to the unique circumstances for any particular tribal nation.

> *This chapter will demonstrate. . .*
>
> • *The operation of the Oklahoma Indian Welfare Act*
>
> • *The operation of the Alaska Native Claims Settlement Act*
>
> • *The status of Native Hawaiians*

OKLAHOMA

In 2008 the state of Oklahoma redesigned its license plates to depict a bronze sculpture of a Native man using his bow to shoot an arrow into the sky. The sculpture, created by famed Native artist Allen Houser and housed at the Gilcrease Museum in Tulsa, was accompanied by the words "Native America" at the center bottom of the plate. In the bottom right hand corner a Native battle shield is crossed by a peace pipe and an olive branch.

This extensive Native imagery on the Oklahoma license plate is a nod to the state's significantly intermingled history with and connection to Native peoples. Already home to many tribal nations, the federal government used what was to become the state of Oklahoma as a common destination for several tribal nations that were removed throughout the nineteenth century (see Chapter 3). Consequently, today there are thirty-eight federally recognized tribal nations in Oklahoma. In addition, before it became a state, what was to become Oklahoma was comprised of two territories: Oklahoma territory in the west and Indian Territory in the east. In the early twentieth century, there was a movement within Indian Territory to convert the area into a state of the union named Sequoyah. Statehood bills were introduced into Congress but were ultimately defeated and Indian Territory was shortly thereafter joined with Oklahoma Territory to become the state of Oklahoma in 1907. Tribal land loss was rampant at this time as non-Native "sooners" crossed into the region before they were legally permitted to claim homesteads in what was soon to be the 46th state. The experiences of Native peoples in Oklahoma is also roughly bisected into the eastern half, which has tended to have more involvement with non-Natives, and the western half, which had tended to have less involvement with non-Natives.

Comprising a significant portion of the population, Native peoples have been able to influence Oklahoma politics in a greater degree than in most other states of the union, whether directly through voting and running for office or indirectly as a matter of additional concern for non-Native leaders and voters. The large number of tribal nations has also meant that, on occasion, the federal government has had to give Indian Country in Oklahoma extra or different consideration. Perhaps the most prominent example is the Oklahoma Indian Welfare Act (OIWA), a companion piece of legislation to the Indian Reorganization Act (IRA).

Oklahoma's congressional delegation was able to exempt tribal nations within the state from the IRA in 1934. The IRA is given greater attention in Chapter 8; for the purposes of this chapter it suffices to note that it was a major legislative effort aimed at undoing many of the destructive polices of the Allotment Era (see Chapter 5). The IRA sought to accomplish this lofty goal by, among other things, ending the allotment process, creating a pathway for tribal constitutional governments, and also creating a pathway for the establishment of tribal corporations. In order to better understand the OIWA, it is useful to review the excerpt of the IRA in Chapter 8.

Two years after they successfully fought against the inclusion of the state's tribal nations into the IRA, the Oklahoma congressional delegation successfully fought for the passage of the OIWA. Very similar to the IRA, the OIWA nonetheless speaks more directly to the issues facing tribal nations in Oklahoma. As you read the excerpt of the statute, ask yourself what it seeks to accomplish. How does it compare and contrast to the IRA? Who remains excluded?

OKLAHOMA INDIAN WELFARE ACT

25 U.S.C.A. Ch. 45A

§ 5201. Acquisition of agricultural and grazing lands for Indians; title to lands; tax exemption

The Secretary of the Interior is authorized, in his discretion, to acquire by purchase, relinquishment, gift, exchange, or assignment, any interest in lands, water rights, or surface rights to lands, within or without existing Indian reservations, including trust or otherwise restricted lands now in Indian ownership: *Provided*, That such lands shall be agricultural and grazing lands of good character and quality in proportion to the respective needs of the particular Indian or Indians for whom such purchases are made. Title to all lands so acquired shall be taken in the name of the United States, in trust for the tribe, band, group, or individual Indian for whose benefit such land is so acquired, and while the title thereto is held by the United States said lands shall be free from any and all taxes, save that the State of Oklahoma is authorized to levy and collect a gross-production tax. . . .

§ 5202. Purchase of restricted Indian lands; preference to Secretary of the Interior; waiver of preference

Whenever any restricted Indian land or interests in land, other than sales or leases of oil, gas, or other minerals therein, are offered for sale, pursuant to the terms of this chapter or any other Act of Congress, the Secretary of the Interior shall have a preference right, in his discretion, to purchase the same for or in behalf of any other Indian or Indians of the same or any other tribe, at a fair valuation to be fixed by the appraisement satisfactory to the Indian owner or owners, or if offered for sale at auction said Secretary shall have a preference right, in his discretion, to purchase the same for or in behalf of any other Indian or Indians by meeting the highest bid otherwise offered therefor. . . .

§ 5203. Organization of tribes or bands; constitution; charter; right to participate in revolving credit fund

Any recognized tribe or band of Indians residing in Oklahoma shall have the right to organize for its common welfare and to adopt a constitution and bylaws, under such rules and regulations as the Secretary of the Interior may prescribe. . . . *Provided, however,* That such election shall be void unless the total vote cast be at least 30 per centum of those entitled to vote. . . .

§ 5204. Cooperative associations; charter; purposes; voting rights

Any ten or more Indians . . . who reside within the State of Oklahoma in convenient proximity to each other may receive from the Secretary of the Interior a charter as a local cooperative association for any one or more of the following purposes: Credit administration, production, marketing, consumers' protection, or land management. . . .

§ 5205. Amendment or revocation of charters; suits by and against associations

The charters of any cooperative association organized pursuant to section 5204 of this title shall not be amended or revoked by the Secretary except after a majority vote of the membership. Such cooperative associations may sue and be sued in any court of the State of Oklahoma or of the United States having jurisdiction of the cause of action, but a certified copy of all papers filed in any action against a cooperative association in a court of Oklahoma shall be served upon the Secretary of the Interior. . . . [T]he Secretary of the Interior may intervene in such action or may remove such action to the United States district court.

§ 5206. Loans to individuals and groups; appropriation

The Secretary is authorized to make loans to individual Indians and to associations or corporate groups organized pursuant to this chapter. . . .

§ 5207. Availability and allocation of funds; royalties from mineral deposits

All funds appropriated under the several grants of authority contained in [the IRA] are hereby made available for use under the provisions of this chapter, and Oklahoma Indians shall be accorded and allocated a fair and just share of any and all funds appropriated. . . .

§ 5208. Application of provisions to Osage County

This chapter shall not relate to or affect Osage County, Oklahoma.

§ 5209. Rules and regulations; repeals

The Secretary of the Interior is authorized to prescribe such rules and regulations as may be necessary to carry out the provisions of this chapter. All Acts or parts of Acts inconsistent with this chapter are repealed.

* * *

Some of the spirit and much of the text of the OIWA follows the IRA, although there are some subtle but important differences between the two. One of those differences involves one of the most controversial elements of both pieces of legislation: the provisions that have authorized the federal government to buy land back for Native peoples.

The "buy back" provisions have been controversial for a number of reasons, but primarily because of their effects on states. In both pieces of legislation, once land is purchased on behalf of tribal nations, it is no longer taxable by the state. Consequently, states have objected, under both the IRA and OIWA about the reduction of the taxable land base within their borders.

A good deal of the language of the "buy back" provisions of the IRA and OIWA is identical, but there is an important distinction in the OIWA that is not present in the IRA. In the following case, a Pawnee couple owned several tracts of land that were validly taxed by the state of Oklahoma. At a certain point, acting under the advice of the federal government, the couple turned over four tracts of land to be held in trust for their minor children under OIWA. For two years after the land had been given over to the federal government, the state, acting through one of its counties, sought to continue to tax the four tracts of land while the federal government argued that they were no longer taxable by the state. As you read the case, ask yourself about the nature of the state's arguments. What distinction does the OIWA make in its "buy back" provision that is missing from the IRA? How does it affect the case? What authority does Congress have to pass the OIWA?

BOARD OF COM'RS OF PAWNEE COUNTY, OKL. V. U.S.
139 F.2d 248 (1943)

MURRAH, CIRCUIT JUDGE:

* * *

On the merits, it is urged that . . . the Oklahoma Indian Welfare Act is invalid as an unconstitutional delegation of legislative power; that the Act "has delegated to the Secretary of the Interior not the power to enforce the law, but to determine in effect what the law shall be." It is of course true that Congress may not, within the constitutional framework, grant lawmaking power to the executive branch of the government, to be exercised under the guise of administrative discretion. In other words, Congress must prescribe the standards or declare the legislative policy which is to be administered by the executive. It must be conceded, however, that within reasonable limits, Congress may delegate to the executive, authority to exercise appropriate discretion in the administration and effectuation of the declared Congressional policy. The discretionary power granted to the Secretary to acquire lands, and to hold the same in trust for the benefit of the Indian is not limitless. It is subject to the Congressional command that the lands shall be "agricultural and grazing lands of good character and quality in proportion to the respective needs of the particular Indian.". . . Historically, the Secretary of the Interior has been the delegated arm of the Federal government to act as the guardian of the Indian ward; to administer the affairs of its Indians, and to that end has been granted wide discretionary powers in the enforcement of the declared Congressional policy.

Assuming the Act to be a valid delegation of power to the Secretary, the [state] next argues that the Secretary has not exercised that power in accordance with the declared legislative policy. In effect, it is contended that the lands in question are not agricultural and grazing lands of good character and quality in proportion to the respective needs of the particular Indian, for whose benefit they are now held, but rather it is insisted that the dominant purpose of the entire transaction was to effect a nontaxable status of otherwise taxable lands . . . and the [OIWA] was merely a hand device by which the Secretary was enabled to accomplish that result. . . . The selection of lands to be acquired is an administrative detail which must necessarily be left to the exercise of the Secretary's discretion, and the courts are not authorized to substitute their judgment for that of the Secretary, unless it clearly appears that he arbitrarily exercised his discretion in a manner wholly unrelated to the legislative design.

The trial court found that the lands in question were agricultural and grazing lands of good character and quality in proportion to the respective needs of the particular Indians, and . . . we are unable to hold that the Secretary has exercised his discretion in a manner wholly inconsistent to the legislative purpose. It may be conceded that the primary purpose of the [federal government] was to effect a nontaxable status of taxable lands . . . yet, if in accomplishing that result, the Secretary acted in accordance with constitutionally delegated power, we are not at liberty to annul his actions merely because he may have been initially prompted by some purpose not within the contemplation of the Act. Furthermore we are unable to say . . . that the secretary was not actuated by a desire to protect the lands from loss by tax foreclosure and sale and thus preserve the same for the benefit of the Indians for whom the lands were acquired. If this be so, both the purpose and the result are wholly within the legislative design. It should be noted that as respects Indian affairs, the United States, acting through the Secretary of the Interior, is guardian of the Indian wards, and in the discharge of this duty, the Government acts in a proprietary capacity, and its discretion, when exercised in respect to an Indian ward, is less limitable than an ordinary Congressional delegation of power.

* * *

In one sense, the result in the case demonstrates the similarities between IRA and the OIWA. Both have "buy back" provisions and, since the tribal interests prevailed in this case then the tribal interests assuredly would have also prevailed had the IRA applied instead.

In another sense, the case also demonstrates the differences between the IRA and the OIWA. Whereas the "buy back" provision in the IRA is very robust and lacking in conditions, the one in the OIWA, as noted by the Court, is limited by the fact that the lands need to be "agricultural and grazing lands of good character and quality in proportion to the respective needs of the particular Indian." Put another way, the "buy back" provision of the OIWA continues to envision tribal peoples and lands in terms of their capacity to engage in farming and ranching, which was the dominant framework of thinking for federal officials in the

Allotment Era. Consequently, it is fair to wonder whether to what extent the OIWA sought to perpetuate the full spirit of the IRA and to what extent tribal nations in Oklahoma remain beholden to Allotment Era understandings to this day. It also operates as one prominent example of a different context that tribal nations in Oklahoma sometimes have to navigate in the larger field of federal Indian law and policy.

ALASKA

The federal government's history and engagement with the Native peoples of what is now Alaska has been characterized by confusion and contradiction. This is due, in some part, to the fact that the state of Alaska is both large in size and rich in resources, yet also small in population and remote in location. To demonstrate, as of 2018 there were 229 federally recognized tribal nations in Alaska, or approximately 40% of all of the federally recognized tribal nations. These astounding numbers have and do necessitate a fair amount of attention from the federal government. However, many of the federally recognized tribal nations are quite small, and as a whole each Alaskan tribal nation averages a citizenry of about 350 people. Many are also a significant distance from the larger population centers in the state or otherwise difficult to access. Consequently, there are often fewer federal services or opportunities for Alaskan tribal nations than the raw numbers would indicate.

The unique experience for Alaskan tribal nations is also due to a somewhat different colonial experience than what occurred in the lower forty-eight states. In the mid-1700s Russia began serious colonization efforts in North America, primarily in what is now Alaska but reaching as far south as what is now northern California. By the mid-1800s, Russia's colonies were waning and in 1867, Russia sold its land claims in North America to the United States in a treaty. Regarding the Native peoples of Alaska, Article III of the treaty stated that, "The uncivilized tribes will be subject to such laws and regulations as the United States may, from time to time, adopt in regard to aboriginal tribes of that country."[1]

After gaining colonial authority over Alaska, the United States did not extensively engage with the Native peoples of the territory, nor did the United States significantly pursue tribal lands. Most strikingly—and most differently from many tribal nations in the lower forty-eight (although not all)—the United States did not engage in treaties with the Native peoples of Alaska. Two different acts of Congress in the late nineteenth century that established a governing structure for Alaska stated that Native peoples were not to be disturbed in their use of the lands that they claimed. The enormity of Alaska and the remoteness of many Native settlements limited the non-Native desires for tribally claimed lands.

By the mid-twentieth century, however, circumstances began to change for Alaska and its Native inhabitants. The resource-rich region was becoming of greater interest to those who wanted to develop and profit from those resources, and the territory was moving increasingly closer to statehood. These developments led to a question of major significance for both Native peoples and those who wanted access to Alaska's resources: what rights did Native peoples have to Alaskan lands? On one hand, neither the political autonomy of Native peoples nor their claims to lands had been recognized by the United States through treaties. On the other hand, a few federal statutes stated that Native peoples were not to be disturbed in the use of their land. Were these statutes enough of an acknowledgment to tribal land claims, and the right to control, or at least profit, from the resources upon them?

The Supreme Court took up this question in 1955 in *Tee-Hit-Ton Indians v. U.S.* The case is given fuller consideration in Chapter 15. For the purposes of this chapter it suffices to note that the Supreme Court ruled that "every American schoolboy knows" that tribal nations could not assert land claims unless the federal government has acknowledged those claims in some manner—which was typically done through a treaty. Since the federal government had not negotiated treaties with the Native peoples of Alaska, the ruling was particularly bleak from the tribal perspective. And yet, the question of tribal land rights was not completely closed after *Tee-Hit-Ton*. The Alaska Statehood Act of 1958 seemed to admit to the existence of legitimate tribal land claims and set them under the jurisdiction of the United States.

By the early 1970s there was a strong desire among the interested parties to find some resolution to the situation. To that end, Congress received input from a number of stakeholders, including Native peoples, and passed the Alaska Native Claims Settlement Act (ANCSA) in 1971. The purpose of the Act was to settle Alaskan tribal land claims in a manner that was acceptable for all parties involved. As you read the excerpt from the statute, ask yourself what Native peoples give and what they get from the legislation. What structure does ANCSA establish for Alaskan tribal nations? How is this arrangement different from your understanding of the typical arrangement for a tribal nation in the lower forty-eight states?

ALASKA NATIVE CLAIMS SETTLEMENT ACT
43 U.S.C.A. Ch. 33

§ 1601—Congressional findings and declaration of policy

Congress finds and declares that—

(a) there is an immediate need for a fair and just settlement of all claims by Native and Native groups of Alaska, based on aboriginal land claims;

(b) the settlement should be accomplished rapidly, with certainty, in conformity with the real economic and social needs of Natives, without litigation, with maximum participation by Natives in decisions affecting their rights and property, without establishing any permanent racially defined institutions, rights, privileges, or obligations, without creating a reservation system or lengthy wardship or trusteeship, and without adding to the categories of property and institutions enjoying special tax privileges or to the legislation establishing special relationships between the United States Government and the State of Alaska;

(c) No provision of this chapter shall replace or diminish any right, privilege, or obligation of Natives as citizens of the United State or of Alaska, or relieve, replace, or diminish any obligation or the United States or of the State [of] Alaska to protect and promote the rights or welfare of Native as citizens of the United States or of Alaska. . . .

* * *

§ 1603—Declaration of settlement

(a) Aboriginal title extinguishment through prior land and water area conveyances

All prior conveyances of public land and water areas in Alaska . . . shall be regarded as an extinguishment of the aboriginal title thereto. . . .

(b) Aboriginal title and claim extinguishment where based on use and occupancy. . . .

All aboriginal titles, if any, and claims of aboriginal title in Alaska based on use and occupancy . . . are hereby extinguished.

(c) . . . pending claims

All claims against the United States, the State, and all other persons that are based on claims of aboriginal title . . . are hereby extinguished.

* * *

§ 1605   Alaska Native Fund

(a)   Establishment in Treasury. . . .

There is hereby established in the United States Treasury an Alaska Native fund into which the following moneys shall be deposited:

(1) $462,500,000 from the general fund of the Treasury. . . .

(2)   Four percent interest per annum. . . .

(3) $500,000,000 pursuant to the revenue sharing provisions of . . . this title

* * *

§ 1606—Regional Corporations

(a)   Division of Alaska into twelve geographic regions. . . .

For purposes of this chapter, the State of Alaska shall be divided by the Secretary . . . into twelve geographic regions, with each region composed as far as practicable of Natives having a common heritage and sharing common interests. . . .

(d)   Incorporation. . . .

Five incorporators within each region, named by the Native association in the region, shall incorporate . . . to conduct business for profit, which shall be eligible for the benefits of this chapter so long as it is organized and functions in accordance with this chapter. . . .

* * *

§ 1607   Village Corporations

(a)   Organization of Corporation prerequisite. . . .

The Native residents of each Native village entitled to receive lands and benefits under this chapter shall organize as a business for profit or nonprofit corporation . . . before the Native village may receive patent to lands or benefits under this chapter. . . .

> (b)   Regional Corporation: approval of initial articles. . . .
>
> The initial articles of incorporation for each Village Corporation shall be subject to the approval of the Regional Corporation for the region in which the village is located. . . .
>
> * * *
>
> § 1610—Withdrawal of public lands
>
> (a)   Description of withdrawn public lands. . . .
>
> > (1)   The following public lands are withdrawn . . . from all forms of appropriation under the public land laws . . . and from selection under the Alaska Statehood Act. . . .
> >
> > > (A) The lands in each township that encloses all or part of any Native village. . . .
> > >
> > > (B) The lands in each township that is contiguous to or corners on the township that encloses all or part of such Native village. . . .
>
> * * *

At its most basic, ANCSA extinguished all tribal rights to lands or any other claims within the state for the price of almost one billion dollars. It also established more of a corporate structure, as opposed to a more typically governmental structure, to exercise authority within Native communities. Individual Native villages—each essentially a separate federally recognized tribal nation—govern themselves under the umbrella of one of the twelve regional corporations established under ANCSA (ANCSA also established a thirteenth regional corporation for Alaskan Natives who are not residents of the state). The purpose of this structure was to manage tribal land and resources in a manner that was intended to be profitable and self-fulfilling. Stock in both the regional and village corporations was issued to Native individuals with restrictions on the capacity for individuals to sell that stock. ANCSA and its amendments have established additional rules and procedures to perpetuate itself and maintain a sense of fairness among the village corporations, regional corporations, and the state.

ANCSA also set aside lands for the various tribal villages. However, this raised a related but slightly different question than before: what is the status of the tribally held lands under ANCSA? Put differently, to what extent are those lands like reservations or other forms of "Indian Country"?

The Supreme Court wrestled with this question in the following case. In 1943 the federal government established a reservation north of the Arctic Circle for the Native Village of Venetie. Under ANCSA, the Village was able to convert the reservation land to fee land, or land over which they held more control then typical reservation lands. In the 1980s, a dispute arose when the Village sought to collect a tax against a private contractor doing business on tribal lands on behalf of the state. The validity of the tax, according to the courts who heard the case, turned on whether the Village's land was or was not "Indian Country."

Indian Country is defined by a federal statute, which is given greater attention in Chapter 13. For the purposes of this chapter, it suffices to know that the statute (which the opinion refers to as § 1151) identifies three categories of land that is "Indian Country": (a) reservations, (b) "dependent Indian communities," and (c) allotments. As you read the case, ask yourself what conditions, according to the Supreme Court, are necessary for determining what is a dependent Indian community. Would the lands in question have qualified as Indian Country before ANCSA? What is their status after ANCSA? How does this ruling benefit and/or burden the Native Village of Venetie?

AK V. NATIVE VILLAGE OF VENETIE TRIBAL GOV'T
522 U.S. 520 (1998)

JUSTICE THOMAS, delivered the opinion of the Court.

* * *

. . . ANCSA revoked "the various reserves set aside . . . for Native use" by legislative or Executive action . . . and completely extinguished all aboriginal claims to Alaska land. In return, Congress authorized the transfer of $962.5 million in state and federal funds and approximately 44 million acres of Alaska land to state-chartered private business corporations that were to be formed pursuant to the statute; all of the shareholders of these corporations were required to be Alaska Natives. The ANCSA corporations received title to the transferred land in fee simple, and no federal restrictions applied to subsequent land transfers by them.

* * *

Because ANCSA revoked the Venetie Reservation, and because no Indian allotments are at issue, whether the Tribe's land is Indian country depends on whether it falls within the "dependent Indian communities" prong of the statute. Since 18 U.S.C. § 1151 was enacted in 1948, we have not had an occasion to interpret the term "dependent Indian communities." We now hold that it refers to a limited category of Indian lands that are neither reservations nor allotments, and that satisfy two requirements—first, they must have been set aside by the Federal Government for the use of the Indians as Indian land; second, they must be under federal superintendence. Our holding is based on our conclusion that in enacting § 1151, Congress codified these two requirements, which previously we had held necessary for a finding of "Indian country" generally.

* * *

The Tribe's ANCSA lands do not satisfy either of these requirements. After the enactment of ANCSA, the Tribe's lands are neither "validly set apart for the use of the Indians as such," nor are they under the superintendence of the Federal Government.

With respect to the federal set-aside requirement, it is significant that ANCSA, far from designating Alaskan lands for Indian use, revoked the existing Venetie Reservation, and indeed revoked all existing reservations in Alaska "set aside by legislation or by Executive or Secretarial Order for Native use," save one. In no clearer fashion could Congress have departed from its traditional practice of setting aside Indian lands.

* * *

Equally clearly, ANCSA ended federal superintendence over the Tribe's lands. As noted above, ANCSA revoked the Venetie Reservation along with every other reservation in Alaska but one, and Congress stated explicitly that ANCSA's settlement provisions were intended to avoid a "lengthy wardship or trusteeship." After ANCSA, federal protection of the Tribe's land is essentially limited to a statutory declaration that the land is exempt from adverse possession claims, real property taxes, and certain judgments as long as it has not been sold, leased, or developed. These protections, if they can be called that, simply do not approach the level of superintendence over the Indians' land that existed in our prior cases. . . .

* * *

Justice Clarence Thomas's opinion set forth two criteria for determining if land is considered Indian Country as a dependent Indian Community: (1) The land must have been set aside by the federal government for the use of the Indians as Indian land, and (2) the land must be under federal superintendence. ANCSA, according to Thomas, operated against both of those purposes. Thus, the land base for the Native Village of Venetie—and many other Alaska Native nations—is not Indian Country.

Consequently, Alaska Natives find themselves in a much different set of circumstances than tribal nations in the lower forty-eight states. Those who live within the territory of a tribal nation in Alaska live under a corporate structure on lands that are not considered Indian Country. Much of this difference has been brought about by ANCSA, but much of it has been the product of a unique history that began with Russian colonization and included no Native treaty history with the United States. It is a reminder that the legal and political status of a tribal nation is tied to its location, history, and engagement with the federal government.

HAWAII

When you conceptualize a traditional Native American what comes to mind? When you conceptualize a traditional Native Hawaiian what comes to mind? What are the differences between those two conceptualizations? Do they have any similarities? What distinctions, if any, should American law make between the two?

On the one hand, there are important differences between traditional Native Hawaiians and their mainland Native American counterparts. For example, Native Hawaiians employed a more hierarchical governing structure than most Native American tribal nations, with high chiefs, and then eventually a single monarch, having significant—although not unfettered—control over land use rights. In addition, the multi-linguistic and cultural groupings on the mainland necessitated a greater network of diplomatic relations, including trade, political alignments, and warfare than was possible on the relatively isolated Hawaiian Islands—although Native Hawaiians hardly lacked their share of diplomatic engagements among the several islands.

On the other hand, there are important parallels between the Native Hawaiian and the Native American experience as well. Europeans first made contact with Native Hawaiians in 1778. Shortly thereafter, in 1810, the people of Hawaii consolidated their political authority in a single monarch and began operating under a constitution beginning in 1840 in reaction to their contacts with colonizers. Nonetheless, by the mid-1800s, as colonial efforts were taking increasing root on the Islands, title to lands began to quickly fall from Hawaiian hands into those of Westerners. In 1893, American forces overthrew the constitutional monarchy of Hawaii and established the Islands as a territory of the United States. The Hawaiian experience of land loss, governmental overthrow, colonialism, military suppression, and the disruption of a way of life is a story that is very familiar to mainland Native America.

This very brief summation does not do justice to the complex and tragic history of the indigenous peoples of Hawaii, but it does allow us to return to an important question that began this section: what distinction, if any, should American law make between Native Hawaiians and Native Americans? Put another way, are Native Hawaiians the same as "Indians" for the purposes of American law?

The answer to this question is, of course, complicated. Since the beginning of the Self-Determination Era (see Chapter 10), Congress has often included Native Hawaiians in legislation directly targeting or otherwise including provisions for Native Americans. For example, the Native American Graves Protection and Repatriation Act, which seeks to protect tribal burial sites and cultural remains (see Chapter 25), includes Native Hawaiian remains and artifacts under its protections. Yet these deliberate inclusions within legislation do not necessarily cover the full scope of the federal government's obligations to tribal nations, nor the status that American law places upon tribal nations and their citizens.

In the following case, *Rice v. Cayetano*, the Supreme Court was given the opportunity to measure the difference between Native Hawaiians and Native Americans. Under its constitution, the state of Hawaii established an Office for Hawaiian Affairs (OHA), a state agency devoted to administering programing for descendants of indigenous Hawaiians—people who could trace their ancestry to the original inhabitants of the Hawaiian Islands. The trustees for the OHA are elected state officials. However, voting for these state officials was limited to descendants of indigenous Hawaiians. A citizen of the state of Hawaii who was not a descendant of indigenous Hawaiians sued the state, claiming that the voting scheme for the OHA violated the U.S. Constitution. The state of Hawaii argued, among other things, that it was fulfilling a trust responsibility to the descendants of indigenous Hawaiians in a manner similar to the federal government's trust responsibility to Native Americans (see Chapter 14).

In order to understand the decision in *Rice v. Cayetano*, it is important to have some knowledge of the 1974 case *Morton v. Mancari*. A fuller discussion of *Mancari* can be found in Chapter 10. For the purposes of this chapter, it suffices to know that the Supreme Court ruled in *Mancari* that a hiring preference for Native individuals in the Bureau of Indian Affairs was based on a political classification and not a racial one. Consequently, as a general proposition, legislation that directly targets Native peoples or nations, such as the Indian Child Welfare Act (see Chapter 23), is understood to be constitutionally valid whereas legislation that directly targets other seemingly racial groupings, such as African Americans or Asian Americans, is considered constitutionally suspect. The state of Hawaii argued that the voting scheme for the OHA paralleled the hiring preference in *Mancari* and should not be regarded as a racial classification.

As you read the case, ask yourself how the Court distinguishes *Mancari* from this case. What does the Court actually decide and what does it decline to decide? Does this case offer any clarity on the status of Native Hawaiians under American law? How would the dissent rule on the question of trust responsibilities to descendants of indigenous Hawaiians?

Rice v. Cayetano

528 U.S. 495 (2000)

Justice Kennedy, delivered the opinion of the Court.

* * *

The most far reaching of the State's arguments is that exclusion of non-Hawaiians from voting is permitted under our cases allowing the differential treatment of certain members of Indian tribes. The decisions of this Court, interpreting the effect of treaties and congressional enactments on the subject, have held that various tribes retained some elements of quasi-sovereign authority, even after cession of their lands to the United States. The retained tribal authority relates to self-governance. In reliance on that theory the Court has sustained a federal provision giving employment preferences to persons of tribal ancestry. The *Mancari* case, and the theory upon which it rests, are invoked by the State to defend its decision to restrict voting for the OHA trustees, who are charged so directly with protecting the interests of native Hawaiians.

If Hawaii's restriction were to be sustained under *Mancari* we would be required to accept some beginning premises not yet established in our case law. Among other postulates, it would be necessary to conclude that Congress . . . has determined that native Hawaiians have a status like that of Indians in organized tribes, and that it may, and has, delegated to the State a broad authority to preserve that status. These propositions would raise questions of considerable moment and difficulty. It is a matter of some dispute, for instance, whether Congress may treat the native Hawaiians as it does the Indian tribes. We can stay far off that difficult terrain, however.

The State's argument fails for a more basic reason. Even were we to take the substantial step of finding authority in Congress, delegated to the State, to treat Hawaiians or native Hawaiians as tribes, Congress may not authorize a State to create a voting scheme of this sort.

Of course, as we have established in a series of cases, Congress may fulfill its treaty obligations and its responsibilities to the Indian tribes by enacting legislation dedicated to their circumstances and needs. As we have observed, "every piece of legislation dealing with Indian tribes and reservations . . . single[s] out for special treatment a constituency of tribal Indians."

Mancari . . . presented the somewhat different issue of a preference in hiring and promoting at the federal Bureau of Indian Affairs. . . . Although the classification had a racial component, the Court found it important that the preference was "not directed towards a 'racial' group consisting of 'Indians,' " but rather "only to members of 'federally recognized' tribes." "In this sense," the Court held, "the preference [was] political rather than racial in nature.". . .

Hawaii would extend the limited exception of *Mancari* to a new and larger dimension. The State contends that "one of the very purposes of OHA—and the challenged voting provision—is to afford Hawaiians a measure of self-governance," and so it fits the model of *Mancari*. It does not follow from *Mancari*, however, that Congress may authorize a State to establish a voting scheme that limits the electorate for its public officials to a class of tribal Indians, to the exclusion of all non-Indian citizens.

. . . If a non-Indian lacks a right to vote in tribal elections, it is for the reason that such elections are the internal affair of a quasi sovereign. The OHA elections, by contrast, are the affair of the State of Hawaii. . . .

* * *

. . . [T]he elections for OHA trustee are elections of the State, not of a separate quasi sovereign, and they are elections to which the [U.S. Constitution] applies. To extend *Mancari* to this context would be to permit a State, by racial classification, to fence out whole classes of its citizens from decisionmaking in critical state affairs. The [U.S. Constitution] forbids this result.

* * *

JUSTICE STEVENS dissenting.

The Court's holding today rests largely on the repetition of glittering generalities that have little, if any, application to the compelling history of the State of Hawaii. When that history is held up against . . . two centuries of this

Court's federal Indian law, it is clear to me that Hawaii's election scheme should be upheld.

* * *

. . . [T]he Federal Government must be, and had been, afforded wide latitude in carrying out its obligations arising from the special relationship it has with the aboriginal peoples, a category that includes the native Hawaiians, whose lands are now a part of the territory of the United States. . . .

Throughout our Nation's history, this Court has recognized both the plenary power of Congress over the affairs of Native Americans and the fiduciary character of the special federal relationship with descendants of those once sovereign peoples. . . .

As our cases have consistently recognized, Congress' plenary power over these peoples has been exercised time and again to implement a federal duty to provide native peoples with special " 'care and protection.' "

Critically, neither the extent of Congress' sweeping power nor the character of the trust relationship with indigenous peoples has depended on the ancient racial origins of the people, the allotment of tribal lands, the coherence or existence of tribal self-government, or the varying definitions of "Indian" Congress has chosen to adopt. . . .

As the history . . . reveals, the grounds for recognizing the existence of federal trust power here are overwhelming. . . .

. . . Among the many and varied laws passed by Congress in carrying out its duty to indigenous peoples, more than 150 today expressly include native Hawaiians as part of the class of Native Americans benefitted.

While splendidly acknowledging this history . . . the majority fails to recognize its import. The descendants of the native Hawaiians share with the descendants of the Native Americans on the mainland or in the Aleutian Islands not only a history of subjugation at the hands of colonial forces, but also a purposefully created and specialized "guardian-ward" relationship with the Government of the United States. It follows that legislation targeting the native Hawaiians must be evaluated according to the same understanding of the equal protection that this Court has long applied to the Indians on the continental United States: that "special treatment . . . be tied rationally to the fulfillment of Congress' unique obligation" toward the native peoples.

* * *

> Membership in a tribe, the majority suggest, rather than membership in a race or class of descendants, has been the [essential element] of governmental power in the realm of Indian law; *Mancari* itself, the majority contends, makes this proposition clear. But as scholars have often pointed out, tribal membership cannot be seen as the decisive factor in this Court's opinion upholding the [governmental] preferences in *Mancari*. . . . Indeed, the Federal Government simply has not been limited in its special dealings with the native peoples to laws affecting tribes or tribal Indians alone. In light of this precedent, it is a painful irony indeed to conclude that native Hawaiians are not entitled to special benefits designed to restore a measure of native self-governance because they currently lack any vestigial native government—a possibility of which history and the actions of this Nation have deprived them.
>
> . . . As I have explained, OHA and its trustee elections can hardly be characterized simply as an "affair of the State" alone; they are the instruments for implementing the Federal Government's trust relationship with a once sovereign indigenous people. This Court has held more than once that the federal power to pass laws fulfilling the federal trust relationship with the Indians may be delegated to the States. . . .
>
> * * *

Whereas the facts of *Rice v. Cayetano* offered the Supreme Court the opportunity to make a definitive ruling on the status of Native Hawaiians, Justice Anthony Kennedy's majority opinion sought to sidestep the issue, stating that it "would raise questions of considerable moment and difficulty," and that, "It is a matter of some dispute . . . whether Congress may treat the native Hawaiians as it does the Indian tribes." Further claiming that, "We can stay far off that difficult terrain," Kennedy's opinion revolved primarily around the fact that the OHA was an arm of the state, not of a tribal nation. Since it was a state election, the U.S. Constitution did not allow this type of "racial classification" as it concerned voting. Furthermore, Kennedy strongly implied, even if Native Hawaiians were regarded the same as Native Americans under American law, the reasoning in *Mancari* would not apply to this case since this was a state and not a tribal election.

Justice John Paul Stevens's dissent, on the other hand, would have made a determination that Native Hawaiians were the same as Native Americans under American law central to the case. More specifically, Stevens would have asserted that the federal government held the same trust responsibility to Native Hawaiians that it holds for Native Americans, stating that "the grounds for recognizing the existence of federal trust power here are overwhelming." With the trust responsibility firmly established, under Stevens's reasoning, the elections at dispute in *Rice v. Cayetano* should be assessed with an eye toward the federal government's broad authority to legislate for Native America.

Stevens's view did not win the day, however, and the status of Native Hawaiians under American law remains "a matter of some dispute," as described by Kennedy's majority opinion. To that end, there have been a number of attempts to pass legislation in Congress that would recognize Native Hawaiians as having the same political relationship with the federal government that Native nations and individuals on the mainland have. Put another way, under these bills Native Hawaiians would have federal recognition (see Chapter 13). To date, none of these efforts have been enacted into law, nor are they universally accepted by the people that they seek to cover. The bills provoke considerable debate and controversy within the Native Hawaiian population, as many wonder whether living under the trust responsibility would actually be to their benefit.

Each one of these case studies—the Oklahoma Indian Welfare Act, the Alaskan Native Claims Settlement Act, and the status of Native Hawaiians—is a noteworthy example of the tremendous diversity in Native America generally and in federal Indian law and policy more specifically. The case studies are not meant to, nor could they, give a complete picture of the totality of the different challenges and statuses that Native nations face. Rather, they describe some of the most prominent diversions from the more typical tribal experience that any student of the field should be aware of. Most important, they are a reminder that every tribal nation has its own unique political and legal status that must be understood on its own terms.

SUGGESTED READINGS

- *Oklahoma's Indian New Deal.* Jon S. Blackman. Norman, OK: University of Oklahoma Press, 2013.

- "Sovereignty and Subsistence: Native Self-Government and Rights to Hunt, Fish, and Gather after ANCSA." Robert T. Anderson. 33 *Alaska Law Review* 187 (December 2016).

- "Government of the People, by the People, for the People: Cultural Sovereignty, Civil Rights, and Good Native Hawaiian Governance." Breann Swann Nu'uhiwa. 14 *Asian-Pacific Law and Policy Journal* 57 (2013).

---

[1]   Act of Mar. 30, 1867, art. 3, 15 Stat. 539, 542.

CHAPTER 29

Tribal Law and Courts

Any introduction to federal Indian law would be incomplete without some discussion of tribal law. This is in part because, despite ample evidence to the contrary, the federal government has justified its colonial efforts in Indian Country on the premise that Native peoples lacked law, governing structures, or any sense of basic human rights. For example, in listing grievances against the King of England, the Declaration of Independence stated that the King "excited domestic insurrections" against the colonists by the "merciless Indian savages, whose known rule of warfare, is an undistinguished destruction of all ages, sexes and conditions." In addition, the adherence to a Western style of law and governance has perpetually been a measure of civilization for colonial forces. For example, in his 1855 Annual Report, the Commissioner of Indian Affairs argued in favor of a reservation for the Seminole, claiming that with a reservation and "the right and responsibility of governing themselves, they would gradually lose their present sense of degradation and their disposition to lawlessness, and soon become a better people."[1]

A discussion of tribal law, and specifically tribal courts, is also necessary because perhaps no other branch of government in the United States—whether federal, state, or tribal—faces such a disparate array of challenges: to their legitimacy, to the development of a body of law that is adequate for a community, to jurisdictional issues, or to a whole host of other complications. In addition, no other branch of government in the United States has engaged in as much development, innovation, and adaptation over the last fifty years.

Tribal law and tribal courts operate both inside and outside of federal Indian law. They operate within this regime because their reach is defined within the scope of federal Indian law; for example through legislation like the Indian Civil Rights Act (see Chapter 22) and the Indian Child Welfare Act (see Chapter 23). There have also been a number of important Supreme Court and Circuit Appellate Court decisions that originated in tribal courts. Yet, they operate outside of this regime because they must be responsive to their home communities and the legal traditions of their people. Tribal courts must also resolve some of the most difficult internal issues for a tribal nation that are not found in other American jurisdictions and that are dependent on tribal law, not federal or state law, for their resolution.

This chapter will demonstrate. . .

- *The history of tribal courts*

- *The efforts and challenges to incorporating tribal common law into tribal legal culture*

- *The unique challenges tribal law and courts face*

A BRIEF HISTORY OF TRIBAL COURTS

What is the purpose of a court, or adjudicatory, system? At its most basic, the purpose of a court system is to resolve disputes or other issues that members of a society cannot, or perhaps should not, resolve by themselves. Without the benefit of a court system, neighbors who are feuding over the boundaries of their respective properties might resort to behavior or actions that society normally seeks to discourage. Similarly, victims of crimes might also engage in self-help measures that create more problems than they solve. Put another way, if there were no court system to resolve the dispute, how might you react to a neighbor encroaching on your property or a thief who has burglarized your home? To what extent are these situations and others like them likely to escalate into violent or dangerous episodes without the benefit of a court system? And what about those who are unable or unwilling to engage with the pushy neighbor or the criminal offender? Should the weak and powerless be victimized merely because they are weak and powerless? An adjudicatory system offers a societally sanctioned opportunity to manage these types of conflicts in a manner that minimizes the potential for greater harm.

And yet, adequately resolving disputes that members of a society cannot resolve themselves cannot be accomplished merely by the presence of a court or adjudicatory system. That system must be accompanied by a set of principles or rules that governs the decisions of the court system. Adjudicatory structures that lack a set of rules or that are otherwise arbitrary or have no foundation for their decisions will quickly lose the respect of the communities for which they ostensibly function. In short, every court system must be accompanied by law. The rules by which a society lives—its law—and a system to enforce those rules exist in a symbiotic relationship.

Traditional tribal communities neither lacked in adjudicatory systems nor in law. One of the most straightforward examples of this understanding is the dispute between Crow Dog and Spotted Tail, which led to the *Ex parte Crow Dog* Supreme Court case. The decision in *Ex parte Crow Dog* and the circumstances surrounding the decision are discussed in greater detail in Chapter 6. For the purposes of this chapter, a brief retelling of the pertinent facts will suffice.

In the summer of 1881 Crow Dog killed Spotted Tail. Both men were leaders of the Brule Lakota and were rivals, and the killing caused a great amount of disruption within the community. Employing their own adjudicatory process (and one which was common in Native America), the Brule Lakota brought members of the families of both Crow Dog and Spotted Tail together to negotiate a settlement between the parties. The family of Crow Dog agreed to provide the family of Spotted Tail $600, eight horses, and a blanket in exchange for forgiveness and communal harmony.

To the federal officials who sought greater control over Indian Country, the situation between Crow Dow and Spotted Tail and its resolution within the community was, at best, a murderer buying his way out of justice. However, the community had managed the situation through an adjudicatory process that utilized the principles of the community. Members of both families were active participants in the resolution of the dispute. There was a negotiation that was managed by leaders within the community. And, unlike Western systems of justice which tend to focus on punishing the offender, the underlying goal of the Brule Lakota system was focused on making the victim, or the victim's family, as whole as possible. By doing so, the Brule Lakota—and many other tribal nations that operated in a very similar manner—sought, after the disruption caused by a crime, to recreate an environment in which all parties could continue to live with one another and in a sense of harmony and well-being. To that end, the $600, eight horses, and a blanket was not "blood money" as some outside observers at the time suggested, but rather the cost of repairing Spotted Tail's family to as whole as possible. The steep price testified to Spotted Tail's high standing in the community and the great loss for his family. The federal government, on the other hand, was concerned with enacting capital punishment against Crow Dog.

In the midst of the Allotment Era and in the wake of the *Ex parte Crow Dog* decision, the federal government became increasingly concerned with "lawlessness" in Indian Country—despite the successful resolution to the dispute among the Brule Lakota and other examples of tribal law and adjudication. In 1885 Congress passed the Major Crimes Act, a piece of legislation in which the federal government gave itself criminal jurisdiction over "major" crimes in Indian Country. A year later, the Supreme Court found the Major Crimes Act to be constitutional despite failing to find a textual basis in the Constitution for the Congressional authority to pass the Major Crimes Act (see Chapters 6 and 7).

To further combat the perceived problem of "lawlessness," the federal government also established what were called the Indian Police and Indian Courts on reservations during the Allotment Era. Both the Indian Police and Indian Courts (also known as CFR courts) are described in greater detail in Chapter 5. For the purposes of this chapter, it is useful to note a few important points about the Indian Courts. They functioned more like a Western style court, with a judge and sometimes a jury presiding over the proceedings, and they were generally staffed by Native peoples. Despite their Native participation, the Indian Courts were instruments to further Allotment Era policies. For example, Indian Courts sanctioned not only typical, smaller crimes on reservations but also cultural activities that the federal government was trying to eradicate, such as engaging in traditional medicinal practices and dancing. The dual purposes of maintaining law and order on a reservation and eradicating tribal practices meant that CFR courts were regarded in the eyes of federal officials as more like a finishing school than an actual court of law. One federal judge described them as "mere educational and disciplinary instrumentalities, by which the government of the United States is endeavoring to improve and elevate the condition of these dependent tribes to whom it sustains the relation of guardian" (see Chapter 5). Nor were the decisions of the CFR courts ever truly in the hands of the Native judges who presided over them. The superintendent of the Turtle Mountain Band of Chippewa Indians reservation reported in 1926 that he "sits with the judges, hears the evidence, and approves or disapproves of the decisions."[2]

Many of these Indian or CFR Courts were the first introduction to Western style adjudication within Native communities. Today, some tribal nations still maintain their CFR courts, although they have significantly more control over them than they did during the Allotment Era. After the Allotment Era, there was little further development of Western-style court systems on reservations. The governments that were established under constitutions under the Indian Reorganization Act (see Chapter 8) generally lacked court systems. And many of the tribal efforts during the Termination Era (see Chapter 9) were focused on preserving the governmental systems that did exist, as opposed to growing or expanding them.

In the Self-Determination Era (see Chapter 10), however, many tribal nations sought out ways to increase their sovereignty and self-governance. Consequently, many tribal nations began seriously investing in their court systems, including developing tribal codes, or bodies of written law. These noteworthy efforts are one of the primary reasons why issues of jurisdiction have become increasingly important in federal Indian law (see Chapters 18 and 19). It is also why many of the most important cases of the last half-century—such as *Oliphant v. Suquamish Indian Tribe*, *Nevada v. Hicks*, and *U.S. v. Lara*—began in tribal courtrooms. Tribal nations have increasingly recognized that a robust court system is critical to good governance and increased legitimacy, both internally and externally, under the present legal and political circumstances.

Despite the time and resources that tribal nations have invested, tribal courts face more constraints than any other branch of government within the United States. The Self-Determination Era continues to produce a complicated and contradictory situation for tribal nations, in which one arm of the federal government's efforts to foster self-governance in Native America is often undermined by another arm of the federal government. Presently, tribal courts are limited in their authority by both federal legislation and decisions of the Supreme Court. The most prominent piece of federal legislation to temper the authority of tribal courts is the Indian Civil Rights Act. This important legislation is discussed in greater detail in Chapter 22. For the purposes of this chapter it suffices to note that the Indian Civil Rights Act limits the amount of criminal punishment that a tribal court can bestow to one year in jail and a $5,000 fine. A handful of key Supreme Court decisions have limited the scope of tribal court jurisdiction, particularly over non-Natives. Consequently, tribal courts have to assess and monitor the scope of their jurisdiction to a much greater degree than any other court in the United States.

It is also difficult to describe tribal courts as a singular whole. As noted many places elsewhere in this text, there is a tremendous diversity within Indian Country, and no single text could describe the wide range of development of court systems among the many tribal nations today. Many smaller tribal nations do not have any court system at all, whereas other tribal nations have very well developed and sophisticated court systems that take great care to center traditional knowledge and law. As a general proposition, today many tribal courts resemble a typical rural state court system and they apply traditional knowledge and law to varying degrees. Some tribal nations require practitioners to pass a tribal bar exam and most, if not all, require that at least some of the officers of the court have Western-style legal training. Thus, a great number of tribal judges have graduated from law school and passed a bar exam for at least one state jurisdiction. However, many tribal nations lack the resources or population to have a readily available pool of licensed attorneys at their disposal. Thus, some tribal nations do not require that their trial judges have graduated from law school and some also employ "advocates"—persons who do not have Western-style legal training but who are nonetheless trained in and familiar with tribal law and procedure—to represent individuals before the court in the way that licensed attorneys otherwise would. Each court system has its own rules and requirements and anyone needing or seeking to engage with a particular tribal court system should become familiar with those specific rules and regulations.

Tribal court systems have also benefitted from a willingness and ability to innovate to meet the needs of the community. A number of tribal nations, in addition to their more Western-style court system, have what are often called Peacemaker Courts or Alternative Dispute Resolution Courts. These courts align more closely to traditional methods of adjudication. Typically, an offender and a victim, along with their families and other interested parties, meet to talk through an issue and come to a mutually agreeable resolution. Everyone in the process is allowed to speak, including the offender and the victim—which is not a characteristic of the Western system, where criminal defendants are often advised not to speak and victims are regularly excluded from the proceedings. A mediator participates, but does not act as a judge or hand down rulings. The mediator helps all of the parties to craft a meaningful plan of action for the offender to rectify the bad behavior. If an offender fails to follow through or complete the agreed upon plan of action, then the offender is typically redirected into the Western-style court system.

Peacemaker Courts have proven to be more successful in some situations and less effective or appropriate in others. For example, they have been particularly useful with juvenile offenders, as they have shifted the focus from punishment to a plan of action for a young person to atone for her or his mistakes. They have proven less successful in resolving issues of domestic or sexual violence, where a victim may feel afraid to participate in a process with an offender or otherwise coerced into perpetuating a difficult or dangerous situation.

There are any number of other examples of tribal courts that have evolved to meet the needs of the nation in unique and important ways within the constraints in which they find themselves. For example, some tribal nations share a trial level court or an appellate court to minimize the financial burden for each nation while maximizing the adjudicatory authority and capabilities of each nation. This brief summation testifies to the understanding that no other branch of government within the United States has engaged in more growth, development, and innovation than tribal courts over the last half-century. A number of challenges remain, and tribal courts are not without their own difficulties nor are they immune to critique. However, they are becoming an ever more important part of tribal governance and an increasingly necessary tool in the fight for greater sovereignty. In addition, these developments are merely the next step of a long-standing commitment within Native America to the rule of law and to maintaining an adjudicatory system for the benefit of the community.

NATIVE PERSPECTIVES IN TRIBAL LAW

One of the major challenges facing tribal courts today is striking a proper balance between a Western-style court system and more traditional understandings of law and dispute resolution. On the one hand, tribal courts are increasingly expected to reproduce Western systems and standards. As noted above, most tribal courts systems already resemble rural state court systems, and they are increasingly incentivized to operate like their other American counterparts. For example, the Violence Against Women Act (see Chapter 18) and the Tribal Law and Order Act (see Chapter 22) allow tribal courts to expand their authority over criminal defendants, but only if they guarantee those defendants many of the same protections and processes found in American courts. For a tribal court to exercise the authority to increase the penalties for criminal defendants under the Tribal Law and Order Act, that court must, among other things, "at the expense of the tribal government, provide an indigent defendant the assistance of a defense attorney licensed to practice law by any jurisdiction in the United States." Many tribal courts already provide council for indigent defendants, which means that the Tribal Law and Order Act perhaps speaks more to outside perceptions of tribal courts than the actual practice on the ground. Nonetheless, recent federal and state recognition of expanded tribal court authority has generally included conditions such as these.

On the other hand, the primary responsibility of any tribal court is to interpret tribal law for a tribal nation. This includes not just a tribal constitution and/or code, but what might also be called tribal common law as well. To understand what the tribal common law is, it is easiest to start with the understanding of the "common law" in the Western context.

Beginning with the English and then continuing with the American court traditions, the common law is the body of law created by judges as they resolved the disputes that came before them. The common law, or judge-made law as it is sometimes called, is often distinguished from the civil law tradition, in which the source of law is in written form and passed by a legislature. Each decision that a judge made in a given case would carry importance for the next judge that made a decision in a similar fact scenario. In essence, the theory behind the common law regime is that the collective wisdom of judges making many decisions in similar cases over a number of years and referring to past precedent would eventually lead to the correct legal principle. In keeping with that understanding, many of the major rules of American (and English) law that exist today first emerged from the common law tradition. Today, many common law principles have been codified, or put in writing, through statutes by Congress and state legislatures, and American legal regimes today are best understood as a mix of primarily statutory, or written, law with the common law filling in the gaps.

Somewhat like the English and American traditions, tribal nations have historically generated rules to live by and principles to resolve disputes. While these rules can and have been conceptualized in different ways—such as the traditions of a people, or its cosmology—it can also be understood as a tribal common law. When there was a dispute to be resolved, such as with Crow Dog and Spotted Tail, there was a method with which to resolve it and rules by which to govern the outcome of the decision. As with the Western common law, the major principles to emerge from this dispute resolution process have been handed down through the generations and have guided actions and behaviors thereafter.

Any tribal court must be aware of and sensitive to the common law of its nation. Failure to heed this legal source can and has produced friction and called the legitimacy of courts into question. Any tribal court that appears to merely mimic an American court, with no regard for the unique characteristics, understandings, and common law of its community, not only flirts with disaster but also loses out on a valuable resource with which to make meaningful decisions. Even so, the diversity in Native America can make this a challenging proposition. Respecting and adhering to tribal common law is easier for those court systems whose nations have managed to maintain a strong connection to their teachings than for other tribal nations that have suffered greater historical loss.

Further muddying the waters, the balance that tribal courts have to find is in some ways helped and in some ways hindered by the fact that one can find more overlap in Western and Native legal traditions than perhaps at first glance. One of the difficulties in discussing "Native" versus "Western" legal traditions is that it can suggest or imply that the two are diametrical opposites. But any righteous system of justice will find some commonalities with other similarly oriented regimes. The concept of "due process" is illustrative. There are many iterations of due process in the American legal system, but they all essentially seek to guarantee that every person in the American court system receives the same basic treatment throughout a legal process. In short, it is a promise to be fair to everyone.

Fairness was not and is not outside of Native legal traditions and regimes. To that end, tribal courts are benefitted by the overlap because they do not have to extend themselves beyond Native understandings of law when they are required to provide due process under the Indian Civil Rights Act. However, "due process" is a decidedly Western term. Consequently, tribal courts run the risk of merely mimicking the American legal regime when discussing or filtering issues of fairness through the lens of due process. Put differently, since fairness is not a foreign concept to tribal nations, how might a tribal community interpret a court's rulings if that court only speaks of "due process" or of other terms or ideas that come from outside of the community? What might that say to the community about tribal law and the court's willingness to invoke it?

These types of complications do not end at a reservation's borders, as non-Natives are sometimes participants in tribal courts. Reconsider the underlying question: if there is an available Native word or term or idea that conveys the same basic understanding of fairness that "due process" invokes, is it more to a tribal court's benefit to use the Native terminology or the due process terminology? This question might seem merely semantic, but one of the most steadfast issues that tribal courts face is the fear from outsiders that tribal courts are unfair or unprincipled. This is coupled with a sense that Native law (often conceptualized as traditional or insider knowledge) is mysterious or unknowable to outsiders. Many scholars have argued that tribal jurisdiction, particularly over non-Natives, has been curtailed by these fears and perceptions—which are largely unfounded as tribal courts have proven to often be more fair than their state counterparts. Nonetheless, if it is the case that non-Native fear of "unknowable" tribal law has curtailed tribal jurisdiction, is it to the benefit of tribal courts to resolve issues of fairness through the lens of Native terminology and concepts, or would they be better off resolving conflicts, particularly when non-Natives are involved, with terminology and concepts that will be familiar to non-Natives?

One more wrinkle is worthy of consideration. Just because one can find parallels between Native and Western concepts of justice, those parallels are not necessarily equals. Due process can be managed differently and with equal validity under different regimes. For example, one jurisdiction may require twelve members to sit on a jury whereas another may only require six members for a jury. So long as each of the trials in each jurisdiction has the requisite number of jurors, each is fulfilling its due process obligations.[3] Since there can be variations in the exercise of due process, is it more important for a tribal court to more closely adhere to a Native understanding of fairness or more closely adhere to American understandings of due process? What might be the consequences of both choices? This is, of course, a very broad and open-ended line of inquiry. Certainly additional factors will sway the choices, but considering the question helps to encapsulate the intense challenges and decisions that tribal courts face every day.

The challenges that tribal courts confront are tricky and in greater number than for other court systems in the United States, but they have not proven to be insurmountable. One of the leading examples in Native America of negotiating this difficult terrain is the Navajo court system. Over the course of more than a century, a few key events have been especially noteworthy to the development of the Navajo court system that exists today. In 1892 the federal government established a CFR court on the Navajo reservation. In 1958 the Navajo Tribal Council established its own court system under its own rules as part of a plan to reassert its sovereignty and to combat the threats engendered by the Termination Era. In 1985 the Navajo court system underwent major reform in an effort to secure its independence from the rest of the government and to create a distinct tribal legal culture. Today, the Navajo court system includes a supreme court, which is the court of last resort on the reservation and which sits above eleven judicial districts. Each judicial district includes a trial court, a family court, and a peacemaker court.

Navajo courts, and the Navajo Supreme Court in particular, have developed a well-founded reputation for purposefully developing and relying upon tribal law. This is often to the exclusion of other sources of law, particularly federal law. This is not to suggest that Navajo tribal court decisions completely ignore or otherwise violate other applicable sources of law. Rather, the idea behind these efforts is that the Navajo Nation and its court system function more effectively and perpetuate a greater sense of validity among the citizenry when it roots its decisions within the soil of its own law.

The following case, *Means v. District Court of Chinle Judicial Dist.*, is a helpful example of the Navajo Supreme Court's efforts to base its decisions within its own legal regime. Russell Means, a well-known figure in Native America for his activism and artistic endeavors, was living on the Navajo reservation with his Navajo wife when he was accused of assaulting his father-in-law while within the territorial limits of the reservation. When brought before the Navajo court, Means, a citizen of the Oglala Lakota Nation, argued that the Navajo Nation did not have jurisdiction over him because he was not a Navajo citizen.

Knowing the basic history of tribal criminal jurisdiction and recognizing the timing of the case, which was decided in 1999, are integral in understanding the importance of the Navajo Supreme Court's decision in *Means*. As described in greater detail in Chapter 18, the U.S. Supreme Court decided *Oliphant v. Suquamish Indian Tribe* in 1978. *Oliphant* stands for the proposition that tribal nations (with some narrow exceptions described in the *Means* case) do not have criminal jurisdiction over non-Natives. In 1990, the U.S. Supreme Court decided *Duro v. Reina*, which took the principle of *Oliphant* one step further and stated that tribal nations did not have criminal jurisdiction over Native individuals who are not citizens of that particular tribal nation. One year later, in 1991, Congress passed what is colloquially known as the "*Duro* Fix," which "recognized and affirmed" the right of tribal nations to criminally prosecute non-citizen Natives and which sought to undo the result in *Duro*. This was not the end of the matter, however, as many questioned whether Congress had the authority to pass the *Duro* Fix. In 2004, the Supreme Court took up the issue in *U.S. v. Lara*, deciding Congress did have the authority to pass the *Duro* Fix.

Thus, the Navajo Supreme Court's decision in *Means* occurred in the period after Congress had passed the *Duro* Fix, but before the U.S. Supreme Court settled the debate about the validity of the *Duro* Fix in *Lara*. Put another way, *Means* was decided in a point in time when the validity of the *Duro* Fix was still an open question. As you read the case, ask yourself what is the basis for the decision. How does the Navajo Supreme Court justify its jurisdiction over Russell Means? What are the sources of this authority? How does this decision circumvent the potential problem with the *Duro* Fix?

MEANS V. DISTRICT COURT OF CHINLE JUDICIAL DIST.

2 Am. Tribal Law 439, 7 Nav. R. 383 (1999)

YAZZIE, CHIEF JUSTICE.

* * *

The petition alleges that the Navajo Nation lacks criminal jurisdiction over the petitioner, who is a member of the Oglala Sioux Nation. . . . The petitioner . . . broadly asserts that the Navajo Nation has no criminal jurisdiction over non-Navajo Indians under the Treaty of June 1, 1868 between the United States of America and the Navajo Nation [and] that the petitioner has not consented to criminal jurisdiction by virtue of his marriage to a Navajo and residence within the Navajo Nation. . . .

***

Given the United States Indian education policy of sending Indian children to boarding schools, Indians in the armed services, modern population mobility, and other factors, there are high rates of intertribal intermarriage among American Indians. . . . [A]t least 9,327 "other" or nonmember Indians resided within the Navajo Nation in 1990. . . . We must sadly take judicial notice of the fact that, with a few exceptions, non-Indians and nonmember Indians who commit crimes within the Navajo Nation escape punishment for the crimes they commit. The social health of the Navajo Nation is at risk in addressing the petitioners personal issues, as is the actual health and well-being of thousands of people.

***

The petitioner complained of a lack of hospitality toward him when he resided within the Navajo Nation. He said he could not vote, run for Navajo Nation office (including judicial office), become a Navajo Nation Council delegate, the president, vice-president, or be a member of a farm board. In sum, he could not attain any Navajo Nation political position. That may be because the petitioner was not on any Navajo Nation registration or voter list and he was not on the voter registration list for Apache County, Arizona. He complained at length about his inability to get a job or start a business because of Navajo Nation employment and contracting preference laws.

The petitioner's national reputation as an activist is well-known. On cross-examination, the prosecution attempted to develop the petitioner's active participation in the public and political life of the Navajo Nation. The prosecution highlighted the petitioner's attendance at chapter meetings and elicited the fact that subsequent to a 1989 incident when Navajos were shot by Navajos, he led a march to the court house for a demonstration to make a "broad statement" about political activities of the Navajo Nation.

The "facts" the petitioner related during his testimony are only partially correct. While it is true that there are preference laws for employment and contracting in the Navajo Nation, they are not an absolute barrier to either employment or the ability to do business. There are many non-Navajo employees of the Navajo Nation (some of whom hold high positions in the Navajo Nation government), and non-Navajo businesses operate within the Navajo Nation. The ability to work or do business within the Navajo Nation has a great deal more to do with individual initiative and talent than preference laws. The petitioner was most likely not called for jury duty because he did not register to vote in Arizona. Non-Navajos have been called for jury duty since at least 1979. The 126 Sioux Indians listed in the 1990 Census can be called for jury duty if they are on a voter list and are called. If the petitioner was an indigent at the time of his arraignment, he would have been eligible for the appointment of an attorney.

* * *

There is a general and false assumption that Indian nations have no criminal jurisdiction over non-Indians and nonmember Indians. While the United States Supreme Court ruled that Indian nations have no *inherent* criminal jurisdiction over non-Indians in *Oliphant v. Suquamish Indian Tribe,* and that there is no inherent criminal jurisdiction over nonmember Indians in *Duro v. Reina,* criminal jurisdiction over nonmembers can rest upon a treaty or federal statute. . . . Therefore, we will examine whether the Navajo Nation Treaty of 1868 is a source of Navajo Nation criminal jurisdiction over nonmember Indians. . . .

* * *

. . . We are primarily interested in language found in Article II of the Treaty, which we will call the "set apart for the use and occupation" clause, and that in Article I, which we will call the "bad men" clause.

* * *

The plain language of Article II indicates that the Navajo Reservation exists for the exclusive use of not only Navajos, but other Indians, either as tribes or individuals, where both the Navajo Nation and the United States agree to their admission. Given that the jurisdiction of our courts is recognized in the Article II language, Indians such as the petitioner who are permitted to reside within the Navajo Nation fall within the same grouping as Navajo Indians in terms of the Treaty's coverage.

* * *

. . . The "bad men" clause has been used as the basis for . . . civil jurisdiction in Navajo Nation courts.

* * *

Therefore, we conclude that the [Navajo Nation] has criminal jurisdiction over the petitioner by virtue of the 1868 Treaty. The petitioner entered the Navajo Nation, married a Navajo woman, conducted business activities, engaged in political activities by expressing his right to free speech, and otherwise satisfied the . . . conditions for . . . Articles I and II court jurisdiction.

* * *

We previously held . . . that the Navajo Nation has criminal jurisdiction over individuals who "assume tribal relations.". . .

We have previously ruled that our 1997 Navajo Nation Criminal Code will be construed in light of Navajo common law. . . . While there is a formal process to obtain membership as a Navajo, that is not the only kind of "membership" under Navajo Nation law. An individual who marries or has an intimate relationship with a Navajo is a *hadane* (in-law). . . . A *hadane* or in-law assumes a clan relation to a Navajo when an intimate relationship forms, and when that relationship is conducted within the Navajo Nation, there are reciprocal obligations to and from family and clan members under Navajo common law. Among those obligations is the duty to avoid threatening or assaulting a relative by marriage (or any other person).

We find that the petitioner, by reason of his marriage to a Navajo, longtime residence within the Navajo Nation, his activities here, and his status as a *hadane*, consented to Navajo Nation criminal jurisdiction. This is not done by "adoption" in any formal or customary sense, but by assuming tribal relations and establishing familial and community relationships under Navajo common law.

There is another aspect to consent by conduct. . . . The "bad men" clause is not confined to United States Government employees, but extends "to people subject to the authority of the United States.". . .

. . . The thrust of the "bad men" clause was to avoid conflict. . . . It would be absurd to conclude that our *hadane* relatives can enter the Navajo Nation, offend, and remain among us, and we can do nothing to protect Navajos and others from them. . . . While there are those who may think that the remedies offered by the United States Government are adequate, it is plain and clear to us that federal enforcement of criminal law is deficient. Potential state remedies are impractical, because law enforcement personnel in nearby areas have their own law enforcement problems. We must have the rule of peaceful law . . . so we conclude that the petitioner has assumed tribal relations with Navajos and he is thus subject to the jurisdiction of our courts.

* * *

The Navajo Supreme Court faced a difficult choice in *Means*. At the time, it could have based its assertion of jurisdiction over Means under the *Duro* Fix. The benefit for a tribal court in grounding a decision in federal law is that any such decision is much less likely to automatically arouse suspicions among outsiders (and sometimes for insiders as well), particularly if the dispute should wind up in another court in the United States. Put another way, federal and state courts and the lawyers who litigate in them are much more likely to respect tribal court decisions or assertions of jurisdiction that are authorized or somehow condoned by American law. Resting Navajo jurisdiction on the *Duro* Fix would have cleared a major hurdle for outsiders, such as federal and state judges, who sometimes have to consider the scope of tribal jurisdiction and law. However, as noted above, it was unclear at the time of the *Means* decision if the *Duro* Fix would survive a challenge in the Supreme Court. Thus, any benefit that the Navajo Supreme Court might have gained under the *Duro* Fix could have quickly crumbled. If the Navajo Supreme Court had based its decision on the *Duro* Fix and then the U.S. Supreme Court had ruled that the *Duro* Fix was invalid, then the foundation for Navajo jurisdiction over Means and others like him would have disappeared. Without the recourse to criminally prosecute those like Means—and since, according to the Navajo Supreme Court, federal law enforcement on the reservation was "deficient" and state remedies were "impractical"—offenders were unlikely to be punished and were a menace to all, regardless of tribal affiliation, on the reservation.

Rather than relying on the *Duro* Fix, the Navajo Supreme Court based its decision on two other tribally-centered sources of law: the 1868 Treaty and Navajo common law. According to the Navajo Supreme Court, under both the terms of the 1868 Treaty and his status as a *hadane*, Means consented to Navajo court jurisdiction by marrying a tribal citizen, living on the reservation, and participating in public life. By using these sources of law, the Navajo Supreme Court not only avoided the potential issue tribal courts faced under the *Duro* Fix, it also further developed its own body of law and legal reasoning for the nation. Although the opinion lacked the benefit of reference to federal law that tends to lessen the fears of outsiders, it nonetheless established a more stable basis for its ruling. Both the 1868 Treaty and Navajo common law would continue to exert their authority, and the *Means* decision had the capacity to operate as precedent, regardless of the status of the *Duro* Fix. The well-written, deeply developed explanation for jurisdiction was also designed to operate as a shield against those who might otherwise argue that tribal law is unknowable or mysterious.

In some ways, the Navajo are uniquely situated, with a large land base, a large citizenry, a number of Navajo language speakers, as well as other resources and opportunities that are not available to every tribal nation. Many tribal courts have less access and capacity to engage with and develop their common law. In addition, reasonable minds within tribal nations, including within the Navajo, can and do come to different conclusions about the common law of a tribal nation as well as the outcomes that such law will produce (as is the case with other actors in other court systems in the United States).

Nonetheless, the decision in *Means*, as well as other decisions by the Navajo Supreme Court, offers a useful example of how a tribal court might meet the myriad of difficulties that it faces. The challenge of finding a proper balance between a Western style court system and more traditional understandings of law and dispute resolution, as well as fostering respect for a tribal court and its decisions, is not likely to abate anytime soon. But careful attention to the development of tribal law, as is displayed in *Means*, will be critical to meeting the challenge.

CITIZENSHIP AND INTERNAL TRIBAL POLITICS

The historical and ongoing experience of colonialism has, as this chapter has sought to demonstrate, created a number of distinct problems for tribal nations, their law, and their courts. Sometimes those problems are manifested externally, such as the limitations that American law places on tribal jurisdiction over non-Natives. And sometimes those problems are manifested internally within tribal nations, such as the disputes that have occurred around tribal citizenship in recent years. In one sense, issues of citizenship are hardly unique to tribal nations, as any government has to determine the scope of its own citizenry. Nonetheless, tribal nations regularly face distinct complications stemming from their histories and involvement with colonial forces and law.

At the most basic level, every tribal nation is primarily responsible for determining its citizenry. To that end, every tribal nation has some criteria for making citizenship assessments. However, these criteria have been shaped by a number of factors, many of which have originated outside of Native America and which raise serious questions. For example, a certain amount of blood quantum is a requirement for citizenship for many tribal nations. Blood quantum is considered in greater detail in Chapter 13. For the purposes of this chapter, it suffices to note that blood quantum is a tool to measure an individual's race and was originally used by the federal government in earlier eras to, among other things, assess authority over individuals as "wards" of the federal government. The idea behind these sorts of assessments was that one's race contained immutable characteristics that determined their capacities and proclivities. Thus, the more racially Indian an individual was, the more that individual was in need of oversight by the federal government. As time went by, blood quantum became increasingly important to many Native peoples and nations themselves, and it made its way the into citizenship requirements of a number of tribal nations. Consequently, today a tribal nation may require that an individual have, for example, a ¼ blood quantum, or be one-quarter Native—usually one-quarter of that particular tribal nation—to be a citizen. The tremendous influence that the idea of blood quantum holds within Native America, coupled with the federal government's influence in this and other matters, makes it overly simplistic to claim that tribal nations alone control their citizenship requirements.

The fact that many tribal nations continue to perpetuate the link between earlier conceptions of race and present day citizenship through blood quantum requirements raises issues about the nature of tribal government. For example, what are the limits of the authority any government can legitimately claim over those who are excluded from its citizenry based on their race? On the other hand, there is no shortage of examples, both historical and contemporary, of individuals with loose or no connections to tribal nations claiming Native ancestry or citizenry for their personal gain. In the past, some have falsely pretended to be Indian to earn allotments or access to treaty annuities. More recently, some have falsely claimed Native ancestry or citizenry to gain from federal or state programs designed to benefit Native individuals. Tribal nations understandably want to prevent such unscrupulous individuals from profiting from their misrepresentations of their connections to Native America. Does blood quantum aid in this fight? If not blood quantum, what criteria or standards for tribal citizenship would be appropriate under tribal law?

Further complicating the matter, blood quantum is hardly the only troublesome quandary facing tribal citizenship. The legacy of colonialism has produced other unique dilemmas as well. The saga of the Cherokee Freedmen offers one such example. The long story of the Cherokee Freedmen, and the many perspectives that it has produced, can only be briefly touched upon in this chapter. Nonetheless, a concise recounting of the dispute will demonstrate the challenges that tribal law and tribal courts face.

Prior to the Civil War, some Cherokee individuals, as well as some individuals from other Southeastern tribal nations, owned enslaved persons of African descent. In fact, many of the Cherokee who owned these persons brought them along on the infamous Trail of Tears that relocated many Cherokee peoples from the Southeast to present-day Oklahoma. In 1866, after the Civil War, the Cherokee of Oklahoma, who primarily sided with and signed a treaty with the Confederacy (although there was great debate within the community on the subject), signed a new treaty with the United States. The 1866 treaty provided that the formerly enslaved persons of the Cherokee were granted citizenship within the Cherokee Nation.

The incorporation of formerly enslaved peoples into the Cherokee Nation met with some success and some failure. While there was some representation of formerly enslaved peoples within Cherokee government early on and some familial and intimate relations between groups, there was also segregation and resentment from some Cherokee who were aggrieved by the treaty stipulations with the United States and wary of associating with formerly enslaved peoples. In the early twentieth century, during the Allotment Era, the federal government created a tribal census of the Cherokee for the purposes of allotting tribal lands, known as the Dawes Commission Roll. Reflecting the attitudes of the Allotment Era, the roll distinguished between Cherokee, Whites who had intermarried, and Freedmen. Also in keeping with the times, the roll was not overly precise and did not measure the potential Native ancestry of the Freedmen. Nonetheless, the Dawes Commission Roll became the basis for determining Cherokee citizenship, which included those who have come to be known as the Cherokee Freedmen.

In the Self-Determination Era, a number of tribal nations, including the Cherokee, began reassessing the status of their tribal governments on a number of different fronts, including citizenship. In 1975, the Cherokee adopted a new constitution, which, in Article III, defined Cherokee citizenship as those "proven by reference to the Dawes Commission Roll." However, by the 1980s, there was enough political support among enough Cherokee to attempt to exclude the Freedmen. In 1983 the Cherokee Tribal Council amended the tribal code, or body of tribal law, to allow only citizenship to those who had "proof of Cherokee blood," based on the Dawes Commission Rolls. This law was directly targeted at the Cherokee Freedmen, and even though a number of Cherokee Freedmen did have some degree of Cherokee blood, they were also excluded since that part of their ancestry was not recorded during the creation of the Dawes Commission Roll. A number of Cherokee Freedmen immediately began seeking reinstatement into the Cherokee Nation, resulting in a number of cases in both tribal and federal courts.

For some who were deeply invested in the outcome of this dispute, the issue was a matter of tribal sovereignty. Many argued that the inclusion of the Cherokee

Freedmen into the Cherokee Nation was an imposition by the federal government, and that the Cherokee should be free to determine their own citizenry. For others who were equally deeply invested in the outcome of the dispute, the actions of the Cherokee government amounted to little more than blatant racism. Despite well over a century of legal and political inclusion, the Freedmen were being treated as less than second-class citizens. The matter was further complicated by the fact that members of other tribal nations, the Shawnee and Delaware, were incorporated into the Cherokee Nation at the time of the Dawes Commission Rolls and would not have been excluded by the amendment to the code.

The Cherokee Supreme Court directly confronted the issue in 2006. The question before the Court was whether the 1983 provision in the tribal code that limited citizenship to Cherokees "by blood" violated the 1975 Constitution and the 1866 treaty. As you read the case, ask yourself how the majority opinion frames the issue? How does the dissent frame the issue? What are the critical differences between the two? How does the majority engage with the underlying issue of race in this case?

ALLEN V. CHEROKEE NATION TRIBAL COUNCIL
6 Am. Tribal Law 18 (2006)

STACY L. LEEDS, JUSTICE.

Petitioner Lucy Allen is a descendent of individuals listed on the Dawes Commission Rolls as "Cherokee Freedmen." To become a tribal member under the current legislation, she must prove she is "Cherokee by blood." She asks this Court to declare [the amendment to the tribal code] unconstitutional because it is more restrictive than the membership criteria set forth in . . . the 1975 Constitution.

* * *

The Cherokee citizenry has the ultimate authority to define tribal citizenship. When they adopted the 1975 Constitution, they did not limit membership to people who possess Cherokee blood. Instead, they extended membership to all the people who were "citizens" of the Cherokee Nation as listed on the Dawes Commission Rolls.

The Constitution could be amended to require that all tribal members possess Cherokee blood. The people could also choose to set a minimum Cherokee blood quantum. However, if the Cherokee people wish to limit tribal citizenship, and such limitation would terminate the preexisting citizenship of even one Cherokee citizen, then it must be done in the open. It cannot be accomplished through silence.

The Council lacks the power to redefine tribal membership absent a constitutional amendment. . . . The current legislation is contrary to the plain language of the 1975 Constitution.

. . . [T]he 1975 Constitution defines eligibility for tribal membership very broadly. . . .

There is simply no "by blood" requirement. . . . There is no ambiguity to resolve. The words "by blood" or "Cherokee by blood" do not appear.

* * *

It is important to note that the phrase "Dawes Commission Rolls" is plural. While the overwhelming majority of people on the Dawes rolls are Cherokee by blood, the rolls also include other people who the Cherokee Nation recognized as citizens at the time the Dawes roll were compiled. Membership is not limited . . . to those individuals only appearing on the "Cherokee by blood" pages of the Dawes rolls.

* * *

If the Freedmen's citizenship rights existed on the very night before the 1975 Constitution was approved, then they must necessarily survive today. These rights were not terminated by the adoption of the 1975 Constitution. In fact, the 1975 Constitution affirms these rights by linking citizenship to one single document: the Dawes Commission Rolls.

* * *

[The Constitution] expressly includes all people, who can prove they were "citizens" on the Dawes Commission Rolls with no mention (one way or the other) about Cherokee or Indian blood quantum. The Cherokee Freedmen, the Shawnee and the Delaware were all citizens at the time the Dawes rolls were finalized and they all continue as citizens to this day.

* * *

Individual Shawnees are actually listed on the "Cherokee by blood" pages of the Dawes Commission Rolls. . . .

Individual Delaware are listed on separate pages in the Dawes Commission Rolls with the caption "Delaware Cherokee" at the top. . . .

Individual Freedmen, like the Delaware, appear on separate pages with the caption "Cherokee Freedmen" at the top. . . .

The Dawes Commission had their own federal purposes for including a blood degree on their documents. The federal government continues to use these blood degrees for their own purposes today. It is not clear that the Dawes Commission had any appreciation for the fact that Indian blood, of the various tribes, is different. Shawnee blood is not Cherokee blood. Delaware blood is not Cherokee blood. It is important for this Court to question whether all these federal blood degrees really matter today, for the purpose of Cherokee citizenship laws.

* * *

The only time a legal right, under Cherokee law, depends on Cherokee blood, is when a person decides to run for elected office. . . . This guarantees Cherokee control of government, but that government is ultimately elected by a larger and more diverse constituency of citizens.

The Cherokee Nation is a Sovereign. The Cherokee Nation is much more than just a group of families with a common ancestry. For almost 150 years, the Cherokee Nation has included not only citizens that are Cherokee by blood, but also citizens who have origins in other Indian nations and/or African and/or European ancestry. Many of these citizens are mixed race and a small minority of these citizens possess no Cherokee blood at all.

People will always disagree on who is culturally Cherokee and who possesses enough Cherokee blood to be "racially" Indian. It is not the role of this Court to engage in these political or social debates. This Court must interpret the law as it is plainly written in our Constitution.

* * *

Dissenting Opinion of CHIEF JUSTICE MATLOCK:

* * *

The majority opinion goes to great lengths of historical rhetoric to prove what is obvious; that the Cherokee Freedmen were citizens of the Cherokee Nation prior to the adoption of the [1975 Constitution] because of the [Treaty of 1866]. However, the majority opinion fails to point out that the Treaty of 1866 . . . was brought about by duress from the United States Federal Government after the Cherokee Nation chose the losing side of the Civil War. The Dawes Rolls were a product of the United States Government and not the Cherokee Nation. My colleagues in the majority opinion have failed to cite any

instance where the Cherokee Nation voluntarily granted citizenship to the
Cherokee Freedman prior to and after 1866.

* * *

The decision in *Allen* was far from the end of the dispute. Among the many
important events, the Cherokee Nation amended their constitution to exclude the
Freedmen in response to the decision in *Allen*. Thereafter, further challenges to
the constitutional amendment made their way through both tribal and federal
courts with the federal government taking notice and occasionally acting. In 2017,
a federal court ruled that the 1866 Treaty granted citizenship rights to the
Cherokee Freedman and the Cherokee Nation declared shortly thereafter that it
would abide by the ruling.[4] Presently, the Freedmen are Cherokee citizens.

The Cherokee Freedmen dispute is indicative of the difficult types of
controversies that tribal courts and tribal law sometimes have to face. The history
of colonialism forged a multilayered issue for the Cherokee Supreme Court. The
majority opinion sought to move beyond the issue of race by focusing on the
political nature of the dispute. More specifically, the majority opinion measured
the dispute in terms of the political construction of citizenship within the
Cherokee Nation, as opposed to the racial characteristics of the citizenry. The
dissent, somewhat in keeping with the majority opinion, framed the issue in terms
of sovereignty. For the dissent, the inclusion of the Freedmen in the 1866 Treaty
was not a sovereign choice (which the majority disputed in parts of the opinion
that were not excerpted), but one forced upon the Cherokee. And yet, despite the
efforts of both the majority opinion and the dissent, the issue of race is, at a
minimum, an undeniable undercurrent in the issue. Consequently, the colonial
antecedents of this dispute led to a clash between race, citizenship, and
sovereignty.

The decisions in *Means* and *Allen* offer a useful cross section of some of the
more difficult quandaries, originating both inside and outside of reservation
boundaries, that tribal courts and tribal law have to confront. Each case speaks to
the unique challenges to the development and perpetuation of tribal law created
by the colonial experience. Each also demonstrates how tribal courts exist both
inside and outside of federal Indian law, responding to the needs of their home
community while also having to be aware of federal engagements—such as
treaties—that shape their own legal culture. And yet, like any case that reaches any
supreme court, they are also outliers that exist at the extremes.

Like most other courts in the United States (particularly like the
aforementioned typical rural state court), tribal courts primarily deal with everyday

cases that are likely to be found in any other jurisdiction: traffic accidents, drug crimes, employment disputes, divorce and custody proceedings, domestic violence, shoplifting, broken contracts, and bar fights to name a few. These mundane cases, which occur in far greater numbers than cases like *Means* or *Allen*, are just as important in exercising and fostering tribal sovereignty. Through each and every one of these cases, tribal law and tribal courts are playing an increasingly central role within their nations and within federal Indian law.

SUGGESTED READINGS

- *Navajo Courts and Navajo Common Law: A Tradition of Tribal Self-Governance.* Raymond D. Austin. Minneapolis, MN: University of Minnesota Press, 2009.

- *Arguing with Tradition: The Language of Law in Hopi Tribal Court.* Justin B. Richland. Chicago: University of Chicago Press, 2008.

- *American Indian Tribal Law.* Matthew L.M. Fletcher. Austin, TX: Wolters Kluwer Law & Business, 2011.

---

[1] Annual Report of the Commissioner of Indian Affairs to the Secretary of the Interior. Washington D.C.: Government Printing Office, 1855, 329–30.

[2] Henry J. McQuigg. 1926 Annual Report, 642. Annual Narrative and Statistical Reports from Field Jurisdictions of the Bureau of Indian Affairs, 1907–38. Record Group 75. National Archives, Washington D.C. Frames 55–56.

[3] This assertion assumes that the difference in the number of jurors—six as opposed to twelve—does not materially affect one's due process rights.

[4] Cherokee Nation v. Nash, 267 F.Supp.3d 86 (2017).

CHAPTER 30

International Law

The first chapter of this text outlined a few of the prominent legal and political instruments and debates that the Western world engaged in at the beginning of colonialism in the Americas: the *Requerimiento*, de Victoria's *On the Indians Lately Discovered*, and a 1685 English treaty with a tribal nation. The second chapter of this text discussed the adoption of the Doctrine of Discovery, an international legal principle that justified colonization, into American law in the famous 1823 *Johnson v. McIntosh* case. Testifying to its status as a principle of international law, Chief Justice John Marshall noted that the Doctrine of Discovery not only affected the Indigenous peoples of the Americas, but also operated "against all other European governments," and that, "The history of America, from its discovery to the present day, proves, we think, the universal recognition of these principles." In short, for hundreds of years the Western world regarded the Indigenous peoples of the Americas as a matter of international law.

By the second half of the nineteenth century, the United States started to separate its law and policy away from these origins, and began to increasingly treat Indigenous peoples and issues as domestic concerns. Perhaps most prominently, in 1871 the federal government declared that it would no longer engage in treaty making with Native nations (see Chapter 6). The end of treaty making signaled the beginning of the Allotment Era (see Chapter 5) and a major shift in federal Indian law. For example, the federal government passed the Major Crimes Act, in which it gave itself jurisdiction over major crimes in Indian Country, and sanctified the legislation in *U.S. v. Kagama* (see Chapters 6 and 7). This shift, from international to domestic law, was a significant contributor to what many consider the darkest policy period for Indigenous peoples in the United States.

Law is in a constant state of development, however, and what was once old can become new again. Today, many scholars in federal Indian law regard international law as the most promising avenue to direct tribal legal efforts. Furthering this understanding, Native peoples have found some success in international law tribunals and the United States has taken some small steps toward once again engaging with Native America in an international law context. It will take more time to see if international law regimes fulfill the promise that they hold for Indigenous peoples, but it is increasingly important for students of federal Indian law and policy to have some understanding of their existence and operation.

This chapter will demonstrate. . .

- *The basic structure of international law*

- *The development of the case of the Dann sisters from domestic to international tribunals*

- *The creation and promise of the United Nations Declaration on the Rights of Indigenous Peoples*

A BASIC PRIMER ON INTERNATIONAL LAW AND INDIGENOUS PEOPLES

International law, both as a concept and as a practical matter, can be difficult to understand. At its most basic, international law is the law of countries—as opposed to domestic law, which regulates the actions of individuals and companies and other groups within the defined jurisdiction of a country. Also unlike domestic legal regimes—where it is relatively easy to identify a body of law that applies to a dispute and the bodies that make, interpret, and apply that law—international regimes are more fluid and operate on a slightly different model.

Although still governed by custom and traditional standards, today international law is primarily established through treaties. Part of what makes international law seemingly so complicated to many is that there is no single treaty that purports to speak to all of international law. Rather, there are many treaties that cover a wide range of subject areas—trade, mutual protection, environmental policy, or human rights, to name a few examples. In addition, not every country is a participant in every treaty, nor does every country participate in every aspect of every treaty. Consequently, different countries can be held to different standards depending on which treaties, and which parts of which treaties, they have agreed to. Further complicating the matter, sometimes a treaty practice or general practice can become so widespread and entrenched that it can become a standard to which every country is held, regardless of whether a particular country is a party to the treaty or situation from which it originated. Thus, any individual or group seeking to enforce an international law principle on a country must have a strong understanding of not only the present treaty status of the country in question, but also of the customary practices of countries in the subject area of law in question.

Perhaps the biggest criticism that many have of international law is the relative lack of enforceability of its rules. Unlike domestic law, in which the nation (or subdivision of a nation, like a state) is in charge of enforcing the law, there is no easy equivalent in the international law scheme. Put another way, if an individual commits a criminal act, then the government can prosecute that individual for the crime and put her or him in prison. However, there is no prison for countries. To that end, individual countries themselves, and their own citizenry and political processes, are primarily responsible for abiding by international law rules. Flagrant or repeat violators may suffer some rebuke from the rest of the international community, such as sanctions or other economic, diplomatic, or political pressures. In rare instances, the international community may take military action, such as when the United Nations and the North Atlantic Treaty Organization (NATO) intervened during the Kosovo War in the 1990s.

The relative unenforceability of international law rules have led some to suggest that international law is not really law at all. From this perspective, any standard that rises to the level of law must also be accompanied by some direct method of making sure that it is abided by. However, not everyone shares this view and even without the type of enforcement found in the domestic realm, international law can exert a tremendous amount of force. For example, economic sanctions or limited access to the rest of the international community can be particularly devastating to some countries. For other countries, the shame of rebuke from its international brethren is a powerful motivator. The United States is a world leader and an economic powerhouse; consequently, the full scope of international law's potential to shape behavior is muted as compared to the rest of the world. Regardless, even the United States is not completely immune from international pressures, and as technology, travel, worldwide trade, environmental concern and other factors make the world smaller, international law is growing in importance.

A number of treaties establish independent bodies or organizations to perpetuate and maintain the purposes of treaties. The most prominent example is the United Nations. Another useful example for the purposes of this chapter is the Organization of American States (OAS). Although there were a number of intergovernmental precursors that led to its establishment, the OAS was formally founded in 1948 when a number of countries in the Americas, including the United States, signed its charter in 1948. Designed to maintain mutual protection and cooperation among the nations of the Americas, the organization created by the OAS charter and its subsidiary organizations have focused a significant amount of attention on the subject of human rights. In 1959 the OAS created the Inter-American Commission on Human Rights (IACHR) to further this mission. In 1979 the OAS established the Inter-American Court of Human Rights to create a forum to hear disputes against countries concerning human rights violations.

At the same time as the creation of the OAS in 1948, the member nations also adopted the American Declaration on the Rights and Duties of Man. This declaration outlines the basic human rights understandings among the member states of the OAS. As you read the excerpt of the American Declaration, ask yourself to whom it applies. What balance is the American Declaration trying to make? What are the expectations of governments under the American Declaration? What are the expectations of individuals? What might this mean for Indigenous peoples?

AMERICAN DECLARATION ON THE RIGHTS AND DUTIES OF MAN

Ratified May 2, 1948

Preamble

All men are born free and equal, in dignity and in rights, and, being endowed by nature with reason and conscience, they should conduct themselves as brothers one to another.

The fulfillment of duty by each individual is a prerequisite to the rights of all. Rights and duties are interrelated in every social and political activity of man. While rights exalt individual liberty, duties express the dignity of that liberty.

* * *

Chapter 1—Rights

Article I. Every human being has the right to life, liberty, and the security of his person.

Article II. All persons are equal before the law and have the rights and duties established in this Declaration, without distinction as to race, sex, language, creed, or any other factor.

Article III. Every person has the right freely to profess a religious faith, and to manifest and practice it both in public and in private.

* * *

Article VI. Every person has the right to establish a family, the basic element of society, and to receive protection therefore.

* * *

Article XIV. Every person has the right to work, under proper conditions, and to follow his vocation freely, insofar as existing conditions of employment permit.

Every person who works has the right to receive such remuneration as will, in proportion to his capacity and skill, assure him a standard of living suitable for himself and for his family.

* * *

Article XVIII. Every person may resort to the courts to ensure respect for his legal rights. There should likewise be available to him a simple, brief procedure whereby the courts will protect him from acts of authority that, to his prejudice, violate any fundamental constitutional rights.

* * *

Article XXIII. Every person has a right to own such private property as meets the essential needs of decent living and helps to maintain the dignity of the individual and of the home.

* * *

Chapter 2—Duties

Article XXIX. It is the Duty of the individual so to conduct himself in relation to others that each and every one may fully form and develop his personality.

Article XXX. It is the duty of every person to aid, support, educate and protect his minor children, and it is the duty of children to honor their parents always and to aid, support and protect them when they need it.

Article XXXI. It is the duty of every person to acquire at least an elementary education.

Article XXXII. It is the duty of every person to vote in the popular elections of the country of which he is a national, when he is legally capable of doing so.

* * *

> Article XXXVII. It is the duty of every person to work, as far as his capacity and possibilities permit, in order to obtain the means of livelihood or to benefit his community.
>
> Article XXXVIII. It is the duty of every person to refrain from taking part in political activities that, according to law, are reserved exclusively to the citizens of the state in which he is an alien.

In the last few decades, Indigenous peoples around the world have been increasingly looking to international treaties and agreements such as the American Declaration on the Rights and Duties of Man to protect themselves in their domestic spheres, and they have been finding some success. For example, in 2001 the Awas Tingni won an important victory against Nicaragua regarding their land rights in the IACHR.[1] Tribal nations in the United States have taken note of these efforts and have begun to act accordingly.

ANATOMY OF AN INTERNATIONAL LAW CASE: THE DANN SISTERS

Perhaps the most famous example of Native individuals in the United States pursuing an international law remedy is that of Mary and Carrie Dann. The long history of this important dispute can only be recounted in brief in this chapter. Nonetheless, tracing the development of the dispute from domestic channels through a decision by the IACHR offers a helpful example of the challenges, promises, and limitations of international law for Indigenous peoples.

A few pieces of background information are necessary to most fully understand the story of the Danns. First, most international tribunals, such as the IACHR, require that individuals exhaust their domestic remedies before they will entertain a case. This is out of respect for the sovereignty of the nation in which the dispute takes place.

Second, the United States established the Indian Claims Commission (ICC) in 1948 to settle ongoing tribal land claims. The ICC is given greater attention in Chapter 9. For the purposes of this chapter, it suffices to note that the ICC, in seeking to finalize tribal land disputes, only authorized payment for lands that were henceforth considered ceded by tribal litigants. It did not allow for the return of tribal lands to Native nations and individuals. Consequently, ICC decisions were generally focused on answering two questions: what was the land base for a particular tribal nation and when was it taken? By assessing both how much land was taken and when it was taken, the ICC could then assess the value of the land for the purposes of compensating the tribal nation.

Finally, the Danns, sisters and Western Shoshones, were ranchers who grazed cattle on the traditional lands of the Western Shoshone. The federal government regarded the lands on which the Danns operated to be public lands and fined the Dann sisters for grazing the cattle without a permit. The Danns countered that the Shohone had never ceded the land in question to the United States. Decades worth of disputes between the Danns and the federal government led to massive fines for the Danns and the confiscation of their cattle. The Danns responded by aggressively fighting against the fines in court.

Adequately tracing this history requires beginning several years before the federal government and the Dann sisters engaged in litigation, however. The story begins with the ICC decision concerning the Shoshone. Like many ICC decisions, there were a number of complications to determining both the scope of tribal lands claimed and when it was purchased or otherwise taken from the Shoshone. A number of smaller Shoshone units had signed some treaties with the federal government that ceded some lands. However, the larger Shoshone collective claimed a significant portion of land in the West, much of which that had not been formally ceded in a treaty or other instrument. Thus, the ICC—under its structure that only allowed for monetary payments and not for the return of land—had to decide how much land the Shoshone could actually claim and when it was taken from them. As you read the decision, ask yourself what conclusions the ICC comes to on these issues. What problems do the events in this case create for the decisions that the ICC needed to make under its structure?

SHOSHONE TRIBE OF INDIANS V. U.S.
11 Ind. Cl. Comm. 387 (1962)

Findings of Fact

The Commission makes the following findings of fact:

1. Petitioners ... are the Shoshone Tribe of Indians of the Wind River Reservation, Wyoming suing as representatives of [a number of other related tribal nations]. ...

* * *

3. Within a broad area covering eastern Nevada, southern Idaho, northern Utah and western Wyoming, the major Indian population is that known generically as Shoshone. ...

***

5.   Within the broad area described in Finding 3 and in a small part of California lived Shoshonean speaking people.... Disruption of the native economy during the 1850's and 1860's by the whites emigrating through and settling on the lands of these Indians caused strife and the previously independent villages in certain areas united into military bands....

***

7.   Following the advent of the Mormons into Utah in 1847, and their spread into arable valleys in the southeastern portion of Idaho and the establishment of the overland trails to California and Oregon and to the mining regions of California, Idaho, and Montana, through the country inhabited by the Shoshone Indians, trouble between some of the Indians and emigrants and settlers arose. This was occasioned by the driving away by the emigrants and white settlers of the sparse game supply of the Indians and the destruction of other natural resources which provided the Indians' source of livelihood...

***

26. The Commission further finds that ... the Western Shoshone ... exclusively used and occupied their respective territories ... until by gradual encroachment by whites, settlers and others, and the acquisition, disposition or taking of their lands by the United States for its own use and benefit, or the use and benefit of its citizens, the way of life of these Indians was disrupted and they were deprived of their lands....

***

While the ICC did acknowledge that the Shoshone could claim to have once possessed a wide swath of land, its determination on when that land was taken was shakier. Ultimately, the ICC could not point to a singular document (such as a treaty), event, or moment that marked a formal or official transfer of land from the larger Shoshone collective to the federal government. Instead, the ICC stated that the land moved from tribal to non-tribal hands "by gradual encroachment." Eventually, the legal representation for the Shoshone and the federal government decided on an 1872 date for the taking of the land and the ICC awarded the Shoshone $26 million. The Shoshone have yet to accept the award.

In the mid-1970s the federal government began taking action against the Dann sisters for their cattle grazing. The Danns responded to the legal proceedings against them by arguing that the lands upon which their cattle were grazing was theirs, it had been in their family from time immemorial, and it did not belong to the federal government because it had never been formally transferred to the federal government. They also argued that they were not adequately represented in the ICC process, which, according to them, had been taken over by a small, unrepresentative group and the legal representation for that group.

By the time the case was heard in the Supreme Court in the mid-1980s, the terms of the dispute had changed, and not in the favor of the Danns. While the underlying question of whether Shoshone title to the land had been extinguished was still present in the background, the focus for Supreme Court was whether or not the Shoshone had been paid for their land. This was in question because although Congress had appropriated money for the ICC award and placed it in the U.S. Treasury, it had not yet developed a plan for distribution to the tribal nation—primarily because the Shoshone were uncooperative and sought to keep the issue of their land rights alive. Thus, if the Shoshone had received "payment" according to the framework of how the Supreme Court was engaging with the case, then tribal title to the land was extinguished and the Danns could no longer argue that they owned the lands on which they grazed their cattle. If the Shoshone had not yet been paid, then the Danns could hold onto the possibility that tribal title to the land had never been extinguished.

Put another way, the Supreme Court was not deciding about whether Shoshone title to the land had been extinguished, but rather if the Shoshone had yet been paid for the extinguishment of the title to the land. As you read the opinion, ask yourself why the Supreme Court frames the dispute in these terms. How does the Court describe the role of the ICC? How does this description speak to the federal government's understanding of the role of the ICC? Why might this understanding be troublesome to the Danns, the Shoshone, and other Indigenous peoples?

U.S. V. DANN
470 U.S. 39 (1985)

JUSTICE BRENNAN delivered the opinion of the Court.

* * *

This case is an episode in a longstanding conflict between the United States and the Shoshone Tribe over title to lands in the western United States. In 1951 certain members of the Shoshone Tribe sought compensation for the loss of aboriginal title to lands located in California, Colorado, Idaho, Nevada, Utah, and Wyoming. Eleven years later, the Indian Claims Commission entered an . . . order holding that the aboriginal title of the Western Shoshone had been extinguished in the latter part of the 19th century, and later awarded the Western Shoshone in excess of $26 million in compensation. . . .

Under [federal statutes], the Secretary of the Interior is required, after consulting with the Tribe, to submit to Congress within a specified period of time a plan for the distribution of the fund. In this case, the Secretary has yet to submit a plan of distribution of the $26 million owing to the refusal of the Western Shoshone in devising the plan. . . .

In 1974, the United States brought an action in trespass against two sisters, Mary and Carrie Dann, members of . . . the Western Shoshone, alleging that the Danns, in grazing livestock without a permit from the United States, were acting in violation of [a federal statute]. The 5120 acres at issue in the suit are located in the northeast corner of Nevada. In response to the United States' suit, the Danns claimed that the land has been in the possession of their family from time immemorial and that their aboriginal title to the land precluded the Government from requiring grazing permits. The United States District Court for the District of Nevada rejected the Danns' argument and ruled that aboriginal title had been extinguished by . . . the Indian Claims Commission's judgment in 1962. The Court of Appeals for the Ninth Circuit reversed . . . on the ground that "[w]hatever may have been the implicit assumptions of both the United States and the Shoshone Tribes during the litigation. . ., the extinguishment question was not necessarily in issue, it was not actually litigated, and it has not been decided."

On remand, the District Court held that aboriginal title was extinguished when the final award of the Indian Claims Commission was certified for payment. . . . On appeal, the Government defended the judgment of the District Court on the ground that the "full discharge" language of . . . the Indian Claims Commission Act, precluded the Danns from raising the defense of aboriginal title. Although Congress had not approved a plan for the distribution of the funds to the Western Shoshone, the United States maintained that the requirement of a "payment" . . . was satisfied by the congressional appropriation of the $26 million award into the Treasury account. The Danns argued that until Congress approved a plan for the distribution of the money to the Tribe, "payment" was not satisfied.

The Court of Appeals held that "payment" had not occurred within the meaning of [the federal statute]. . . .

The legislative purposes of the Indian Claims Commission Act and the principles of payment under the common law of trust as they have been applied to the context of relations between native American communities and the United States requires that we hold that "payment" occurs . . . when funds are placed by the United States into an account in the Treasury. . . .

The Indian Claims Commission Act had two purposes. The "chief purpose of the [Act was] to dispose of the Indian claims problem with finality.". . . To hold . . . that payment does not occur until a final plan of distribution has been approved by Congress would frustrate the purpose of finality. . . .

The second purpose of the Indian Claims Commission Act was to transfer from Congress to the Indian Claims Commission the responsibility for determining the merits of native American claims. . . .

The court below justified its decision on the ground that in making "payment" turn on the submission and approval of a final plan of distribution, Congress would have one last opportunity to review the merits of claims litigated before the Indian Claims Commission. This justification for delay obviously conflicts with the purpose of relieving Congress of the burden of having to resolve these claims.

* * *

The Danns also claim to possess individual as well as tribal aboriginal rights and that because only the latter were before the Indian Claims Commission, the "final discharge" . . . does not bar the Danns from raising individual aboriginal title as a defense in this action. Though we have recognized that individual aboriginal rights may exist in certain contexts, this contention has not been addressed by the lower courts and, if open, should first be addressed below. We express no opinion as to its merits.

* * *

According to Justice William Brennan's opinion, the purpose of the ICC was to essentially finalize any and all tribal land claims. In one sense, this is a noble and noteworthy endeavor. Large-scale, systemic efforts to rectify the wrongs committed during the colonial process were and are relatively rare.

On the other hand, if achieving finality is the singular or dominant purpose of such an effort, it runs the risk of satisfying its goals at the expense of justice or reconciliation, particularly for ongoing wrongs. The structure of the ICC, which only permitted monetary payments for extinguished land claims, was unable to contemplate or tolerate the possibility of the type of ongoing dispute raised by the Danns. To that end, the ICC, and the courts that came after it, were constantly seeking an endpoint with which to assess the dispute, whether that endpoint was "by gradual encroachment" or through "payment." The Danns, for their part, argued against the acknowledgment of any endpoint. They primarily sought to argue that there was no endpoint because the land on which their cattle grazed had not yet been ceded to the federal government, but they were also forced to argue that they had not received payment in an effort to keep the litigation alive in the hopes of somehow getting back to the question of whether the land had truly been ceded.

The Supreme Court did offer one alternative theory for the Danns—individual aboriginal rights. The case was remanded, or returned to a lower court, for further consideration on this point. As you read the case, ask yourself how the 9th Circuit Court of Appeals engages with the idea of individual aboriginal rights. What are they? How are they established? How might an individual Native person assert these rights in a U.S. court? How did the Danns engage with this concept?

U.S. v. Dann
873 F.2d 1189 (1989)

Canby, Circuit Judge:

* * *

Individual aboriginal title is by no means a well-defined concept. The common view of aboriginal title is that it is held by tribes. . . . Nevertheless, the Supreme Court has pointed out . . . that it has "recognized that individual aboriginal rights may exist in certain contexts." We therefore consider the possible nature and scope of such an individual title.

There is no theoretical reason why individuals could not establish aboriginal title in much the same manner that a tribe does. An individual might be able to show that his or her lineal ancestors held and occupied, *as individuals*, a particular tract of land, to the exclusion of all others, from time immemorial, and that this title has never been extinguished.

Whether any such individual aboriginal title has existed or could exist, we need not decide, for it is clear that the Danns make no such individual claim to these lands from time immemorial. . . . [T]he Danns pleaded that the lands in issue were beneficially owned "by the defendants and other members of the Western Shoshone Tribe," and requested a declaration that "the Western

Shoshone tribes of Indians are the recognized beneficial owners of the land.". . . [T]he Danns disavow any claim of individual possessory interests. . . . Indeed, the Danns' entire attack on the claims proceeding is directed toward rescuing the aboriginal title of the Western Shoshone to these lands from the effect of the claims award. . . .

It is beyond question, then, that the aboriginal rights to these lands were tribal until they were extinguished. As individual tribal members occupying land under tribal original title, the Danns or their lineal ancestors could assert not rights excluding the tribe or its members from the land they were occupying. And because the rights they assert are tribal, the Danns could just as easily lay claim to any of the 22 million acres of aboriginal Western Shoshone land in Nevada as they do to the tracts at issue in this case. The problem with the claim . . . is that the Western Shoshone have been paid for that title, and it must be deemed extinguished. . . .

* * *

As noted by the 9th Circuit Court of Appeals, individual aboriginal rights are "by no means a well-defined concept." As briefly explained by the Court, an individual could, in theory, establish certain rights to land in the same way that Native nations have asserted their rights to land in ICC cases. Is this realistic? Tribal nations were forced to expend a tremendous amount of time, money, and energy on expert witnesses who went to great lengths to write detailed reports about tribal land claims. And those tribal nations also had to endure governmental lawyers who challenged every witness, report, and claim. Could an individual create and defend such a record? Would this have truly been a viable alternative for the Danns? If it is not a viable alternative, then what purpose does it serve for the courts to raise it as a possibility?

More pertinent for this chapter, the Danns decided not to pursue this avenue of legal argument. Doing so might have resulted in a victory for them, but it would not have addressed the larger issue of Shoshone land rights. The Dann sisters once again appealed to the Supreme Court, but this time they were not granted a hearing, thus exhausting their domestic remedies. To that end, the Danns appealed to the IACHR. They alleged that the United States violated, among other things, Articles II, III, VI, XIV, XVIII, and XXIII of the American Declaration of the Rights and Duties of Man. Before reading the decision of the IACHR, reread the articles cited by the Danns. As you read the decision, ask yourself why the IACHR chose to focus on the articles of the American Declaration that it chose. What makes those articles different from the others the Danns alleged that the U.S. violated? How does this decision fundamentally differ from the previous decisions in the U.S. court system? What is the source of the IACHR's reasoning for the decision?

CASE OF MARY AND CARRIE DANN V. UNITED STATES
Case No. 11.140, Inter Am. C. H. R. No. 75/02, Doc. 5, rev. 1 (2002)

* * *

2. ... The Petitioners ... contend that the State has interfered with the Danns' use and occupation of their ancestral lands by purporting to have appropriated the lands as federal property through an unfair procedure before the Indian Claims Commission ("ICC"). ...

3. ... [T]he state submits that the Danns and other Western Shoshone lost any interest in the lands in question in 1872 as a result of encroachment by non-Native Americans, and that this determination was properly made through fair proceedings before the ICC, a quasi-judicial body established by the United States for the very purpose of determining Indian land claims issues. ...

* * *

5. In the present report, having examined the evidence and arguments present on behalf of the parties to the proceedings, the Commission concluded that the State has failed to ensure the Danns' right to property under conditions of equality contrary to Articles II, XVIII and XXIII of the American Declaration in connection with their claims to property rights in the Western Shoshone ancestral lands.

* * *

54. The Petitioners ... contend that the theory upon which the ICC determined the extinguishment of Western Shoshone, namely "gradual encroachment" by non-indigenous settlers, miners, and others, constitutes a nonconsensual and discriminatory transfer of property rights in land away from indigenous people who continue in possession of their land and in favor of non-indigenous interests. They claim that this is a "lawless concept that simply rewards trespassers and relieves the United States of its own legal obligation to uphold Indian land rights."

* * *

73. ... the Petitioners point out that the domestic courts ultimately disposed of proceedings regarding the Danns' interests in the Western Shoshone

ancestral lands without determining the actual existence of historical acts of extinguishment.... Rather ... the Supreme Court ... ruled that the Danns were barred as a result of the judgment of the ICC and subsequent money award ... from asserting such title.

* * *

88. The State ... contends that regardless of whether there was a trial on the status of title to Western Shoshone ancestral lands, a final decision was reached by the ICC that the Western Shoshone had been deprived of their lands as of 1872.... The State argues that merely because the Danns disagree with the final decision of the ICC and believe it to be wrong does not mean that the decision is incorrect.

* * *

91. The State therefore argues that in effect, the Petitioners are seeking to have the Commission second-guess decisions made many years ago by their fellow Western Shoshone and their attorney in deciding to seek compensation rather than litigate land title rights, by the ICC in its handling of the matters, and by U.S. courts that endorsed the ICC decision.

* * *

112. The nature and breadth of the ICC's jurisdiction was further developed through judicial interpretations of the ICC legislation.... [I]t was established ... that the ICC Act limited the relief that could be ordered by the ICC to that which was compensable in money and did not include recovery of land where that would be plausible.

113. The Commission notes that ... publicists have over the years since its establishment and dissolution criticized the ICC on various grounds. Among the subjects of these criticisms have been ... the narrowing of the ICC jurisdiction to award only monetary compensation and accordingly to preclude claimants from recovering lands.

* * *

128. Perhaps most fundamentally, the Commission and other international authorities have recognized the collective aspect of indigenous rights, in the sense of rights that are realized in part of in whole through their guarantee to groups or organizations of people. And this recognition has extended to acknowledgment of a particular connection between communities of indigenous peoples and the lands and resources that they have traditionally occupied and used, the preservation of which is fundamental to the effective

realization of the human rights of indigenous peoples more generally and therefore warrants special measures of protection. . . .

* * *

138. . . . [T]he Commission first wishes to expressly recognize and acknowledge that the State, through the development and implementation of the Indian Claims Commission process, has taken significant measures to recognize and account for historic deprivations suffered by indigenous communities living within the United States and commends the State for this initiative. . . .

139. Upon evaluating these processes in the facts as disclosed by the record in this case, however, the Commission concludes that these processes were not sufficient to comply with contemporary international human rights norms, principles and standards that govern the determination of indigenous property interests.

* * *

142. The insufficiency of this process was augmented by the fact that, on the evidence, the issue of extinguishment was not litigated before or determined by the ICC, in that the ICC did not conduct an independent review of historical and other evidence to determine as a matter of fact whether the Western Shoshone properly claimed title to all or some of their traditional lands. . . . [I]t cannot be said that the Danns' claims to property rights in the Western Shoshone ancestral lands were determined through an effective and fair process in compliance with the norms and principles under Articles XVIII and XXIII of the American Declaration.

143. Further, the Commission concludes that to the extent the State has asserted as against the Danns' title in the property in issue based upon the ICC proceedings, the Danns have not been afforded their right to equal protection of the law under Article II of the American Declaration. . . .

144. The record before the Commission indicates that under prevailing common law in the United States, including the Fifth Amendment to the U.S. Constitution, the taking of property by the government ordinarily requires a valid public purpose and the entitlement of owners to notice, just compensation, and judicial review. In the present case, however, the Commission cannot find that the same prerequisites have been extended to the Danns in regard to the determination of their property claims to the Western Shoshone ancestral lands, and no proper justification for the distinction in their treatment has been established by the State. . . .

***

148. In accordance with the analysis and conclusions in the present report, the Inter-American Commission on Human Rights recommends to the United States that it

    1.   Provide Mary and Carrie Dann with an effective remedy, which includes adopting the legislative or other measures necessary to ensure respect for the Danns' right to property in accordance with Articles II, XVIII and XXIII of the American Declaration in connection with their claims to property rights in the Western Shoshone ancestral lands.

    2.   Review its laws, procedures and practices to ensure that the property rights of indigenous persons are determined in accordance with the rights established in the American Declaration, including Articles II, XVIII and XXIII of the Declaration.

***

Understanding the differences in the multiple opinions among various courts regarding the Danns, and ultimately the nature of the IACHR's decision, requires some reflection on the nature of the different tribunals. As noted above, international law is the law that applies against nations, whereas domestic law is the law that applies against individuals and other groups with less sovereignty than nations. Consequently, the two different court systems—U.S. courts and the IACHR—were trying the actions of two different entities.

In the U.S. court system, the Danns were on trial. They were judged to be in violation of federal law because they grazed their cattle on lands that the United States no longer regarded as belonging to the Shoshone, primarily because of the 1962 decision of the ICC. The land in question had been, from the U.S. perspective, divested from the Shoshone by "gradual encroachment."

However, in the IACHR, the ICC was essentially on trial and was deemed inadequate. The purpose of the ICC, the IACHR noted, was part of the "significant measures to recognize and account for historic deprivations suffered by indigenous communities living within the United States." Nonetheless, the ICC was "not sufficient to comply with contemporary international human rights norms, principles and standards that govern the determination of indigenous property interests." As such, the IACHR recommended that the United States provide the Danns with an "effective remedy" and to review its laws and procedures to come into compliance with the American Declaration on the Rights and Duties of Man.

The Dann sisters' victory at the IACHR was a major milestone for Indigenous peoples in the international law context. Nonetheless, the United States has chosen not to honor the ruling, stating, among other things, that the ICC was a fair process, that the situation was not a human rights violation, and that it "respectfully declines to take any further actions to comply" with the IACHR's recommendations.[2] Consequently, it is fair to ask what, exactly, the Dann sisters and Indigenous peoples have achieved in this case.

On the one hand, from the Indigenous perspective, it is easy to be pessimistic. After decades of litigation and a positive ruling from an international tribunal, the Dann sisters had no tangible benefit to show for it. The United States' decision to basically ignore the IACHR's ruling exposes the weaknesses in international law, particularly for Native peoples in the United States. On the other hand, massive changes to law and policy rarely occur in just one pivotal step or moment. For example, many people are aware of *Brown v. Board of Education*, the landmark 1954 case that ended segregation in public schools in the United States. Yet, far fewer are aware of the long series of cases that led to *Brown*, which was the culmination of years of effort. Put another way, *Brown* did not occur in a vacuum but was the most famous in a series of steps toward a larger goal. As of now, the Danns in particular and Indigenous peoples more generally have a positive decision that has the potential to be a building block for the future.

UNDRIP

There are a number of other potential and actualized sources of international law that are available to Indigenous peoples beyond the American Declaration and the IACHR. This chapter cannot do justice to them all. However, it is necessary to note what is, by far, the biggest development in international law for Indigenous peoples in the 21st century: the United Nations Declaration on the Rights of Indigenous Peoples (UNDRIP). The UNDRIP was adopted by the United Nations in 2007.

Decades in the making, the UNDRIP is the most definitive statement ever in favor of Indigenous rights from the United Nations, perhaps the most important international organization ever established. As you read this excerpt from the UNDRIP, ask yourself what standards it sets for Indigenous peoples. What standards does it set for governments? How might the UNDRIP have applied to the Dann sisters? How might the UNDRIP speak to many of the issues that you have encountered in other chapters of this text?

UNITED NATIONS DECLARATION ON THE RIGHTS OF INDIGENOUS PEOPLES

U.N. Doc. A/61/L.67, Adopted Sep. 13, 2007

* * *

Article 1

Indigenous peoples have the right to the full enjoyment, as a collective or as individuals, of all human rights and fundamental freedoms as recognized in the Charter of the United Nations, the Universal Declaration of Human Rights and international human rights law.

Article 2

Indigenous peoples and individuals are free and equal to all other peoples and individuals and have the right to be free from any kind of discrimination, in the exercise of their rights, in particular that based on their indigenous origin or identity.

Article 3

Indigenous peoples have the right to self-determination. By virtue of that right they freely determine their political status and freely pursue their economic, social and cultural development.

Article 4

Indigenous peoples, in exercising their right to self-determination, have the right to autonomy or self-government in matters relating to their internal and local affairs, as well as ways and means for financing their autonomous functions.

Article 5

Indigenous peoples have the right to maintain and strengthen their distinct political, legal, economic, social and cultural institutions, while retaining their right to participate fully, if they so choose, in the political, economic, social and cultural life of the State.

* * *

Article 7

. . .

2.   Indigenous peoples have the collective right to live in freedom, peace and security as distinct peoples and shall not be subjected to any act of genocide or

any other act of violence, including forcibly removing children of the group to another group.

* * *

Article 10

Indigenous peoples shall not be forcibly removed from their lands or territories. No relocation shall take place without the free, prior and informed consent of the indigenous peoples concerned and after agreement on just and fair compensation and, where possible, with the option to return.

Article 11

1.   Indigenous peoples have the right to practise and revitalize their cultural traditions and customs. This includes the right to maintain, protect and develop the past, present and future manifestations of their cultures, such as archaeological and historical sites, artefacts, designs, ceremonies, technologies and visual and performing arts and literature. . . .

* * *

Article 18

Indigenous peoples have the right to participate in decision-making in matters which would affect their rights, through representatives chosen by themselves in accordance with their own procedures, as well as to maintain and develop their own indigenous decision-making institutions.

Article 19

States shall consult and cooperate in good faith with the indigenous peoples concerned through their own representative institutions in order to obtain their free, prior and informed consent before adopting and implementing legislative or administrative measures that may affect them.

* * *

Article 25

Indigenous peoples have the right to maintain and strengthen their distinctive spiritual relationship with their traditionally owned or otherwise occupied and used lands, territories, waters and coastal seas and other resources and to uphold their responsibilities to future generations in this regard.

Article 26

1.   Indigenous peoples have the right to the lands, territories and resources which they have traditionally owned, occupied or otherwise used or acquired. . . .

Article 27

States shall establish and implement, in conjunction with indigenous peoples concerned, a fair, independent, impartial, open and transparent process, giving due recognition to indigenous peoples' laws, traditions, customs and land tenure systems, to recognize and adjudicate the rights of indigenous peoples pertaining to their lands, territories and resources, including those which were traditionally owned or otherwise occupied or used. Indigenous peoples shall have the right to participate in this process.

* * *

Article 29

1.   Indigenous peoples have the right to the conservation and protection of the environment and the productive capacity of their lands or territories and resources. . . .

* * *

Article 33

1.   Indigenous peoples have the right to determine their own identity or membership in accordance with their customs and traditions. . . .

* * *

Article 37

1.   Indigenous peoples have the right to the recognition, observance and enforcement of treaties, agreements and other constructive arrangements concluded with States or their successors and to have States honour and respect such treaties, agreements and other constructive arrangements.

* * *

Article 43

The rights recognized herein constitute the minimum standards for the survival, dignity and well-being of the indigenous peoples of the world.

* * *

When voted upon by the members of the United Nations, the UNDRIP received overwhelming support, with over 140 nations voting in support of the Declaration. Four nations voted against it. Those four nations—the United States, Canada, Australia, and New Zealand—all share a common legal tradition, a relatively similar colonial history, and a significant Indigenous population. Put another way, four of the most prominent nations to which the UNDRIP would apply did not support it.

Despite these initial votes, all four countries did change their positions and endorsed the UNDRIP within just a few years. Yet at least with the United States, that support has been qualified. The position paper of the State Department—the department within the executive branch that engages with the affairs of the United States in the international sphere—on UNDRIP stated that, "The United States supports the Declaration, which—while not legally binding or a statement of current international law—has both moral and political force."[3] Furthermore, it is well established that the UNDRIP does not, by itself, create legal obligations on its own.

Thus, it is fair to ask, as it was considering the Dann sisters, what Indigenous peoples in the United States have gained with the United States' endorsement of the UNDRIP. In one sense, it is still too early to tell. Change in international law is often methodical, at best. However, the early results have not produced promising returns for Native peoples. The small handful of U.S. courts that have encountered the UNDRIP have been much more mindful of its lack of authority rather than its "moral and political force." As noted by a prominent federal court in one step of the noteworthy efforts to protect water rights at the Standing Rock Reservation in 2018, "courts have consistently held that UNDRIP is a non-binding declaration that does not create a federal cause of action."[4]

Yet, Native nations and peoples are increasingly turning to the UNDRIP as a source of authority and are regularly making it a part of their arguments before the courts. As noted above, the type of change that the UNDRIP might portend does not usually happen quickly or with one single event, but rather in incremental steps that rarely ever always move forward. And as Native nations and peoples increasingly imagine a world where the UNDRIP does have more than "moral and political force," it becomes that much more possible for others to imagine the world in this way as well. At present, the UNDRIP is, at minimum, a beacon of hope that we might more justly and fairly address the issues created and perpetuated by the history and law found elsewhere in this text.

SUGGESTED READINGS

- *In the Light of Justice: The Rise of Human Rights in Native America and the UN Declaration on the Rights of Indigenous Peoples.* Walter R. Echo-Hawk. Golden, CO: Fulcrum Publishing, 2013.

- *Indigenous Peoples in International Law,* 2nd ed. S. James Anaya. New York: Oxford University Press, 2004.

- "The Dann Litigation and International Human Rights Law: The Proceedings and Decision of Inter-American Commission on Human Rights." Brian D. Tittemore. 31 *American Indian Law Review* 593 (2006–2007).

---

[1] Case of the Mayagna (Sumo) Awas Tingni Community v. Nicaragua, Inter-Am. Ct. H. R., Case No. 11.577 (2001).

[2] Case of Mary and Carrie Dann v. United States, Case No. 11.140, Inter Am. C. H. R. No. 75/02, Doc. 1, rev. 1 (2002), para. 150, 176.

[3] https://2009-2017.state.gov/documents/organization/184099.pdf (accessed July 14, 2019).

[4] Standing Rock Sioux Tribe v. U.S. Army Corps of Engineers, 301 F.Supp.3d 50, 60 (2018).

State civil law powers and Williams v. Lee
case
Generally, 195
Worcester v. Georgia distinguished,
197
Talton v. Mayes, 241
Taxation rights
Generally, 418
Federal taxation, 421
State taxation, 432
Third government concept, 6
Treaties and, 115
Tribal courts' roles, 374

STATE LAW
Federal vs State Law, this index

TAKINGS OF PROPERTY
Property Rights, this index

TAXATION
Generally, 417 et seq.
Cherokee Tobacco tax case, 87 et seq.
Coexistence of state and federal taxes, 437
Constitution reference to Indians not taxed,
418
Double taxation issues, 437
Federal preemption of state taxation, 432
Federal taxing authority
Generally, 418
Coexistence of state taxes, 437
Indian tribes, taxation of, 419
Native individuals, 419
Squire v. Capoeman, 420
Highway taxes, state, 229, 433
Indian Mineral and Leasing Act of 1938,
432
Interest-balancing approach to federal vs
state taxation, 437
Native individuals
Federal taxation, 419
State taxation, 428
Tribal taxation, 421
Non-Indians engaging in activity on
reservation, state taxation, 436
Non-Indians, tribal taxation authority, 398
Non-natives and non-citizen natives, tribal
taxation, 422
Non-natives entities and individuals in
Indian Country, state taxation, 428
Public Law 280 transfer of jurisdiction to
states, 363
Sovereignty and right to tax, 418, 421

State taxation authority
Generally, 428 et seq.
Coexistence of federal taxes, 437
Cotton Petroleum Corp. v. NM, 432
Federal preemption, 432
Highway taxes, 229, 433, 439
Indian Mineral and Leasing Act of
1938, 432
Non-native entities and individuals in
Indian Country, 428
Non-natives engaging in activity on
reservation, 436
Treaty provisions affecting, 440
Tribal sovereignty, 432
Wagnon v. Prairie Band of
Potawatomi Indians, 436
Washington v. Cougar Den, 439
White Mountain Apache v. Bracker,
428
States, tribal taxation of, 428
Treaty provisions affecting state taxation,
440
Treaty provisions, canons of construction,
229
Tribal taxation authority
Generally, 421 et seq.
Atkinson Trading Company, Inc. v.
Shirley, 426
Merrion v. Jicarilla Apache Tribe, 422
Native individuals, 428
Non-natives and non-citizen natives,
422
States, 428
Tribal citizens, 421
Who/where issues, 438

TERMINATION ERA
Generally, 173
Allotment era compared, 182
Cold War influences on policies, 180, 352
Definition, 178
Emancipation and freedom policies, 180
Failures of, 182, 193
House Concurrent Resolution 108
establishing, 180
Hunting and fishing rights, 189
Indian Claims Commission, 178
"Indian Problem," search for solution of,
173
Laws reforming impacts, 203